Ten Cosmic Forms of the Divine Mother – Volume 2

(Integrated *Daśa Mahā Vidyā*)

*

Kamalātmānanda Nāthaḥ @ **Dr. Ramamurthy N.**

M.Sc., B.G.L., CAIIB, CCP, DSADP, CISA, PMP, CGBL, Ph.D.

*

*

Name: Ten Cosmic Forms of the Divine Mother Volume 2 (Integrated *Daśa Mahā Vidyā*)

First Edition: 2025

Series: Volume 2 of 2

Author: *Kamalātmānanda Nāthaḥ* @ **Dr. Ramamurthy N,** http://ramamurthy.jaagruti.co.in/

Copyright ©:   With the author (No part of this book may be reproduced in any manner whatsoever without the written permission from the author).

ISBN (13):   978-93-343-0077-2

Number of pages: 678

Price: ₹ 600.00

Printed at:

Published by:

*****

Table of Contents

Dedication

Oṃ Sadāshiva Samārambām Śankarāchārya Madhyamām |

Asmad Achārya Paranthām Vande Guru Paramparām ‖

ॐ सदाशिव समारंभां शङ्कराचार्य मध्यमां।
अस्मद आचार्य पर्यन्तां वन्दे गुरु परंपराम्॥

This book is dedicated with devotion to all Sri Vidya Upasakas throughout the world. There is no doubt that they all will be showered with the blessings by the divine mother.

Kamalātmānanda Nāthaḥ @ Dr. Ramamurthy N

*****

Blessings

Hrīṅkārāṅkita Mantra Rāja Nilayam Śrī Sarva Saṅkṣōbhiṇī

Mukyābhiścala Kuntalābhiruṣitam Maṉvasra Cakrē Śubhē |

Yatra Śrī Pura Vāsiṉī Vijayatē Śrī Sarva Saubhāgyadē

Śrī Cakram Śaraṇam Vrajāmi Satatam Sarvēṣṭa Siddhipradam ||

Sri Bhuvaneshwari Devi, in the form of all Gods, lives in Manidveepam and playfully creates, protects, destroys and blesses the entire universe. With Her fullest compassions, our disciple Dr. Ramamurthy has written an integrated book about all the ten Devis of *Dasha Maha Vidya*.

Sri Lalita Sahasranama says *Athma Vidya, Maha Vidya, Sri Vidya* and so on. *Athma Vidya* and *Sri Vidya* are not different, they are one and the same. The text called *Lalitopākyānam* says the *Sri Lalita Tripura Sundari* lives in *Sripuram*. In that *Sripuram*, in the middle of the house called *Chintāmaṇi*, in the royal assembly made of nine gems, in a beautiful throne, *Ambikā* sits alongwith *Mahākāmeshwarar*. She shines like crores of rising Suns. That *Sripuram* is being worshipped in the form of *Srichakra* by *Srividya upasakas*. In the center of that *Srichakra*, called *Bindu*, Sri *Lalitāmbikā* sits and performs the five tasks viz., creation, protection, destruction, *tirodhāna* and *anugrahā*.

That *Sri chakra* is our body. It has to be imagined that nine *Āvaranās* are available in our body, *Sri Devi* has to be meditated in the *Sasarara Chakra*. Once that meditation matures, body is filled with nectar and the worshipper reaches an unlimited bliss.

The same is mentioned in *Bhavanopanishat* as; *Tayōḥ Kāmēśvarī Sadāṉaṉda Ghaṉā Paripūrṇa Svātmaikya Rūpā Dēvatā Lalitā |*

How many ever *upāsanas* are there, *Srividya* is something distinctly special. Gods like *Mahesha, Mādava, Vidātru, Manmata* (Cupid), *Skanda, Nandi, Indra, Manu, Chandra, Kubera, Agastya, Krodabattāraka* – right from

Brahma, Vishnu, Maheshar everyone including Gods worship *Sri Lalita Tripura Sundari* only.

Everyone will not get the blessing to worship that, *Ambika*. As per the saying – *Sri Sundari Pungavānām Bhogashca Mokshahca Karasya Eva* – the *Srividya Upasakas* live with every possible wealth in this world and also get salvation (*moksham*) after death. To whomsoever this is the last birth, those people will only able to perform *Srividya Upasana*.

This book encompasses various *stotrams, Ashtotra, Trishati, Sahasranama archanas* and various other minute details relating to all the 10 *Devis*.

We also bless **Dr. Ramamurthy N** and his family, who has compiled this book to get the grace of *Jaganmata Sri Bhuvaneswari Devi*.

Āṇandam	*Śupam*	*Maṅgaḷam* l
Bliss	Propitious	Auspicious
	Jaya Bhuvaneshwari	

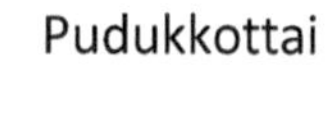

2025   *Śrī Praṇavānanta Svāmiṇaḥ*
Sri Bhuvaneswari Avadhoota Vidhya Peetam,   Pudukkottai

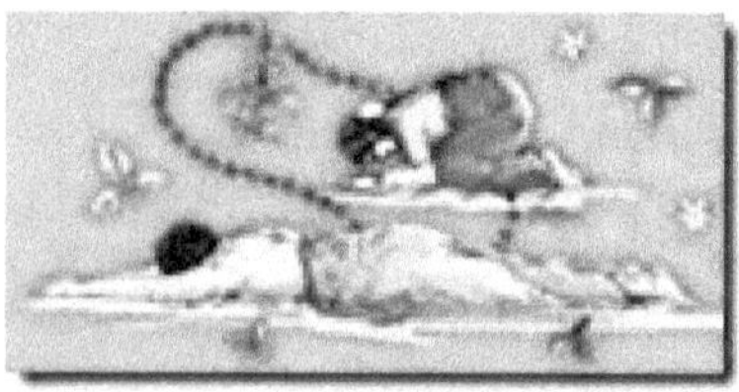

****

Introduction

Oṃ Śrī Gurubhyo Namaḥ ॥ ॐ श्री गुरुभ्यो नम: ॥

A story goes. Once during their numerous love games, things got out of hand between Lord Shiva and Paarvatee. What had started in jest turned into a serious matter with an incensed Shiva threatening to walk out on Paarvatee. No amount of coaxing or cajoling by Paarvatee could reverse matters. Left with no choice, Paarvatee multiplied herself into ten different forms for each of the ten directions. Thus, however hard Shiva might try to escape from his beloved Paarvatee, he would find her standing as a guardian, guarding all the escape routes.

Each of the Devee's manifested forms made Shiva realise essential truths, made him aware of the eternal nature of their mutual love and most significantly established for always in the cannons of Indian thought the Goddess's superiority over her male counterpart. Not that Shiva in any way felt belittled by this awareness, only spiritually awakened. This is true as much for this Great Lord as for us ordinary mortals. Befittingly thus they are referred to as the Great Goddess of Wisdom, known in Samskrutam as the *Maha Vidyas*. Indeed, in the process of spiritual learning, the Goddess is the muse who guides and inspires us. **She** is the high priestess who unfolds the inner truths.

In their strong associations with death, violence, pollution and despised marginal social roles, they call into question such normative social 'goods' as worldly comfort, security, respect, and honor. The worship of these goddesses suggests that the devotee experiences a refreshing and liberating spirituality in all that is forbidden by established social orders.

The central aim here is to stretch one's consciousness beyond the conventional, to break away from approved social norms. By rejecting conventional social norms, the adept seeks to liberate his consciousness from the inherited, imposed, and probably inhibiting categories of proper and improper, good and bad, polluted and pure. Perhaps the more marginal, bizarre, 'outsider' goddesses among the *Maha Vidyas* facilitate this escape. By identifying with the forbidden or the marginalised, an adept may acquire a new and refreshing perspective on the cage of respectability and predictability. Indeed, a mystical adventure, without the experience of which, any spiritual quest would remain incomplete.

For every *Devee*, *Nyasa mantras* have been mentioned. It was thought that it would befit to explain a little about *Nyasa* here. Different schools use different methods for *Nyasa*. The method taught by the appropriate guru should be used.

a. *Bīja* – naval button, *Śakti* – the secret organ and *Kīlakam* – the feet.
b. *Bīja* – right shoulder, *Śakti* – left shoulder and *Kīlakam* – the secret organ.
c. *Bīja* – the secret organ, *Śakti* – the feet and *Kīlakam* – the naval.

Kara-ṣaḍanga-nyāsa-s (six *naysays* in hands) – thumb, fore finger, middle finger, ring finger, little finger and palm & back of the palm.

Nyāsas of Six organs

The organ to be touched	The offering *mantra*	The hand to be used	Finger(s) to be used
Heart	*Hrudayāya Namaḥ*	Right	Ring, middle and fore-fingers
Head	*Sirase Svāhā*	Right	Middle and ring fingers
The hair knot at the back of the head or its place, if it is not there.	*Śikāyai Vashat*	Right	Thumb
Shoulders – both right and left	*Kavacāya hoom*	Both the hands at a time	All the five fingers

The organ to be touched	The offering *mantra*	The hand to be used	Finger(s) to be used
Two eyes and the middle of the eye brows	*Netratrayāya Voushat*	Right	Ring, middle and fore-fingers (at a time to be touched)
Left Palm	*Astrāyapaṭ*	Right	Middle and fore-fingers
Around the head from right to left	*Bhūḥ Bhuvaḥ Suvaḥ*	Right	By knuckling middle and fore-fingers.

Worship of the Divine Mother dates back to *Vedic* period. Every being naturally is attached and turns towards the mother who not only gives birth but also protects the child by giving milk and food to sustain. Thus, worship of the mother has the earliest origins. Everybody in India is virtually a worshipper of the Divine Mother in one form or other. The first three castes were given the ceremony of *Upanayana* or sacred thread ceremony around eight years of age. The Holy *Gāyatrī mantra* is given to him to repeat. By mere chanting of the same it yields all the benefits herein and after. *Gaayatree* is said to be supreme *mantra* and there is no *mantra* equal to the same as per *Vedic* teaching. It is called the mother of all *mantras* and meters. "*Gāyatrīm Candasām Mātaḥ*" it is said. It is a license to repeat all the *mantras* in the *Vedas*. Unless one repeats this *Gāyatrī mantra*, one will not be able to learn other *Vedic mantras*. *Vedas* contain *mantras*, which are useful to remove all the miseries and problems in life from birth to death. Thus, *Gāyatrī* occupies a prime place in the system of *mantra Vidya*.

But all are not eligible to do japam of the *Gāyatrī mantra*. Only males and only those who are born in the first three castes are permitted to learn and repeat the *mantra*. *Tāntric* system wanted to cure this defect. It had found many *mantras* that are more powerful and at the same time could be followed by all sections of society irrespective of their position with regard to sex, creed and belief. Many *tantras* were found out and elaborate systems of worship came into being. They were practiced by the great *rishis* like Agastya,

Lopamudra, Hayagreeva and Kamaraja. Even deities like Indra and Chandra too followed them and obtained equanimity of mind.

Worship of the Divine Mother being oldest had branched into many forms. From the village deities to the Supreme Brahmam many forms came into being. Different methods of worship called *ācaras* also came into being. Those *ācaras* which are not against the *Vedic* methods of worship are called *Samaya ācaras* and those that are opposed to the *Vedic* methods are called *Koula ācaras* and *Vāma ācaras*. All of them are permitted in *Tantras*. After all, since mother is being worshipped by all sections of society, each worship according to his nature and with objects, which he consumes. Thus, even liquor and meat are being offered to the Divine Mother by persons who willingly consume them. Nothing is wrong, as long as the mind is pure and offered with devotion and without ill-will. But if one consumes them to please his senses, he becomes a *pashu* or an animal. Even for the five 'M's that are peculiar to this *tantric* system, substitutes are given so that one will not become an outcaste by consuming them. It is the *Bhāvana* that is important. Hence Mother is known *"Bhāvanā Gamyā"*. Mother appreciates only the language of *Bhakti* even though **She** is omniscient and knows all the languages. In fact, **she** dwells in the hearts of all her devotees. Nobody needs to tell the problems or seek anything from **Her**. **She** knows the needs of everyone and offers them more than their requirements. *"Phalamapi Vancā Samādhikam"* says *Soundaryalaharee*. But persons in their ignorance make all sorts of demands and prayers.

Different regions of the country developed worship of different forms of deities. *Lalitā* and *Sundarī* are famous in South India; *Chandee* in Mysore; *Vindhyā Vāsini* in Vindhya regions. *Kāli Mātā* is worshipped mainly in Kolkata, *Bagalāmukhī* in Bihar, etc. But all these systems were neatly formulated and integrated into a single system by the great *Ādi Śankarācārya* in the great *tantra* called *Prapancasāra*. He had synthesised not only the various forms of the Divine mother but also the *upasanas* of *Vishnu, Shiva, Ganapati, Subrahmanya* and *Sun* God. He is thus called the *Shanmata Sthāpanācāryar*.

Kālī, Bagalāmukhī, Tārā, Chinnamastā, Mātangī, Lalitā, are some of the ten *Maha Vidyās*. These are ten Cosmic powers. Worship of these forms is found in the *Vedic* system itself. In 1980s research was undertaken and a paper was written in Tamil by Dr. *Goda Venkateshwara Sastri* citing the *Vedic* references also, which was later printed as a book *"Daśa Mahā Vidyā Rahasyam"* and published by the Gnana Bhaskara Sangham, Chennai. This Tamil book was translated into English by this author during August 2011. It was a very concise, gist of all the 10 Devis. Later, as per the instructions of my Guru HH *ŚrīŚrī Pranavānanda Swāmijee*, individual books were written detailing each of the 10 Devis. There were requests from different corners to write an integrated book combining all the 10 Devis and hence this attempt.

Writing meanings and comments for Samskruta verses is not an easy task. The meaning and beauty of the source should not be fragmented but the clarity of the words should captivate the mind of the readers. The readers should dissolve and melt in the mind of the author of the source. The comments should be written in such a way that the readers can enjoy the sweet juice in it.

Conventions – Wherever **She** is used, it indicates *Sri Devi.* The transliterated Samskrutam or other language words are written in *italics*. When Samskruta words are transliterated in English diacritical marks are used for proper pronunciation like;

> *ā* – as in R<u>a</u>ma *ḍ* – as in mu<u>d</u>
> *ḍh* – as in go<u>dh</u>ood *ḥ* – visarga in as in *Rāmaḥ*
> *ī* – as in p<u>ee</u>l *ṇ* – as in pu<u>n</u>
> *ṛ* – as in st<u>r</u>ewn *ś* – as in <u>Sh</u>ankar
> *ṣ* – as in fi<u>sh</u> *ṭ* – as in cu<u>t</u>
> *ṭh* – as in an<u>th</u>ill *ū* – as in r<u>oo</u>t

Humble pranams to HH *ŚrīŚrī **Pranavānanda Swāmijee***, who has blessed me and the readers with his nice introduction and some pleasantries. I am fortunate to have association with people like ***Swāmijīs***, who are my *Gurus*. Sincere thanks are due to all who helped me in bringing this book so nicely. It is only because of the blessings of such gurus that I am able to continue my efforts to write books. It is because of their kindness that this 107th book has been written. I pray at the feet of the gurus to continue such efforts.

Appreciation and acknowledgements are due to all those who supported in this noble cause. The readers are requested to feel free in providing feedback. Let all the readers be blessed with glory of Gods.

With the splendid blessings of our forefathers, priests and Sri Devi, this 107th book has been completed. My humble salutations to all of them. May their blessings continue.

Due to the bulk size of the book, this is being published in 2 volumes. This is the second volume covering second five of the ten vidyas (Devis) viz., *Dhūmāvatī* – धूमावती, *Chinna Mastā* – छिन्नमस्ता, *Bagalāmukhī* – बगलामुखी, *Mātangī* – मातंगी and *Ṣodaśī* – षोडशी. The first five Devis have already been dealt with in the previous volume.

Om Tat Sat

Chennai
2025   **Dr. *Ramamurthy N***

*****

Daśa Mahā Vidyā Devis

काली तारा महाविद्या षोडशी भुवनेश्वरी । भैरवी धूमावती च विद्या धूमावती तथा ॥

बगला सिद्ध विद्या च मातंगी कमलात्मिका । एता विद्या महेशानि महाविद्या प्रकीर्तिता ॥

Kāli Tārā Mahāvidya Şodaśī Bhuvaneśwarī ।

Bhairavī Kamalātmikā Ca Vidyā Kamalātmikā Tathā ॥

Bagalā Siddha Vidyā Cha Kamalātmikā Baggala ।

Etā Vidyā Maheśāni Mahāvidyā Prakīrtitā ॥   *Śyāmā Rahasyam*

Each form of the divine mother is a *Maha Vidya*. The ten *Maha Vidyas* are;

1. *Kāli* – काली
2. *Tārā* – तारा
3. *Tripurasundarī* – त्रिपुरसुन्दरी
4. *Bhuvaneśwarī* – भुवनेश्वरी
5. *Bhairavī* – भैरवी
6. *Dhūmāvatī* – धूमावती
7. *Chinna Mastā* – छिन्नमस्ता
8. *Bagalāmukhī* – बगलामुखी
9. *Mātangī* – मातंगी
10. *Şodaśī* – षोडशी [1]

The *Dasha Maha Vidyas* are wisdom goddesses. Dasha means ten, maha means great and vidya means wisdom. The Dasha Maha Vidyas are considered forms of divine mother kali, who is the first of the ten Maha Vidyas.

These ten forms of divine mother are known as the *Dasha Maha Vidyas*. Each form (wisdom goddess) has own name, story, quality, and *mantras*.

---

[1] These names are mentioned differently in various schools. In particular, Kamalatmika is also called as *Şodaśī*. These are further being discussed in the relevant places.

In *tantra*, worship of *devi-shakti* is referred to as a *vidya*. of the hundreds of tantrik practices, the worship of the ten major devis is called the *Dasha Maha Vidyas*. These major forms of the goddess are described in the text called *Todala Tantra*. These ten aspects of *shakti* are the epitome of the entire creation.

There are several 'levels' at which these devis can be worshiped with the prescribed *mantras* and *yantras*. Like a simple worship of the *yantra* with recitation of the relevant mantras, as a remedial astrological measure, elaborate worship with all tantrik rituals for attaining various *siddhis* associated with these tantras and for spiritual salvation.

Successful *sadhana* of these *Vidyas* gives several boons to the practitioner. The tantrik-yogi who has control over his senses and positively inclined, uses the boons to guide people and for the benefit of mankind. The ones whose head starts spinning with success use them for the gratification of the senses, gather a bunch of disciples around them and become fake gurus.

The last chapter of Todala Tantra equates Vishnu's ten incarnations with the ten *Maha Vidyas* as below;

"*Sri Devi* said – lord of devas, guru of the universe, tell me of the ten incarnations. Now I want to hear of this, tell me of their true nature. *Parameshvara*, reveal to me which avatar goes with which devi. The worship of these devis is also prescribed as an astrological remedy. As per – Todala Tantra, chapter 10 – As told by Shri Shiva – the Avatar of Sri Vishnu and the Navagrahas corresponding to each of the *Dasha Maha Vidyas* is tabulated below;

#	Dasha Maha Vidya	Vishnu Avatar	Navagraha
1.	*Kālī* – काली	Krishna	Saturn
2.	*Tārā* – तारा	Matsya	Jupitar
3.	*Tripurasundarī* – त्रिपुरसुन्दरी	Parashurama	Mercury
4.	*Bhuvaneśwarī* – भुवनेश्वरी	Vamana	Moon
5.	*Bhairavī* – भैरवी	Balarama	Lagna
6.	*Dhūmāvatī* – धूमावती	Varaha	Ketu

#	Dasha Maha Vidya	Vishnu Avatar	Navagraha
7.	Chinna Mastā – छिन्नमस्ता	Narasimha	Rahu
8.	Bagalāmukhī – बगलामुखी	Koorma	Mars
9.	Mātangī – मातंगी	Rama	Sun
10.	Şodaśī – षोडशी	Bhuddha	Venus

The tantrik worship of these most powerful *Vidyas* must be practiced only under the guidance of a siddha guru. At the cost of repetition, it is stressed that the books cannot be gurus. They can only be guides.

As Swamiji has mentioned in his blessings, the *chakras* in our body are the 9 *Avaranas* of the *Sri Chakra*. Various texts on Ambika, like *Sri Lalita Sahasranama, Sri Lalita Trishati, Soundaryalahari,* etc., deal in detail about the connection between *Sri Devi* and the *chakras/ Grantis* in our body. *Sri Chakra* is *Sri Devi*. Hence, our body is *Ambika* herself. In different *chakras* of our body, Ambika resides in various forms. These Vidya Devis also reside in the *chakras* of the human body, in lotuses with different number of petals. The details can be found in this list;

Dasha Maha Vidya	Chakra	No. of petals
1. Kālī – काली	Mūlādhāram	4
2. Tārā – तारा	Maṇipūrakam	10
3. Tripurasundarī – त्रिपुरसुन्दरी	Sahasrāram	1,000
4. Bhuvaneśwarī – भुवनेश्वरी	Anāhatam	12
5. Bhairavī – भैरवी	Mūlādhāram	4
6. Dhūmāvatī – धूमावती	Ajnā	2
7. Chinna Mastā – छिन्नमस्ता	Anāhatam	12
8. Bagalāmukhī – बगलामुखी	Anāhatam	12
9. Mātangī – मातंगी	Viśuddhi	16
10. Şodaśī – षोडशी	Anāhatam	12

More than one Goddess resides in the *Anahata Chakra*, i.e. the Heart. Almost all the deities should be meditated upon in the heart. There could be some exceptions.

There are 'n' number of images of *devi*-s worshipped by sages for quite a long time. The most significant ten among them are being considered here.

Each of these ten *vidya*-s, itself is called as *Brahma Vidya*. *Tantra sastras* describe in detail the worshipping methods of these *Devis*.

Out of these 10 *vidya*-s, the *Bhuvaneshvari Vidya* also called as *Sri Vidya* is more famous in South India.

The *mantras, yantra, dhyana*, worshipping methods, results, forms, etc., of these ten *vidya*-s can be read in the tantra texts in Samskrutam. Sir Arthur Avalon, has also explained in detail in English.

There are different types, in the worship of *Sri Devi* – like *Vāmācāra, Dakshinācāra, Samayācāra* and *Koulacāra. Sri Lalita Sahasranama* (98ᵗʰ name – *Samayācāratatparā*, 441ˢᵗ name – *Koulamārga Tatpara Sevitā*) accepts all these methods.

One of the 10 sons of Lord Brahma was *Dakshan*. He was called as *Daksha Prajapati*. The destruction of *Daksha*'s *yagna* by *Sati Devi* has been described in the 4ᵗʰ *Skanda* of *Shrimad Bhagavatam*. This has also been described in detail in *Bruhat Dharma Purana*.

Once when *Daksha Prajapati* was proceeding towards the *yagna-Shala* (the place where the holy fire was being conducted), Lord *Shiva* (his son-in-law), who was in meditation did not get up as a respect. On account of this *Daksha* got wild and gave a curse that Lord Shiva will not get any share from his *yagna*. From that moment onwards, Lord Shiva does not even see Daksha.

In another instance, Daksha Prajapati himself started a *yagna*. All his daughters were invited with their husbands excepting *Sati Devi*. Knowing this, **she** asked permission from her husband Lord Shiva to attend the *yagna*, executed by her father. When Lord Shiva did not permit her, **she** took the form of *Mahā Kālī*, the first of Dasha Maha Vidya in a ferocious form.

Surprised by the most terrified form of peaceful *Sati Devi*, Lord *Shiva* started running in all directions from that place. But in whichever direction he ran, *Devi* was before him with the terrified form. The ten forms **She** took in all the ten directions (8 directions + upward + downward) are *Dasha Maha Vidyas* of *Sri Devi*.

Surprised by this Lord Shiva stood stunned. Though *Devi* tried to console him stating that **She** is *Sati Devi* only, Lord *Shiva* could not get away from the fear immediately. Then *Devi* explained the specialties and purposes of all the ten *Vidya*-s to her husband.

Further **She** mentioned – "the *Vedas* and sacred writings (*Agamas*) told by you to this world are my two hands. I wear moveable and immoveable things of this world with those two hands. These ten forms will help to bless the worshippers. People should reach me by secretly following the *mantra*, *yantra*, verses, *kavacha*, etc., as taught by the teacher (Guru). I am telling you with the affection on you. Please permit me to attend the *yagna*" – **She** requested.

The directions in which the ten *Maha Vidyas* originated are described in the below diagram;

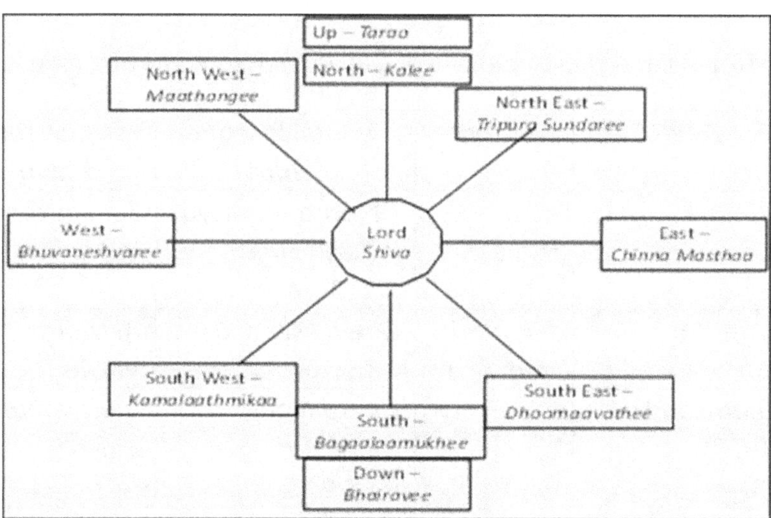

After getting his permission, **she** reached the *yagna* place of Daksha, which was protected by Nandi, Brungi and others. **She** could not tolerate the reprimands on Lord Shiva and hence disappeared in the fire of *yagna*. Knowing this Lord Shiva created *Veerabhadra* from his entangled locks of hair and sent him to destroy the *yagna* of Daksha. *Devi* also took the form of *Bhadra Kālī* and with the help of *Veerabhadra* destroyed Daksha and all the opponents of Lord Shiva. This is the origin of *Dasha Maha Vidyas*.

Out of the three qualities of illusion, the pure *sattva* quality related with *Brahmam* (the Supreme Being) is called *Vidya*. Sir Arthur Avalon feels that even in this the fourth and which is beyond any *tattva* is the blissful form of *Devi* is called *Maha Vidya*.

The relation of *Brahmam* to the pure Sattva quality, of the three qualities of *Maya*, is called *Vidya*. The fourth (transcendental) philosophy is the blissful form of the Goddess, which is called *Maha Vidya*. *Camuṇḍa Tattva* splits these ten *Maha Vidyas* into *Maha Vidyas*, *Siddha Vidyas* and *Vidyas*. But the text *Shyāmā Rahasya* mentions all these as *Maha Vidyas* only. We also follow this and call all the ten as *Maha Vidyas*.

The presiding deity(ies) of the 10th Chapter of *Sri Devi Mahatmyam* is said to be these *Dasha Maha Vidyas*.

Let us try to understand a little more about each of these 10 Devis. Books about the first Nine Devis have already been written. Now this is about the Tenth Sri Kamalātmikā Devi.

The Tattvas and the evidences of Dasha Maha Vidyas at a glance;

Devi	Tattva	Evidence from Vedas	Upaniṣat Vidya
Kālī – काली	*Kāla* (time)	*Orvapra Amartyā* – (*Rātri Sūkta*) RV 10:127:2	*Samvarga Vidya*
Tārā – तारा	*Paṣyantī Vāg*	*Gowrī Mimāya* – RV 1:164:41	*Akshara Vidya*
Tripurasundarī – त्रिपुरसुन्दरी		*Gourdayati Marutām* – RV 8:94:1	*Vaishvanara Vidya*
Bhuvaneśwarī – भुवनेश्वरी	*Aakāsh* (ether)	*Atitir Dyoutiti* – RV 1:89:10	*Parovarīyaśī Vidya*
Bhairavī – भैरवी	*Parā Vāg*	*Jātavedase* – RV 1:99:1	*Chāndilya Vidya*
Dhūmāvatī – धूमावती	*Ṣuśumnā*	*Samhotram Sm Purā* – RV x: 86:10	Jyotir Vidya

Devi	Tattva	Evidence from *Vedas*	*Upaniṣat Vidya*
Chinna Mastā – छिन्नमस्ता		*Mokśuna Parāvarā –* RV 1:38:6	*Bhūma Vidya*
Bhagalātmukhī – बगलामुखी		*Tatitaasa Bhuvaneshu –* RV X: 120:1	*Indrayoni Vidya*
Mātangī – मातंगी	*Vaikharī Vāg*	*Maho Arnāḥ Sarasvatī* – RV 1:3:12	*Udgīta Vidya*
Ṣodaśī – षोडशी		*Tat Saviturvarenyam* – RV 111:62:10	*Madhu Vidya*

Self-Dedication with *Dasha Maha Vidyas*;

Ma!

- Whatever my tongue speaks, let it be your prayer.
- Whatever my hands act, let it symbolise your signet.
- If I walk with my legs, let it be circumambulation around you.
- Whatever food I take, let it be a fire-offering to you.
- If I relaxedly lie down, let it be a bowing to you.

<u>Note</u>; Sri Adi Shankara prays like this in his *Soundaryalahari.*

Sri Dasha Maha Vidya Prayers

1. Let *Kali*, who is in the form of time, protect us from the darkness of ignorance.
2. Let *Sri Tarambika* bless us to easily cross the ocean of birth.
3. Let *Sri Maha Tripura Sundari* bless us with a fruitful life in this birth itself by offering us the knowledge of *Sri Vidya.*
4. Let us get all the wealth by the blessings of *Sri Bhuvaneswari.*
5. Let *Sri Tripura Bhairavi* offer knowledge by destroying pride, arrogance and illusion.
6. Let all the sorrows of our life be destructed with the blessings of *Sri Dhoomavati.*
7. Let the *Sri Chinnamasthaa,* who is the sixth *devi,* bless us to control all our five senses and the mind.
8. Let *Sri Bagalamukhī* protect the rightfulness by extinguishing the requite of the enemies.

9. Let *Sri Raja Mātangī* bless us to get the light of knowledge spread in all directions.

10. Let *Sri Kamaladhārini* offer her complete blessings to –
    - Obtain all the eight types of wealth in the life
    - Remove poverty and obligations
    - Get complete wealth
    - Everyone to get everything
    - Make this world peaceful and remain equal

Thus Let Sri Devi take Ten Incarnations and blesse the devotees with many kinds of blessings and material wealth to lead them to blissful life in this world and then she also bestows Moksha (liberation) with her great grace.

Let us dvelve something more about the last devis from 6th to 10th viz. *Dhūmāvatī* – धूमावती, *Chinna Mastā* – छिन्नमस्ता, *Bagalāmukhī* – बगलामुखी, *Mātangī* – मातंगी and *Ṣodaśī* – षोडशी.

*****

Mantra, Tantra, Yantras

It is usual to worship Gods through *mantras*, *tantras* and *yantras*. Worshipping through *mantras* is called *Māntrīka* method. Worshipping through *tantras* is called *Tāntrīka* method. Worshipping through *yantras* is called *Vaidhīka* method. Whichever be the method *mantras* are definitely used to worship. But which is predominant is to be considered.

Mantras, the sound form of deities, are integral to *Sādhanas* (worship). *Mantra* pertaining to each God/ Goddess will have different number of letters called *chandas*. Similarly, each God/ Goddess will have various *mantras* – probably each one for a particular purpose/ satiating a desire.

Chanting *Mantras* create vibrations in the human body, which can only be felt by the concerned individuals and cannot be explained in words. For instance, if anyone asks how sugar will taste, it can be said that it is sweet. On the other hand, if someone asks how the sweet will be, no one can explain. It has to be enjoyed individually. In the same way the vibrations of the mantras can only be felt. However, to get complete result, it should be chant with proper pronunciation with clear words entirely focusing on the deity and not as a routine. Lalita Sahasranama (206th name) is *Sarvamantra Svarūpiṇī*. *Sri Lalita Devi* is in the form of all the mantras.

Tantras (Looms or Weavings) refer to numerous and varied scriptures pertaining to any of several esoteric traditions rooted in philosophy of the religion. The religious culture of the *Tantras* is essentially *Tāntric* material can be shown to have been derived from earlier *Vedic* sources. And although *Tantras* of different religions have many similarities from the outside, internally they do have some clear distinctions.

Yantras are some mathematical drawings/ patterns used for worship. There are mathematical construction methods explaining the drawing of *yantras*. *Yantras* mean originally the mechanical, mnemonic and musical contraption in the macrocosm. It is a graphic symbol of the contemplative meditation in the tradition, which was intended to be unified with the Gods/ goddesses. *Yantras* area also called as *cakras*. In a human body itself we have seven cakras thought to be an energy point or node in the subtle body viz., *Mūlādhārā, Swādhiṣṭānā, Maṇipūrakā, Anāhatā, Viśuddha, Agjnā* and *Sahasrārā*.

Sri Lalita Sahasranama, names 204, 205 and 206, *Sarva Mantra Svarūpiṇī, Sarva Yantrātmikā* and *Sarva Tantrarūpā*. That is, Sri Lalita herself is in the form of all the *Mantras, Yantras* and *Tantras*.

Usually when consecrating an idol of a deity, it is customary to place the *yantras* of the respective deity beneath the respective idol, duly drawn on copper or five-metals or silver or gold, etc. Properly drawn *yantras* emit micro-vibrations. Those vibrations are not feelable by human beings. However, they have a huge impact on our body, mainly positive impact. It is customary to worship the concerned deity alongwith the respective *chakras/ yantras*.

Yantras are great cosmic conductors of energy, an antenna of Nature, a powerful tool for harmony, prosperity, success, good health, yoga and meditation. *Yantras* are usually made out of copper and consist of a series of geometric patterns. The eyes and mind concentrate at the center of the yantra to achieve higher levels of consciousness.

<u>The Yantric Contour</u>

Every Yantra is delimited from the exterior by a line or a group of lines forming its perimeter. These marginal lines have the function to maintain, contain and prevent the loss of the magical forces represented by the core structure of the Yantra, usually the central dot. They also have the function to increase its magical and subtle force.

The core of the Yantra is composed of one or several simple geometrical shapes – dots, lines, triangles, squares, circles and lotus petals, representing in different ways the subtle energies.

<u>The Dot (Bindu)</u> – For example the dot (Bindu) signifies the focalized energy and its intense concentration. It can be envisaged as a kind of energy deposit which can in turn radiate energy under other forms. The dot is usually surrounded by different surfaces, either a triangle, a hexagon, a circle etc. These forms depend on the characteristic of the deity or aspect represented by the Yantra. In the tantric iconography, the dot is named Bindu; in tantra Bindu is symbolically considered to be Shiva himself, the source of the whole creation.

<u>The Triangle (Trikona)</u> – The triangle (Trikona) is the symbol of Shakti, the feminine energy or aspect of Creation. The triangle pointing down represents the Yoni, the feminine sexual organ and the symbol of the supreme source of the Universe and when the triangle is pointing upwards it signifies intense spiritual aspiration, the sublimation of one's nature into the most subtle planes and the element of fire (Agni Tattva). The fire is always oriented upwards, thus the correlation with the upward triangle – Shiva Kona. On the other hand, the downward pointing triangle signifies the element of water which always tends to flown and occupy the lowest possible position. This triangle is known as Shakti Kona.

The intersection of two geometric forms (lines, triangles, circles, etc.) represents forces that are even more intense than those generated by the simple forms. Such an interpenetration indicates a high level in the dynamic interaction of the correspondent energies. The empty spaces generated by such combinations are described as very efficient operational fields of the forces emanating from the central point of the Yantra. That is why we can very often encounter representations of Mantras in such spaces. Yantra and Mantra are complementary aspects of Shiva and their use together is much more efficient than the use of one alone.

<u>The Six-Pointed Star (Shatkona)</u> – A typical combination often found in the graphical structure of a Yantra is the superposition of two triangles, one pointing upwards and the other downwards, forming a star with six points (Shatkona), also known as David's Star. This form symbolically represents the union of Purusha and Prakriti or Shiva-Shakti, without which there could be no creation.

The Hexagon also known as the Shatkona is an archetypal amalgamation of two triangles structured in all the *Yantra*. It characteristically signifies the divine unification of Shiva (male energy) and Shakti (Female energy) which is the cause of all creation and the triangle also known as the Trikona is the emblem of Shakti, the absolute female energy of the Divine. It completes the creation or manifestation of both, material as well as spiritual worlds. The triangle pointing down characterises the Yoni, which is the source of all creations. A triangle pointing downwards represents the Water Element, since water flows down. Water Element represents Shakti.

<u>The Circle (Chakra)</u> – Another simple geometrical shape often used in Yantras is the circle, representing the rotation, a movement closely linked to the shape of spiral which is fundamental in the Macrocosmic evolution. At the same time, the circle represents perfection and the blissful creative void. In the series of the five fundamental elements, it represents air (Vayu Tattva). The circle also known as the chakra stands for rotation which is central to the functioning of the macrocosmic progression. At the same time, the circle signified perfection and the peaceful creative void of the *Vishudha Chakra*.

<u>The Square (Bhoopura)</u> – Between the simple geometrical elements that compose Yantras there is also the square (Bhoopura). The square is usually the exterior limit of the Yantra and symbolically, it represents the element earth (Prithivi Tattva).

<u>The Lotus (Padma)</u> – The lotus symbol (or its petals) is both a symbol of purity and variety, every lotus petal representing a distinct aspect. The

inclusion of a lotus in a Yantra represents freedom from multiple interference with the exterior (purity) and expresses the absolute force of the Supreme Self. A lotus in the Yantra represents the unconditional force of the Supreme Absolute truth. The lotus serves as a divine seat for Devas. It also represents detachment. It grows in the mud but never touches even a tinge of mud, representing detachment to the external forces (material world) and maintaining the original nature of pure and divine.

In conclusion, a Yantra is a very complex spiritual instrument in the tantric practice (Sadhana). It can calm and focus the activities of the mind, and by its positive auto-suggestion it has a beneficial impact on the health and psychic well-being of a person.

Every Yantra starts from the center, often marked by a central dot (Bindu) and ends with the outer square. This represents the sense of universal evolution, starting from the subtle and ending with the course, starting from 'ether' and ending with 'earth'.

Even though most of the times Yantras are composed of these simple geometrical shapes, sometimes we encounter other elements such as arrow points, tridents, swords, spikes included in the design of a Yantra with the purpose of representing vectors and directions of action for the Yantric energies.

A Yantra alone represents nothing. Only when it is awakened by mental concentration and meditation will the process of Resonance appear and the beneficial macrocosmic energies will manifest themselves in the practitioner's Microcosm.

A *Kavacam* is a shield protecting the body during wars. There are mantra shields to protect our body, mind and soul. We chant *Kavachams* on various lords like, *Skanda Shashti Kavacham* (about Lord Kumara), *Vishnu Kavacham, Sri Devi Kavacham*, etc. Among them, his *Kavacams* on Sri Devis are infallible weapons to receive the blessings of *Sri Devi* and to protect one's body and home. These Kavachas can be read daily and the results can be seen by self, how effective it is.

6. *Chinna Mastā* – छिन्नमस्ता

Śrī Chinna Masthā Devī

Adiparasakti, Paradevata, Sarva Loka Jaganmata, Sri Devi creates, preserves and destroys all the worlds. In addition, she performs the tasks of Anugraham and Tirodanam also, in accordance with one of the names in Sri Lalita Sahasranama *"Pancha Krutya Parayana"*. As a *Parabrahma Mahishi*, she, after creating lives, has taken many divine incarnations for the state and has been regularly doing *sishta* maintenance and evil discipline.

Among the various incarnations of Sriman Narayana described by Sri Vishnu Bhagavatam, ten avatars are prominent. Similarly, to protect the entire world, Sri Devi has manifested herself in ten different forms known as Dasha Maha Vidyas, as described in the previous chapter. Among those ten, Sri Chinna Masthā Devi Vidya is the sixth one.

Out of the ten the sixth one is *Chinna Masta Vidya*. Only this *Devi* is called as *Prachanda Chandee*. This *Chinna Masta Devi* shines in the *Aagnaa chakra* between the two eye brows in our body. Since *Chinna Masta* acts more furious and faster than *Kaalee* **she** is called *Prachanda Chandee*. **She** completes the tasks swiftly without the help of time (*kalam*).

Among the 10 incarnations of Sri Maha Vishnu, Sri Chinna Masta Devi is compared to Narasimha Avatar and Rahu among the Navagrahas.

We can compare **her** to the current. Electricity passes into our body so fast through the nerves and completes its activities. Similarly, *Chinna Masta* also spreads the entire body within a second before the eyes wink. The Seven petals in the *Aagnaa chakra* indicate *icchaa* (wish) and *Gnana* (knowledge). The *Chinna Masta Devi* in that place is also in those forms.

Though there are many *naadis* (pulses) in our body, the 101 *naadis* around the heart are considered as important –
    "Śadam Ca Ekā Ca Hrudyasya Nādyāḥ" (*Kāṭaka Upanishat* 3-2-16).

Still important are the three viz., *Idaa, Pingala* and *Sushumnaa*. *Sushumnaa* is the one which moves in the mid of the spine at the back of our body. *Idaa* and *pingala* coil themselves around both the sides and join the *Sushumnaa* at the *Aagnaa chakra*. This is *Triveni sangama* (meeting of three – as meeting of three rivers Ganga, Yamuna and Saraswathi in Allahabad). *Idaa* is Ganga, *Pingala* – Yamuna and *Sushumnaa* is invisible Saraswathi. This is what is told in *Vedas* as –
    "Sitaa Sito Sarito Yatra Sangate".

The energy (*Shakti*) called *atipeekara* running in *Sushumna* is called *Chinna Masta* or *Prachanda Chandee* or *Vajra Virochanee*. *Idaa Varninee Devi* shines like beautiful Moon and **she** carries the nectar. *Daakinee Devi* is in Red colour and shines like Sun. These *Varninee* and *Daakinee Devis* are close aides of *Chinna Masta Devi*.

Chinnamasta Jayanti is the birth anniversary or first appearance day of Goddess Chinnamasta is the Chitra Pournami day (the Full Moon Day of the first month of Tamil Calendar).

She is identified as Adi Para Shakti in the Devi Bhagavatam.

Worshiping male gods is called mantra. The method of worshiping female deities is called Vidya. Worshiping Sri Vidya, the unison of Shiva and Shakti. So, this also comes under Mantra group. Sri Vidya is said to be the best of all mantras.

That Devi is also known as Tripura Sundari, Rajarajeshwari, Shodasee, Kamakshi, Lalita and so on. She is also an important Maha Vidya. She is glorified in many Shakta texts like Sri Lalitha Sahasranamam, Soundarya-lahari, etc. She is called Adi Para Shakti in the Lalithopakyanam of Brahmanda Purana.

According to the Srikula tradition in Shaktaism, Chinna Masthā is the Shakta's supreme deity of Hinduism and the principal deity of Sri Vidya. The Tripura Upanishad places her as the ultimate Shakti (energy, power) of the universe. She is described as the Supreme Consciousness ruling from above Brahma, Vishnu and Shiva.

May the Divine Mother guide us all in our every action and thought. And may She remove the veil of maya and bestow upon us the greatest gift of all, moksha (liberation).

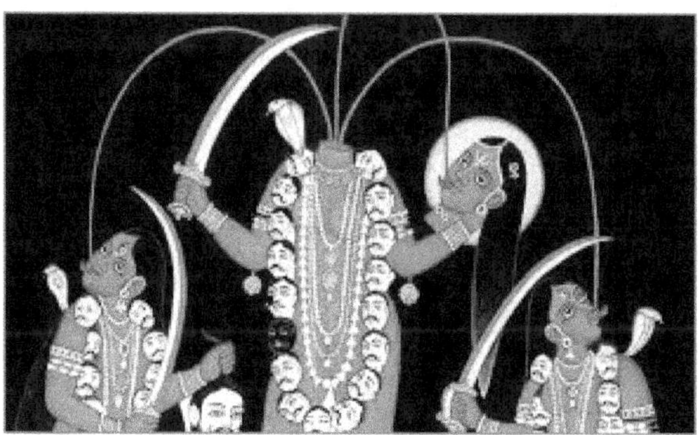

Form(s) of *Śrī Chinna Masthā Devī*

Usually meditative hymns (*dhyana shlokas*) about the gods are figurative of the concerned God or Goddess.

The meditation hymn of *Śrī Chinna Masthā Devī* is;

भास्वन्मन्डलमध्यगां निजशिरच्छिन्नं विकीर्णलकं
स्फारास्यं प्रपिबद्कलात्स्वरुधिरं वामेकरे बिभ्रतीम् ।
य्रा भासक्त रतिस्मरोपरिगतां सख्यौ निजेडाकिनी
वर्णिन्यौ परिदृश्यमोद कलिताम् श्रीचिन्नमस्ताम् भजे ॥

Bhāsvanmandalamadhyagām Nijaśiracchinnam Vikīrṇālakam
Sphārāsyam Prapibadkalātsvarudhiram Vāmekare Bibhratīm |
Yā Bhāsakta Ratismaroparigatām Sakhyou Nijedākinī
Varninyou Paridrushyamoda Kalitām Śrī Chinnamastām Bhaje ||

Her name and images show her own severed head, which she holds in her hands, is drinking one stream of blood spurting from the arteries of her neck and while at her sides are two naked Shaktis each of whom drinks another stream of blood.

Goddess Chinnamasta is been generally shown as if she is standing on the body of Manmatha (Cupid) God of love.

Chinna Mastaa Devee lives in the galaxy of Sun. **She** stands on *Rati* (wife of *Manmata*) and Manmata (Cupid) with **her** left leg stretched and her right leg folded. **She** holds an axe in the right hand and her own cut skull in the left hand. Her hair is elongated. **Her** form is so frightening that **she** drinks the blood oozing out of her neck through the mouth in **her** head in **her** own hand. **She** wears a garland of skulls in her body and a snake as a cross belt (*yagnopaveeda*). **She** is in the form 16 years old girl called *Vivastrai*. *Varninee* and *Daakinee devees*, the close aides shining on both the sides seem to be 12 years old. These two are also *Vivastrais* only. They are in the form holding hammer and axe in left hands and skull in the right hand and they drink the blood oozing out of the neck of *Chinna Mastaa Devee*. Out of these close aides *Varninee devee* is in the right side of *Chinna Mastaa Devee* with a beautiful form and *Daakinee devees* is in the left side of *Chinna Mastaa Devee* with a horrific form.

The *tatva* of *Chinna Masta* is to cut the *Brahma*, *Vishnu* and *Rudra grantis* (knots) and to join the energy in the *Brahmaanda* to *Pindaanda*. Between the gaps in the skull the energy reaches the human body. The same message is conveyed by *Taitreeya Upanishad* (1-6-1) as the soul after breaking of head, worships the *Brahmam* with the spiritual character and reaches the spirit of universal soul.

The head of a man indicates the intellect. The Supreme Being is beyond intellect and energy. "This is not to be recognised by intellect nor energy", says *Veda* (*Ka.U.*2-1-9). The indication that this is apart from intellect and energy is the form of censored head. Overpowering the organs is indicated by standing on Rati and Cupid. This *Devee* is also called as *Indiraani* energy of Indra. The sage *Vaashista Ganapathi* in his book *Prachanda Chandi Trishatee* says that the form of *Kaalee*, *Sundaree* and *Bhuvaneshee* is called *Gowree* and *Indranee*, who are middle *Devees*. *Vaashishta Vaibhavam* written by *Kabaali Saastrigal* says that *Vaashista Ganapathi* reached the feet of *Shakti* even while living because of his *Devee* worship.

Some call *Chinna Mastaa Devee* as *Renukaa Devee*. *Parashuraama* (one of the 10 incarnations of Lord Vishnu), son of sage *Jamadagni*, cut his mother's head with his axe, obeying the order of his father. Later, when his father was delighted, *Parashuraama* got his mother back as a boon from his father. Since **she** is the energy of *Parashuraama*, the sixth incarnation of Lord Vishnu, **she** is also called as *Shashti Devee*. Since **she** has the capability of winning everything in this world, **she** is also called as *Ekaveeraa*. The important part of the *mantra* of this *Devee* is *Denu Beeja* (*Hūm*). With this the worshipper gets control over his organs and the mind.

If there are any goddesses in Hinduism who are equally depicted as fierce as Mahakali and as kind-hearted as Mahadev (aka, Lord Shiva), it'd be none other than Goddess Chinnamasta. She is an important figure in tantric traditions and sadhanas because she is the sixth manifestation of Dasa Maha Vidyas. Her role as a goddess is to halt all negativities.

Chinna Masta Devi can be easily identified by her fearsome iconography. The self-decapitated goddess holds her own severed head in one hand, a scimitar in another. Three jets of blood spurt out of her bleeding neck and are drunk by her severed head and two attendants. Chinna Masta is usually depicted standing on a copulating couple.

Chhinnamasta is associated with the concept of self-sacrifice as well as the awakening of the kundalini - spiritual energy.

Once while she bathes within the river Mandakini Mata Parvati is excited while her Dakini and Varnini (Jaya and Vijaya) wanted to eat any eatable. They are very hungry. Mata Parvati promises to give them meals when they reach Kailasa but then merciful Parvati Mata beheads herself with her nails and her 'Raktam' (blood) is consumed via Jaya and Vijaya and they are satiated. Then they return home and Mata Parvati rejoins her head.

Mata Chhinnamasta is reddish like Hibiscus flower and radiant like millions of Suns. She is slim and 16-year-old who is decorated with one lotus. Her one hand has her separated head and other hand has scimitar. One hand of hers has the skull bowl. Sometimes she has swords within her hand. Ma Chhinnamasta is the bestower of salvation.

Chhinnamasta (She whose head is severed) also called as Prachanda Chandika and Jogani Maa (in western states of India). She is one of the Mahavidyas, ten goddesses from the esoteric tradition of Tantra and a ferocious aspect of Mahadevi, the Hindu Mother goddess.

Chhinnamasta is a goddess of contradictions. She symbolises both aspects of Devi; a life-giver and a life-taker. She is considered both a symbol of sexual self-control and an embodiment of sexual energy, depending upon interpretation. She represents death, temporality, and destruction as well as life, immortality, and recreation. The goddess conveys spiritual self-realization and the awakening of the kundalini – spiritual energy. The legends of Chhinnamasta emphasise her self-sacrifice – sometimes coupled with a maternal element – sexual dominance, and self-destructive fury.

Chhinnamasta is worshipped in the Kalikula sect of Shaktism, the Goddess-centric tradition of Hinduism. Though Chhinnamasta enjoys patronage as one of the Mahavidyas, temples devoted to her (found mostly in Nepal and eastern India) and her public worship are rare. However, she is a significant Tantric deity, well known and worshipped among esoteric Tantric practitioners. Chhinnamasta is closely related to Chinnamunda – the severed-headed form of the Tibetan Buddhist goddess Vajrayogini.

Temples for Chinnamasta Devi –

The Chintpurni ("She who fulfills one's wishes"), Himachal Pradesh temple of Chhinnamastika, is one of the Shakti Peethas (considered the holiest goddess temples) and is where the goddess Sati's forehead (mastaka) fell. Here, Chhinnamasta is interpreted as the severed-headed one as well as the fore headed-one. The central icon is a pindi, an abstract form of Devi. While householders worship the goddess as a form of the goddess Durga, ascetic sadhus view her as the Tantric severed-headed goddess.

An important shrine is the Chhinnamasta Temple near Rajrappa in Jharkhand, where a natural rock covered with an ashta dhatu (eight-metal alloy) *kavacha* (cover) is worshipped as the goddess. Though well-established as a centre of Chhinnamasta by the 18th century, the site is a popular place of worship among tribals since ancient times. Kheer and animal sacrifice are offered to the goddess.

A shrine dedicated to Chhinnamasta was built by a Tantric sadhu in the Durga Temple complex, Ramnagar, near Varanasi, Uttar Pradesh, where tantrikas worship her using corpses. Kanpur, Uttar Pradesh, has a shrine of the goddess that is open only three days a year, around Chaitra Navaratri. Her shrines are also situated in the Kamakhya Temple complex, Assam and Basukinath temple complex, Jharkhand along with other Mahavidyas. There is a Chhinnamasta temple at Bishnupur, West Bengal. The goddess Manikeswari, a popular goddess in Odisha, is often identified with Chhinnamasta.

Chhinnamasta's shrines are also found in Nepal's Kathmandu Valley. A shrine in the Changu Narayan Temple holds a 13th-century icon of Chhinnamasta. A chariot festival in the Nepali month of Baishakh is held in honour of the goddess. In the fields near the temple sits a small shrine to Chhinnamasta. A temple of the goddess in Patan built in 1732 contains her images in different postures and enjoys active worship.

Chhinnamasta is typically worshipped at midnight along with the other Mahavidyas at Kali Puja, the festival of Kali. The Bakhrabad area of Cuttack district and the 86 Palli pandal of Kolkata have unique traditions of worshipping Chhinnamasta, instead of Kali, on Kali Puja.

By the grace of this Goddess, the devotee will attain whatever legally pray for including the nature of Shiva. Devi also bestows poetry and erudition.

This Goddess should be meditated upon in the seven petalled lotus at the Ajnaa Chakra between the two eye-brows of the human body. Let us all cry at her feet to be able to meditate her.

*****

Śrī Chinna Masthā Devī Mantras

Śrī Chinna Masthā Vidyā

In Samskrutam, in general *Vidyā* means mantra. Vidya means knowledge. Here is a very powerful *Srī Chinna Masthā Devī Mantra*.

Om Asya Śrī Chinna Mastā Mahā Mantrasya Dakṣinā Mūrti Rishiḥ |
Panktī Chandaḥ | Śrī Chinna Masthā Devatā |
Aim Bījam, Souḥ Śaktiḥ Kleem Kīlakam |
Śrī Chinna Masthā Prasāda Siddhyarte Jape Viniyogaḥ |

Om Aam Katkaaya Hreem Hreem Bat Angushtaabhyaam Namaḥ
Om Eem Sukatkaaya Hreem Hreem Bat Darjaneebhyaam Namaḥ
Om Oom Vajraaya Hreem Hreem Bat Madhymaabhyaam Namaḥ
Om Im Paashaaya Hreem Hreem Bat Anaamikaabhyaam Namaḥ
Om Oum Angushaaya Hreem Hreem Bat Kanishtikaabhyaam Namaḥ
Om Aha Suraksharaha Hreem Hreem Bat Karatala Karabrushtaabhyaam
Namaḥ

Om Aam Katkaaya Hreem Hreem Bat Hrudayāya Namaḥ
Om Eem Sukatkaaya Hreem Hreem Bat Sirase Svāhā
Om Oom Vajraaya Hreem Hreem Bat Shikāyai Vashat
Om Im Paashaaya Hreem Hreem Bat Kavachāya Hūm
Om Oum Angushaaya Hreem Hreem Bat Netratrayāya Vouśaṭ
Om Aha Suraksharaha Hreem Hreem Bat Astrāyaphaṭ
Bhūrbhuvasuvaromiti Digbandhaḥ |

Chinna Masthā Dhyāna *Mantram*

भास्वन्मन्डलमध्यगां निजशिरच्छिन्नं विकीर्णलिकं
स्फारास्यं प्रपिबद्कलात्स्वरुधिरं वामेकरे बिभ्रतीम् ।
य्रा भासक्त रतिस्मरोपरिगतां सख्यौ निजेडाकिनी
वर्णिन्यौ परिदृश्यमोद कलिताम् श्रीचिन्नमस्ताम् भजे ॥

Bhāsvanmanḍalamadhyagām Nijaśiracchinnam Vikīrṇālakam
Sphārāsyam Prapibadkalātsvarudhiram Vāmekare Bibhratīm |
Yā Bhāsakta Ratismaroparigatām Sakhyou Nijedākinī
Varninyou Paridruśyamoda Kalitām Śrī Chinnamastām Bhaje ||

Lam Pritviyātmikāyai Gandham Samarpayāmi |
Ham Ākashātmikāyai Puśpaiḥ Pūjayāmi |
Yam Vaivātmikāyai Dhūpam Āgrāpayāmi |
Ram Vahniyātmikāyai Dhīpam Dharśayāmi |
Vam Amrutātmikāyai Amrutam Mahāneivedhyam Nivedayāmi |
Sam Sarvātmikāyai Sarvopahāra Pūjām Samarpayāmi ||

Chinna Masthā Mūla Mantras

Śrī Chinna Masthā Mahā Mantrāḥ |

ॐ श्रीं ह्रीं क्लीं ऐं वज्र वैरोचनीये हूं हूं फट् (स्वाहा) |

Oṃ Śrīm Hrīm Klīm Aim Vajra Vairocanīye Hūm Hūm Phat (Svāhā) |

Oṃ Aam Katkaaya Hreem Hreem Bat Hrudayāya Namaḥ

Oṃ Eem Sukatkaaya Hreem Hreem Bat Sirase Svāhā

Oṃ Oom Vajraaya Hreem Hreem Bat Shikāyai Vashat

Oṃ Im Paashaaya Hreem Hreem Bat Kavachāya Hūm

Oṃ Oum Angushaaya Hreem Hreem Bat Netratrayāya Vouśaṭ

Oṃ Aha Suraksharaha Hreem Hreem Bat Astrāyaphaṭ

Bhūrbhuvasuvaromiti Digvimogaḥ |

Chinna Masthā Dhyāna Mantram

भास्वन्मन्डलमध्यगां निजशिरच्छिन्नं विकीर्णालकं
स्फारास्यं प्रपिबद्कलात्स्वरुधिरं वामेकरे बिभ्रतीम् ।
य्रा भासक्त रतिस्मरोपरिगतां सख्यौ निजेडाकिनी
वर्णिन्यौ परिदृश्यमोद कलिताम् श्रीचिन्नमस्ताम् भजे ॥

Bhāsvanmanḍalamadhyagām Nijaśiracchinnam Vikīrṇālakam

Sphārāsyam Prapibadkalātsvarudhiram Vāmekare Bibhratīm |

Yā Bhāsakta Ratismaroparigatām Sakhyou Nijedākinī

Varninyou Paridruśyamoda Kalitām Śrī Chinnamastām Bhaje ||

Lam Pritviyātmikāyai Gandham Samarpayāmi |
Ham Ākashātmikāyai Puśpaiḥ Pūjayāmi |
Yam Vaivātmikāyai Dhūpam Āgrāpayāmi |
Ram Vahniyātmikāyai Dhīpam Dharśayāmi |
Vam Amrutātmikāyai Amrutam Mahāneivedhyam Nivedayāmi |
Sam Sarvātmikāyai Sarvopahāra Pūjām Samarpayāmi ||

Some more important mantras on **Sri Chinna Masthā Devi**;

1. *Ekākśara Mantra* (1 Syllable *Mantra*) – हूं॥ *Hūm*॥

2. *Tryakśara Mantra (3 Syllables Mantra)* – ॐ हूं ॐ॥ *Oṃ Hūm Oṃ*॥

3. *Chaturakśara Mantra (4 Syllables Mantra)* –
ॐ हूं स्वाहा॥ *Oṃ Hūm Svāhā*॥

4. *Panchakśara Mantra (5 Syllables Mantra)*
ॐ हूं स्वाहा ॐ॥ *Oṃ Hūm Svāhā Oṃ* ॥

5. *Shadakśara Mantra (6 Syllables Mantra)*
ह्रीं क्लीं श्रीं ऐं हूं फट्॥ *Hrīm Klīm Śrīm Aim Hum Phat*॥

6. *Chhinnamastā Gāyatri Mantras* –
ॐ वैरोचन्ये च विद्महे छिन्नमस्तायै च धीमहि तन्नो देवी प्रचोदयात्॥
Oṃ Vairochanye Ca Vidmahe Chhinnamastayai Ca Dhīmahi Tanno Devī
Prachodayāt॥
ॐ छिन्नमस्तायै च विद्महे जमदग्नियै च धीमहि तन्नो मारी प्रचोदयात्॥
Oṃ Chhinnamastayai Ca Vidmahe Jamadagniyai Ca Dhīmahi Tanno Mārī
Prachodayāt॥

This goddess is not as widely worshiped as other popular goddesses such as Kali and Durga, to name a few. However, if any tantric sadhak is asked about Devi Chinnamasta, we will hear a lot of praise for her being a goddess who is equally difficult to please and violent if not worshiped correctly. It can be noticed that the majority of Hindus are afraid of Chinnamasta Devi and other tantric goddesses. They don't even want any pictures of this goddess in their home. Tantric practitioners, on the other hand, worship her in order to gain siddhis and supernatural powers.

Only the most advanced tantric practitioners have access to the mantra's full potential (Sadhaks). There is no hard rule in normal recitation, but please do not chant the mantra with any unusual desire, as this can easily backfire.

There are numerous other mantras and stotrams dedicated to Devi Chinnamasta. However, these are the most popular and can be chanted by the average person without any extreme tantric rituals.
Prescribed process;

Devotees have to carefully worship *Chinna Mastaa Devee*. The worshipper has to see the brightness when he sees objects. He has to always imagine that the electric energy passes from ether through his head. With this the worshipper can realise *Devee* (*Prachanda Chanda Trishatee*). *Tantra, Hrudaya, Ashtotra* and *Sahasranaama* texts are available on *Chinna Mastaa Devee* (have been provided in different chapters of this book).

Tantric practitioners' worship Chhinnamasta for acquiring siddhis or supernatural powers.

One should be interested in the words of the teacher. The four — self, teacher, *mantra* and the God should be treated as same. One should not reprimand other religions. One should always think of himself as Lord *Shiva*. One should not rebuke ladies.

Shakta ideologies affirm — *Shree Devee* in the form of, *kundalini* energy has to be brought from *Mūlādhāra Chakra* to *Sahasrāra Chakra* through *Brahma Granti, Swādhiṣṭāna Chakra, Maṇipūraka Chakra, Vishnu Granti, Anāhata Chakra, Visuddhi Chakra, Rudra Granti* and *Agjna Chakra*. At the *Sahasrāra Chakra*, in a *Sahasradala Padma* (1000 petalled lotus), the unison of *Shiva-Shakti* has to be inwardly looked (*antharmukha* — inwardly imagined) into and the devotee should be soaked in the rain of nectar (*Amruta Tara*).

Important results of worshipping *Śrī Chinna Masthā*;

With the blessings of this *Devee*, the worshipper gets the state of *Shiva*. He will get children, wealth and grains very early. With the blessings of *Shree Devee,* he becomes wealthy and becomes expert poet. Nothing is impossible to get through the worship of this *Devee*. After getting all the wealth, he gets the knowledge of *Vedantas* and hence the benefit of liberation through desireless meditation.

By worshipping this *Devee*, the devotee can obtain the art of speech, clear knowledge of *shastras*, wealth like Kubera, energy to win anything in this world and at last liberation.

Progress is the only in the life, if the grace of *Devī* is given to a devotee. Motivation comes naturally in the actions that are done. There is nothing he cannot achieve by her grace. She is interested in removing the sins of her devotees and showing him the right way. She lovingly bestows grace on those who are active, solid, and engaged in worship.

Let us all get initiated with these mantras from an appropriate guru and reap all the benefits.

*****

Śrī Chinna Masthā Devī Yantram

Sri Chinna Masthā Devi Yantra

Goddess Sri Chinna Masta Devi is the fierce avatar of Goddess Shakti, the Mother Goddess. She is the destroyer of evil and the supreme protector of Her devotees. Worshipping the Chinna Masta Devi Yantra provides spiritual upliftment, prosperity, victory over enemies and protection.

The perfectly etched Goddess Chinnamasta Devi Yantra in Gold plated copper has an image and Her Mantra etched on its surface.

The ideal place is to hang it on the wall of puja room, living room or office facing North or East direction. The North-East region is ideally suited for Yantras because this direction is where the energies flowing from the North magnetic pole and sun rays of the East meet. Yantras placed here get charged with the divine energies leading to overall benefits.

Chinnamasta Yantra is a powerful and effective one that overcomes the negative planetary implications of Planet Rahu. All doshas related to planet Rahu can be overcome by worshipping this yantra. It symbolises proliferation, be it progeny, wealth or success. The yantra removes problems and protects people from abject poverty, frees limitations of the mind, improves perception, helps to find solutions to problems, grants great focus of mind for meditation etc.

The presiding deity of this yantra is Goddess Chhinnamasta. This Yantra is been used for overcoming the evil impact of Rahu. This Yantra is very powerful and effective. Blesses one with progeny, removes the troubles and protects one from poverty.

Yantra for worshippers of Goddess Chinnamasta, the Shakti or power of Indra;

- Helps to free from the limitations of the mind,
- helps successful meditation
- improves perception
- free from troubles or find solutions to problems.
- Diminishes negative or dark energies.
- Helps to get peace, prosperity, and growth in life.
- It gives energy and Courage to get all work done against all odds and getting success in each work

How to Use this Chinnamasta Yantra?

- The Yantra can be kept in the prayer altar.
- Wash the copper plate with rose water/ pure water on a periodical basis
- Place Sandal and Vermillion paste on all the 4 corners and the centre of the Yantra
- Pray sincerely to the Yantra and offer flowers and incense stick in front of it
- Any type of Prasad can be offered to the Yantra considering as the deity who is going to fill the life with whatever asked for.
- This Yantra can be carried with while travelling in a safe pouch/ wallet, so that it can be ensured that the God's protection follows.

One of most powerful Yantras to achieve protection against all sorts of negative energies and for self-control. Chinna Masthā – The Goddess of decay. It can be noticed certain symbols that are engraved or printed on the Chinna Masthā *Yantra*. It characteristically signifies the divine unification of Shiva (Male energy) and Shakti (Female energy) which is the cause of all creation.

Care should always be taken while installing the *yantra*. Because it is very important to place the Yantra in the right direction. When the device is installed, it energizes the place where it is installed or placed. It can be placed near entrance of the house/ offices/ shops or in reception/ office room. The best place to keep the Chinna Masthā Yantra is inside the house facing the East direction. It is powered by the growing rays of the Sun. With the divine vibrations of the Eastern corner, this Chinna Masthā Yantram through its mystical geometry imparts positive transformative energies to the abode.

Prosperity, good health, peace, beauty, influence, protection from all forms of evils, etc., and so on, are the known benefits that the devotees of this *yantra* are granted with. The Chinna Masta Yantra is meant for the enhancement of one's well-being. Whatever one does, that can be done in a much better way with the assistance of the Bhairavi Yantra. It is a very powerful, personalised tool that creates a certain space and an atmosphere so that one's wellbeing is naturally taken care of.

Those who bear Chinna Masthā Yantra and worship it with complete devotion and true belief are bestowed with safety and happiness. Such people are blessed with expressive and persuasive speech. Those with Chinna Masthā Yantra always remain under the protective sight of the deity and have safe journeys. Bearing Chinna Masthā Yantra also fades away all the negative energies, fears, uncertainties, nervousness and malefic spirits. Chinna Masthā takes care of all circumstances which could cause fear, tensions, worries, accidents and disrepute. The methods for the worship of Tripura-Bhairavi have been described in the sacred texts for the attainment of victory over the sensual desires and all-round development.

The *yantras* pertaining to most of the Gods are kept beneath or in front of the deities in temples. One *yantra* is a drawing of lines or circles or angles drawn in a prescribed measurements and ratios. There cannot be any deviation plus or minus. If a *mantra* is wrongly chant, it can result in negative impact or even end up with destruction. In the same manner, if there is an error in drawing of a *yantra*, it may end up in devastation.

In modern days, lot many worship *Śrī Chakra* in their houses. In general, this is very good. But many do it as a pride, some do it as a style and some with ignorance. But the customs are not strictly followed. Resultantly, they suffer for want of peace.

It is not enough if one wants to follow the bigger things. Exact rules prescribed by *Śāstras* have to be clearly understood, absorbed and followed. These are time tested and handed over to us by our ancestors. It is our duty to stringently follow the same and get benefited. Definitely *Śrī Chakra* has been raised upto the sky by the *Śāstras*. But the same *Śāstras* have recommended lots of dos and don'ts, lots of processes. The approach that "I will do the pooja in my way" is not acceptable, the expected fruits will be missed. Sometimes that may result in negative angle.

One *yantra* is not a place of dwelling for the deity; It is the deity her/himself. It is not an alternative to the deity. It is not a representation – it the deity. It is all the more apt in the case of *Śrī Devī*.

The radiations of the Yantra will bring the devotee and the Goddess into direct contact. The energy will soothe the inner peace and will gift with beauty, happiness and prosperity. These power lines attract the amiability of the Goddess opening doors for harmony and success.

This Yantra is a great cosmic conductor of energy, an antenna of Nature, a powerful tool for harmony, prosperity, success, good health, yoga and meditation! Yantras consist of a series of geometric patterns. The eyes and mind concentrate at the center of the yantra to achieve higher levels of consciousness. Yantras are usually made out of copper.

Let us all choose an appropriate guru, get initiated and worship this yantra to exploit maximum benefits.

*****

Śrī Chinna Masthā Dhyānaṃ

Pratyālīḍhapadāṃ Sadaiva Dadhatīṃ Chinnaṃ Śiraḥ Kartrikāṃ
Digvastrāṃ Svakabandhaśoṇitasudhādhārāṃ Pibantīṃ Mudā |
Nāgābaddhaśiromaṇiṃ Trinayanāṃ Hṛdyutpalālaṅkṛtāṃ
Ratyāsaktamanobhavopari Dṛḍhāṃ Vande Japāsannibhām ‖ 1

Dakṣe Cātisitā Vimuktacikurā Kartrīṃ Tathā Kharparam |
Hastābhyāṃ Dadhatī Rajoguṇabhavā Nāmnāpi Sā Varṇinī ‖
Devyāśchinnakabandhataḥ Patadasṛgdhārāṃ Pibantī Mudā |
Nāgābaddhaśiromaṇirmanuvidā Dhyeyā Sadā Sā Suraiḥ ‖ 2

Pratyālīḍhapadā Kabandhavigaladraktaṃ Pibantī Mudā |
Saiṣā Yā Pralaye Samastabhuvanaṃ Bhoktuṃ Kṣamā Tāmasī ‖
Śaktiḥ Sāpi Parātparā Bhagavatī Nāmnā Parā Ḍākinī |
Dhyeyā Dhyānaparaiḥ Sadā Savinayaṃ Bhakteṣṭabhūtipradā ‖ 3

Bhāsvanmaṇḍalamadhyagāṃ Nijaśiraśchinnaṃ Vikīrṇālakam |
Sphārāsyaṃ Prapibadgalātsvarudhiraṃ Vāme Kare Bibhratīṃ ‖
Yābhāsaktaratismaroparigatāṃ Sakhyau Nije Ḍākinī-
Varṇinyau Paridṛśya Modakalitāṃ Śrīchinnamastāṃ Bhaje ‖ 4

Svanābhau Nīrajaṃ Dhyāyāmyardhaṃ Vikasitaṃ Sitam |
Tatpadmakośamadhye Tu Maṇḍalaṃ Caṇḍarociṣaḥ ‖ 5

Japākusumasaṅkāśaṃ Raktabandhūkasannibham |
Rajassatvatamorekhā Yonimaṇḍalamaṇḍitam ‖ 6

Tanmadhye Tāṃ Mahādevīṃ Sūryakoṭisamaprabhām |
Chinnamastāṃ Kare Vāme Dhārayantīṃ Svamastakam ‖ 7

Prasāritamukhīṃ Devīṃ Lelihānāgrajihvikām |
Pibantīṃ Raudhirīṃ Dhārāṃ Nijakaṇṭhavinirgatām ‖ 8

Vikīrṇakeśapāśaṃ Ca Nānāpuṣpasamanvitām |
Dakṣiṇe Ca Kare Kartrīṃ Muṇḍamālāvibhūṣitām ‖ 9

Digambarāṃ Mahāghorāṃ Pratyālīḍhapade Sthitām |
Asthimālādharāṃ Devīṃ Nāgayajñepavītinīm ‖ 10

Ratikāmoparişţhāṃ Ca Sadā Dhyātāṃ Ca Mantribhiḥ |
Sadā Şoḍaśavarşīyāṃ Pīnonnatapayodharām || 11

Viparītaratāsaktau Dhyāyāmi Ratimanmathau |
Śākinīvarṇinīyuktāṃ Vāmadakṣiṇayogataḥ || 12

Devīgalocchaladraktadhārāpānaṃ Prakurvatīm |
Varṇinīṃ Lohitāṃ Saumyāṃ Muktakeśīṃ Digambarām || 13

Kapālakartrikāhastāṃ Vāmadakṣiṇayogataḥ |
Nāgayajñepavītāḍhyāṃ Jvalattejomayīmiva || 14

Pratyālīḍhapadāṃ Vidyāṃ Nānālaṅkārabhūṣitām |
Sadā Dvādaśavarşīyāṃ Asthimālāvibhūṣitām || 15

Ḍākinīṃ Vāmapārśve Tu Kalpasūryānalopamām |
Vidyujjaṭāṃ Trinayanāṃ Dantapaṅktibalākinīm || 16

Daṃşţrākarālavadanāṃ Pīnonnatapayodharām |
Mahādevīṃ Mahāghorāṃ Muktakeśīṃ Digambarām || 17

Lelihānamahājihvāṃ Muṇḍamālāvibhūṣitām |
Kapālakartrikāhastāṃ Vāmadakṣiṇayogataḥ || 18

Devīgalocchaladraktadhārāpānaṃ Prakurvatīm |
Karasthitakapālena Bhīṣaṇenātibhīṣaṇām |
Ābhyāṃ Nişevyamāṇāṃ Tāṃ Kalaye Jagadīśvarīm || 19

Iti Chinnamastādhyānam ||

छिन्नमस्ताध्यानम्

प्रत्यालीढपदां सदैव दधतीं छिन्नं शिरः कर्त्रिकां
दिग्वस्त्रां स्वकबन्धशोणितसुधाधारां पिबन्तीं मुदा ।
नागाबद्धशिरोमणिं त्रिनयनां हृद्युत्पलालङ्कृतां
रत्यासक्तमनोभवोपरि दृढां वन्दे जपासन्निभाम् ॥ १

दक्षे चातिसिता विमुक्तचिकुरा कर्त्री तथा खर्परम् ।
हस्ताभ्यां दधती रजोगुणभवा नाम्नापि सा वर्णिनी ॥

देव्याश्छिन्नकबन्धतः पतदसृग्धारां पिबन्ती मुदा ।
नागाबद्धशिरोमणिर्मनुविदा ध्येया सदा सा सुरैः ॥ २

प्रत्यालीढपदा कबन्धविगलद्रक्तं पिबन्ती मुदा ।
सैषा या प्रलये समस्तभुवनं भोक्तुं क्षमा तामसी ॥
शक्तिः सापि परात्परा भगवती नाम्ना परा डाकिनी ।
ध्येया ध्यानपरैः सदा सविनयं भक्तेष्टभूतिप्रदा ॥ ३

भास्वन्मण्डलमध्यगां निजशिरश्छिन्नं विकीर्णालकम् ।
स्फारास्यं प्रपिबद्गलात्स्वरुधिरं वामे करे बिभ्रतीम् ॥
याभासक्तरतिस्मरोपरिगतां सख्यौ निजे डाकिनी-
वर्णिन्यौ परिदृश्य मोदकलितां श्रीछिन्नमस्तां भजे ॥ ४

स्वनाभौ नीरजं ध्यायाम्यर्धं विकसितं सितम् ।
तत्पद्मकोशमध्ये तु मण्डलं चण्डरोचिषः ॥ ५

जपाकुसुमसङ्काशं रक्तबन्धूकसन्निभम् ।
रजस्सत्वतमोरेखा योनिमण्डलमण्डितम् ॥ ६

तन्मध्ये तां महादेवीं सूर्यकोटिसमप्रभाम् ।
छिन्नमस्तां करे वामे धारयन्तीं स्वमस्तकम् ॥ ७

प्रसारितमुखीं देवीं लेलिहानाग्रजिह्विकाम् ।
पिबन्तीं रौधिरीं धारां निजकण्ठविनिर्गताम् ॥ ८

विकीर्णकेशपाशां च नानापुष्पसमन्विताम् ।
दक्षिणे च करे कर्त्रीं मुण्डमालाविभूषिताम् ॥ ९

दिगम्बरां महाघोरां प्रत्यालीढपदे स्थिताम् ।
अस्थिमालाधरां देवीं नागयज्ञेपवीतिनीम् ॥ १०

रतिकामोपरिष्ठां च सदा ध्यातां च मन्त्रिभिः ।
सदा षोडशवर्षीयां पीनोन्नतपयोधराम् ॥ ११

विपरीतरतासक्तौ ध्यायामि रतिमन्मथौ ।
शाकिनीवर्णिनीयुक्तां वामदक्षिणयोगतः ॥ १२

देवीगलोच्छलद्रक्तधारापानं प्रकुर्वतीम् ।
वर्णिनीं लोहितां सौम्यां मुक्तकेशीं दिगम्बराम् ॥ १३

कपालकर्त्रिकाहस्तां वामदक्षिणयोगतः ।
नागयज्ञेपवीताद्यां ज्वलत्तेजोमयीमिव ॥ १४

प्रत्यालीढपदां विद्यां नानालङ्कारभूषिताम् ।
सदा द्वादशवर्षीयां अस्थिमालाविभूषिताम् ॥ १५

डाकिनीं वामपार्श्वे तु कल्पसूर्यानिलोपमाम् ।
विद्युज्जटां त्रिनयनां दन्तपङ्क्तिबलाकिनीम् ॥ १६

दंष्ट्राकरालवदनां पीनोन्नतपयोधराम् ।
महादेवीं महाघोरां मुक्तकेशीं दिगम्बराम् ॥ १७

लेलिहानमहाजिह्वां मुण्डमालाविभूषिताम् ।
कपालकर्त्रिकाहस्तां वामदक्षिणयोगतः ॥ १८

देवीगलोच्छलद्रक्तधारापानं प्रकुर्वतीम् ।
करस्थितकपालेन भीषणेनातिभीषणाम् ।
आभ्यां निषेव्यमाणां तां कलये जगदीश्वरीम् ॥ १९

इति छिन्नमस्ताध्यानम् ॥

*****

Śrī Chinna Masthā Kavacaṃ

Śrīgaṇeśāya Namaḥ | *Devyuvāca |*

Kathitācchinnamastāyā Yā Yā Vidyā Sugopitāḥ |
Tvayā Nāthena Jīveśa Śrutāścādhigatā Mayā ‖ 1

Idānīṃ Śrotumicchāmi Kavacaṃ Sarvasūcitam |
Trailokyavijayaṃ Nāma Kṛpayā Kathyatāṃ Prabho ‖ 2

Bhairava Uvāca |

Śruṇu Vakṣyāmi Deveśi Sarvadevanamaskṛte |
Trailokyavijayaṃ Nāma Kavacaṃ Sarvamohanam ‖ 3

Sarvavidyāmayaṃ Sākṣātsurātsurajayapradam |
Dhāraṇātpaṭhanādīśastrailokyavijayī Vibhuḥ ‖ 4

Brahmā Nārāyaṇo Rudro Dhāraṇātpaṭhanādyataḥ |
Kartā Pātā Ca Saṃhartā Bhuvanānāṃ Sureśvari ‖ 5

Na Deyaṃ Paraśiṣyebhyo'bhaktebhyo'pi Viśeṣataḥ |
Deyaṃ Śiṣyāya Bhaktāya Prāṇebhyo'pyadhikāya Ca ‖ 6

Devyāśca Cchinnamastāyāḥ Kavacasya Ca Bhairavaḥ |
Ṛṣistu Syādvirāṭ Chando Devatā Cchinnamastakā ‖ 7

Trailokyavijaye Muktau Viniyogaḥ Prakīrtitaḥ |
Huṃkāro Me Śiraḥ Pātu Chinnamastā Balapradā ‖ 8

Hrāṃ Hrūṃ Aiṃ Tryakṣarī Pātu Bhālaṃ Vaktraṃ Digambarā |
Śrīṃ Hrīṃ Hrūṃ Aiṃ Dṛśau Pātu Muṇḍaṃ Kartridharāpi Sā ‖ 9

Sā Vidyā Praṇavādyantā Śrutiyugmaṃ Sadā'vatu |
Vajravairocanīye Huṃ Phaṭ Svāhā Ca Dhruvādikā ‖ 10

Ghrāṇaṃ Pātu Cchinnamastā Muṇḍakartrividhāriṇī |
Śrīmāyākūrcavāgbījairvajravairocanīyahrūṃ ‖ 11

Hūṃ Phaṭ Svāhā Mahāvidyā Ṣoḍaśī Brahmarūpiṇī |
Svapārśrve Varṇinī Cāsṛgdhārāṃ Pāyayatī Mudā || 12

Vadanaṃ Sarvadā Pātu Cchinnamastā Svaśaktikā |
Muṇḍakartridharā Raktā Sādhakābhīṣṭadāyinī || 13

Varṇinī Ḍākinīyuktā Sāpi Māmabhito'vatu |
Rāmādyā Pātu Jihvāṃ Ca Lajjādyā Pātu Kaṇṭhakam || 14

Kūrcādyā Hṛdayaṃ Pātu Vāgādyā Stanayugmakam |
Ramayā Puṭitā Vidyā Pārśvau Pātu Sureśrvarī || 15

Māyayā Puṭitā Pātu Nābhideśe Digambarā |
Kūrceṇa Puṭitā Devī Pṛṣṭhadeśe Sadā'vatu || 16

Vāgbījapuṭitā Caiṣā Madhyaṃ Pātu Saśaktikā |
Īśvarī Kūrcavāgbījairvajravairocanīyahrūm || 17

Hūṃphaṭ Svāhā Mahāvidyā Koṭisūryyasamaprabhā |
Chinnamastā Sadā Pāyāduruyugmaṃ Saśaktikā || 18

Hrīṃ Hrūṃ Varṇinī Jānuṃ Śrīṃ Hrīṃ Ca Ḍākinī Padam |
Sarvavidyāsthitā Nityā Sarvāṅgaṃ Me Sadā'vatu || 19

Prācyāṃ Pāyādekaliṅgā Yoginī Pāvake'vatu |
Ḍākinī Dakṣiṇe Pātu Śrīmahābhairavī Ca Mām || 20

Nairṛtyāṃ Satataṃ Pātu Bhairavī Paścime'vatu |
Indrākṣī Pātu Vāyavye'sitāṅgī Pātu Cottare || 21

Saṃhāriṇī Sadā Pātu Śivakoṇe Sakartrikā |
Ityaṣṭaśaktayaḥ Pāntu Digvidikṣu Sakartrikāḥ || 22

Krīṃ Krīṃ Krīṃ Pātu Sā Pūrvaṃ Hrīṃ Hrīṃ Māṃ Pātu Pāvake |
Hrūṃ Hrūṃ Māṃ Dakṣiṇe Pātu Dakṣiṇe Kālikā'vatu || 23

Krīṃ Krīṃ Krīṃ Caiva Nairṛtyāṃ Hrīṃ Hrīṃ Ca Paścime'vatu |
Hrūṃ Hrūṃ Pātu Marutkoṇe Svāhā Pātu Sadottare || 24

Mahākālī Khaḍgahastā Rakṣahkoṇe Sadā'vatu |
Tāro Māyā Vadhūḥ Kūrcaṃ Phaṭ Kāro'yaṃ Mahāmanuḥ ‖ 25

Khaḍgakartridharā Tārā Cordhvadeśaṃ Sadā'vatu |
Hrīṃ Strīṃ Hūṃ Phaṭ Ca Pātāle Māṃ Pātu Caikajaṭā Satī |
Tārā Tu Sahitā Khe'vyānmahānīlasarasvatī ‖ 26

Iti Te Kathitaṃ Devyāḥ Kavacaṃ Mantravigraham |
Yaddhṛtvā Paṭhanānbhīmaḥ Krodhākhyo Bhairavaḥ Smṛtaḥ ‖ 27

Surāsuramunīndrāṇāṃ Kartā Hartā Bhavetsvayam |
Yasyājñayā Madhumatī Yāti Sā Sādhakālayam ‖ 28

Bhūtinyādyāśca Ḍākinyo Yakṣiṇyādyāśca Khecarāḥ |
Ājñāṃ Gṛhṇaṃti Tāstasya Kavacasya Prasādataḥ ‖ 29

Etadevaṃ Paraṃ Brahmakavacaṃ Manmukhoditam |
Devīmabhyarca Gandhādyairmūlenaiva Paṭhetsakṛt ‖ 30

Saṃvatsarakṛtāyāstu Pūjāyāḥ Phalamāpnuyāt |
Bhūrje Vilikhitaṃ Caitadguṭikāṃ Kāñcanasthitām ‖ 31

Dhārayeddakṣiṇe Bāhau Kaṇṭhe Vā Yadi Vānyataḥ |
Sarvaiśvaryayuto Bhūtvā Trailokyaṃ Vaśamānayet ‖ 32

Tasya Gehe Vasellakṣmīrvāṇī Ca Vadanāmbuje |
Brahmāstrādīni Śastrāṇi Tadgātre Yānti Saumyatām ‖ 33

Idaṃ Kavacamajñātvā Yo Bhajecchinnamastakām |
So'pi Śatraprahāreṇa Mṛtyumāpnoti Satvaram ‖ 34

‖ Iti Śrībhairavatantre Bhairavabhairavīsaṃvāde Trailokya Vijayaṃ Nāma
Chinnamastā Kavacaṃ Sampūrṇam ‖

श्रीछिन्नमस्ता कवचम्

श्रीगणेशाय नमः ।   देव्युवाच ।

कथिताच्छिन्नमस्ताया या या विद्या सुगोपिताः ।
त्वया नाथेन जीवेश श्रुताश्चाधिगता मया ॥ १

इदानीं श्रोतुमिच्छामि कवचं सर्वसूचितम् ।
त्रैलोक्यविजयं नाम कृपया कथ्यतां प्रभो ॥ २

भैरव उवाच ।

श्रुणु वक्ष्यामि देवेशि सर्वदेवनमस्कृते ।
त्रैलोक्यविजयं नाम कवचं सर्वमोहनम् ॥ ३

सर्वविद्यामयं साक्षात्सुरात्सुरजयप्रदम् ।
धारणात्पठनादीशस्त्रैलोक्यविजयी विभुः ॥ ४

ब्रह्मा नारायणो रुद्रो धारणात्पठनाद्यतः ।
कर्ता पाता च संहर्ता भुवनानां सुरेश्वरि ॥ ५

न देयं परशिष्येभ्योऽभक्तेभ्योऽपि विशेषतः ।
देयं शिष्याय भक्ताय प्राणेभ्योऽप्यधिकाय च ॥ ६

देव्याश्च छिन्नमस्तायाः कवचस्य च भैरवः ।
ऋषिस्तु स्याद्विराट् छन्दो देवता छिन्नमस्तका ॥ ७

त्रैलोक्यविजये मुक्तौ विनियोगः प्रकीर्तितः ।
हुंकारो मे शिरः पातु छिन्नमस्ता बलप्रदा ॥ ८

हां हूं ऐं त्र्यक्षरी पातु भालं वक्त्रं दिगम्बरा ।
श्रीं ह्रीं हूं ऐं दृशौ पातु मुण्डं कर्त्रिधरापि सा ॥ ९

सा विद्या प्रणवाद्यन्ता श्रुतियुग्मं सदाऽवतु ।
वज्रवैरोचनीये हुं फट् स्वाहा च ध्रुवादिका ॥ १०

घ्राणं पातु च्छिन्नमस्ता मुण्डकर्त्रिविधारिणी ।
श्रीमायाकूर्चवाग्बीजैर्वज्रवैरोचनीयहूं म् ॥ ११

हूं फट् स्वाहा महाविद्या षोडशी ब्रह्मरूपिणी ।
स्वपार्श्वे वर्णिनी चासृग्धारां पाययती मुदा ॥ १२

वदनं सर्वदा पातु च्छिन्नमस्ता स्वशक्तिका ।
मुण्डकर्त्रिधरा रक्ता साधकाभीष्टदायिनी ॥ १३

वर्णिनी डाकिनीयुक्ता सापि मामभितोऽवतु ।
रामाद्या पातु जिह्वां च लज्जाद्या पातु कण्ठकम् ॥ १४

कूर्चाद्या हृदयं पातु वागाद्या स्तनयुग्मकम् ।
रमया पुटिता विद्या पार्श्वौ पातु सुरेश्वरी ॥ १५

मायया पुटिता पातु नाभिदेशे दिगम्बरा ।
कूर्चेण पुटिता देवी पृष्ठदेशे सदाऽवतु ॥ १६

वाग्बीजपुटिता चैषा मध्यं पातु सशक्तिका ।
ईश्वरी कूर्चवाग्बीजैर्वज्रवैरोचनीयहूम् ॥ १७

हूंफट् स्वाहा महाविद्याकोटिसूर्य्यसमप्रभा ।
छिन्नमस्ता सदा पायादुरुयुग्मं सशक्तिका ॥ १८

ह्रीं हूं वर्णिनी जानुं श्रीं ह्रीं च डाकिनी पदम् ।
सर्वविद्यास्थिता नित्या सर्वाङ्गं मे सदाऽवतु ॥ १९

प्राच्यां पायादेकलिङ्गा योगिनी पावकेऽवतु ।
डाकिनी दक्षिणे पातु श्रीमहाभैरवी च माम् ॥ २०

नैरृत्यां सततं पातु भैरवी पश्चिमेऽवतु ।
इन्द्राक्षी पातु वायव्येऽसिताङ्गी पातु चोत्तरे ॥ २१

संहारिणी सदा पातु शिवकोणे सकर्त्रिका ।
इत्यष्टशक्तयः पान्तु दिग्विदिक्षु सकर्त्रिकाः ॥ २२

क्रीं क्रीं क्रीं पातु सा पूर्व ह्रीं ह्रीं मां पातु पावके ।
हूं हूं मां दक्षिणे पातु दक्षिणे कालिकाऽवतु ॥ २३

क्रीं क्रीं क्रीं चैव नैरृत्यां ह्रीं ह्रीं च पश्चिमेऽवतु ।
हूं हूं पातु मरुत्कोणे स्वाहा पातु सदोत्तरे ॥ २४

महाकाली खड्गहस्ता रक्षःकोणे सदाऽवतु ।
तारो माया वधूः कूर्च फट्कारोऽयं महामनुः ॥ २५

खड्गकर्त्रिधरा तारा चोर्ध्वदेशं सदाऽवतु ।
ह्रीं स्त्रीं हूं फट् च पाताले मां पातु चैकजटा सती ।
तारा तु सहिता खेऽव्यान्महानीलसरस्वती ॥ २६

इति ते कथितं देव्याः कवचं मन्त्रविग्रहम् ।
यद्धृत्वा पठनान्भीमः क्रोधाख्यो भैरवः स्मृतः ॥ २७

सुरासुरमुनीन्द्राणां कर्ता हर्ता भवेत्स्वयम् ।
यस्याज्ञया मधुमती याति सा साधकालयम् ॥ २८

भूतिन्याद्याश्च डाकिन्यो यक्षिण्याद्याश्च खेचराः ।
आज्ञां गृह्णंति तास्तस्य कवचस्य प्रसादतः ॥ २९

एतदेवं परं ब्रह्मकवचं मन्मुखोदितम् ।
देवीमभ्यर्च गन्धाद्यैर्मूलेनैव पठेत्सकृत् ॥ ३०

संवत्सरकृतायास्तु पूजायाः फलमाप्नुयात् ।
भूर्जे विलिखितं चैतद्धु टिकां काञ्चनस्थिताम्
॥ ३१

धारयेद्दक्षिणे बाहौ कण्ठे वा यदि वान्यतः ।
सर्वैश्वर्ययुतो भूत्वा त्रैलोक्यं वशमानयेत् ॥ ३२

तस्य गेहे वसेल्लक्ष्मीर्वाणी च वदनाम्बुजे ।
ब्रह्मास्त्रादीनि शस्त्राणि तद्गात्रे यान्ति सौम्यताम्
॥ ३३

इदं कवचमज्ञात्वा यो भजेच्छिन्नमस्तकाम् ।
सोऽपि शत्रप्रहारेण मृत्युमाप्नोति सत्वरम् ॥ ३४

॥ इति श्रीभैरवतन्त्रे भैरव भैरवी संवादे त्रैलोक्य विजयं नाम छिन्नमस्ता कवचं
सम्पूर्णम् ॥

*****

Śrī Chinna Masthā Stotram

Chinnagrīvā Chinnamastā Chinnamuṇḍadharā'kṣatā |

Kṣodakṣemakarī Svakṣā Kṣoṇīśācchādanakṣamā || 1

Vairocanī Varārohā Balidānapraharṣitā |

Balipūjitapādābjā Vāsudevaprapūjitā || 2

Iti Dvādaśanāmāni Chinnamastāpriyāṇi Yaḥ |

Smaretprātaḥ Samutthāya Tasya Naśyanti Śatravaḥ || 3

Iti Chinna Mastā Dvādaśa Nāma Stotraṃ Sampūrṇam |

Twelve Names of Goddess *Chinnamasta* (From *Chinnamasta* Hridayam)

1. *Chinnagriva* (Whose Neck is Severed),
2. *Chinnamasta* (Whose Head is Severed),
3. *Chinnamundadhara* (One Who Holds a Severed Head),
4. *Akshata* (Who is Whole or Uninjured),
5. *Kshodakshemakari* (Who Is Skillful In Causing Peace),
6. *Svaksha* (Who Has Beautiful Eyes),
7. *Kshonisachchadanakshama* (Who Protects the Kings of the Earth),
8. *Vairochani* (Indra's Wife),
9. *Vararoha* (Fine [Beautiful] Thighed),
10. *Balidanapraharshita* (Who Delights Those Who Perform Sacrificial Offering),
11. *Balipujatapadabja* (Whose Lotus Feet are Honoured with Sacrificial Offerings), and
12. *Vasudevaprapujita* (Who is Worshipped by Vasudeva, i.e., Krsna) |

छिन्नमस्ताद्वादशनामस्तोत्रम्

छिन्नग्रीवा छिन्नमस्ता छिन्नमुण्डधराऽक्षता ।
क्षोदक्षेमकरी स्वक्षा क्षोणीशाच्छादनक्षमा ॥ १

वैरोचनी वरारोहा बलिदानप्रहर्षिता ।
बलिपूजितपादाब्जा वासुदेवप्रपूजिता ॥ २

इति द्वादशनामानि छिन्नमस्ताप्रियाणि यः ।
स्मरेत्प्रातः समुत्थाय तस्य नश्यन्ति शत्रवः ॥ ३

इति छिन्नमस्ताद्वादशनामस्तोत्रं सम्पूर्णम् ।

छिन्नमस्ता
अष्टोत्तर शतनाम
स्तोत्रम्

*****

Śrī Chinna Masthā Hṛdayam

Śrīgaṇeśāya Namaḥ | Śrī Pārvatyuvāca |

Śrutaṃ Pūjādikaṃ Samyagbhavadvaktrābjaniḥsṛtam |
Hṛdayaṃ Chinnamastāyāḥ Śrotumicchāmi Sāmpratam || 1

Oṃ Mahādeva Uvāca |

Nādyāvadhi Mayā Proktaṃ Kasyāpi Prāṇavallabhe |
Yatvayā Paripṛṣṭo'haṃ Vakṣye Prītyai Tava Priye || 2

Oṃ Asya Śrīchinnamastāhṛdayastotramantrasya Bhairava Ṛṣiḥ ,
Samrāṭ Chandaḥ , Chinnamastā Devatā , Hūṃ Bījam ,
Oṃ Śaktiḥ , Hrīṃ Kīlakam , Śatrukṣayakaraṇārthe Pāṭhe Viniyogaḥ ||

Ṛṣyādinyāsaḥ |

Oṃ Bhairavarṣaye Namaḥ Śirasi |
Oṃ Samrāṭchandase Namo Mukhe |
Oṃ Chinnamastādevatāyai Namo Hṛdi |
Oṃ Hūṃ Bījāya Namo Guhye |
Oṃ Oṃ Śaktaye Namaḥ Pādayoḥ |
Oṃ Hrīṃ Kīlakāya Namo Nābhau |
Oṃ Viniyogāya Namaḥ Sarvāṅge |

Karanyāsaḥ |

Oṃ Oṃ Aṅguṣṭhābhyāṃ Namaḥ |
Oṃ Hūṃ Tarjanībhyāṃ Namaḥ |
Oṃ Hrīṃ Madhyamābhyāṃ Namaḥ |
Oṃ Aiṃ Anāmikābhyāṃ Namaḥ |
Oṃ Klīṃ Kaniṣṭhikābhyāṃ Namaḥ |
Oṃ Hūṃ Karatalakaraprṣṭhābhyāṃ Namaḥ |

Hṛdayādiṣaḍaṅganyāsaḥ |

Oṃ Oṃ Hṛdayāya Namaḥ |　　　*Oṃ Hūṃ Śirase Svāhā |*

Oṃ Hrīṃ Śikhāyai Vaṣaṭ |　　　*Oṃ Aiṃ Kavacāya Hum |*

Oṃ Klīṃ Netratrayāya Vauṣaṭ |　　　*Oṃ Hūṃ Astrāya Phaṭ |*

Dhyānam |

*Raktābhāṃ Raktakeśīṃ Karakamalalasatkartrikāṃ Kālakāntiṃ
Vicchinnātmīyamuṇḍāsṛgaruṇabahulodagradhārāṃ Pibantīm |
Vighnābhraughapracaṇḍaśvasanasamanibhāṃ Sevitāṃ Siddhasaṅghaiḥ
Padmākṣīṃ Chinnamastāṃ Chalakaraditijacchedinīṃ Saṃsmarāmi ||*

*Vande'haṃ Chinnamastāṃ Tāṃ Chinnamuṇḍadharāṃ Parām |
Chinnagrīvocchaṭācchannāṃ Kṣaumavastraparicchadām || 2*

*Sarvadā Surasaṅghena Sevitāṅghrisaroruhām |
Seve Sakalasampattyai Chinnamastāṃ Śubhapradām || 3*

*Yajñānāṃ Yogayajñāya Yā Tu Jātā Yuge Yuge |
Dānavāntakarīṃ Devīṃ Chinnamastāṃ Bhajāmi Tām || 4*

*Vairocanīṃ Varārohāṃ Vāmadevavivarddhitām |
Koṭisūryyaprabhāṃ Vande Vidyudvarṇākṣimaṇḍitām || 5*

*Nijakaṇṭhocchaladraktadhārayā Yā Muhurmuhuḥ |
Yoginīstarpayantyugrā Tasyāścaraṇamāśraye || 6*

*Hūmityekākṣaraṃ Mantraṃ Yadīyaṃ Yuktamānasaḥ |
Yo Japettasya Vidveṣī Bhasmatāṃ Yāti Tāṃ Bhaje || 7*

*Hūṃ Svāheti Manuṃ Samyagyaḥ Smaratyartimānnaraḥ |
Chinatti Cchinnamastāyā Tasya Bādhāṃ Namāmi Tām || 8*

*Yasyāḥ Kaṭākṣamātreṇa Krūrabhūtādayo Drutam |
Dūrataḥ Sampalāyante Cchinnamastāṃ Bhajāmi Tām || 9*

Kṣititalaparirakṣākṣāntaroṣā Sudakṣā
Chalayutakhalakakṣācchedane Kṣāntilakṣyā |
Kṣitiditijasupakṣā Kṣoṇipākṣayyaśikṣā
Jayatu Jayatu Cākṣā Cchinnamastāribhakṣā || 10

Kalikaluṣakalānāṃ Karttane Kartrihastā
Surakuvalayakāśā Mandabhānuprakāśā |
Asurakulakalāpatrāsikā'mlānamūrti
Jayatu Jayatu Kālī Cchinnamastā Karālī || 11

Bhuvanabharaṇabhūribhrājamānānubhāvā
Bhavabhavavibhavānāṃ Bhāraṇodbhātabhūtiḥ |
Dvijakulakamalānāṃ Bhāsinī Bhānumūrti
Bhavatu Bhavatu Vāṇī Cchinnamastā Bhavānī || 12

Mama Ripugaṇamāśu Cchettumugraṃ Kṛpāṇaṃ
Sapadi Janani Tīkṣṇaṃ Chinnamuṇḍaṃ Gṛhāṇa |
Bhavatu Tava Yaśo'laṃ Chindhi Śatrūnkhalānme
Mama Ca Paridiśeṣṭaṃ Chinnamaste Kṣamasva || 13

Chinnagrīvā Chinnamastā Chinnamuṇḍadharā'kṣatā |
Kṣodakṣemakarī Svakṣā Kṣoṇīśācchādanakṣamā || 14

Vairocanī Varārohā Balidānapraharṣitā |
Balipūjitapādābjā Vāsudevaprapūjitā || 15

Iti Dvādaśanāmāni Cchinnamastāpriyāṇi Yaḥ |
Smaretprātaḥ Samutthāya Tasya Naśyanti Śatravaḥ || 16

Yāṃ Smṛtvā Santi Sadyaḥ Sakalasuragaṇāḥ Sarvadā Sampadāḍhyāḥ
Śatrūṇāṃ Saṅghamāhatya Viśadavadanāḥ Svasthacittāḥ Śrayanti |
Tasyāḥ Saṅkalpavantaḥ Sarasijacaraṇāṃ Satataṃ Saṃśrayanti Sā''dyā
Śrīśādisevyā Suphalatu Sutaraṃ Chinnamastā Praśastā || 17

Idaṃ Hṛdayamajñātvā Hantumicchati Yo Dviṣam |
Kathaṃ Tasyāciraṃ Śatrurnāśameṣyati Pārvati || 18

Yadīcchennāśanaṃ Śatroḥ Śīghrametatpaṭhennaraḥ |
Chinnamastā Prasannā Hi Dadāti Phalamīpsitam || 19

Śatrupraśamanaṃ Puṇyaṃ Samīpsitaphalapradam |

Āyurārogyadaṃ Caiva Paṭhatāṃ Puṇyasādhanam || 20

|| Iti Śrīnandyāvarte Mahādevapārvatīsaṃvāde

Śrīchinnamastāhṛdayastotraṃ Sampūrṇam ||

श्रीछिन्नमस्ताहृदयम्

श्रीगणेशाय नमः ।   श्रीपार्वत्युवाच ।

श्रुतं पूजादिकं सम्यग्भवद्वक्त्राब्जनिःसृतम् ।
हृदयं छिन्नमस्तायाः श्रोतुमिच्छामि साम्प्रतम् ॥ १

ॐ महादेव उवाच ।

नाद्यावधि मया प्रोक्तं कस्यापि प्राणवल्लभे ।
यत्त्वया परिपृष्टोऽहं वक्ष्ये प्रीत्यै तव प्रिये ॥ २

ऋष्यादिन्यासः ।

ॐ अस्य श्रीछिन्नमस्ताहृदयस्तोत्रमन्त्रस्य भैरव ऋषिः,
सम्राट् छन्दः, छिन्नमस्ता देवता, हूं बीजम्
ॐ शक्तिः, ह्रीं कीलकं, शत्रुक्षयकरणार्थे पाठे विनियोगः ॥

ॐ भैरवऋषये नमः शिरसि ।   ॐ सम्राट्छन्दसे नमो मुखे ।
ॐ छिन्नमस्तादेवतायै नमो हृदि ।   ॐ हूं बीजाय नमो गुह्ये ।
ॐ ॐ शक्तये नमः पादयोः ।   ॐ ह्रीं कीलकाय नमो नाभौ ।
ॐ विनियोगाय नमः सर्वाङ्गे ।

करन्यासः ।

ॐ ॐ अङ्गुष्ठाभ्यां नमः ।   ॐ हूं तर्जनीभ्यां नमः ।
ॐ ह्रीं मध्यमाभ्यां नमः ।   ॐ ऐं अनामिकाभ्यां नमः ।
ॐ क्लीं कनिष्ठिकाभ्यां नमः ।   ॐ हूं करतलकरपृष्ठाभ्यां नमः ।

हृदयादिषडङ्गन्यासः ।

ॐ ॐ हृदयाय नमः ।   ॐ हूं शिरसे स्वाहा ।
ॐ ह्रीं शिखायै वषट् ।   ॐ ऐं कवचाय हुम् ।

ॐ क्लीं नेत्रत्रयाय वौषट् ।   ॐ हूं अस्त्राय फट् ।

ध्यानम् ।

रक्ताभां रक्तकेशीं करकमललसत्कर्त्रिकां कालकान्तिं
विच्छिन्नात्मीयमुण्डासृगरुणबहुलोदग्रधारां पिबन्तीम् ।
विघ्नाभ्रौघप्रचण्डश्वसनसमनिभां सेवितां सिद्धसङ्घैः
पद्माक्षीं छिन्नमस्तां छलकरदितिजच्छेदिनीं संस्मरामि ॥

वन्देऽहं छिन्नमस्तां तां छिन्नमुण्डधरां पराम् ।
छिन्नग्रीवोच्छटाच्छिन्नां क्षौमवस्त्रपरिच्छदाम् ॥ २

सर्वदा सुरसङ्घेन सेविताङ्घ्रिसरोरुहाम् ।
सेवे सकलसम्पत्त्यै छिन्नमस्तां शुभप्रदाम् ॥ ३

यज्ञानां योगयज्ञाय या तु जाता युगे युगे ।
दानवान्तकरीं देवीं छिन्नमस्तां भजामि ताम् ॥ ४

वैरोचनीं वरारोहां वामदेवविवर्द्धिताम् ।
कोटिसूर्य्यप्रभां वन्दे विद्युद्वर्णाक्षिमण्डिताम् ॥ ५

निजकण्ठोच्छलद्रक्तधारया या मुहुर्मुहुः ।
योगिनीस्तर्पयन्त्युग्रा तस्याश्शरणमाश्रये ॥ ६

हूमित्येकाक्षरं मन्त्रं यदीयं युक्तमानसः ।
यो जपेत्तस्य विद्वेषी भस्मतां याति तां भजे ॥ ७

हूं स्वाहेति मनुंसम्यग्यः स्मरत्यर्तिमान्नरः ।
छिनत्ति च्छिन्नमस्ताया तस्य बाधां नमामि ताम् ॥ ८

यस्याः कटाक्षमात्रेण क्रूरभूतादयो द्रुतम् ।
दूतः सम्पलायन्ते च्छिन्नमस्तां भजामि ताम् ॥ ९

क्षितितलपरिरक्षाक्षान्तरोषा सुदक्षा
छलयुतखलकक्षाच्छेदने क्षान्तिलक्ष्या ।
क्षितिदितिजसुपक्षा क्षोणिपाक्षय्यशिक्षा
जयतु जयतु चाक्षा च्छिन्नमस्तारिभिक्षा ॥ १०

कलिकलुषकलानां कर्त्तने कर्त्रिहस्ता
सुरकुवलयकाशा मन्दभानुप्रकाशा ।
असुरकुलकलापत्रासिकाऽम्लानमूर्ति
जयतु जयतु काली च्छिन्नमस्ता कराली ॥ ११

भुवनभरणभूरिभ्राजमानानुभावा
भवभवविभवानां भारणोद्द्रातभूतिः ।
द्विजकुलकमलानां भासिनी भानुमूर्ति
भवतु भवतु वाणी च्छिन्नमस्ता भवानी ॥ १२

मम रिपुगणमाशु च्छेत्तुमुग्रं कृपाणं
सपदि जननि तीक्ष्णं छिन्नमुण्डं गृहाण ।
भवतु तव यशोऽलं छिन्धि शत्रून्खलान्मे
मम च परिदिशेषं छिन्नमस्ते क्षमस्व ॥ १३

छिन्नग्रीवा छिन्नमस्ता छिन्नमुण्डधराऽक्षता ।
क्षोदक्षेमकरी स्वक्षा क्षोणीशाच्छादनक्षमा ॥ १४

वैरोचनी वरारोहा बलिदानप्रहर्षिता ।
बलिपूजितपादाब्जा वासुदेवप्रपूजिता ॥ १५

इति द्वादशनामानि च्छिन्नमस्ताप्रियाणि यः ।
स्मरेत्प्रातः समुत्थाय तस्य नश्यन्ति शत्रवः ॥ १६

यां स्मृत्वा सन्ति सद्यः सकलसुरगणाः सर्वदा सम्पदाढ्याः
शत्रूणां सङ्घमाहत्य विशदवदनाः स्वस्थचित्ताः श्रयन्ति ।
तस्याः सङ्कल्पवन्तः सरसिजचरणां सततं संश्रयन्ति साऽऽढ्या
श्रीशादिसेव्या सुफलतु सुतरं छिन्नमस्ता प्रशस्ता ॥ १७

इदं हृदयमज्ञात्वा हन्तुमिच्छति यो द्विषम् ।
कथं तस्याचिरं शत्रुर्नाशमेष्यति पार्वति ॥ १८

यदीच्छेन्नाशनं शत्रोः शीघ्रमेतत्पठेन्नरः ।
छिन्नमस्ता प्रसन्ना हि ददाति फलमीप्सितम् ॥ १९

शत्रुप्रशमनं पुण्यं समीप्सितफलप्रदम् ।
आयुरारोग्यदं चैव पठतां पुण्यसाधनम् ॥ २०

॥ इति श्रीनन्द्यावर्ते महादेवपार्वतीसंवादे
श्रीछिन्नमस्ताहृदयस्तोत्रं सम्पूर्णम् ॥

*****

Śrī Chinna Masthā Aṣtotra Śata Nāma Stotram

Śrīpārvatyuvāca --

Nāmnāṃ Sahasramaṃ Paramaṃ Chinnamastā-Priyaṃ Śubham |
Kathitaṃ Bhavatā Śambho Sadyaḥ Śatru-Nikṛntanam || 1

Punaḥ Pṛcchāmyahaṃ Deva Kṛpāṃ Kuru Mamopari |
Sahasra-Nāma-Pāṭhe Ca Aśakto Yaḥ Pumān Bhavet || 2

Tena Kiṃ Paṭhyate Nātha Tanme Brūhi Kṛpā-Maya |

Śrī Sadāśiva Uvāca -

Aṣṭottara-Śataṃ Nāmnāṃ Paṭhyate Tena Sarvadā || 3

Sahasra-Nāma-Pāṭhasya Phalaṃ Prāpnoti Niścitam |

Oṃ Asya Śrīchinnamastāṣṭottara-Śata-Nāma-Stotrasya Sadāśiva Ṛṣiḥ
Anuṣṭup Chandaḥ Śrīchinnamastā Devatā
Mama-Sakala-Siddhi-Prāptaye Jape Viniyogaḥ ||

Oṃ Chinnamastā Mahāvidyā Mahābhīmā Mahodarī |
Caṇḍeśvarī Caṇḍa-Mātā Caṇḍa-Muṇḍ-Prabhañjinī || 4

Mahācaṇḍā Caṇḍa-Rūpā Caṇḍikā Caṇḍa-Khaṇḍinī |
Krodhinī Krodha-Jananī Krodha-Rūpā Kuhū Kalā || 5

Kopāturā Kopayutā Jopa-Saṃhāra-Kāriṇī |
Vajra-Vairocanī Vajrā Vajra-Kalpā Ca Ḍākinī || 6

Ḍākinī Karma-Niratā Ḍākinī Karma-Pūjitā |
Ḍākinī Saṅga-Niratā Ḍākinī Prema-Pūritā || 7

Khaṭvāṅga-Dhāriṇī Kharvā Khaḍga-Khappara-Dhāriṇī |
Pretāsanā Preta-Yutā Preta-Saṅga-Vihāriṇī || 8

Chinna-Muṇḍa-Dharā Chinna-Caṇḍa-Vidyā Ca Citriṇī |
Ghora-Rūpā Ghora-Dṛṣṭarghora-Rāvā Ghanovarī || 9

Yoginī Yoga-Niratā Japa-Yajña-Parāyaṇā |
Yoni-Cakra-Mayī Yoniryoni-Cakra-Pravartinī || 10

Yoni-Mudrā-Yoni-Gamyā Yoni-Yantra-Nivāsinī |
Yantra-Rūpā Yantra-Mayī Yantreśī Yantra-Pūjitā || 11

Kīrtyā Karpādanī Kālī Kaṅkālī Kala-Kāriṇī |
Āraktā Rakta-Nayanā Rakta-Pāna-Parāyaṇā || 12

Bhavānī Bhūtidā Bhūtirbhūti-Dātrī Ca Bhairavī |
Bhairavācāra-Niratā Bhūta-Bhairava-Sevitā || 13

Bhīmā Bhīmeśvarī Devī Bhīma-Nāda-Parāyaṇā |
Bhavārādhyā Bhava-Nutā Bhava-Sāgara-Tāriṇī || 14

Bhadra-Kālī Bhadra-Tanurbhadra-Rūpā Ca Bhadrikā |
Bhadra-Rūpā Mahā-Bhadrā Subhadrā Bhadrapālinī || 15

Subhavyā Bhavya-Vadanā Sumukhī Siddha-Sevitā |
Siddhidā Siddhi-Nivahā Siddhāsiddha-Niṣevitā || 16

Śubhadā Śubhafgā Śuddhā Śuddha-Satvā-Śubhāvahā |
Śreṣṭhā Dṛṣṭhi-Mayī Devī Dṛṣṭhi-Saṃhāra-Kāriṇī || 17

Śarvāṇī Sarvagā Sarvā Sarva-Maṅgala-Kāriṇī |
Śivā Śāntā Śānti-Rūpā Mṛḍānī Madānaturā || 18

Iti Te Kathitaṃ Devi Stotraṃ Parama-Durlabhamaṃ |
Guhyād-Guhya-Taraṃ Gopyaṃ Gopaniyaṃ Prayatnataḥ || 19

Kimatra Bahunoktena Tvadagraṃ Prāṇa-Vallabhe |
Māraṇaṃ Mohanaṃ Devi Hyuccāṭanamataḥ Paramam || 20

Stambhanādika-Karmāṇi Ṛddhayaḥ Siddhayo'pi Ca |
Trikāla-Paṭhanādasya Sarve Sidhyantyasaṃśayaḥ || 21

Mahottamaṃ Stotramidaṃ Varānane Mayeritaṃ Nitya Mananya-

Buddhayaḥ |

Paṭhanti Ye Bhakti-Yutā Narottamā Bhavenna Teṣāṃ Ripubhiḥ

Parājayaḥ || 22

|| *Iti Śrī Chinnamastāṣṭottara Śatanāma Stotram* ||

श्रीछिन्नमस्ताष्टोत्तर शत नामस्तोत्रम्

श्रीपार्वत्युवाच --

नाम्नां सहस्रमं परमं छिन्नमस्ताःप्रियं शुभम् ।
कथितं भवता शाम्भो सद्यः शत्रु-निकृन्तनम् ॥ १

पुनः पृच्छाम्यहं देव कृपां कुरु ममोपरि ।
सहस्र-नाम-पाठे च अशक्तो यः पुमान् भवेत् ॥ २

तेन किं पठ्यते नाथ तन्मे ब्रूहि कृपा-मय ।

श्रीसदाशिव उवाच -

अष्टोत्तर-शतं नाम्नां पठ्यते तेन सर्वदा ॥ ३

सहस्र-नाम-पाठस्य फलं प्राप्नोति निश्चितम् ।

ॐ अस्य श्रीछिन्नमस्ताष्टोत्तर-शत-नाम-स्तोत्रस्य सदाशिव ऋषि:
अनुष्टुप् छन्दः श्रीछिन्नमस्ता देवता
मम-सकल-सिद्धि-प्राप्तये जपे विनियोगः ॥

ॐ छिन्नमस्ता महाविद्या महाभीमा महोदरी ।
चण्डेश्वरी चण्ड-माता चण्ड-मुण्ड-प्रभञ्जिनी ॥ ४

महाचण्डा चण्ड-रूपा चण्डिका चण्ड-खण्डिनी ।
क्रोधिनी क्रोध-जननी क्रोध-रूपा कुहू कला ॥ ५

कोपातुरा कोपयुता जोफ-संहार-कारिणी ।
वज्र-वैरोचनी वज्रा वज्र-कल्पा च डाकिनी ॥ ६

डाकिनी कर्म-निरता डाकिनी कर्म-पूजिता ।
डाकिनी सङ्ग-निरता डाकिनी प्रेम-पूरिता ॥ ७

खट्वाङ्ग-धारिणी खर्वा खड्ग-खप्पर-धारिणी ।
प्रेतासना प्रेत-युता प्रेत-सङ्ग-विहारिणी ॥ ८

छिन्न-मुण्ड-धरा छिन्न-चण्ड-विद्या च चित्रिणी ।
घोर-रूपा घोर-दृष्टिर्घोर-रावा घनोदरी ॥ ९

योगिनी योग-निरता जप-यज्ञ-परायणा ।
योनि-चक्र-मयी योनिर्योनि-चक्र-प्रवर्तिनी ॥ १०

योनि-मुद्रा-योनि-गम्या योनि-यन्त्र-निवासिनी ।
यन्त्र-रूपा यन्त्र-मयी यन्त्रेशी यन्त्र-पूजिता ॥ ११

कीर्त्या कर्पादनी काली कङ्काली कल-कारिणी ।
आरक्ता रक्त-नयना रक्त-पान-परायणा ॥ १२

भवानी भूतिदा भूतिर्भूति-दात्री च भैरवी ।
भैरवाचार-निरता भूत-भैरव-सेविता ॥ १३

भीमा भीमेश्वरी देवी भीम-नाद-परायणा ।
भवाराध्या भव-नुता भव-सागर-तारिणी ॥ १४

भद्र-काली भद्र-तनुर्भद्र-रूपा च भद्रिका ।
भद्र-रूपा महा-भद्रा सुभद्रा भद्रपालिनी ॥ १५

सुभव्या भव्य-वदना सुमुखी सिद्ध-सेविता ।
सिद्धिदा सिद्धि-निवहा सिद्धासिद्ध-निषेविता ॥ १६

शुभदा शुभगा शुद्धा शुद्धसत्वा-शुभावहा ।
श्रेष्ठा दृष्टि-मयी देवी दृष्टि-संहार-कारिणी ॥ १७

शर्वाणी सर्वगा सर्वा सर्व-मङ्गल-कारिणी ।
शिवा शान्ता शान्ति-रूपा मृडानी मदानतुरा ॥ १८

इति ते कथितं देवि स्तोत्रं परम-दुर्लभम् ।
गुह्याद्-गुह्य-तरं गोप्यं गोपनियं प्रयत्नतः ॥ १९

किमत्र बहुनोक्तेन त्वदग्रं प्राण-वल्लभे ।
मारणं मोहनं देवि ह्युच्चाटनमतः परमम् ॥ २०

स्तम्भनादिक-कर्माणि ऋद्धयः सिद्धयोऽपि च।
त्रिकाल-पठनादस्य सर्वे सिध्यन्त्यसंशयः ॥ २१

महोत्तमं स्तोत्रमिदं वरानने मयेरितं नित्य मनन्यबुद्धयः।
पठन्ति ये भक्ति-युता नरोत्तमा भवेन्न तेषां रिपुभिः पराजयः ॥ २२

॥ इति श्रीछिन्नमस्ताष्टोत्तरशतनाम स्तोत्रम् ॥

*****

Śrī Chinna Masthā Aṣtotra Śata Nāmāvaliḥ

108 divine names of *Śrī Chinna Masthā Devi*.

श्री छिन्नमस्ताष्टोत्तर शत नामावली

1.	Oṃ Śrī Chinnamastāyai Namaḥ ǀ	ॐ श्री छिन्नमस्तायै नमः ǀ
2.	Oṃ Śrī Mahāvidyāyai Namaḥ ǀ	ॐ श्री महाविद्यायै नमः ǀ
3.	Oṃ Śrī Mahābhīmāyai Namaḥ ǀ	ॐ श्री महाभीमायै नमः ǀ
4.	Oṃ Śrī Mahodaryai Namaḥ ǀ	ॐ श्री महोदर्यै नमः ǀ
5.	Oṃ Śrī Caṇḍeśvaryai Namaḥ ǀ	ॐ श्री चण्डेश्वर्यै नमः ǀ
6.	Oṃ Śrī Caṇḍamātre Namaḥ ǀ	ॐ श्री चण्डमात्रे नमः ǀ
7.	Oṃ Śrī Caṇḍamuṇḍa Prabhañjinyai Namaḥ ǀ	ॐ श्री चण्डमुण्डप्रभञ्जिन्यै नमः ǀ
8.	Oṃ Śrī Mahācaṇḍāyai Namaḥ ǀ	ॐ श्री महाचण्डायै नमः ǀ
9.	Oṃ Śrī Caṇḍarūpāyai Namaḥ ǀ	ॐ श्री चण्डरूपायै नमः ǀ
10	Oṃ Śrī Caṇḍikāyai Namaḥ ǀ	ॐ श्री चण्डिकायै नमः ǀ
11	Oṃ Śrī Caṇḍakhaṇḍinyai Namaḥ	ॐ श्री चण्डखण्डिन्यै नमः ǀ
12	Oṃ Śrī Krodhinyai Namaḥ ǀ	ॐ श्री क्रोधिन्यै नमः ǀ
13	Oṃ Śrī Krodhajananyai Namaḥ ǀ	ॐ श्री क्रोधजनन्यै नमः ǀ
14	Oṃ Śrī Krodharūpāyai Namaḥ ǀ	ॐ श्री क्रोधरूपायै नमः ǀ
15	Oṃ Śrī Kuhave Namaḥ ǀ	ॐ श्री कुहवे नमः ǀ
16	Oṃ Śrī Kalāyai Namaḥ ǀ	ॐ श्री कलायै नमः ǀ
17	Oṃ Śrī Kopāturāyai Namaḥ ǀ	ॐ श्री कोपातुरायै नमः ǀ
18	Oṃ Śrī Kopayutāyai Namaḥ ǀ	ॐ श्री कोपयुतायै नमः ǀ
19	Oṃ Śrī Kopasaṃhārakāriṇyai Namaḥ ǀ	ॐ श्री कोपसंहारकारिण्यै नमः ǀ
20	Oṃ Śrī Vajravairocanyai Namaḥ	ॐ श्री वज्रवैरोचन्यै नमः ǀ
21	Oṃ Śrī Vajrāyai Namaḥ ǀ	ॐ श्री वज्रायै नमः ǀ
22	Oṃ Śrī Vajrakalpāyai Namaḥ ǀ	ॐ श्री वज्रकल्पायै नमः ǀ
23	Oṃ Śrī Ḍākinyai Namaḥ ǀ	ॐ श्री डाकिन्यै नमः ǀ
24	Oṃ Śrī Ḍākinīkarmaniratāyai Namaḥ ǀ	ॐ श्री डाकिनीकर्मनिरतायै नमः ǀ

25	*Oṃ Śrī Ḍākinīkarmapūjitāyai Namaḥ*	ॐ श्री डाकिनीकर्मपूजितायै नमः ।
26	*Oṃ Śrī Ḍākinīsaṅganiratāyai Namaḥ*	ॐ श्री डाकिनीसङ्गनिरतायै नमः ।
27	*Oṃ Śrī Ḍākinīpremapūritāyai Namaḥ*	ॐ श्री डाकिनीप्रेमपूरितायै नमः ।
28	*Oṃ Śrī Khaṭvāṅgadhāriṇyai Namaḥ*	ॐ श्री खट्वाङ्गधारिण्यै नमः ।
29	*Oṃ Śrī Kharvāyai Namaḥ*	ॐ श्री खर्वायै नमः ।
30	*Oṃ Śrī Khaḍgadhāriṇyai Namaḥ*	ॐ श्री खड्गधारिण्यै नमः ।
31	*Oṃ Śrī Khapparadhāriṇyai Namaḥ*	ॐ श्री खप्परधारिण्यै नमः ।
32	*Oṃ Śrī Pretāsanāyai Namaḥ*	ॐ श्री प्रेतासनायै नमः ।
33	*Oṃ Śrī Pretayutāyai Namaḥ*	ॐ श्री प्रेतयुतायै नमः ।
34	*Oṃ Śrī Pretasaṅgavihāriṇyai Namaḥ*	ॐ श्री प्रेतसङ्गविहारिण्यै नमः ।
35	*Oṃ Śrī Chinnamuṇḍadharāyai Namaḥ*	ॐ श्री छिन्नमुण्डधरायै नमः ।
36	*Oṃ Śrī Chinnacaṇḍavidyāyai Namaḥ*	ॐ श्री छिन्नचण्डविद्यायै नमः ।
37	*Oṃ Śrī Citriṇyai Namaḥ*	ॐ श्री चित्रिण्यै नमः ।
38	*Oṃ Śrī Ghorarūpāyai Namaḥ*	ॐ श्री घोररूपायै नमः ।
39	*Oṃ Śrī Ghoradṛṣṭyai Namaḥ*	ॐ श्री घोरदृष्ट्यै नमः ।
40	*Oṃ Śrī Ghorarāvāyai Namaḥ*	ॐ श्री घोररावायै नमः ।
41	*Oṃ Śrī Ghanodaryai Namaḥ*	ॐ श्री घनोदर्यै नमः ।
42	*Oṃ Śrī Yoginyai Namaḥ*	ॐ श्री योगिन्यै नमः ।
43	*Oṃ Śrī Yoganiratāyai Namaḥ*	ॐ श्री योगनिरतायै नमः ।
44	*Oṃ Śrī Japayajñaparāyaṇāyai Namaḥ*	ॐ श्री जपयज्ञपरायणायै नमः ।
45	*Oṃ Śrī Yonicakramayyai Namaḥ*	ॐ श्री योनिचक्रमय्यै नमः ।
46	*Oṃ Śrī Yonaye Namaḥ*	ॐ श्री योनये नमः ।
47	*Oṃ Śrī Yonicakrapravartinyai Namaḥ*	ॐ श्री योनिचक्रप्रवर्तिन्यै नमः ।

48	Oṃ Śrī Yonimudrāyai Namaḥ		ॐ श्री योनिमुद्रायै नमः ।
49	Oṃ Śrī Yonigamyāyai Namaḥ		ॐ श्री योनिगम्यायै नमः ।
50	Oṃ Śrī Yoniyantranivāsinyai Namaḥ		ॐ श्री योनियन्त्रनिवासिन्यै नमः ।
51	Oṃ Śrī Yantrarūpāyai Namaḥ		ॐ श्री यन्त्ररूपायै नमः ।
52	Oṃ Śrī Yantramayyai Namaḥ		ॐ श्री यन्त्रमय्यै नमः ।
53	Oṃ Śrī Yantreśyai Namaḥ		ॐ श्री यन्त्रेश्यै नमः ।
54	Oṃ Śrī Yantrapūjitāyai Namaḥ		ॐ श्री यन्त्रपूजितायै नमः ।
55	Oṃ Śrī Kīrtyāyai Namaḥ		ॐ श्री कीर्त्यायै नमः ।
56	Oṃ Śrī Kapardinyai Namaḥ		ॐ श्री कपर्दिन्यै नमः ।
57	Oṃ Śrī Kālyai Namaḥ		ॐ श्री काल्यै नमः ।
58	Oṃ Śrī Kaṅkālyai Namaḥ		ॐ श्री कङ्काल्यै नमः ।
59	Oṃ Śrī Kalakāriṇyai Namaḥ		ॐ श्री कलकारिण्यै नमः ।
60	Oṃ Śrī Āraktāyai Namaḥ		ॐ श्री आरक्तायै नमः ।
61	Oṃ Śrī Raktanayanāyai Namaḥ		ॐ श्री रक्तनयनायै नमः ।
62	Oṃ Śrī Raktapānaparāyaṇāyai Namaḥ		ॐ श्री रक्तपानपरायणायै नमः ।
63	Oṃ Śrī Bhavānyai Namaḥ		ॐ श्री भवान्यै नमः ।
64	Oṃ Śrī Bhūtidāyai Namaḥ		ॐ श्री भूतिदायै नमः ।
65	Oṃ Śrī Bhūtyai Namaḥ		ॐ श्री भूत्यै नमः ।
66	Oṃ Śrī Bhūtidātryai Namaḥ		ॐ श्री भूतिदात्र्यै नमः ।
67	Oṃ Śrī Bhairavyai Namaḥ		ॐ श्री भैरव्यै नमः ।
68	Oṃ Śrī Bhairavācāraniratāyai Namaḥ		ॐ श्री भैरवाचारनिरतायै नमः ।
69	Oṃ Śrī Bhūtasevitāyai Namaḥ		ॐ श्री भूतसेवितायै नमः ।
70	Oṃ Śrī Bhairavasevitāyai Namaḥ	ॐ श्री भैरवसेवितायै नमः ।
71	Oṃ Śrī Bhīmāyai Namaḥ		ॐ श्री भीमायै नमः ।
72	Oṃ Śrī Bhīmeśvarīdevyai Namaḥ	ॐ श्री भीमेश्वरीदेव्यै नमः ।
73	Oṃ Śrī Bhīmanādaparāyaṇāyai Namaḥ		ॐ श्री भीमनादपरायणायै नमः ।
74	Oṃ Śrī Bhavārādhyāyai Namaḥ		ॐ श्री भवाराध्यायै नमः ।

75.	Oṃ Śrī Bhavanutāyai Namaḥ		ॐ श्री भवनुतायै नमः ।
76.	Oṃ Śrī Bhavasāgaratāriṇyai Namaḥ		ॐ श्री भवसागरतारिण्यै नमः ।
77.	Oṃ Śrī Bhadrakālyai Namaḥ		ॐ श्री भद्रकाल्यै नमः ।
78.	Oṃ Śrī Bhadratanave Namaḥ		ॐ श्री भद्रतनवे नमः ।
79.	Oṃ Śrī Bhadrarūpāyai Namaḥ		ॐ श्री भद्ररूपायै नमः ।
80.	Oṃ Śrī Bhadrikābhadrarūpāyai Namaḥ		ॐ श्री भद्रिकाभद्ररूपायै नमः ।
81.	Oṃ Śrī Mahābhadrāyai Namaḥ		ॐ श्री महाभद्रायै नमः ।
82.	Oṃ Śrī Subhadrāyai Namaḥ		ॐ श्री सुभद्रायै नमः ।
83.	Oṃ Śrī Bhadrapālinyai Namaḥ		ॐ श्री भद्रपालिन्यै नमः ।
84.	Oṃ Śrī Subhavyāyai Namaḥ		ॐ श्री सुभव्यायै नमः ।
85.	Oṃ Śrī Bhavyavadanāyai Namaḥ	ॐ श्री भव्यवदनायै नमः ।
86.	Oṃ Śrī Sumukhyai Namaḥ		ॐ श्री सुमुख्यै नमः ।
87.	Oṃ Śrī Siddhasevitāyai Namaḥ		ॐ श्री सिद्धसेविताये नमः ।
88.	Oṃ Śrī Siddhidāyai Namaḥ		ॐ श्री सिद्धिदायै नमः ।
89.	Oṃ Śrī Siddhinivahāyai Namaḥ		ॐ श्री सिद्धिनिवहायै नमः ।
90.	Oṃ Śrī Siddhaniṣevitāyai Namaḥ	ॐ श्री सिद्धनिषेविताये नमः ।
91.	Oṃ Śrī Asiddhaniṣevitāyai Namaḥ		ॐ श्री असिद्धनिषेविताये नमः ।
92.	Oṃ Śrī Śubhadāyai Namaḥ		ॐ श्री शुभदायै नमः ।
93.	Oṃ Śrī Śubhagāyai Namaḥ		ॐ श्री शुभगायै नमः ।
94.	Oṃ Śrī Śuddhāyai Namaḥ		ॐ श्री शुद्धायै नमः ।
95.	Oṃ Śrī Śuddhasattvāyai Namaḥ		ॐ श्री शुद्धसत्त्वायै नमः ।
96.	Oṃ Śrī Śubhāvahāyai Namaḥ		ॐ श्री शुभावहायै नमः ।
97.	Oṃ Śrī Śreṣṭhāyai Namaḥ		ॐ श्री श्रेष्ठायै नमः ।
98.	Oṃ Śrī Dṛṣṭimayīdevyai Namaḥ		ॐ श्री दृष्टिमयीदेव्यै नमः ।
99.	Oṃ Śrī Dṛṣṭisaṃhārakāriṇyai Namaḥ	ॐ श्री दृष्टिसंहारकारिण्यै नमः ।
100.	Oṃ Śrī Sarvāṇyai Namaḥ		ॐ श्री शर्वाण्यै नमः ।
101.	Oṃ Śrī Sarvagāyai Namaḥ		ॐ श्री सर्वगायै नमः ।

102.	Oṃ Śrī Sarvāyai Namaḥ		ॐ श्री सर्वायै नमः ।
103.	Oṃ Śrī Sarvamaṅgalakāriṇyai Namaḥ		ॐ श्री सर्वमङ्गलकारिण्यै नमः ।
104.	Oṃ Śrī Śivāyai Namaḥ		ॐ श्री शिवायै नमः ।
105.	Oṃ Śrī Śāntāyai Namaḥ		ॐ श्री शान्तायै नमः ।
106.	Oṃ Śrī Śāntirūpāyai Namaḥ		ॐ श्री शान्तिरूपायै नमः ।
107.	Oṃ Śrī Mṛḍānyai Namaḥ		ॐ श्री मृडान्यै नमः ।
108.	Oṃ Śrī Madanāturāyai Namaḥ		ॐ श्री मदनातुरायै नमः ।

Iti Śrī Chinnamastā Aṣṭottara Śata Nāmāvaliḥ Sampūrṇā ‖

‖ इति श्रीच्छिन्न मस्ताष्टोत्तरशत नामावलिः सम्पूर्णम् ‖

*****

Śrī Chinna Masthā Sahasranāma Stotram

Śrī Gaṇeśāya Namaḥ |　　　　Śrī Devyuvāca |

Devadeva Mahādeva Sarvaśāstravidāṃvara |
Kṛpāṃ Kuru Jagannātha Kathayasva Mama Prabho || 1

Pracaṇḍacaṇḍikā Devī Sarvalokahitaiṣiṇī |
Tasyāśca Kathitaṃ Sarvaṃ Stavaṃ Ca Kavacādikam || 2

Idānīṃ Chinnamastāyā Nāmnāṃ Sāhasrakaṃ Śubham |
Tvaṃ Prakāśaya Me Deva Kṛpayā Bhaktavatsala || 3

Śrī Śiva Uvāca |

Śṛnu Devi Pravakṣyāmi Cchinnāyāḥ Sumanoharam |
Gopanīyaṃ Prayatnena Yadīcchedātmano Hitam || 4

Na Vaktavyaṃ Ca Kutrāpi Prāṇaiḥ Kaṇṭhagatairapi |
Tacchṛnuṣva Maheśāni Sarvaṃ Tatkathayāmi Te || 5

Vinā Pūjāṃ Vinā Dhyānaṃ Vinā Jāpyena Siddhyati |
Vinā Dhyānaṃ Tathā Devi Vinā Bhūtādiśodhanam || 6

Paṭhanādeva Siddhiḥ Syātsatyaṃ Satyaṃ Varānane |
Purā Kailāsaśikhare Sarvadevasabhālaye || 7

Paripapraccha Kathitaṃ Tathā Śṛnu Varānane |

Atha Sahasranāma Stotram

Oṃ Asya Śrīpracaṇḍacaṇḍikāsahasranāmastotrasya Bhairava Ṛṣiḥ ,
Samrāṭ Chandaḥ , Pracaṇḍacaṇḍikā Devatā ,
Dharmārtha Kāma Mokṣārthe Pāṭhe Viniyogaḥ || 8

Oṃ Pracaṇḍacaṇḍikā Caṇḍā Caṇḍadaityavināśinī |
Cāmuṇḍā Ca Sacaṇḍā Ca Capalā Cārudehinī || 9

Lalajihvā Caladraktā Cārucandranibhānanā |
Cakorākṣī Caṇḍanādā Cañcalā Ca Manonmadā || 10

Cetanā Citisaṃsthā Ca Citkalā Jñānarūpiṇī |
Mahābhayaṅkarī Devī Varadābhayadhāriṇī || 11

Bhavāḍhyā Bhavarūpā Ca Bhavabandhavimocinī |
Bhavānī Bhuvaneśī Ca Bhavasaṃsāratāriṇī || 12

Bhavābdhirbhavamokṣā Ca Bhavabandhavighātinī |
Bhāgīrathī Bhagasthā Ca Bhāgyabhogapradāyinī || 13

Kamalā Kāmadā Durgā Durgabandhavimocinī |
Durddarśanā Durgarūpā Durjñeyā Durganāśinī || 14

Dīnaduḥkhaharā Nityā Nityaśokavināśinī |
Nityānandamayā Devī Nityaṃ Kalyāṇakāriṇī || 15

Sarvārthasādhanakarī Sarvasiddhisvarūpiṇī |
Sarvakṣobhaṇaśaktiśca Sarvavidrāviṇī Parā || 16

Sarvarañjanaśaktiśca Sarvonmādasvarūpiṇī |
Sarvadā Siddhidātrī Ca Siddhavidyāsvarūpiṇī || 17

Sakalā Niṣkalā Siddhā Kalātītā Kalāmayī |
Kulajñā Kularūpā Ca Cakṣurānandadāyinī || 18

Kulīnā Sāmarūpā Ca Kāmarūpā Manoharā |
Kamalasthā Kañjamukhī Kuñjareśvaragāminī || 19

Kularūpā Koṭarākṣī Kamalaiśvaryadāyinī |
Kuntī Kakudminī Kullā Kurukullā Karālikā || 20

Kāmeśvarī Kāmamātā Kāmatāpavimocinī |
Kāmarūpā Kāmasatvā Kāmakautukakāriṇī || 21

Kāruṇyahṛdayā Krīṃkrīṃmantrarūpā Ca Koṭarā |
Kaumodakī Kumudinī Kaivalyā Kulavāsinī || 22

Keśavī Keśavārādhyā Keśidaityaniṣūdinī |
Kleśahā Kleśarahitā Kleśasaṅghavināśinī || 23

Karālī Ca Karālāsyā Karālāsuranāśinī |

Karālacarmāsidharā Karālakalanāśinī ‖ 24

Kaṅkinī Kaṅkaniratā Kapālavaradhāriṇī |

Khaḍgahastā Trinetrā Ca Khaṇḍamuṇḍāsidhāriṇī ‖ 25

Khalahā Khalahantrī Ca Kṣarantī Khagatā Sadā |

Gaṅgāgautamapūjyā Ca Gaurī Gandharvavāsinī ‖ 26

Gandharvā Gagaṇārādhyā Gaṇā Gandharvasevitā |

Gaṇatkāragaṇā Devī Nirguṇā Ca Guṇātmikā ‖ 27

Guṇatā Guṇadātrī Ca Guṇagauravadāyinī |

Gaṇeśamātā Gambhīrā Gagaṇā Jyotikāriṇī ‖ 28

Gaurāṅgī Ca Gayā Gamyā Gautamasthānavāsinī |

Gadādharapriyā Jñeyā Jñānagamyā Guheśvarī ‖ 29

Gāyatrī Ca Guṇavatī Guṇātītā Guṇeśvarī |

Gaṇeśajananī Devī Gaṇeśavaradāyinī ‖ 30

Gaṇādhyakṣanutā Nityā Gaṇādhyakṣaprapūjitā |

Girīśaramaṇī Devī Girīśaparivanditā ‖ 31

Gatidā Gatihā Gītā Gautamī Gurusevitā |

Gurupūjyā Guruyutā Gurusevanatatparā ‖ 32

Gandhadvārā Ca Gandhāḍhyā Gandhātmā Gandhakāriṇī |

Gīrvāṇapatisampūjyā Gīrvāṇapatituṣṭidā ‖ 33

Gīrvāṇādhiśaramaṇī Gīrvāṇādhiśavanditā |

Gīrvāṇādhiśasaṃsevyā Gīrvāṇādhiśaharṣadā ‖ 34

Gānaśaktirgānagamyā Gānaśaktipradāyinī |
Gānavidyā Gānasiddhā Gānasantuṣṭamānasā ‖ 35

Gānātītā Gānagītā Gānaharṣaprapūritā |
Gandharvapatisaṃhṛṣṭā Gandharvaguṇamaṇḍitā ‖ 36

Gandharvagaṇasaṃsevyā Gandharvagaṇamadhyagā |
Gandharvagaṇakuśalā Gandharvagaṇapūjitā || 37

Gandharvagaṇaniratā Gandharvagaṇabhūṣitā |
Ghargharā Ghorarūpā Ca Ghoraghurghuranādinī || 38

Gharmabindusamudbhūtā Gharmabindusvarūpiṇī |
Ghaṇṭāravā Ghanaravā Ghanarūpā Ghanodarī || 39

Ghorasatvā Ca Ghanadā Ghaṇṭānādavinodanī |
Ghoracāṇḍālinī Ghorā Ghoracaṇḍavināśinī || 40

Ghoradānavadamanī Ghoradānavanāśinī |
Ghorakarmādirahitā Ghorakarmaniṣevitā || 41

Ghoratatvamayī Devī Ghoratatvavimocanī |
Ghorakarmādirahitā Ghorakarmādipūritā || 42

Ghorakarmādiniratā Ghorakarmapravarddhinī |
Ghorabhūtapramathinī Ghoravetālanāśinī || 43

Ghoradāvāgnidamanī Ghoraśatruniṣūdinī |
Ghoramantrayutā Caiva Ghoramantraprapūjitā || 44

Ghoramantramanobhijñā Ghoramantraphalapradā |
Ghoramantranidhiścaiva Ghoramantrakṛtāspadā || 45

Ghoramantreśvarī Devī Ghoramantrārthamānasā |
Ghoramantrārthatatvajñā Ghoramantrārthapāragā || 46

Ghoramantrārthavibhavā Ghoramantrārthabodhinī |
Ghoramantrārthanicayā Ghoramantrārthajanmabhūḥ || 47

Ghoramantrajaparatā Ghoramantrajapodyatā |
Ṅakāravarṇānilayā Ṅakārākṣaramaṇḍitā || 48

Ṅakārāpararūpā Ṅakārākṣararūpiṇī |
Citrarūpā Citranāḍī Cārukeśī Cayaprabhā || 49

Cañcalā Cañcalākārā Cārurūpā Ca Caṇḍikā |

Caturvedamayī Caṇḍā Caṇḍālagaṇamaṇḍitā || 50

Cāṇḍālacchedinī Caṇḍataponirmūlakāriṇī |

Caturbhujā Caṇḍarūpā Caṇḍamuṇḍavināśinī || 51

Candrikā Candrakīrtiśca Candrakāntistathaiva Ca |

Candrāsyā Candrarūpā Ca Candramaulisvarūpiṇī || 52

Candramaulipriyā Candramaulisantuṣṭamānasā |

Cakorabandhuramaṇī Cakorabandhupūjitā || 53

Cakrarūpā Cakramayī Cakrākārasvarūpiṇī |

Cakrapāṇipriyā Cakrapāṇiprītidāyinī || 54

Cakrapāṇirasābhijñā Cakrapāṇivarapradā |

Cakrapāṇivaronmattā Cakrapāṇisvarūpiṇī || 55

Cakrapāṇiśvarī Nityaṃ Cakrapāṇinamaskṛtā |

Cakrapāṇisamudbhūtā Cakrapāṇiguṇāspadā || 56

Candrāvalī Candravatī Candrakoṭisamaprabhā |

Candanārcitapādābjā Candanānvitamastakā || 57

Cārukīrtiścārunetrā Cārucandravibhūṣaṇā |

Cārubhūṣā Cāruveṣā Cāruveṣapradāyinī || 58

Cārubhūṣābhūṣitāṅgī Caturvaktravarapradā |

Caturvaktrasamārādhyā Caturvaktrasamāśritā || 59

Caturvaktracaturvāhā Caturthī Ca Caturdaśī |

Citrā Carmaṇvatī Caitrī Candrabhāgā Ca Campakā || 60

Caturddaśayamākārā Caturdaśayamānugā |

Caturdaśayamaprītā Caturdaśayamapriyā || 61

Chalasthā Cchidrarūpā Ca Cchadmadā Cchadmarājikā |

Chinnamastā Tathā Cchinnā Cchinnamuṇḍavidhāriṇī || 62

Jayadā Jayarūpā Ca Jayantī Jayamohinī |

Jayā Jīvanasaṃsthā Ca Jālandharanivāsinī || 63

Jvālāmukhī Jvāladātrī Jājvalyadahanopamā |

Jagadvandyā Jagatpūjyā Jagattrāṇaparāyaṇā || 64

Jagatī Jagatādhārā Janmamṛtyujarāpahā |

Jananī Janmabhūmiścajanmadā Jayaśālinī || 65

Jvararogaharā Jvālā Jvālāmālāprapūritā |

Jambhārātīśvarī Jambhārātivaibhavakāriṇī || 66

Jambhārātistutā Jambhārātiśatruniṣūdinī |

Jayadurgā Jayārādhyā Jayakālī Jayeśvarī || 67

Jayatārā Jayātītā Jayaśaṅkaravallabhā |

Jayadā Jahnutanayā Jaladhitrāsakāriṇī || 68

Jaladhivyādhidamanī Jaladhijvaranāśinī |

Jaṅgameśī Jāḍyaharā Jāḍyasaṅghanivāriṇī || 69

Jāḍyagrastajanātītā Jāḍyaroganivāriṇī |

Janmadātrī Janmahartrī Jayaghoṣasamanvitā || 70

Japayogasamāyuktā Japayogavinodinī |

Japayogapriyā Jāpyā Japātītā Jayasvanā || 71

Jāyābhāvasthitā Jāyā Jāyābhāvaprapūraṇī |

Japākusumasaṅkāśā Japākusumapūjitā || 72

Japākusumasamprītā Japākusumamaṇḍitā |

Japākusumavadbhāsā Japākusumarūpiṇī || 73

Jamadagnisvarūpā Ca Jānakī Janakātmajā |

Jhañjhāvātapramuktāṅgi Jhorajhaṅkāravāsinī || 74

Jhaṅkārakāriṇī Jhañjhāvātarūpā Ca Jhaṅkarī |

Ñakārāṇusvarūpā Ca Ṭanaṭaṅkāranādinī || 75

Ṭaṅkārī Ṭakuvāṇī Ca Ṭhakārākṣararūpiṇī |
Ḍiṇḍimā Ca Tathā Ḍimbhā Ḍiṇḍuḍiṇḍimanādinī || 76

Ḍhakkāmayī Ḍhilamayī Nṛtyaśabdā Vilāsinī |
Ḍhakkā Ḍhakkeśvarī Ḍhakkāśabdarūpā Tathaiva Ca || 77

Ḍhakkānādapriyā Ḍhakkānādasantuṣṭamānasā |
Ṇaṅkārā Ṇākṣaramayī Ṇākṣarādisvarūpiṇī || 78

Tripurā Tripuramayī Caiva Triśaktistriguṇātmikā |
Tāmasī Ca Trilokeśī Tripurā Ca Trayīśvarī || 79

Trividyā Ca Trirūpā Ca Trinetrā Ca Trirūpiṇī |
Tāriṇī Taralā Tārā Tārakāriprapūjitā || 80

Tārakārisamārādhyā Tārakārivarapradā |
Tārakāriprasūstanvī Taruṇī Taralaprabhā || 81

Trirūpā Ca Tripuragā Triśūlavaradhāriṇī |
Triśūlinī Tantramayī Tantraśāstraviśāradā || 82

Tantrarūpā Tapomūrtistantramantrasvarūpiṇī |
Taḍittaḍillatākārā Tattvajñānapradāyinī || 83

Tattvajñāneśvarī Devī Tattvajñānaprabodhinī |
Trayīmayī Trayīsevyā Tryakṣarī Tryakṣareśvarī || 84

Tāpavidhvaṃsinī Tāpasaṅghanirmūlakāriṇī |
Trāsakartrī Trāsahartrī Trāsadātrī Ca Trāsahā || 85

Tithīśā Tithirūpā Ca Tithisthā Tithipūjitā |
Tilottamā Ca Tiladā Tilapritā Tileśvarī || 86

Triguṇā Triguṇākārā Tripurī Tripurātmikā |
Trikuṭā Trikuṭākārā Trikuṭācalamadhyagā || 87

Trijaṭā Ca Trinetrā Ca Trinetravarasundarī |
Tṛtīyā Ca Trivarṣā Ca Trividhā Trimateśvarī || 88

Trikoṇasthā Trikoṇeśī Trikoṇayantramadhyagā |
Trisandhyā Ca Trisandhyārcyā Tripadā Tripadāspadā || 89

Sthānasthitā Sthalasthā Ca Dhanyasthalanivāsinī |
Thakārākṣararūpā Ca Sthalarūpā Tathaiva Ca || 90

Sthūlahastā Tathā Sthūlā Sthairyarūpaprakāśinī |
Durgā Durgārtihantrī Ca Durgabandhavimocinī || 91

Devī Dānavasaṃhantrī Danujyeṣthaniṣūdinī |
Dārāpatyapradā Nityā Śaṅkarārddhāṅgadhāriṇī || 92

Divyāṅgī Devamātā Ca Devaduṣṭavināśinī |
Dīnaduḥkhaharā Dīnatāpanirmūlakāriṇī || 93

Dīnamātā Dīnasevyā Dīnadambhavināśinī |
Danujadhvaṃsinī Devī Devakī Devavallabhā || 94

Dānavāripriyā Dīrghā Dānavāriprapūjitā |
Dīrghasvarā Dīrghatanurddīrghadurgatināśinī || 95

Dīrghanetrā Dīrghacakṣurddīrghakeśī Digambarā |
Digambarapriyā Dāntā Digambarasvarūpiṇī || 96

Duḥkhahīnā Duḥkhaharā Duḥkhasāgaratāriṇī |
Duḥkhadāridryaśamanī Duḥkhadāridryakāriṇī || 97

Duḥkhadā Dussahā Duṣṭakhaṇḍanaikasvarūpiṇī |
Devavāmā Devasevyā Devaśaktipradāyinī || 98

Dāminī Dāminīprītā Dāminīśatasundarī |
Dāminīśatasaṃsevyā Dāminīdāmabhūṣitā || 99

Devatābhāvasantuṣṭā Devatāśatamadhyagā |
Dayārddarā Ca Dayārūpā Dayādānaparāyaṇā || 100

Dayāśīlā Dayāsārā Dayāsāgarasaṃsthitā |
Daśavidyātmikā Devī Daśavidyāsvarūpiṇī || 101

Dharaṇī Dhanadā Dhātrī Dhanyā Dhanyaparā Śivā |
Dharmarūpā Dhaniṣṭhā Ca Dheyā Ca Dhīragocarā ‖ 102

Dharmarājeśvarī Dharmakarmarūpā Dhaneśvarī |
Dhanurvidyā Dhanurgamyā Dhanurddharavarapradā ‖ 103

Dharmaśīlā Dharmalīlā Dharmakarmavivarjitā |
Dharmadā Dharmaniratā Dharmapākhaṇḍakhaṇḍinī ‖ 104

Dharmeśī Dharmarūpā Ca Dharmarājavarapradā |
Dharmiṇī Dharmagehasthā Dharmādharmasvarūpiṇī ‖ 105

Dhanadā Dhanadaprītā Dhanadhānyasamṛddhidā |
Dhanadhānyasamṛddhisthā Dhanadhānyavināśinī ‖ 106

Dharmaniṣṭhā Dharmadhīrā Dharmamārgaratā Sadā |
Dharmabījakṛtasthānā Dharmabījasurakṣiṇī ‖ 107

Dharmabījeśvarī Dharmabījarūpā Ca Dharmagā |
Dharmabījasamudbhūtā Dharmabījasamāśritā ‖ 108

Dharādharapatiprāṇā Dharādharapatistutā |
Dharādharendratanujā Dharādharendravanditā ‖ 109

Dharādharendragehasthā Dharādharendrapālinī |
Dharādharendrasarvārtināśinī Dharmapālinī ‖ 110

Navīnā Nirmmalā Nityā Nāgarājaprapūjitā |
Nāgeśvarī Nāgamātā Nāgakanyā Ca Nagnikā ‖ 111

Nirlepā Nirvikalpā Ca Nirlomā Nirupadravā |
Nirāhārā Nirākārā Nirañjanasvarūpiṇī ‖ 112

Nāginī Nāgavibhavā Nāgarājaparistutā |
Nāgarājaguṇajñā Ca Nāgarājasukhapradā ‖ 113

Nāgalokagatā Nityaṃ Nāgalokanivāsinī |
Nāgalokeśvarī Nāgabhāginī Nāgapūjitā ‖ 114

Nāgamadhyasthitā Nāgamohasaṃkṣobhadāyinī |
Nṛtyapriyā Nṛtyavatī Nṛtyagītaparāyaṇā || 115

Nṛtyeśvarī Nartakī Ca Nṛtyarūpā Nirāśrayā |
Nārāyaṇī Narendrasthā Naramuṇḍāsthimālinī || 116

Naramāṃsapriyā Nityā Nararaktapriyā Sadā |
Nararājeśvarī Nārīrūpā Nārīsvarūpiṇī || 117

Nārīgaṇārcitā Nārīmadhyagā Nūtanāmbarā |
Narmadā Ca Nadīrūpā Nadīsaṅgamasaṃsthitā || 118

Narmadeśvarasamprītā Narmadeśvararūpiṇī |
Padmāvatī Padmamukhī Padmakiñjalkavāsinī || 119

Paṭṭavastraparīdhānā Padmarāgavibhūṣitā |
Paramā Prītidā Nityaṃ Pretāsananivāsinī || 120

Paripūrṇarasonmattā Premavihvalavallabhā |
Pavitrāsavaniṣpūtā Preyasī Paramātmikā || 121

Priyavratuparā Nityaṃ Paramapremadāyinī |
Puṣpapriyā Padmakośā Padmadharmanivāsinī || 122

Phetkāriṇī Tantrarūpā Pherupheravanādinī |
Vaṃśinī Vaṃśarūpā Ca Bagalā Vāmarūpiṇī || 123

Vāṅmayī Vasudhā Dhṛṣyā Vāgbhavākhyā Varā Narā |
Buddhidā Buddhirūpā Ca Vidyā Vādasvarūpiṇī || 124

Bālā Vṛddhamayīrūpā Vāṇī Vākyanivāsinī |
Varuṇā Vāgvatī Vīrā Vīrabhūṣaṇabhūṣitā || 125

Vīrabhadrārcitapadā Vīrabhadraprasūrapi |
Vedamārgaratā Vedamantrarūpā Vaṣaṭ Priyā || 126

Vīṇāvādyasamāyuktā Vīṇāvādyaparāyaṇā |
Vīṇāravā Tathā Vīṇāśabdarūpā Ca Vaiṣṇavī || 127

Vaiṣṇavācāniratā Vaiṣṇavācāratatparā |
Viṣṇusevyā Viṣṇupatnī Viṣṇurūpā Varānanā || 128

Viśveśvarī Viśvamātā Viśvanirmāṇakāriṇī |
Viśvarūpā Ca Viśveśī Viśvasaṃhārakāriṇī || 129

Bhairavī Bhairavārādhyā Bhūtabhairavasevitā |
Bhairaveśī Tathā Bhīmā Bhairaveśvaratuṣṭidā || 130

Bhairavādhiśaramaṇī Bhairavādhiśapālinī |
Bhīmeśvarī Bhīmamātā Bhīmaśabdaparāyaṇā || 131

Bhīmarūpā Ca Bhīmeśī Bhīmā Bhīmavarapradā |
Bhīmapūjitapādābjā Bhīmabhairavapālinī || 132

Bhīmāsuradhvaṃsakarī Bhīmaduṣṭavināśinī |
Bhuvanā Bhuvanārādhyā Bhavānī Bhūtidā Sadā || 133

Bhayadā Bhayahantrī Ca Abhayā Bhayarūpiṇī |
Bhīmanādā Vihvalā Ca Bhayabhītivināśinī || 134

Mattā Pramattarūpā Ca Madonmattasvarūpiṇī |
Mānyā Manojñā Mānā Ca Maṅgalā Ca Manoharā || 135

Mānanīyā Mahāpūjyā Mahāmahiṣamarddinī |
Mahiṣāsurahantrī Ca Mātaṅgī Mayavāsinī || 136

Mādhvī Madhumayī Mudrā Mudrikā Mantrarūpiṇī |
Mahāviśveśvarī Dūtī Maulicandraprakāśinī || 137

Yaśaḥsvarūpiṇī Devī Yogamārgapradāyinī |
Yoginī Yogagamyā Ca Yāmyeśī Yogarūpiṇī || 138

Yajñāṅgī Ca Yogamayī Japarūpā Japātmikā |
Yugākhyā Ca Yugāntā Ca Yonimaṇḍalavāsinī || 139

Ayonijā Yoganidrā Yogānandapradāyinī |
Ramā Ratipriyā Nityaṃ Ratirāgavivarddhinī || 140

Ramaṇī Rāsasambhūtā Ramyā Rāsapriyā Rasā |
Raṇotkaṇṭhā Raṇasthā Ca Varā Raṅgapradāyinī ‖ 141

Revatī Raṇajaitrī Ca Rasodbhūtā Raṇotsavā |
Latā Lāvaṇyarūpā Ca Lavaṇābdhisvarūpiṇī ‖ 142

Lavaṅgakusumārādhyā Lolajihvā Ca Lelihā |
Vaśinī Vanasaṃsthā Ca Vanapuṣpapriyā Varā ‖ 143

Prāṇeśvarī Buddhirūpā Buddhidātrī Budhātmikā |
Śamanī Śvetavarṇā Ca Śāṅkarī Śivabhāṣiṇī ‖ 144

Śyāmyarūpā Śaktirūpā Śaktibindunivāsinī |
Sarveśvarī Sarvadātrī Sarvamātā Ca Śarvarī ‖ 145

Śāmbhavī Siddhidā Siddhā Suṣumnā Surabhāsinī |
Sahasradalamadhyasthā Sahasradalavarttinī ‖ 146

Harapriyā Haradhyeyā Hūṁkārabījarūpiṇī |
Laṅkeśvarī Ca Taralā Lomamāṃsaprapūjitā ‖ 147

Kṣemyā Kṣemakarī Kṣāmā Kṣīrabindusvarūpiṇī |
Kṣiptacittapradā Nityaṃ Kṣaumavastravilāsinī ‖ 148

Chinnā Ca Cchinnarūpā Ca Kṣudhā Kṣautkārarūpiṇī |
Sarvavarṇamayī Devī Sarvasampatpradāyinī ‖ 149

Sarvasampatpradātrī Ca Sampadāpadvibhūṣitā |
Sattvarūpā Ca Sarvārthā Sarvadevaprapūjitā ‖ 150

Sarveśvarī Sarvamātā Sarvajñā Surasṛtmikā |
Sindhurmandākinī Gaṅgā Nadīsāgararūpiṇī ‖ 151

Sukeśī Muktakeśī Ca Ḍākinī Varavarṇinī |
Jñānadā Jñānagaganā Somamaṇḍalavāsinī ‖ 152

Ākāśanilayā Nityā Paramākāśarūpiṇī |
Annapūrṇā Mahānityā Mahādevarasodbhavā ‖ 153

Maṅgalā Kālikā Caṇḍā Caṇḍanādātibhīṣaṇā |
Caṇḍāsurasya Mathinī Cāmuṇḍā Capalātmikā || 154

Caṇḍī Cāmarakeśī Ca Calatkuṇḍaladhāriṇī |
Muṇḍamālādharā Nityā Khaṇḍamuṇḍavilāsinī || 155

Khaḍgahastā Muṇḍahastā Varahastā Varapradā |
Asicarmadharā Nityā Pāśāṅkuśadharā Parā || 156

Śūlahastā Śivahastā Ghaṇṭānādavilāsinī |
Dhanurbāṇadharā"dityā Nāgahastā Nagātmajā || 157

Mahiṣāsurahantrī Ca Raktabījavināśinī |
Raktarūpā Raktagā Ca Raktahastā Bhayapradā || 158

Asitā Ca Dharmadharā Pāśāṅkuśadharā Parā |
Dhanurbāṇadharā Nityā Dhūmralocananāśinī || 159

Parasthā Devatāmūrtiḥ Śarvāṇī Śāradā Parā |
Nānāvarṇavibhūṣāṅgī Nānārāgasamāpinī || 160

Paśuvastraparīdhānā Puṣpāyudhadharā Parā |
Muktarañjitamālāḍhyā Muktāhāravilāsinī || 161

Svarṇakuṇḍalabhūṣā Ca Svarṇasiṃhāsanasthitā |
Sundarāṅgī Suvarṇābhā Śāmbhavī Śakaṭātmikā || 162

Sarvalokeśavidyā Ca Mohasammohakāriṇī |
Śreyasī Sṛṣṭirūpā Ca Cchinnacchadmamayī Cchalā || 163

Chinnamuṇḍadharā Nityā Nityānandavidhāyinī |
Nandā Pūrṇā Ca Riktā Ca Tithayaḥ Pūrṇaṣoḍaśī || 164

Kuhūḥ Saṅkrāntirūpā Ca Pañcaparvavilāsinī |
Pañcabāṇadharā Nityā Pañcamaprītidā Parā || 165

Pañcapatrābhilāṣā Ca Pañcāmṛtavilāsinī |
Pañcālī Pañcamī Devī Pañcaraktaprasāriṇī || 166

Pañcabāṇadharā Nityā Nityadātrī Dayāparā |
Palalādipriyā Nityā'paśugamyā Pareśitā || 167

Parā Pararahasyā Ca Paramapremavihvalā |
Kulinā Keśimārgasthā Kulamārgaprakāśinī || 168

Kulākulasvarūpā Ca Kulārṇavamayī Kulā |
Rukmā Ca Kālarūpā Ca Kālakampanakāriṇī || 169

Vilāsarūpiṇī Bhadrā Kulākulanamaskṛtā |
Kuberavittadhātrī Ca Kumārajananī Parā || 170

Kumārīrūpasaṃsthā Ca Kumārīpūjanāmbikā |
Kuraṅganayanā Devī Dineśāsyā'parājitā || 171

Kuṇḍalīkadalī Senā Kumārgarahitā Varā |
Anatarūpā'nantasthā Ānandasindhuvāsinī || 172

Ilāsvarūpiṇī Devī lībhedabhayaṅkarī |
Iḍā Ca Piṅgalā Nāḍī Ikārākṣararūpiṇī || 173

Umā Cotpattirūpā Ca Uccabhāvavināśinī |
Ṛgvedā Ca Nirārādhyā Yajurvedaprapūjitā || 174

Sāmavedena Saṅgītā Atharvavedabhāṣiṇī |
Ṛkārarūpiṇī Ṛkṣā Nirakṣarasvarūpiṇī || 175

Ahidurgāsamācārā Ikārārṇasvarūpiṇī |
Oṃkārā Praṇavasthā Ca Oṃkārādisvarūpiṇī || 176

Anulomavilomasthā Thakāravarṇasambhavā |
Pañcāśadvarṇabījāḍhyā Pañcāśanmuṇḍamālikā || 177

Pratyekā Daśasaṃkhyā Ca Ṣoḍaśī Cchinnamastakā |
Ṣaḍaṅgayuvatīpūjyā Ṣaḍaṅgarūpavarjitā || 178

Ṣaḍvaktrasaṃśritā Nityā Viśveśī Khaḍgadālayā |
Mālāmantramayī Mantrajapamātā Madālasā || 179

Sarvaviśveśvarī Śaktiḥ Sarvānandapradāyinī || 180

Iti Śrī Chinnamastāyā Nāma Sahasramuttamam ||

Phala Śrutiḥ

Pūjākrameṇa Kathitaṃ Sādhakānāṃ Sukhāvaham |
Gopanīyaṃ Gopanīyaṃ Gopanīyaṃ Na Saṃśayaḥ || 181

Arddharātre Muktakeśo Bhaktiyukto Bhavennaraḥ |
Japitvā Pūjayitvā Ca Paṭhennāmasahasrakam || 182

Vidyāsiddhirbhavettasya Ṣaṇmāsābhyāsayogataḥ |
Yena Kena Prakāreṇa Devībhaktiparo Bhavet || 183

Akhilānstambhayellokāṃrājño'pi Mohayetsadā |
Ākarṣayeddevaśaktiṃ Mārayeddevi Vidviṣam || 184

Śatravo Dāsatāṃ Yānti Yānti Pāpāni Saṃkṣayam |
Mṛtyuśca Kṣayatāṃ Yāti Paṭhanādbhāṣaṇātpriye || 185

Praśastāyāḥ Prasādena Kiṃ Na Siddhyati Bhūtale |
Idaṃ Rahasyaṃ Paramaṃ Paraṃ Svastyayanaṃ Mahat || 186

Dhṛtvā Bāhau Mahāsiddhiḥ Prāpyate Nātra Saṃśayaḥ |
Anayā Sadṛśī Vidyā Vidyate Na Maheśvari || 187

Vāramekaṃ Tu Yo'dhīte Sarvasiddhīśvaro Bhavet |
Kulavāre Kulāṣṭamyāṃ Kuhūsaṅkrāntiparvasu || 188

Yaścemaṃ Paṭhate Vidyāṃ Tasya Samyakphalaṃ Śṛṇu |
Aṣṭottaraśataṃ Japtvā Paṭhennāmasahasrakam || 189

Bhaktyā Stutvā Mahādevi Sarvapāpātpramucyate |
Sarvapāpairvinirmuktaḥ Sarvasiddhīśvaro Bhavet || 190

Aṣṭamyāṃ Vā Niśīthe Ca Catuṣpathagato Naraḥ |
Māṣabhaktabaliṃ Datvā Paṭhennāmasahasrakam || 191

Sudarśavāmavedyāṃ Tu Māsatrayavidhānataḥ |
Durjayaḥ Kāmarūpaśca Mahābalaparākramaḥ || 192

Kumārīpūjanam Nāma Mantramātraṃ Paṭhennaraḥ |
Etanmantrasya Paṭhanātsarvasiddhīśvaro Bhavet || 193

Iti Te Kathitaṃ Devi Sarvasiddhiparaṃ Naraḥ |
Japtvā Stutvā Mahādevīṃ Sarvapāpaiḥ Pramucyate || 194

Na Prakāśyamidaṃ Devi Sarvadevanamaskṛtam |
Idaṃ Rahasyaṃ Paramaṃ Goptavyaṃ Paśusaṅkaṭe || 195

Iti Sakalavibhūterhetubhūtaṃ Praśastaṃ Paṭhati
Ya Iha Marttyaśchinnamastāstavaṃ Ca |

Dhanada Iva Dhanāḍhyo Mānanīyo Nṛpāṇāṃ Sa Bhavati
Ca Janānāmāśrayaḥ Siddhivettā || 196

|| Iti Śrīviśvasāratantre Śivapārvatīsaṃvāde Śrī Chinnamastā
Sahasranāma Stotraṃ Sampūrṇam ||

****

श्रीछिन्न मस्ता सहस्रनाम स्तोत्रम्

श्री गणेशाय नमः ।   श्री देव्युवाच ।

देवदेव महादेव सर्वशास्त्रविदां वर ।
कृपां कुरु जगन्नाथ कथयस्व मम प्रभो ॥ १

प्रचण्डचण्डिका देवी सर्वलोकहितैषिणी ।
तस्याश्च कथितं सर्वं स्तवं च कवचादिकम् ॥ २

इदानीं छिन्नमस्ताया नाम्नां साहस्रकं शुभम् ।
त्वं प्रकाशय मे देव कृपया भक्तवत्सल ॥ ३

श्रीशिव उवाच ।

शृणु देवि प्रवक्ष्यामि च्छिन्नायाः सुमनोहरम् ।
गोपनीयं प्रयत्नेन यदीच्छेदात्मनो हितम् ॥ ४

न वक्तव्यं च कुत्रापि प्राणैः कण्ठगतैरपि ।
तच्छृणुष्व महेशानि सर्वं तत्कथयामि ते ॥ ५

विना पूजां विना ध्यानं विना जाप्येन सिद्ध्यति ।
विना ध्यानं तथा देवि विना भूतादिशोधनम् ॥ ६

पठनादेव सिद्धिः स्यात्सत्यं सत्यं वरानने ।
पुरा कैलासशिखरे सर्वदेवसभालये ॥ ७

परिपप्रच्छ कथितं तथा शृणु वरानने ।

<h2 style="text-align:center">अथ सहस्रनाम स्तोत्रम्</h2>

ॐ अस्य श्रीप्रचण्डचण्डिकासहस्रनामस्तोत्रस्य भैरव ऋषिः ,
सम्राट् छन्दः , प्रचण्डचण्डिका देवता ,
धर्मार्थ काम मोक्षार्थे पाठे विनियोगः ॥ ८

ॐ प्रचण्डचण्डिका चण्डा चण्डदैत्यविनाशिनी ।
चामुण्डा च सचण्डा च चपला चारुदेहिनी ॥ ९

ललजिह्वा चलद्रक्ता चारुचन्द्रनिभानना ।
चकोराक्षी चण्डनादा चञ्चला च मनोन्मदा ॥ १०

चेतना चितिसंस्था च चित्कला ज्ञानरूपिणी ।
महाभयङ्करी देवी वरदाभयधारिणी ॥ ११

भवाढ्या भवरूपा च भवबन्धविमोचिनी ।
भवानी भुवनेशी च भवसंसारतारिणी ॥ १२

भवाब्धिर्भवमोक्षा च भवबन्धविघातिनी ।
भागीरथी भगस्था च भाग्यभोगप्रदायिनी ॥ १३

कमला कामदा दुर्गा दुर्गबन्धविमोचिनी ।
दुर्दर्शना दुर्रूपा दुर्ज्ञेया दुर्गनाशिनी ॥ १४

दीनदुःखहरा नित्या नित्यशोकविनाशिनी ।
नित्यानन्दमया देवी नित्यं कल्याणकारिणी ॥ १५

सर्वार्थसाधनकरी सर्वसिद्धिस्वरूपिणी ।
सर्वक्षोभणशक्तिश्च सर्वविद्राविणी परा ॥ १६

सर्वरञ्जनशक्तिश्च सर्वोन्मादस्वरूपिणी ।
सर्वदा सिद्धिदात्री च सिद्धविद्यास्वरूपिणी ॥ १७

सकला निष्कला सिद्धा कलातीता कलामयी ।
कुलज्ञा कुलरूपा च चक्षु रानन्ददायिनी ॥ १८

कुलीना सामरूपा च कामरूपा मनोहरा ।
कमलस्था कञ्जमुखी कुञ्जरेश्वरगामिनी ॥ १९

कुलरूपा कोटराक्षी कमलैश्वर्यदायिनी ।
कुन्ती ककुद्मिनी कुल्ला कुरुकुल्ला करालिका ॥ २०

कामेश्वरी काममाता कामतापविमोचिनी ।
कामरूपा कामसत्वा कामकौतुककारिणी ॥ २१

कारुण्यहृदया क्रींक्रींमन्त्ररूपा च कोटरा ।
कौमोदकी कुमुदिनी कैवल्या कुलवासिनी ॥ २२

केशवी केशवाराध्या केशिदैत्यनिषूदिनी ।
क्लेशहा क्लेशरहिता क्लेशसङ्घविनाशिनी ॥ २३

कराली च करालास्या करालासुरनाशिनी ।
करालचर्मासिधरा करालकलनाशिनी ॥ २४

कङ्किनी कङ्कनिरता कपालवरधारिणी ।
खड्गहस्ता त्रिनेत्रा च खण्डमुण्डासिधारिणी ॥ २५

खलहा खलहन्त्री च क्षरन्ती खगता सदा ।
गङ्गागौतमपूज्या च गौरी गन्धर्ववासिनी ॥ २६

गन्धर्वा गगणाराध्या गणा गन्धर्वसेविता ।
गणत्कारगणा देवी निर्गुणा च गुणात्मिका ॥ २७

गुणता गुणदात्री च गुणगौरवदायिनी ।
गणेशमाता गम्भीरा गगणा ज्योतिकारिणी ॥ २८

गौराङ्गी च गया गम्या गौतमस्थानवासिनी ।
गदाधरप्रिया ज्ञेया ज्ञानगम्या गुहेश्वरी ॥ २९

गायत्री च गुणवती गुणातीता गुणेश्वरी ।
गणेशजननी देवी गणेशवरदायिनी ॥ ३०

गणाध्यक्षनुता नित्या गणाध्यक्षप्रपूजिता ।
गिरीशरमणी देवी गिरीशपरिवन्दिता ॥ ३१

गतिदा गतिहा गीता गौतमी गुरुसेविता ।
गुरुपूज्या गुरुयुता गुरुसेवनतत्परा ॥ ३२

गन्धद्वारा च गन्धाढ्या गन्धात्मा गन्धकारिणी ।
गीर्वाणपतिसम्पूज्या गीर्वाणपतितुष्टिदा ॥ ३३

गीर्वाणाधिशरमणी गीर्वाणाधिशवन्दिता ।
गीर्वाणाधिशसंसेव्या गीर्वाणाधिशहर्षदा ॥ ३४

गानशक्तिर्गानगम्या गानशक्तिप्रदायिनी ।
गानविद्या गानसिद्धा गानसन्तुष्टमानसा ॥ ३५

गानातीता गानगीता गानहर्षप्रपूरिता ।
गन्धर्वपतिसंहृष्टा गन्धर्वगुणमण्डिता ॥ ३६

गन्धर्वगणसंसेव्या गन्धर्वगणमध्यगा ।
गन्धर्वगणकुशला गन्धर्वगणपूजिता ॥ ३७

गन्धर्वगणनिरता गन्धर्वगणभूषिता ।
घर्घरा घोररूपा च घोरघुर्घुरनादिनी ॥ ३८

घर्मबिन्दुसमुद्भूता घर्मबिन्दुस्वरूपिणी ।
घण्टारवा घनरवा घनरूपा घनोदरी ॥ ३९

घोरसत्त्वा च घनदा घण्टानादविनोदनी ।
घोरचाण्डालिनी घोरा घोरचण्डविनाशिनी ॥ ४०

घोरदानवदमनी घोरदानवनाशिनी ।
घोरकर्मादिरहिता घोरकर्मनिषेविता ॥ ४१

घोरतत्त्वमयी देवी घोरतत्त्वविमोचनी ।
घोरकर्मादिरहिता घोरकर्मादिपूरिता ॥ ४२

घोरकर्मादिनिरता घोरकर्मप्रवर्द्धिनी ।
घोरभूतप्रमथिनी घोरवेतालनाशिनी ॥ ४३

घोरदावाग्निदमनी घोरशत्रुनिषूदिनी ।
घोरमन्त्रयुता चैव घोरमन्त्रप्रपूजिता ॥ ४४

घोरमन्त्रमनोभिज्ञा घोरमन्त्रफलप्रदा ।
घोरमन्त्रनिधिश्चैव घोरमन्त्रकृतास्पदा ॥ ४५

घोरमन्त्रेश्वरी देवी घोरमन्त्रार्थमानसा ।
घोरमन्त्रार्थतत्त्वज्ञा घोरमन्त्रार्थपारगा ॥ ४६

घोरमन्त्रार्थविभवा घोरमन्त्रार्थबोधिनी ।
घोरमन्त्रार्थनिचया घोरमन्त्रार्थजन्मभूः ॥ ४७

घोरमन्त्रजपरता घोरमन्त्रजपोद्यता ।
ङकारवर्णनिलया ङकाराक्षरमण्डिता ॥ ४८

ङकारापररूपा ङकाराक्षररूपिणी ।
चित्ररूपा चित्रनाडी चारुकेशी चयप्रभा ॥ ४९

चञ्चला चञ्चलाकारा चारुरूपा च चण्डिका ।
चतुर्वेदमयी चण्डा चण्डालगणमण्डिता ॥ ५०

चाण्डालच्छेदिनी चण्डतपोनिर्मूलकारिणी ।
चतुर्भुजा चण्डरूपा चण्डमुण्डविनाशिनी ॥ ५१

चन्द्रिका चन्द्रकीर्तिश्च चन्द्रकान्तिस्तथैव च ।
चन्द्रास्या चन्द्ररूपा च चन्द्रमौलिस्वरूपिणी ॥ ५२

चन्द्रमौलिप्रिया चन्द्रमौलिसन्तुष्टमानसा ।
चकोरबन्धुरमणी चकोरबन्धुपूजिता ॥ ५३

चक्ररूपा चक्रमयी चक्राकारस्वरूपिणी ।
चक्रपाणिप्रिया चक्रपाणिप्रीतिदायिनी ॥ ५४

चक्रपाणिरसाभिज्ञा चक्रपाणिवरप्रदा ।
चक्रपाणिवरोन्मत्ता चक्रपाणिस्वरूपिणी ॥ ५५

चक्रपाणिश्वरी नित्यं चक्रपाणिनमस्कृता ।
चक्रपाणिसमुद्धूता चक्रपाणिगुणास्पदा ॥ ५६

चन्द्रावली चन्द्रवती चन्द्रकोटिसमप्रभा ।
चन्दनार्चितपादाब्जा चन्दनान्वितमस्तका ॥ ५७

चारुकीर्तिश्वारुनेत्रा चारुचन्द्रविभूषणा ।
चारुभूषा चारुवेषा चारुवेषप्रदायिनी ॥ ५८

चारुभूषाभूषिताङ्गी चतुर्वक्त्रवरप्रदा ।
चतुर्वक्त्रसमाराध्या चतुर्वक्त्रसमाश्रिता ॥ ५९

चतुर्वक्त्रचतुर्वाहा चतुर्थी च चतुर्दशी ।
चित्रा चर्मण्वती चैत्री चन्द्रभागा च चम्पका ॥ ६०

चतुर्दशयमाकारा चतुर्दशयमानुगा ।
चतुर्दशयमप्रीता चतुर्दशयमप्रिया ॥ ६१

छलस्था च्छिद्ररूपा च च्छद्मदा च्छद्मराजिका ।
छिन्नमस्ता तथा च्छिन्ना च्छिन्नमुण्डविधारिणी ॥ ६२

जयदा जयरूपा च जयन्ती जयमोहिनी ।
जया जीवनसंस्था च जालन्धरनिवासिनी ॥ ६३

ज्वालामुखी ज्वालदात्री जाज्वल्यदहनोपमा ।
जगद्वन्द्या जगत्पूज्या जगत्राणपरायणा ॥ ६४

जगती जगताधारा जन्ममृत्युजरापहा ।
जननी जन्मभूमिश्वजन्मदा जयशालिनी ॥ ६५

ज्वररोगहरा ज्वाला ज्वालामालाप्रपूरिता ।
जम्भारातीश्वरी जम्भारातिवैभवकारिणी ॥ ६६

जम्भारातिस्तुता जम्भारातिशत्रुनिषूदिनी ।
जयदुर्गा जयाराध्या जयकाली जयेश्वरी ॥ ६७

जयतारा जयातीता जयशङ्करवल्लभा ।
जयदा जह्नुतनया जलधित्रासकारिणी ॥ ६८

जलधिव्याधिदमनी जलधिज्वरनाशिनी ।
जङ्गमेशी जाड्यहरा जाड्यसङ्घनिवारिणी ॥ ६९

जाड्यग्रस्तजनातीता जाड्यरोगनिवारिणी ।
जन्मदात्री जन्महर्त्री जयघोषसमन्विता ॥ ७०

जपयोगसमायुक्ता जपयोगविनोदिनी ।
जपयोगप्रिया जाप्या जपातीता जयस्वना ॥ ७१

जायाभावस्थिता जाया जायाभावप्रपूरणी ।
जपाकुसुमसङ्काशा जपाकुसुमपूजिता ॥ ७२

जपाकुसुमसम्प्रीता जपाकुसुममण्डिता ।
जपाकुसुमवद्धासा जपाकुसुमरूपिणी ॥ ७३

जमदग्निस्वरूपा च जानकी जनकात्मजा ।
झञ्झावातप्रमुक्ताङ्गी झोरझङ्कारवासिनी ॥ ७४

झङ्कारकारिणी झञ्झावातरूपा च झङ्करी ।
अकाराणुस्वरूपा च टनटङ्कारनादिनी ॥ ७५

टङ्कारी टकुवाणी च ठकाराक्षररूपिणी ।
डिण्डिमा च तथा डिम्भा डिण्डुडिण्डिमनादिनी ॥ ७६

ढक्कामयी ढिलमयी नृत्यशब्दा विलासिनी ।
ढक्का ढक्केश्वरी ढक्काशब्दरूपा तथैव च ॥ ७७

ढक्कानादप्रिया ढक्कानादसन्तुष्टमानसा ।
णङ्कारा णाक्षरमयी णाक्षरादिस्वरूपिणी ॥ ७८

त्रिपुरा त्रिपुरमयी चैव त्रिशक्तिस्त्रिगुणात्मिका ।
तामसी च त्रिलोकेशी त्रिपुरा च त्रयीश्वरी ॥ ७९

त्रिविद्या च त्रिरूपा च त्रिनेत्रा च त्रिरूपिणी ।
तारिणी तरला तारा तारकारिप्रपूजिता ॥ ८०

तारकारिसमाराध्या तारकारिवरप्रदा ।
तारकारिप्रसूस्तन्वी तरुणी तरलप्रभा ॥ ८१

त्रिरूपा च त्रिपुरगा त्रिशूलवरधारिणी ।
त्रिशूलिनी तन्त्रमयी तन्त्रशास्त्रविशारदा ॥ ८२

तन्त्ररूपा तपोमूर्तिस्तन्त्रमन्त्रस्वरूपिणी ।
तडित्तडिल्लताकारा तत्त्वज्ञानप्रदायिनी ॥ ८३

तत्त्वज्ञानेश्वरी देवी तत्त्वज्ञानप्रबोधिनी ।
त्रयीमयी त्रयीसेव्या त्र्यक्षरी त्र्यक्षरेश्वरी ॥ ८४

तापविध्वंसिनी तापसङ्घनिर्मूलकारिणी ।
त्रासकर्त्री त्रासहर्त्री त्रासदात्री च त्रासहा ॥ ८५

तिथीशा तिथिरूपा च तिथिस्था तिथिपूजिता ।
तिलोत्तमा च तिलदा तिलप्रिता तिलेश्वरी ॥ ८६

त्रिगुणा त्रिगुणाकारा त्रिपुरी त्रिपुरात्मिका ।
त्रिकुटा त्रिकुटाकारा त्रिकुटाचलमध्यगा ॥ ८७

त्रिजटा च त्रिनेत्रा च त्रिनेत्रवरसुन्दरी ।
तृतीया च त्रिवर्षा च त्रिविधा त्रिमतेश्वरी ॥ ८८

त्रिकोणस्था त्रिकोणेशी त्रिकोणयन्त्रमध्यगा ।
त्रिसन्ध्या च त्रिसन्ध्याच्र्या त्रिपदा त्रिपदास्पदा ॥ ८९

स्थानस्थिता स्थलस्था च धन्यस्थलनिवासिनी ।
थकाराक्षररूपा च स्थलरूपा तथैव च ॥ ९०

स्थूलहस्ता तथा स्थूला स्थैर्यरूपप्रकाशिनी ।
दुर्गा दुर्गार्तिहन्त्री च दुर्गबन्धविमोचिनी ॥ ९१

देवी दानवसंहन्त्री दनुज्येष्ठनिषूदिनी ।
दारापत्यप्रदा नित्या शङ्कराद्धाङ्गधारिणी ॥ ९२

दिव्याङ्गी देवमाता च देवदुष्टविनाशिनी ।
दीनदुःखहरा दीनतापनिर्मूलकारिणी ॥ ९३

दीनमाता दीनसेव्या दीनदम्भविनाशिनी ।
दनुजध्वंसिनी देवी देवकी देववल्लभा ॥ ९४

दानवारिप्रिया दीर्घा दानवारिप्रपूजिता ।
दीर्घस्वरा दीर्घतनुर्दीर्घदुर्गतिनाशिनी ॥ ९५

दीर्घनेत्रा दीर्घचक्षु र्दीर्घकेशी दिगम्बरा ।
दिगम्बरप्रिया दान्ता दिगम्बरस्वरूपिणी ॥ ९६

दुःखहीना दुःखहरा दुःखसागरतारिणी ।
दुःखदारिद्र्यशमनी दुःखदारिद्र्यकारिणी ॥ ९७

दुःखदा दुस्सहा दुष्टखण्डनैकस्वरूपिणी ।
देववामा देवसेव्या देवशक्तिप्रदायिनी ॥ ९८

दामिनी दामिनीप्रीता दामिनीशतसुन्दरी ।
दामिनीशतसंसेव्या दामिनीदामभूषिता ॥ ९९

देवताभावसन्तुष्टा देवताशतमध्यगा ।
दयार्द्रा च दयारूपा दयादानपरायणा ॥ १००

दयाशीला दयासारा दयासागरसंस्थिता ।
दशविद्यात्मिका देवी दशविद्यास्वरूपिणी ॥ १०१

धरणी धनदा धात्री धन्या धन्यपरा शिवा ।
धर्मरूपा धनिष्ठा च धेया च धीरगोचरा ॥ १०२

धर्मराजेश्वरी धर्मकर्मरूपा धनेश्वरी ।
धनुर्विद्या धनुर्गम्या धनुर्द्धरवरप्रदा ॥ १०३

धर्मशीला धर्मलीला धर्मकर्मविवर्जिता ।
धर्मदा धर्मनिरता धर्मपाखण्डखण्डिनी ॥ १०४

धर्मेशी धर्मरूपा च धर्मराजवरप्रदा ।
धर्मिणी धर्मगेहस्था धर्माधर्मस्वरूपिणी ॥ १०५

धनदा धनदप्रीता धनधान्यसमृद्धिदा ।
धनधान्यसमृद्धिस्था धनधान्यविनाशिनी ॥ १०६

धर्मनिष्ठा धर्मधीरा धर्ममार्गरता सदा ।
धर्मबीजकृतस्थाना धर्मबीजसुरक्षिणी ॥ १०७

धर्मबीजेश्वरी धर्मबीजरूपा च धर्मगा ।
धर्मबीजसमुद्भूता धर्मबीजसमाश्रिता ॥ १०८

धराधरपतिप्राणा धराधरपतिस्तुता ।
धराधरेन्द्रतनुजा धराधरेन्द्रवन्दिता ॥ १०९

धराधरेन्द्रगेहस्था धराधरेन्द्रपालिनी ।
धराधरेन्द्रसर्वार्तिनाशिनी धर्मपालिनी ॥ ११०

नवीना निर्म्मला नित्या नागराजप्रपूजिता ।
नागेश्वरी नागमाता नागकन्या च नग्निका ॥ १११

निर्लेपा निर्विकल्पा च निर्लोमा निरुपद्रवा ।
निराहारा निराकारा निरञ्जनस्वरूपिणी ॥ ११२

नागिनी नागविभवा नागराजपरिस्तुता ।
नागराजगुणज्ञा च नागराजसुखप्रदा ॥ ११३

नागलोकगता नित्यं नागलोकनिवासिनी ।
नागलोकेश्वरी नागभागिनी नागपूजिता ॥ ११४

नागमध्यस्थिता नागमोहसंक्षोभदायिनी ।
नृत्यप्रिया नृत्यवती नृत्यगीतपरायणा ॥ ११५

नृत्येश्वरी नर्तकी च नृत्यरूपा निराश्रया ।
नारायणी नरेन्द्रस्था नरमुण्डास्थिमालिनी ॥ ११६

नरमांसप्रिया नित्या नररक्तप्रिया सदा ।
नरराजेश्वरी नारीरूपा नारीस्वरूपिणी ॥ ११७

नारीगणार्चिता नारीमध्यगा नूतनाम्बरा ।
नर्मदा च नदीरूपा नदीसङ्गमसंस्थिता ॥ ११८

नर्मदेश्वरसम्प्रीता नर्मदेश्वररूपिणी ।
पद्मावती पद्ममुखी पद्मकिञ्जल्कवासिनी ॥ ११९

पट्टवस्त्रपरीधाना पद्मरागविभूषिता ।
परमा प्रीतिदा नित्यं प्रेतासननिवासिनी ॥ १२०

परिपूर्णरसोन्मत्ता प्रेमविह्वलवल्लभा ।
पवित्रासवनिष्पूता प्रेयसी परमात्मिका ॥ १२१

प्रियव्रतपरा नित्यं परमप्रेमदायिनी ।
पुष्पप्रिया पद्मकोशा पद्मधर्मनिवासिनी ॥ १२२

फेत्कारिणी तन्त्ररूपा फेरुफेरवनादिनी ।
वंशिनी वंशरूपा च बगला वामरूपिणी ॥ १२३

वाङ्मयी वसुधा धृष्या वाग्भवाख्या वरा नरा ।
बुद्धिदा बुद्धिरूपा च विद्या वादस्वरूपिणी ॥ १२४

बाला वृद्धमयीरूपा वाणी वाक्यनिवासिनी ।
वरुणा वाग्वती वीरा वीरभूषणभूषिता ॥ १२५

वीरभद्रार्चितपदा वीरभद्रप्रसूरपि ।
वेदमार्गरता वेदमन्त्ररूपा वषट् प्रिया ॥ १२६

वीणावाद्यसमायुक्ता वीणावाद्यपरायणा ।
वीणारवा तथा वीणाशब्दरूपा च वैष्णवी ॥ १२७

वैष्णवाचारनिरता वैष्णवाचारतत्परा ।
विष्णुसेव्या विष्णुपत्नी विष्णुरूपा वरानना ॥ १२८

विश्वेश्वरी विश्वमाता विश्वनिर्माणकारिणी ।
विश्वरूपा च विश्वेशी विश्वसंहारकारिणी ॥ १२९

भैरवी भैरवाराध्या भूतभैरवसेविता ।
भैरवेशी तथा भीमा भैरवेश्वरतुष्टिदा ॥ १३०

भैरवाधिशरमणी भैरवाधिशपालिनी ।
भीमेश्वरी भीममाता भीमशब्दपरायणा ॥ १३१

भीमरूपा च भीमेशी भीमा भीमवरप्रदा ।
भीमपूजितपादाब्जा भीमभैरवपालिनी ॥ १३२

भीमासुरध्वंसकरी भीमदुष्टविनाशिनी ।
भुवना भुवनाराध्या भवानी भूतिदा सदा ॥ १३३

भयदा भयहन्त्री च अभया भयरूपिणी ।
भीमनादा विह्वला च भयभीतिविनाशिनी ॥ १३४

मत्ता प्रमत्तरूपा च मदोन्मत्तस्वरूपिणी ।
मान्या मनोज्ञा माना च मङ्गला च मनोहरा ॥ १३५

माननीया महापूज्या महामहिषमर्दिनी ।
महिषासुरहन्त्री च मातङ्गी मयवासिनी ॥ १३६

माध्वी मधुमयी मुद्रा मुद्रिका मन्त्ररूपिणी ।
महाविश्वेश्वरी दूती मौलिचन्द्रप्रकाशिनी ॥ १३७

यशःस्वरूपिणी देवी योगमार्गप्रदायिनी ।
योगिनी योगगम्या च याम्येशी योगरूपिणी ॥ १३८

यज्ञाङ्गी च योगमयी जपरूपा जपात्मिका ।
युगाख्या च युगान्ता च योनिमण्डलवासिनी ॥ १३९

अयोनिजा योगनिद्रा योगानन्दप्रदायिनी ।
रमा रतिप्रिया नित्यं रतिरागविवर्द्धिनी ॥ १४०

रमणी राससम्भूता रम्या रासप्रिया रसा ।
रणोत्कण्ठा रणस्था च वरा रङ्गप्रदायिनी ॥ १४१

रेवती रणजैत्री च रसोद्भूता रणोत्सवा ।
लता लावण्यरूपा च लवणाब्धिस्वरूपिणी ॥ १४२

लवङ्गकुसुमाराध्या लोलजिह्वा च लेलिहा ।
वशिनी वनसंस्था च वनपुष्पप्रिया वरा ॥ १४३

प्राणेश्वरी बुद्धिरूपा बुद्धिदात्री बुधात्मिका ।
शमनी श्वेतवर्णा च शाङ्करी शिवभाषिणी ॥ १४४

श्याम्यरूपा शक्तिरूपा शक्तिबिन्दुनिवासिनी ।
सर्वेश्वरी सर्वदात्री सर्वमाता च शर्वरी ॥ १४५

शाम्भवी सिद्धिदा सिद्धा सुषुम्ना सुरभासिनी ।
सहस्रदलमध्यस्था सहस्रदलवर्त्तिनी ॥ १४६

हरप्रिया हरध्येया हूँकारबीजरूपिणी ।
लङ्केश्वरी च तरला लोममांसप्रपूजिता ॥ १४७

क्षेम्या क्षेमकरी क्षामा क्षीरबिन्दुस्वरूपिणी ।
क्षिप्रचित्तप्रदा नित्यं क्षौमवस्त्रविलासिनी ॥ १४८

छिन्ना च च्छिन्नरूपा च क्षुधा क्षौत्काररूपिणी ।
सर्ववर्णमयी देवी सर्वसम्पत्प्रदायिनी ॥ १४९

सर्वसम्पत्प्रदात्री च सम्पदापद्विभूषिता ।
सत्त्वरूपा च सर्वार्था सर्वदेवप्रपूजिता ॥ १५०

सर्वेश्वरी सर्वमाता सर्वज्ञा सुरसृत्मिका ।
सिन्धुर्मन्दाकिनी गङ्गा नदीसागररूपिणी ॥ १५१

सुकेशी मुक्तकेशी च डाकिनी वरवर्णिनी ।
ज्ञानदा ज्ञानगगना सोममण्डलवासिनी ॥ १५२

आकाशनिलया नित्या परमाकाशरूपिणी ।
अन्नपूर्णा महानित्या महादेवरसोद्भवा ॥ १५३

मङ्गला कालिका चण्डा चण्डनादातिभीषणा ।
चण्डासुरस्य मथिनी चामुण्डा चपलात्मिका ॥ १५४

चण्डी चामरकेशी च चलत्कुण्डलधारिणी ।
मुण्डमालाधरा नित्या खण्डमुण्डविलासिनी ॥ १५५

खड्गहस्ता मुण्डहस्ता वरहस्ता वरप्रदा ।
असिचर्मधरा नित्या पाशाङ्कुशधरा परा ॥ १५६

शूलहस्ता शिवहस्ता घण्टानादविलासिनी ।
धनुर्बाणधराऽऽदित्या नागहस्ता नगात्मजा ॥ १५७

महिषासुरहन्त्री च रक्तबीजविनाशिनी ।
रक्तरूपा रक्तगा च रक्तहस्ता भयप्रदा ॥ १५८

असिता च धर्मधरा पाशाङ्कुशधरा परा ।
धनुर्बाणधरा नित्या धूम्रलोचननाशिनी ॥ १५९

परस्था देवतामूर्तिः शर्वाणी शारदा परा ।
नानावर्णविभूषाङ्गी नानारागसमापिनी ॥ १६०

पशुवस्त्रपरीधाना पुष्पायुधधरा परा ।
मुक्तरञ्जितमालाद्या मुक्ताहारविलासिनी ॥ १६१

स्वर्णकुण्डलभूषा च स्वर्णसिंहासनस्थिता ।
सुन्दराङ्गी सुवर्णाभा शाम्भवी शकटात्मिका ॥ १६२

सर्वलोकेशविद्या च मोहसम्मोहकारिणी ।
श्रेयसी सृष्टिरूपा च च्छिन्नच्छद्ममयी च्छला ॥ १६३

छिन्नमुण्डधरा नित्या नित्यानन्दविधायिनी ।
नन्दा पूर्णा च रिक्ता च तिथयः पूर्णषोडशी ॥ १६४

कुहूः सङ्क्रान्तिरूपा च पञ्चपर्वविलासिनी ।
पञ्चबाणधरा नित्या पञ्चमप्रीतिदा परा ॥ १६५

पञ्चपत्राभिलाषा च पञ्चामृतविलासिनी ।
पञ्चाली पञ्चमी देवी पञ्चरक्तप्रसारिणी ॥ १६६

पञ्चबाणधरा नित्या नित्यदात्री दयापरा ।
पललादिप्रिया नित्याऽपशुगम्या परेशिता ॥ १६७

परा पररहस्या च परमप्रेमविह्वला ।
कुलिना केशिमार्गस्था कुलमार्गप्रकाशिनी ॥ १६८

कुलाकुलस्वरूपा च कुलार्णवमयी कुला ।
रुक्मा च कालरूपा च कालकम्पनकारिणी ॥ १६९

विलासरूपिणी भद्रा कुलाकुलनमस्कृता ।
कुबेरवित्तधात्री च कुमारजननी परा ॥ १७०

कुमारीरूपसंस्था च कुमारीपूजनाम्बिका ।
कुरङ्गनयना देवी दिनेशास्याऽपराजिता ॥ १७१

कुण्डलीकदली सेना कुमार्गरहिता वरा ।
अनतरूपाऽनन्तस्था आनन्दसिन्धुवासिनी ॥ १७२

इलास्वरूपिणी देवी ईईभेदभयङ्करी ।
इडा च पिङ्गला नाडी इकाराक्षररूपिणी ॥ १७३

उमा चोत्पत्तिरूपा च उच्चभावविनाशिनी ।
ऋग्वेदा च निराराध्या यजुर्वेदप्रपूजिता ॥ १७४

सामवेदेन सङ्गीता अथर्ववेदभाषिणी ।
ऋकाररूपिणी ऋक्षा निरक्षरस्वरूपिणी ॥ १७५

अहिदुर्गासिमाचारा इकाराण्स्वरूपिणी ।
ॐकारा प्रणवस्था च ॐकारादिस्वरूपिणी ॥ १७६

अनुलोमविलोमस्था थकारवर्णसम्भवा ।
पञ्चाशद्वर्णबीजाद्या पञ्चाशन्मुण्डमालिका ॥ १७७

प्रत्येका दशसंख्या च षोडशी च्छिन्नमस्तका ।
षडङ्गयुवतीपूज्या षडङ्गरूपवर्जिता ॥ १७८

षड्वक्त्रसंश्रिता नित्या विश्वेशी खड्गदालया ।
मालामन्त्रमयी मन्त्रजपमाता मदालसा ॥ १७९

सर्वविश्वेश्वरी शक्तिः सर्वानन्दप्रदायिनी ॥ १८०

इति श्रीच्छिन्नमस्ताया नामसहस्रमुत्तमम् ॥

फलश्रुति:

पूजाक्रमेण कथितं साधकानां सुखावहम् ।
गोपनीयं गोपनीयं गोपनीयं न संशयः ॥ १८१

अर्द्धरात्रे मुक्तकेशो भक्तियुक्तो भवेन्नरः ।
जपित्वा पूजयित्वा च पठेन्नामसहस्रकम् ॥ १८२

विद्यासिद्धिर्भवेत्तस्य षण्मासाभ्यासयोगतः ।
येन केन प्रकारेण देवीभक्तिपरो भवेत् ॥ १८३

अखिलान्स्तम्भयेल्लोकांराज्ञोऽपि मोहयेत्सदा ।
आकर्षयेद्देवशक्तिं मारयेद्देवि विद्विषम् ॥ १८४

शत्रवो दासतां यान्ति यान्ति पापानि संक्षयम् ।
मृत्युश्च क्षयतां याति पठनाद्भाषणात्प्रिये ॥ १८५

प्रशस्तायाः प्रसादेन किं न सिद्ध्यति भूतले ।
इदं रहस्यं परमं परं स्वस्त्ययनं महत् ॥ १८६

धृत्वा बाहौ महासिद्धिः प्राप्यते नात्र संशयः ।
अनया सदृशी विद्या विद्यते न महेश्वरि ॥ १८७

वारमेकं तु योऽधीते सर्वसिद्धीश्वरो भवेत् ।
कुलवारे कुलाष्टम्यां कुहूसङ्क्रान्तिपर्वसु ॥ १८८

यश्चेमं पठते विद्यां तस्य सम्यक्फलं शृणु ।
अष्टोत्तरशतं जप्त्वा पठेन्नामसहस्रकम् ॥ १८९

भक्त्या स्तुत्वा महादेवि सर्वपापात्प्रमुच्यते ।
सर्वपापैर्विनिर्मुक्तः सर्वसिद्धीश्वरो भवेत् ॥ १९०

अष्टम्यां वा निशीथे च चतुष्पथगतो नरः ।
माषभक्तबलिं दत्वा पठेन्नामसहस्रकम् ॥ १९१

सुदर्शवामवेद्यां तु मासत्रयविधानतः ।
दुर्जयः कामरूपश्च महाबलपराक्रमः ॥ १९२

कुमारीपूजनं नाम मन्त्रमात्रं पठेन्नरः ।
एतन्मन्त्रस्य पठनात्सर्वसिद्धीश्वरो भवेत् ॥ १९३

इति ते कथितं देवि सर्वसिद्धिपरं नरः ।
जप्त्वा स्तुत्वा महादेवीं सर्वपापैः प्रमुच्यते ॥ १९४

न प्रकाश्यमिदं देवि सर्वदेवनमस्कृतम् ।
इदं रहस्यं परमं गोप्तव्यं पशुसङ्कटे ॥ १९५

इति सकलविभूतेर्हेतुभूतं प्रशस्तं पठति इह मर्त्यश्छिन्नमस्तास्तवं च ।
धनद इव धनाढ्यो माननीयो नृपाणां स भवति च जनानामाश्रयः सिद्धिवेत्ता ॥ १९६

॥ इति श्रीविश्वसारतन्त्रे शिवपार्वतीसंवादे श्रीच्छिन्नमस्ता सहस्रनाम
स्तोत्रं सम्पूर्णम् ॥

*****

Śrī Chinna Masthā Sahasra Nāmāvaliḥ

1,000 divine names on *Śrī Chinna Masthā Devi.*

Dhyānam |

Pratyālīḍhapadāṁ Sadaiva Dadhatīṁ Chinnaṁ Śiraḥ Kartrikāṁ
Digvastrāṁ Svakabandhaśoṇitasudhādhārāṁ Pibantīṁ Mudā |
Nāgābaddhaśiromaṇiṁ Trinayanāṁ Hṛdyutpalālaṅkṛtāṁ
Ratyāsaktamanobhavopari Dṛḍhāṁ Vande Japāsannibhām ||

श्रीछिन्न मस्ता सहस्रनामावलिः

ध्यानम् ।

प्रत्यालीढपदां सदैव दधतीं छिन्नं शिरः कर्त्रिकां
दिग्वस्त्रां स्वकबन्धशोणितसुधाधारां पिबन्तीं मुदा ।
नागाबद्धशिरोमणिं त्रिनयनां हृद्युत्पलालङ्कृतां
रत्यासक्तमनोभवोपरि दृढां वन्दे जपासन्निभाम् ॥

1.	Oṁ Pracaṇḍacaṇḍikāyai Namaḥ	ॐ प्रचण्डचण्डिकायै नमः ।
2.	Oṁ Caṇḍāyai Namaḥ	ॐ चण्डायै नमः ।
3.	Oṁ Caṇḍadevyai Namaḥ	ॐ चण्डदेव्यै नमः ।
4.	Oṁ Avināśinyai Namaḥ	ॐ अविनाशिन्यै नमः ।
5.	Oṁ Cāmuṇḍāyai Namaḥ	ॐ चामुण्डायै नमः ।
6.	Oṁ Sucaṇḍāyai Namaḥ	ॐ सुचण्डायै नमः ।
7.	Oṁ Capalāyai Namaḥ	ॐ चपलायै नमः ।
8.	Oṁ Cārudehinyai Namaḥ	ॐ चारुदेहिन्यै नमः ।
9.	Oṁ Lalajjihvāyai Namaḥ	ॐ ललज्जिह्वायै नमः ।
10.	Oṁ Caladraktāyai Namaḥ	ॐ चलद्रक्तायै नमः ।
11.	Oṁ Cārucandranibhānanāyai Namaḥ	ॐ चारुचन्द्रनिभाननायै नमः ।
12.	Oṁ Cakorākṣyai Namaḥ	ॐ चकोराक्ष्यै नमः ।
13.	Oṁ Caṇḍanādāyai Namaḥ	ॐ चण्डनादायै नमः ।
14.	Oṁ Cañcalāyai Namaḥ	ॐ चञ्चलायै नमः ।

15.	*Oṃ Manonmadāyai Namaḥ* ǀ	ॐ मनोन्मदायै नमः ǀ
16.	*Oṃ Cetanāyai Namaḥ* ǀ	ॐ चेतनायै नमः ǀ
17.	*Oṃ Citisaṃsthāyai Namaḥ* ǀ	ॐ चितिसंस्थायै नमः ǀ
18.	*Oṃ Citkalāyai Namaḥ* ǀ	ॐ चित्कलायै नमः ǀ
19.	*Oṃ Jñānarūpiṇyai Namaḥ* ǀ	ॐ ज्ञानरूपिण्यै नमः ǀ
20.	*Oṃ Mahābhayaṅkarīdevyai Namaḥ* ǀ	ॐ महाभयङ्करीदेव्यै नमः ǀ
21.	*Oṃ Varadābhayadhāriṇyai Namaḥ* ǀ	ॐ वरदाभयधारिण्यै नमः ǀ
22.	*Oṃ Bhayāḍhyāyai Namaḥ* ǀ	ॐ भयाढ्यायै नमः ǀ
23.	*Oṃ Bhavarūpāyai Namaḥ* ǀ	ॐ भवरूपायै नमः ǀ
24.	*Oṃ Bhavabandhavimocinyai Namaḥ* ǀ	ॐ भवबन्धविमोचिन्यै नमः ǀ
25.	*Oṃ Bhavānyai Namaḥ* ǀ	ॐ भवान्यै नमः ǀ
26.	*Oṃ Bhuvaneśyai Namaḥ* ǀ	ॐ भुवनेश्यै नमः ǀ
27.	*Oṃ Bhavasaṃsāratāriṇyai Namaḥ* ǀ	ॐ भवसंसारतारिण्यै नमः ǀ
28.	*Oṃ Bhavābdhaye Namaḥ* ǀ	ॐ भवाब्धये नमः ǀ
29.	*Oṃ Bhavamokṣāyai Namaḥ* ǀ	ॐ भवमोक्षायै नमः ǀ
30.	*Oṃ Bhavabandhavighātinyai Namaḥ* ǀ	ॐ भवबन्धविघातिन्यै नमः ǀ
31.	*Oṃ Bhāgīrathyai Namaḥ* ǀ	ॐ भागीरथ्यै नमः ǀ
32.	*Oṃ Bhagasthāyai Namaḥ* ǀ	ॐ भगस्थायै नमः ǀ
33.	*Oṃ Bhāgyabhogyapradāyinyai Namaḥ* ǀ	ॐ भाग्यभोग्यप्रदायिन्यै नमः ǀ
34.	*Oṃ Kamalāyai Namaḥ* ǀ	ॐ कमलायै नमः ǀ
35.	*Oṃ Kāmadāyai Namaḥ* ǀ	ॐ कामदायै नमः ǀ
36.	*Oṃ Durgāyai Namaḥ* ǀ	ॐ दुर्गायै नमः ǀ
37.	*Oṃ Durgabandhavimocinyai Namaḥ* ǀ	ॐ दुर्गबन्धविमोचिन्यै नमः ǀ
38.	*Oṃ Durdarśanāyai Namaḥ* ǀ	ॐ दुर्दर्शनायै नमः ǀ
39.	*Oṃ Durgarūpāyai Namaḥ* ǀ	ॐ दुर्गरूपायै नमः ǀ
40.	*Oṃ Durjñeyāyai Namaḥ* ǀ	ॐ दुर्ज्ञेयायै नमः ǀ

41	Oṃ Durganāśinyai Namaḥ ǀ	ॐ दुर्नाशिन्यै नमः ǀ
42	Oṃ Dīnaduḥkhaharāyai Namaḥ ǀ	ॐ दीनदुःखहरायै नमः ǀ
43	Oṃ Nityāyai Namaḥ ǀ	ॐ नित्यायै नमः ǀ
44	Oṃ Nityaśokavināśinyai Namaḥ ǀ	ॐ नित्यशोकविनाशिन्यै नमः ǀ
45	Oṃ Nityānandamayyai Devyai Namaḥ ǀ	ॐ नित्यानन्दमय्यै देव्यै नमः ǀ
46	Oṃ Nityakalyāṇarupiṇyai Namaḥ ǀ	ॐ नित्यकल्याणरूपिण्यै नमः ǀ
47	Oṃ Sarvārthasādhanakaryai Namaḥ ǀ	ॐ सर्वार्थसाधनकर्यै नमः ǀ
48	Oṃ Sarvasiddhi Svarūpiṇyai Namaḥ ǀ	ॐ सर्वसिद्धि स्वरूपिण्यै नमः ǀ
49	Oṃ Sarvakṣobhaṇaśaktyai Namaḥ ǀ	ॐ सर्वक्षोभणशक्त्यै नमः ǀ
50	Oṃ Sarvavidrāviṇyai Namaḥ ǀ	ॐ सर्वविद्राविण्यै नमः ǀ
51	Oṃ Parāyai Namaḥ ǀ	ॐ परायै नमः ǀ
52	Oṃ Sarvarañjanaśaktyai Namaḥ	ॐ सर्वरञ्जनशक्त्यै नमः ǀ
53	Oṃ Sarvonmādasvarūpiṇyai Namaḥ ǀ	ॐ सर्वोन्मादस्वरूपिण्यै नमः ǀ
54	Oṃ Sarvajñāyai Namaḥ ǀ	ॐ सर्वज्ञायै नमः ǀ
55	Oṃ Siddhidātryai Namaḥ ǀ	ॐ सिद्धिदात्र्यै नमः ǀ
56	Oṃ Siddhividyāsvarūpiṇyai Namaḥ ǀ	ॐ सिद्धिविद्या स्वरूपिण्यै नमः ǀ
57	Oṃ Sakalāyai Namaḥ ǀ	ॐ सकलायै नमः ǀ
58	Oṃ Niṣkalāyai Namaḥ ǀ	ॐ निष्कलायै नमः ǀ
59	Oṃ Siddhāyai Namaḥ ǀ	ॐ सिद्धायै नमः ǀ
60	Oṃ Kalātītāyai Namaḥ ǀ	ॐ कलातीतायै नमः ǀ
61	Oṃ Kalāmayyai Namaḥ ǀ	ॐ कलामय्यै नमः ǀ

62.	Oṃ Kulajñāyai Namaḥ		ॐ कुलज्ञायै नमः ।
63.	Oṃ Kularūpāyai Namaḥ		ॐ कुलरूपायै नमः ।
64.	Oṃ Cakṣurānandadāyinyai Namaḥ		ॐ चक्षुरानन्ददायिन्यै नमः
65.	Oṃ Kulīnāyai Namaḥ		ॐ कुलीनायै नमः ।
66.	Oṃ Sāmarūpāyai Namaḥ		ॐ सामरूपायै नमः ।
67.	Oṃ Kāmarūpāyai Namaḥ		ॐ कामरूपायै नमः ।
68.	Oṃ Manoharāyai Namaḥ		ॐ मनोहरायै नमः ।
69.	Oṃ Kamalasthāyai Namaḥ		ॐ कमलस्थायै नमः ।
70.	Oṃ Kañjamukhyai Namaḥ		ॐ कञ्जमुख्यै नमः ।
71.	Oṃ Kuñjareśvaragāminyai Namaḥ		ॐ कुञ्जरेश्वरगामिन्यै नमः
72.	Oṃ Kularūpāyai Namaḥ		ॐ कुलरूपायै नमः ।
73.	Oṃ Koṭarākṣyai Namaḥ		ॐ कोटराक्ष्यै नमः ।
74.	Oṃ Kamalāyai Namaḥ		ॐ कमलायै नमः ।
75.	Oṃ Aiśvaryadāyinyai Namaḥ		ॐ ऐश्वर्यदायिन्यै नमः ।
76.	Oṃ Kuntyai Namaḥ		ॐ कुन्त्यै नमः ।
77.	Oṃ Kakudminyai Namaḥ		ॐ ककुद्मिन्यै नमः ।
78.	Oṃ Kullāyai Namaḥ		ॐ कुल्लायै नमः ।
79.	Oṃ Kurukullāyai Namaḥ		ॐ कुरुकुल्लायै नमः ।
80.	Oṃ Karālikāyai Namaḥ		ॐ करालिकायै नमः ।
81.	Oṃ Kāmeśvaryai Namaḥ		ॐ कामेश्वर्यै नमः ।
82.	Oṃ Kāmamātre Namaḥ		ॐ काममात्रे नमः ।
83.	Oṃ Kāmatāpavimocinyai Namaḥ		ॐ कामतापविमोचिन्यै नमः ।
84.	Oṃ Kāmarūpāyai Namaḥ		ॐ कामरूपायै नमः ।
85.	Oṃ Kāmasattvāyai Namaḥ		ॐ कामसत्त्वायै नमः ।
86.	Oṃ Kāmakautukakāriṇyai Namaḥ		ॐ कामकौतुककारिण्यै नमः ।
87.	Oṃ Kāruṇyahṛdayāyai Namaḥ		ॐ कारुण्यहृदयायै नमः ।
88.	Oṃ Krīṃ Namaḥ		ॐ क्रीं नमः ।
89.	Oṃ Krīṃ Mantrarūpāyai Namaḥ		ॐ क्रीं मन्त्ररूपायै नमः ।

90.	Oṃ Koṭarāyai Namaḥ ǀ	ॐ कोटरायै नमः ǀ
91.	Oṃ Kaumodakyai Namaḥ ǀ	ॐ कौमोदक्यै नमः ǀ
92.	Oṃ Kumudinyai Namaḥ ǀ	ॐ कुमुदिन्यै नमः ǀ
93.	Oṃ Kaivalyāyai Namaḥ ǀ	ॐ कैवल्यायै नमः ǀ
94.	Oṃ Kulavāsinyai Namaḥ ǀ	ॐ कुलवासिन्यै नमः ǀ
95.	Oṃ Keśavyai Namaḥ ǀ	ॐ केशव्यै नमः ǀ
96.	Oṃ Keśavārādhyāyai Namaḥ ǀ	ॐ केशवाराध्यायै नमः ǀ
97.	Oṃ Keśidaityaniṣūdinyai Namaḥ	ॐ केशिदैत्यनिषूदिन्यै नमः
98.	Oṃ Kleśahāyai Namaḥ ǀ	ॐ क्लेशहायै नमः ǀ
99.	Oṃ Kleśarahitāyai Namaḥ ǀ	ॐ क्लेशरहितायै नमः ǀ
100.	Oṃ Kleśasaṅghavināśinyai Namaḥ ǀ	ॐ क्लेशसङ्घ विनाशिन्यै नमःǀ
101.	Oṃ Karālyai Namaḥ ǀ	ॐ कराल्यै नमः ǀ
102.	Oṃ Karālāsyāyai Namaḥ ǀ	ॐ करालास्यायै नमः ǀ
103.	Oṃ Karālāsuranāśinyai Namaḥ ǀ	ॐ करालासुरनाशिन्यै नमः
104.	Oṃ Karālacarmāsidharāyai Namaḥ ǀ	ॐ करालचर्मासिधरायै नमः ǀ
105.	Oṃ Karālakulanāśinyai Namaḥ ǀ	ॐ करालकुलनाशिन्यै नमः ǀ
106.	Oṃ Kaṅkinyai Namaḥ ǀ	ॐ कङ्किन्यै नमः ǀ
107.	Oṃ Kaṅkaniratāyai Namaḥ ǀ	ॐ कङ्कनिरतायै नमः ǀ
108.	Oṃ Kapālavaradhāriṇyai Namaḥ	ॐ कपालवरधारिण्यै नमः ǀ
109.	Oṃ Khaḍgahastāyai Namaḥ ǀ	ॐ खड्गहस्तायै नमः ǀ
110.	Oṃ Trinetrāyai Namaḥ ǀ	ॐ त्रिनेत्रायै नमः ǀ
111.	Oṃ Khaḍgamuṇḍāsidhāriṇyai Namaḥ ǀ	ॐ खड्गमुण्डासि धारिण्यै नमः ǀ
112.	Oṃ Khalahāyai Namaḥ ǀ	ॐ खलहायै नमः ǀ

113.	Oṃ Khalahantryai Namaḥ I	ॐ खलहन्त्र्यै नमः I
114.	Oṃ Kṣaratyai Namaḥ I	ॐ क्षरत्यै नमः I
115.	Oṃ Sadā Khagatyai Namaḥ I	ॐ सदा खगत्यै नमः I
116.	Oṃ Gaṅgāyai Namaḥ I	ॐ गङ्गायै नमः I
117.	Oṃ Gautamapūjyāyai Namaḥ I	ॐ गौतमपूज्यायै नमः I
118.	Oṃ Gauryai Namaḥ I	ॐ गौर्यै नमः I
119.	Oṃ Gandharvavāsinyai Namaḥ I	ॐ गन्धर्ववासिन्यै नमः I
120.	Oṃ Gandharvāyai Namaḥ I	ॐ गन्धर्वायै नमः I
121.	Oṃ Gagaṇārādhyāyai Namaḥ I	ॐ गगणाराध्यायै नमः I
122.	Oṃ Gaṇāyai Namaḥ I	ॐ गणायै नमः I
123.	Oṃ Gandharvasevitāyai Namaḥ I	ॐ गन्धर्वसेविताये नमः
124.	Oṃ Gaṇatkāragaṇādevyai Namaḥ I	ॐ गणत्कारगणादेव्यै नमः I
125.	Oṃ Nirguṇāyai Namaḥ I	ॐ निर्गुणायै नमः I
126.	Oṃ Guṇātmikāyai Namaḥ I	ॐ गुणात्मिकायै नमः I
127.	Oṃ Guṇatāyai Namaḥ I	ॐ गुणतायै नमः I
128.	Oṃ Guṇadātryai Namaḥ I	ॐ गुणदात्र्यै नमः I
129.	Oṃ Guṇagauravadāyinyai Namaḥ I	ॐ गुणगौरवदायिन्यै नमः I
130.	Oṃ Gaṇeśamātre Namaḥ I	ॐ गणेशमात्रे नमः I
131.	Oṃ Gambhīrāyai Namaḥ I	ॐ गम्भीरायै नमः I
132.	Oṃ Gagaṇāyai Namaḥ I	ॐ गगणायै नमः I
133.	Oṃ Jyotikāriṇyai Namaḥ I	ॐ ज्योतिकारिण्यै नमः I
134.	Oṃ Gaurāṅgyai Namaḥ I	ॐ गौराङ्ग्यै नमः I
135.	Oṃ Gayāyai Namaḥ I	ॐ गयायै नमः I
136.	Oṃ Gamyāyai Namaḥ I	ॐ गम्यायै नमः I
137.	Oṃ Gautamasthānavāsinyai Namaḥ I	ॐ गौतमस्थानवासिन्यै नमः I
138.	Oṃ Gadādharapriyāyai Namaḥ I	ॐ गदाधरप्रियायै नमः I
139.	Oṃ Jñeyāyai Namaḥ I	ॐ ज्ञेयायै नमः I

140.	Om Jñānagamyāyai Namaḥ ǀ	ॐ ज्ञानगम्यायै नमः ǀ
141.	Om Guheśvaryai Namaḥ ǀ	ॐ गुहेश्वर्यै नमः ǀ
142.	Om Gāyatryai Namaḥ ǀ	ॐ गायत्र्यै नमः ǀ
143.	Om Guṇavatyai Namaḥ ǀ	ॐ गुणवत्यै नमः ǀ
144.	Om Guṇātītāyai Namaḥ ǀ	ॐ गुणातीतायै नमः ǀ
145.	Om Guṇeśvaryai Namaḥ ǀ	ॐ गुणेश्वर्यै नमः ǀ
146.	Om Gaṇeśajananyai Devyai Namaḥ ǀ	ॐ गणेशजनन्यै देव्यै नमः ǀ
147.	Om Gaṇeśavaradāyinyai Namaḥ	ॐ गणेशवरदायिन्यै नमः ǀ
148.	Om Gaṇādhyakṣanutāyai Nityāyai Namaḥ ǀ	ॐ गणाध्यक्षनुतायै नित्यायै नमः ǀ
149.	Om Gaṇādhyakṣaprapūjitāyai Namaḥ ǀ	ॐ गणाध्यक्षप्रपूजितायै नमः ǀ
150.	Om Girīśaramaṇyai Devyai Namaḥ ǀ	ॐ गिरीशरमण्यै देव्यै नमः ǀ
151.	Om Girīśaparivanditāyai Namaḥ	ॐ गिरीशपरिवन्दितायै नमः ǀ
152.	Om Gatidāyai Namaḥ ǀ	ॐ गतिदायै नमः ǀ
153.	Om Gatihāyai Namaḥ ǀ	ॐ गतिहायै नमः ǀ
154.	Om Gītāyai Namaḥ ǀ	ॐ गीतायै नमः ǀ
155.	Om Gautamyai Namaḥ ǀ	ॐ गौतम्यै नमः ǀ
156.	Om Gurusevitāyai Namaḥ ǀ	ॐ गुरुसेवितायै नमः ǀ
157.	Om Gurupūjyāyai Namaḥ ǀ	ॐ गुरुपूज्यायै नमः
158.	Om Guruyutāyai Namaḥ ǀ	ॐ गुरुयुतायै नमः
159.	Om Gurusevanatatparāyai Namaḥ ǀ	ॐ गुरुसेवनतत्परायै नमः ǀ
160.	Om Gandhadvārāyai Namaḥ ǀ	ॐ गन्धद्वारायै नमः ǀ
161.	Om Gandhāḍhyāyai Namaḥ ǀ	ॐ गन्धाढ्यायै नमः ǀ
162.	Om Gandhātmane Namaḥ ǀ	ॐ गन्धात्मने नमः ǀ

163.	Oṃ Gandhakāriṇyai Namaḥ ।	ॐ गन्धकारिण्यै नमः ।
164.	Oṃ Gīrvāṇapatisampūjyāyai Namaḥ ।	ॐ गीर्वाणपति सम्पूज्यायै नमः ।
165.	Oṃ Gīrvāṇapatituṣṭidāyai Namaḥ ।	ॐ गीर्वाणपतितुष्टिदायै नमः ।
166.	Oṃ Gīrvāṇādhīśaramaṇyai Namaḥ ।	ॐ गीर्वाणाधीशरमण्यै नमः ।
167.	Oṃ Gīrvāṇādhīśavanditāyai Namaḥ ।	ॐ गीर्वाणाधीश वन्दितायै नमः ।
168.	Oṃ Gīrvāṇādhīśasaṃsevyāyai Namaḥ ।	ॐ गीर्वाणाधीश संसेव्यायै नमः ।
169.	Oṃ Gīrvāṇādhīśaharṣadāyai Namaḥ ।	ॐ गीर्वाणाधीशहर्षदायै नमः ।
170.	Oṃ Gānaśaktyai Namaḥ ।	ॐ गानशक्त्यै नमः ।
171.	Oṃ Gānagamyāyai Namaḥ ।	ॐ गानगम्यायै नमः ।
172.	Oṃ Gānaśaktipradāyinyai Namaḥ ।	ॐ गानशक्तिप्रदायिन्यै नमः ।
173.	Oṃ Gānavidyāyai Namaḥ ।	ॐ गानविद्यायै नमः ।
174.	Oṃ Gānasiddhāyai Namaḥ ।	ॐ गानसिद्धायै नमः ।
175.	Oṃ Gānasantuṣṭamānasāyai Namaḥ ।	ॐ गानसन्तुष्टमानसायै नमः ।
176.	Oṃ Gānātītāyai Namaḥ ।	ॐ गानातीतायै नमः ।
177.	Oṃ Gānagītāyai Namaḥ ।	ॐ गानगीतायै नमः ।
178.	Oṃ Gānaharṣaprapūritāyai Namaḥ ।	ॐ गानहर्षप्रपूरितायै नमः ।
179.	Oṃ Gandharvapatisaṃhṛṣṭāyai Namaḥ ।	ॐ गन्धर्वपतिसंहृष्टायै नमः ।
180.	Oṃ Gandharvaguṇamaṇḍitāyai Namaḥ ।	ॐ गन्धर्वगुणमण्डितायै नमः ।
181.	Oṃ Gandharvagaṇasaṃsevyāyai Namaḥ ।	ॐ गन्धर्वगणसंसेव्यायै नमः ।

182.	*Oṃ Gandharva Gaṇa Madhyagāyai Namaḥ* ।	ॐ गन्धर्वगणमध्यगायै नमः ।
183.	*Oṃ Gandharvagaṇakuśalāyai Namaḥ* ।	ॐ गन्धर्वगणकुशलायै नमः ।
184.	*Oṃ Gandharvagaṇapūjitāyai Namaḥ* ।	ॐ गन्धर्वगणपूजितायै नमः ।
185.	*Oṃ Gandharvagaṇaniratāyai Namaḥ* ।	ॐ गन्धर्वगणनिरतायै नमः ।
186.	*Oṃ Gandharvagaṇabhūṣitāyai Namaḥ* ।	ॐ गन्धर्वगणभूषितायै नमः ।
187.	*Oṃ Ghargharāyai Namaḥ* ।	ॐ घर्घरायै नमः ।
188.	*Oṃ Ghorarūpāyai Namaḥ* ।	ॐ घोररूपायै नमः ।
189.	*Oṃ Ghoraghurghuranādinyai Namaḥ* ।	ॐ घोरघुर्घुरनादिन्यै नमः
190.	*Oṃ Gharma Bindu Samudbhūtāyai Namaḥ* ।	ॐ घर्मबिन्दुसमुद्भूतायै नमः ।
191.	*Oṃ Gharmabindusvarūpiṇyai Namaḥ* ।	ॐ घर्मबिन्दुस्वरूपिण्यै नमः ।
192.	*Oṃ Ghaṇṭāravāyai Namaḥ* ।	ॐ घण्टारवायै नमः ।
193.	*Oṃ Ghanaravāyai Namaḥ* ।	ॐ घनरवायै नमः ।
194.	*Oṃ Ghanarūpāyai Namaḥ* ।	ॐ घनरूपायै नमः ।
195.	*Oṃ Ghanodaryai Namaḥ* ।	ॐ घनोदर्यै नमः ।
196.	*Oṃ Ghorasattvāyai Namaḥ* ।	ॐ घोरसत्त्वायै नमः ।
197.	*Oṃ Ghanadāyai Namaḥ* ।	ॐ घनदायै नमः ।
198.	*Oṃ Ghaṇṭānādavinodinyai Namaḥ* ।	ॐ घण्टानादविनोदिन्यै नमः ।
199.	*Oṃ Ghoracāṇḍālinyai Namaḥ* ।	ॐ घोरचाण्डालिन्यै नमः ।
200.	*Oṃ Ghorāyai Namaḥ* ।	ॐ घोरायै नमः ।
201.	*Oṃ Ghoracaṇḍavināśinyai Namaḥ* ।	ॐ घोरचण्डविनाशिन्यै नमः ।

202.	Oṃ Ghoradānavadamanyai Namaḥ |	ॐ घोरदानवदमन्यै नमः
203.	Oṃ Ghoradānavanāśinyai Namaḥ |	ॐ घोरदानवनाशिन्यै नमः |
204.	Oṃ Ghorakarmādirahitāyai Namaḥ |	ॐ घोरकर्मादिरहितायै नमः |
205.	Oṃ Ghorakarmaniṣevitāyai Namaḥ |	ॐ घोरकर्मनिषेवितायै नमः |
206.	Oṃ Ghoratattvamayyai Devyai Namaḥ |	ॐ घोरतत्त्वमय्यै देव्यै नमः |
207.	Oṃ Ghoratattvavimocinyai Namaḥ |	ॐ घोरतत्त्वविमोचिन्यै नमः |
208.	Oṃ Ghorakarmādirahitāyai Namaḥ |	ॐ घोरकर्मादिरहितायै नमः |
209.	Oṃ Ghorakarmādipūritāyai Namaḥ |	ॐ घोरकर्मादिपूरितायै नमः |
210.	Oṃ Ghorakarmādiniratāyai Namaḥ |	ॐ घोरकर्मादिनिरतायै नमः |
211.	Oṃ Ghorakarmapravardhinyai Namaḥ |	ॐ घोरकर्मप्रवर्धिन्यै नमः |
212.	Oṃ Ghorabhūtapramathanyai Namaḥ |	ॐ घोरभूतप्रमथन्यै नमः |
213.	Oṃ Ghoravetālanāśinyai Namaḥ	ॐ घोरवेतालनाशिन्यै नमः |
214.	Oṃ Ghoradāvāgnidamanyai Namaḥ |	ॐ घोरदावाग्निदमन्यै नमः |
215.	Oṃ Ghoraśatruniṣūdinyai Namaḥ |	ॐ घोरशत्रुनिषूदिन्यै नमः |
216.	Oṃ Ghoramantrayutāyai Namaḥ	ॐ घोरमन्त्रयुतायै नमः |
217.	Oṃ Ghoramantraprapūjitāyai Namaḥ |	ॐ घोरमन्त्रप्रपूजितायै नमः |

218.	*Oṃ Ghora Mantramano' Bhijñāyai Namaḥ* |	ॐ घोरमन्त्रमनोऽभिज्ञायै नमः ।
219.	*Oṃ Ghoramantraphalapradāyai Namaḥ* |	ॐ घोरमन्त्रफलप्रदायै नमः ।
220.	*Oṃ Ghoramantranidhaye Namaḥ* |	ॐ घोरमन्त्रनिधये नमः ।
221.	*Oṃ Ghoramantrakṛtāspadāyai Namaḥ* |	ॐ घोरमन्त्रकृतास्पदायै नमः ।
222.	*Oṃ Ghoramantreśvaryai Devyai Namaḥ* |	ॐ घोरमन्त्रेश्वर्यै देव्यै नमः ।
223.	*Oṃ Ghoramantrārthamānasāyai Namaḥ* |	ॐ घोरमन्त्रार्थमानसायै नमः ।
224.	*Oṃ Ghora Mantrārtha Tattvajñāyai Namaḥ* |	ॐ घोरमन्त्रार्थतत्त्वज्ञायै नमः ।
225.	*Oṃ Ghoramantrārthapāragāyai Namaḥ* |	ॐ घोरमन्त्रार्थपारगायै नमः ।
226.	*Oṃ Ghoramantrārthavibhavāyai Namaḥ* |	ॐ घोरमन्त्रार्थविभवायै नमः ।
227.	*Oṃ Ghoramantrārthabodhinyai Namaḥ* |	ॐ घोरमन्त्रार्थबोधिन्यै नमः ।
228.	*Oṃ Ghoramantrārthanicayāyai Namaḥ* |	ॐ घोरमन्त्रार्थनिचयायै नमः ।
229.	*Oṃ Ghora Mantrārtha Janma Bhuve Namaḥ* |	ॐ घोरमन्त्रार्थजन्मभुवे नमः ।
230.	*Oṃ Ghoramantrajaparatāyai Namaḥ* |	ॐ घोरमन्त्रजपरतायै नमः ।
231.	*Oṃ Ghoramantrajapodyatāyai Namaḥ* |	ॐ घोरमन्त्रजपोद्यतायै नमः ।
232.	*Oṃ Ṅakāravarṇanilayāyai Namaḥ* |	ॐ ङकारवर्णनिलयायै नमः ।
233.	*Oṃ Ṅakārākṣaramaṇḍitāyai Namaḥ* |	ॐ ङकाराक्षरमण्डितायै नमः ।

234.	Oṃ Ṅakārāpararūpāyai Namaḥ ǀ	ॐ ङकारापररूपायै नमः
235.	Oṃ Ṅakārākṣararūpiṇyai Namaḥ	ॐ ङकाराक्षररूपिण्यै नमः ǀ
236.	Oṃ Citrarūpāyai Namaḥ ǀ	ॐ चित्ररूपायै नमः ǀ
237.	Oṃ Citranāḍyai Namaḥ ǀ	ॐ चित्रनाड्यै नमः ǀ
238.	Oṃ Cārukeśyai Namaḥ ǀ	ॐ चारुकेश्यै नमः ǀ
239.	Oṃ Cayaprabhāyai Namaḥ ǀ	ॐ चयप्रभायै नमः ǀ
240.	Oṃ Cañcalāyai Namaḥ ǀ	ॐ चञ्चलायै नमः ǀ
241.	Oṃ Cañcalākārāyai Namaḥ ǀ	ॐ चञ्चलाकारायै नमः
242.	Oṃ Cārurūpāyai Namaḥ ǀ	ॐ चारुरूपायै नमः ǀ
243.	Oṃ Caṇḍikāyai Namaḥ ǀ	ॐ चण्डिकायै नमः ǀ
244.	Oṃ Caturvedamayyai Namaḥ ǀ	ॐ चतुर्वेदमय्यै नमः ǀ
245.	Oṃ Caṇḍāyai Namaḥ ǀ	ॐ चण्डायै नमः ǀ
246.	Oṃ Cāṇḍālagaṇamaṇḍitāyai Namaḥ ǀ	ॐ चाण्डालगण मण्डितायै नमः ǀ
247.	Oṃ Cāṇḍālacchedinyai Namaḥ ǀ	ॐ चाण्डालच्छेदिन्यै नमः ǀ
248.	Oṃ Caṇḍatāpanirmūlakāriṇyai Namaḥ ǀ	ॐ चण्डतापनिर्मूल कारिण्यै नमः ǀ
249.	Oṃ Caturbhujāyai Namaḥ ǀ	ॐ चतुर्भुजायै नमः ǀ
250.	Oṃ Caṇḍarūpāyai Namaḥ ǀ	ॐ चण्डरूपायै नमः ǀ
251.	Oṃ Caṇḍamuṇḍavināśinyai Namaḥ ǀ	ॐ चण्डमुण्डविनाशिन्यै नमः ǀ
252.	Oṃ Candrikāyai Namaḥ ǀ	ॐ चन्द्रिकायै नमः ǀ
253.	Oṃ Candrakīrtaye Namaḥ ǀ	ॐ चन्द्रकीर्तये नमः ǀ
254.	Oṃ Candrakāntyai Namaḥ ǀ	ॐ चन्द्रकान्त्यै नमः ǀ
255.	Oṃ Ṅandrāsyāyai Namaḥ ǀ	ॐ चन्द्रास्यायै नमः ǀ
256.	Oṃ Candrarūpāyai Namaḥ ǀ	ॐ चन्द्ररूपायै नमः ǀ
257.	Oṃ Candramaulisvarūpiṇyai Namaḥ ǀ	ॐ चन्द्रमौलिस्वरूपिण्यै नमः ǀ

258.	*Oṃ Candramaulipriyāyai Namaḥ*	ॐ चन्द्रमौलिप्रियायै नमः ।
259.	*Oṃ Candra Mauli Santuṣṭa Mānasāyai Namaḥ* |	ॐ चन्द्रमौलिसन्तुष्ट मानसायै नमः ।
260.	*Oṃ Cakorabandhuramaṇyai Namaḥ* |	ॐ चकोरबन्धुरमण्यै नमः ।
261.	*Oṃ Cakorabandhupūjitāyai Namaḥ* |	ॐ चकोरबन्धुपूजितायै नमः ।
262.	*Oṃ Cakrarūpāyai Namaḥ* |	ॐ चक्ररूपायै नमः ।
263.	*Oṃ Cakramayyai Namaḥ* |	ॐ चक्रमय्यै नमः ।
264.	*Oṃ Cakrākārasvarūpiṇyai Namaḥ* |	ॐ चक्राकारस्वरूपिण्यै नमः ।
265.	*Oṃ Cakrapāṇipriyāyai Namaḥ* |	ॐ चक्रपाणिप्रियायै नमः ।
266.	*Oṃ Cakrapāṇiprītipradāyinyai Namaḥ* |	ॐ चक्रपाणिप्रीति प्रदायिन्यै नमः ।
267.	*Oṃ Cakrapāṇirasābhijñāyai Namaḥ* |	ॐ चक्रपाणिरसाभिज्ञायै नमः ।
268.	*Oṃ Cakrapāṇivarapradāyai Namaḥ* |	ॐ चक्रपाणिवरप्रदायै नमः ।
269.	*Oṃ Cakrapāṇivaronmattāyai Namaḥ* |	ॐ चक्रपाणिवरोन्मत्तायै नमः ।
270.	*Oṃ Cakrapāṇisvarūpiṇyai Namaḥ* |	ॐ चक्रपाणिस्वरूपिण्यै नमः ।
271.	*Oṃ Cakrapāṇīśvaryai Namaḥ* |	ॐ चक्रपाणीश्वर्यै नमः ।
272.	*Oṃ Nityaṃ Cakrapāṇi Namaskṛtāyai Namaḥ* |	ॐ नित्यं चक्रपाणि नमस्कृतायै नमः ।
273.	*Oṃ Cakrapāṇisamudbhūtāyai Namaḥ* |	ॐ चक्रपाणिसमुद्भूतायै नमः ।
274.	*Oṃ Cakrapāṇiguṇāspadāyai Namaḥ* |	ॐ चक्रपाणिगुणास्पदायै नमः ।

275.	Oṃ Candrāvalyai Namaḥ ǀ	ॐ चन्द्रावल्यै नमः ।
276.	Oṃ Candravatyai Namaḥ ǀ	ॐ चन्द्रवत्यै नमः ।
277.	Oṃ Candrakoṭisamaprabhāyai Namaḥ ǀ	ॐ चन्द्रकोटिसमप्रभायै नमः ।
278.	Oṃ Candanārcitapādābjāyai Namaḥ ǀ	ॐ चन्दनार्चित पादाब्जायै नमः ।
279.	Oṃ Candanānvitamastakāyai Namaḥ ǀ	ॐ चन्दनान्वित मस्तकायै नमः ।
280.	Oṃ Cārukīrtaye Namaḥ ǀ	ॐ चारुकीर्तये नमः ।
281.	Oṃ Cārunetrāyai Namaḥ ǀ	ॐ चारुनेत्रायै नमः ।
282.	Oṃ Cārucandravibhūṣaṇāyai Namaḥ ǀ	ॐ चारुचन्द्रविभूषणायै नमः ।
283.	Oṃ Cārubhūṣāyai Namaḥ ǀ	ॐ चारुभूषायै नमः ।
284.	Oṃ Cāruveṣāyai Namaḥ ǀ	ॐ चारुवेषायै नमः ।
285.	Oṃ Cāruveṣapradāyinyai Namaḥ	ॐ चारुवेषप्रदायिन्यै नमः ।
286.	Oṃ Cārubhūṣābhūṣitāṅgyai Namaḥ ǀ	ॐ चारुभूषाभूषिताङ्ग्यै नमः ।
287.	Oṃ Caturvaktravarapradāyai Namaḥ ǀ	ॐ चतुर्वक्त्रवरप्रदायै नमः ।
288.	Oṃ Caturvaktrasamārādhyāyai Namaḥ ǀ	ॐ चतुर्वक्त्रसमाराध्यायै नमः ।
289.	Oṃ Caturvaktrasamāśritāyai Namaḥ ǀ	ॐ चतुर्वक्त्रसमाश्रितायै नमः ।
290.	Oṃ Caturvaktrāyai Namaḥ ǀ	ॐ चतुर्वक्त्रायै नमः ।
291.	Oṃ Caturbāhāyai Namaḥ ǀ	ॐ चतुर्बाहायै नमः ।
292.	Oṃ Caturthyai Namaḥ ǀ	ॐ चतुर्थ्यै नमः ।
293.	Oṃ Caturdaśyai Namaḥ ǀ	ॐ चतुर्दश्यै नमः ।
294.	Oṃ Citrāyai Namaḥ ǀ	ॐ चित्रायै नमः ।
295.	Oṃ Carmaṇvatyai Namaḥ ǀ	ॐ चर्मण्वत्यै नमः ।

296.	Oṃ Caitryai Namaḥ		ॐ चैत्र्यै नमः	
297.	Oṃ Candrabhāgāyai Namaḥ		ॐ चन्द्रभागायै नमः	
298.	Oṃ Campakāyai Namaḥ		ॐ चम्पकायै नमः	
299.	Oṃ Caturdaśayamākārāyai Namaḥ		ॐ चतुर्दशयमाकारायै नमः	
300.	Oṃ Caturdaśayamānugāyai Namaḥ		ॐ चतुर्दशयमानुगायै नमः	
301.	Oṃ Caturdaśayamaprītāyai Namaḥ		ॐ चतुर्दशयमप्रीतायै नमः	
302.	Oṃ Caturdaśayamapriyāyai Namaḥ		ॐ चतुर्दशयमप्रियायै नमः	
303.	Oṃ Chalasthāyai Namaḥ		ॐ छलस्थायै नमः	
304.	Oṃ Chidrarūpāyai Namaḥ		ॐ छिद्ररूपायै नमः	
305.	Oṃ Chadmadāyai Namaḥ		ॐ छद्मदायै नमः	
306.	Oṃ Chadmarājikāyai Namaḥ		ॐ छद्मराजिकायै नमः	
307.	Oṃ Chinnamastāyai Namaḥ		ॐ छिन्नमस्तायै नमः	
308.	Oṃ Chinnāyai Namaḥ		ॐ छिन्नायै नमः	
309.	Oṃ Chinnamuṇḍavidhāriṇyai Namaḥ		ॐ छिन्नमुण्डविधारिण्यै नमः	
310.	Oṃ Jayadāyai Namaḥ		ॐ जयदायै नमः	
311.	Oṃ Jayarūpāyai Namaḥ		ॐ जयरूपायै नमः	
312.	Oṃ Jayantyai Namaḥ		ॐ जयन्त्यै नमः	
313.	Oṃ Jayamohinyai Namaḥ		ॐ जयमोहिन्यै नमः	
314.	Oṃ Jayāyai Namaḥ		ॐ जयायै नमः	
315.	Oṃ Jīvanasaṃsthāyai Namaḥ		ॐ जीवनसंस्थायै नमः	
316.	Oṃ Jālandharanivāsinyai Namaḥ	ॐ जालन्धरनिवासिन्यै नमः	
317.	Oṃ Jvālāmukhyai Namaḥ		ॐ ज्वालामुख्यै नमः	
318.	Oṃ Jvāladātryai Namaḥ		ॐ ज्वालदात्र्यै नमः	

319.	Oṃ Jājjvalyadahanopamāyai Namaḥ |	ॐ जाज्ज्वल्य दहनोपमायै नमः ।
320.	Oṃ Jagadvandyāyai Namaḥ|	ॐ जगद्वन्द्यायै नमः ।
321.	Oṃ Jagatpūjyāyai Namaḥ |	ॐ जगत्पूज्यायै नमः ।
322.	Oṃ Jagattrāṇaparāyaṇāyai Namaḥ |	ॐ जगत्त्राणपरायणायै नमः ।
323.	Oṃ Jagatyai Namaḥ |	ॐ जगत्यै नमः ।
324.	Oṃ Jagadādhārāyai Namaḥ |	ॐ जगदाधारायै नमः ।
325.	Oṃ Janmamṛtyujarāpahāyai Namaḥ |	ॐ जन्ममृत्युजरापहायै नमः ।
326.	Oṃ Jananyai Namaḥ |	ॐ जनन्यै नमः ।
327.	Oṃ Janmabhūmyai Namaḥ |	ॐ जन्मभूम्यै नमः ।
328.	Oṃ Janmadāyai Namaḥ |	ॐ जन्मदायै नमः ।
329.	Oṃ Jayaśālinyai Namaḥ |	ॐ जयशालिन्यै नमः ।
330.	Oṃ Jvararogaharāyai Namaḥ |	ॐ ज्वररोगहरायै नमः ।
331.	Oṃ Jvālāyai Namaḥ |	ॐ ज्वालायै नमः ।
332.	Oṃ Jvālāmālāprapūritāyai Namaḥ |	ॐ ज्वालामाला प्रपूरितायै नमः ।
333.	Oṃ Jambhārātīśvaryai Namaḥ |	ॐ जम्भारातीश्वर्यै नमः ।
334.	Oṃ Jambhārātivaibhavakāriṇyai Namaḥ |	ॐ जम्भारातिवैभव कारिण्यै नमः ।
335.	Oṃ Jambhārātistutāyai Namaḥ |	ॐ जम्भारातिस्तुतायै नमः ।
336.	Oṃ Jambhārātiśatruniṣūdinyai Namaḥ |	ॐ जम्भारातिशत्रु निषूदिन्यै नमः ।
337.	Oṃ Jayadurgāyai Namaḥ |	ॐ जयदुर्गायै नमः ।
338.	Oṃ Jayārādhyāyai Namaḥ |	ॐ जयाराध्यायै नमः ।
339.	Oṃ Jayakālyai Namaḥ |	ॐ जयकाल्यै नमः ।
340.	Oṃ Jayeśvaryai Namaḥ |	ॐ जयेश्वर्यै नमः ।
341.	Oṃ Jayatārāyai Namaḥ |	ॐ जयतारायै नमः ।

342.	Oṃ Jayātītāyai Namaḥ		ॐ जयातीतायै नमः ।
343.	Oṃ Jayaśaṅkaravallabhāyai Namaḥ		ॐ जयशङ्कर वल्लभायै नमः ।
344.	Oṃ Jaladāyai Namaḥ		ॐ जलदायै नमः ।
345.	Oṃ Jahnutanayāyai Namaḥ		ॐ जह्नुतनयायै नमः ।
346.	Oṃ Jaladhitrāsakāriṇyai Namaḥ		ॐ जलधित्रासकारिण्यै नमः ।
347.	Oṃ Jaladhivyādhidamanyai Namaḥ		ॐ जलधिव्याधिदमन्यै नमः ।
348.	Oṃ Jaladhijvaranāśinyai Namaḥ		ॐ जलधिज्वरनाशिन्यै नमः ।
349.	Oṃ Jaṅgameśyai Namaḥ		ॐ जङ्गमेश्यै नमः ।
350.	Oṃ Jāḍyaharāyai Namaḥ		ॐ जाड्यहरायै नमः ।
351.	Oṃ Jāḍyasaṅghanivāriṇyai Namaḥ		ॐ जाड्यसङ्घ निवारिण्यै नमः ।
352.	Oṃ Jāḍyagrastajanātītāyai Namaḥ		ॐ जाड्यग्रस्त जनातीतायै नमः ।
353.	Oṃ Jāḍyaroganivāriṇyai Namaḥ		ॐ जाड्यरोगनिवारिण्यै नमः ।
354.	Oṃ Janmadātryai Namaḥ		ॐ जन्मदात्र्यै नमः ।
355.	Oṃ Janmahartryai Namaḥ		ॐ जन्महत्र्यै नमः ।
356.	Oṃ Jayaghoṣasamanvitāyai Namaḥ		ॐ जयघोषसमन्वितायै नमः ।
357.	Oṃ Japayogasamāyuktāyai Namaḥ		ॐ जपयोगसमायुक्तायै नमः ।
358.	Oṃ Japayogavinodinyai Namaḥ		ॐ जपयोगविनोदिन्यै नमः ।
359.	Oṃ Japayogapriyāyai Namaḥ		ॐ जपयोगप्रियायै नमः
360.	Oṃ Jāpyāyai Namaḥ		ॐ जाप्यायै नमः ।
361.	Oṃ Japātītāyai Namaḥ		ॐ जपातीतायै नमः ।

362.	Oṃ Jayasvanāyai Namaḥ		ॐ जयस्वनायै नमः ।
363.	Oṃ Jāyābhāvasthitāyai Namaḥ		ॐ जायाभावस्थितायै नमः ।
364.	Oṃ Jāyāyai Namaḥ		ॐ जायायै नमः ।
365.	Oṃ Jāyābhāvaprapūriṇyai Namaḥ		ॐ जायाभावप्रपूरिण्यै नमः ।
366.	Oṃ Japākusumasaṅkāśāyai Namaḥ		ॐ जपाकुसम सङ्काशायै नमः ।
367.	Oṃ Japākusumapūjitāyai Namaḥ	ॐ जपाकुसुमपूजितायै नमः ।
368.	Oṃ Japākusumasamprītāyai Namaḥ		ॐ जपाकुसुमसम्प्रीतायै नमः ।
369.	Oṃ Japākusumamaṇḍitāyai Namaḥ		ॐ जपाकुसुममण्डितायै नमः ।
370.	Oṃ Japākusumavadbhāsāyai Namaḥ		ॐ जपाकुसुमवद्भासायै नमः ।
371.	Oṃ Japākusumarūpiṇyai Namaḥ	ॐ जपाकुसुमरूपिण्यै नमः ।
372.	Oṃ Jamadagnisvarūpāyai Namaḥ		ॐ जमदग्निस्वरूपायै नमः ।
373.	Oṃ Jānakyai Namaḥ		ॐ जानक्यै नमः ।
374.	Oṃ Janakātmajāyai Namaḥ		ॐ जनकात्मजायै नमः ।
375.	Oṃ Jhañjhāvātapramuktāṅgyai Namaḥ		ॐ झञ्झावात प्रमुक्ताङ्ग्यै नमः ।
376.	Oṃ Jhorajhaṅkāravāsinyai Namaḥ		ॐ झोरझङ्कारवासिन्यै नमः ।
377.	Oṃ Jhaṅkārakāriṇyai Namaḥ		ॐ झङ्कारकारिण्यै नमः ।
378.	Oṃ Jhañjhāvātarūpāyai Namaḥ|	ॐ झञ्झावातरूपायै नमः ।
379.	Oṃ Jhaṅkaryai Namaḥ		ॐ झङ्कर्यै नमः ।

380.	Oṁ Ñakārāṇusvarūpāyai Namaḥ		ॐ अकाराणुस्वरूपायै नमः ।
381.	Oṁ Ṭavaṭṭaṅkāranādinyai Namaḥ		ॐ टवट्टङ्कारनादिन्यै नमः ।
382.	Oṁ Ṭaṅkāryai Namaḥ		ॐ टङ्कार्यै नमः ।
383.	Oṁ Ṭakuvāṇyai Namaḥ		ॐ टकुवाण्यै नमः ।
384.	Oṁ Ṭhakārākṣararūpiṇyai Namaḥ		ॐ ठकाराक्षररूपिण्यै नमः ।
385.	Oṁ Ḍiṇḍimāyai Namaḥ		ॐ डिण्डिमायै नमः ।
386.	Oṁ Ḍimbhāyai Namaḥ		ॐ डिम्भायै नमः ।
387.	Oṁ Ḍiṇḍuḍiṇḍimavādinyai Namaḥ		ॐ डिण्डुडिण्डिम वादिन्यै नमः ।
388.	Oṁ Ḍhakkāmayyai Namaḥ		ॐ ढक्कामय्यै नमः ।
389.	Oṁ Ḍhilamayyai Namaḥ		ॐ ढिलमय्यै नमः ।
390.	Oṁ Nṛtyaśabdavilāsinyai Namaḥ		ॐ नृत्यशब्दविलासिन्यै नमः ।
391.	Oṁ Ḍhakkāyai Namaḥ		ॐ ढक्कायै नमः ।
392.	Oṁ Ḍhakkeśvaryai Namaḥ		ॐ ढक्केश्वर्यै नमः ।
393.	Oṁ Ḍhakkāśabdarūpāyai Namaḥ		ॐ ढक्काशब्दरूपायै नमः ।
394.	Oṁ Ḍhakkānādapriyāyai Namaḥ	ॐ ढक्कानादप्रियायै नमः ।
395.	Oṁ Ḍhakkānāda Santuṣṭa Mānasāyai Namaḥ		ॐ ढक्कानाद सन्तुष्टमानसायै नमः ।
396.	Oṁ Ṇakārāyai Namaḥ		ॐ णकारायै नमः ।
397.	Oṁ Ṇākṣaramayyai Namaḥ		ॐ णाक्षरमय्यै नमः ।
398.	Oṁ Ṇākṣarādisvarūpiṇyai Namaḥ		ॐ णाक्षरादिस्वरूपिण्यै नमः ।
399.	Oṁ Tripurāyai Namaḥ		ॐ त्रिपुरायै नमः ।
400.	Oṁ Tripuramayyai Namaḥ		ॐ त्रिपुरमय्यै नमः ।

401.	Oṃ Triśaktyai Namaḥ l	ॐ त्रिशक्त्यै नमः।
402.	Oṃ Triguṇātmikāyai Namaḥ l	ॐ त्रिगुणात्मिकायै नमः
403.	Oṃ Tāmasyai Namaḥ l	ॐ तामस्यै नमः।
404.	Oṃ Trilokeśyai Namaḥ l	ॐ त्रिलोकेश्यै नमः।
405.	Oṃ Tripurāyai Namaḥ l	ॐ त्रिपुरायै नमः।
406.	Oṃ Trayīśvaryai Namaḥ l	ॐ त्रयीश्वर्यै नमः।
407.	Oṃ Trividyāyai Namaḥ l	ॐ त्रिविद्यायै नमः।
408.	Oṃ Trirūpāyai Namaḥ l	ॐ त्रिरूपायै नमः।
409.	Oṃ Trinetrāyai Namaḥ l	ॐ त्रिनेत्रायै नमः।
410.	Oṃ Trirūpiṇyai Namaḥ l	ॐ त्रिरूपिण्यै नमः।
411.	Oṃ Tāriṇyai Namaḥ l	ॐ तारिण्यै नमः।
412.	Oṃ Taralāyai Namaḥ l	ॐ तरलायै नमः।
413.	Oṃ Tārāyai Namaḥ l	ॐ तारायै नमः।
414.	Oṃ Tārakāriprapūjitāyai Namaḥ	ॐ तारकारिप्रपूजितायै नमः।
415.	Oṃ Tārakārisamārādhyāyai Namaḥ l	ॐ तारकारिसमाराध्यायै नमः।
416.	Oṃ Tārakārivarapradāyai Namaḥ l	ॐ तारकारिवरप्रदायै नमः।
417.	Oṃ Tārakāriprasuve Namaḥ l	ॐ तारकारिप्रसुवे नमः।
418.	Oṃ Tanvyai Namaḥ l	ॐ तन्व्यै नमः।
419.	Oṃ Taruṇyai Namaḥ l	ॐ तरुण्यै नमः।
420.	Oṃ Taralaprabhāyai Namaḥl	ॐ तरलप्रभायै नमः।
421.	Oṃ Trirūpāyai Namaḥ l	ॐ त्रिरूपायै नमः।
422.	Oṃ Tripuragāyai Namaḥ l	ॐ त्रिपुरगायै नमः।
423.	Oṃ Triśūlavaradhāriṇyai Namaḥ	ॐ त्रिशूलवरधारिण्यै नमः।
424.	Oṃ Triśūlinyai Namaḥ l	ॐ त्रिशूलिन्यै नमः।
425.	Oṃ Tantramayyai Namaḥ l	ॐ तन्त्रमय्यै नमः।

426.	Oṃ Tantraśāstraviśāradāyai Namaḥ |	ॐ तन्त्रशास्त्रविशारदायै नमः ।
427.	Oṃ Tantrarūpāyai Namaḥ |	ॐ तन्त्ररूपायै नमः ।
428.	Oṃ Tapomūrtaye Namaḥ |	ॐ तपोमूर्तये नमः ।
429.	Oṃ Tantramantrasvarūpiṇyai Namaḥ |	ॐ तन्त्रमन्त्रस्वरूपिण्यै नमः ।
430.	Oṃ Taḍite Namaḥ |	ॐ तडिते नमः ।
431.	Oṃ Taḍillatākārāyai Namaḥ |	ॐ तडिल्लताकारायै नमः ।
432.	Oṃ Tattvajñānapradāyinyai Namaḥ	ॐ तत्त्वज्ञानप्रदायिन्यै नमः ।
433.	Oṃ Tattvajñāneśvaryai Devyai Namaḥ |	ॐ तत्त्वज्ञानेश्वर्यै देव्यै नमः ।
434.	Oṃ Tattvajñānapramodinyai Namaḥ |	ॐ तत्त्वज्ञानप्रमोदिन्यै नमः ।
435.	Oṃ Trayīmayyai Namaḥ |	ॐ त्रयीमय्यै नमः ।
436.	Oṃ Trayīsevyāyai Namaḥ |	ॐ त्रयीसेव्यायै नमः ।
437.	Oṃ Tryakṣaryai Namaḥ |	ॐ त्र्यक्षर्यै नमः ।
438.	Oṃ Tryakṣareśvaryai Namaḥ |	ॐ त्र्यक्षरेश्वर्यै नमः ।
439.	Oṃ Tāpavidhvaṃsinyai Namaḥ |	ॐ तापविध्वंसिन्यै नमः ।
440.	Oṃ Tāpasaṅghanirmūlakāriṇyai Namaḥ |	ॐ तापसङ्घनिर्मूलकारिण्यै नमः ।
441.	Oṃ Trāsakartryai Namaḥ |	ॐ त्रासकर्त्र्यै नमः ।
442.	Oṃ Trāsahartryai Namaḥ |	ॐ त्रासहर्त्र्यै नमः ।
443.	Oṃ Trāsadātryai Namaḥ |	ॐ त्रासदात्र्यै नमः ।
444.	Oṃ Trāsahāyai Namaḥ |	ॐ त्रासहायै नमः ।
445.	Oṃ Tithīśāyai Namaḥ |	ॐ तिथीशायै नमः ।
446.	Oṃ Tithirūpāyai Namaḥ |	ॐ तिथिरूपायै नमः ।
447.	Oṃ Tithisthāyai Namaḥ |	ॐ तिथिस्थायै नमः ।
448.	Oṃ Tithipūjitāyai Namaḥ |	ॐ तिथिपूजितायै नमः ।
449.	Oṃ Tilottamāyai Namaḥ |	ॐ तिलोत्तमायै नमः ।
450.	Oṃ Tiladāyai Namaḥ |	ॐ तिलदायै नमः ।
451.	Oṃ Tilaprītāyai Namaḥ |	ॐ तिलप्रीतायै नमः ।

452.	Oṃ Tileśvaryai Namaḥ		ॐ तिलेश्वर्यै नमः	
453.	Oṃ Triguṇāyai Namaḥ		ॐ त्रिगुणायै नमः	
454.	Oṃ Triguṇākārāyai Namaḥ		ॐ त्रिगुणाकारायै नमः	
455.	Oṃ Tripuryai Namaḥ		ॐ त्रिपुर्यै नमः	
456.	Oṃ Tripurātmikāyai Namaḥ		ॐ त्रिपुरात्मिकायै नमः	
457.	Oṃ Trikūṭāyai Namaḥ		ॐ त्रिकूटायै नमः	
458.	Oṃ Trikūṭākārāyai Namaḥ		ॐ त्रिकूटाकारायै नमः	
459.	Oṃ Trikūṭācalamadhyagāyai Namaḥ		ॐ त्रिकूटाचलमध्यगायै नमः	
460.	Oṃ Trijaṭāyai Namaḥ		ॐ त्रिजटायै नमः	
461.	Oṃ Trinetrāyai Namaḥ		ॐ त्रिनेत्रायै नमः	
462.	Oṃ Trinetravarasundaryai Namaḥ		ॐ त्रिनेत्रवरसुन्दर्यै नमः	
463.	Oṃ Tṛtīyāyai Namaḥ		ॐ तृतीयायै नमः	
464.	Oṃ Trivarṣāyai Namaḥ		ॐ त्रिवर्षायै नमः	
465.	Oṃ Trividhāyai Namaḥ		ॐ त्रिविधायै नमः	
466.	Oṃ Trimateśvaryai Namaḥ		ॐ त्रिमतेश्वर्यै नमः	
467.	Oṃ Trikoṇasthāyai Namaḥ		ॐ त्रिकोणस्थायै नमः	
468.	Oṃ Trikoṇeśyai Namaḥ		ॐ त्रिकोणेश्यै नमः	
469.	Oṃ Trikoṇayantramadhyagāyai Namaḥ		ॐ त्रिकोणयन्त्रमध्यगायै नमः	
470.	Oṃ Trisandhyāyai Namaḥ		ॐ त्रिसन्ध्यायै नमः	
471.	Oṃ Trisandhyārcyāyai Namaḥ		ॐ त्रिसन्ध्याच्यायै नमः	
472.	Oṃ Tripadāyai Namaḥ		ॐ त्रिपदायै नमः	
473.	Oṃ Tripadāspadāyai Namaḥ		ॐ त्रिपदास्पदायै नमः	
474.	Oṃ Sthānasthitāyai Namaḥ		ॐ स्थानस्थितायै नमः	
475.	Oṃ Sthalasthāyai Namaḥ		ॐ स्थलस्थायै नमः	
476.	Oṃ Dhanyasthalanivāsinyai Namaḥ	ॐ धन्यस्थलनिवासिन्यै नमः	
477.	Oṃ Thakārākṣararūpāyai Namaḥ		ॐ थकाराक्षररूपायै नमः	
478.	Oṃ Sthūlarūpāyai Namaḥ		ॐ स्थूलरूपायै नमः	
479.	Oṃ Sthūlahastāyai Namaḥ		ॐ स्थूलहस्तायै नमः	
480.	Oṃ Sthūlāyai Namaḥ		ॐ स्थूलायै नमः	

481.	*Oṃ Sthairyarūpaprakāśinyai Namaḥ*	ॐ स्थैर्यरूपप्रकाशिन्यै नमः ।
482.	*Oṃ Durgāyai Namaḥ*	ॐ दुर्गायै नमः ।
483.	*Oṃ Durgārtihantryai Namaḥ*	ॐ दुर्गार्तिहन्त्र्यै नमः ।
484.	*Oṃ Durgabandhavimocinyai Namaḥ*	ॐ दुर्गबन्धविमोचिन्यै नमः ।
485.	*Oṃ Devyai Namaḥ*	ॐ देव्यै नमः ।
486.	*Oṃ Dānavasaṃhantryai Namaḥ*	ॐ दानवसंहन्त्र्यै नमः ।
487.	*Oṃ Danujeśaniṣūdinyai Namaḥ*	ॐ दनुजेशनिषूदिन्यै नमः
488.	*Oṃ Dārāpatyapradāyai Nityāyai Namaḥ*	ॐ दारापत्यप्रदायै नित्यायै नमः ।
489.	*Oṃ Śaṅkarārdhāṅgadhāriṇyai Namaḥ*	ॐ शङ्करार्धाङ्गधारिण्यै नमः ।
490.	*Oṃ Divyāṅgyai Namaḥ*	ॐ दिव्याङ्ग्यै नमः ।
491.	*Oṃ Devamātre Namaḥ*	ॐ देवमात्रे नमः ।
492.	*Oṃ Devaduṣṭavināśinyai Namaḥ*	ॐ देवदुष्टविनाशिन्यै नमः ।
493.	*Oṃ Dīnaduḥkhaharāyai Namaḥ*	ॐ दीनदुःखहरायै नमः ।
494.	*Oṃ Dīnatāpanirmūlakāriṇyai Namaḥ*	ॐ दीनतापनिर्मूलकारिण्यै नमः ।
495.	*Oṃ Dīnamātre Namaḥ*	ॐ दीनमात्रे नमः ।
496.	*Oṃ Dīnasevyāyai Namaḥ*	ॐ दीनसेव्यायै नमः ।
497.	*Oṃ Dīnadambhavināśinyai Namaḥ*	ॐ दीनदम्भविनाशिन्यै नमः ।
498.	*Oṃ Danujadhvaṃsinyai Namaḥ*	ॐ दनुजध्वंसिन्यै नमः
499.	*Oṃ Devyai Namaḥ*	ॐ देव्यै नमः ।
500.	*Oṃ Devakyai Namaḥ*	ॐ देवक्यै नमः ।
501.	*Oṃ Devavallabhāyai Namaḥ*	ॐ देववल्लभायै नमः ।
502.	*Oṃ Dānavāripriyāyai Namaḥ*	ॐ दानवारिप्रियायै नमः ।
503.	*Oṃ Dīrghāyai Namaḥ*	ॐ दीर्घायै नमः ।
504.	*Oṃ Dānavāriprapūjitāyai Namaḥ*	ॐ दानवारिप्रपूजितायै नमः ।
505.	*Oṃ Dīrghasvarāyai Namaḥ*	ॐ दीर्घस्वरायै नमः ।
506.	*Oṃ Dīrghatanvyai Namaḥ*	ॐ दीर्घतन्व्यै नमः ।

507.	Oṃ Dīrghadurgatināśinyai Namaḥ ।	ॐ दीर्घदुर्गतिनाशिन्यै नमः ।
508.	Oṃ Dīrghanetrāyai Namaḥ ।	ॐ दीर्घनेत्रायै नमः ।
509.	Oṃ Dīrghacakṣuṣe Namaḥ ।	ॐ दीर्घचक्षुषे नमः ।
510.	Oṃ Dīrghakeśyai Namaḥ ।	ॐ दीर्घकेश्यै नमः ।
511.	Oṃ Digambarāyai Namaḥ ।	ॐ दिगम्बरायै नमः ।
512.	Oṃ Digambarapriyāyai Namaḥ ।	ॐ दिगम्बरप्रियायै नमः ।
513.	Oṃ Dāntāyai Namaḥ ।	ॐ दान्तायै नमः ।
514.	Oṃ Digambarasvarūpiṇyai Namaḥ	ॐ दिगम्बरस्वरूपिण्यै नमः ।
515.	Oṃ Duḥkhahīnāyai Namaḥ ।	ॐ दुःखहीनायै नमः ।
516.	Oṃ Duḥkhaharāyai Namaḥ ।	ॐ दुःखहरायै नमः ।
517.	Oṃ Duḥkhasāgaratāriṇyai Namaḥ ।	ॐ दुःखसागरतारिण्यै नमः ।
518.	Oṃ Duḥkhadāridryaśamanyai Namaḥ ।	ॐ दुःखदारिद्र्यशमन्यै नमः ।
519.	Oṃ Duḥkhadāridryakāriṇyai Namaḥ ।	ॐ दुःखदारिद्र्यकारिण्यै नमः ।
520.	Oṃ Duḥkhadāyai Namaḥ ।	ॐ दुःखदायै नमः ।
521.	Oṃ Dussahāyai Namaḥ ।	ॐ दुस्सहायै नमः ।
522.	Oṃ Duṣṭa Khaṇḍanaika Svarūpiṇyai Namaḥ ।	ॐ दुष्खण्डनैकस्वरूपिण्यै नमः ।
523.	Oṃ Devavāmāyai Namaḥ ।	ॐ देववामायै नमः ।
524.	Oṃ Devasevyāyai Namaḥ ।	ॐ देवसेव्यायै नमः ।
525.	Oṃ Devaśaktipradāyinyai Namaḥ ।	ॐ देवशक्तिप्रदायिन्यै नमः ।
526.	Oṃ Dāminyai Namaḥ ।	ॐ दामिन्यै नमः ।
527.	Oṃ Dāminīprītāyai Namaḥ ।	ॐ दामिनीप्रीतायै नमः ।
528.	Oṃ Dāminīśatasundaryai Namaḥ ।	ॐ दामिनीशतसुन्दर्यै नमः ।
529.	Oṃ Dāminīśatasaṃsevyāyai Namaḥ ।	ॐ दामिनीशतसंसेव्यायै नमः ।
530.	Oṃ Dāminīdāmabhūṣitāyai Namaḥ	ॐ दामिनीदामभूषितायै नमः ।
531.	Oṃ Devatābhāvasantuṣṭāyai Namaḥ ।	ॐ देवताभावसन्तुष्टायै नमः ।
532.	Oṃ Devatāśatamadhyagāya Namaḥ ।	ॐ देवताशतमध्यगायै नमः ।

533.	Oṃ Dayārdrāyai Namaḥ		ॐ दयार्द्रायै नमः ।
534.	Oṃ Dayārūpāyai Namaḥ		ॐ दयारूपायै नमः ।
535.	Oṃ Dayāyai Namaḥ		ॐ दयायै नमः ।
536.	Oṃ Dānaparāyaṇāyai Namaḥ		ॐ दानपरायणायै नमः ।
537.	Oṃ Dayāśīlāyai Namaḥ		ॐ दयाशीलायै नमः ।
538.	Oṃ Dayāsārāyai Namaḥ		ॐ दयासारायै नमः ।
539.	Oṃ Dayāsāgarasaṃsthitāyai Namaḥ		ॐ दयासागरसंस्थितायै नमः ।
540.	Oṃ Daśavidyātmikāyai Namaḥ		ॐ दशविद्यात्मिकायै नमः ।
541.	Oṃ Devyai Namaḥ		ॐ देव्यै नमः ।
542.	Oṃ Daśavidyāsvarūpiṇyai Namaḥ		ॐ दशविद्यास्वरूपिण्यै नमः ।
543.	Oṃ Dharaṇyai Namaḥ		ॐ धरण्यै नमः ।
544.	Oṃ Dhanadāyai Namaḥ		ॐ धनदायै नमः ।
545.	Oṃ Dhātryai Namaḥ		ॐ धात्रै नमः ।
546.	Oṃ Dhanyāyai Namaḥ		ॐ धन्यायै नमः ।
547.	Oṃ Dhanyaparāyai Namaḥ		ॐ धन्यपरायै नमः ।
548.	Oṃ Śivāyai Namaḥ		ॐ शिवायै नमः ।
549.	Oṃ Dharmarūpāyai Namaḥ		ॐ धर्मरूपायै नमः ।
550.	Oṃ Dhaniṣṭhāyai Namaḥ		ॐ धनिष्ठायै नमः ।
551.	Oṃ Dheyāyai Namaḥ		ॐ धेयायै नमः ।
552.	Oṃ Dhīragocarāyai Namaḥ		ॐ धीरगोचरायै नमः ।
553.	Oṃ Dharmarājeśvaryai Namaḥ		ॐ धर्मराजेश्वर्यै नमः ।
554.	Oṃ Dharmakarmarūpāyai Namaḥ		ॐ धर्मकर्मरूपायै नमः ।
555.	Oṃ Dhaneśvaryai Namaḥ		ॐ धनेश्वर्यै नमः ।
556.	Oṃ Dhanurvidyāyai Namaḥ		ॐ धनुर्विद्यायै नमः ।
557.	Oṃ Dhanurgamyāyai Namaḥ		ॐ धनुर्गम्यायै नमः ।
558.	Oṃ Dhanurdharavarapradāyai Namaḥ		ॐ धनुर्धरवरप्रदायै नमः ।
559.	Oṃ Dharmaśīlāyai Namaḥ		ॐ धर्मशीलायै नमः ।
560.	Oṃ Dharmalīlāyai Namaḥ		ॐ धर्मलीलायै नमः ।

561.	Oṃ Dharmakarmavivarjitāyai Namaḥ ǀ	ॐ धर्मकर्मविवर्जितायै नमः ǀ
562.	Oṃ Dharmadāyai Namaḥ ǀ	ॐ धर्मदायै नमः ǀ
563.	Oṃ Dharmaniratāyai Namaḥ ǀ	ॐ धर्मनिरतायै नमः ǀ
564.	Oṃ Dharma Pākhaṇḍa Khaṇḍinyai Namaḥ ǀ	ॐ धर्मपाखण्डखण्डिन्यै नमः ǀ
565.	Oṃ Dharmeśyai Namaḥ ǀ	ॐ धर्मेश्यै नमः ǀ
566.	Oṃ Dharmarūpāyai Namaḥ ǀ	ॐ धर्मरूपायै नमः ǀ
567.	Oṃ Dharmarājavarapradāyai Namaḥ ǀ	ॐ धर्मराजवरप्रदायै नमः ǀ
568.	Oṃ Dharmiṇyai Namaḥ ǀ	ॐ धर्मिण्यै नमः ǀ
569.	Oṃ Dharmagehasthāyai Namaḥ	ॐ धर्मगेहस्थायै नमः ǀ
570.	Oṃ Dharmādharmasvarūpiṇyai Namaḥ ǀ	ॐ धर्माधर्मस्वरूपिण्यै नमः ǀ
571.	Oṃ Dhanadāyai Namaḥ ǀ	ॐ धनदायै नमः ǀ
572.	Oṃ Dhanadaprītāyai Namaḥ ǀ	ॐ धनदप्रीतायै नमः ǀ
573.	Oṃ Dhanadhānyasamṛddhidāyai Namaḥ ǀ	ॐ धनधान्यसमृद्धिदायै नमः ǀ
574.	Oṃ Dhana Dhānya Samṛddhisthāyai Namaḥ ǀ	ॐ धनधान्यसमृद्धिस्थायै नमः ǀ
575.	Oṃ Dhanadhānyavināśinyai Namaḥ	ॐ धनधान्यविनाशिन्यै नमः ǀ
576.	Oṃ Dharmaniṣṭhāyai Namaḥ ǀ	ॐ धर्मनिष्ठायै नमः ǀ
577.	Oṃ Dharmadhīrāyai Namaḥ ǀ	ॐ धर्मधीरायै नमः ǀ
578.	Oṃ Sadā Dharmamārgaratāyai Namaḥ ǀ	ॐ सदा धर्ममार्गरतायै नमः ǀ
579.	Oṃ Dharmabījakṛtasthānāyai Namaḥ ǀ	ॐ धर्मबीजकृतस्थानायै नमः ǀ
580.	Oṃ Dharmabījasurakṣiṇyai Namaḥ	ॐ धर्मबीजसुरक्षिण्यै नमः ǀ
581.	Oṃ Dharmabījeśvaryai Namaḥ ǀ	ॐ धर्मबीजेश्वर्यै नमः ǀ
582.	Oṃ Dharmabījarūpāyai Namaḥ ǀ	ॐ धर्मबीजरूपायै नमः ǀ
583.	Oṃ Dharmagāyai Namaḥ ǀ	ॐ धर्मगायै नमः ǀ
584.	Oṃ Dharmabījasamudbhūtāyai Namaḥ ǀ	ॐ धर्मबीजसमुद्भूतायै नमः ǀ

585.	*Oṃ Dharmabījasamāśritāyai Namaḥ* |	ॐ धर्मबीजसमाश्रितायै नमः ।
586.	*Oṃ Dharādharapatiprāṇāyai Namaḥ* |	ॐ धराधरपतिप्राणायै नमः ।
587.	*Oṃ Dharādharapatistutāyai Namaḥ* |	ॐ धराधरपतिस्तुतायै नमः ।
588.	*Oṃ Dharādharendratanujāyai Namaḥ* |	ॐ धराधरेन्द्रतनुजायै नमः ।
589.	*Oṃ Dharādharendravanditāyai Namaḥ* |	ॐ धराधरेन्द्रवन्दितायै नमः ।
590.	*Oṃ Dharādharendragehasthāyai Namaḥ* |	ॐ धराधरेन्द्रगेहस्थायै नमः ।
591.	*Oṃ Dharādharendrapālinyai Namaḥ* |	ॐ धराधरेन्द्रपालिन्यै नमः ।
592.	*Oṃ Dharādharendra Sarvārtināśinyai Namaḥ* |	ॐ धराधरेन्द्रसर्वार्तिनाशिन्यै नमः ।
593.	*Oṃ Dharmapālinyai Namaḥ* |	ॐ धर्मपालिन्यै नमः ।
594.	*Oṃ Navīnāyai Namaḥ* |	ॐ नवीनायै नमः ।
595.	*Oṃ Nirmalāyai Namaḥ* |	ॐ निर्मलायै नमः ।
596.	*Oṃ Nityāyai Namaḥ* |	ॐ नित्यायै नमः ।
597.	*Oṃ Nagarājaprapūjitāyai Namaḥ* |	ॐ नगराजप्रपूजितायै नमः ।
598.	*Oṃ Nāgeśvaryai Namaḥ* |	ॐ नागेश्वर्यै नमः ।
599.	*Oṃ Nāgamātre Namaḥ* |	ॐ नागमात्रे नमः ।
600.	*Oṃ Nāgakanyāyai Namaḥ* |	ॐ नागकन्यायै नमः ।
601.	*Oṃ Nagnikāyai Namaḥ* |	ॐ नग्निकायै नमः ।
602.	*Oṃ Nirlepāyai Namaḥ* |	ॐ निर्लेपायै नमः ।
603.	*Oṃ Nirvikalpāyai Namaḥ* |	ॐ निर्विकल्पायै नमः ।
604.	*Oṃ Nirlomāyai Namaḥ* |	ॐ निर्लोमायै नमः ।
605.	*Oṃ Nirupadravāyai Namaḥ* |	ॐ निरुपद्रवायै नमः ।
606.	*Oṃ Nirāhārāyai Namaḥ* |	ॐ निराहारायै नमः ।
607.	*Oṃ Nirākārāyai Namaḥ* |	ॐ निराकारायै नमः ।
608.	*Oṃ Nirañjanasvarūpiṇyai Namaḥ* |	ॐ निरञ्जनस्वरूपिणयै नमः ।
609.	*Oṃ Nāginyai Namaḥ* |	ॐ नागिन्यै नमः ।

610.	Oṃ Nāgavibhavāyai Namaḥ	ॐ नागविभवायै नमः ।
611.	Oṃ Nāgarājaparistutāyai Namaḥ	ॐ नागराजपरिस्तुतायै नमः ।
612.	Oṃ Nāgarājaguṇajñāyai Namaḥ	ॐ नागराजगुणज्ञायै नमः ।
613.	Oṃ Nāgarājasukhapradāyai Namaḥ	ॐ नागराजसुखप्रदायै नमः ।
614.	Oṃ Nāgalokagatāyai Namaḥ	ॐ नागलोकगतायै नमः ।
615.	Oṃ Nityaṃ Nāgalokanivāsinyai Namaḥ	ॐ नित्यं नागलोकनिवासिन्यै नमः ।
616.	Oṃ Nāgalokeśvaryai Namaḥ	ॐ नागलोकेश्वर्यै नमः ।
617.	Oṃ Nāgabhaginyai Namaḥ	ॐ नागभगिन्यै नमः ।
618.	Oṃ Nāgapūjitāyai Namaḥ	ॐ नागपूजितायै नमः ।
619.	Oṃ Nāgamadhyasthitāyai Namaḥ	ॐ नागमध्यस्थितायै नमः ।
620.	Oṃ Nāga Mohasaṅkṣobha Dāyinyai Namaḥ	ॐ नागमोहसङ्क्षोभदायिन्यै नमः ।
621.	Oṃ Nṛtyapriyāyai Namaḥ	ॐ नृत्यप्रियायै नमः ।
622.	Oṃ Nṛtyavatyai Namaḥ	ॐ नृत्यवत्यै नमः ।
623.	Oṃ Nṛtyagītaparāyaṇāyai Namaḥ	ॐ नृत्यगीतपरायणायै नमः ।
624.	Oṃ Nṛtyeśvaryai Namaḥ	ॐ नृत्येश्वर्यै नमः ।
625.	Oṃ Nartakyai Namaḥ	ॐ नर्तक्यै नमः ।
626.	Oṃ Nṛtyarūpāyai Namaḥ	ॐ नृत्यरूपायै नमः ।
627.	Oṃ Nirāśrayāyai Namaḥ	ॐ निराश्रयायै नमः ।
628.	Oṃ Nārāyaṇyai Namaḥ	ॐ नारायण्यै नमः ।
629.	Oṃ Narendrasthāyai Namaḥ	ॐ नरेन्द्रस्थायै नमः ।
630.	Oṃ Naramuṇḍāsthimālinyai Namaḥ	ॐ नरमुण्डास्थिमालिन्यै नमः ।
631.	Oṃ Nityaṃ Naramāṃsapriyāyai Namaḥ	ॐ नित्यं नरमांसप्रियायै नमः ।
632.	Oṃ Sadā Nararaktapriyāyai Namaḥ	ॐ सदा नररक्तप्रियायै नमः ।
633.	Oṃ Nararājeśvaryai Namaḥ	ॐ नरराजेश्वर्यै नमः ।
634.	Oṃ Nārīrūpāyai Namaḥ	ॐ नारीरूपायै नमः ।
635.	Oṃ Nārīsvarūpiṇyai Namaḥ	ॐ नारीस्वरूपिण्यै नमः ।

636.	*Oṃ Nārīgaṇārcitāyai Namaḥ*	ॐ नारीगणार्चिताये नमः।
637.	*Oṃ Nārīmadhyagāyai Namaḥ*	ॐ नारीमध्यगाये नमः।
638.	*Oṃ Nūtanāmbarāyai Namaḥ*	ॐ नूतनाम्बराये नमः।
639.	*Oṃ Narmadāyai Namaḥ*	ॐ नर्मदाये नमः।
640.	*Oṃ Nadīrūpāyai Namaḥ*	ॐ नदीरूपाये नमः।
641.	*Oṃ Nadīsaṅgamasaṃsthitāyai Namaḥ*	ॐ नदीसङ्गमसंस्थिताये नमः।
642.	*Oṃ Narmadeśvarasamprītāyai Namaḥ*	ॐ नर्मदेश्वरसम्प्रीताये नमः।
643.	*Oṃ Narmadeśvararūpiṇyai Namaḥ*	ॐ नर्मदेश्वररूपिण्यै नमः।
644.	*Oṃ Padmāvatyai Namaḥ*	ॐ पद्मावत्यै नमः।
645.	*Oṃ Padmamukhyai Namaḥ*	ॐ पद्ममुख्यै नमः।
646.	*Oṃ Padmakiñjalkavāsinyai Namaḥ*	ॐ पद्मकिञ्जल्कवासिन्यै नमः
647.	*Oṃ Paṭṭavastraparidhānāyai Namaḥ*	ॐ पट्टवस्त्रपरिधानाये नमः।
648.	*Oṃ Padmarāgavibhūṣitāyai Namaḥ*	ॐ पद्मरागविभूषिताये नमः।
649.	*Oṃ Paramāyai Namaḥ*	ॐ परमाये नमः।
650.	*Oṃ Nityaṃ Prītidāyai Namaḥ*	ॐ नित्यं प्रीतिदाये नमः।
651.	*Oṃ Pretāsananivāsinyai Namaḥ*	ॐ प्रेतासननिवासिन्यै नमः।
652.	*Oṃ Paripūrṇarasonmattāyai Namaḥ*	ॐ परिपूर्णरसोन्मत्ताये नमः।
653.	*Oṃ Premavihvalavallabhāyai Namaḥ*	ॐ प्रेमविह्वलवल्लभाये नमः।
654.	*Oṃ Pavitrāsavaniṣpūtāyai Namaḥ*	ॐ पवित्रासवनिष्पूताये नमः।
655.	*Oṃ Preyasyai Namaḥ*	ॐ प्रेयस्यै नमः।
656.	*Oṃ Paramātmikāyai Namaḥ*	ॐ परमात्मिकाये नमः।
657.	*Oṃ Priyavrataparāyai Namaḥ*	ॐ प्रियव्रतपराये नमः।
658.	*Oṃ Nityaṃ Parama Prema Dāyinyai Namaḥ*	ॐ नित्यं परमप्रेमदायिन्यै नमः।
659.	*Oṃ Puṣpapriyāyai Namaḥ*	ॐ पुष्पप्रियाये नमः।
660.	*Oṃ Padmakośāyai Namaḥ*	ॐ पद्मकोशाये नमः।

661.	*Oṃ Padmadharmanivāsinyai Namaḥ* |	ॐ पद्मधर्मनिवासिन्यै नमः ।
662.	*Oṃ Phetkāriṇītantrarūpāyai Namaḥ* |	ॐ फेत्कारिणीतन्त्ररूपाये नमः ।
663.	*Oṃ Pherupheravanādinyai Namaḥ*	ॐ फेरुफेरवनादिन्यै नमः ।
664.	*Oṃ Vaṃśinyai Namaḥ* |	ॐ वंशिन्यै नमः ।
665.	*Oṃ Veśarūpāyai Namaḥ* |	ॐ वेशरूपायै नमः ।
666.	*Oṃ Bagalāyai Namaḥ* |	ॐ बगलायै नमः ।
667.	*Oṃ Vāmarūpiṇyai Namaḥ* |	ॐ वामरूपिण्यै नमः ।
668.	*Oṃ Vāṅmayyai Namaḥ* |	ॐ वाङ्मय्यै नमः ।
669.	*Oṃ Vasudhāyai Namaḥ* |	ॐ वसुधायै नमः ।
670.	*Oṃ Vṛṣyāyai Namaḥ* |	ॐ वृष्यायै नमः ।
671.	*Oṃ Vāgbhavākhyāyai Namaḥ* |	ॐ वाग्भवाख्यायै नमः ।
672.	*Oṃ Varānanāyai Namaḥ* |	ॐ वराननायै नमः ।
673.	*Oṃ Buddhidāyai Namaḥ* |	ॐ बुद्धिदायै नमः ।
674.	*Oṃ Buddhirūpāyai Namaḥ* |	ॐ बुद्धिरूपायै नमः ।
675.	*Oṃ Vidyāyai Namaḥ* |	ॐ विद्यायै नमः ।
676.	*Oṃ Vādasvarūpiṇyai Namaḥ* |	ॐ वादस्वरूपिण्यै नमः ।
677.	*Oṃ Bālāyai Namaḥ* |	ॐ बालायै नमः ।
678.	*Oṃ Vṛddhamayīrūpāyai Namaḥ* |	ॐ वृद्धमयीरूपायै नमः ।
679.	*Oṃ Vāṇyai Namaḥ* |	ॐ वाण्यै नमः ।
680.	*Oṃ Vākyanivāsinyai Namaḥ* |	ॐ वाक्यनिवासिन्यै नमः ।
681.	*Oṃ Varuṇāyai Namaḥ* |	ॐ वरुणायै नमः ।
682.	*Oṃ Vāgvatyai Namaḥ* |	ॐ वाग्वत्यै नमः ।
683.	*Oṃ Vīrāyai Namaḥ* |	ॐ वीरायै नमः ।
684.	*Oṃ Vīrabhūṣaṇabhūṣitāyai Namaḥ*	ॐ वीरभूषणभूषितायै नमः ।
685.	*Oṃ Vīrabhadrārcitapadāyai Namaḥ*	ॐ वीरभद्रार्चितपदायै नमः ।
686.	*Oṃ Vīrabhadraprasuve Namaḥ* |	ॐ वीरभद्रप्रसुवे नमः ।
687.	*Oṃ Vedamārgaratāyai Namaḥ* |	ॐ वेदमार्गरतायै नमः ।
688.	*Oṃ Vedamantrarūpāyai Namaḥ* |	ॐ वेदमन्त्ररूपायै नमः ।
689.	*Oṃ Vaṣaṭpriyāyai Namaḥ* |	ॐ वषट्प्रियायै नमः ।

690.	Oṃ Vīṇāvādyasamāyuktāyai Namaḥ |	ॐ वीणावाद्यसमायुक्तायै नमः ।
691.	Oṃ Vīṇāvādyaparāyaṇāyai Namaḥ	ॐ वीणावाद्यपरायणायै नमः ।
692.	Oṃ Vīṇāravāyai Namaḥ |	ॐ वीणारवायै नमः ।
693.	Oṃ Vīṇāśabdarūpāyai Namaḥ |	ॐ वीणाशब्दरूपायै नमः ।
694.	Oṃ Vaiṣṇavyai Namaḥ |	ॐ वैष्णव्यै नमः ।
695.	Oṃ Vaiṣṇavācāraniratāyai Namaḥ |	ॐ वैष्णवाचारनिरतायै नमः ।
696.	Oṃ Vaiṣṇavācāratatparāyai Namaḥ |	ॐ वैष्णवाचारतत्परायै नमः ।
697.	Oṃ Viṣṇusevyāyai Namaḥ |	ॐ विष्णुसेव्यायै नमः ।
698.	Oṃ Viṣṇupatnyai Namaḥ |	ॐ विष्णुपत्न्यै नमः ।
699.	Oṃ Viṣṇurūpāyai Namaḥ |	ॐ विष्णुरूपायै नमः ।
700.	Oṃ Varānanāyai Namaḥ |	ॐ वराननायै नमः ।
701.	Oṃ Viśveśvaryai Namaḥ |	ॐ विश्वेश्वर्यै नमः ।
702.	Oṃ Viśvamātre Namaḥ |	ॐ विश्वमात्रे नमः ।
703.	Oṃ Viśvanirmāṇakāriṇyai Namaḥ |	ॐ विश्वनिर्माणकारिण्यै नमः ।
704.	Oṃ Viśvarūpāyai Namaḥ |	ॐ विश्वरूपायै नमः ।
705.	Oṃ Viśveśyai Namaḥ |	ॐ विश्वेश्यै नमः ।
706.	Oṃ Viśvasaṃhārakāriṇyai Namaḥ |	ॐ विश्वसंहारकारिण्यै नमः ।
707.	Oṃ Bhairavyai Namaḥ |	ॐ भैरव्यै नमः ।
708.	Oṃ Bhairavārādhyāyai Namaḥ |	ॐ भैरवाराध्यायै नमः ।
709.	Oṃ Bhūtabhairavasevitāyai Namaḥ	ॐ भूतभैरवसेवितायै नमः ।
710.	Oṃ Bhairaveśyai Namaḥ |	ॐ भैरवेश्यै नमः ।
711.	Oṃ Bhīmāyai Namaḥ |	ॐ भीमायै नमः ।
712.	Oṃ Bhairaveśvaratuṣṭidāyai Namaḥ |	ॐ भैरवेश्वरतुष्टिदायै नमः ।
713.	Oṃ Bhairavādhīśaramaṇyai Namaḥ	ॐ भैरवाधीशरमण्यै नमः ।
714.	Oṃ Bhairavādhīśapālinyai Namaḥ |	ॐ भैरवाधीशपालिन्यै नमः ।
715.	Oṃ Bhīmeśvaryai Namaḥ |	ॐ भीमेश्वर्यै नमः ।
716.	Oṃ Bhīmamātre Namaḥ |	ॐ भीममात्रे नमः ।

717.	Oṃ Bhīmaśabdaparāyaṇāyai Namaḥ		ॐ भीमशब्दपरायणायै नमः ।
718.	Oṃ Bhīmarūpāyai Namaḥ		ॐ भीमरूपायै नमः ।
719.	Oṃ Bhīmeśyai Namaḥ		ॐ भीमेश्यै नमः ।
720.	Oṃ Bhīmāyai Namaḥ		ॐ भीमायै नमः ।
721.	Oṃ Bhīmavarapradāyai Namaḥ		ॐ भीमवरप्रदायै नमः ।
722.	Oṃ Bhīmapūjitapādābjāyai Namaḥ	ॐ भीमपूजितपादाब्जायै नमः
723.	Oṃ Bhīmabhairavapālinyai Namaḥ	ॐ भीमभैरवपालिन्यै नमः ।
724.	Oṃ Bhīmāsuradhvaṃsakaryai Namaḥ		ॐ भीमासुरध्वंसकर्यै नमः ।
725.	Oṃ Bhīmaduṣṭavināśinyai Namaḥ		ॐ भीमदुष्टविनाशिन्यै नमः ।
726.	Oṃ Bhuvanāyai Namaḥ		ॐ भुवनायै नमः ।
727.	Oṃ Bhuvanārādhyāyai Namaḥ		ॐ भुवनाराध्यायै नमः ।
728.	Oṃ Bhavānyai Namaḥ		ॐ भवान्यै नमः ।
729.	Oṃ Bhūtidāyai Namaḥ		ॐ भूतिदायै नमः ।
730.	Oṃ Bhayadāyai Namaḥ		ॐ भयदायै नमः ।
731.	Oṃ Bhayahantryai Namaḥ		ॐ भयहन्त्र्यै नमः ।
732.	Oṃ Abhayāyai Namaḥ		ॐ अभयायै नमः ।
733.	Oṃ Bhayarūpiṇyai Namaḥ		ॐ भयरूपिण्यै नमः ।
734.	Oṃ Bhīmanādāvihvalāyai Namaḥ		ॐ भीमनादाविह्वलायै नमः ।
735.	Oṃ Bhayabhītivināśinyai Namaḥ	ॐ भयभीतिविनाशिन्यै नमः ।
736.	Oṃ Mattāyai Namaḥ		ॐ मत्तायै नमः ।
737.	Oṃ Pramattarūpāyai Namaḥ		ॐ प्रमत्तरूपायै नमः ।
738.	Oṃ Madonmattasvarūpiṇyai Namaḥ		ॐ मदोन्मत्तस्वरूपिण्यै नमः ।
739.	Oṃ Mānyāyai Namaḥ		ॐ मान्यायै नमः ।
740.	Oṃ Manojñāyai Namaḥ		ॐ मनोज्ञायै नमः ।
741.	Oṃ Mānāyai Namaḥ		ॐ मानायै नमः ।
742.	Oṃ Maṅgalāyai Namaḥ		ॐ मङ्गलायै नमः ।
743.	Oṃ Manoharāyai Namaḥ		ॐ मनोहरायै नमः ।
744.	Oṃ Mānanīyāyai Namaḥ		ॐ माननीयायै नमः ।

745.	Oṃ Mahāpūjyāyai Namaḥ ।	ॐ महापूज्याये नमः ।
746.	Oṃ Mahiṣīduṣṭamardinyai Namaḥ ।	ॐ महिषीदुष्टमर्दिन्ये नमः ।
747.	Oṃ Mahiṣāsurahantryai Namaḥ	ॐ महिषासुरहन्त्र्ये नमः ।
748.	Oṃ Mātaṅgyai Namaḥ ।	ॐ मातङ्ग्ये नमः ।
749.	Oṃ Mayavāsinyai Namaḥ ।	ॐ मयवासिन्ये नमः ।
750.	Oṃ Mādhvyai Namaḥ ।	ॐ माध्व्ये नमः ।
751.	Oṃ Madhumayyai Namaḥ ।	ॐ मधुमय्ये नमः ।
752.	Oṃ Mudrāyai Namaḥ ।	ॐ मुद्राये नमः ।
753.	Oṃ Mudrikāmantrarūpiṇyai Namaḥ ।	ॐ मुद्रिकामन्त्ररूपिण्ये नमः ।
754.	Oṃ Mahāviśveśvarīdūtyai Namaḥ ।	ॐ महाविश्वेश्वरीदूत्ये नमः ।
755.	Oṃ Maulicandraprakāśinyai Namaḥ ।	ॐ मौलिचन्द्रप्रकाशिन्ये नमः ।
756.	Oṃ Yaśaḥsvarūpiṇyai Devyai Namaḥ ।	ॐ यशःस्वरूपिण्ये देव्ये नमः ।
757.	Oṃ Yogamārgapradāyinyai Namaḥ	ॐ योगमार्गप्रदायिन्ये नमः ।
758.	Oṃ Yoginyai Namaḥ ।	ॐ योगिन्ये नमः ।
759.	Oṃ Yogagamyāyai Namaḥ ।	ॐ योगगम्याये नमः ।
760.	Oṃ Yāmyeśyai Namaḥ ।	ॐ याम्येश्ये नमः ।
761.	Oṃ Yogarūpiṇyai Namaḥ ।	ॐ योगरूपिण्ये नमः ।
762.	Oṃ Yajñāṅgyai Namaḥ ।	ॐ यज्ञाङ्ग्ये नमः ।
763.	Oṃ Yogamayyai Namaḥ ।	ॐ योगमय्ये नमः ।
764.	Oṃ Japarūpāyai Namaḥ ।	ॐ जपरूपाये नमः ।
765.	Oṃ Japātmikāyai Namaḥ ।	ॐ जपात्मिकाये नमः ।
766.	Oṃ Yugākhyāyai Namaḥ ।	ॐ युगाख्याये नमः ।
767.	Oṃ Yugāntāyai Namaḥ ।	ॐ युगान्ताये नमः ।
768.	Oṃ Yonimaṇḍalavāsinyai Namaḥ	ॐ योनिमण्डलवासिन्ये नमः ।
769.	Oṃ Ayonijāyai Namaḥ ।	ॐ अयोनिजाये नमः ।
770.	Oṃ Yoganidrāyai Namaḥ ।	ॐ योगनिद्राये नमः ।
771.	Oṃ Yogānandapradāyinyai Namaḥ	ॐ योगानन्दप्रदायिन्ये नमः ।
772.	Oṃ Ramāyai Namaḥ ।	ॐ रमाये नमः ।

773.	Oṃ Nityaṃ Ratipriyāyai Namaḥ	ॐ नित्यं रतिप्रियायै नमः ।
774.	Oṃ Ratirāgavivardhinyai Namaḥ	ॐ रतिरागविवर्धिन्यै नमः ।
775.	Oṃ Ramaṇyai Namaḥ	ॐ रमण्यै नमः ।
776.	Oṃ Rāsasambhūtāyai Namaḥ	ॐ राससम्भूतायै नमः ।
777.	Oṃ Ramyāyai Namaḥ	ॐ रम्यायै नमः ।
778.	Oṃ Rāsapriyāyai Namaḥ	ॐ रासप्रियायै नमः ।
779.	Oṃ Rasāyai Namaḥ	ॐ रसायै नमः ।
780.	Oṃ Raṇotkaṇṭhāyai Namaḥ	ॐ रणोत्कण्ठायै नमः ।
781.	Oṃ Raṇasthāyai Namaḥ	ॐ रणस्थायै नमः ।
782.	Oṃ Varāraṅgapradāyinyai Namaḥ	ॐ वरारङ्गप्रदायिन्यै नमः ।
783.	Oṃ Revatyai Namaḥ	ॐ रेवत्यै नमः ।
784.	Oṃ Raṇajaitryai Namaḥ	ॐ रणजैत्र्यै नमः ।
785.	Oṃ Rasodbhūtāyai Namaḥ	ॐ रसोद्भूतायै नमः ।
786.	Oṃ Raṇotsavāyai Namaḥ	ॐ रणोत्सवायै नमः ।
787.	Oṃ Latāyai Namaḥ	ॐ लतायै नमः ।
788.	Oṃ Lāvaṇyarūpāyai Namaḥ	ॐ लावण्यरूपायै नमः ।
789.	Oṃ Lavaṇābdhisvarūpiṇyai Namaḥ	ॐ लवणाब्धिस्वरूपिण्यै नमः
790.	Oṃ Lavaṅgakusumārādhyāyai Namaḥ	ॐ लवङ्गकुसुमाराध्यायै नमः।
791.	Oṃ Lolajihvāyai Namaḥ	ॐ लोलजिह्वायै नमः ।
792.	Oṃ Lelihāyai Namaḥ	ॐ लेलिहायै नमः ।
793.	Oṃ Vaśinyai Namaḥ	ॐ वशिन्यै नमः ।
794.	Oṃ Vanasaṃsthāyai Namaḥ	ॐ वनसंस्थायै नमः ।
795.	Oṃ Vanapuṣpapriyāyai Namaḥ	ॐ वनपुष्पप्रियायै नमः ।
796.	Oṃ Varāyai Namaḥ	ॐ वरायै नमः ।
797.	Oṃ Prāṇeśvaryai Namaḥ	ॐ प्राणेश्वर्यै नमः ।
798.	Oṃ Buddhirūpāyai Namaḥ	ॐ बुद्धिरूपायै नमः ।
799.	Oṃ Buddhidātryai Namaḥ	ॐ बुद्धिदात्र्यै नमः ।
800.	Oṃ Budhātmikāyai Namaḥ	ॐ बुधात्मिकायै नमः ।
801.	Oṃ Śamanyai Namaḥ	ॐ शमन्यै नमः ।

802.	Oṃ Śvetavarṇāyai Namaḥ		ॐ श्वेतवर्णायै नमः ।
803.	Oṃ Śāṅkaryai Namaḥ		ॐ शाङ्कर्यै नमः ।
804.	Oṃ Śivabhāṣiṇyai Namaḥ		ॐ शिवभाषिण्यै नमः ।
805.	Oṃ Śāmyarūpāyai Namaḥ		ॐ शाम्यरूपायै नमः ।
806.	Oṃ Śaktirūpāyai Namaḥ		ॐ शक्तिरूपायै नमः ।
807.	Oṃ Śaktibindunivāsinyai Namaḥ	ॐ शक्तिबिन्दुनिवासिन्यै नमः
808.	Oṃ Sarveśvaryai Namaḥ		ॐ सर्वेश्वर्यै नमः ।
809.	Oṃ Sarvadātryai Namaḥ		ॐ सर्वदात्र्यै नमः ।
810.	Oṃ Sarvamātre Namaḥ		ॐ सर्वमात्रे नमः ।
811.	Oṃ Śarvaryai Namaḥ		ॐ शर्वर्यै नमः ।
812.	Oṃ Śāmbhavyai Namaḥ		ॐ शाम्भव्यै नमः ।
813.	Oṃ Siddhidāyai Namaḥ		ॐ सिद्धिदायै नमः ।
814.	Oṃ Siddhāyai Namaḥ		ॐ सिद्धायै नमः ।
815.	Oṃ Suṣumnāyai Namaḥ		ॐ सुषुम्नायै नमः ।
816.	Oṃ Svarabhāsinyai Namaḥ		ॐ स्वरभासिन्यै नमः ।
817.	Oṃ Sahasradalamadhyasthāyai Namaḥ		ॐ सहस्रदलमध्यस्थायै नमः ।
818.	Oṃ Sahasradalavartinyai Namaḥ		ॐ सहस्रदलवर्तिन्यै नमः ।
819.	Oṃ Harapriyāyai Namaḥ		ॐ हरप्रियायै नमः ।
820.	Oṃ Haradhyeyāyai Namaḥ		ॐ हरध्येयायै नमः ।
821.	Oṃ Huṅkārabījarūpiṇyai Namaḥ	ॐ हुङ्कारबीजरूपिण्यै नमः ।
822.	Oṃ Laṅkeśvaryai Namaḥ		ॐ लङ्केश्वर्यै नमः ।
823.	Oṃ Taralāyai Namaḥ		ॐ तरलायै नमः ।
824.	Oṃ Lomamāmsaprapūjitāyai Namaḥ		ॐ लोममांसप्रपूजितायै नमः ।
825.	Oṃ Kṣemyāyai Namaḥ		ॐ क्षेम्यायै नमः ।
826.	Oṃ Kṣemakaryai Namaḥ		ॐ क्षेमकर्यै नमः ।
827.	Oṃ Kṣāmāyai Namaḥ		ॐ क्षामायै नमः ।
828.	Oṃ Kṣīrabindusvarūpiṇyai Namaḥ		ॐ क्षीरबिन्दुस्वरूपिण्यै नमः ।
829.	Oṃ Kṣiptacittapradāyai Namaḥ		ॐ क्षिप्तचित्तप्रदायै नमः ।

830.	Oṃ Nityaṃ Kṣauma Vastra Vilāsinyai Namaḥ		ॐ नित्यं क्षौमवस्त्रविलासिन्यै नमः ।
831.	Oṃ Chinnāyai Namaḥ		ॐ छिन्नायै नमः ।
832.	Oṃ Chinnarūpāyai Namaḥ		ॐ छिन्नरूपायै नमः ।
833.	Oṃ Kṣudhāyai Namaḥ		ॐ क्षुधायै नमः ।
834.	Oṃ Kṣautkārarūpiṇyai Namaḥ		ॐ क्षौत्काररूपिण्यै नमः ।
835.	Oṃ Sarvavarṇamayyai Devyai Namaḥ		ॐ सर्ववर्णमय्यै देव्यै नमः ।
836.	Oṃ Sarvasampatpradāyinyai Namaḥ		ॐ सर्वसम्पत्प्रदायिन्यै नमः ।
837.	Oṃ Sarvasampatpradātryai Namaḥ		ॐ सर्वसम्पत्प्रदात्र्यै नमः ।
838.	Oṃ Sampadāpadabhūṣitāyai Namaḥ		ॐ सम्पदापदभूषितायै नमः ।
839.	Oṃ Sattvarūpāyai Namaḥ		ॐ सत्त्वरूपायै नमः ।
840.	Oṃ Sarvārthāyai Namaḥ		ॐ सर्वार्थ्यै नमः ।
841.	Oṃ Sarvadevaprapūjitāyai Namaḥ		ॐ सर्वदेवप्रपूजितायै नमः ।
842.	Oṃ Sarveśvaryai Namaḥ		ॐ सर्वेश्वर्यै नमः ।
843.	Oṃ Sarvamātre Namaḥ		ॐ सर्वमात्रे नमः ।
844.	Oṃ Sarvajñāyai Namaḥ		ॐ सर्वज्ञायै नमः ।
845.	Oṃ Surasātmikāyai Namaḥ		ॐ सुरसात्मिकायै नमः ।
846.	Oṃ Sindhave Namaḥ		ॐ सिन्धवे नमः ।
847.	Oṃ Mandākinyai Namaḥ		ॐ मन्दाकिन्यै नमः ।
848.	Oṃ Gaṅgāyai Namaḥ		ॐ गङ्गायै नमः ।
849.	Oṃ Nadīsāgararūpiṇyai Namaḥ		ॐ नदीसागररूपिण्यै नमः ।
850.	Oṃ Sukeśyai Namaḥ		ॐ सुकेश्यै नमः ।
851.	Oṃ Muktakeśyai Namaḥ		ॐ मुक्तकेश्यै नमः ।
852.	Oṃ Ḍākinyai Namaḥ		ॐ डाकिन्यै नमः ।
853.	Oṃ Varavarṇinyai Namaḥ		ॐ वरवर्णिन्यै नमः ।
854.	Oṃ Jñānadāyai Namaḥ		ॐ ज्ञानदायै नमः ।
855.	Oṃ Jñānagaganāyai Namaḥ		ॐ ज्ञानगगनायै नमः ।
856.	Oṃ Somamaṇḍalavāsinyai Namaḥ		ॐ सोममण्डलवासिन्यै नमः ।

857.	*Oṃ Ākāśanilayāyai Namaḥ ।*	ॐ आकाशनिलयायै नमः ।
858.	*Oṃ Nityaṃ Paramākāśarūpiṇyai Namaḥ ।*	ॐ नित्यं परमाकाशरूपिण्यै नमः ।
859.	*Oṃ Annapūrṇāyai Namaḥ ।*	ॐ अन्नपूर्णायै नमः ।
860.	*Oṃ Mahānityāyai Namaḥ ।*	ॐ महानित्यायै नमः ।
861.	*Oṃ Mahādevarasodbhavāyai Namaḥ ।*	ॐ महादेवरसोद्भवायै नमः ।
862.	*Oṃ Maṅgalāyai Namaḥ ।*	ॐ मङ्गलायै नमः ।
863.	*Oṃ Kālikāyai Namaḥ ।*	ॐ कालिकायै नमः ।
864.	*Oṃ Caṇḍāyai Namaḥ ।*	ॐ चण्डायै नमः ।
865.	*Oṃ Caṇḍanādātibhīṣaṇāyai Namaḥ*	ॐ चण्डनादातिभीषणायै नमः
866.	*Oṃ Caṇḍāsurasya Mathanyai Namaḥ ।*	ॐ चण्डासुरस्य मथन्यै नमः ।
867.	*Oṃ Cāmuṇḍāyai Namaḥ ।*	ॐ चामुण्डायै नमः ।
868.	*Oṃ Capalātmikāyai Namaḥ ।*	ॐ चपलात्मिकायै नमः ।
869.	*Oṃ Caṇḍyai Namaḥ ।*	ॐ चण्ड्यै नमः ।
870.	*Oṃ Cāmarakeśyai Namaḥ ।*	ॐ चामरकेश्यै नमः ।
871.	*Oṃ Calatkuṇḍaladhāriṇyai Namaḥ*	ॐ चलत्कुण्डलधारिण्यै नमः ।
872.	*Oṃ Muṇḍamālādharāyai Namaḥ ।*	ॐ मुण्डमालाधरायै नमः ।
873.	*Oṃ Nityaṃ Khaṇḍamuṇḍa Vilāsinyai Namaḥ ।*	ॐ नित्यं खण्डमुण्डविलासिन्यै नमः।
874.	*Oṃ Khaḍgahastāyai Namaḥ ।*	ॐ खड्गहस्तायै नमः ।
875.	*Oṃ Muṇḍahastāyai Namaḥ ।*	ॐ मुण्डहस्तायै नमः ।
876.	*Oṃ Varahastāyai Namaḥ ।*	ॐ वरहस्तायै नमः ।
877.	*Oṃ Varapradāyai Namaḥ ।*	ॐ वरप्रदायै नमः ।
878.	*Oṃ Nityamasicarmadharāyai Namaḥ ।*	ॐ नित्यमसिचर्मधरायै नमः ।
879.	*Oṃ Pāśāṅkuśadharāyai Parāyai Namaḥ ।*	ॐ पाशाङ्कुशधरायै परायै नमः ।
880.	*Oṃ Śūlahastāyai Namaḥ ।*	ॐ शूलहस्तायै नमः ।
881.	*Oṃ Śivahastāyai Namaḥ ।*	ॐ शिवहस्तायै नमः ।

882.	Oṃ Ghaṇṭānādavilāsinyai Namaḥ ǀ	ॐ घण्टानादविलासिन्यै नमः ǀ
883.	Oṃ Dhanurbāṇadharāyai Namaḥ ǀ	ॐ धनुर्बाणधरायै नमः ǀ
884.	Oṃ Ādityāyai Namaḥ ǀ	ॐ आदित्यायै नमः ǀ
885.	Oṃ Nāgahastāyai Namaḥ ǀ	ॐ नागहस्तायै नमः ǀ
886.	Oṃ Nagātmajāyai Namaḥ ǀ	ॐ नगात्मजायै नमः ǀ
887.	Oṃ Mahiṣāsurahantryai Namaḥ	ॐ महिषासुरहन्त्र्यै नमः ǀ
888.	Oṃ Raktabījavināśinyai Namaḥ ǀ	ॐ रक्तबीजविनाशिन्यै नमः ǀ
889.	Oṃ Raktarūpāyai Namaḥ ǀ	ॐ रक्तरूपायै नमः ǀ
890.	Oṃ Raktagātrāyai Namaḥ ǀ	ॐ रक्तगात्रायै नमः ǀ
891.	Oṃ Raktahastāyai Namaḥ ǀ	ॐ रक्तहस्तायै नमः ǀ
892.	Oṃ Bhayapradāyai Namaḥ ǀ	ॐ भयप्रदायै नमः ǀ
893.	Oṃ Asitāyai Namaḥ ǀ	ॐ असितायै नमः ǀ
894.	Oṃ Dharmadharāyai Namaḥ ǀ	ॐ धर्मधरायै नमः ǀ
895.	Oṃ Pāśāṅkuśadharāyai Parāyai Namaḥ ǀ	ॐ पाशाङ्कुशधरायै परायै नमः ǀ
896.	Oṃ Nityaṃ Dhanur Bāṇa Dharāyai Namaḥ ǀ	ॐ नित्यं धनुर्बाणधरायै नमः ǀ
897.	Oṃ Dhūmralocananāśinyai Namaḥ	ॐ धूम्रलोचननाशिन्यै नमः ǀ
898.	Oṃ Parasthāyai Namaḥ ǀ	ॐ परस्थायै नमः ǀ
899.	Oṃ Devatāmūrtyai Namaḥ ǀ	ॐ देवतामूर्त्यै नमः ǀ
900.	Oṃ Śarvāṇyai Namaḥ ǀ	ॐ शर्वाण्यै नमः ǀ
901.	Oṃ Śāradāyai Parāyai Namaḥ ǀ	ॐ शारदायै परायै नमः ǀ
902.	Oṃ Nānāvarṇavibhūṣāṅgyai Namaḥ ǀ	ॐ नानावर्णविभूषाङ्ग्यै नमः ǀ
903.	Oṃ Nānārāgasamāpinyai Namaḥ ǀ	ॐ नानारागसमापिन्यै नमः ǀ
904.	Oṃ Paśuvastraparidhānāyai Namaḥ ǀ	ॐ पशुवस्त्रपरिधानायै नमः ǀ
905.	Oṃ Puṣpāyudhadharāyai Parāyai Namaḥ ǀ	ॐ पुष्पायुधधरायै परायै नमः ǀ
906.	Oṃ Muktārañjitamālāḍhyāyai Namaḥ ǀ	ॐ मुक्तारञ्जितमालाढ्यायै नमः ǀ
907.	Oṃ Muktāhāravilāsinyai Namaḥ	ॐ मुक्ताहारविलासिन्यै नमः ǀ

908.	Oṃ Svarṇakuṇḍalabhūṣāyai Namaḥ	ॐ स्वर्णकुण्डलभूषायै नमः ।
909.	Oṃ Svarṇasiṃhāsanasthitāyai Namaḥ ।	ॐ स्वर्णसिंहासनस्थितायै नमः ।
910.	Oṃ Sundarāṅgyai Namaḥ ।	ॐ सुन्दराङ्ग्यै नमः ।
911.	Oṃ Suvarṇābhāyai Namaḥ ।	ॐ सुवर्णाभायै नमः ।
912.	Oṃ Śāmbhavyai Namaḥ ।	ॐ शाम्भव्यै नमः ।
913.	Oṃ Śakaṭātmikāyai Namaḥ ।	ॐ शकटात्मिकायै नमः ।
914.	Oṃ Sarvalokeśavidyāyai Namaḥ	ॐ सर्वलोकेशविद्यायै नमः ।
915.	Oṃ Mohasammohakāriṇyai Namaḥ	ॐ मोहसम्मोहकारिण्यै नमः ।
916.	Oṃ Śreyasyai Namaḥ ।	ॐ श्रेयस्यै नमः ।
917.	Oṃ Sṛṣṭirūpāyai Namaḥ ।	ॐ सृष्टिरूपायै नमः ।
918.	Oṃ Chinnachadmamayyai Namaḥ ।	ॐ छिन्नछद्ममय्यै नमः ।
919.	Oṃ Chalāyai Namaḥ ।	ॐ छलायै नमः ।
920.	Oṃ Nityaṃ Chinna Muṇḍa Dharāyai Namaḥ ।	ॐ नित्यं छिन्नमुण्डधरायै नमः।
921.	Oṃ Nityānanda Vidhāyinyai Namaḥ	ॐ नित्यानन्द विधायिन्यै नमः
922.	Oṃ Nandāyai Namaḥ ।	ॐ नन्दायै नमः ।
923.	Oṃ Pūrṇāyai Namaḥ ।	ॐ पूर्णायै नमः ।
924.	Oṃ Riktāyai Namaḥ ।	ॐ रिक्तायै नमः ।
925.	Oṃ Tithibhyo Namaḥ ।	ॐ तिथिभ्यो नमः ।
926.	Oṃ Pūrṇaṣoḍaśyai Namaḥ ।	ॐ पूर्णषोडश्यै नमः ।
927.	Oṃ Kuhvai Namaḥ ।	ॐ कुह्वै नमः ।
928.	Oṃ Saṅkrāntirūpāyai Namaḥ ।	ॐ सङ्क्रान्तिरूपायै नमः ।
929.	Oṃ Pañcaparvavilāsinyai Namaḥ	ॐ पञ्चपर्वविलासिन्यै नमः ।
930.	Oṃ Nityaṃ Pañcabāṇadharāyai Namaḥ ।	ॐ नित्यं पञ्चबाणधरायै नमः ।
931.	Oṃ Pañcamaprītidāyai Parāyai Namaḥ ।	ॐ पञ्चमप्रीतिदायै परायै नमः ।
932.	Oṃ Pañcapatrābhilāṣāyai Namaḥ ।	ॐ पञ्चपत्राभिलाषायै नमः ।
933.	Oṃ Pañcāmṛtavilāsinyai Namaḥ।	ॐ पञ्चामृतविलासिन्यै नमः ।

934.	Oṃ Pāñcālyai Namaḥ		ॐ पाञ्चाल्यै नमः ।
935.	Oṃ Pañcamīdevyai Namaḥ		ॐ पञ्चमीदेव्यै नमः ।
936.	Oṃ Pañcaraktaprasāriṇyai Namaḥ	ॐ पञ्चरक्तप्रसारिण्यै नमः ।
937.	Oṃ Nityaṃ Pañcabāṇadharāyai Namaḥ		ॐ नित्यं पञ्चबाणधरायै नमः ।
938.	Oṃ Nityadātryai Namaḥ		ॐ नित्यदात्र्यै नमः ।
939.	Oṃ Dayāparāyai Namaḥ		ॐ दयापरायै नमः ।
940.	Oṃ Palalādipriyāyai Nityāyai Namaḥ		ॐ पललादिप्रियायै नित्यायै नमः ।
941.	Oṃ Apaśugamyāyai Namaḥ		ॐ अपशुगम्यायै नमः ।
942.	Oṃ Pareśitāyai Namaḥ		ॐ परेशितायै नमः ।
943.	Oṃ Parāyai Namaḥ		ॐ परायै नमः ।
944.	Oṃ Pararahasyāyai Namaḥ		ॐ पररहस्यायै नमः ।
945.	Oṃ Paramapremavihvalāyai Namaḥ		ॐ परमप्रेमविह्वलायै नमः ।
946.	Oṃ Kulīnāyai Namaḥ		ॐ कुलीनायै नमः ।
947.	Oṃ Keśimārgasthāyai Namaḥ		ॐ केशिमार्गस्थायै नमः ।
948.	Oṃ Kulamārgaprakāśinyai Namaḥ		ॐ कुलमार्गप्रकाशिन्यै नमः ।
949.	Oṃ Kulākulasvarūpāyai Namaḥ		ॐ कुलाकुलस्वरूपायै नमः ।
950.	Oṃ Kulārṇavamayyai Namaḥ		ॐ कुलार्णवमय्यै नमः ।
951.	Oṃ Kulāyai Namaḥ		ॐ कुलायै नमः ।
952.	Oṃ Rukmāyai Namaḥ		ॐ रुक्मायै नमः ।
953.	Oṃ Kālarūpāyai Namaḥ		ॐ कालरूपायै नमः ।
954.	Oṃ Kālakampanakāriṇyai Namaḥ		ॐ कालकम्पनकारिण्यै नमः ।
955.	Oṃ Vilāsarūpiṇyai Namaḥ		ॐ विलासरूपिण्यै नमः ।
956.	Oṃ Bhadrāyai Namaḥ		ॐ भद्रायै नमः ।
957.	Oṃ Kulākulanamaskṛtāyai Namaḥ		ॐ कुलाकुलनमस्कृतायै नमः
958.	Oṃ Kuberavittadhātryai Namaḥ		ॐ कुबेरवित्तधात्र्यै नमः ।
959.	Oṃ Kumārajananyai Parāyai Namaḥ		ॐ कुमारजनन्यै परायै नमः ।

960.	Oṃ Kumārīrūpasaṃsthāyai Namaḥ	ॐ कुमारीरूपसंस्थायै नमः ।
961.	Oṃ Kumārīpūjanāmbikāyai Namaḥ	ॐ कुमारीपूजनाम्बिकायै नमः
962.	Oṃ Kuraṅganayanāyai Devyai Namaḥ		ॐ कुरङ्गनयनायै देव्यै नमः ।
963.	Oṃ Dineśāsyāparājitāyai Namaḥ	ॐ दिनेशास्यापराजितायै नमः
964.	Oṃ Kuṇḍalyai Namaḥ		ॐ कुण्डल्यै नमः ।
965.	Oṃ Kadalīsenāyai Namaḥ		ॐ कदलीसेनायै नमः ।
966.	Oṃ Kumārgarahitāyai Namaḥ		ॐ कुमार्गरहितायै नमः ।
967.	Oṃ Varāyai Namaḥ		ॐ वरायै नमः ।
968.	Oṃ Anantarūpāyai Namaḥ		ॐ अनन्तरूपायै नमः ।
969.	Oṃ Anantasthāyai Namaḥ		ॐ अनन्तस्थायै नमः ।
970.	Oṃ Ānandasindhuvāsinyai Namaḥ		ॐ आनन्दसिन्धुवासिन्यै नमः
971.	Oṃ Ilāsvarūpiṇyai Devyai Namaḥ		ॐ इलास्वरूपिण्यै देव्यै नमः ।
972.	Oṃ Ibhedabhayaṅkaryai Namaḥ	ॐ इभेदभयङ्कर्यै नमः ।
973.	Oṃ Iṅgalāyai Namaḥ		ॐ इङ्गलायै नमः ।
974.	Oṃ Piṅgalāyai Nāḍyai Namaḥ		ॐ पिङ्गलायै नाड्यै नमः ।
975.	Oṃ Ikārākṣararūpiṇyai Namaḥ		ॐ इकाराक्षररूपिण्यै नमः ।
976.	Oṃ Umāyai Namaḥ		ॐ उमायै नमः ।
977.	Oṃ Utpattirūpāyai Namaḥ		ॐ उत्पत्तिरूपायै नमः ।
978.	Oṃ Uccabhāvavināśinyai Namaḥ	ॐ उच्चभावविनाशिन्यै नमः ।
979.	Oṃ Ṛgvedāyai Namaḥ		ॐ ऋग्वेदायै नमः ।
980.	Oṃ Nirārādhyāyai Namaḥ		ॐ निराराध्यायै नमः ।
981.	Oṃ Yajurvedaprapūjitāyai Namaḥ		ॐ यजुर्वेदप्रपूजितायै नमः ।
982.	Oṃ Sāmavedena Saṅgītāyai Namaḥ	ॐ सामवेदेन सङ्गीतायै नमः
983.	Oṃ Atharvavedabhāṣiṇyai Namaḥ		ॐ अथर्ववेदभाषिण्यै नमः ।
984.	Oṃ Ṛkārarūpiṇyai Namaḥ		ॐ ऋकाररूपिण्यै नमः ।
985.	Oṃ Ṛkṣāyai Namaḥ		ॐ ऋक्षायै नमः ।
986.	Oṃ Nirakṣarasvarūpiṇyai Namaḥ		ॐ निरक्षरस्वरूपिण्यै नमः ।
987.	Oṃ Ahidurgāsamācārāyai Namaḥ		ॐ अहिदुर्गासमाचारायै नमः ।
988.	Oṃ Ikārārṇasvarūpiṇyai Namaḥ		ॐ इकारार्णस्वरूपिण्यै नमः ।
989.	Oṃ Oṅkārāyai Namaḥ		ॐ ओङ्कारायै नमः ।

990.	Oṃ Praṇavasthāyai Namaḥ	ॐ प्रणवस्थायै नमः ।
991.	Oṃ Oṅkārādi Svarūpiṇyai Namaḥ	ॐ ओङ्कारादि स्वरूपिण्यै नमः ।
992.	Oṃ Anulomavilomasthāyai Namaḥ	ॐ अनुलोमविलोमस्थायै नमः
993.	Oṃ Thakāravarṇasambhavāyai Namaḥ	ॐ थकारवर्णसम्भवायै नमः ।
994.	Oṃ Pañcāśadvarṇabījāḍhyāyai Namaḥ	ॐ पञ्चाशद्वर्णबीजाढ्यायै नमः ।
995.	Oṃ Pañcāśanmuṇḍamālikāyai Namaḥ	ॐ पञ्चाशन्मुण्डमालिकायै नमः ।
996.	Oṃ Pratyekādaśasaṅkhyāyai Namaḥ	ॐ प्रत्येकादशसङ्ख्यायै नमः ।
997.	Oṃ Ṣoḍaśyai Namaḥ	ॐ षोडश्यै नमः ।
998.	Oṃ Chinnamastakāyai Namaḥ	ॐ छिन्नमस्तकायै नमः ।
999.	Oṃ Ṣaḍaṅgayuvatīpūjyāyai Namaḥ	ॐ षडङ्गयुवतीपूज्यायै नमः
1000.	Oṃ Ṣaḍaṅgarūpavarjitāyai Namaḥ	ॐ षडङ्गरूपवर्जितायै नमः ।
1001.	Oṃ Ṣaḍvaktrasaṃśritāyai Nityāyai Namaḥ	ॐ षड्वक्त्रसंश्रितायै नित्यायै नमः ।
1002.	Oṃ Viśveśyai Namaḥ	ॐ विश्वेश्यै नमः ।
1003.	Oṃ Ṣaṅgadālayāyai Namaḥ	ॐ षङ्गदालयायै नमः ।
1004.	Oṃ Mālāmantramayyai Namaḥ	ॐ मालामन्त्रमय्यै नमः ।
1005.	Oṃ Mantrajapamātre Namaḥ	ॐ मन्त्रजपमात्रे नमः ।
1006.	Oṃ Madālasāyai Namaḥ	ॐ मदालसायै नमः ।
1007.	Oṃ Sarvaviśveśvarīśaktyai Namaḥ	ॐ सर्वविश्वेश्वरीशक्त्यै नमः ।
1008.	Oṃ Sarvānandapradāyinyai Namaḥ	ॐ सर्वानन्दप्रदायिन्यै नमः

Iti Śrī Chinnamastā Sahasranāmāvaliḥ Sampūrṇā ॥

इति श्रीछिन्नमस्ता सहस्र नामावलिः सम्पूर्णा ॥

*****

7. *Dhūmāvatī* – धूमावती

Śrī Dhūmāvatī Devī

Adiparasakti, Paradevata, Sarva Loka Jaganmata, Sri Devi creates, preserves and destroys all the worlds. In addition, she performs the tasks of Anugraham and Tirodanam also, in accordance with one of the names in Sri Lalita Sahasranama *"Pancha Krutya Parayana"*. As a *Parabrahma Mahishi*, she, after creating lives, has taken many divine incarnations for the state and has been regularly doing *sishta* maintenance and evil discipline.

Among the various incarnations of Sriman Narayana described by Sri Vishnu Bhagavatam, ten avatars are prominent. Similarly, to protect the entire world, Sri Devi has manifested herself in ten different forms known as Dasha Maha Vidyas, as described in the previous chapter. Among those ten, Sri *Dhūmāvatī* Devi Vidya is the seventh one.

This Dhoomavati *Devi* shines in the *Swadhishtana chakra* in the secret organ of our body. Among the 10 incarnations of Sri Maha Vishnu, Sri *Dhūma*vati Devi is compared to Varaha Avatar and Ketu among the Navagrahas.

Dhūmāvatī, literally "the smoky one", represents the fearsome aspect of Mahadevi, the supreme goddess. She is often portrayed as an old, ugly widow and is associated with things considered inauspicious and unattractive in Hinduism, such as the crow and the Chaturmas period. The goddess is often depicted carrying a winnowing basket on a horseless chariot or riding a crow, usually in a cremation ground.

This goddess is also known as *Jyeṣṭā* because of the presence of darkness even earlier to the creation of this world (Jagat Srushti). Jyeshta means elder. Hence, she is called as elder sister of all the gods.

In *tantra shastras* the word energy will always indicate one with that energy. *Kali* to *Kalee*, *Akshobya* to *Taara* and *Bhairava* to *Bhairavee*. But *Dhūmāvatī* is taking a deviation to this convention. Hence *tantras* mention that **she** is spouseless. *Dhūmāvatī Devee* indicates smoke, darkness and innocence. But when there is a smoke there should be fire. The concepts dark and innocence hide light and wisdom. Hence with the blessings of *Dhūmāvatī Devee* we can easily reach knowledge by removing the darkness of innocence and by destroying the enemies like obstructions, who are friends of darkness. This is the essence of *Dhūmāvatī Vidhya*. That is the reason, the important result of *Dhūmāvatī Vidhya* is destruction of enemies. When we say enemies, that does not mean outside enemies. Enemies are within one self. Once the enemies of knowledge namely suspicion and diversity have been uprooted, the blessings of the *guru* through belief and devotion and the liberation can easily be reached through the knowledge of *Brahmam*.

When *Dākṣāyaṇī* fired herself in the fire of *yagna*, this *Dhūmāvatī* originated from the smoke of the fire and hence this name (*Dhūma* = smoke). **She** has crow in her flag and in some places, **she** sits on a crow.

The *tattva* of *Dhūmāvatī Devī*:

Dhūmāvatī Devee can also be called as *Pralaya Kālī* or *Yoga Nitra*. *Paraman* was in the state of *samādhi* (one's own spiritual nature) and hence was not aware of the impact of self-broken commodities by *Dhūmāvatī*. Only on account of this *Samādhi* every soul gets liberation. Only because of this *Devi*, the state of ignorance, sleep for the family, unconsciousness and forgetfulness are all happen. *Shastras* mention that the family do not recognise their real form, because of ignorance. The energy of such a hiding is *Dhūmāvatī*. The special effect of showing one as many is called illusion. This *tattva* is called as *Ratri* in *Rig Veda* and the same is in the form of *Brandi* in *puranas*. Since **she** is there even before this world is created, in the form of darkness, **she** is called *Jyeshta* (senior). One who wants to attain the knowledge of *Brahmam* and resultantly attain *moksha*, can worship this, *Devee*. The easy way for this worship is sacrificing all the wishes from the mind. There cannot be a difference between our form and thought. That will create damages. This *Vidya* is called as *Bhūmā Vidya* in *Upanishats* as – where nothing else other than self is visible, where nothing else other than self is heard.... (*Cha.* 7.24.1.). The state that there nothing else other than self, is created.

Ganapathi Muni in his *Mahavidya Sootra Paata*, feels that knowledge, ignorance and aggregation mentioned in *Eesaavaasya Upanishad* is this *Vidya* itself.

Hence, it is clear that by worshipping *Dhūmāvatī Devee* – one can get rid of fear from enemies, get plenty of wealth, money and grains, lead a decent life, respectively win over the inner enemies like desire, anger, wishes, etc., get a clean state of mind on account of daily chores and worshipping, lead an endless life with the benefit of the state of *samadhi*.

It is due to the grace of this goddess that the state of ignorance, sleep, fainting, forgetfulness, etc. are created for the samsari. The shastras say that the reason why samsaris do not know their true self is *avidya*. The *Avarana Shakti* (concealing) of this *Avidya* is called *Dhūmāvatī Devi*. The special power of manifesting something is called *Maya*. This form is called as *Ratri* in *Devi Suktam* of *Rig Veda* and *Branti Rupa* in Puranas.

Jayanti *Dhūmāvatī Devi* is the birth anniversary or first appearance day of Goddess is the *Ashtami* day of *Jyeshta Shukla* (as per Tamil Calendar).

Though there are many *naadis* (pulses) in our body, the 101 *naadis* around the heart are considered as important –
    "*Śadam Ca Ekā Ca Hrudyasya Nādyāḥ*" (*Kāṭaka Upanishat* 3-2-16).

Still important are the three viz., *Idaa, Pingala* and *Sushumnaa*. *Sushumnaa* is the one which moves in the mid of the spine at the back of our body. *Idaa* and *pingala* coil themselves around both the sides and join the *Sushumnaa* at the *Aagnaa chakra*. This is *Triveni sangama* (meeting of three – as meeting of three rivers Ganga, Yamuna and Saraswathi in Allahabad). *Idaa* is Ganga, *Pingala* – Yamuna and *Sushumnaa* is invisible Saraswathi. This is what is told in *Vedas* as –
    "*Sitaa Sito Sarito Yatra Sangate*".

The energy (*Shakti*) called *atipeekara* running in *Sushumna* is called *Dhūmāvatī*.

She is identified as Adi Para Shakti in the Devi Bhagavatam.

Worshiping male gods is called mantra. The method of worshiping female deities is called Vidya. Worshiping Sri Vidya, the unison of Shiva and Shakti. So, this also comes under Mantra group. Sri Vidya is said to be the best of all mantras.

That Devi is also known as Tripura Sundari, Raja Rajeshwari, Shodasee, Kamakshi, Lalita and so on. She is also an important Maha Vidya. She is glorified in many Shakta texts like Sri Lalitha Sahasranamam, Soundarya-lahari, etc. She is called Adi Para Shakti in the Lalithopakyanam of Brahmanda Purana.

According to the Srikula tradition in Shaktaism, *Dhūmāvatī* is the Shakta's supreme deity of Hinduism and the principal deity of Sri Vidya. The Tripura Upanishad places her as the ultimate Shakti (energy, power) of the universe. She is described as the Supreme Consciousness ruling from above Brahma, Vishnu and Shiva.

May the Divine Mother guide us all in our every action and thought. And may She remove the veil of maya and bestow upon us the greatest gift of all, moksha (liberation).

*****

Form(s) of *Śrī Dhūmāvatī Devī*

Usually Meditative Hymns (*Dhyana Shlokas*) about the Gods are figurative of the concerned God or Goddess.

The Meditation Hymn of *Śrī Dhūmāvatī Devī* is;

विवर्णा चरम्चला दुष्टा दीर्घा च मलिम्नाम्बरा ।
विमुक्त कुन्दला रुक्षा विधवा विरलद्विजा ॥
काकध्वज रथारूढा विलम्बित पयोधरा ।
शूर्प हस्तादि रक्ताक्षी धृतहस्ता वरान्विता ॥
प्रवृद्ध घोणा तु भृशम् कुटिला कुटिलेक्षणा ।
क्षु त्पिपासार्दिता नित्यम् भयदा कलहास्पदा ॥

Vivarṇā Caramcalā Duṣṭā Dīrghā Ca Malimnāmbarā ।
Vimukta Kundalā Rukṣa Vidhavā Viraladvijā ॥
Kākadhvaja Rathārūḍhā Vilambita Payodharā ।
Śūrpa Hastādi Raktākṣī Dhṛtahastā Varānvitā ॥
Pravṛddha Ghoṇā Tu Bhṛśam Kuṭilā Kuṭilekṣaṇā ।
Kṣutpipāsārditā Nityam Bhayadā Kalahāspadā ॥

She wears pale, moving, ugly, tall and dirty clothes. Her earrings are loose and clumsy and she is a widow and hardly a Brahmin. She rides in a chariot with a crow's flag and breasts hanging down. She is very beautiful with red eyes like a ghostly hand. The grown-up horse is so crooked and has crooked eyes that she is always tormented by hunger and thirst and is a source of fear and strife.

She holds a winnowing fan in one hand and fearlessness signet in another hand and with a look that **she** is suffering from hunger and thirst. **She** is black in colour and also not in such a beautiful form. **She** has an elongated long hair.

She is the only Maha Vidya who does not have any consort. Goddess Dhumavati is prominently illustrated as a widow who acquires supreme powers without masculine aid. The mahavidya is demonstrated to ride on a chariot whose emblem is a crow. She is pictured as a tall and robust standing older woman. She possesses messy hair and a heavily wrinkled face. She has grey hair and crooked teeth and some of the teeth are missing while others are enormous. She wears old and unpleasant clothes and acquires an ugly and big nose. The goddess holds a winnowing basket in her left hand and clenches skull-cup and sword with other indicators. The chief deity also has one of her hands in a posture to give blessings of wisdom and immense knowledge. Goddess Dhumavati adorns a garland of shredded heads.

It has been explained that by worshiping Goddess Dhoomavati Devi, one can escape from the evils of life, achieve self-realisation in life, live a good life, get rid of lust, anger, etc., and achieve eternal life sans death through the benefits of samadhi.

Dhumavati is worshipped in the Kalikula sect of Shaktism, the Goddess-centric tradition of Hinduism. Though *Dhumavati* enjoys patronage as one of the Mahavidyas, there are not much temples devoted to her and her public worship are rare. However, she is a significant Tantric deity, well known and worshipped among esoteric Tantric practitioners.

Dhumavati is described as a giver of siddhis (supernatural powers), a rescuer from all troubles, and a granter of all desires and rewards, including ultimate knowledge and moksha (salvation). Her worship is also prescribed for those who wish to defeat their foes. Dhumavati' s worship is considered ideal for unpaired members of society, such as bachelors, widows, and world renouncers as well as Tantrikas. In her Varanasi temple, however, she transcends her inauspiciousness and acquires the status of a local protective deity. There, even married couples worship her. Although she has very few dedicated temples, her worship by Tantric ritual continues in private in secluded places like cremation grounds and forests.

Dhumavati hardly has an independent existence outside the Mahavidya group. There is no historical mention of her before she is included among the Mahavidyas. As a goddess of poverty, frustration and despair, associates Dhumavati with Nirruti, the goddess of disease and misery, and Alakshmi, the goddess of misfortune and poverty. Kinsley adds another goddess to the list: Jyestha.

Jyeshta means elder. Lakshmi's elder (sister) is Alakshmi. Goddess Dhoomavati is also called Jyeshta. Hence, this goddess is compared to Alakshmi.

Dhumavati' s worship is performed in the night in a cremation ground, bare-bodied with the exception of a loincloth. The fourth lunar day of the dark fortnight (Krishna Paksha) is considered the special day to perform her puja (worship). The worshipper should observe a fast and remain silent for a whole day and night. They should also perform a homa ("fire sacrifice"), wearing wet clothes and a turban, repeating the goddess' mantra in a cremation ground, forest, or any lonely place.

Temples for *Dhumavati* Devi –

Dhumavati temples are extremely rare. At a temple in Varanasi, Dhumavati is the main deity. Smaller Dhumavati temples exist in Rajrappa in Bihar and near the Kamakya Temple near Guwahati. At the Varanasi temple, which claims to be a Shakti Peetha, Dhumavati's idol rides a chariot and holds a winnowing fan, a broom, and a pot, while the fourth hand makes the fear-not gesture (abhaya-mudra). The goddess is offered usual offerings like flowers and fruit, but also liquor, bhang, cigarettes, meat, and sometimes even blood sacrifices. Though traditional devotees of Dhumavati (world renouncers and Tantrikas) worship at the Varanasi temple, here the goddess transcends her traditional role as "the inauspicious, dangerous goddess who can be approached only by heroic tantric adepts". Dhumavati acquires the role of a local guardian deity, or village deity, who protects the locals and even married couples worship her. There is also a temple dedicated to the goddess in Pitambara Peeth temple complex, Datia.

By the grace of this Goddess, the devotee will attain whatever legally pray for including the nature of Shiva. Devi also bestows poetry and erudition.

This Goddess should be meditated upon in the six petalled lotus at the Swadishitana Chakra at the secret organ of the human body. Let us all cry at her feet to be able to meditate her.

Śrī Dhūmāvatī Devī Mantras

Śrī Dhūmāvatī Vidyā

In Samskrutam, in general *Vidyā* means mantra. Vidya means knowledge. Here is a very powerful *Sri Dhūmāvatī Devī Mantra*.

Om Asya Śrī Dhūmāvatī Mahā Mantrasya Pippalāta Riśiḥ |
Niśrut Chandaḥ | Śrī Dhūmāvatī Devatā |
Dhūm Bījam, Svāhā Śaktiḥ Dhūmāvatī Kīlakam |
Śrī Dhūmāvatī Prasāda Siddhyarte Jape Viniyogaḥ |

Om Dhūm Dhūm Angushṭābhyām Namaḥ
Om Dhūm Darjanībhyām Namaḥ   Om Mām Madhymābhyām Namaḥ
Om Vam Anāmikābhyām Namaḥ   Om Tim Kanishṭikābhyām Namaḥ
Om Svāhā Karatala Karabrushṭābhyām Namaḥ

Om Dhūm Dhūm Hrudayāya Namaḥ
Om Dhūm Sirase Svāhā   Om Mām Shikāyai Vashat
Om Vam Kavachāya Hūm   Om Tim Netratrayāya Vouśaṭ
Om Svāhā Astrāyaphaṭ   Bhūrbhuvasuvaromiti Digbandhaḥ |

Dhyānam

विवर्णा चरम्चला दुष्टा दीर्घा च मलिम्नाम्बरा ।
विमुक्त कुन्दला रुक्षा विधवा विरलद्विजा ॥
काकध्वज रथारूढा विलम्बित पयोधरा ।
शूर्प हस्तादि रक्ताक्षी धृतहस्ता वरान्विता ॥
प्रवृद्ध घोणा तु भृशम् कुटिला कुटिलेक्षणा ।
क्षु त्पिपासार्दिता नित्यम् भयदा कलहास्पदा ॥

Vivarṇā Caramcalā Duṣṭā Dīrghā Ca Malimnāmbarā |
Vimukta Kundalā Rukṣā Vidhavā Viraladvijā ॥
Kākadhvaja Rathārūḍhā Vilambita Payodharā |
Śūrpa Hastādi Raktākṣī Dhṛtahastā Varānvitā ॥
Pravṛddha Ghoṇā Tu Bhṛśam Kuṭilā Kuṭilekṣaṇā |
Kṣutpipāsārditā Nityam Bhayadā Kalahāspadā ॥

Lam Pritviyātmikāyai Gandham Samarpayāmi |
Ham Ākashātmikāyai Puṣpaiḥ Pūjayāmi |

Yam Vaivātmikāyai Dhūpam Āgrāpayāmi |
Ram Vahniyātmikāyai Dhīpam Dharśayāmi |
Vam Amrutātmikāyai Amrutam Mahāneivedhyam Nivedayāmi |
Sam Sarvātmikāyai Sarvopahāra Pūjām Samarpayāmi ||

Dhūmāvatī Mūla Mantras

Śrī Dhūmāvatī Mahā Mantrāḥ |

ॐ धूं धूं धूमावती(स्वाहा)   *Om Dhūm Dhūm Dhūmāvatī (Svāhā)*

Om Dhūm Dhūm Hrudayāya Namaḥ
Om Dhūm Sirase Svāhā
Om Mām Shikāyai Vashat
Om Vam Kavachāya Hūm
Om Tim Netratrayāya Vouśaṭ
Om Svāhā Astrāyaphaṭ
Bhūrbhuvasuvaromiti Digvimogaḥ |

Dhūmāvatī Dhyānam

विवर्णा चरम्चला दुष्टा दीर्घा च मलिम्नाम्बरा ।
विमुक्त कुन्दला रुक्षा विधवा विरलद्विजा ॥
काकध्वज रथारूढा विलम्बित पयोधरा ।
शूर्प हस्तादि रक्ताक्षी धृतहस्ता वरान्विता ॥
प्रवृद्ध घोणा तु भृशम् कुटिला कुटिलेक्षणा ।
क्षु त्पिपासार्दिता नित्यम् भयदा कलहास्पदा ॥

Vivarṇā Caramcalā Duṣṭā Dīrghā Ca Malimnāmbarā |
Vimukta Kundalā Rukṣā Vidhavā Viraladvijā ||
Kākadhvaja Rathārūḍhā Vilambita Payodharā |
Śūrpa Hastādi Raktākṣī Dhṛtahastā Varānvitā ||
Pravṛddha Ghoṇā Tu Bhṛśam Kuṭilā Kuṭilekṣaṇā |
Kṣutpipāsārditā Nityam Bhayadā Kalahāspadā ||

Lam Pritviyātmikāyai Gandham Samarpayāmi |
Ham Ākashātmikāyai Puśpaiḥ Pūjayāmi |
Yam Vaivātmikāyai Dhūpam Āgrāpayāmi |
Ram Vahniyātmikāyai Dhīpam Dharśayāmi |
Vam Amrutātmikāyai Amrutam Mahāneivedhyam Nivedayāmi |
Sam Sarvātmikāyai Sarvopahāra Pūjām Samarpayāmi ||

The *mantra* and the process of worshipping *Dhūmāvatī* has been clearly explained in *Bhetkārinī tantra*. It is seen there that this *mantra* will result in destroying the enemies –

Dhūmāvatī Manuḥ Prokto Vairī Vigraha Karakaḥ ||

The golden voice of *Meru Tantra* is that the devotee who worships this *Maha Vidya*, which has eight letters, can get complete attainment.

Dhūmāvatī stotra is mentioned in *Ūrdvāmnāya tantra*. In the results (*phalashruti*) part of this *tantra* it has been mentioned that even in deep trouble or profound distress or suffering from chronic disease or whenever thought of destroying enemies, chanting the *stotra* of *Dhūmāvatī* will come handy. It has to be noted that liberation can also be reached through the knowledge of this *Vidhya – Ande Nivānatām Vrajet*.

The *Kavaca, Hrudaya* and 1000 names of *Dhūmāvatī* have been mentioned in the 10th chapter of a rare book called *Śākta Pramodam* written by *Deva Nandana Simha Bahadur*. There are *Aṣṭotra* and *Sahasranāmas*[2] on this *Devī*.

Some schools have the habit of worshipping in a nude form, on the *Caturdaśi* (14th day) of black lunar fortnight, this *Devī* in a deserted temple. Worshipping this *Devī* is like walking on the edge of a sword – needs more caution. To protect her devotees, **she** takes the forms of buffalo, or eagle or pig.

This goddess is not as widely worshiped as other popular goddesses such as Kali and Durga, to name a few. However, if any tantric sadhak is asked about Devi Dhoomavati, we will hear a lot of praise for her being a goddess who is equally difficult to please and violent if not worshiped correctly. It can be noticed that the majority of Hindus are afraid of Dhoomavati Devi and other tantric goddesses. They don't even want any pictures of this goddess in their home. Tantric practitioners, on the other hand, worship her in order to gain siddhis and supernatural powers.

Only the most advanced tantric practitioners have access to the mantra's full potential (Sadhaks). There is no hard rule in normal recitation, but please do not chant the mantra with any unusual desire, as this can easily backfire.

There are numerous other mantras and stotrams dedicated to Devi Dhoomavati. However, the most popular one and that can be chant by the average person without any extreme tantric rituals is discussed here.

---

[2] These have been provided in different chapters of this book.

Prescribed process;

Devotees have to carefully worship *Dhoomavati Devi*. The worshipper has to see the brightness when he sees objects. He has to always imagine that the electric energy passes from ether through his head. With this the worshipper can realise *Devee*. *Tantra*, *Hrudaya*, *Ashtotra* and *Sahasranama* texts are available on *Dhoomavati Devee* (have been provided in different chapters of this book).

Tantric practitioners' worship *Dhoomavati* for acquiring siddhis or supernatural powers.

One should be interested in the words of the teacher. The four – self, teacher, *mantra* and the God should be treated as same. One should not reprimand other religions. One should always think of himself as Lord *Shiva*. One should not rebuke ladies.

Shakta ideologies affirm – *Shree Devee* in the form of, *kundalini* energy has to be brought from *Mūlādhāra Chakra* to *Sahasrāra Chakra* through *Brahma Granti*, *Swādhiṣṭāna Chakra*, *Maṇipūraka Chakra*, *Vishnu Granti*, *Anāhata Chakra*, *Viśuddhi Chakra*, *Rudra Granti and Agjna Chakra*. At the *Sahasrāra Chakra*, in a *Sahasradala Padma* (1000 petalled lotus), the unison of *Shiva-Shakti* has to be inwardly looked (*antharmukha* – inwardly imagined) into and the devotee should be soaked in the rain of nectar (*Amruta Tara*).

Important results of worshipping *Śrī Dhūmāvatī*;

With the blessings of this *Devee*, the worshipper gets the state of *Shiva*. He will get children, wealth and grains very early. With the blessings of *Shree Devee,* he becomes wealthy and becomes expert poet. Nothing is impossible to get through the worship of this *Devee*. After getting all the wealth, he gets the knowledge of *Vedantas* and hence the benefit of liberation through desireless meditation.

By worshipping this *Devee*, the devotee can obtain the art of speech, clear knowledge of *shastras*, wealth like Kubera, energy to win anything in this world and at last liberation.

Progress is the only in the life, if the grace of *Devī* is given to a devotee. Motivation comes naturally in the actions that are done. There is nothing he cannot achieve by her grace. She is interested in removing the sins of her devotees and showing him the right way. She lovingly bestows grace on those who are active, solid, and engaged in worship.

Let us all get initiated with these mantras from an appropriate guru and reap all the benefits.

*****

Śrī Dhūmāvatī Devī Yantram

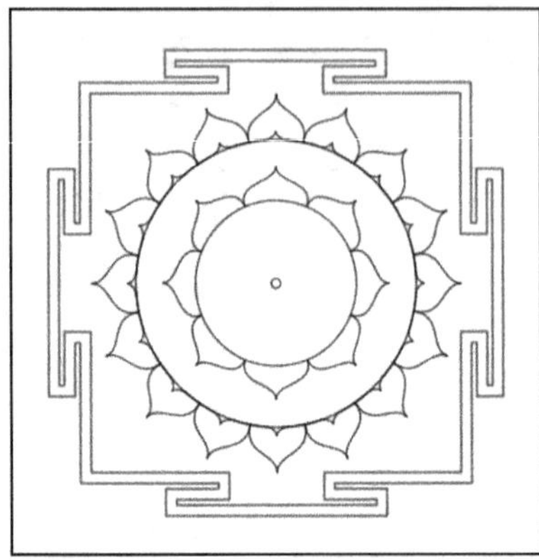

When this yantra is looked at, it can be noticed that certain symbols are engraved on it. The symbol of the lotus petals is known as the Padma. A lotus in an Yantra represents the unconditional force of the Supreme Absolute Truth. The lotus serves as a divine seat for Gods. It also represents detachment. It grows in the mud, but never touches even a tinge of mud, representing detachment of the macrocosmic progression. At the same time, the circle signifies perfection and the peaceful creating void of the Swadhishtana Chakra. In the group five fundamental elements it represents air and the dot or Bindu indicates the energy and its extreme concentration at the center. It is the center of cosmic radiation. Bounded by different surfaces such as a triangle, a hexagon, a circle, the Bindu represents the union with the force or creative energy ruling the Yantra.

This Yantra of Goddess Dhoomavati is worshipped for overcoming sadness, sorrow, depression, tragedy, disease, poverty and to eliminate the evil impact of Ketu from one's horoscope. This Yantra is not commonly known. It is worshipped for all round success and spiritual upliftment. This Yantra yields quick results.

The perfectly etched Goddess Dhoomavati Devi Yantra in Gold plated copper has an image and Her Mantra etched on its surface.

The ideal place is to hang it on the wall of puja room, living room or office facing North or East direction. The North-East region is ideally suited for Yantras because this direction is where the energies flowing from the North magnetic pole and sun rays of the East meet. Yantras placed here get charged with the divine energies leading to overall benefits.

Dhoomavati Yantra is a powerful and effective one that overcomes the negative planetary implications of Planet Ketu. All doshas related to planet Ketu can be overcome by worshipping this yantra. It symbolises proliferation, be it progeny, wealth or success. The yantra removes problems and protects people from abject poverty, frees limitations of the mind, improves perception, helps to find solutions to problems, grants great focus of mind for meditation etc.

The presiding deity of this yantra is Goddess Dhoomavati. This Yantra is been used for overcoming the evil impact of Rahu. This Yantra is very powerful and effective. Blesses one with progeny, removes the troubles and protects one from poverty.

Yantra for worshippers of Goddess Dhoomavati;

- Dhumavati yantra brings the blessings of supreme Dhoomavati.
- It protects devotees from enemies.
- One can combat hostile forces and evils by admiring Dhumavati Yantra.
- The yantra guides worshippers towards the path of ultimate truce, stability, and peace.
- It enlightens devotees with the power of silence and calmness.
- The yantra blesses worshippers with supreme knowledge and intellect.
- It assists by empowering with intelligence and consciousness.
- The yantra guides devotees towards salvation or moksha.
- It enlightens life with fulfilment and abundance.

How to Use this Dhoomavati Yantra?

- The Yantra can be kept in the prayer altar.
- Wash the copper plate with rose water/ pure water on a periodical basis
- Place Sandal and Vermillion paste on all the 4 corners and the centre of the Yantra
- Pray sincerely to the Yantra and offer flowers and incense stick in front of it
- Any type of Prasad can be offered to the Yantra considering as the deity who is going to fill the life with whatever asked for.
- This Yantra can be carried with while travelling in a safe pouch/ wallet, so that it can be ensured that the God's protection follows.

One of most powerful Yantras to achieve protection against all sorts of negative energies and for self-control. *Dhūmāvatī* – The Goddess of decay. It can be noticed certain symbols that are engraved or printed on the *Dhūmāvatī Yantra*. It characteristically signifies the divine unification of

Shiva (Male energy) and Shakti (Female energy) which is the cause of all creation.

Care should always be taken while installing the *yantra*. Because it is very important to place the Yantra in the right direction. When the device is installed, it energizes the place where it is installed or placed. It can be placed near entrance of the house/ offices/ shops or in reception/ office room. The best place to keep the *Dhūmāvatī* Yantra is inside the house facing the East direction. It is powered by the growing rays of the Sun. With the divine vibrations of the Eastern corner, this *Dhūmāvatī* Yantram through its mystical geometry imparts positive transformative energies to the abode.

Prosperity, good health, peace, beauty, influence, protection from all forms of evils, etc., and so on, are the known benefits that the devotees of this *yantra* are granted with. The Dhoomavati Yantra is meant for the enhancement of one's well-being. Whatever one does, that can be done in a much better way with the assistance of the Dhoomavati Yantra. It is a very powerful, personalised tool that creates a certain space and an atmosphere so that one's wellbeing is naturally taken care of.

Those who bear *Dhūmāvatī* Yantra and worship it with complete devotion and true belief are bestowed with safety and happiness. Such people are blessed with expressive and persuasive speech. Those with *Dhūmāvatī* Yantra always remain under the protective sight of the deity and have safe journeys. Bearing *Dhūmāvatī* Yantra also fades away all the negative energies, fears, uncertainties, nervousness and malefic spirits. *Dhūmāvatī* takes care of all circumstances which could cause fear, tensions, worries, accidents and disrepute. The methods for the worship of *Dhūmāvatī* have been described in the sacred texts for the attainment of victory over the sensual desires and all-round development.

The *yantras* pertaining to most of the Gods are kept beneath or in front of the deities in temples. One *yantra* is a drawing of lines or circles or angles drawn in a prescribed measurements and ratios. There cannot be any deviation plus or minus. If a *mantra* is wrongly chant, it can result in negative impact or even end up with destruction. In the same manner, if there is an error in drawing of a *yantra*, it may end up in devastation.

In modern days, lot many worship *Śrī Chakra* in their houses. In general, this is very good. But many do it as a pride, some do it as a style and some with ignorance. But the customs are not strictly followed. Resultantly, they suffer for want of peace.

It is not enough if one wants to follow the bigger things. Exact rules prescribed by *Śāstras* have to be clearly understood, absorbed and followed. These are time tested and handed over to us by our ancestors. It is our duty to stringently follow the same and get benefited. Definitely *Śrī Chakra* has been raised upto the sky by the *Śāstras*. But the same *Śāstras* have recommended lots of dos and don'ts, lots of processes. The approach that "I will do the pooja in my way" is not acceptable, the expected fruits will be missed. Sometimes that may result in negative angle.

One *yantra* is not a place of dwelling for the deity; It is the deity her/himself. It is not an alternative to the deity. It is not a representation – it the deity. It is all the more apt in the case of *Śrī Devī*.

The radiations of the Yantra will bring the devotee and the Goddess into direct contact. The energy will soothe the inner peace and will gift with beauty, happiness and prosperity. These power lines attract the amiability of the Goddess opening doors for harmony and success.

This Yantra is a great cosmic conductor of energy, an antenna of Nature, a powerful tool for harmony, prosperity, success, good health, yoga and meditation! Yantras consist of a series of geometric patterns. The eyes and mind concentrate at the center of the yantra to achieve higher levels of consciousness. Yantras are usually made out of copper.

Let us all choose an appropriate guru, get initiated and worship this yantra to exploit maximum benefits.

*****

Śrī Dhūmāvatī Dhyānam

Pratyālīḍhapadāṃ Sadaiva Dadhatīṃ Chinnaṃ Śiraḥ Kartrikāṃ
Digvastrāṃ Svakabandhaśoṇitasudhādhārāṃ Pibantīṃ Mudā |
Nāgābaddhaśiromaṇiṃ Trinayanāṃ Hṛdyutpalālaṅkṛtāṃ
Ratyāsaktamanobhavopari Dṛḍhāṃ Vande Japāsannibhām || 1

Dakṣe Cātisitā Vimuktacikurā Kartrīṃ Tathā Kharparam |
Hastābhyāṃ Dadhatī Rajoguṇabhavā Nāmnāpi Sā Varṇinī ||
Devyāśchinnakabandhataḥ Patadasṛgdhārāṃ Pibantī Mudā |
Nāgābaddhaśiromaṇirmanuvidā Dhyeyā Sadā Sā Suraiḥ || 2

Pratyālīḍhapadā Kabandhavigaladraktaṃ Pibantī Mudā |
Saiṣā Yā Pralaye Samastabhuvanaṃ Bhoktuṃ Kṣamā Tāmasī ||
Śaktiḥ Sāpi Parātparā Bhagavatī Nāmnā Parā Ḍākinī |
Dhyeyā Dhyānaparaiḥ Sadā Savinayaṃ Bhakteṣṭabhūtipradā || 3

Bhāsvanmaṇḍalamadhyagāṃ Nijaśiraśchinnaṃ Vikīrṇālakam |
Sphārāsyaṃ Prapibadgalātsvarudhiraṃ Vāme Kare Bibhratīm ||
Yābhāsaktaratismaroparigatāṃ Sakhyau Nije Ḍākinī-
Varṇinyau Paridṛśya Modakalitāṃ Śrīdhūmāvatī M Bhaje || 4

Svanābhau Nīrajaṃ Dhyāyāmyardhaṃ Vikasitaṃ Sitam |
Tatpadmakośamadhye Tu Maṇḍalaṃ Caṇḍarociṣaḥ || 5

Japākusumasaṅkāśaṃ Raktabandhūkasannibham |
Rajassatvatamorekhā Yonimaṇḍalamaṇḍitam || 6

Tanmadhye Tāṃ Mahādevīṃ Sūryakoṭisamaprabhām |
Dhūmāvatī M Kare Vāme Dhārayantīṃ Svamastakam || 7

Prasāritamukhīṃ Devīṃ Lelihānāgrajihvikām |
Pibantīṃ Raudhirīṃ Dhārāṃ Nijakaṇṭhavinirgatām || 8

Vikīrṇakeśapāśāṃ Ca Nānāpuṣpasamanvitām |
Dakṣiṇe Ca Kare Kartrīṃ Muṇḍamālāvibhūṣitām || 9

Digambarāṃ Mahāghorāṃ Pratyālīḍhapade Sthitām |
Asthimālādharāṃ Devīṃ Nāgayajñepavītinīm || 10

Ratikāmoparişthāṃ Ca Sadā Dhyātāṃ Ca Mantribhiḥ |
Sadā Şoḍaśavarşīyāṃ Pīnonnatapayodharām ‖ 11

Viparītaratāsaktau Dhyāyāmi Ratimanmathau |
Śākinīvarṇinīyuktāṃ Vāmadakşiṇayogataḥ ‖ 12

Devīgalocchaladraktadhārāpānaṃ Prakurvatīm |
Varṇinīṃ Lohitāṃ Saumyāṃ Muktakeśīṃ Digambarām ‖ 13

Kapālakartrikāhastāṃ Vāmadakşiṇayogataḥ |
Nāgayajñepavītāḍhyāṃ Jvalattejomayīmiva ‖ 14

Pratyālīḍhapadāṃ Vidyāṃ Nānālaṅkārabhūşitām |
Sadā Dvādaśavarşīyāṃ Asthimālāvibhūşitām ‖ 15

Ḍākinīṃ Vāmapārśve Tu Kalpasūryānalopamām |
Vidyujjaṭāṃ Trinayanāṃ Dantapaṅktibalākinīm ‖ 16

Daṃşṭrākarālavadanāṃ Pīnonnatapayodharām |
Mahādevīṃ Mahāghorāṃ Muktakeśīṃ Digambarām ‖ 17

Lelihānamahājihvāṃ Muṇḍamālāvibhūşitām |
Kapālakartrikāhastāṃ Vāmadakşiṇayogataḥ ‖ 18

Devīgalocchaladraktadhārāpānaṃ Prakurvatīm |
Karasthitakapālena Bhīşaṇenātibhīşaṇām |
Ābhyāṃ Nişevyamāṇāṃ Tāṃ Kalaye Jagadīśvarīm ‖ 19

Iti Dhūmāvatī Dhyānam ‖

धूमावती ध्यानम्

प्रत्यालीढपदां सदैव दधतीं छिन्नं शिरः कर्त्रिकां
दिग्वस्त्रां स्वकबन्धशोणितसुधाधारां पिबन्तीं मुदा ।
नागाबद्धशिरोमणिं त्रिनयनां हृद्युत्पलालङ्कृतां
रत्यासक्तमनोभवोपरि दृढां वन्दे जपासन्निभाम् ‖ १

दक्षे चातिसिता विमुक्तचिकुरा कर्त्री तथा खर्परम् ।
हस्ताभ्यां दधती रजोगुणभवा नाम्नापि सा वर्णिनी ‖

देव्याश्छिन्नकबन्धतः पतदसृग्धारां पिबन्ती मुदा ।
नागाबद्धशिरोमणिर्मनुविदा ध्येया सदा सा सुरैः ॥ २

प्रत्यालीढपदा कबन्धविगलद्रक्तं पिबन्ती मुदा ।
सैषा या प्रलये समस्तभुवनं भोक्तुं क्षमा तामसी ॥
शक्तिः सापि परात्परा भगवती नाम्ना परा डाकिनी ।
ध्येया ध्यानपरैः सदा सविनयं भक्तेष्टभूतिप्रदा ॥ ३

भास्वन्मण्डलमध्यगां निजशिरश्छिन्नं विकीर्णालिकम् ।
स्फारास्यं प्रपिबद्गलात्स्वरुधिरं वामे करे बिभ्रतीम् ॥
याभासक्तरतिस्मरोपरिगतां सख्यौ निजे डाकिनी-
वर्णिन्यौ परिदृश्य मोदकलितां श्रीछिन्नमस्तां भजे ॥ ४

स्वनाभौ नीरजं ध्यायाम्यर्धं विकसितं सितम् ।
तत्पद्मकोशमध्ये तु मण्डलं चण्डरोचिषः ॥ ५

जपाकुसुमसङ्काशं रक्तबन्धूकसन्निभम् ।
रजस्सत्वतमोरेखा योनिमण्डलमण्डितम् ॥ ६

तन्मध्ये तां महादेवीं सूर्यकोटिसमप्रभाम् ।
छिन्नमस्तां करे वामे धारयन्तीं स्वमस्तकम् ॥ ७

प्रसारितमुखीं देवीं लेलिहानाग्रजिह्विकाम् ।
पिबन्तीं रौधिरीं धारां निजकण्ठविनिर्गताम् ॥ ८

विकीर्णकेशपाशां च नानापुष्पसमन्विताम् ।
दक्षिणे च करे कर्त्रीं मुण्डमालाविभूषिताम् ॥ ९

दिगम्बरां महाघोरां प्रत्यालीढपदे स्थिताम् ।
अस्थिमालाधरां देवीं नागयज्ञोपवीतिनीम् ॥ १०

रतिकामोपरिष्ठां च सदा ध्यातां च मन्त्रिभिः ।
सदा षोडशवर्षीयां पीनोन्नतपयोधराम् ॥ ११

विपरीतरतासक्तौ ध्यायामि रतिमन्मथौ ।
शाकिनीवर्णिनीयुक्तां वामदक्षिणयोगतः ॥ १२

देवीगलोच्छलद्रक्तधारापानं प्रकुर्वतीम् ।
वर्णिनीं लोहितां सौम्यां मुक्तकेशीं दिगम्बराम् ॥ १३

कपालकर्त्रिकाहस्तां वामदक्षिणयोगतः ।
नागयज्ञेपवीताद्द्यां ज्वलत्तेजोमयीमिव ॥ १४

प्रत्यालीढपदां विद्यां नानालङ्कारभूषिताम् ।
सदा द्वादशवर्षीयां अस्थिमालाविभूषिताम् ॥ १५

डाकिनीं वामपार्श्वे तु कल्पसूर्यानलोपमाम् ।
विद्युज्जटां त्रिनयनां दन्तपङ्क्तिबलाकिनीम् ॥ १६

दंष्ट्राकरालवदनां पीनोन्नतपयोधराम् ।
महादेवीं महाघोरां मुक्तकेशीं दिगम्बराम् ॥ १७

लेलिहानमहाजिह्वां मुण्डमालाविभूषिताम् ।
कपालकर्त्रिकाहस्तां वामदक्षिणयोगतः ॥ १८

देवीगलोच्छलद्रक्तधारापानं प्रकुर्वतीम् ।
करस्थितकपालेन भीषणेनातिभीषणाम् ।
आभ्यां निषेव्यमाणां तां कलये जगदीश्वरीम् ॥ १९

इति धूमावती ध्यानम् ॥

*****

Śrī Dhūmāvatī Kavacaṃ

A *kavacam* is a shield protecting the body. This is a mantra shield to protect our body, mind and soul. We chant *kavacams* on various lords like, *Skanda Shashti Kavacam* (about lord *Kumara*), *Narayana Kavacam, Sri Devi Kavacam*, etc. Among them, this *Śrī Dhūmāvatī Kavacam* is an infallible weapon to receive the blessings of *Śrī Dhūmāvatī* and to protect one's body and soul. This *kavaca* can be read daily and the results can be seen by self, how effective it is.

Śrī Dhūmāvatī Kavacam

Śrī Gaṇeśāya Namaḥ |

Atha Dhūmāvatī Kavacam |

Śrī Pārvatyuvāca -

Dhūmāvatyarcanaṃ Śambho Śrutaṃ Vistaratomayā |
Kavacaṃ Śrotumicchāmi Tasyā Deva Vadasva Me || 1

Śrībhairava Uvāca -

Śṛṇudevi Paraṃ Guhyaṃ Na Prakāśyaṃ Kalauyuge |
Kavacaṃ Śrīdhūmāvatyāśśatrunigrahakārakam || 2

Brahmādyādevi Satataṃ Yadvaśādarighātinaḥ |
Yoginobhavachatrughnā Yasyādhyāna Prabhāvataḥ || 3

Oṃ Asya Śrīdhūmāvatīkavacasya Pippalāda Ṛṣiḥ Anuṣṭupchandaḥ Śrīdhūmāvatī Devatā Dhūṃ Bījam Svāhāśaktiḥ Dhūmāvatī Kīlakam Śatruhanane Pāṭhe Viniyogaḥ |

Oṃ Dhūṃ Bījaṃ Me Śiraḥ Pātu Dhūṃ Lalāṭaṃ Sadāvatu |
Dhūmānetrayugaṃ Pātu Vatī Karṇausadāvatu || 4

Dīrghātūdaramadhye Tu Nābhiṃ Me Malināmbarā |
Śūrpahastā Pātu Guhyaṃ Rūkṣārakṣatu Jānunī || 5

Mukhaṃ Me Pātu Bhīmākhyā Svāhā Rakṣatu Nāsikām |
Sarvaṃ Vidyāvatu Kaṣṭaṃ Vivarṇā Bāhuyugmakam || 6

Cañcalā Hṛdayaṃ Pātu Duṣṭā Pārśvaṃ Sadāvatu |
Dhūtahastā Sadā Pātu Pādau Pātu Bhayāvahā || 7

Pravṛddharomā Tu Bhṛśaṃ Kuṭilā Kuṭilekṣaṇā |
Kṣṛtpipāsārditā Devī Bhayadā Kalahapriyā || 8

Sarvāṅgaṃ Pātu Me Devī Sarvaśatruvināśinī |
Iti Te Kavacaṃ Puṇyaṃ Kathitaṃ Bhuvi Durlabham || 9

Na Prakāśyaṃ Na Prakāśyaṃ Na Prakāśyaṃ Kalau Yuge |
Paṭhanīyaṃ Mahādevi Trisandhyaṃ Dhyānatatparaiḥ |
Duṣṭābhicāro Deveśi Tadgātraṃ Naiva Saṃspṛśet || 10

Iti Bhairavī Bhairava Saṃvāde Dhūmāvatī Tattve Dhūmāvatī Kavacaṃ
Sampūrṇam |

श्री धूमावती कवचम्

श्री गणेशाय नमः ।

अथ धूमावती कवचम् ।

श्रीपार्वत्युवाच -

धूमावत्यर्चनं शम्भो श्रुतं विस्तरतोमया ।
कवचं श्रोतुमिच्छामि तस्या देव वदस्व मे ॥ १

श्रीभैरव उवाच –

शृणुदेवि परं गुह्यं न प्रकाश्यं कलौयुगे ।
कवचं श्रीधूमावत्याश्शत्रुनिग्रहकारकम् ॥ २

ब्रह्माद्यादेवि सततं यद्द्वशादरिघातिनः ।
योगिनोभवच्छत्रुघ्ना यस्याध्यान प्रभावतः ॥ ३

ॐ अस्य श्रीधूमावतीकवचस्य पिप्पलाद ऋषिः
अनुष्टुप्छन्दः श्रीधूमावती देवता धूं बीजम् स्वाहाशक्तिः
धूमावती कीलकम् शत्रुहनने पाठे विनियोगः ।

ॐ धूं बीजं मे शिरः पातु धूं ललाटं सदावतु ।
धूमानेत्रयुगं पातु वती कर्णौसदावतु ॥ ४

दीर्घातूदरमध्ये तु नाभिं मे मलिनाम्बरा ।
शूर्पहस्ता पातु गुह्यं रूक्षारक्षतु जानुनी ॥ ५

मुखं मे पातु भीमाख्या स्वाहा रक्षतु नासिकाम् ।
सर्वं विद्यावतु कष्टं विवर्णा बाहुयुग्मकम् ॥ ६

चञ्चला हृदयं पातु दुष्टा पार्श्वं सदावतु ।
धूतहस्ता सदा पातु पादौ पातुभयावहा ॥ ७

प्रवृद्धरोमा तु भृशं कुटिला कुटिलेक्षणा ।
क्षुत्पिपासार्दिता देवी भयदा कलहप्रिया ॥ ८

सर्वाङ्गं पातु मे देवी सर्वशत्रुविनाशिनी ।
इति ते कवचं पुण्यं कथितं भुवि दुर्लभम् ॥ ९

न प्रकाश्यं न प्रकाश्यं न प्रकाश्यं कलौ युगे ।
पठनीयं महादेवि त्रिसन्ध्यं ध्यानतत्परैः ।
दुष्टाभिचारो देवेशि तद्गात्रं नैव संस्पृशेत् ॥ १०

इति भैरवी भैरव संवादे धूमावती तत्त्वे धूमावती कवचं सम्पूर्णम् ।

*****

Śrī Dhūmāvatī Stotram

This is a stotram on goddess *Dhūmāvatī* and it is also called as *Aṣṭakam*, since it has 8 verses.

Śrī Dhūmāvatī Stotram Dhūmāvaty Aṣṭakam Ca

Śrīgaṇeśāya Namaḥ |

Dhūmāyāḥ Stotram |

Prātaryāsyāt Kumārī Kusumakalikayā Jāpamālāṃ Japantī
Madhyāhne Prauḍharūpā Vikasitavadanā Cārunetrā Niśāyām |
Sandhyāyāṃ Vṛddharūpā Galitakucayugā Muṇḍamālāṃ Vahantī
Sā Devī Devadevī Tribhuvanajananī Kālikāpātu Yuṣmān ‖ 1

Baddhvā Khaṭvāṅgakoṭau Kapilavarajaṭā Maṇḍalampadmayoneḥ
Kṛtvādaityottamāṅgaiḥ Srajamurasiśiraśśekharaṃ Tārkṣyapakṣaiḥ |
Pūrṇamraktaiḥ Surāṇāṃ Yamamahiṣamahāśṛṅgamādāyapāṇau
Pāyādvovandyamānaḥ Pralayamuditayā Bhairavaḥ Kālarātryām ‖ 2

Carvantīmasthikhaṇḍaṃ Prakaṭa Kaṭakaṭā Śabdasaṅghātamugraṃ
Kurvāṇi Pretamadhye Kahahakahakahā Hāsyamugraṃ Kṛśāṃṅgī |
Nityaṃ Nnityaprasaktāṃ Ḍamaruḍimaḍimāṃ Sphārayantīṃ Mukhābjaṃ
Pāyānnaścaṇḍikeyaṃ Jhajhamajhamajhamā Jalpamānā Bhramantī ‖ 3

Ṭaṇṭaṇṭaṇṭaṇṭaṭaṇṭā Nrakaṭa Tamaṭamā Nāṭaghaṇṭāṃ Vahantī
Sphem Sphem Sphem Sphārakārā Ṭakaṭakitahasā Nādasaṅghaṭṭa Bhīmā |
Lolammuṇḍāgramālā Lalahalahalahā Lolalolāgravācaṃ
Carvantīcaṇḍamuṇḍaṃ Maṭamaṭamaṭite Caryaṣantī Punātu ‖ 4

Vāme Karṇe Mṛgāṅkaṃ Palayaparigataṃ Dakṣiṇe Sūryabimbaṃ
Kaṇṭhe Nakṣatrahāraṃ Varavikaṭajaṭājūṭake Muṇḍamālām |
Skandhekṛtvoragendradhvajanikarayutaṃ Brahmakaṅkālabhāraṃ
Saṃhāre Dhārayantī Mamaharatubhayaṃ Bhadradā Bhadrakālī ‖ 5

Tailābhyaktaikaveṇī Trapumayavilasat Karṇikākrāntakarṇā
Lauhenaikena Kṛtvācaraṇanalinakāmātmanaḥ Pādaśobhām |
Digvāsā Rāsabhena Grasatijagadidaṃ Māyayā Karṇapūrā
Varṣiṇyātiprabaddhā Dhvajavitatabhujā Sāsidevitvameva ‖ 6

Saṅgrāme Hetikṛtvaissarudhiradaśanairyadbhaṭānāṃ
Śirobhirmālāmābaddhyamūrdhni Dhvajavitatabhujā Tvaṃ Śmaśāne

                                Praviṣṭā |

Dṛṣṭā Bhūtaprabhūtaiḥ Pṛthutarajaghanā Baddhanāgendra Kāñcī
Śūlagravyagrahastā Madhurudhirasadā Tāmranetrā Niśāyām || 7

Daṃṣṭrā Raudremukhe'smiṃstavaviśatijagaddevi Sarvaṃ Kṣaṇārdhāt
Saṃsārasyāntakāle Nararudhiravaśāsamplavebhūmadhūmre |
Kālīkāpālikī Sā Śavaśayanatarā Yoginī Yogamudrā
Raktāruddhiḥ Sabhāsthā Maraṇabhayaharā Tvaṃ Śivā Caṇḍaghaṇṭā || 8

Dhūmāvatyaṣṭakaṃ Puṇyaṃ Sarvāpadvinivārakam |
Yaḥ Paṭhet Sādhako Bhaktyā Siddhiṃ Vindati Vāñchitām || 9

Mahāpadi Mahāghore Mahāroge Mahāraṇe |
Śatrūccāṭe Māraṇādau Jantūnāṃ Mohane Tathā || 10

Paṭhet Stotramidaṃ Devi Sarvatra Siddhibhāgbhavet |
Devadānavagandharvā Yakṣarākṣasapannagāḥ || 11

Siṃha Vyāghrādikāssarve Stotra Smaraṇamātrataḥ |
Dūrāddūrataraṃ Yānti Kiṃ Punarmānuṣādayaḥ || 12

Stotreṇānena Deveśi Kiṃ Na Siddhyati Bhūtale |
Sarvaśāntirbhaveddevihyante Nirvāṇatāṃ Vrajet || 13

        Ityūrdhvāmnāye Dhūmāvatī Stotram Samāptam ||

श्री धूमावती स्तोत्रम् धूमावत्यष्टकम् च

श्रीगणेशाय नमः ।

धूमायाः स्तोत्रम् ।

प्रातर्यास्यात् कुमारी कुसुमकलिकया जापमालां जपन्ती
मध्याह्ने प्रौढरूपा विकसितवदना चारुनेत्रा निशायाम् ।
सन्ध्यायां वृद्धरूपा गलितकुचयुगा मुण्डमालां वहन्ती
सा देवी देवदेवी त्रिभुवनजननी कालिकापातु युष्मान् ॥ १

बद्ध्वा खट्वाङ्गकोटौ कपिलवरजटा मण्डलम्पद्वयोनेः
कृत्वादैत्योत्तमाङ्गैः स्रजमुरसिशिरश्शेखरं ताक्ष्यपक्षैः ।
पूर्णरक्तैः सुराणां यममहिषमहाशृङ्गमादायपाणौ
पायाद्द्रोवन्द्यमानः प्रलयमुदितया भैरवः कालरात्र्याम् ॥ २

चर्वन्तीमस्थिखण्डं प्रकट कटकटा शब्दसङ्घातमुग्रं
कुर्वाणि प्रेतमध्ये कहहकहकहा हास्यमुग्रं कृशांङ्गी ।
नित्यं न्नित्यप्रसक्तां डमरुडिमडिमां स्फारयन्तीं मुखाब्जं
पायान्नश्रणिडकेयं झझमझमझमा जल्पमाना भ्रमन्ती ॥ ३

टण्टण्टण्टण्टटण्टा प्रकट टमटमा नाटघण्टां वहन्ती
स्फें स्फें स्फें स्फारकारा टकटकितहसा नादसङ्घट्ट भीमा ।
लोलम्मुण्डाग्रमाला ललहलहलहा लोललोलाग्रवाचं
चर्वन्तीचण्डमुण्डं मटमटमटिते चर्यषन्ती पुनातु ॥ ४

वामे कर्णे मृगाङ्कं पलयपरिगतं दक्षिणे सूर्यबिम्बं
कण्ठे नक्षत्रहारं वरविकटजटाजूटके मुण्डमालाम् ।
स्कन्धेकृत्वोरगेन्द्रध्वजनिकरयुतं ब्रह्मकङ्कालभारं
संहारे धारयन्ती ममहरतुभयं भद्रदा भद्रकाली ॥ ५

तैलाभ्यक्तैकवेणी त्रपुमयविलसत् कर्णिकाक्रान्तकर्णा
लौहेनैकेन कृत्वाचरणनलिनकामात्मनः पादशोभाम् ।
दिग्वासा रासभेन ग्रसतिजगदिदं मायया कर्णपूरा
वर्षिण्यातिप्रबद्धा ध्वजविततभुजा सासिदेवित्वमेव ॥ ६

सङ्ग्रामे हेतिकृत्वैस्सरुधिरदशनैर्यद्वटानां
शिरोभिर्मालामाबद्ध्यमूर्धिं ध्वजविततभुजा त्वं शमशाने प्रविष्टा ।
दृष्टा भूतप्रभूतैः पृथुतरजघना बद्धनागेन्द्र काञ्ची
शूलग्रव्यग्रहस्ता मधुरुधिरसदा ताम्रनेत्रा निशायाम् ॥ ७

दंष्ट्रा रौद्रेमुखेऽस्मिंस्तवविशतिजगद्देवि सर्वं क्षणार्धात्
संसारस्यान्तकाले नररुधिरवशासम्प्लवेभूमधूम्रे ।
कालीकापालिकी सा शवशयनतरा योगिनी योगमुद्रा
रक्तारुद्धिः सभास्था मरणभयहरा त्वं शिवा चण्डघण्टा ॥ ८

धूमावत्यष्टकं पुण्यं सर्वापद्विनिवारकम् ।
यः पठेत् साधको भक्त्या सिद्धिं विन्दति वाञ्छिताम् ॥ ९

महापदि महाघोरे महारोगे महारणे ।
शत्रूच्चाटे मारणादौ जन्तूनां मोहने तथा ॥ १०

पठेत् स्तोत्रमिदं देवि सर्वत्र सिद्धिभाग्भवेत् ।
देवदानवगन्धर्वा यक्षराक्षसपन्नगाः ॥ ११

सिंह व्याघ्रादिकास्सर्वे स्तोत्र स्मरणमात्रतः ।
दूराद्दूरतरं यान्ति किं पुनर्मानुषादयः ॥ १२

स्तोत्रेणानेन देवेशि किं न सिद्ध्यति भूतले ।
सर्वशान्तिर्भवेद्देविहह्यन्ते निर्वाणतां व्रजेत् ॥ १३

इत्यूर्ध्वाम्नाये धूमावती स्तोत्रं समाप्तम् ॥

*****

Śrī Dhūmāvatī Hṛdayam

Śrī Gaṇeśāya Namaḥ || Śrī Umāmaheśvarābhyāṃ Namaḥ ||

Śrī Dhūmāvatyai Namaḥ ||

Oṃ Asya Śrīdhūmāvatīhṛdayastotramantrasya Pippalāda Ṛṣiḥ |
Anuṣṭupchandaḥ | Śrīdhūmāvatī Devatā | Dhūṃ Bījam | Hrīṃ Śaktiḥ |
Klīṃ Kīlakam | Sarvaśatrusaṃharaṇe Pāṭhe Viniyogaḥ ||

Hṛdayādi Ṣaḍaṅganyāsaḥ |

Oṃ Dhāṃ Hṛdayāya Namaḥ | Oṃ Dhīṃ Śirase Svāhā |
Oṃ Dhūṃ Śikhāyai Vaṣaṭ | Oṃ Dhaiṃ Kavacāya Hum |
Oṃ Dhauṃ Netratrayāya Vauṣaṭ | Oṃ Dhaḥ Astrāya Phaṭ |

Karanyāsaḥ |

Oṃ Dhāṃ Aṅguṣṭhābhyāṃ Namaḥ |
Oṃ Dhīṃ Tarjanībhyāṃ Namaḥ |
Oṃ Dhūṃ Madhyamābhyāṃ Namaḥ |
Oṃ Dhaiṃ Anāmikābhyāṃ Namaḥ |
Oṃ Dhauṃ Kaniṣṭhikābhyāṃ Namaḥ |
Oṃ Dhaḥ Karatalakarapṛṣṭhābhyāṃ Namaḥ |

Dhyānam |

Oṃ Dhūmrābhāṃ Dhūmravastrāṃ Prakaṭitadaśanāṃ
                              Muktavālāmbarāḍhyāṃ
Kākāṅkasyandanasthāṃ Dhavalakarayugāṃ Śūrpahastātirūkṣām |
Nityaṃ Kṣutkṣāntadehāṃ Muhuratikuṭilāṃ Vārivāñchāvicitrāṃ
Dhyāyeddhūmāvatīṃ Vāmanayanayugalāṃ Bhītidāṃ Bhīṣaṇāsyām || 1

Kalpādau Yā Kālikādyā'cīkalanmadhukaiṭabhau |
Kalpānte Trijagatsarvaṃ Dhūmāvatīṃ Bhajāmi Tām || 2

Guṇāgārā'gamyaguṇā Yā Guṇā Guṇavarddhinī |
Gītāvedārthatattvajñairdhūmāvatīṃ Bhajāmi Tām ǁ 3

Khaṭvāṅgadhāriṇī Kharvā Khaṇḍinī Khalarakṣasām |
Dhāriṇī Kheṭakasyāpi Dhūmāvatīṃ Bhajāmi Tām ǁ 4

Ghūrṇā Ghūrṇakarā Ghorā Ghūrṇitākṣī Ghanasvanā |
Ghātinī Ghātakānāṃ Yā Dhūmāvatīṃ Bhajāmi Tām ǁ 5

Carvantīmasthikhaṇḍānāṃ Caṇḍamuṇḍavidāriṇīm |
Caṇḍāṭṭahāsinīṃ Devīṃ Bhaje Dhūmāvatīmaham ǁ 6

Chinnagrīvāṃ Kṣatācchannāṃ Chinnamastāsvarūpiṇīm |
Chedinīṃ Duṣṭasaṅghānāṃ Bhaje Dhūmāvatīmaham ǁ 7

Jātā Yā Yācitā Devairasuraṇāṃ Vighātinī |
Jalpantī Bahu Garjantī Bhaje Tāṃ Dhūmrarūpiṇīm ǁ 8

Jhaṅkārakāriṇīṃ Jhañjhāṃ Jhañjhamājhamavādinīm |
Jhaṭityākarṣiṇīṃ Devīṃ Bhaje Dhūmāvatīmaham ǁ 9

Ṭīpaṭaṅkārasaṃyuktāṃ Dhanuṣṭaṅkārakāriṇīm |
Ghorāṃ Ghanaghaṭāṭopāṃ Vande Dhūmāvatīmaham ǁ 10

Ṭhaṃ Ṭhaṃ Ṭhaṃ Ṭhaṃ Manuprītiṃ Ṭhaḥ Ṭhaḥ Mantrasvarūpiṇīm |
Ṭhamakāhvagatiprītāṃ Bhaje Dhūmāvatīmaham ǁ 11

Ḍamarūḍiṇḍimārāvāṃ Ḍākinīgaṇamaṇḍitām |
Ḍākinībhogasantuṣṭāṃ Bhaje Dhūmāvatīmaham ǁ 12

Ḍhakkānādena Santuṣṭāṃ Ḍhakkāvādakasiddhidām |
Ḍhakkāvādacalaccittāṃ Bhaje Dhūmāvatīmaham ǁ 13

Tattvavārttāpriyaprāṇāṃ Bhavapāthodhitāriṇīm |
Tārasvarūpiṇīṃ Tārāṃ Bhaje Dhūmāvatīmaham ǁ 14

Thāṃ Thīṃ Thūṃ Theṃ Mantrarūpāṃ Thaiṃ Thauṃ Thaṃ Thaḥ

Svarūpiṇīm |

Thakāravarṇasarvasvāṃ Bhaje Dhūmāvatīmaham || 15

Dūrgāsvarūpiṇīṃ Devīṃ Duṣṭadānavadāriṇīm |
Devadaityakṛtadhvaṃsāṃ Vande Dhūmāvatīmaham || 16

Dhvāntākārāndhakadhvaṃsāṃ Muktadhammilladhāriṇīm |
Dhūmadhārāprabhāṃ Dhīrāṃ Bhaje Dhūmāvatīmaham || 17

Narttakīnaṭanaprītāṃ Nāṭyakarmavivarddhinīm |
Nārasiṃhīnnarārādhyāṃ Naumi Dhūmāvatīmaham || 18

Pārvatīpatisampūjyāṃ Parvatoparivāsinīm |
Padmārūpāṃ Padmapūjyāṃ Naumi Dhūmāvatīmaham || 19

Phūtkārasahitaśvāsāṃ Phaṭ Mantraphaladāyinīm |
Phetkāriganasaṃsevyāṃ Seve Dhūmāvatīmaham || 20

Balipūjyāṃ Balārādhyāṃ Bagalārūpiṇīṃ Varām |
Brahmādivanditāṃ Vidyāṃ Vande Dhūmāvatīmaham || 21

Bhavyarūpāṃ Bhavārādhyāṃ Bhuvaneśīsvarūpiṇīm |
Bhaktabhavyapradāndevīṃ Bhaje Dhūmāvatīmaham || 22

Māyāṃ Madhumatīṃ Mānyāṃ Makaradhvajamānitām |
Matsyamāṃsamadāsvādāṃ Manye Dhūmāvatīmaham || 23

Yogayajñaprasannāsyāṃ Yoginīparisevitām |
Yaśodāṃ Yajñaphaladāṃ Yaje Dhūmāvatīmaham || 24

Rāmārādhyapadadvandvāṃ Rāvaṇadhvaṃsakāriṇīm |
Rameśaramaṇīṃ Pūjyāmahaṃ Dhūmāvatīṃ Śraye || 25

Lakṣalīlākalālakṣyāṃ Lokavandyapadāmbujām |
Lambitāṃ Bījakośāḍhyāṃ Vande Dhūmāvatīmaham || 26

Bakapūjyapadāmbhojāṃ Bakadhyānaparāyaṇām |
Bālāṃ Bakārisandhyeyāṃ Vande Dhūmāvatīmaham || 27

Śaṅkarīṃ Śaṅkaraprāṇāṃ Saṅkaṭadhvaṃsakāriṇīm |
Śatrusaṃhāriṇīṃ Śuddhāṃ Śraye Dhūmāvatīmaham || 28

Ṣaḍānanārisaṃhantrīṃ Ṣoḍaśīrūpadhāriṇīm |
Ṣaḍrasāsvādinīṃ Saumyāṃ Seve Dhūmāvatīmaham || 29

Surasevitapādābjāṃ Surasaukhyapradāyinīm |
Sundarīgaṇasaṃsevyāṃ Seve Dhūmāvatīmaham || 30

Herambajananīṃ Yogyāṃ Hāsyalāsyavihāriṇīm |
Hāriṇīṃ Śatrusaṅghānāṃ Seve Dhūmāvatīmaham || 31

Kṣīrodatīrasaṃvāsāṃ Kṣīrapānapraharṣitām |
Kṣaṇadeśejyapādābjāṃ Seve Dhūmāvatīmaham || 32

Catustriṃśadvarṇakānāṃ Prativarṇādināmabhiḥ |
Kṛtaṃ Tu Hṛdayastotraṃ Dhūmāvatyāṃ Susiddhidam || 33

Ya Idaṃ Paṭhati Stotraṃ Pavitraṃ Pāpanāśanam |
Sa Prāpnoti Parāṃ Siddhiṃ Dhūmāvatyāḥ Prasādataḥ || 34

Paṭhannekāgracitto Yo Yadyadicchati Mānavaḥ |
Tatsarvaṃ Samavāpnoti Satyaṃ Satyaṃ Vadāmyaham || 35

Iti Dhūmāvatī Hṛdayaṃ Samāptam ||

श्री धूमावती हृदयम्

श्री गणेशाय नमः ||

श्री उमामहेश्वराभ्यां नमः ||

श्री धूमावत्यै नमः ||

ॐ अस्य श्रीधूमावतीहृदयस्तोत्रमन्त्रस्य पिप्पलाद ऋषिः | अनुष्टुप्छन्दः |
श्रीधूमावती देवता | धूं बीजम् | ह्रीं शक्तिः |क्लीं कीलकम् |
सर्व शत्रु संहरणे पाठे विनियोगः ||

हृदयादि षडङ्गन्यासः ।

ॐ धां हृदयाय नमः ।　　　　ॐ धीं शिरसे स्वाहा ।
ॐ धूं शिखायै वषट् ।　　　　ॐ धैं कवचाय हुम् ।
ॐ धौं नेत्रत्रयाय वौषट् ।　　　　ॐ धः अस्त्राय फट् ।

करन्यासः ।

ॐ धां अङ्गुष्ठाभ्यां नमः ।　　　　ॐ धीं तर्जनीभ्यां नमः ।
ॐ धूं मध्यमाभ्यां नमः ।　　　　ॐ धैं अनामिकाभ्यां नमः ।
ॐ धौं कनिष्ठिकाभ्यां नमः ।　　　　ॐ धः करतलकरपृष्ठाभ्यां नमः ।

ध्यानम् ।

ॐ धूम्राभां धूम्रवस्त्रां प्रकटितदशनांमुक्तवालाम्बराद्यां
काकाङ्कस्यन्दनस्थां धवलकरयुगां शूर्पहस्तातिरूक्षाम् ।

नित्यं क्षुत्क्षान्तदेहां मुहुरतिकुटिलां वारिवाञ्छाविचित्रां
ध्यायेद्धूमावतीं वामनयनयुगलां भीतिदां भीषणास्याम् ॥ १

कल्पादौ या कालिकाद्याऽचीकलन्मधुकैटभौ ।
कल्पान्ते त्रिजगत्सर्वं धूमावतीं भजामि ताम् ॥ २

गुणागाराऽगम्यगुणा या गुणा गुणवर्द्धिनी ।
गीतावेदार्थतत्त्वज्ञैर्धूमावतीं भजामि ताम् ॥ ३

खट्वाङ्गधारिणी खर्वा खण्डिनी खलरक्षसाम् ।
धारिणी खेटकस्यापि धूमावतीं भजामि ताम् ॥ ४

घूर्णा घूर्णकरा घोरा घूर्णिताक्षी घनस्वना ।
घातिनी घातकानां या धूमावतीं भजामि ताम् ॥ ५

चर्वन्तीमस्थिखण्डानां चण्डमुण्डविदारिणीम् ।
चण्डाट्टहासिनीं देवीं भजे धूमावतीमहम् ॥ ६

छिन्नग्रीवां क्षताच्छन्नां छिन्नमस्तास्वरूपिणीम् ।
छेदिनीं दुष्टसङ्घानां भजे धूमावतीमहम् ॥ ७

जाता या याचिता देवैरसुरणां विघातिनी ।
जल्पन्ती बहु गर्जन्ती भजे तां धूम्ररूपिणीम् ॥ ८

झङ्कारकारिणीं झञ्झां झञ्झमाझमवादिनीम् ।
झटित्याकर्षिणीं देवीं भजे धूमावतीमहम् ॥ ९

टीपटङ्कारसंयुक्तां धनुष्टङ्कारकारिणीम् ।
घोरां घनघटाटोपां वन्दे धूमावतीमहम् ॥ १०

ठं ठं ठं ठं मनुप्रीतिं ठः ठःमन्त्रस्वरूपिणीम् ।
ठमकाह्वगतिप्रीतां भजे धूमावतीमहम् ॥ ११

डमरूडिण्डिमारावां डाकिनीगणमण्डिताम् ।
डाकिनीभोगसन्तुष्टां भजे धूमावतीमहम् ॥ १२

ढक्कानादेन सन्तुष्टां ढक्कावादकसिद्धिदाम् ।
ढक्कावादचलच्चित्तां भजे धूमावतीमहम् ॥ १३

तत्त्ववार्त्ताप्रियप्राणां भवपाथोधितारिणीम् ।
तारस्वरूपिणीं तारां भजे धूमावतीमहम् ॥ १४

थां थीं थूं थें मन्त्ररूपां थैं थौं थं थः स्वरूपिणीम् ।
थकारवर्णसर्वस्वां भजे धूमावतीमहम् ॥ १५

दूर्गास्वरूपिणीं देवीं दुष्टदानवदारिणीम् ।
देवदैत्यकृतध्वंसां वन्दे धूमावतीमहम् ॥ १६

ध्वान्ताकारान्धकध्वंसां मुक्तधम्मिल्ललधारिणीम् ।
धूमधाराप्रभां धीरां भजे धूमावतीमहम् ॥ १७

नर्त्तकीनटनप्रीतां नाट्यकर्मविवर्द्धिनीम् ।
नारसिंहीन्नराराध्यां नौमि धूमावतीमहम् ॥ १८

पार्वतीपतिसम्पूज्यां पर्वतोपरिवासिनीम् ।
पद्मारूपां पद्मपूज्यां नौमि धूमावतीमहम् ॥ १९

फूत्कारसहितश्वासां फट् मन्त्रफलदायिनीम् ।
फेत्कारिगणसंसेव्यां सेवे धूमावतीमहम् ॥ २०

बलिपूज्यां बलाराध्यां बगलारूपिणीं वराम् ।
ब्रह्मादिवन्दितां विद्यां वन्दे धूमावतीमहम् ॥ २१

भव्यरूपां भवाराध्यां भुवनेशीस्वरूपिणीम् ।
भक्तभव्यप्रदान्देवीं भजे धूमावतीमहम् ॥ २२

मायां मधुमतीं मान्यां मकरध्वजमानिताम् ।
मत्स्यमांसमदास्वादां मन्ये धूमावतीमहम् ॥ २३

योगयज्ञप्रसन्नास्यां योगिनीपरिसेविताम् ।
यशोदां यज्ञफलदां यजे धूमावतीमहम् ॥ २४

रामाराध्यपदद्वन्द्वां रावणध्वंसकारिणीम् ।
रमेशरमणीं पूज्यामहं धूमावतीं श्रये ॥ २५

लक्षलीलाकलालक्ष्यां लोकवन्द्यपदाम्बुजाम् ।
लम्बितां बीजकोशाढ्यां वन्दे धूमावतीमहम् ॥ २६

बकपूज्यपदाम्भोजां बकध्यानपरायणाम् ।
बालां बकारिसन्ध्येयां वन्दे धूमावतीमहम् ॥ २७

शाङ्करीं शङ्करप्राणां सङ्कटध्वंसकारिणीम् ।
शत्रुसंहारिणीं शुद्धां श्रये धूमावतीमहम् ॥ २८

षडाननारिसंहन्त्रीं षोडशीरूपधारिणीम् ।
षड्रसास्वादिनीं सौम्यां सेवे धूमावतीमहम् ॥ २९

सुरसेवितपादाब्जां सुरसौख्यप्रदायिनीम् ।
सुन्दरीगणसंसेव्यां सेवेधूमावतीमहम् ॥ ३०

हेरम्बजननीं योग्यां हास्यलास्यविहारिणीम् ।
हारिणीं शत्रुसङ्घानां सेवे धूमावतीमहम् ॥ ३१

क्षीरोदतीरसंवासां क्षीरपानप्रहर्षिताम् ।
क्षणदेशेज्यपादाब्जां सेवे धूमावतीमहम् ॥ ३२

चतुस्त्रिंशद्वर्णकानां प्रतिवर्णादिनामभिः ।
कृतं तु हृदयस्तोत्रं धूमावत्यां सुसिद्धिदम् ॥ ३३

य इदं पठति स्तोत्रं पवित्रं पापनाशनम् ।
स प्राप्नोति परां सिद्धिं धूमावत्याः प्रसादतः ॥ ३४

पठन्नेकाग्रचित्तो यो यद्यदिच्छति मानवः ।
तत्सर्वं समवाप्नोति सत्यं सत्यं वदाम्यहम् ॥ ३५

इति धूमावतीहृदयं समाप्तम् ॥

*****

य इदं पठति स्तोत्रं पवित्रं पापनाशनम् ।
स प्राप्नोति परां सिद्धिं धूमावत्याः प्रसादतः ॥ ३४

पठन्नेकाग्रचित्तो यो यद्यदिच्छति मानवः ।
तत्सर्वं समवाप्नोति सत्यं सत्यं वदाम्यहम् ॥ ३५

इति धूमावतीहृदयं समाप्तम् ॥

Śrī Dhūmāvatī Aṣtotra Śata Nāma Stotram

Iśvara Uvaca:-

Dhūmāvati Dhūmravarṇā Dhūmrapāna Parayaṇā |
Dhūmrākśamathinī Dhanyā Dhanyasthānanivāsini || 1

Aghorā Cāra Santusṭā Aghorā Cāra Maṇḍitā |
Aghora Mantra Samprītā Aghora Mantrapūjitā || 2

Aṭṭaṭṭahāsaniratā Malinām Baradhāriṇī |
Vruddhā Virūpā Vidhavā Vidyā Ca Viraladvijā || 3

Pravrddhaghoṇā Kumukhī Kuṭilā Kuṭilekśaṇā |
Karālī Ca Karālāsyā Kankālī Śurpadhārinī || 4

Kākadhvaja Rathārūḍhā Kevalā Kaṭhinā Kuhūḥ |
Kśutpipāsārditā Nityā Lalajjihvā Digambarī || 5

Dīrghodarī Dīrgharavā Dīrghangī Dīrghamastakā |
Vimukta Kuntalā Kīrtyā Kailasasthānavāsinī || 6

Krūrā Kālasvarūpā Ca Kālacakrapravartinī |
Vivarṇā Cañcalā Duṣṭā Duṣṭavidhvaṃsakāriṇī || 7

Caṇḍī Caṇḍasvarūpā Ca Cāmuṇḍā Caṇḍanisvanā |
Caṇḍavegā Caṇḍagatiścaṇḍamuṇḍavināśinī || 8

Cāṇḍālinī Citrarekhā Citrāṅgī Citrarūpiṇī |
Kṛṣṇā Kapardinī Kullā Kṛṣṇārūpā Kriyāvatī || 9

Kumbhastanī Mahonmattā Maḍirāpānavihvalā |
Caturbhujā Lalajjihvā Śatrusaṃhārakāriṇī || 10

Śavārūḍhā Śavagatā Śmaśānasthānavāsinī |
Durārādhyā Durācārā Durjanaprītidāyinī || 11

Nirmāṃsā Ca Nirākārā Dhūtahastā Varānvitā |

Kalahā Ca Kaliprītā Kalikalmaṣanāśinī || 12

Mahākālasvarūpā Ca Mahākālaprapūjitā |

Mahādevapriyā Medhā Mahāsaṅkaṭanāśinī || 13

Bhaktapriyā Bhaktagatirbhaktaśatruvināśinī |

Bhairavī Bhuvanā Bhīmā Bhāratī Bhuvanātmikā || 14

Bheruṇḍā Bhīmanayanā Trinetrā Bahurūpiṇī |

Trilokeśī Trikālajñā Trisvarūpā Trayītanuḥ || 15

Trimūrtiśca Tathā Tanvī Triśaktiśca Triśūlinī |

Iti Dhūmāmahatstotraṃ Nāmnāmaṣṭottarātmakam || 16

Mayā Te Kathitaṃ Devi Śatrusaṅghavināśanam |

Kārāgāre Ripugraste Mahotpāte Mahābhaye || 17

Idaṃ Stotraṃ Paṭhenmartyo Mucyate Sarvasaṅkaṭaiḥ |

Guhyādguhyataraṃ Guhyaṃ Gopanīyaṃ Prayatnataḥ || 18

Catuṣpadārthadaṃ Nṝṇāṃ Sarvasampatpradāyakam || 19

Iti Śrī Dhūmāvatyaṣṭottara Śata Nāma Stotram Sampūrṇam ||

धूमावती अष्टोत्तर शतनाम स्तोत्रम्

ईश्वर उवाच:-

धूमावती धूम्रवर्णा धूम्रपानपरायणा ।
धूम्राक्षमथिनी धन्या धन्यस्थाननिवासिनी ॥ १

अघोराचारसन्तुष्टा अघोराचारमण्डिता ।
अघोरमन्त्रसम्प्रीता अघोरमन्त्रपूजिता ॥ २

अट्टाट्टहासनिरता मलिनाम्बरधारिणी ।
वृद्धा विरूपा विधवा विद्या च विरलद्विजा ॥ ३

प्रवृद्धघोणा कुमुखी कुटिला कुटिलेक्षणा ।
कराली च करालास्या कङ्काली शूर्पधारिणी ॥ ४

काकध्वजरथारूढा केवला कठिना कुहूः ।
क्षुत्पिपासार्दिता नित्या ललज्जिह्वा दिगम्बरी ॥ ५

दीर्घोदरी दीर्घरवा दीर्घाङ्गी दीर्घमस्तका ।
विमुक्तकुन्तला कीर्या कैलासस्थानवासिनी ॥ ६

क्रूरा कालस्वरूपा च कालचक्रप्रवर्तिनी ।
विवर्णा चञ्चला दुष्टा दुष्टविध्वंसकारिणी ॥ ७

चण्डी चण्डस्वरूपा च चामुण्डा चण्डनिस्वना ।
चण्डवेगा चण्डगतिश्चण्डमुण्डविनाशिनी ॥ ८

चाण्डालिनी चित्ररेखा चित्राङ्गी चित्ररूपिणी ।
कृष्णा कपर्दिनी कुल्ला कृष्णारूपा क्रियावती ॥ ९

कुम्भस्तनी महोन्मत्ता मदिरापानविह्वला ।
चतुर्भुजा ललज्जिह्वा शत्रुसंहारकारिणी ॥ १०

शवारूढा शवगता श्मशानस्थानवासिनी ।
दुराध्या दुराचारा दुर्जनप्रीतिदायिनी ॥ ११

निर्मांसा च निराकारा धूतहस्ता वरान्विता ।
कलहा च कलिप्रीता कलिकल्मषनाशिनी ॥ १२

महाकालस्वरूपा च महाकालप्रपूजिता ।
महादेवप्रिया मेधा महासङ्कटनाशिनी ॥ १३

भक्तप्रिया भक्तगतिर्भक्तशत्रुविनाशिनी ।
भैरवी भुवना भीमा भारती भुवनात्मिका ॥ १४

भेरुण्डा भीमनयना त्रिनेत्रा बहुरूपिणी ।
त्रिलोकेशी त्रिकालज्ञा त्रिस्वरूपा त्रयीतनुः ॥ १५

त्रिमूर्तिश्च तथा तन्वी त्रिशक्तिश्च त्रिशूलिनी ।
इति धूमामहत्स्तोत्रं नाम्नामष्टोत्तरात्मकम् ॥ १६

मया ते कथितं देवि शत्रुसङ्घविनाशनम् ।
कारागारे रिपुग्रस्ते महोत्पाते महाभये ॥ १७

इदं स्तोत्रं पठेन्मर्त्यो मुच्यते सर्वसङ्कटैः ।
गुह्याद्गुह्यतरं गुह्यं गोपनीयं प्रयत्नतः ॥ १८

चतुष्पदार्थदं नॄणां सर्वसम्पत्प्रदायकम् ॥ १९

इति श्री धूमावत्यष्टोत्तर शत नाम स्तोत्रं सम्पूर्णम् ॥

*****

Śrī Dhūmāvatī Aṣtotra Śata Nāmāvaliḥ

108 Divine Names of *Śrī Dhūmāvatī Devi.*

1.	ॐ धूमावत्यै नमः।	Oṃ Dhūmāvatyai Namaḥ।
2.	ॐ धूम्रवर्णायै नमः।	Oṃ Dhūmravarṇāyai Namaḥ।
3.	ॐ धूम्रपानपरायणायै नमः।	Oṃ Dhūmrapānaparāyaṇāyai Namaḥ।
4.	ॐ धूम्राक्षमथिन्यै नमः।	Oṃ Dhūmrākṣamathinyai Namaḥ।
5.	ॐ धन्यायै नमः।	Oṃ Dhanyāyai Namaḥ।
6.	ॐ धन्यस्थाननिवासिन्यै नमः।	Oṃ Dhanyasthānanivāsinyai Namaḥ।
7.	ॐ अघोराचारसन्तुष्टायै नमः।	Oṃ Aghorāchārasantushṭāyai Namaḥ।
8.	ॐ अघोराचारमण्डितायै नमः।	Oṃ Aghorāchāramaṇḍitāyai Namaḥ।
9.	ॐ अघोरमन्त्रसम्प्रीतायै नमः।	Oṃ Aghoramantrasamprītāyai Namaḥ।
10.	ॐ अघोरमन्त्रपूजितायै नमः।	Oṃ Aghoramantrapujitāyai Namaḥ।
11.	ॐ अट्टाट्टहासनिरतायै नमः।	Oṃ Aṭṭāṭṭahāsaniratāyai Namaḥ।
12.	ॐ मलिनाम्बरधारिण्यै नमः।	Oṃ Malināmbaradhāriṇyai Namaḥ।
13.	ॐ वृद्धायै नमः।	Oṃ Vruddhāyai Namaḥ।
14.	ॐ विरूपायै नमः।	Oṃ Virupāyai Namaḥ।
15.	ॐ विधवायै नमः।	Oṃ Vidhavāyai Namaḥ।
16.	ॐ विद्यायै नमः।	Oṃ Vidyāyai Namaḥ।
17.	ॐ विरलद्विजायै नमः।	Oṃ Viraladvijāyai Namaḥ।
18.	ॐ प्रवृद्धघोणायै नमः।	Oṃ Pravriddhaghoṇāyai Namaḥ।
19.	ॐ कुमुख्यै नमः।	Oṃ Kumukhyai Namaḥ।
20.	ॐ कुटिलायै नमः।	Oṃ Kuṭilāyai Namaḥ।
21.	ॐ कुटिलेक्षणायै नमः।	Oṃ Kuṭilekṣaṇāyai Namaḥ।

22.	ॐ कराल्यै नमः।	Oṃ Karālyai Namaḥ।
23.	ॐ करालास्याये नमः।	Oṃ Karālāsyāyai Namaḥ।
24.	ॐ कङ्कराल्यै नमः।	Oṃ Kankālyai Namaḥ।
25.	ॐ शूर्पधारिण्यै नमः।	Oṃ Śurpadhāriṇyai Namaḥ।
26.	ॐ काकध्वजरथारूढायै नमः।	Oṃ Kākadhvajarathārūḍhāyai Namaḥ।
27.	ॐ केवलायै नमः।	Oṃ Kevalāyai Namaḥ।
28.	ॐ कठिनायै नमः।	Oṃ Kaṭhināyai Namaḥ।
29.	ॐ कुह्वै नमः।	Oṃ Kuhvai Namaḥ।
30.	ॐ क्षुत्पिपासार्दितायै नमः।	Oṃ Kṣutpipāsārditāyai Namaḥ।
31.	ॐ नित्यायै नमः।	Oṃ Nityāyai Namaḥ।
32.	ॐ ललज्जिह्वायै नमः।	Oṃ Lalajjihvāyai Namaḥ।
33.	ॐ दिगम्बर्यै नमः।	Oṃ Digambaryai Namaḥ।
34.	ॐ दीर्घोदर्यै नमः।	Oṃ Dirghodaryai Namaḥ।
35.	ॐ दीर्घरवायै नमः।	Oṃ Dirgharavāyai Namaḥ।
36.	ॐ दीर्घाङ्ग्यै नमः।	Oṃ Dirghāngyai Namaḥ।
37.	ॐ दीर्घमस्तकायै नमः।	Oṃ Dirghamastakāyai Namaḥ।
38.	ॐ विमुक्तकुन्तलायै नमः।	Oṃ Vimuktakuntalāyai Namaḥ।
39.	ॐ कीर्त्यायै नमः।	Oṃ Kirtyāyai Namaḥ।
40.	ॐ कैलासस्थानवासिन्यै नमः।	Oṃ Kailāsasthānavāsinyai Namaḥ।
41.	ॐ क्रूरायै नमः।	Oṃ Krurāyai Namaḥ।
42.	ॐ कालस्वरूपायै नमः।	Oṃ Kālasvarupāyai Namaḥ।
43.	ॐ कालचक्रप्रवर्तिन्यै नमः।	Oṃ Kālachakrapravartinyai Namaḥ।
44.	ॐ विवर्णायै नमः।	Oṃ Vivarṇāyai Namaḥ।
45.	ॐ चञ्चलायै नमः।	Oṃ Chanchalāyai Namaḥ।
46.	ॐ दुष्टायै नमः।	Oṃ Duṣṭāyai Namaḥ।
47.	ॐ दुष्टविध्वंसकारिण्यै नमः।	Oṃ Duṣṭavidhvamsakāriṇyai Namaḥ।
48.	ॐ चण्ड्यै नमः।	Oṃ Caṇḍyai Namaḥ।
49.	ॐ चण्डस्वरूपायै नमः।	Oṃ Caṇḍasvarupāyai Namaḥ।

50.	ॐ चामुण्डायै नमः।	Oṃ Camuṇḍāyai Namaḥ।
51.	ॐ चण्डनिःस्वनायै नमः।	Oṃ Caṇḍaniḥ Svanāyai Namaḥ।
52.	ॐ चण्डवेगायै नमः।	Oṃ Caṇḍavegāyai Namaḥ।
53.	ॐ चण्डगत्यै नमः।	Oṃ Caṇḍagatyai Namaḥ।
54.	ॐ चण्डविनाशिन्यै नमः।	Oṃ Caṇḍavināśinyai Namaḥ।
55.	ॐ मुण्डविनाशिन्यै नमः।	Oṃ Muṇḍavināśinyai Namaḥ।
56.	ॐ चाण्डालिन्यै नमः।	Oṃ Cāṇḍālinyai Namaḥ।
57.	ॐ चित्ररेखायै नमः।	Oṃ Citrarekhḍyai Namaḥ।
58.	ॐ चित्राङ्ग्यै नमः।	Oṃ Citrḍngyai Namaḥ।
59.	ॐ चित्ररूपिण्यै नमः।	Oṃ Citrarupiṇyai Namaḥ।
60.	ॐ कृष्णायै नमः।	Oṃ Kriṣṇāyai Namaḥ।
61.	ॐ कपर्दिन्यै नमः।	Oṃ Kapardinyai Namaḥ।
62.	ॐ कुल्लायै नमः।	Oṃ Kullayāi Namaḥ।
63.	ॐ कृष्णरूपायै नमः।	Oṃ Kriṣṇarūpāyai Namaḥ।
64.	ॐ क्रियावत्यै नमः।	Oṃ Kriyāvatyai Namaḥ।
65.	ॐ कुम्भस्तन्यै नमः।	Oṃ Kumbhastanyai Namaḥ।
66.	ॐ महोन्मत्तायै नमः।	Oṃ Mahonmattāyai Namaḥ।
67.	ॐ मदिरापानविह्वलायै नमः।	Oṃ Madirāpānavihvalāyai Namaḥ।
68.	ॐ चतुर्भुजायै नमः	Oṃ Caturbhujāyai Namaḥ।
69.	ॐ ललज्जिह्वायै नमः	Oṃ Lalajjihvāyai Namaḥ।
70.	ॐ शत्रुसंहारकारिण्यै नमः।	Oṃ Śatrusamhārakāriṇyai Namaḥ।
71.	ॐ शवारूढायै नमः।	Oṃ Śavārudhāyai Namaḥ।
72.	ॐ शवगतायै नमः।	Oṃ Śavagatāyai Namaḥ।
73.	ॐ शमशानस्थानवासिन्यै नमः।	Oṃ Śmaśānasthānavāsinyai Namaḥ।
74.	ॐ दुराराध्यायै नमः।	Oṃ Durārādhyāyai Namaḥ।
75.	ॐ दुराचारायै नमः।	Oṃ Durācārayai Namaḥ।
76.	ॐ दुर्जनप्रीतिदायिन्यै नमः।	Oṃ Durjanapritidāyinyai Namaḥ।
77.	ॐ निर्मांसायै नमः।	Oṃ Nirmāmsāyai Namaḥ।

78.	ॐ निराकारायै नमः।	Oṃ Nirākārayai Namaḥ।
79.	ॐ धूमहस्तायै नमः।	Oṃ Dhūmahastāyai Namaḥ।
80.	ॐ वरान्वितायै नमः।	Oṃ Varānvitāyai Namaḥ।
81.	ॐ कलहायै नमः।	Oṃ Kalahāyai Namaḥ।
82.	ॐ कलिप्रीतायै नमः।	Oṃ Kaliprītāyai Namaḥ।
83.	ॐ कलिकल्मषनाशिन्यै नमः।	Oṃ Kalikalmaṣanāśinyai Namaḥ।
84.	ॐ महाकालस्वरूपायै नमः।	Oṃ Mahākālasvarupāyai Namaḥ।
85.	ॐ महाकालप्रपूजितायै नमः।	Oṃ Mahākālaprapujitāyai Namaḥ।
86.	ॐ महादेवप्रियायै नमः।	Oṃ Mahādevapriyāyai Namaḥ।
87.	ॐ मेधायै नमः।	Oṃ Medhāyai Namaḥ।
88.	ॐ महासङ्कटनाशिन्यै नमः।	Oṃ Mahāsankaṭanāśinyai Namaḥ।
89.	ॐ भक्तप्रियायै नमः।	Oṃ Bhaktapriyāyai Namaḥ।
90.	ॐ भक्तगत्यै नमः।	Oṃ Bhaktagatyai Namaḥ।
91.	ॐ भक्तशत्रुविनाशिन्यै नमः।	Oṃ Bhaktaśatruvināśinyai Namaḥ।
92.	ॐ भैरव्यै नमः।	Oṃ Bhairavyai Namaḥ।
93.	ॐ भुवनायै नमः।	Oṃ Bhuvanāyai Namaḥ।
94.	ॐ भीमायै नमः।	Oṃ Bhīmāyai Namaḥ।
95.	ॐ भारत्यै नमः।	Oṃ Bhāratyai Namaḥ।
96.	ॐ भुवनात्मिकायै नमः।	Oṃ Bhuvānatmikāyai Namaḥ।
97.	ॐ भेरूण्डायै नमः।	Oṃ Bheruṇḍāyai Namaḥ।
98.	ॐ भीमनयनायै नमः।	Oṃ Bhīmanayanāyai Namaḥ।
99.	ॐ त्रिनेत्रायै नमः।	Oṃ Trinetrāyai Namaḥ।
100.	ॐ बहुरूपिण्यै नमः।	Oṃ Bahurūpiṇyai Namaḥ।
101.	ॐ त्रिलोकेश्यै नमः।	Oṃ Trilokeśyai Namaḥ।
102.	ॐ त्रिकालज्ञायै नमः।	Oṃ Trikālagyāyai Namaḥ।
103.	ॐ त्रिस्वरूपायै नमः।	Oṃ Trisvarupāyai Namaḥ।
104.	ॐ त्रयीतनवे नमः।	Oṃ Trayitanave Namaḥ।
105.	ॐ त्रिमूर्त्यै नमः।	Oṃ Trimūrtyai Namaḥ।
106.	ॐ तन्व्यै नमः।	Oṃ Tanvyai Namaḥ।
107.	ॐ त्रिशक्त्यै नमः।	Oṃ Triśaktyai Namaḥ।

| 108. | ॐ त्रिशूलिन्यै नमः। | *Oṃ Triśulinyai Namaḥ।* |

॥ इति धूमावतियष्टोत्तरशत नामावलिः सम्पूर्णम् ॥

*****

Śrī Dhūmāvatī Sahasranāma Stotram

Śrī Dhūmāvatī Sahasranāma Stotram

Śrī Bhairavy Uvāca

Dhūmāvatyā Dharmarātryāḥ Kathayasva Maheśvara |
Sahasranāmastotramme Sarvasiddhipradāyakam ‖ 1

Śrī Bhairava Uvāca

Śṛṇu Devi Mahāmāye Priye Prāṇasvarūpiṇi |
Sahasranāmastotramme Bhavaśatruvināśam ‖ 2

*Oṃ Asya Śrīdhūmāvatīsahasranāmastotrasya Pippalāda Ṛṣiḥ
Paṅktiśchando Dhūmāvatī Devatā Śatruvinigrahe Pāṭhe Viniyogaḥ*

Sahasranama Stotram

Dhumā Dhūmavatī Dhūmā Dhūmapānaparāyaṇā |
Dhautā Dhautagirā Dhāmnī Dhūmeśvaranivāsinī ‖ 3

Anantā'nantarūpā Ca Akārākārarūpiṇī |
Ādyā Ānandadānandā Ikārā Indrarūpiṇī ‖ 4

Dhanadhānyārtthavāṇīdā Yaśodharmapriyeṣṭadā |
Bhāgyasaubhāgyabhaktisthā Gṛhaparvatavāsinī ‖ 5

Rāmarāvaṇasugrīvamohadā Hanumatpriyā |
Vedaśāstrapurāṇajñā Jyotiśchandaḥsvarūpiṇī ‖ 6

Cāturyacārurucirā Rañjanaprematoṣadā |
Kamalāsanasudhāvaktrā Candrahāsā Smitānanā ‖ 7

Caturā Cārukeśī Ca Caturvargapradā Mudā |
Kalā Kāladharā Dhīrā Dhāriṇī Vasunīradā ‖ 8

Hīrā Hīrakavarṇābhā Hariṇāyatalocanā |
Dambhamohakrodhalobhasnehadveṣaharā Parā ‖ 9

Nāradevakarī Rāmā Rāmānandamanoharā |
Yogabhogakrodhalobhaharā Haranamaskṛtā || 10

Dānamānajñānamāna-Pānagānasukhapradā |
Gajagośvapadāgañjā Bhūtidā Bhūtanāśinī || 11

Bhavabhāvā Tathā Bālā Varadā Haravallabhā |
Bhagabhaṅgabhayā Mālā Mālatī Tālanāhṛdā || 12

Jālavālahālakālakapālapriyavādinī |
Karañjaśīlaguñjāḍhyā Cūtāṅkuranivāsinī || 13

Panasasthā Pānasaktā Panaseśakuṭumbinī |
Pāvanī Pāvanādhārā Pūrṇā Pūrṇamanorathā || 14

Pūtā Pūtakalā Paurā Purāṇasurasundarī |
Pareśī Paradā Pārā Parātmā Paramohinī || 15

Jaganmāyā Jagatkarttrī Jagatkīrttirjaganmayī |
Jananī Jayinī Jāyā Jitā Jinajayapradā || 16

Kīrttirjñānadhyānamānadāyinī Dānaveśvarī |
Kāvyavyākaraṇajñānā Prajñāprajñānadāyinī || 17

Vijñājñā Vijñajayadā Vijñā Vijñaprapūjitā |
Parāvarejyā Varadā Pāradā Śāradā Darā || 18

Dāriṇī Devadūtī Ca Madanā Madanāmadā |
Paramajñānagamyā Ca Ṣareśī Paragā Parā || 19

Yajñā Yajñapradā Yajñajñānakāryakarī Śubhā |
Śobhinī Śubhramathinī Niśumbhāsuramarddinī || 20

Śāmbhavī Śambhupatnī Ca Śambhujāyā Śubhānanā |
Śāṅkarī Śaṅkarārādhyā Sandhyā Sandhyāsudharmiṇī || 21

Śatrughnī Śatruhā Śatrupradā Śātravanāśinī |
Śaivī Śivalayā Śailā Śailarājapriyā Sadā || 22

Śarvarī Śavarī Śambhuḥ Sudhāḍhyā Saudhavāsinī |
Saguṇā Guṇarūpā Ca Gauravī Bhairavīravā || 23

Gaurāṅgī Gauradehā Ca Gaurī Gurumatī Guruḥ |
Gaurggaurgavyasvarūpā Ca Guṇānandasvarūpiṇī || 24

Gaṇeśagaṇadā Guṇyā Guṇā Gauravavāñchitā |
Gaṇamātā Gaṇārādhyā Gaṇakoṭivināśinī || 25

Durgā Durjjanahantrī Ca Durjjanaprītidāyinī |
Svargāpavargadā Dātrī Dīnā Dīnadayāvatī || 26

Durnnirīkṣyā Durāduḥsthā Dauḥsthabhañjanakāriṇī |
Śvetapāṇḍurakṛṣṇābhā Kāladā Kālanāśinī || 27

Karmanarmakarī Narmā Dharmādharmavināśinī |
Gaurī Gauravadā Godā Gaṇadā Gāyanapriyā || 28

Gaṅgā Bhāgīrathī Bhaṅgā Bhagā Bhāgyavivarddhinī |
Bhavānī Bhavahantrī Ca Bhairavī Bhairavīsamā || 29

Bhīmā Bhīmaravā Bhaimī Bhīmānandapradāyinī |
Śaraṇyā Śaraṇā Śamyā Śaśinī Śaṅkhanāśinī || 30

Guṇā Guṇakarī Gauṇī Priyāprītipradāyinī |
Janamohanakarttrī Ca Jagadānandadāyinī || 31

Jitā Jāyā Ca Vijayā Vijayā Jayadāyinī |
Kāmā Kālī Karālāsyā Kharvā Khañjā Kharā Gadā || 32

Garvā Garutmatī Dharmā Gharggharā Ghoranādinī |
Carācarī Carārādhyā Chinā Chinnamanorathā || 33

Chinnamastā Jayā Jāpyā Jagajjāyā Ca Jharjjharī |
Jhakārā Jhīṣkṛtiṣṭīkā Ṭaṅkā Ṭaṅkāranādinī || 34

Ṭhīkā Ṭhakkuraṭhakkāṅgī Ṭhaṭhaṭhāṅkāraḍhuṇḍhurā |
Ḍhuṇḍhītārājatīrṇā Ca Tālasthābhramanāśinī || 35

Thakārā Thakarā Dātrī Dīpā Dīpavināśinī |

Dhanyā Dhanā Dhanavatī Narmadā Narmamodinī || 36

Padmā Padmāvatī Pītā Sphāntā Phūtkārakāriṇī |

Phullā Brahmamayī Brāhmī Brahmānandapradāyinī || 37

Bhavārādhyā Bhavādhyakṣā Bhagālī Mandagāminī |

Madirā Madirekṣā Ca Yaśodā Yamapūjitā || 38

Yāmyā Rāmyā Rāmarūpā Ramaṇī Lalitā Latā |

Laṅkeśvarī Vākpradā Vācyā Sadāśramavāsinī || 39

Śrāntā Śakārarūpā Ca Ṣakārakharavāhanā |

Sahyādrirūpā Sānandā Hariṇī Harirūpiṇī || 40

Harārādhyā Vālavācalavaṅgaprematoṣitā |

Kṣapā Kṣayapradā Kṣīrā Akārādisvarūpiṇī || 41

Kālikā Kālamūrttiśca Kalahā Kalahapriyā |

Śivā Śandāyinī Saumyā Śatrunigrahakāriṇī || 42

Bhavānī Bhavamūrttiśca Śarvāṇī Sarvamaṅgalā |

Śatruviddrāviṇī Śaivī Śumbhāsuravināśinī || 43

Dhakāramantrarūpā Ca Dhūmbījaparitoṣitā |

Dhanādhyakṣastutā Dhīrā Dharārūpā Dharāvatī || 44

Carviṇī Candrapūjyā Ca Cchandorūpā Chaṭāvatī |

Chāyā Chāyāvatī Svacchā Chedinī Medinī Kṣamā || 45

Valginī Varddhinī Vandyā Vedamātā Budhastutā |

Dhārā Dhārāvatī Dhanyā Dharmadānaparāyaṇā || 46

Garviṇī Gurupūjyā Ca Jñānadātrī Guṇānvitā |

Dharmiṇī Dharmarūpā Ca Ghaṇṭānādaparāyaṇā ||| 47

Ghaṇṭāninādinī Ghūrṇā Ghūrṇitā Ghorarūpiṇī |

Kalighnī Kalidūtī Ca Kalipūjyā Kalipriyā || 48

Kālanirṇāśinī Kālyā Kāvyadā Kālarūpiṇī |
Varṣiṇī Vṛṣṭidā Vṛṣṭirmahāvṛṣṭinivāriṇī || 49

Ghāṭinī Ghāṭinī Ghoṇṭā Ghātakī Ghanarūpiṇī |
Dhūmbījā Dhūñjapānandā Dhūmbījajapatoṣitā || 50

Dhūndhūmbījajapāsaktā Dhūndhūmbījaparāyaṇā |
Dhūṅkāraharṣiṇī Dhūmā Dhanadā Dhanagarvitā || 51

Padmāvatī Padmamālā Padmayoniprapūjitā |
Apārā Pūraṇī Pūrṇā Pūrṇimāparivanditā || 52

Phaladā Phalabhoktrī Ca Phalinī Phaladāyinī |
Phūtkāriṇī Phalāvāptrī Phalabhoktrī Phalānvitā || 53

Vāriṇī Varaṇaprītā Vāripāthodhipāragā |
Vivarṇā Dhūmranayanā Dhūmrākṣī Dhūmrarūpiṇī || 54

Nītirnītisvarūpā Ca Nītijñā Nayakovidā |
Tāriṇī Tārarūpā Ca Tattvajñānaparāyaṇā || 55

Sthūlā Sthūlādharā Sthātrī Uttamasthānavāsinī |
Sthūlā Padmapadasthānā Sthānabhraṣṭā Sthalasthitā || 56

Śoṣiṇī Śobhinī Śītā Śītapānīyapāyinī |
Śāriṇī Śāṅkhinī Śuddhā Śaṅkhāsuravināśinī || 57

Śarvarī Śarvarīpūjyā Śarvarīśaprapūjitā |
Śarvarījāgritā Yogyā Yoginī Yogivanditā || 58

Yoginīgaṇasaṃsevyā Yoginī Yogabhāvitā |
Yogamārgaratāyuktā Yogamārgānusāriṇī || 59

Yogabhāvā Yogayuktā Yāminīpativanditā |
Ayogyā Yoghinī Yoddhrī Yuddhakarmaviśāradā || 60

Yuddhamārgaratānāntā Yuddhasthānanivāsinī |
Siddhā Siddheśvarī Siddhiḥ Siddhigehanivāsinī || 61

Siddharītissiddhaprītiḥ Siddhā Siddhāntakāriṇī |

Siddhagamyā Siddhapūjyā Siddhabandyā Susiddhidā || 62

Sādhinī Sādhanaprītā Sādhyā Sādhanakāriṇī |

Sādhanīyā Sādhyasādhyā Sādhyasaṅghasuśobhinī || 63

Sādhvī Sādhusvabhāvā Sā Sādhusantatidāyinī |

Sādhupūjyā Sādhuvandyā Sādhusandarśanodyatā || 64

Sādhudṛṣṭā Sādhupṛṣṭhā Sādhupoṣaṇatatparā |

Sāttvikī Sattvasaṃsiddhā Sattvasevyā Sukhodayā || 65

Sattvavṛddhikarī Śāntā Sattvasaṃharṣamānasā |

Sattvajñānā Sattvavidyā Sattvasiddhāntakāriṇī || 66

Sattvavṛddhissattvasiddhissattvasampannamānasā |

Cārurūpā Cārudehā Cārucañcalalocanā || 67

Chadminī Chadmasaṅkalpā Chadmavārttā Kṣamāpriyā |

Haṭhinī Haṭhasamprītirhaṭhavārttā Haṭhodyamā || 68

Haṭhakāryā Haṭhadharmā Haṭhakarmaparāyaṇā |

Haṭhasambhoganiratā Haṭhātkāraratipriyā || 69

Haṭhasambhedinī Hṛdyā Hṛdyavārttā Haripriyā |

Hariṇī Hariṇīdṛṣṭirhariṇīmāṃsabhakṣaṇā || 70

Hariṇākṣī Hariṇapā Hariṇīgaṇaharṣadā |

Hariṇīgaṇasaṃhartrī Hariṇīparipoṣikā || 71

Hariṇīmṛgayāsaktā Hariṇīmānapurassarā |

Dīnā Dīnākṛtirdūnā Drāviṇī Draviṇapradā || 72

Draviṇācalasaṃvvāsā Dravitā Dravyasaṃyyutā |

Dīrgghā Dīrgghapadā Dṛśyā Darśanīyā Dṛḍhākṛtiḥ || 73

Dṛḍhā Dviṣṭamatirddduṣṭā Dveṣiṇī Dveṣibhañjinī |

Doṣiṇī Doṣasaṃyyuktā Duṣṭaśatruvināśinī || 74

Devatārttiharā Duṣṭadaityasaṅghavidāriṇī |

Duṣṭadānavahantrī Ca Duṣṭadaityaniṣūdinī ‖ 75

Devatāprāṇadā Devī Devadurgatināśinī |

Naṭanāyakasaṃsevyā Narttakī Narttakapriyā ‖ 76

Nāṭyavidyā Nāṭyakartrī Nādinī Nādakāriṇī |

Navīnanūtanā Navyā Navīnavastradhāriṇī ‖ 77

Navyabhūṣā Navyamālyā Navyālaṅkāraśobhitā |

Nakāravādinī Namyā Navabhūṣaṇabhūṣitā ‖ 78

Nīcamārgā Nīcabhūmirnīcamārgagatirgatiḥ |

Nāthasevyā Nāthabhaktā Nāthānandapradāyinī ‖ 79

Namrā Namragatirnnetrī Nidānavākyavādinī |

Nārīmadhyasthitā Nārī Nārīmadhyagatā'naghā ‖ 80

Nārīprīti Narārādhyā Naranāmaprakāśinī |

Ratī Ratipriyā Ramyā Ratipremā Ratipradā ‖ 81

Ratisthānasthitārādhyā Ratiharṣapradāyinī |

Ratirūpā Ratidhyānā Ratirītisudhāriṇī ‖ 82

Ratirāsamahollāsā Ratirāsavihāriṇī |

Ratikāntastutā Rāśī Rāśirakṣaṇakāriṇī ‖ 83

Arūpā Śuddharūpā Ca Surūpā Rūpagarvitā |

Rūpayauvanasampannā Rūparāśī Ramāvatī ‖ 84

Rodhinī Roṣiṇī Ruṣṭā Roṣiruddhā Rasapradā |

Mādinī Madanaprītā Madhumattā Madhupradā ‖ 85

Madyapā Madyapadhyeyā Madyapaprāṇarakṣiṇī |

Madyapānandasandātrī Madyapaprematoṣitā ‖ 86

Madyapānaratā Mattā Madyapānavihāriṇī |

Madirā Madirāraktā Madirāpānaharṣiṇī ‖ 87

Madirāpānasantuṣṭā Madirāpānamohinī |
Madirāmānasāmugdhā Mādhvīpā Madirāpradā ‖ 88

Mādhvīdānasadānandā Mādhvīpānaratā Madā |
Modinī Modasandātrī Muditā Modamānasā ‖ 89

Modakartrī Modadātrī Modamaṅgalakāriṇī |
Modakādānasantuṣṭā Modakagrahaṇakṣamā ‖ 90

Modakālabdhisaṅkruddhā Modakaprāptitoṣiṇī |
Māṃsādā Māṃsasambhakṣā Māṃsabhakṣaṇaharṣiṇī ‖ 91

Māṃsapākaparapremā Māṃsapākālayasthitā |
Matsyamāṃsakṛtāsvādā Makārapañcakānvitā ‖ 92

Mudrā Mudrānvitā Mātā Mahāmohā Manasvinī |
Mudrikā Mudrikāyuktā Mudrikākṛtalakṣaṇā ‖ 93

Mudrikālaṅkṛtā Mādrī Mandarācalavāsinī |
Mandarācalasaṃsevyā Mandarācalavāsinī ‖ 94

Mandaradhyeyapādābjā Mandarāraṇyavāsinī |
Mandurāvāsinī Mandā Māriṇī Mārikāmitā ‖ 95

Mahāmārī Mahāmārīśaminī Śavasaṃsthitā |
Śavamāṃsakṛtāhārā Śmaśānālayavāsinī ‖ 96

Śmaśānasiddhisaṃhṛṣṭā Śmaśānabhavanasthitā |
Śmaśānaśayanāgārā Śmaśānabhasmalepitā ‖ 97

Śmaśānabhasmabhīmāṅgī Śmaśānāvāsakāriṇī |
Śāminī Śamanārādhyā Śamanastutivanditā ‖ 98

Śamanācārasantuṣṭā Śamanāgāravāsinī |
Śamanasvāminī Śāntiḥ Śāntasajjanapūjitā ‖ 99

Śāntapūjāparā Śāntā Śāntāgāraprabhojinī |
Śāntapūjyā Śāntavandyā Śāntagrahasudhāriṇī ‖ 100

Śāntarūpā Śāntiyuktā Śāntacandraprabhā'malā |
Amalā Vimalā Mlānā Mālatī Kuñjavāsinī || 101

Mālatīpuṣpasamprītā Mālatīpuṣpapūjitā |
Mahogrā Mahatī Madhyā Madhyadeśanivāsinī || 102

Madhyamadhvanisamprītā Madhyamadhvanikāriṇī |
Madhyamā Madhyamaprītirmadhyamapremapūritā || 103

Madhyāṅgacitravasanā Madhyakhinnā Mahoddhatā |
Mahendrakṛtasampūjā Mahendraparivanditā || 104

Mahendrajālasaṃyyuktā Mahendrajālakāriṇī |
Mahendramānitā'mānā Māninīgaṇamadhyagā || 105

Māninīmānasamprītā Mānavidhvaṃsakāriṇī |
Māninyākarṣiṇī Muktirmuktidātrī Sumuktidā || 106

Muktidveṣakarī Mūlyakāriṇī Mūlyahāriṇī |
Nirmalā Mūlasaṃyyuktā Mūlinī Mūlamantriṇī || 107

Mūlamantrakṛtārhādyā Mūlamantrārgghyaharṣiṇī |
Mūlamantrapratiṣṭhātrī Mūlamantrapraharṣiṇī || 108

Mūlamantraprasannāsyā Mūlamantraprapūjitā |
Mūlamantrapraṇetrī Ca Mūlamantrakṛtārccanā || 109

Mūlamantraprahṛṣṭātmā Mūlavidyā Malāpahā |
Vidyā'vidyā Vaṭasthā Ca Vaṭavṛkṣanivāsinī || 110

Vaṭavṛkṣakṛtasthānā Vaṭapūjāparāyaṇā |
Vaṭapūjāpariprītā Vaṭadarśanalālasā || 111

Vaṭapūjā Kṛtā Hlādā Vaṭapūjāvivarddhinī |
Vaśinī Vivaśārādhyā Vaśīkaraṇamantriṇī || 112

Vaśīkaraṇasamprītā Vaśīkārakasiddhidā |
Baṭukā Baṭukārādhyā Baṭukāhāradāyinī || 113

Baṭukārccāparā Pūjyā Baṭukārccāvivarddhinī |

Baṭukānandakarttrī Ca Baṭukaprāṇarakṣiṇī || 114

Baṭukejyāpradā'pārā Pāriṇī Pārvatīpriyā |

Parvatāgrakṛtāvāsā Parvatendraprapūjitā || 115

Pārvatīpatipūjyā Ca Pārvatīpatiharṣadā |

Pārvatīpatibuddhisthā Pārvatīpatimohinī || 116

Pārvatīyaddvijārādhyā Parvatasthā Pratāriṇī |

Padmalā Padminī Padmā Padmamālāvibhūṣitā || 117

Padmajeḍyapadā Padmamālālaṅkṛtamastakā |

Padmārccitapadadvandvā Padmahastapayodhijā || 118

Payodhipāragantrī Ca Pāthodhiparikīrttitā |

Pāthodhipāragāpūtā Palvalāmbupratarpitā || 119

Palvalāntaḥ Payomagnā Pavamānagatirgatiḥ |

Payaḥ Pānā Payodātrī Pānīyaparikāṅkṣiṇī || 120

Payojamālābharaṇā Muṇḍamālāvibhūṣaṇā |

Muṇḍinī Muṇḍahantrī Ca Muṇḍitā Muṇḍaśobhitā || 121

Maṇibhūṣā Maṇigrīvā Maṇimālāvirājitā |

Mahāmohā Mahāmarṣā Mahāmāyā Mahāhavā || 122

Mānavī Mānavīpūjyā Manuvaṃśavivarddhinī |

Maṭhinī Maṭhasaṃhantrī Maṭhasampattihāriṇī || 123

Mahākrodhavatī Mūḍhā Mūḍhaśatruvināśinī |

Pāṭhīnabhojinī Pūrṇā Pūrṇahāravihāriṇī || 124

Pralayānalatulyābhā Pralayānalarūpiṇī |

Pralayārṇavasammagnā Pralayābdhivihāriṇī || 125

Mahāpralayasambhūtā Mahāpralayakāriṇī |

Mahāpralayasamprītā Mahāpralayasādhinī || 126

Mahāmahāpralayejyā Mahāpralayamodinī |
Chedinī Chinnamuṇḍogrā Chinnā Chinnaruhārtthinī || 127

Śatrusañchedinī Channā Kṣodinī Kṣodakāriṇī |
Lakṣiṇī Lakṣasampūjyā Lakṣitā Lakṣaṇānvitā || 128

Lakṣaśastrasamāyuktā Lakṣabāṇapramocinī |
Lakṣapūjāparā'lakṣyā Lakṣakodaṇḍakhaṇḍinī || 129

Lakṣakodaṇḍasaṃyyuktā Lakṣakodaṇḍadhāriṇī |
Lakṣalīlālayālabhyā Lākṣāgāranivāsinī || 130

Lakṣalobhaparā Lolā Lakṣabhaktaprapūjitā |
Lokinī Lokasampūjyā Lokarakṣaṇakāriṇī || 131

Lokavanditapādābjā Lokamohanakāriṇī |
Lalitā Lālitālīnā Lokasaṃhārakāriṇī || 132

Lokalīlākarī Lokyālokasambhavakāriṇī |
Bhūtaśuddhikarī Bhūtarakṣiṇī Bhūtatoṣiṇī || 133

Bhūtavetālasaṃyyuktā Bhūtasenāsamāvṛtā |
Bhūtapretapiśācādisvāminī Bhūtapūjitā || 134

Ḍākinī Śākinī Ḍeyā Ḍiṇḍimārāvakāriṇī |
Ḍamarūvādyasantuṣṭā Ḍamarūvādyakāriṇī || 135

Huṅkārakāriṇī Hotrī Hāvinī Hāvanārtthinī |
Hāsinī Hvāsinī Hāsyaharṣiṇī Haṭhavādinī || 136

Aṭṭāṭṭahāsinī Ṭīkā Ṭīkānirmāṇakāriṇī |
Ṭaṅkinī Ṭaṅkitā Ṭaṅkā Ṭaṅkamātrasuvarṇadā || 137

Ṭaṅkāriṇī Ṭakārādhyā Śatrutroṭanakāriṇī |
Truṭitā Truṭirūpā Ca Truṭisandehakāriṇī || 138

Tarṣiṇa Tṛṭpariklāntā Kṣutkṣāmā Kṣutpariplutā |
Akṣiṇī Takṣiṇī Bhikṣāprārtthinī Śatrubhakṣiṇī || 139

Kāṅkṣiṇī Kuṭṭanī Krūrā Kuṭṭanīveśmavāsinī |

Kuṭṭanīkoṭisampūjyā Kuṭṭanīkulamārgiṇī || 140

Kuṭṭanīkulasaṃrakṣā Kuṭṭanīkularakṣiṇī |

Kālapāśāvṛtā Kanyā Kumārīpūjanapriyā || 141

Kaumudī Kaumudīhṛṣṭā Karuṇādṛṣṭisamyyutā |

Kautukācāranipuṇā Kautukāgāravāsinī || 142

Kākapakṣadharā Kākarakṣiṇī Kākasaṃvvṛtā |

Kākāṅkarathasaṃsthānā Kākāṅkasyandanāsthitā || 143

Kākinī Kākadṛṣṭiśca Kākabhakṣaṇadāyinī |

Kākamātā Kākayoniḥ Kākamaṇḍalamaṇḍitā || 144

Kākadarśanasaṃśīlā Kākasaṅkīrṇamandirā |

Kākadhyānasthadehādidhyānagamyā Dhamāvṛtā || 145

Dhaninī Dhanisaṃsevyā Dhanacchedanakāriṇī |

Dhundhurā Dhundhurākārā Dhūmralocanaghātinī || 146

Dhūṅkāriṇī Ca Dhūmmantrapūjitā Dharmanāśinī |

Dhūmravarṇinī Dhūmrākṣī Dhūmrākṣāsuraghātinī || 147

Dhūmbījajapasantuṣṭā Dhūmbījajapamānasā |

Dhūmbījajapapūjārhā Dhūmbījajapakāriṇī || 148

Dhūmbījākarṣitā Dhṛṣyā Dharṣiṇī Dhṛṣṭamānasā |

Dhūlīprakṣepiṇī Dhūlīvyāptadhammilladhāriṇī || 149

Dhūmbījajapamālāḍhyā Dhūmbījanindakāntakā |

Dharmavidveṣiṇī Dharmarakṣiṇī Dharmatoṣitā || 150

Dhārāstambhakarī Dhūrtā Dhārāvārivilāsinī |

Dhāṃdhīṃdhūṃdhaimmantravarṇā Dhauṃdhaḥsvāhāsvarūpiṇī || 151

Dharitrīpūjitā Dhūrvā Dhānyacchedanakāriṇī |

Dhikkāriṇī Sudhīpūjyā Dhāmodyānanivāsinī || 152

Dhāmodyānapayodātrī Dhāmadhūlīpradhūlitā |

Mahādhvanimatī Dhūpyā Dhūpāmodapraharṣiṇī ‖ 153

Dhūpādānamatiprītā Dhūpadānavinodinī |

Dhīvarīgaṇasampūjyā Dhīvarīvaradāyinī ‖ 154

Dhīvarīgaṇamadhyasthā Dhīvarīdhāmavāsinī |

Dhīvarīgaṇagoptrī Ca Dhīvarīgaṇatoṣitā ‖ 155

Dhīvarīdhanadātrī Ca Dhīvarīprāṇarakṣiṇī |

Dhātrīśā Dhātṛsampūjyā Dhātrīvṛkṣasamāśrayā ‖ 156

Dhātrīpūjanakartrī Ca Dhātrīropaṇakāriṇī |

Dhūmrapānaratāsaktā Dhūmrapānarateṣṭadā ‖ 157

Dhūmrapānakarānandā Dhūmravarṣaṇakāriṇī |

Dhanyaśabdaśrutiprītā Dhundhukārījanacchidā ‖ 158

Dhundhukārīṣṭasandātrī Thundhukārisumuktidā |

Dhundhukāryārādhyarūpā Dhundhukārimanassthitā ‖ 159

Dhundhukārihitākāṅkṣā Dhundhukārihitaiṣiṇī |

Dhindhimārāviṇī Dhyātrī Dhyānagamyā Dhanārthinī ‖ 160

Dhoriṇī Dhoraṇaprītā Dhāriṇī Ghorarūpiṇī |

Dharitrīrakṣiṇī Devī Dharāpralayakāriṇī ‖ 161

Dharādharasutā'śeṣadhārādharasamadyutiḥ |

Dhanādhyakṣā Dhanaprāptirddhanadhānyavivarddhinī ‖ 162

Dhanākarṣaṇakarttrī Ca Dhanāharaṇakāriṇī |

Dhanacchedanakartrī Ca Dhanahīnā Dhanapriyā ‖ 163

Dhanasam̐vvṛddhisampannā Dhanadānaparāyaṇā ‖ 164

Dhanahṛṣṭā Dhanapuṣṭā Dānādhyayanakāriṇī |

Dhanarakṣā Dhanaprāṇā Dhanānandakarī Sadā ‖ 165

Śatruhantrī Śavārūḍhā Śatrusaṃhārakāriṇī |

Śatrupakṣakṣatiprītā Śatrupakṣaniṣūdinī || 166

Śatrugrīvācchidāchāyā Śatrupaddhatikhaṇḍinī |

Śatruprāṇaharāhāryā Śatrūnmūlanakāriṇī || 167

Śatrukāryavihantrī Ca Sāṅgaśatruvināśinī |

Sāṅgaśatrukulacchetrī Śatrusadmapradāyinī || 168

Sāṅgasāyudhasarvāri-Sarvasampattināśinī |

Sāṅgasāyudhasarvāri-Dehagehapradāhinī || 169

Phalaśrutiḥ |

Itīdandhūmarūpiṇyāsstotrannāma Sahasrakam |

Yaḥ Paṭhecchūnyabhavane Sadhvānte Yatamānasaḥ || 170

Madirāmodayukto Vai Devīdhyānaparāyaṇaḥ |

Tasya Śatruḥ Kṣayaṃ Yāti Yadi Śakrasamo'pi Vai || 171

Bhavapāśaharampuṇyandhūmāvatyāḥ Priyammahat |

Stotraṃ Sahasranāmākhyammama Vaktrādvinirgatam || 172

Paṭhedvā Śṛṇuyādvāpi Satrughātakaro Bhavet |

Na Deyamparaśiṣyāyā'bhaktāya Prāṇavallabhe || 173

Deyaṃ Śiṣyāya Bhaktāya Devībhaktiparāya Ca |

Idaṃ Rahasyamparamandurllabhanduṣṭacetasām || 174

Iti Dhūmāvatī Sahasranāma Stotraṃ Sampūrṇam

श्री धूमावती सहस्रनाम स्तोत्रम्

श्रीभैरव्युवाच

धूमावत्या धर्मरात्र्याः कथयस्व महेश्वर ।
सहस्रनामस्तोत्रम्मे सर्वसिद्धिप्रदायकम् ॥ १

श्रीभैरव उवाच

शृणु देवि महामाये प्रिये प्राणस्वरूपिणि ।
सहस्रनामस्तोत्रम्मे भवशत्रुविनाशम् ॥ २

ॐ अस्य श्रीधूमावतीसहस्रनामस्तोत्रस्य पिप्पलाद ऋषिः
पङ्क्तिश्छन्दो धूमावती देवता शत्रुविनिग्रहे पाठे विनियोगः

सहस्रनाम स्तोत्रम्

धुमा धूमवती धूमा धूमपानपरायणा ।
धौता धौतगिरा धाम्नी धूमेश्वरनिवासिनी ॥ ३

अनन्ताऽनन्तरूपा च अकाराकाररूपिणी ।
आद्या आनन्ददानन्दा इकारा इन्द्ररूपिणी ॥ ४

धनधान्यार्थवाणीदा यशोधर्मप्रियेष्टदा ।
भाग्यसौभाग्यभक्तिस्था गृहपर्वतवासिनी ॥ ५

रामरावणसुग्रीवमोहदा हनुमत्प्रिया ।
वेदशास्त्रपुराणज्ञा ज्योतिश्छन्दःस्वरूपिणी ॥ ६

चातुर्यचारुरुचिरा रञ्जनप्रेमतोषदा ।
कमलासनसुधावक्त्रा चन्द्रहासा स्मितानना ॥ ७

चतुरा चारुकेशी च चतुर्वर्गप्रदा मुदा ।
कला कालधरा धीरा धारिणी वसुनीरदा ॥ ८

हीरा हीरकवर्णाभा हरिणायतलोचना ।
दम्भमोहक्रोधलोभस्नेहद्वेषहरा परा ॥ ९

नारदेवकरी रामा रामानन्दमनोहरा ।
योगभोगक्रोधलोभहरा हरनमस्कृता ॥ १०

दानमानज्ञानमान-पानगानसुखप्रदा । गजगोश्वपदागञ्ज्ञा भूतिदा भूतनाशिनी ॥ ११

भवभावा तथा बाला वरदा हरवल्लभा ।
भगभङ्गभया माला मालती तालनाहदा ॥ १२

जाल्विवालहालकालकपालप्रियवादिनी ।
करञ्जशीलगुञ्जाद्या चूताङ्कुरनिवासिनी ॥ १३

पनसस्था पानसक्ता पनसेशकुटुम्बिनी ।
पावनी पावनाधारा पूर्णा पूर्णमनोरथा ॥ १४

पूता पूतकला पौरा पुराणसुरसुन्दरी ।
परेशी परदा पारा परात्मा परमोहिनी ॥ १५

जगन्माया जगत्कर्त्री जगत्कीर्त्तिर्जगन्मयी ।
जननी जयिनी जाया जिता जिनजयप्रदा ॥ १६

कीर्त्तिर्ज्ञानध्यानमानदायिनी दानवेश्वरी ।
काव्यव्याकरणज्ञाना प्रज्ञाप्रज्ञानदायिनी ॥ १७

विज्ञाज्ञा विज्ञजयदा विज्ञा विज्ञप्रपूजिता ।
परावरेज्या वरदा पारदा शारदा दरा ॥ १८

दारिणी देवदूती च मदना मदनामदा ।
परमज्ञानगम्या च षरेशी परगा परा ॥ १९

यज्ञा यज्ञप्रदा यज्ञज्ञानकार्यकरी शुभा ।
शोभिनी शुभ्रमथिनी निशुम्भासुरमर्दिनी ॥ २०

शाम्भवी शम्भुपत्नी च शम्भुजाया शुभानना ।
शाङ्करी शङ्करराध्या सन्ध्या सन्ध्यासुधर्मिणी ॥ २१

शत्रुघ्नी शत्रुहा शत्रुप्रदा शात्रवनाशिनी ।
शैवी शिवलया शैला शैलराजप्रिया सदा ॥ २२

शर्वरी शवरी शम्भुः सुधाढ्या सौधवासिनी ।
सगुणा गुणरूपा च गौरवी भैरवीरवा ॥ २३

गौराङ्गी गौरदेहा च गौरी गुरुमती गुरुः ।
गौग्गौर्गव्यस्वरूपा च गुणानन्दस्वरूपिणी ॥ २४

गणेशगणदा गुण्या गुणा गौरववाञ्छिता ।
गणमाता गणाराध्या गणकोटिविनाशिनी ॥ २५

दुर्गा दुर्जनहन्त्री च दुर्जनप्रीतिदायिनी ।
स्वर्गापवर्गदा दात्री दीना दीनदयावती ॥ २६

दुर्निरीक्ष्या दुरादुःस्था दौःस्थभञ्जनकारिणी ।
श्वेतपाण्डुरकृष्णाभा कालदा कालनाशिनी ॥ २७

कर्मनर्मकरी नर्मा धर्माधर्मविनाशिनी ।
गौरी गौरवदा गोदा गणदा गायनप्रिया ॥ २८

गङ्गा भागीरथी भङ्गा भगा भाग्यविवर्द्धिनी ।
भवानी भवहन्त्री च भैरवी भैरवीसमा ॥ २९

भीमा भीमरवा भैमी भीमानन्दप्रदायिनी ।
शरण्या शरणा शम्या शशिनी शङ्खनाशिनी ॥ ३०

गुणा गुणकरी गौणी प्रियाप्रीतिप्रदायिनी ।
जनमोहनकत्त्री च जगदानन्ददायिनी ॥ ३१

जिता जाया च विजया विजया जयदायिनी ।
कामा काली करालास्या खर्वा खञ्जा खरा गदा ॥ ३२

गर्वा गरुत्मती धर्मा घर्घरा घोरनादिनी ।
चराचरी चराराध्या छिना छिन्नमनोरथा ॥ ३३

छिन्नमस्ता जया जाप्या जगज्जाया च झर्झरी ।
झकारा झीष्कृतिष्ठीका टङ्का टङ्कारनादिनी ॥ ३४

ठीका ठक्कुरठक्काङ्गी ठठठाङ्कारढुण्डुरा ।
ढुण्ढीताराजतीर्णा च तालस्थाभ्रमनाशिनी ॥ ३५

थकारा थकरा दात्री दीपा दीपविनाशिनी ।
धन्या धना धनवती नर्मदा नर्ममोदिनी ॥ ३६

पद्मा पद्मावती पीता स्फान्ता फूत्कारकारिणी ।
फुल्ला ब्रह्ममयी ब्राह्मी ब्रह्मानन्दप्रदायिनी ॥ ३७

भवाराध्या भवाध्यक्षा भगाली मन्दगामिनी ।
मदिरा मदिरेक्षा च यशोदा यमपूजिता ॥ ३८

याम्या राम्या रामरूपा रमणी ललिता लता ।
लङ्केश्वरी वाक्प्रदा वाच्या सदाश्रमवासिनी ॥ ३९

श्रान्ता शकाररूपा च षकारखरवाहना ।
सह्याद्रिरूपा सानन्दा हरिणी हरिरूपिणी ॥ ४०

हराराध्या वालवाचलवङ्गप्रेमतोषिता ।
क्षपा क्षयप्रदा क्षीरा अकारादिस्वरूपिणी ॥ ४१

कालिका कालमूर्त्तिश्च कलहा कलहप्रिया ।
शिवा शन्दायिनी सौम्या शत्रुनिग्रहकारिणी ॥ ४२

भवानी भवमूर्त्तिश्च शर्वाणी सर्वमङ्गला ।
शत्रुविद्द्राविणी शैवी शुम्भासुरविनाशिनी ॥ ४३

धकारमन्त्ररूपा च धूम्बीजपरितोषिता ।
धनाध्यक्षस्तुता धीरा धरारूपा धरावती ॥ ४४

चर्विणी चन्द्रपूज्या च च्छन्दोरूपा छटावती ।
छाया छायावती स्वच्छा छेदिनी मेदिनी क्षमा ॥ ४५

वल्गिनी वर्द्धिनी वन्द्या वेदमाता बुधस्तुता ।
धारा धारावती धन्या धर्मदानपरायणा ॥ ४६

गर्विणी गुरुपूज्या च ज्ञानदात्री गुणान्विता ।
धर्मिणी धर्मरूपा च घण्टानादपरायणा ॥। ४७

घण्टानिनादिनी घूर्णा घूर्णिता घोररूपिणी ।
कलिघ्नी कलिदूती च कलिपूज्या कलिप्रिया ॥ ४८

कालनिर्णाशिनी काल्या काव्यदा कालरूपिणी ।
वर्षिणी वृष्टिदा वृष्टिर्महावृष्टिनिवारिणी ॥ ४९

घातिनी घाटिनी घोण्टा घातकी घनरूपिणी ।
धूम्बीजा धूञ्जपानन्दा धूम्बीजजपतोषिता ॥ ५०

धून्धूम्बीजजपासक्ता धून्धूम्बीजपरायणा ।
धूङ्कारहर्षिणी धूमा धनदा धनगर्विता ॥ ५१

पद्मावती पद्ममाला पद्मयोनिप्रपूजिता ।
अपारा पूरणी पूर्णा पूर्णिमापरिवन्दिता ॥ ५२

फलदा फलभोक्त्री च फलिनी फलदायिनी ।
फूत्कारिणी फलावाप्त्री फलभोक्त्री फलान्विता ॥ ५३

वारिणी वरणप्रीता वारिपाथोधिपारगा ।
विवर्णा धूम्रनयना धूम्राक्षी धूम्ररूपिणी ॥ ५४

नीतिर्नीतिस्वरूपा च नीतिज्ञा नयकोविदा ।
तारिणीताररूपा च तत्त्वज्ञानपरायणा ॥ ५५

स्थूला स्थूलाधरा स्थात्री उत्तमस्थानवासिनी ।
स्थूला पद्मपदस्थाना स्थानभ्रष्टा स्थलस्थिता ॥ ५६

शोषिणी शोभिनी शीता शीतपानीयपायिनी ।
शारिणी शाङ्खिनी शुद्धा शङ्खासुरविनाशिनी ॥ ५७

शर्वरी शर्वरीपूज्या शर्वरीशप्रपूजिता ।
शर्वरीजाग्रिता योग्या योगिनी योगिवन्दिता ॥ ५८

योगिनीगणसंसेव्या योगिनी योगभाविता ।
योगमार्गरतायुक्ता योगमार्गानुसारिणी ॥ ५९

योगभावा योगयुक्ता यामिनीपतिवन्दिता ।
अयोग्या योधिनी योद्ध्री युद्धकर्मविशारदा ॥ ६०

युद्धमार्गरतानान्ता युद्धस्थाननिवासिनी ।
सिद्धा सिद्धेश्वरी सिद्धिः सिद्धिगेहनिवासिनी ॥ ६१

सिद्धरीतिस्सिद्धप्रीतिः सिद्धा सिद्धान्तकारिणी ।
सिद्धगम्या सिद्धपूज्या सिद्धबन्द्या सुसिद्धिदा ॥ ६२

साधिनी साधनप्रीता साध्या साधनकारिणी ।
साधनीया साध्यसाध्या साध्यसङ्घसुशोभिनी ॥ ६३

साध्वी साधुस्वभावा सा साधुसन्ततिदायिनी ।
साधुपूज्या साधुवन्द्या साधुसन्दर्शनोद्यता ॥ ६४

साधुदृष्टा साधुपृष्ठा साधुपोषणतत्परा ।
सात्त्विकी सत्त्वसंसिद्धा सत्त्वसेव्या सुखोदया ॥ ६५

सत्त्ववृद्धिकरी शान्ता सत्त्वसंहर्षमानसा ।
सत्त्वज्ञाना सत्त्वविद्या सत्त्वसिद्धान्तकारिणी ॥ ६६

सत्त्ववृद्धिस्सत्त्वसिद्धिस्सत्त्वसम्पन्नमानसा ।
चारुरूपा चारुदेहा चारुचञ्चललोचना ॥ ६७

छद्मिनी छद्मसङ्कल्पा छद्मवार्त्ता क्षमाप्रिया ।
हठिनी हठसम्प्रीतिर्हठवार्त्ता हठोद्यमा ॥ ६८

हठकार्या हठधर्मा हठकर्मपरायणा ।
हठसम्भोगनिरता हठात्काररतिप्रिया ॥ ६९

हठसम्भेदिनी हृद्या हृद्यवार्त्ता हरिप्रिया ।
हरिणी हरिणीदृष्टिर्हरिणीमांसभक्षणा ॥ ७०

हरिणाक्षी हरिणपा हरिणीगणहर्षदा ।
हरिणीगणसंहर्त्री हरिणीपरिपोषिका ॥ ७१

हरिणीमृगयासक्ता हरिणीमानपुरस्सरा ।
दीना दीनाकृतिर्दूना द्राविणी द्रविणप्रदा ॥ ७२

द्रविणाचलसंव्वासा द्रविता द्रव्यसंय्युता ।
दीर्घा दीर्घपदा दृश्या दर्शनीया दृढाकृतिः ॥ ७३

दृढा द्विष्टमतिर्दुष्टा द्वेषिणी द्वेषिभञ्जिनी ।
दोषिणी दोषसंय्युक्ता दुष्टशत्रुविनाशिनी ॥ ७४

देवतार्त्तिहरा दुष्टदैत्यसङ्घविदारिणी ।
दुष्टदानवहन्त्री च दुष्टदैत्यनिषूदिनी ॥ ७५

देवताप्राणदा देवी देवदुर्गतिनाशिनी ।
नटनायकसंसेव्या नर्त्तकी नर्त्तकप्रिया ॥ ७६

नाट्यविद्या नाट्यकर्त्री नादिनी नादकारिणी ।
नवीननूतना नव्या नवीनवस्त्रधारिणी ॥ ७७

नव्यभूषा नव्यमाल्या नव्यालङ्कारशोभिता ।
नकारवादिनी नम्या नवभूषणभूषिता ॥ ७८

नीचमार्गा नीचभूमिर्नीचमार्गगतिर्गतिः ।
नाथसेव्या नाथभक्ता नाथानन्दप्रदायिनी ॥ ७९

नम्रा नम्रगतिर्नेत्री निदानवाक्यवादिनी ।
नारीमध्यस्थिता नारी नारीमध्यगताऽनघा ॥ ८०

नारीप्रीति नराराध्या नरनामप्रकाशिनी ।
रती रतिप्रिया रम्या रतिप्रेमा रतिप्रदा ॥ ८१

रतिस्थानस्थिताराध्या रतिहर्षप्रदायिनी ।
रतिरूपा रतिध्याना रतिरीतिसुधारिणी ॥ ८२

रतिरासमहोल्लासा रतिरासविहारिणी ।
रतिकान्तस्तुता राशी राशिरक्षणकारिणी ॥ ८३

अरूपा शुद्धरूपा च सुरूपा रूपगर्विता ।
रूपयौवनसम्पन्ना रूपराशी रमावती ॥ ८४

रोधिनी रोषिणी रुष्टा रोषिरुद्धा रसप्रदा ।
मादिनी मदनप्रीता मधुमत्ता मधुप्रदा ॥ ८५

मद्यपा मद्यपध्येया मद्यपप्राणरक्षिणी ।
मद्यपानन्दसन्दात्री मद्यपप्रेमतोषिता ॥ ८६

मद्यपानरता मत्ता मद्यपानविहारिणी ।
मदिरा मदिरारक्ता मदिरापानहर्षिणी ॥ ८७

मदिरापानसन्तुष्टा मदिरापानमोहिनी ।
मदिरामानसामुग्धा माध्वीपा मदिराप्रदा ॥ ८८

माध्वीदानसदानन्दा माध्वीपानरता मदा ।
मोदिनी मोदसन्दात्री मुदिता मोदमानसा ॥ ८९

मोदकर्त्री मोददात्री मोदमङ्गलकारिणी ।
मोदकादानसन्तुष्टा मोदकग्रहणक्षमा ॥ ९०

मोदकालब्धिसङ्क्रुद्धा मोदकप्राप्तितोषिणी ।
मांसादा मांससम्भक्षा मांसभक्षणहर्षिणी ॥ ९१

मांसपाकपरप्रेमा मांसपाकालयस्थिता ।
मत्स्यमांसकृतास्वादा मकारपञ्चकान्विता ॥ ९२

मुद्रा मुद्रान्विता माता महामोहा मनस्विनी ।
मुद्रिका मुद्रिकायुक्ता मुद्रिकाकृतलक्षणा ॥ ९३

मुद्रिकालङ्कृता मान्द्री मन्दराचलवासिनी ।
मन्दराचलसंसेव्या मन्दराचलवासिनी ॥ ९४

मन्दरध्येयपादाब्जा मन्दरारण्यवासिनी ।
मन्दुरावासिनी मन्दा मारिणी मारिकामिता ॥ ९५

महामारी महामारीशमिनी शवसंस्थिता ।
शवमांसकृताहारा श्मशानालयवासिनी ॥ ९६

श्मशानसिद्धिसंहृष्टा श्मशानभवनस्थिता ।
श्मशानशयनागारा श्मशानभस्मलेपिता ॥ ९७

श्मशानभस्मभीमाङ्गी श्मशानावासकारिणी ।
शामिनी शमनाराध्या शमनस्तुतिवन्दिता ॥ ९८

शमनाचारसन्तुष्टा शमनागारवासिनी ।
शमनस्वामिनी शान्तिः शान्तसज्जनपूजिता ॥ ९९

शान्तपूजापरा शान्ता शान्तागारप्रभोजिनी ।
शान्तपूज्या शान्तवन्द्या शान्तग्रहसुधारिणी ॥ १००

शान्तरूपा शान्तियुक्ता शान्तचन्द्रप्रभाऽमला ।
अमला विमला म्लाना मालती कुञ्जवासिनी ॥ १०१

मालतीपुष्पसम्प्रीता मालतीपुष्पपूजिता ।
महोग्रा महती मध्या मध्यदेशनिवासिनी ॥ १०२

मत्स्यमध्वनिसम्प्रीता मध्यमध्वनिकारिणी ।
मध्यमा मध्यमप्रीतिर्मध्यमप्रेमपूरिता ॥ १०३

मध्याङ्गचित्रवसना मध्यखिन्ना महोद्धता ।
महेन्द्रकृतसम्पूजा महेन्द्रपरिवन्दिता ॥ १०४

महेन्द्रजालसंय्युक्ता महेन्द्रजालकारिणी ।
महेन्द्रमानिताऽमाना मानिनीगणमध्यगा ॥ १०५

मानिनीमानसम्प्रीता मानविध्वंसकारिणी ।
मानिन्याकर्षिणी मुक्तिर्मुक्तिदात्री सुमुक्तिदा ॥ १०६

मुक्तिद्वेषकरी मूल्यकारिणी मूल्यहारिणी ।
निर्मला मूलसंय्युक्ता मूलिनी मूलमन्त्रिणी ॥ १०७

मूलमन्त्रकृताहार्द्या मूलमन्त्राग्र्यहर्षिणी ।
मूलमन्त्रप्रतिष्ठात्री मूलमन्त्रप्रहर्षिणी ॥ १०८

मूलमन्त्रप्रसन्नास्या मूलमन्त्रप्रपूजिता ।
मूलमन्त्रप्रणेत्री च मूलमन्त्रकृताच्र्चना ॥ १०९

मूलमन्त्रप्रहृष्टात्मा मूलविद्या मलापहा ।
विद्याऽविद्या वटस्था च वटवृक्षनिवासिनी ॥ ११०

वटवृक्षकृतस्थाना वटपूजापरायणा ।
वटपूजापरिप्रीता वटदर्शनलालसा ॥ १११

वटपूजा कृता ह्लादा वटपूजाविवर्द्धिनी ।
वशिनी विवशाराध्या वशीकरणमन्त्रिणी ॥ ११२

वशीकरणसम्प्रीता वशीकारकसिद्धिदा ।
बटुका बटुकाराध्या बटुकाहारदायिनी ॥ ११३

बटुकाच्र्चापरा पूज्या बटुकाच्र्चाविवर्द्धिनी ।
बटुकानन्दकर्त्री च बटुकप्राणरक्षिणी ॥ ११४

बटुकेज्याप्रदाऽपारा पारिणी पार्वतीप्रिया ।
पर्वताग्रकृतावासा पर्वतेन्द्रप्रपूजिता ॥ ११५

पार्वतीपतिपूज्या च पार्वतीपतिहर्षदा ।
पार्वतीपतिबुद्धिस्था पार्वतीपतिमोहिनी ॥ ११६

पार्वतीयद्द्विजाराध्या पर्वतस्था प्रतारिणी ।
पद्मला पद्मिनी पद्मा पद्ममालाविभूषिता ॥ ११७

पद्मजेड्रयपदा पद्ममालालङ्कृतमस्तका ।
पद्माच्चिर्वतपदद्वन्द्वा पद्महस्तपयोधिजा ॥ ११८

पयोधिपारगन्त्री च पाथोधिपरिकीर्त्तिता ।
पाथोधिपारगापूता पल्वलाम्बुप्रतर्पिता ॥ ११९

पल्वलान्तः पयोमग्ना पवमानगतिर्गतिः ।
पयः पाना पयोदात्री पानीयपरिकाङ्क्षिणी ॥ १२०

पयोजमालाभरणा मुण्डमालाविभूषणा ।
मुण्डिनी मुण्डहन्त्री च मुण्डिता मुण्डशोभिता ॥ १२१

मणिभूषा मणिग्रीवा मणिमालाविराजिता ।
महामोहा महामर्षा महामाया महाहवा ॥ १२२

मानवी मानवीपूज्या मनुवंशविवर्द्धिनी ।
मठिनी मठसंहन्त्री मठसम्पत्तिहारिणी ॥ १२३

महाक्रोधवती मूढा मूढशत्रुविनाशिनी ।
पाठीनभोजिनी पूर्णा पूर्णहारविहारिणी ॥ १२४

प्रलयानलतुल्याभा प्रलयानलरूपिणी ।
प्रलयार्णवसम्मग्ना प्रलयाब्धिविहारिणी ॥ १२५

महाप्रलयसम्भूता महाप्रलयकारिणी ।
महाप्रलयसम्प्रीता महाप्रलयसाधिनी ॥ १२६

महामहाप्रलयेज्या महाप्रलयमोदिनी ।
छेदिनी छिन्नमुण्डोग्रा छिन्ना छिन्नरुहार्त्थिनी ॥ १२७

शत्रुसञ्छेदिनी छन्ना क्षोदिनी क्षोदकारिणी ।
लक्षिणी लक्षसम्पूज्या लक्षिता लक्षणान्विता ॥ १२८

लक्षशस्त्रसमायुक्ता लक्षबाणप्रमोचिनी ।
लक्षपूजापराऽलक्ष्या लक्षकोदण्डखण्डिनी ॥ १२९

लक्षकोदण्डसंय्युक्ता लक्षकोदण्डधारिणी ।
लक्षलीलालयालभ्या लाक्षागारनिवासिनी ॥ १३०

लक्षलोभपरा लोला लक्षभक्तप्रपूजिता ।
लोकिनी लोकसम्पूज्या लोकरक्षणकारिणी ॥ १३१

लोकवन्दितपादाब्जा लोकमोहनकारिणी ।
ललिता लालितालीना लोकसंहारकारिणी ॥ १३२

लोकलीलाकरी लोक्यालोकसम्भवकारिणी ।
भूतशुद्धिकरी भूतरक्षिणी भूततोषिणी ॥ १३३

भूतवेतालसंय्युक्ता भूतसेनासमावृता ।
भूतप्रेतपिशाचादिस्वामिनी भूतपूजिता ॥ १३४

डाकिनी शाकिनी डेया डिण्डिमारावकारिणी ।
डमरूवाद्यसन्तुष्टा डमरूवाद्यकारिणी ॥ १३५

हुङ्कारकारिणी होत्री हाविनी हावनार्थिनी ।
हासिनी ह्वासिनी हास्यहर्षिणी हठवादिनी ॥ १३६

अट्टाट्टहासिनी टीका टीकानिर्माणकारिणी ।
टङ्किनी टङ्किता टङ्का टङ्कमात्रसुवर्णदा ॥ १३७

टङ्कारिणी टकाराद्या शत्रुत्रोटनकारिणी ।
त्रुटिता त्रुटिरूपा च त्रुटिसन्देहकारिणी ॥ १३८

तर्षिण तृट्परिक्लान्ता क्षुत्क्षामा क्षुत्परिप्लुता ।
अक्षिणी तक्षिणी भिक्षाप्रार्थिनी शत्रुभक्षिणी ॥ १३९

काङ्क्षिणी कुट्टनी क्रूरा कुट्टनीवेश्मवासिनी ।
कुट्टनीकोटिसम्पूज्या कुट्टनीकुलमार्गिणी ॥ १४०

कुट्टनीकुलसंरक्षा कुट्टनीकुलरक्षिणी ।
कालपाशावृता कन्या कुमारीपूजनप्रिया ॥ १४१

कौमुदी कौमुदीहृष्टा करुणादृष्टिसंय्युता ।
कौतुकाचारनिपुणा कौतुकागारवासिनी ॥ १४२

काकपक्षधरा काकरक्षिणी काकसंव्वृता ।
काकाङ्करथसंस्थाना काकाङ्कस्यन्दनास्थिता ॥ १४३

काकिनी काकदृष्टिश्च काकभक्षणदायिनी ।
काकमाता काकयोनि: काकमण्डलमण्डिता ॥ १४४

काकदर्शनसंशीला काकसङ्कीर्णमन्दिरा ।
काकध्यानस्थदेहादिध्यानगम्या धमावृता ॥ १४५

धनिनी धनिसंसेव्या धनच्छेदनकारिणी ।
धुन्धुरा धुन्धुराकारा धूम्रलोचनघातिनी ॥ १४६

धूङ्कारिणी च धूम्मन्त्रपूजिता धर्मनाशिनी ।
धूम्रवर्णिनी धूम्राक्षी धूम्राक्षासुरघातिनी ॥ १४७

धूम्बीजजपसन्तुष्टा धूम्बीजजपमानसा ।
धूम्बीजजपपूजाहा धूम्बीजजपकारिणी ॥ १४८

धूम्बीजाकर्षिता धृष्या धर्षिणी धृष्टमानसा ।
धूलीप्रक्षेपिणी धूलीव्याप्तधम्मिल्लधारिणी ॥ १४९

धूम्बीजजपमालाढ्या धूम्बीजनिन्दकान्तका ।
धर्मविद्वेषिणी धर्मरक्षिणी धर्मतोषिता ॥ १५०

धारास्तम्भकरी धूर्ता धारावारिविलासिनी ।
धांधींधूंधैम्मन्त्रवर्णा धौंध:स्वाहास्वरूपिणी ॥ १५१

धरित्रीपूजिता धूर्वा धान्यच्छेदनकारिणी ।
धिक्कारिणी सुधीपूज्या धामोद्याननिवासिनी ॥ १५२

धामोद्यानपयोदात्री धामधूलीप्रधूलिता ।
महाध्वनिमती धूप्या धूपामोदप्रहर्षिणी ॥ १५३

धूपादानमतिप्रीता धूपदानविनोदिनी ।
धीवरीगणसम्पूज्या धीवरीवरदायिनी ॥ १५४

धीवरीगणमध्यस्था धीवरीधामवासिनी ।
धीवरीगणगोप्त्री च धीवरीगणतोषिता ॥ १५५

धीवरीधनदात्री च धीवरीप्राणरक्षिणी ।
धात्रीशा धातृसम्पूज्या धात्रीवृक्षसमाश्रया ॥ १५६

धात्रीपूजनकर्त्री च धात्रीरोपणकारिणी ।
धूम्रपानरतासक्ता धूम्रपानरतेष्टदा ॥ १५७

धूम्रपानकरानन्दा धूम्रवर्षणकारिणी ।
धन्यशब्दश्रुतिप्रीता धुन्धुकारीजनच्छिदा ॥ १५८

धुन्धुकारीष्टसन्दात्री धुन्धुकारिसुमुक्तिदा ।
धुन्धुकार्याराध्यरूपा धुन्धुकारिमनस्स्थिता ॥ १५९

धुन्धुकारिहिताकाङ्क्षा धुन्धुकारिहितैषिणी ।
धिन्धिमाराविणी ध्यात्री ध्यानगम्या धनार्थिनी ॥ १६०

धोरिणी धोरणप्रीता धारिणी घोररूपिणी ।
धरित्रीरक्षिणी देवी धराप्रलयकारिणी ॥ १६१

धराधरसुताऽशेषधाराधरसमद्युतिः ।
धनाध्यक्षा धनप्राप्तिर्द्धनधान्यविवर्द्धिनी ॥ १६२

धनाकर्षणकर्त्री च धनाहरणकारिणी ।
धनच्छेदनकर्त्री च धनहीना धनप्रिया ॥ १६३

धनसँव्वृद्धिसम्पन्ना धनदानपरायणा ॥ १६४

धनहृष्टा धनपुष्टा दानाध्ययनकारिणी ।
धनरक्षा धनप्राणा धनानन्दकरी सदा ॥ १६५

शत्रुहन्त्री शवारूढा शत्रुसंहारकारिणी ।
शत्रुपक्षक्षतिप्रीता शत्रुपक्षनिषूदिनी ॥ १६६

शत्रुग्रीवाच्छिदाछाया शत्रुपद्धतिखण्डिनी ।
शत्रुप्राणहराहार्या शत्रून्मूलनकारिणी ॥ १६७

शत्रुकार्यविहन्त्री च साङ्गशत्रुविनाशिनी ।
साङ्गशत्रुकुलच्छेत्री शत्रुसद्मप्रदायिनी ॥ १६८

साङ्गसायुधसर्वारि-सर्वसम्पत्तिनाशिनी ।
साङ्गसायुधसर्वारि-देहगेहप्रदाहिनी ॥ १६९

फलश्रुति:

इतीदन्धूमरूपिण्यास्स्तोत्रन्नाम सहस्रकम् ।
यः पठेच्छून्यभवने सध्वान्ते यतमानसः ॥ १७०

मदिरामोदयुक्तो वै देवीध्यानपरायणः ।
तस्य शत्रुः क्षयं याति यदि शक्रसमोऽपि वै ॥ १७१

भवपाशहरम्पुण्यन्धूमावत्याः प्रियम्महत् ।
स्तोत्रं सहस्रनामाख्यम्मम वक्त्राद्विनिर्गतम् ॥ १७२

पठेद्वा शृणुयाद्वापि शत्रुघातकरो भवेत् ।
न देयम्परशिष्यायाऽभक्ताय प्राणवल्लभे ॥ १७३

देयं शिष्याय भक्ताय देवीभक्तिपराय च ।
इदं रहस्यम्परमन्दुर्ल्लभन्दुष्टचेतसाम् ॥ १७४

इति धूमावती सहस्रनाम स्तोत्रं सम्पूर्णम् ॥

*****

Śrī Dhūmāvatī Sahasra Nāmāvaliḥ

1,000 divine names on *Śrī Dhūmāvatī Devi.*

Dhyānam |

Vivarṇā Cañcalā Duṣṭā Dīrghā Ca Malināmbarā |
Vimuktakuntalā Rūkṣā Vidhavā Viraladvijā || 1

Kākadhvajarathārūḍhā Vilambitapayodharā |
Śūrpahastātirūkṣākṣā Dhūtahastā Varānvitā || 2

Pravṛddhaghoṇā Tu Bhṛśam Kuṭilā Kuṭilekṣaṇā |
Kṣutpipāsārdi Tā Dhyeyā Bhayadā Kalahāspadā || 3

Atyuccā Malināmbarā'khilajanodvegāvahā Durmanā
Rūkṣākṣitritayā Viśāladaśanā Sūryodarī Cañcalā |
Prasvedāmbucitā Kṣudhākulatanuḥ Kṛṣṇā'tirūkṣaprabhā
Dhyeyā Muktakacā Sadāpriyakalirdhūmāvatī Mantriṇā || 4

श्री धूमावती सहस्रनामावलिः |

ध्यानम् |

विवर्णा चञ्चला दुष्टा दीर्घा च मलिनाम्बरा |
विमुक्तकुन्तला रूक्षा विधवा विरलद्विजा || १

काकध्वजरथारूढा विलम्बितपयोधरा |
शूर्पहस्तातिरूक्षाक्षा धूतहस्ता वरान्विता || २

प्रवृद्धघोणा तु भृशं कुटिला कुटिलेक्षणा |
क्षुत्पिपासार्दि ता ध्येया भयदा कलहास्पदा || ३

अत्युच्चा मलिनाम्बराऽखिलजनोद्वेगावहा दुर्मना
रूक्षाक्षित्रितया विशालदशना सूर्योदरी चञ्चला |
प्रस्वेदाम्बुचिता क्षुधाकुलतनुः कृष्णाऽतिरूक्षप्रभा
ध्येया मुक्तकचा सदाप्रियकलिर्धूमावती मन्त्रिणा || ४

Sahasra Nāmāvaliḥ - सहस्रनामावलिः ।

1.	Oṃ Dhūmāyai Namaḥ ।	ॐ धूमायै नमः ।
2.	Oṃ Dhūmavatyai Namaḥ ।	ॐ धूमवत्यै नमः ।
3.	Oṃ Dhūmāyai Namaḥ ।	ॐ धूमायै नमः ।
4.	Oṃ Dhūmapānaparāyaṇāyai Namaḥ ।	ॐ धूमपानपरायणायै नमः ।
5.	Oṃ Dhautādhautagirāṃ Dhāmnyai Namaḥ ।	ॐ धौताधौतगिरां धाम्न्यै नमः ।
6.	Oṃ Dhūmeśvaranivāsinyai Namaḥ ।	ॐ धूमेश्वरनिवासिन्यै नमः ।
7.	Oṃ Anantāyai Namaḥ ।	ॐ अनन्तायै नमः ।
8.	Oṃ Anantarūpāyai Namaḥ ।	ॐ अनन्तरूपायै नमः ।
9.	Oṃ Akārākārarūpiṇyai Namaḥ ।	ॐ अकाराकाररूपिण्यै नमः
10.	Oṃ Ādyāyai Namaḥ ।	ॐ आद्यायै नमः ।
11.	Oṃ Ānandadānandāyai Namaḥ ।	ॐ आनन्ददानन्दायै नमः ।
12.	Oṃ Ikārāyai Namaḥ ।	ॐ इकारायै नमः ।
13.	Oṃ Indrarūpiṇyai Namaḥ ।	ॐ इन्द्ररूपिण्यै नमः ।
14.	Oṃ Dhanadhānyārthavāṇīdāyai Namaḥ ।	ॐ धनधान्यार्थवाणीदाये नमः ।
15.	Oṃ Yaśodharmapriyeṣṭadāyai Namaḥ ।	ॐ यशोधर्मप्रियेष्टदाये नमः ।
16.	Oṃ Bhāgyasaubhāgyabhaktisthāyai Namaḥ ।	ॐ भाग्यसौभाग्यभक्तिस्थाये नमः ।
17.	Oṃ Guhāparvatavāsinyai Namaḥ ।	ॐ गुहापर्वतवासिन्यै नमः ।
18.	Oṃ Rāmarāvaṇasugrīvamohadāyai Namaḥ ।	ॐ रामरावणसुग्रीवमोहदाये नमः ।
19.	Oṃ Hanumatpriyāyai Namaḥ ।	ॐ हनुमत्प्रियायै नमः ।
20.	Oṃ Vedaśāstrapurāṇajñāyai Namaḥ ।	ॐ वेदशास्त्रपुराणज्ञाये नमः
21.	Oṃ Jyotiśchandaḥsvarūpiṇyai Namaḥ ।	ॐ ज्योतिश्छन्दःस्वरूपिण्यै नमः ।
22.	Oṃ Cāturya Cāru Rucirārañjana Prema Toṣadāyai Namaḥ ।	ॐ चातुर्य चारु रुचिरारञ्जन प्रेम तोषदाये नमः ।

23.	Oṃ Kamalāsasudhāvaktrāyai Namaḥ |	ॐ कमलाससुधावक्त्राये नमः ।
24.	Oṃ Candrahāsasmitānanāyai Namaḥ |	ॐ चन्द्रहासस्मिताननाये नमः ।
25.	Oṃ Caturāyai Namaḥ |	ॐ चतुराये नमः ।
26.	Oṃ Cārukeśyai Namaḥ |	ॐ चारुकेश्यै नमः ।
27.	Oṃ Mudā Caturvargapradāyai Namaḥ	ॐ मुदा चतुर्वर्गप्रदाये नमः
28.	Oṃ Kalākāladharāyai Namaḥ |	ॐ कलाकालधराये नमः ।
29.	Oṃ Dhīrāyai Namaḥ |	ॐ धीराये नमः ।
30.	Oṃ Dhāriṇyai Namaḥ |	ॐ धारिण्यै नमः ।
31.	Oṃ Vasunīradāyai Namaḥ |	ॐ वसुनीरदाये नमः ।
32.	Oṃ Hīrāyai Namaḥ |	ॐ हीराये नमः ।
33.	Oṃ Hīrakavarṇābhāyai Namaḥ |	ॐ हीरकवर्णाभाये नमः ।
34.	Oṃ Hariṇāyatalocanāyai Namaḥ |	ॐ हरिणायतलोचनाये नमः ।
35.	Oṃ Dambha Mohakrodhalobha Snehadveṣaharāyai Parāyai Namaḥ |	ॐ दम्भमोह क्रोधलोभ स्नेहद्वेषहराये पराये नमः ।
36.	Oṃ Naradevakaryai Namaḥ |	ॐ नरदेवकर्यै नमः ।
37.	Oṃ Rāmāyai Namaḥ |	ॐ रामाये नमः ।
38.	Oṃ Rāmānandamanoharāyai Namaḥ |	ॐ रामानन्दमनोहराये नमः
39.	Oṃ Yogabhogakrodhalobhaharāyai Namaḥ |	ॐ योगभोगक्रोध लोभहराये नमः ।
40.	Oṃ Haranamaskṛtāyai Namaḥ |	ॐ हरनमस्कृताये नमः ।
41.	Oṃ Dāna Māna Jñāna Māna Pāna Gāna Sukha Pradāyai Namaḥ |	ॐ दान मान ज्ञान मान पान गान सुख प्रदाये नमः ।
42.	Oṃ Gajagośvapadāgañjāyai Bhūtidāyai Namaḥ |	ॐ गजगोश्वपदागञ्जाये भूतिदाये नमः ।
43.	Oṃ Bhūtanāśinyai Namaḥ |	ॐ भूतनाशिन्यै नमः ।
44.	Oṃ Bhavabhāvāyai Namaḥ |	ॐ भवभावाये नमः ।
45.	Oṃ Bālāyai Namaḥ |	ॐ बालाये नमः ।

46.	Oṃ Varadāyai Namaḥ		ॐ वरदायै नमः ।
47.	Oṃ Haravallabhāyai Namaḥ		ॐ हरवल्लभायै नमः ।
48.	Oṃ Bhagabhaṅgabhayāyai Namaḥ		ॐ भगभङ्गभयायै नमः ।
49.	Oṃ Mālāyai Namaḥ		ॐ मालायै नमः ।
50.	Oṃ Mālatyai Namaḥ		ॐ मालत्यै नमः ।
51.	Oṃ Tālanādadāyai Namaḥ		ॐ तालनाददायै नमः ।
52.	Oṃ Jāla Vāla Hāla Kāla Kapāla Priya Vādinyai Namaḥ		ॐ जाल वाल हाल काल कपाल प्रिय वादिन्यै नमः ।
53.	Oṃ Karañjaśīlaguñjāḍhyāyai Namaḥ		ॐ करञ्जशीलगुञ्जाढ्यायै नमः ।
54.	Oṃ Cūtāṅkuranivāsinyai Namaḥ		ॐ चूताङ्कुरनिवासिन्यै नमः
55.	Oṃ Panasasthāyai Namaḥ		ॐ पनसस्थायै नमः ।
56.	Oṃ Pānasaktāyai Namaḥ		ॐ पानसक्तायै नमः ।
57.	Oṃ Panaseśakuṭumbinyai Namaḥ		ॐ पनसेशकुटुम्बिन्यै नमः ।
58.	Oṃ Pāvanyai Namaḥ		ॐ पावन्यै नमः ।
59.	Oṃ Pāvanādhārāyai Namaḥ		ॐ पावनाधारायै नमः ।
60.	Oṃ Pūrṇāyai Namaḥ		ॐ पूर्णायै नमः ।
61.	Oṃ Pūrṇamanorathāyai Namaḥ		ॐ पूर्णमनोरथायै नमः ।
62.	Oṃ Pūtāyai Namaḥ		ॐ पूतायै नमः ।
63.	Oṃ Pūtakalāyai Namaḥ		ॐ पूतकलायै नमः ।
64.	Oṃ Paurāyai Namaḥ		ॐ पौरायै नमः ।
65.	Oṃ Purāṇasurasundaryai Namaḥ		ॐ पुराणसुरसुन्दर्यै नमः
66.	Oṃ Pareśyai Namaḥ		ॐ परेश्यै नमः ।
67.	Oṃ Paradāyai Namaḥ		ॐ परदायै नमः ।
68.	Oṃ Pārāyai Namaḥ		ॐ पारायै नमः ।
69.	Oṃ Parātmane Namaḥ		ॐ परात्मने नमः ।
70.	Oṃ Paramohinyai Namaḥ		ॐ परमोहिन्यै नमः ।
71.	Oṃ Jaganmāyāyai Namaḥ		ॐ जगन्मायायै नमः ।
72.	Oṃ Jagatkartryai Namaḥ		ॐ जगत्कर्त्र्यै नमः ।
73.	Oṃ Jagatkīrtyai Namaḥ		ॐ जगत्कीर्त्यै नमः ।

74.	Oṃ Jaganmayyai Namaḥ |	ॐ जगन्मय्यै नमः ।
75.	Oṃ Jananyai Namaḥ |	ॐ जनन्यै नमः ।
76.	Oṃ Jayinyai Namaḥ |	ॐ जयिन्यै नमः ।
77.	Oṃ Jāyāyai Namaḥ |	ॐ जायायै नमः ।
78.	Oṃ Jitāyai Namaḥ |	ॐ जितायै नमः ।
79.	Oṃ Jinajayapradāyai Namaḥ |	ॐ जिनजयप्रदायै नमः ।
80.	Oṃ Kīrtijñānadhyānamānadāyinyai Namaḥ |	ॐ कीर्तिज्ञानध्यान मानदायिन्यै नमः ।
81.	Oṃ Dānaveśvaryai Namaḥ |	ॐ दानवेश्वर्यै नमः ।
82.	Oṃ Kāvyavyākaraṇajñānāyai Namaḥ |	ॐ काव्यव्याकरणज्ञानायै नमः ।
83.	Oṃ Prajñāprajñānadāyinyai Namaḥ	ॐ प्रज्ञाप्रज्ञानदायिन्यै नमः ।
84.	Oṃ Vijñājñāyai Namaḥ |	ॐ विज्ञाज्ञायै नमः ।
85.	Oṃ Vijñajayadāyai Namaḥ |	ॐ विज्ञजयदायै नमः ।
86.	Oṃ Vijñāvijñaprapūjitāyai Namaḥ |	ॐ विज्ञाविज्ञप्रपूजितायै नमः
87.	Oṃ Parāvarejyāyai Namaḥ |	ॐ परावरेज्यायै नमः ।
88.	Oṃ Varadāyai Namaḥ |	ॐ वरदायै नमः ।
89.	Oṃ Pāradāyai Namaḥ |	ॐ पारदायै नमः ।
90.	Oṃ Śāradādarāyai Namaḥ |	ॐ शारदादरायै नमः । ९
91.	Oṃ Dāriṇyai Namaḥ |	ॐ दारिण्यै नमः ।
92.	Oṃ Devadūtyai Namaḥ |	ॐ देवदूत्यै नमः ।
93.	Oṃ Madanāmadanāmadāyai Namaḥ |	ॐ मदनामदनामदायै नमः ।
94.	Oṃ Paramajñānagamyāyai Namaḥ	ॐ परमज्ञानगम्यायै नमः ।
95.	Oṃ Pareśyai Namaḥ |	ॐ परेश्यै नमः ।
96.	Oṃ Paragāyai Parāyai Namaḥ |	ॐ परगायै परायै नमः ।
97.	Oṃ Yajñāyajñāpradāyai Namaḥ |	ॐ यज्ञायज्ञाप्रदायै नमः ।
98.	Oṃ Yajñajñānakāryakaryai Namaḥ |	ॐ यज्ञज्ञानकार्यकर्यै नमः ।
99.	Oṃ Śubhāyai Namaḥ |	ॐ शुभायै नमः ।
100	Oṃ Śobhinyai Namaḥ |	ॐ शोभिन्यै नमः ।
101	Oṃ Śumbhamathinyai Namaḥ |	ॐ शुम्भमथिन्यै नमः ।

102.	*Oṃ Niśumbhāsuramardinyai Namaḥ*	ॐ निशुम्भासुरमर्दिन्यै नमः
103.	*Oṃ Śāmbhavyai Namaḥ |*	ॐ शाम्भव्यै नमः	
104.	*Oṃ Śambhupatnyai Namaḥ |*	ॐ शम्भुपत्न्यै नमः	
105.	*Oṃ Śambhujāyāyai Namaḥ |*	ॐ शम्भुजायायै नमः	
106.	*Oṃ Śubhānanāyai Namaḥ |*	ॐ शुभाननायै नमः	
107.	*Oṃ Śāṅkaryai Namaḥ |*	ॐ शाङ्कर्यै नमः	
108.	*Oṃ Śaṅkarārādhyāyai Namaḥ |*	ॐ शङ्कराराध्यायै नमः	
109.	*Oṃ Sandhyāyai Namaḥ |*	ॐ सन्ध्यायै नमः	
110.	*Oṃ Sandhyāsudharmiṇyai Namaḥ |*	ॐ सन्ध्यासुधर्मिण्यै नमः	
111.	*Oṃ Śatrughnyai Namaḥ |*	ॐ शत्रुघ्न्यै नमः	
112.	*Oṃ Śatruhāyai Namaḥ |*	ॐ शत्रुहायै नमः	
113.	*Oṃ Śatrupradāyai Namaḥ |*	ॐ शत्रुप्रदायै नमः	
114.	*Oṃ Śātravanāśinyai Namaḥ |*	ॐ शात्रवनाशिन्यै नमः	
115.	*Oṃ Śaivyai Namaḥ |*	ॐ शैव्यै नमः	
116.	*Oṃ Śivalayāyai Namaḥ |*	ॐ शिवलयायै नमः	
117.	*Oṃ Śailāyai Namaḥ |*	ॐ शैलायै नमः	
118.	*Oṃ Sadā Śailarājapriyāyai Namaḥ |*	ॐ सदा शैलराजप्रियायै नमः
119.	*Oṃ Śarvaryai Namaḥ |*	ॐ शर्व्यै नमः	
120.	*Oṃ Śabaryai Namaḥ |*	ॐ शबर्यै नमः	
121.	*Oṃ Śambhave Namaḥ |*	ॐ शम्भवे नमः	
122.	*Oṃ Sudhāḍhyāyai Namaḥ |*	ॐ सुधाढ्यायै नमः	
123.	*Oṃ Saudhavāsinyai Namaḥ |*	ॐ सौधवासिन्यै नमः	
124.	*Oṃ Saguṇāguṇarūpāyai Namaḥ |*	ॐ सगुणागुणरूपायै नमः
125.	*Oṃ Gauravyai Namaḥ |*	ॐ गौरव्यै नमः	
126.	*Oṃ Bhairavīravāyai Namaḥ |*	ॐ भैरवीरवायै नमः	
127.	*Oṃ Gaurāṅgyai Namaḥ |*	ॐ गौराङ्ग्यै नमः	
128.	*Oṃ Gauradehāyai Namaḥ |*	ॐ गौरदेहायै नमः	
129.	*Oṃ Gauryai Namaḥ |*	ॐ गौर्यै नमः	
130	*Oṃ Gurumatyai Gurave Namaḥ |*	ॐ गुरुमत्यै गुरवे नमः	
131	*Oṃ Gave Gave Namaḥ |*	ॐ गवे गवे नमः	

132	Oṃ Gavyasvarūpāyai Namaḥ		ॐ गव्यस्वरूपायै नमः ।
133	Oṃ Guṇānandasvarūpiṇyai Namaḥ		ॐ गुणानन्दस्वरूपिण्यै नमः ।
134	Oṃ Gaṇeśagaṇadāyai Namaḥ		ॐ गणेशगणदायै नमः ।
135	Oṃ Guṇyaguṇāyai Namaḥ		ॐ गुण्यगुणायै नमः
136	Oṃ Gauravavāñchitāyai Namaḥ		ॐ गौरववाञ्छितायै नमः ।
137	Oṃ Gaṇamātre Namaḥ		ॐ गणमात्रे नमः ।
138	Oṃ Gaṇārādhyāyai Namaḥ		ॐ गणाराध्यायै नमः ।
139	Oṃ Gaṇakoṭivināśinyai Namaḥ		ॐ गणकोटिविनाशिन्यै नमः
140	Oṃ Durgāyai Namaḥ		ॐ दुर्गायै नमः ।
141	Oṃ Durjanahantryai Namaḥ		ॐ दुर्जनहन्त्र्यै नमः ।
142	Oṃ Durjanaprītidāyinyai Namaḥ		ॐ दुर्जनप्रीतिदायिन्यै नमः ।
143	Oṃ Svargāpavargadāyai Namaḥ		ॐ स्वर्गापवर्गदायै नमः ।
144	Oṃ Dātryai Namaḥ		ॐ दात्र्यै नमः ।
145	Oṃ Dīnādīnadayāvatyai Namaḥ		ॐ दीनादीनदयावत्यै नमः ।
146	Oṃ Durnirīkṣyāyai Namaḥ		ॐ दुर्निरीक्ष्यायै नमः ।
147	Oṃ Durāduḥsthāyai Namaḥ		ॐ दुरादुःस्थायै नमः ।
148	Oṃ Dausthyabhañjanakāriṇyai Namaḥ		ॐ दौस्थ्यभञ्जनकारिण्यै नमः ।
149	Oṃ Śvetapāṇḍurakṛṣṇābhāyai Namaḥ		ॐ श्वेतपाण्डुरकृष्णाभायै नमः ।
150	Oṃ Kāladāyai Namaḥ		ॐ कालदायै नमः ।
151	Oṃ Kālanāśinyai Namaḥ		ॐ कालनाशिन्यै नमः ।
152	Oṃ Karmanarmakaryai Namaḥ		ॐ कर्मनर्मकर्यै नमः ।
153	Oṃ Narmāyai Namaḥ		ॐ नर्मायै नमः ।
154	Oṃ Dharmādharmavināśinyai Namaḥ		ॐ धर्माधर्मविनाशिन्यै नमः ।
155	Oṃ Gaurīgauravadāyai Namaḥ		ॐ गौरीगौरवदायै नमः ।
156	Oṃ Godāyai Namaḥ		ॐ गोदायै नमः ।
157	Oṃ Gaṇadāyai Namaḥ		ॐ गणदायै नमः ।
158	Oṃ Gāyanapriyāyai Namaḥ		ॐ गायनप्रियायै नमः ।
159	Oṃ Gaṅgāyai Namaḥ		ॐ गङ्गायै नमः ।

160.	Oṃ Bhāgīrathyai Namaḥ |	ॐ भागीरथ्यै नमः ।
161.	Oṃ Bhaṅgāyai Namaḥ |	ॐ भङ्गायै नमः ।
162.	Oṃ Bhagāyai Namaḥ |	ॐ भगायै नमः ।
163.	Oṃ Bhāgyavivardhinyai Namaḥ |	ॐ भाग्यविवर्धिन्यै नमः ।
164.	Oṃ Bhavānyai Namaḥ |	ॐ भवान्यै नमः ।
165.	Oṃ Bhavahantryai Namaḥ |	ॐ भवहन्त्र्यै नमः ।
166.	Oṃ Bhairavyai Namaḥ |	ॐ भैरव्यै नमः ।
167.	Oṃ Bhairavīsamāyai Namaḥ |	ॐ भैरवीसमायै नमः ।
168.	Oṃ Bhīmābhīmaravāyai Namaḥ |	ॐ भीमाभीमरवायै नमः ।
169.	Oṃ Bhaimyai Namaḥ |	ॐ भैम्यै नमः ।
170.	Oṃ Bhīmānandapradāyinyai Namaḥ |	ॐ भीमानन्दप्रदायिन्यै नमः ।
171.	Oṃ Śaraṇyāyai Namaḥ |	ॐ शरण्यायै नमः ।
172.	Oṃ Śaraṇāyai Namaḥ |	ॐ शरणायै नमः ।
173.	Oṃ Śamyāyai Namaḥ |	ॐ शम्यायै नमः ।
174.	Oṃ Śaśinyai Namaḥ |	ॐ शशिन्यै नमः ।
175.	Oṃ Śaṅkhanāśinyai Namaḥ |	ॐ शङ्खनाशिन्यै नमः ।
176.	Oṃ Guṇāguṇakaryai Namaḥ |	ॐ गुणागुणकर्यै नमः ।
177.	Oṃ Gauṇīpriyāyai Namaḥ |	ॐ गौणीप्रियायै नमः ।
178.	Oṃ Prītipradāyinyai Namaḥ |	ॐ प्रीतिप्रदायिन्यै नमः ।
179.	Oṃ Janamohanakartryai Namaḥ |	ॐ जनमोहनकत्र्यै नमः ।
180.	Oṃ Jagadānandadāyinyai Namaḥ |	ॐ जगदानन्ददायिन्यै नमः ।
181.	Oṃ Jitājāyāyai Namaḥ |	ॐ जिताजायायै नमः ।
182.	Oṃ Vijayāyai Namaḥ |	ॐ विजयायै नमः ।
183.	Oṃ Vijayājayadāyinyai Namaḥ |	ॐ विजयाजयदायिन्यै नमः ।
184.	Oṃ Kāmāyai Namaḥ |	ॐ कामायै नमः ।
185.	Oṃ Kālyai Namaḥ |	ॐ काल्यै नमः ।
186.	Oṃ Karālāsyāyai Namaḥ |	ॐ करालास्यायै नमः ।
187.	Oṃ Kharvāyai Namaḥ |	ॐ खर्वायै नमः ।
188.	Oṃ Khañjāyai Namaḥ |	ॐ खञ्जायै नमः ।
189.	Oṃ Kharāyai Namaḥ |	ॐ खरायै नमः ।

190.	Oṃ Gadāyai Namaḥ		ॐ गदायै नमः ।
191.	Oṃ Garvāyai Namaḥ		ॐ गर्वायै नमः ।
192.	Oṃ Garutmatyai Namaḥ		ॐ गरुत्मत्यै नमः ।
193.	Oṃ Gharmāyai Namaḥ		ॐ घर्मायै नमः ।
194.	Oṃ Ghargharāyai Namaḥ		ॐ घर्घरायै नमः ।
195.	Oṃ Ghoranādinyai Namaḥ		ॐ घोरनादिन्यै नमः ।
196.	Oṃ Carācaryai Namaḥ		ॐ चराचर्यै नमः ।
197.	Oṃ Carārādhyāyai Namaḥ		ॐ चराराध्यायै नमः ।
198.	Oṃ Chinnācchinnamanorathāyai Namaḥ		ॐ छिन्नाच्छिन्नमनोरथायै नमः ।
199.	Oṃ Chinnamastāyai Namaḥ		ॐ छिन्नमस्तायै नमः ।
200.	Oṃ Jayājāpyāyai Namaḥ		ॐ जयाजाप्यायै नमः ।
201.	Oṃ Jagajjāyāyai Namaḥ		ॐ जगज्जायायै नमः ।
202.	Oṃ Jharjharyai Namaḥ		ॐ झर्झर्यै नमः ।
203.	Oṃ Jhakārāyai Namaḥ		ॐ झकारायै नमः ।
204.	Oṃ Jhīṣkṛtyai Namaḥ		ॐ झीष्कृत्यै नमः ।
205.	Oṃ Ṭīkāyai Namaḥ		ॐ टीकायै नमः ।
206.	Oṃ Ṭaṅkāyai Namaḥ		ॐ टङ्कायै नमः ।
207.	Oṃ Ṭaṅkāranādinyai Namaḥ		ॐ टङ्कारनादिन्यै नमः ।
208.	Oṃ Ṭhīkāyai Namaḥ		ॐ ठीकायै नमः ।
209.	Oṃ Ṭhakkuraṭhakkāṅgyai Namaḥ		ॐ ठक्कुरठक्काङ्ग्यै नमः ।
210.	Oṃ Ṭhaṭhaṭhāṅkāraḍhuṇḍhurāyai Namaḥ		ॐ ठठठाङ्कारढुण्दुरायै नमः ।
211.	Oṃ Ḍhuṇḍhyai Namaḥ		ॐ ढुण्ढ्यै नमः ।
212.	Oṃ Tārājatīrṇāyai Namaḥ		ॐ ताराजतीर्णायै नमः ।
213.	Oṃ Tālasthabhramaṇāśinyai Namaḥ		ॐ तालस्थभ्रमनाशिन्यै नमः ।
214.	Oṃ Thakārāyai Namaḥ		ॐ थकारायै नमः ।
215.	Oṃ Thakarāyai Namaḥ		ॐ थकरायै नमः ।
216.	Oṃ Dātryai Namaḥ		ॐ दात्र्यै नमः ।

217.	Oṃ Dīpāyai Namaḥ		ॐ दीपायै नमः ।
218.	Oṃ Dīpavināśinyai Namaḥ		ॐ दीपविनाशिन्यै नमः ।
219.	Oṃ Dhanyāyai Namaḥ		ॐ धन्यायै नमः ।
220.	Oṃ Dhanādhanavatyai Namaḥ		ॐ धनाधनवत्यै नमः ।
221.	Oṃ Narmadāyai Namaḥ		ॐ नर्मदायै नमः ।
222.	Oṃ Narmamodinyai Namaḥ		ॐ नर्ममोदिन्यै नमः ।
223.	Oṃ Padmāyai Namaḥ		ॐ पद्मायै नमः ।
224.	Oṃ Padmāvatyai Namaḥ		ॐ पद्मावत्यै नमः ।
225.	Oṃ Pītāsphāntāyai Namaḥ		ॐ पीतास्फान्तायै नमः ।
226.	Oṃ Phūtkārakāriṇyai Namaḥ		ॐ फूत्कारकारिण्यै नमः ।
227.	Oṃ Phullāyai Namaḥ		ॐ फुल्लायै नमः ।
228.	Oṃ Brahmamayyai Namaḥ		ॐ ब्रह्ममय्यै नमः ।
229.	Oṃ Brāhmyai Namaḥ		ॐ ब्राह्म्यै नमः ।
230.	Oṃ Brahmānandapradāyinyai Namaḥ		ॐ ब्रह्मानन्दप्रदायिन्यै नमः ।
231.	Oṃ Bhavārādhyāyai Namaḥ		ॐ भवाराध्यायै नमः ।
232.	Oṃ Bhavādhyakṣāyai Namaḥ		ॐ भवाध्यक्षायै नमः ।
233.	Oṃ Bhagālīmandagāminyai Namaḥ	ॐ भगालीमन्दगामिन्यै नमः
234.	Oṃ Madirāyai Namaḥ		ॐ मदिरायै नमः ।
235.	Oṃ Madirekṣāyai Namaḥ		ॐ मदिरेक्षायै नमः ।
236.	Oṃ Yaśodāyai Namaḥ		ॐ यशोदायै नमः ।
237.	Oṃ Yamapūjitāyai Namaḥ		ॐ यमपूजितायै नमः ।
238.	Oṃ Yāmyāyai Namaḥ		ॐ याम्यायै नमः ।
239.	Oṃ Rāmyāyai Namaḥ		ॐ राम्यायै नमः ।
240.	Oṃ Rāmarūpāyai Namaḥ		ॐ रामरूपायै नमः ।
241.	Oṃ Ramaṇyai Namaḥ		ॐ रमण्यै नमः ।
242.	Oṃ Lalitāyai Namaḥ		ॐ ललितायै नमः ।
243.	Oṃ Latāyai Namaḥ		ॐ लतायै नमः ।
244.	Oṃ Laṅkeśyai Namaḥ		ॐ लङ्केश्यै नमः ।
245.	Oṃ Vākpradāyai Namaḥ		ॐ वाक्प्रदायै नमः ।
246.	Oṃ Vācyāyai Namaḥ		ॐ वाच्यायै नमः ।

247.	Oṃ Sadāśramanivāsinyai Namaḥ |	ॐ सदाश्रमनिवासिन्यै नमः।
248.	Oṃ Śrāntāyai Namaḥ |	ॐ श्रान्तायै नमः।
249.	Oṃ Śakārarūpāyai Namaḥ |	ॐ शकाररूपायै नमः।
250.	Oṃ Ṣakārakharavāhanāyai Namaḥ	ॐ षकारखरवाहनायै नमः।
251.	Oṃ Sahyādrirūpāyai Namaḥ |	ॐ सह्याद्रिरूपायै नमः।
252.	Oṃ Sānandāyai Namaḥ |	ॐ सानन्दायै नमः।
253.	Oṃ Hariṇīharirūpiṇyai Namaḥ |	ॐ हरिणीहरिरूपिण्यै नमः।
254.	Oṃ Harārādhyāyai Namaḥ |	ॐ हराराध्यायै नमः।
255.	Oṃ Bālavācālavaṅga Prematoṣitāyai Namaḥ |	ॐ बालवाचालवङ्ग प्रेमतोषितायै नमः।
256.	Oṃ Kṣapākṣayapradāyai Namaḥ |	ॐ क्षपाक्षयप्रदायै नमः।
257.	Oṃ Kṣīrāyai Namaḥ |	ॐ क्षीरायै नमः।
258.	Oṃ Akārādisvarūpiṇyai Namaḥ |	ॐ अकारादिस्वरूपिण्यै नमः
259.	Oṃ Kālikāyai Namaḥ |	ॐ कालिकायै नमः।
260.	Oṃ Kālamūrtaye Namaḥ |	ॐ कालमूर्तये नमः।
261.	Oṃ Kalahāyai Namaḥ |	ॐ कलहायै नमः।
262.	Oṃ Kalahapriyāyai Namaḥ |	ॐ कलहप्रियायै नमः।
263.	Oṃ Śivāyai Namaḥ |	ॐ शिवायै नमः।
264.	Oṃ Śandāyinyai Namaḥ |	ॐ शन्दायिन्यै नमः।
265.	Oṃ Saumyāyai Namaḥ |	ॐ सौम्यायै नमः।
266.	Oṃ Śatrunigrahakāriṇyai Namaḥ |	ॐ शत्रुनिग्रहकारिण्यै नमः।
267.	Oṃ Bhavānyai Namaḥ |	ॐ भवान्यै नमः।
268.	Oṃ Bhavamūrtaye Namaḥ |	ॐ भवमूर्तये नमः।
269.	Oṃ Śarvāṇyai Namaḥ |	ॐ शर्वाण्यै नमः।
270.	Oṃ Sarvamaṅgalāyai Namaḥ |	ॐ सर्वमङ्गलायै नमः।
271.	Oṃ Śatruvidrāviṇyai Namaḥ |	ॐ शत्रुविद्राविण्यै नमः।
272.	Oṃ Śaivyai Namaḥ |	ॐ शैव्यै नमः।
273.	Oṃ Śumbhāsuravināśinyai Namaḥ |	ॐ शुम्भासुरविनाशिन्यै नमः
274.	Oṃ Dhakāramantrarūpāyai Namaḥ	ॐ धकारमन्त्ररूपायै नमः।
275.	Oṃ Dhūmbījaparitoṣitāyai Namaḥ |	ॐ धूम्बीजपरितोषितायै नमः

276.	Oṃ Dhanādhyakṣastutāyai Namaḥ	ॐ धनाध्यक्षस्तुतायै नमः ।
277.	Oṃ Dhīrāyai Namaḥ		ॐ धीरायै नमः ।
278.	Oṃ Dharārūpāyai Namaḥ		ॐ धरारूपायै नमः ।
279.	Oṃ Dharāvatyai Namaḥ		ॐ धरावत्यै नमः ।
280.	Oṃ Carviṇyai Namaḥ		ॐ चर्विण्यै नमः ।
281.	Oṃ Candrapūjyāyai Namaḥ		ॐ चन्द्रपूज्यायै नमः ।
282.	Oṃ Chandorūpāyai Namaḥ		ॐ छन्दोरूपायै नमः ।
283.	Oṃ Chaṭāvatyai Namaḥ		ॐ छटावत्यै नमः ।
284.	Oṃ Chāyāyai Namaḥ		ॐ छायायै नमः ।
285.	Oṃ Chāyāvatyai Namaḥ		ॐ छायावत्यै नमः ।
286.	Oṃ Svacchāyai Namaḥ		ॐ स्वच्छायै नमः ।
287.	Oṃ Chedinyai Namaḥ		ॐ छेदिन्यै नमः ।
288.	Oṃ Bhedinyai Namaḥ		ॐ भेदिन्यै नमः ।
289.	Oṃ Kṣamāyai Namaḥ		ॐ क्षमायै नमः ।
290.	Oṃ Valginyai Namaḥ		ॐ वल्गिन्यै नमः ।
291.	Oṃ Vardhinyai Namaḥ		ॐ वर्धिन्यै नमः ।
292.	Oṃ Vandyāyai Namaḥ		ॐ वन्द्यायै नमः ।
293.	Oṃ Vedamātre Namaḥ		ॐ वेदमात्रे नमः ।
294.	Oṃ Budhastutāyai Namaḥ		ॐ बुधस्तुतायै नमः
295.	Oṃ Dhārāyai Namaḥ		ॐ धारायै नमः ।
296.	Oṃ Dhārāvatyai Namaḥ		ॐ धारावत्यै नमः ।
297.	Oṃ Dhanyāyai Namaḥ		ॐ धन्यायै नमः ।
298.	Oṃ Dharmadānaparāyaṇāyai Namaḥ		ॐ धर्मदानपरायणायै नमः ।
299.	Oṃ Garviṇyai Namaḥ		ॐ गर्विण्यै नमः ।
300.	Oṃ Gurupūjyāyai Namaḥ		ॐ गुरुपूज्यायै नमः ।
301.	Oṃ Jñānadātryai Namaḥ		ॐ ज्ञानदात्रै नमः ।
302.	Oṃ Guṇānvitāyai Namaḥ		ॐ गुणान्वितायै नमः ।
303.	Oṃ Dharmiṇyai Namaḥ		ॐ धर्मिण्यै नमः ।
304.	Oṃ Dharmarūpāyai Namaḥ		ॐ धर्मरूपायै नमः ।

305.	Oṃ Ghaṇṭānādaparāyaṇāyai Namaḥ |	ॐ घण्टानादपरायणायै नमः ।
306.	Oṃ Ghaṇṭāninādinyai Namaḥ |	ॐ घण्टानिनादिन्यै नमः ।
307.	Oṃ Ghūrṇāghūrṇitāyai Namaḥ |	ॐ घूर्णाघूर्णितायै नमः ।
308.	Oṃ Ghorarūpiṇyai Namaḥ |	ॐ घोररूपिण्यै नमः ।
309.	Oṃ Kalighnyai Namaḥ |	ॐ कलिघ्न्यै नमः ।
310.	Oṃ Kalidūtyai Namaḥ |	ॐ कलिदूत्यै नमः ।
311.	Oṃ Kalipūjyāyai Namaḥ |	ॐ कलिपूज्यायै नमः ।
312.	Oṃ Kalipriyāyai Namaḥ |	ॐ कलिप्रियायै नमः ।
313.	Oṃ Kālanirṇāśinyai Namaḥ |	ॐ कालनिर्णाशिन्यै नमः ।
314.	Oṃ Kālyāyai Namaḥ |	ॐ काल्यायै नमः ।
315.	Oṃ Kāvyadāyai Namaḥ |	ॐ काव्यदायै नमः ।
316.	Oṃ Kālarūpiṇyai Namaḥ |	ॐ कालरूपिण्यै नमः ।
317.	Oṃ Varṣiṇyai Namaḥ |	ॐ वर्षिण्यै नमः ।
318.	Oṃ Vṛṣṭidāyai Namaḥ |	ॐ वृष्टिदायै नमः ।
319.	Oṃ Vṛṣṭirmahāvṛṣṭinivāriṇyai Namaḥ |	ॐ वृष्टिर्महावृष्टिनिवारिण्यै नमः ।
320.	Oṃ Ghātinyai Namaḥ |	ॐ घातिन्यै नमः ।
321.	Oṃ Ghāṭinyai Namaḥ |	ॐ घाटिन्यै नमः ।
322.	Oṃ Ghoṇṭāyai Namaḥ |	ॐ घोण्टायै नमः ।
323.	Oṃ Ghātakyai Namaḥ |	ॐ घातक्यै नमः ।
324.	Oṃ Ghanarūpiṇyai Namaḥ |	ॐ घनरूपिण्यै नमः ।
325.	Oṃ Dhūmbījāyai Namaḥ |	ॐ धूम्बीजायै नमः ।
326.	Oṃ Dhūñjapānandāyai Namaḥ |	ॐ धूञ्जपानन्दायै नमः ।
327.	Oṃ Dhūmbījajapatoṣitāyai Namaḥ |	ॐ धूम्बीजजपतोषितायै नमः ।
328.	Oṃ Dhūndhūmbījajapāsaktāyai Namaḥ |	ॐ धून्धूम्बीजजपासक्तायै नमः ।
329.	Oṃ Dhūndhūmbījajaparāyaṇāyai Namaḥ |	ॐ धून्धूम्बीजजपरायणायै नमः ।

330.	Oṃ Dhūṅkāraharṣiṇyai Namaḥ	ॐ धूङ्कारहर्षिण्यै नमः ।
331.	Oṃ Dhūmāyai Namaḥ	ॐ धूमायै नमः ।
332.	Oṃ Dhanadāyai Namaḥ	ॐ धनदायै नमः ।
333.	Oṃ Dhanagarvitāyai Namaḥ	ॐ धनगर्विताये नमः ।
334.	Oṃ Padmāvatyai Namaḥ	ॐ पद्मावत्यै नमः ।
335.	Oṃ Padmamālāyai Namaḥ	ॐ पद्ममालायै नमः ।
336.	Oṃ Padmayoniprapūjitāyai Namaḥ	ॐ पद्मयोनिप्रपूजितायै नमः
337.	Oṃ Apārāyai Namaḥ	ॐ अपारायै नमः ।
338.	Oṃ Pūraṇyai Namaḥ	ॐ पूरण्यै नमः ।
339.	Oṃ Pūrṇāyai Namaḥ	ॐ पूर्णायै नमः ।
340.	Oṃ Pūrṇimāyai Namaḥ	ॐ पूर्णिमायै नमः ।
341.	Oṃ Parivanditāyai Namaḥ	ॐ परिवन्दितायै नमः ।
342.	Oṃ Phaladāyai Namaḥ	ॐ फलदायै नमः ।
343.	Oṃ Phalabhoktryai Namaḥ	ॐ फलभोक्त्र्यै नमः ।
344.	Oṃ Phalinyai Namaḥ	ॐ फलिन्यै नमः ।
345.	Oṃ Phaladāyinyai Namaḥ	ॐ फलदायिन्यै नमः ।
346.	Oṃ Phūtkāriṇyai Namaḥ	ॐ फूत्कारिण्यै नमः ।
347.	Oṃ Phalāvāptryai Namaḥ	ॐ फलावाप्त्र्यै नमः ।
348.	Oṃ Phalabhoktryai Namaḥ	ॐ फलभोक्त्र्यै नमः ।
349.	Oṃ Phalānvitāyai Namaḥ	ॐ फलान्वितायै नमः ।
350.	Oṃ Vāriṇyai Namaḥ	ॐ वारिण्यै नमः ।
351.	Oṃ Vāraṇaprītāyai Namaḥ	ॐ वारणप्रीतायै नमः ।
352.	Oṃ Vāripāthodhipāragāyai Namaḥ	ॐ वारिपाथोधिपारगायै नमः
353.	Oṃ Vivarṇāyai Namaḥ	ॐ विवर्णायै नमः ।
354.	Oṃ Dhūmranayanāyai Namaḥ	ॐ धूम्रनयनायै नमः ।
355.	Oṃ Dhūmrākṣyai Namaḥ	ॐ धूम्राक्ष्यै नमः ।
356.	Oṃ Dhūmrarūpiṇyai Namaḥ	ॐ धूम्ररूपिण्यै नमः ।
357.	Oṃ Nītyai Namaḥ	ॐ नीत्यै नमः ।
358.	Oṃ Nītisvarūpāyai Namaḥ	ॐ नीतिस्वरूपायै नमः ।
359.	Oṃ Nītijñāyai Namaḥ	ॐ नीतिज्ञायै नमः ।

360.	Oṃ Nayakovidāyai Namaḥ		ॐ नयकोविदायै नमः ।
361.	Oṃ Tāriṇyai Namaḥ		ॐ तारिण्यै नमः ।
362.	Oṃ Tārarūpāyai Namaḥ		ॐताररूपायै नमः ।
363.	Oṃ Tattvajñānaparāyaṇāyai Namaḥ		ॐ तत्त्वज्ञानपरायणायै नमः ।
364.	Oṃ Sthūlāyai Namaḥ		ॐ स्थूलायै नमः ।
365.	Oṃ Sthūlādharāyai Namaḥ		ॐ स्थूलाधरायै नमः ।
366.	Oṃ Sthātryai Namaḥ		ॐ स्थात्र्यै नमः ।
367.	Oṃ Uttamasthānavāsinyai Namaḥ	ॐ उत्तमस्थानवासिन्यै नमः
368.	Oṃ Sthūlāyai Namaḥ		ॐ स्थूलायै नमः ।
369.	Oṃ Padmapadasthānāyai Namaḥ		ॐ पद्मपदस्थानायै नमः ।
370.	Oṃ Sthānabhraṣṭāyai Namaḥ		ॐ स्थानभ्रष्टायै नमः ।
371.	Oṃ Sthalasthitāyai Namaḥ		ॐ स्थलस्थितायै नमः ।
372.	Oṃ Śoṣinyai Namaḥ		ॐ शोषिण्यै नमः ।
373.	Oṃ Śobhinyai Namaḥ		ॐ शोभिन्यै नमः ।
374.	Oṃ Śītāyai Namaḥ		ॐ शीतायै नमः ।
375.	Oṃ Śītapānīyapāyinyai Namaḥ		ॐ शीतपानीयपायिन्यै नमः ।
376.	Oṃ Śāriṇyai Namaḥ		ॐ शारिण्यै नमः ।
377.	Oṃ Śaṅkhinyai Namaḥ		ॐ शङ्खिन्यै नमः ।
378.	Oṃ Śuddhāyai Namaḥ		ॐ शुद्धायै नमः ।
379.	Oṃ Śaṅkhāsuravināśinyai Namaḥ		ॐ शङ्खासुरविनाशिन्यै नमः ।
380.	Oṃ Śarvaryai Namaḥ		ॐ शर्वर्यै नमः ।
381.	Oṃ Śarvarīpūjyāyai Namaḥ		ॐ शर्वरीपूज्यायै नमः ।
382.	Oṃ Śarvarīśaprapūjitāyai Namaḥ		ॐ शर्वरीशप्रपूजितायै नमः ।
383.	Oṃ Śarvarījāgritāyai Namaḥ		ॐ शर्वरीजाग्रितायै नमः ।
384.	Oṃ Yogyāyai Namaḥ		ॐ योग्यायै नमः ।
385.	Oṃ Yoginyai Namaḥ		ॐ योगिन्यै नमः ।
386.	Oṃ Yogavanditāyai Namaḥ		ॐ योगवन्दितायै नमः ।
387.	Oṃ Yoginīgaṇasaṃsevyāyai Namaḥ	ॐ योगिनीगणसंसेव्यायै नमः

388.	Oṁ Yoginīyogabhāvitāyai Namaḥ		ॐ योगिनीयोगभावितायै नमः ।
389.	Oṁ Yogamārgaratāyai Namaḥ		ॐ योगमार्गरतायै नमः ।
390.	Oṁ Yuktāyai Namaḥ		ॐ युक्तायै नमः ।
391.	Oṁ Yogamārgānusāriṇyai Namaḥ		ॐ योगमार्गानुसारिण्यै नमः ।
392.	Oṁ Yogabhāvāyai Namaḥ		ॐ योगभावायै नमः ।
393.	Oṁ Yogayuktāyai Namaḥ		ॐ योगयुक्तायै नमः ।
394.	Oṁ Yāminīpativanditāyai Namaḥ		ॐ यामिनीपतिवन्दितायै नमः ।
395.	Oṁ Ayogyāyai Namaḥ		ॐ अयोग्यायै नमः ।
396.	Oṁ Yodhinyai Namaḥ		ॐ योधिन्यै नमः ।
397.	Oṁ Yoddhrāyai Namaḥ		ॐ योद्ध्रायै नमः ।
398.	Oṁ Yuddhakarmaviśāradāyai Namaḥ		ॐ युद्धकर्मविशारदायै नमः ।
399.	Oṁ Yuddhamārgaratāyai Namaḥ		ॐ युद्धमार्गरतायै नमः ।
400.	Oṁ Nāntāyai Namaḥ		ॐ नान्तायै नमः ।
401.	Oṁ Yuddhasthānanivāsinyai Namaḥ		ॐ युद्धस्थाननिवासिन्यै नमः ।
402.	Oṁ Siddhāyai Namaḥ		ॐ सिद्धायै नमः ।
403.	Oṁ Siddheśvaryai Namaḥ		ॐ सिद्धेश्वर्यै नमः ।
404.	Oṁ Siddhyai Namaḥ		ॐ सिद्ध्यै नमः ।
405.	Oṁ Siddhigehanivāsinyai Namaḥ		ॐ सिद्धिगेहनिवासिन्यै नमः
406.	Oṁ Siddharītyai Namaḥ		ॐ सिद्धरीत्यै नमः ।
407.	Oṁ Siddhaprītyai Namaḥ		ॐ सिद्धप्रीत्यै नमः ।
408.	Oṁ Siddhāyai Namaḥ		ॐ सिद्धायै नमः ।
409.	Oṁ Siddhāntakāriṇyai Namaḥ		ॐ सिद्धान्तकारिण्यै नमः ।
410.	Oṁ Siddhagamyāyai Namaḥ		ॐ सिद्धिगम्यायै नमः ।
411.	Oṁ Siddhapūjyāyai Namaḥ		ॐ सिद्धपूज्यायै नमः ।
412.	Oṁ Siddhavandyāyai Namaḥ		ॐ सिद्धवन्द्यायै नमः ।
413.	Oṁ Susiddhidāyai Namaḥ		ॐ सुसिद्धिदायै नमः ।
414.	Oṁ Sādhinyai Namaḥ		ॐ साधिन्यै नमः ।

415.	Oṃ Sādhanaprītāyai Namaḥ		ॐ साधनप्रीतायै नमः ।
416.	Oṃ Sādhyāyai Namaḥ		ॐ साध्यायै नमः ।
417.	Oṃ Sādhanakāriṇyai Namaḥ		ॐ साधनकारिण्यै नमः ।
418.	Oṃ Sādhanīyāyai Namaḥ		ॐ साधनीयायै नमः ।
419.	Oṃ Sādhyasādhyāyai Namaḥ		ॐ साध्यसाध्यायै नमः ।
420.	Oṃ Sādhyasaṅghasuśobhinyai Namaḥ		ॐ साध्यसङ्घसुशोभिन्यै नमः।
421.	Oṃ Sādhvyai Namaḥ		ॐ साध्व्यै नमः ।
422.	Oṃ Sādhusvabhāvāyai Namaḥ		ॐ साधुस्वभावायै नमः ।
423.	Oṃ Tasyai Namaḥ		ॐ तस्यै नमः ।
424.	Oṃ Sādhusantatidāyinyai Namaḥ		ॐ साधुसन्ततिदायिन्यै नमः
425.	Oṃ Sādhupūjyāyai Namaḥ		ॐ साधुपूज्यायै नमः ।
426.	Oṃ Sādhuvandyāyai Namaḥ		ॐ साधुवन्द्यायै नमः ।
427.	Oṃ Sādhusandarśanodyatāyai Namaḥ		ॐ साधुसन्दर्शनोद्यतायै नमः ।
428.	Oṃ Sādhudṛṣṭāyai Namaḥ		ॐ साधुदृष्टायै नमः ।
429.	Oṃ Sādhupuṣṭāyai Namaḥ		ॐ साधुपुष्टायै नमः ।
430.	Oṃ Sādhupoṣaṇatatparāyai Namaḥ		ॐ साधुपोषणतत्परायै नमः ।
431.	Oṃ Sāttvikyai Namaḥ		ॐ सात्त्विक्यै नमः ।
432.	Oṃ Sattvasaṃsiddhāyai Namaḥ		ॐ सत्त्वसंसिद्धायै नमः ।
433.	Oṃ Sattvasevyāyai Namaḥ		ॐ सत्त्वसेव्यायै नमः ।
434.	Oṃ Sukhodayāyai Namaḥ		ॐ सुखोदयायै नमः ।
435.	Oṃ Sattvavṛddhikaryai Namaḥ		ॐ सत्त्ववृद्धिकर्यै नमः ।
436.	Oṃ Śāntāyai Namaḥ		ॐ शान्तायै नमः ।
437.	Oṃ Sattvasaṃharṣamānasāyai Namaḥ		ॐ सत्त्वसंहर्षमानसायै नमः ।
438.	Oṃ Sattvajñānāyai Namaḥ		ॐ सत्त्वज्ञानायै नमः ।
439.	Oṃ Sattvavidyāyai Namaḥ		ॐ सत्त्वविद्यायै नमः ।
440.	Oṃ Sattvasiddhāntakāriṇyai Namaḥ		ॐ सत्त्वसिद्धान्तकारिण्यै नमः ।
441.	Oṃ Sattvavṛddhyai Namaḥ		ॐ सत्त्ववृद्ध्यै नमः ।

442.	Oṃ Sattvasiddhyai Namaḥ |	ॐ सत्त्वसिद्ध्यै नमः ।
443.	Oṃ Sattvasampannamānasāyai Namaḥ	ॐ सत्त्वसम्पन्नमानसायै नमः ।
444.	Oṃ Cārurūpāyai Namaḥ |	ॐ चारुरूपायै नमः ।
445.	Oṃ Cārudehāyai Namaḥ |	ॐ चारुदेहायै नमः ।
446.	Oṃ Cārucañcalalocanāyai Namaḥ |	ॐ चारुचञ्चललोचनायै नमः ।
447.	Oṃ Chadminyai Namaḥ |	ॐ छद्मिन्यै नमः ।
448.	Oṃ Chadmasaṅkalpāyai Namaḥ |	ॐ छद्मसङ्कल्पायै नमः ।
449.	Oṃ Chadmavārtāyai Namaḥ |	ॐ छद्मवार्तायै नमः ।
450.	Oṃ Kṣamāpriyāyai Namaḥ |	ॐ क्षमाप्रियायै नमः ।
451.	Oṃ Haṭhinyai Namaḥ |	ॐ हठिन्यै नमः ।
452.	Oṃ Haṭhasamprītyai Namaḥ |	ॐ हठसम्प्रीत्यै नमः ।
453.	Oṃ Haṭhavārtāyai Namaḥ |	ॐ हठवार्तायै नमः ।
454.	Oṃ Haṭhodyamāyai Namaḥ |	ॐ हठोद्यमायै नमः ।
455.	Oṃ Haṭhakāryāyai Namaḥ |	ॐ हठकार्यायै नमः ।
456.	Oṃ Haṭhadharmāyai Namaḥ |	ॐ हठधर्मायै नमः ।
457.	Oṃ Haṭhakarmaparāyaṇāyai Namaḥ |	ॐ हठकर्मपरायणायै नमः ।
458.	Oṃ Haṭhasambhoganiratāyai Namaḥ |	ॐ हठसम्भोगनिरतायै नमः ।
459.	Oṃ Haṭhātkāraratipriyāyai Namaḥ	ॐ हठात्काररतिप्रियायै नमः
460.	Oṃ Haṭhasambhedinyai Namaḥ |	ॐ हठसम्भेदिन्यै नमः ।
461.	Oṃ Hṛdyāyai Namaḥ |	ॐ हृद्यायै नमः ।
462.	Oṃ Hṛdyavārtāyai Namaḥ |	ॐ हृद्यवार्तायै नमः ।
463.	Oṃ Haripriyāyai Namaḥ |	ॐ हरिप्रियायै नमः ।
464.	Oṃ Hariṇyai Namaḥ |	ॐ हरिण्यै नमः ।
465.	Oṃ Hariṇīdṛṣṭyai Rhariṇyai Namaḥ	ॐ हरिणीदृष्ट्यै हरिण्यै नमः ।
466.	Oṃ Māṃsabhakṣaṇāyai Namaḥ |	ॐ मांसभक्षणायै नमः ।
467.	Oṃ Hariṇākṣyai Namaḥ |	ॐ हरिणाक्ष्यै नमः ।
468.	Oṃ Hariṇapāyai Namaḥ |	ॐ हरिणपायै नमः ।

469.	Oṃ Hariṇīgaṇaharṣadāyai Namaḥ ।	ॐ हरिणीगणहर्षदायै नमः ।
470.	Oṃ Hariṇīgaṇasaṃhantryai Namaḥ	ॐ हरिणीगणसंहन्त्र्यै नमः ।
471.	Oṃ Hariṇīpariposikāyai Namaḥ ।	ॐ हरिणीपरिपोषिकायै नमः
472.	Oṃ Hariṇīmṛgayāsaktāyai Namaḥ ।	ॐ हरिणीमृगयासक्तायै नमः
473.	Oṃ Hariṇīmānapurassarāyai Namaḥ ।	ॐ हरिणीमानपुरस्सरायै नमः ।
474.	Oṃ Dīnāyai Namaḥ ।	ॐ दीनायै नमः ।
475.	Oṃ Dīnākṛtyai Namaḥ ।	ॐ दीनाकृत्यै नमः ।
476.	Oṃ Dūnāyai Namaḥ ।	ॐ दूनायै नमः ।
477.	Oṃ Drāviṇyai Namaḥ ।	ॐ द्राविण्यै नमः ।
478.	Oṃ Draviṇapradāyai Namaḥ ।	ॐ द्रविणप्रदायै नमः ।
479.	Oṃ Draviṇācalasaṃvāsāyai Namaḥ	ॐ द्रविणाचलसंवासायै नमः
480.	Oṃ Dravitāyai Namaḥ ।	ॐ द्रविताये नमः ।
481.	Oṃ Dravyasaṃyutāyai Namaḥ ।	ॐ द्रव्यसंयुतायै नमः
482.	Oṃ Dīrghāyai Namaḥ ।	ॐ दीर्घायै नमः ।
483.	Oṃ Dīrghapadāyai Namaḥ ।	ॐ दीर्घपदायै नमः ।
484.	Oṃ Dṛśyāyai Namaḥ ।	ॐ दृश्यायै नमः ।
485.	Oṃ Darśanīyāyai Namaḥ ।	ॐ दर्शनीयायै नमः ।
486.	Oṃ Dṛḍhākṛtyai Namaḥ ।	ॐ दृढाकृत्यै नमः ।
487.	Oṃ Dṛḍhāyai Namaḥ ।	ॐ दृढायै नमः ।
488.	Oṃ Dviṣṭamatyai Namaḥ ।	ॐ द्विष्टमत्यै नमः ।
489.	Oṃ Duṣṭāyai Namaḥ ।	ॐ दुष्टायै नमः ।
490.	Oṃ Dveṣiṇyai Namaḥ ।	ॐ द्वेषिण्यै नमः ।
491.	Oṃ Dveṣibhañjinyai Namaḥ ।	ॐ द्वेषिभञ्जिन्यै नमः ।
492.	Oṃ Doṣiṇyai Namaḥ ।	ॐ दोषिण्यै नमः ।
493.	Oṃ Doṣasaṃyuktāyai Namaḥ ।	ॐ दोषसंयुक्तायै नमः
494.	Oṃ Duṣṭaśatruvināśinyai Namaḥ ।	ॐ दुष्टशत्रुविनाशिन्यै नमः ।
495.	Oṃ Devatārtiharāyai Namaḥ ।	ॐ देवतार्तिहरायै नमः ।
496.	Oṃ Duṣṭadaityasaṅghavidāriṇyai Namaḥ ।	ॐ दुष्टदैत्यसङ्घविदारिण्यै नमः ।

497.	Oṃ Duṣṭadānavahantryai Namaḥ		ॐ दुष्टदानवहन्त्र्यै नमः ।
498.	Oṃ Duṣṭadaityaniṣūdinyai Namaḥ		ॐ दुष्टदैत्यनिषूदिन्यै नमः ।
499.	Oṃ Devatāprāṇadāyai Namaḥ		ॐ देवताप्राणदायै नमः ।
500.	Oṃ Devyai Namaḥ		ॐ देव्यै नमः ।
501.	Oṃ Devadurgatināśinyai Namaḥ		ॐ देवदुर्गतिनाशिन्यै नमः ।
502.	Oṃ Naṭanāyakasaṃsevyāyai Namaḥ		ॐ नटनायकसंसेव्यायै नमः ।
503.	Oṃ Nartakyai Namaḥ		ॐ नर्तक्यै नमः ।
504.	Oṃ Nartakapriyāyai Namaḥ		ॐ नर्तकप्रियायै नमः ।
505.	Oṃ Nāṭyavidyāyai Namaḥ		ॐ नाट्यविद्यायै नमः ।
506.	Oṃ Nāṭyakartryai Namaḥ		ॐ नाट्यकर्त्र्यै नमः ।
507.	Oṃ Nādinyai Namaḥ		ॐ नादिन्यै नमः ।
508.	Oṃ Nādakāriṇyai Namaḥ		ॐ नादकारिण्यै नमः ।
509.	Oṃ Navīnanūtanāyai Namaḥ		ॐ नवीननूतनायै नमः ।
510.	Oṃ Navyāyai Namaḥ		ॐ नव्यायै नमः ।
511.	Oṃ Navīnavastradhāriṇyai Namaḥ	ॐ नवीनवस्त्रधारिण्यै नमः ।
512.	Oṃ Navyabhūṣāyai Namaḥ		ॐ नव्यभूषायै नमः ।
513.	Oṃ Navyamālāyai Namaḥ		ॐ नव्यमालायै नमः ।
514.	Oṃ Navyālaṅkāraśobhitāyai Namaḥ		ॐ नव्यालङ्कारशोभितायै नमः ।
515.	Oṃ Nakāravādinyai Namaḥ		ॐ नकारवादिन्यै नमः ।
516.	Oṃ Namyāyai Namaḥ		ॐ नम्यायै नमः ।
517.	Oṃ Navabhūṣaṇabhūṣitāyai Namaḥ	ॐ नवभूषणभूषितायै नमः ।
518.	Oṃ Nīcamārgāyai Namaḥ		ॐ नीचमार्गायै नमः ।
519.	Oṃ Nīcabhūmyai Namaḥ		ॐ नीचभूम्यै नमः ।
520.	Oṃ Nīcamārgagatyai Gatyai Namaḥ		ॐ नीचमार्गगत्यै गत्यै नमः ।
521.	Oṃ Nāthasevyāyai Namaḥ		ॐ नाथसेव्यायै नमः ।
522.	Oṃ Nāthabhaktāyai Namaḥ		ॐ नाथभक्तायै नमः ।
523.	Oṃ Nāthānandapradāyinyai Namaḥ		ॐ नाथानन्दप्रदायिन्यै नमः ।
524.	Oṃ Namrāyai Namaḥ		ॐ नम्रायै नमः ।

525.	Oṃ Namragatyai Namaḥ		ॐ नम्रगत्यै नमः ।
526.	Oṃ Netryai Namaḥ		ॐ नेत्र्यै नमः ।
527.	Oṃ Nidānavākyavādinyai Namaḥ		ॐ निदानवाक्यवादिन्यै नमः
528.	Oṃ Nārīmadhyasthitāyai Namaḥ		ॐ नारीमध्यस्थितायै नमः ।
529.	Oṃ Nāryai Namaḥ		ॐ नार्यै नमः ।
530.	Oṃ Nārīmadhyagatāyai Namaḥ		ॐ नारीमध्यगतायै नमः ।
531.	Oṃ Anaghāyai Namaḥ		ॐ अनघायै नमः ।
532.	Oṃ Nārīprītyai Namaḥ		ॐ नारीप्रीत्यै नमः ।
533.	Oṃ Narārādhyāyai Namaḥ		ॐ नराराध्यायै नमः ।
534.	Oṃ Naranāmaprakāśinyai Namaḥ		ॐ नरनामप्रकाशिन्यै नमः ।
535.	Oṃ Ratyai Namaḥ		ॐ रत्यै नमः ।
536.	Oṃ Ratipriyāyai Namaḥ		ॐ रतिप्रियायै नमः ।
537.	Oṃ Ramyāyai Namaḥ		ॐ रम्यायै नमः ।
538.	Oṃ Ratipremāyai Namaḥ		ॐ रतिप्रेमायै नमः ।
539.	Oṃ Ratipradāyai Namaḥ		ॐ रतिप्रदायै नमः ।
540.	Oṃ Ratisthānasthitārādhyāyai Namaḥ		ॐ रतिस्थानस्थितताराध्याये नमः ।
541.	Oṃ Ratiharṣapradāyinyai Namaḥ		ॐ रतिहर्षप्रदायिन्यै नमः ।
542.	Oṃ Ratirūpāyai Namaḥ		ॐ रतिरूपायै नमः ।
543.	Oṃ Ratidhyānāyai Namaḥ		ॐ रतिध्यानायै नमः ।
544.	Oṃ Ratirītisudhāriṇyai Namaḥ		ॐ रतिरीतिसुधारिण्यै नमः ।
545.	Oṃ Ratirāsamahollāsāyai Namaḥ		ॐ रतिरासमहोल्लासायै नमः ।
546.	Oṃ Ratirāsavihāriṇyai Namaḥ		ॐ रतिरासविहारिण्यै नमः ।
547.	Oṃ Ratikāntastutāyai Namaḥ		ॐ रतिकान्तस्तुतायै नमः ।
548.	Oṃ Rāśyai Namaḥ		ॐ राश्यै नमः ।
549.	Oṃ Rāśirakṣaṇakāriṇyai Namaḥ		ॐ राशिरक्षणकारिण्यै नमः ।
550.	Oṃ Arūpāyai Namaḥ		ॐ अरूपायै नमः ।
551.	Oṃ Śuddharūpāyai Namaḥ		ॐ शुद्धरूपायै नमः ।
552.	Oṃ Surūpāyai Namaḥ		ॐ सुरूपायै नमः ।

553.	Oṃ Rūpagarvitāyai Namaḥ |	ॐ रूपगर्वितायै नमः ।
554.	Oṃ Rūpayauvanasampannāyai Namaḥ |	ॐ रूपयौवनसम्पन्नायै नमः ।
555.	Oṃ Rūparāśyai Namaḥ |	ॐ रूपराश्यै नमः ।
556.	Oṃ Ramāvatyai Namaḥ |	ॐ रमावत्यै नमः ।
557.	Oṃ Rodhinyai Namaḥ |	ॐ रोधिन्यै नमः ।
558.	Oṃ Roṣiṇyai Namaḥ |	ॐ रोषिण्यै नमः ।
559.	Oṃ Ruṣṭāyai Namaḥ |	ॐ रुष्टायै नमः ।
560.	Oṃ Roṣiruddhāyai Namaḥ |	ॐ रोषिरुद्धायै नमः ।
561.	Oṃ Rasapradāyai Namaḥ |	ॐ रसप्रदायै नमः ।
562.	Oṃ Mādinyai Namaḥ |	ॐ मादिन्यै नमः ।
563.	Oṃ Madanaprītāyai Namaḥ |	ॐ मदनप्रीतायै नमः ।
564.	Oṃ Madhumattāyai Namaḥ |	ॐ मधुमत्तायै नमः ।
565.	Oṃ Madhupradāyai Namaḥ |	ॐ मधुप्रदायै नमः ।
566.	Oṃ Madyapāyai Namaḥ |	ॐ मद्यपायै नमः ।
567.	Oṃ Madyapadhyeyāyai Namaḥ |	ॐ मद्यपध्येयायै नमः ।
568.	Oṃ Madyapaprāṇarakṣiṇyai Namaḥ |	ॐ मद्यपप्राणरक्षिण्यै नमः ।
569.	Oṃ Madyapānandasandātryai Namaḥ |	ॐ मद्यपानन्दसन्दात्र्यै नमः ।
570.	Oṃ Madyapaprematoṣitāyai Namaḥ |	ॐ मद्यपप्रेमतोषितायै नमः ।
571.	Oṃ Madyapānaratāyai Namaḥ |	ॐ मद्यपानरतायै नमः ।
572.	Oṃ Mattāyai Namaḥ |	ॐ मत्तायै नमः ।
573.	Oṃ Madyapānavihāriṇyai Namaḥ |	ॐ मद्यपानविहारिण्यै नमः ।
574.	Oṃ Madirāyai Namaḥ |	ॐ मदिरायै नमः ।
575.	Oṃ Madirāsaktāyai Namaḥ |	ॐ मदिरासक्तायै नमः ।
576.	Oṃ Madirāpānaharṣiṇyai Namaḥ |	ॐ मदिरापानहर्षिण्यै नमः ।
577.	Oṃ Madirāpānasantuṣṭāyai Namaḥ	ॐ मदिरापानसन्तुष्टायै नमः ।
578.	Oṃ Madirāpānamohinyai Namaḥ |	ॐ मदिरापानमोहिन्यै नमः ।
579.	Oṃ Madirāmānasāyai Namaḥ |	ॐ मदिरामानसायै नमः ।
580.	Oṃ Mugdhāyai Namaḥ |	ॐ मुग्धायै नमः ।

581.	Oṃ Mādhvīpāyai Namaḥ |	ॐ माध्वीपायै नमः ।
582.	Oṃ Madirāpradāyai Namaḥ |	ॐ मदिराप्रदायै नमः ।
583.	Oṃ Mādhvīdānasadānandāyai Namaḥ |	ॐ माध्वीदानसदानन्दायै नमः ।
584.	Oṃ Mādhvīpānaratāyai Namaḥ |	ॐ माध्वीपानरतायै नमः ।
585.	Oṃ Madāyai Namaḥ |	ॐ मदायै नमः ।
586.	Oṃ Modinyai Namaḥ |	ॐ मोदिन्यै नमः ।
587.	Oṃ Modasandātryai Namaḥ |	ॐ मोदसन्दात्र्यै नमः ।
588.	Oṃ Muditāyai Namaḥ |	ॐ मुदितायै नमः ।
589.	Oṃ Modamānasāyai Namaḥ |	ॐ मोदमानसायै नमः ।
590.	Oṃ Modakartryai Namaḥ |	ॐ मोदकर्त्र्यै नमः ।
591.	Oṃ Modadātryai Namaḥ |	ॐ मोददात्र्यै नमः ।
592.	Oṃ Modamaṅgalakāriṇyai Namaḥ	ॐ मोदमङ्गलकारिण्यै नमः ।
593.	Oṃ Modakādānasantuṣṭāyai Namaḥ |	ॐ मोदकादानसन्तुष्टायै नमः ।
594.	Oṃ Modakagrahaṇakṣamāyai Namaḥ |	ॐ मोदकग्रहणक्षमायै नमः ।
595.	Oṃ Modakālabdhisaṅkruddhāyai Namaḥ |	ॐ मोदकालब्धिसङ्क्रुद्धायै नमः ।
596.	Oṃ Modakaprāptitoṣiṇyai Namaḥ |	ॐ मोदकप्राप्तितोषिण्यै नमः ।
597.	Oṃ Māṃsādāyai Namaḥ |	ॐ मांसादायै नमः ।
598.	Oṃ Māṃsasambhakṣāyai Namaḥ |	ॐ मांससम्भक्षायै नमः ।
599.	Oṃ Māṃsabhakṣaṇaharṣiṇyai Namaḥ |	ॐ मांसभक्षणहर्षिण्यै नमः ।
600.	Oṃ Māṃsapākaparapremāyai Namaḥ |	ॐ मांसपाकपरप्रेमायै नमः ।
601.	Oṃ Māṃsapākālayasthitāyai Namaḥ |	ॐ मांसपाकालयस्थितायै नमः ।
602.	Oṃ Matsyamāṃsakṛtāsvādāyai Namaḥ |	ॐ मत्स्यमांसकृतास्वादायै नमः ।
603.	Oṃ Makārapañcakānvitāyai Namaḥ |	ॐ मकारपञ्चकान्वितायै नमः ।

604.	Oṃ Mudrāyai Namaḥ		ॐ मुद्रायै नमः ।
605.	Oṃ Mudrānvitāyai Namaḥ		ॐ मुद्रान्वितायै नमः ।
606.	Oṃ Mātre Namaḥ		ॐ मात्रे नमः ।
607.	Oṃ Mahāmohāyai Namaḥ		ॐ महामोहायै नमः ।
608.	Oṃ Manasvinyai Namaḥ		ॐ मनस्विन्यै नमः ।
609.	Oṃ Mudrikāyai Namaḥ		ॐ मुद्रिकायै नमः ।
610.	Oṃ Mudrikāyuktāyai Namaḥ		ॐ मुद्रिकायुक्तायै नमः ।
611.	Oṃ Mudrikākṛtalakṣaṇāyai Namaḥ	ॐ मुद्रिकाकृतलक्षणायै नमः
612.	Oṃ Mudrikālaṅkṛtāyai Namaḥ		ॐ मुद्रिकालङ्कृतायै नमः ।
613.	Oṃ Mādryai Namaḥ		ॐ माद्र्यै नमः ।
614.	Oṃ Mandarācalavāsinyai Namaḥ		ॐ मन्दराचलवासिन्यै नमः ।
615.	Oṃ Mandarācalasaṃsevyāyai Namaḥ		ॐ मन्दराचलसंसेव्यायै नमः ।
616.	Oṃ Mandarācalavāsinyai Namaḥ		ॐ मन्दराचलवासिन्यै नमः ।
617.	Oṃ Mandaradhyeyapādābjāyai Namaḥ		ॐ मन्दरध्येयपादाब्जायै नमः ।
618.	Oṃ Mandarāraṇyavāsinyai Namaḥ	ॐ मन्दरारण्यवासिन्यै नमः ।
619.	Oṃ Mandurāvāsinyai Namaḥ		ॐ मन्दुरावासिन्यै नमः ।
620.	Oṃ Mandāyai Namaḥ		ॐ मन्दायै नमः ।
621.	Oṃ Māriṇyai Namaḥ		ॐ मारिण्यै नमः ।
622.	Oṃ Mārikāmitāyai Namaḥ		ॐ मारिकामितायै नमः ।
623.	Oṃ Mahāmāryai Namaḥ		ॐ महामार्यै नमः ।
624.	Oṃ Mahāmārīśamanyai Namaḥ		ॐ महामारीशमन्यै नमः ।
625.	Oṃ Śavasaṃsthitāyai Namaḥ		ॐ शवसंस्थितायै नमः ।
626.	Oṃ Śavamāṃsakṛtāhārāyai Namaḥ	ॐ शवमांसकृताहारायै नमः ।
627.	Oṃ Śmaśānālayavāsinyai Namaḥ		ॐ श्मशानालयवासिन्यै नमः
628.	Oṃ Śmaśānasiddhisaṃhṛṣṭāyai Namaḥ		ॐ श्मशानसिद्धिसंहृष्टायै नमः ।
629.	Oṃ Śmaśānabhavanasthitāyai Namaḥ		ॐ श्मशानभवनस्थितायै नमः ।

630.	Oṃ Śmaśānaśayanāgārāyai Namaḥ	ॐ श्मशानशयनागाराये नमः
631.	Oṃ Śmaśānabhasmalepitāyai Namaḥ		ॐ श्मशानभस्मलेपिताये नमः।
632.	Oṃ Śmaśānabhasmabhīmāṅgyai Namaḥ		ॐ श्मशानभस्मभीमाङ्ग्ये नमः।
633.	Oṃ Śmaśānāvāsakāriṇyai Namaḥ		ॐ श्मशानावासकारिण्ये नमः
634.	Oṃ Śāminyai Namaḥ		ॐ शामिन्ये नमः।
635.	Oṃ Śamanārādhyāyai Namaḥ		ॐ शमनाराध्याये नमः।
636.	Oṃ Śamanastutivanditāyai Namaḥ	ॐ शमनस्तुतिवन्दिताये नमः
637.	Oṃ Śamanācārasantuṣṭāyai Namaḥ		ॐ शमनाचारसन्तुष्टाये नमः।
638.	Oṃ Śamanāgāravāsinyai Namaḥ		ॐ शमनागारवासिन्ये नमः।
639.	Oṃ Śamanasvāminyai Namaḥ		ॐ शमनस्वामिन्ये नमः।
640.	Oṃ Śāntyai Namaḥ		ॐ शान्त्ये नमः।
641.	Oṃ Śāntasajjanapūjitāyai Namaḥ		ॐ शान्तसज्जनपूजिताये नमः
642.	Oṃ Śāntapūjāparāyai Namaḥ		ॐ शान्तपूजापराये नमः।
643.	Oṃ Śāntāyai Namaḥ		ॐ शान्ताये नमः।
644.	Oṃ Śāntāgāraprabhojinyai Namaḥ	ॐ शान्तागारप्रभोजिन्ये नमः
645.	Oṃ Śāntapūjyāyai Namaḥ		ॐ शान्तपूज्याये नमः।
646.	Oṃ Śāntavandyāyai Namaḥ		ॐ शान्तवन्द्याये नमः।
647.	Oṃ Śāntagrahasudhāriṇyai Namaḥ	ॐ शान्तग्रहसुधारिण्ये नमः।
648.	Oṃ Śāntarūpāyai Namaḥ		ॐ शान्तरूपाये नमः।
649.	Oṃ Śāntiyuktāyai Namaḥ		ॐ शान्तियुक्ताये नमः।
650.	Oṃ Śāntacandraprabhāmalāyai Namaḥ		ॐ शान्तचन्द्रप्रभामलाये नमः।
651.	Oṃ Amalāyai Namaḥ		ॐ अमलाये नमः।
652.	Oṃ Vimalāyai Namaḥ		ॐ विमलाये नमः।
653.	Oṃ Mlānāyai Namaḥ		ॐ म्लानाये नमः।
654.	Oṃ Mālatīkuñjavāsinyai Namaḥ		ॐ मालतीकुञ्जवासिन्ये नमः
655.	Oṃ Mālatīpuṣpasamprītāyai Namaḥ		ॐ मालतीपुष्पसम्प्रीताये नमः।

656.	Oṃ Mālatīpuṣpapūjitāyai Namaḥ		ॐ मालतीपुष्पपूजितायै नमः
657.	Oṃ Mahogrāyai Namaḥ		ॐ महोग्रायै नमः	
658.	Oṃ Mahatyai Namaḥ		ॐ महत्यै नमः	
659.	Oṃ Madhyāyai Namaḥ		ॐ मध्यायै नमः	
660.	Oṃ Madhyadeśanivāsinyai Namaḥ	ॐ मध्यदेशनिवासिन्यै नमः	
661.	Oṃ Madhyamadhvanisamprītāyai Namaḥ		ॐ मध्यमध्वनिसम्प्रीतायै नमः	
662.	Oṃ Madhyamadhvanikāriṇyai Namaḥ		ॐ मध्यमध्वनिकारिण्यै नमः	
663.	Oṃ Madhyamāyai Namaḥ		ॐ मध्यमायै नमः	
664.	Oṃ Madhyamaprītyai Namaḥ		ॐ मध्यमप्रीत्यै नमः	
665.	Oṃ Madhyamapremapūritāyai Namaḥ		ॐ मध्यमप्रेमपूरितायै नमः	
666.	Oṃ Madhyāṅgacitravasanāyai Namaḥ		ॐ मध्याङ्गचित्रवसनायै नमः	
667.	Oṃ Madhyakhinnāyai Namaḥ		ॐ मध्यखिन्नायै नमः	
668.	Oṃ Mahoddhatāyai Namaḥ		ॐ महोद्धतायै नमः	
669.	Oṃ Mahendrakṛtasampūjāyai Namaḥ		ॐ महेन्द्रकृतसम्पूजायै नमः	
670.	Oṃ Mahendraparivanditāyai Namaḥ		ॐ महेन्द्रपरिवन्दितायै नमः	
671.	Oṃ Mahendrajālasaṃyuktāyai Namaḥ		ॐ महेन्द्रजालसंयुक्तायै नमः	
672.	Oṃ Mahendrajālakāriṇyai Namaḥ		ॐ महेन्द्रजालकारिण्यै नमः	
673.	Oṃ Mahendramānitā'mānāyai Namaḥ		ॐ महेन्द्रमानिताऽमानायै नमः	
674.	Oṃ Māninīgaṇamadhyagāyai Namaḥ		ॐ मानिनीगणमध्यगायै नमः	
675.	Oṃ Māninīmānasamprītāyai Namaḥ		ॐ मानिनीमानसम्प्रीतायै नमः	
676.	Oṃ Mānavidhvaṃsakāriṇyai Namaḥ		ॐ मानविध्वंसकारिण्यै नमः	
677.	Oṃ Māninyākarṣiṇyai Namaḥ		ॐ मानिन्याकर्षिण्यै नमः	

678.	Oṃ Muktyai Namaḥ |	ॐ मुक्त्यै नमः ।
679.	Oṃ Muktidātryai Namaḥ |	ॐ मुक्तिदात्र्यै नमः ।
680.	Oṃ Sumuktidāyai Namaḥ |	ॐ सुमुक्तिदायै नमः ।
681.	Oṃ Muktidveṣakaryai Namaḥ |	ॐ मुक्तिद्वेषकर्यै नमः ।
682.	Oṃ Mūlyakāriṇyai Namaḥ |	ॐ मूल्यकारिण्यै नमः ।
683.	Oṃ Mūlyahāriṇyai Namaḥ |	ॐ मूल्यहारिण्यै नमः ।
684.	Oṃ Nirmūlāyai Namaḥ |	ॐ निर्मूलायै नमः ।
685.	Oṃ Mūlasaṃyuktāyai Namaḥ |	ॐ मूलसंयुक्तायै नमः
686.	Oṃ Mūlinyai Namaḥ |	ॐ मूलिन्यै नमः ।
687.	Oṃ Mūlamantriṇyai Namaḥ |	ॐ मूलमन्त्रिण्यै नमः ।
688.	Oṃ Mūlamantrakṛtārhādyāyai Namaḥ |	ॐ मूलमन्त्रकृताहाद्यायै नमः ।
689.	Oṃ Mūlamantrārghyaharṣiṇyai Namaḥ |	ॐ मूलमन्त्राघ्र्यहर्षिण्यै नमः ।
690.	Oṃ Mūlamantrapratiṣṭhātryai Namaḥ |	ॐ मूलमन्त्रप्रतिष्ठात्र्यै नमः ।
691.	Oṃ Mūlamantrapraharṣiṇyai Namaḥ |	ॐ मूलमन्त्रप्रहर्षिण्यै नमः ।
692.	Oṃ Mūlamantraprasannāsyāyai Namaḥ |	ॐ मूलमन्त्रप्रसन्नास्यायै नमः ।
693.	Oṃ Mūlamantraprapūjitāyai Namaḥ |	ॐ मूलमन्त्रप्रपूजितायै नमः ।
694.	Oṃ Mūlamantrapraṇetryai Namaḥ	ॐ मूलमन्त्रप्रणेत्र्यै नमः ।
695.	Oṃ Mūlamantrakṛtārcanāyai Namaḥ |	ॐ मूलमन्त्रकृतार्चनायै नमः ।
696.	Oṃ Mūlamantraprahṛṣṭātmane Namaḥ |	ॐ मूलमन्त्रप्रहृष्टात्मने नमः ।
697.	Oṃ Mūlavidyāyai Namaḥ |	ॐ मूलविद्यायै नमः ।
698.	Oṃ Malāpahāyai Namaḥ |	ॐ मलापहायै नमः ।
699.	Oṃ Vidyāyai Namaḥ |	ॐ विद्यायै नमः ।
700.	Oṃ Avidyāyai Namaḥ |	ॐ अविद्यायै नमः ।
701.	Oṃ Vaṭasthāyai Namaḥ |	ॐ वटस्थायै नमः ।
702.	Oṃ Vaṭavṛkṣanivāsinyai Namaḥ |	ॐ वटवृक्षनिवासिन्यै नमः ।

703.	Oṃ Vaṭavṛkṣakṛtasthānāyai Namaḥ	ॐ वटवृक्षकृतस्थानायै नमः।
704.	Oṃ Vaṭapūjāparāyaṇāyai Namaḥ	ॐ वटपूजापरायणायै नमः।
705.	Oṃ Vaṭapūjāpariprītāyai Namaḥ	ॐ वटपूजापरिप्रीतायै नमः।
706.	Oṃ Vaṭadarśanalālasāyai Namaḥ	ॐ वटदर्शनलालसायै नमः।
707.	Oṃ Vaṭapūjākṛtāhlādāyai Namaḥ	ॐ वटपूजाकृताह्लादायै नमः।
708.	Oṃ Vaṭapūjāvivardhinyai Namaḥ	ॐ वटपूजाविवर्धिन्यै नमः।
709.	Oṃ Vaśinyai Namaḥ	ॐ वशिन्यै नमः।
710.	Oṃ Vivaśārādhyāyai Namaḥ	ॐ विवशाराध्यायै नमः।
711.	Oṃ Vaśīkaraṇamantriṇyai Namaḥ	ॐ वशीकरणमन्त्रिण्यै नमः।
712.	Oṃ Vaśīkaraṇasamprītāyai Namaḥ	ॐ वशीकरणसम्प्रीतायै नमः
713.	Oṃ Vaśīkārakasiddhidāyai Namaḥ	ॐ वशीकारकसिद्धिदायै नमः
714.	Oṃ Vaṭukāyai Namaḥ	ॐ वटुकायै नमः।
715.	Oṃ Vaṭukārādhyāyai Namaḥ	ॐ वटुकाराध्यायै नमः।
716.	Oṃ Vaṭukāhāradāyinyai Namaḥ	ॐ वटुकाहारदायिन्यै नमः।
717.	Oṃ Vaṭukārcāparāyai Namaḥ	ॐ वटुकार्चापरायै नमः।
718.	Oṃ Pūjyāyai Namaḥ	ॐ पूज्यायै नमः।
719.	Oṃ Vaṭukārcāvivardhinyai Namaḥ	ॐ वटुकार्चाविवर्धिन्यै नमः।
720.	Oṃ Vaṭukānandakartryai Namaḥ	ॐ वटुकानन्दकर्त्र्यै नमः।
721.	Oṃ Vaṭukaprāṇarakṣiṇyai Namaḥ	ॐ वटुकप्राणरक्षिण्यै नमः।
722.	Oṃ Vaṭukejyāpradāyai Namaḥ	ॐ वटुकेज्याप्रदायै नमः।
723.	Oṃ Apārāyai Namaḥ	ॐ अपारायै नमः।
724.	Oṃ Pāriṇyai Namaḥ	ॐ पारिण्यै नमः।
725.	Oṃ Pārvatīpriyāyai Namaḥ	ॐ पार्वतीप्रियायै नमः।
726.	Oṃ Parvatāgrakṛtāvāsāyai Namaḥ	ॐ पर्वताग्रकृतावासायै नमः।
727.	Oṃ Parvatendraprapūjitāyai Namaḥ	ॐ पर्वतेन्द्रप्रपूजितायै नमः।
728.	Oṃ Pārvatīpatipūjyāyai Namaḥ	ॐ पार्वतीपतिपूज्यायै नमः।
729.	Oṃ Pārvatīpatiharṣadāyai Namaḥ	ॐ पार्वतीपतिहर्षदायै नमः।
730.	Oṃ Pārvatīpatibuddhisthāyai Namaḥ	ॐ पार्वतीपतिबुद्धिस्थाये नमः।
731.	Oṃ Pārvatīpatimohinyai Namaḥ	ॐ पार्वतीपतिमोहिन्यै नमः।

732.	Oṃ Pārvatīyadvijārādhyāyai Namaḥ		ॐ पार्वतीयद्विजाराध्याये नमः ।
733.	Oṃ Parvatasthāyai Namaḥ		ॐ पर्वतस्थाये नमः ।
734.	Oṃ Pratāriṇyai Namaḥ		ॐ प्रतारिण्यै नमः ।
735.	Oṃ Padmalāyai Namaḥ		ॐ पद्मलाये नमः ।
736.	Oṃ Padminyai Namaḥ		ॐ पद्मिन्यै नमः ।
737.	Oṃ Padmāyai Namaḥ		ॐ पद्माये नमः ।
738.	Oṃ Padmamālāvibhūṣitāyai Namaḥ	ॐ पद्ममालाविभूषिताये नमः
739.	Oṃ Padmajeḍyapadāyai Namaḥ		ॐ पद्मजेड्यपदाये नमः ।
740.	Oṃ Padmamālālaṅkṛtamastakāyai Namaḥ		ॐ पद्ममालालङ्कृत मस्तकाये नमः ।
741.	Oṃ Padmārcitapadadvandvāyai Namaḥ		ॐ पद्मार्चितपदद्वन्द्वाये नमः ।
742.	Oṃ Padmahastapayodhijāyai Namaḥ		ॐ पद्महस्तपयोधिजाये नमः ।
743.	Oṃ Payodhipāragantryai Namaḥ		ॐ पयोधिपारगन्त्रये नमः ।
744.	Oṃ Pāthodhiparikīrtitāyai Namaḥ		ॐ पाथोधिपरिकीर्तिताये नमः
745.	Oṃ Pāthodhipāragāyai Namaḥ		ॐ पाथोधिपारगाये नमः ।
746.	Oṃ Pūtāyai Namaḥ		ॐ पूताये नमः ।
747.	Oṃ Palvalāmbupratarpitāyai Namaḥ		ॐ पल्वलाम्बुप्रतर्पिताये नमः ।
748.	Oṃ Palvalāntaḥpayomagnāyai Namaḥ		ॐ पल्वलान्तःपयोमग्नाये नमः ।
749.	Oṃ Pavamānagatyai Namaḥ		ॐ पवमानगत्ये नमः ।
750.	Oṃ Payaḥpānāyai Namaḥ		ॐ पयःपानाये नमः ।
751.	Oṃ Payodātryai Namaḥ		ॐ पयोदात्रये नमः ।
752.	Oṃ Pānīyaparikāṅkṣiṇyai Namaḥ		ॐ पानीयपरिकाङ्क्षिण्ये नमः
753.	Oṃ Payojamālābharaṇāyai Namaḥ	ॐ पयोजमालाभरणाये नमः ।
754.	Oṃ Muṇḍamālāvibhūṣaṇāyai Namaḥ		ॐ मुण्डमालाविभूषणाये नमः ।
755.	Oṃ Muṇḍinyai Namaḥ		ॐ मुण्डिन्ये नमः ।

756.	Oṃ Muṇḍahantryai Namaḥ		ॐ मुण्डहन्त्र्यै नमः ।
757.	Oṃ Muṇḍitāyai Namaḥ		ॐ मुण्डिताये नमः ।
758.	Oṃ Muṇḍaśobhitāyai Namaḥ		ॐ मुण्डशोभिताये नमः ।
759.	Oṃ Maṇibhūṣāyai Namaḥ		ॐ मणिभूषाये नमः ।
760.	Oṃ Maṇigrīvāyai Namaḥ		ॐ मणिग्रीवाये नमः ।
761.	Oṃ Maṇimālāvirājitāyai Namaḥ		ॐ मणिमालाविराजिताये नमः ।
762.	Oṃ Mahāmohāyai Namaḥ		ॐ महामोहाये नमः ।
763.	Oṃ Mahāmarṣāyai Namaḥ		ॐ महामर्षाये नमः ।
764.	Oṃ Mahāmāyāyai Namaḥ		ॐ महामायाये नमः ।
765.	Oṃ Mahāhavāyai Namaḥ		ॐ महाहवाये नमः ।
766.	Oṃ Mānavyai Namaḥ		ॐ मानव्ये नमः ।
767.	Oṃ Mānavīpūjyāyai Namaḥ		ॐ मानवीपूज्याये नमः ।
768.	Oṃ Manuvaṃśavivardhinyai Namaḥ		ॐ मनुवंशविवर्धिन्ये नमः
769.	Oṃ Maṭhinyai Namaḥ		ॐ मठिन्ये नमः ।
770.	Oṃ Maṭhasaṃhantryai Namaḥ		ॐ मठसंहन्त्र्यै नमः ।
771.	Oṃ Maṭhasampattihāriṇyai Namaḥ	ॐ मठसम्पत्तिहारिण्ये नमः ।
772.	Oṃ Mahākrodhavatyai Namaḥ		ॐ महाक्रोधवत्ये नमः ।
773.	Oṃ Mūḍhāyai Namaḥ		ॐ मूढाये नमः ।
774.	Oṃ Mūḍhaśatruvināśinyai Namaḥ		ॐ मूढशत्रुविनाशिन्ये नमः
775.	Oṃ Pāṭhīnabhojinyai Namaḥ		ॐ पाठीनभोजिन्ये नमः ।
776.	Oṃ Pūrṇāyai Namaḥ		ॐ पूर्णाये नमः ।
777.	Oṃ Pūrṇahāravihāriṇyai Namaḥ		ॐ पूर्णहारविहारिण्ये नमः ।
778.	Oṃ Pralayānalatulyābhāyai Namaḥ	ॐ प्रलयानलतुल्याभाये नमः
779.	Oṃ Pralayānalarūpiṇyai Namaḥ		ॐ प्रलयानलरूपिण्ये नमः ।
780.	Oṃ Pralayārṇavasammagnāyai Namaḥ		ॐ प्रलयार्णवसम्मग्नाये नमः ।
781.	Oṃ Pralayābdhivihāriṇyai Namaḥ		ॐ प्रलयाब्धिविहारिण्ये नमः
782.	Oṃ Mahāpralayasambhūtāyai Namaḥ		ॐ महाप्रलयसम्भूताये नमः ।

783.	Oṃ Mahāpralayakāriṇyai Namaḥ |	ॐ महाप्रलयकारिण्यै नमः ।
784.	Oṃ Mahāpralayasamprītāyai Namaḥ |	ॐ महाप्रलयसम्प्रीतायै नमः ।
785.	Oṃ Mahāpralayasādhinyai Namaḥ	ॐ महाप्रलयसाधिन्यै नमः ।
786.	Oṃ Mahāmahāpralayejyāyai Namaḥ |	ॐ महामहाप्रलयेज्यायै नमः ।
787.	Oṃ Mahāpralayamodi Nyainamaḥ	ॐ महाप्रलयमोदि न्यैनमः ।
788.	Oṃ Chedinyai Namaḥ |	ॐ छेदिन्यै नमः ।
789.	Oṃ Chinnamuṇḍāyai Namaḥ |	ॐ छिन्नमुण्डायै नमः ।
790.	Oṃ Ugrāyai Namaḥ |	ॐ उग्रायै नमः ।
791.	Oṃ Chinnāyai Namaḥ |	ॐ छिन्नायै नमः ।
792.	Oṃ Chinnaruhārthinyai Namaḥ |	ॐ छिन्नरुहार्थिन्यै नमः ।
793.	Oṃ Śatrusañchedi Nyai Namaḥ |	ॐ शत्रुसञ्छेदि न्यै नमः ।
794.	Oṃ Channāyai Namaḥ |	ॐ छन्नायै नमः ।
795.	Oṃ Kṣodinyai Namaḥ |	ॐ क्षोदिन्यै नमः ।
796.	Oṃ Kṣodakāriṇyai Namaḥ |	ॐ क्षोदकारिण्यै नमः ।
797.	Oṃ Lakṣiṇyai Namaḥ |	ॐ लक्षिण्यै नमः ।
798.	Oṃ Lakṣasampūjyāyai Namaḥ |	ॐ लक्षसम्पूज्यायै नमः ।
799.	Oṃ Lakṣitāyai Namaḥ |	ॐ लक्षितायै नमः ।
800.	Oṃ Lakṣaṇānvitāyai Namaḥ |	ॐ लक्षणान्वितायै नमः ।
801.	Oṃ Lakṣaśastrasamāyuktāyai Namaḥ |	ॐ लक्षशस्त्रसमायुक्तायै नमः ।
802.	Oṃ Lakṣabāṇapramocinyai Namaḥ	ॐ लक्षबाणप्रमोचिन्यै नमः ।
803.	Oṃ Lakṣapūjāparāyai Namaḥ |	ॐ लक्षपूजापरायै नमः ।
804.	Oṃ Alakṣyāyai Namaḥ |	ॐ अलक्ष्यायै नमः ।
805.	Oṃ Lakṣakodaṇḍakhaṇḍinyai Namaḥ |	ॐ लक्षकोदण्डखण्डिन्यै नमः ।
806.	Oṃ Lakṣakodaṇḍasaṃyuktāyai Namaḥ |	ॐ लक्षकोदण्डसंयुक्तायै नमः ।
807.	Oṃ Lakṣakodaṇḍadhāriṇyai Namaḥ	ॐ लक्षकोदण्डधारिण्यै नमः ।
808.	Oṃ Lakṣalīlālayāyai Namaḥ |	ॐ लक्षलीलालयायै नमः ।

809.	Oṃ Labhyāyai Namaḥ |	ॐ लभ्यायै नमः ।
810.	Oṃ Lākṣāgaranivāsinyai Namaḥ |	ॐ लाक्षागारनिवासिन्यै नमः
811.	Oṃ Lakṣalobhaparāyai Namaḥ |	ॐ लक्षलोभपरायै नमः ।
812.	Oṃ Lolāyai Namaḥ |	ॐ लोलायै नमः ।
813.	Oṃ Lakṣabhaktaprapūjitāyai Namaḥ |	ॐ लक्षभक्तप्रपूजितायै नमः ।
814.	Oṃ Lokinyai Namaḥ |	ॐ लोकिन्यै नमः ।
815.	Oṃ Lokasampūjyāyai Namaḥ |	ॐ लोकसम्पूज्यायै नमः ।
816.	Oṃ Lokarakṣaṇakāriṇyai Namaḥ |	ॐ लोकरक्षणकारिण्यै नमः ।
817.	Oṃ Lokavanditapādābjāyai Namaḥ |	ॐ लोकवन्दितपादाब्जायै नमः ।
818.	Oṃ Lokamohanakāriṇyai Namaḥ |	ॐ लोकमोहनकारिण्यै नमः ।
819.	Oṃ Lalitāyai Namaḥ |	ॐ ललितायै नमः ।
820.	Oṃ Lalitālīnāyai Namaḥ |	ॐ ललितालीनायै नमः ।
821.	Oṃ Lokasaṃhārakāriṇyai Namaḥ |	ॐ लोकसंहारकारिण्यै नमः ।
822.	Oṃ Lokalīlākaryai Namaḥ |	ॐ लोकलीलाकर्यै नमः ।
823.	Oṃ Lokyāyai Namaḥ |	ॐ लोक्यायै नमः ।
824.	Oṃ Lokasambhavakāriṇyai Namaḥ	ॐ लोकसम्भवकारिण्यै नमः
825.	Oṃ Bhūtaśuddhikaryai Namaḥ |	ॐ भूतशुद्धिकर्यै नमः
826.	Oṃ Bhūtarakṣiṇyai Namaḥ |	ॐ भूतरक्षिण्यै नमः ।
827.	Oṃ Bhūtatoṣiṇyai Namaḥ |	ॐ भूततोषिण्यै नमः ।
828.	Oṃ Bhūtavetālasaṃyuktāyai Namaḥ |	ॐ भूतवेतालसंयुक्तायै नमः
829.	Oṃ Bhūtasenāsamāvṛtāyai Namaḥ	ॐ भूतसेनासमावृतायै नमः ।
830.	Oṃ Bhūtapretapiśācādisvāminyai Namaḥ |	ॐ भूतप्रेतपिशाचादि स्वामिन्यै नमः ।
831.	Oṃ Bhūtapūjitāyai Namaḥ |	ॐ भूतपूजितायै नमः ।
832.	Oṃ Ḍākinyai Namaḥ |	ॐ डाकिन्यै नमः ।
833.	Oṃ Śākinyai Namaḥ |	ॐ शाकिन्यै नमः ।
834.	Oṃ Ḍeyāyai Namaḥ |	ॐ डेयायै नमः ।

835.	Oṃ Ḍiṇḍimārāvakāriṇyai Namaḥ		ॐ डिण्डिमारावकारिण्यै नमः
836.	Oṃ Ḍamarūvādyasantuṣṭāyai Namaḥ		ॐ डमरूवाद्यसन्तुष्टायै नमः ।
837.	Oṃ Ḍamarūvādyakāriṇyai Namaḥ		ॐ डमरूवाद्यकारिण्यै नमः ।
838.	Oṃ Huṅkārakāriṇyai Namaḥ		ॐ हुङ्कारकारिण्यै नमः ।
839.	Oṃ Hotryai Namaḥ		ॐ होत्र्यै नमः ।
840.	Oṃ Hāvinyai Namaḥ		ॐ हाविन्यै नमः ।
841.	Oṃ Havanārthinyai Namaḥ		ॐ हवनार्थिन्यै नमः ।
842.	Oṃ Hāsinyai Namaḥ		ॐ हासिन्यै नमः ।
843.	Oṃ Hrāsinyai Namaḥ		ॐ ह्रासिन्यै नमः ।
844.	Oṃ Hāsyaharṣiṇyai Namaḥ		ॐ हास्यहर्षिण्यै नमः ।
845.	Oṃ Haṭhavādinyai Namaḥ		ॐ हठवादिन्यै नमः ।
846.	Oṃ Aṭṭāṭṭahāsinyai Namaḥ		ॐ अट्टाट्टहासिन्यै नमः ।
847.	Oṃ Ṭīkāyai Namaḥ		ॐ टीकायै नमः ।
848.	Oṃ Ṭīkānirmāṇakāriṇyai Namaḥ		ॐ टीकानिर्माणकारिण्यै नमः
849.	Oṃ Ṭaṅkinyai Namaḥ		ॐ टङ्किन्यै नमः ।
850.	Oṃ Ṭaṅkitāyai Namaḥ		ॐ टङ्कितायै नमः ।
851.	Oṃ Ṭaṅkāyai Namaḥ		ॐ टङ्कायै नमः ।
852.	Oṃ Ṭaṅkamātrasuvarṇadāyai Namaḥ		ॐ टङ्कमात्रसुवर्णदायै नमः ।
853.	Oṃ Ṭaṅkāriṇyai Namaḥ		ॐ टङ्कारिण्यै नमः ।
854.	Oṃ Ṭakārāḍhyāyai Namaḥ		ॐ टकाराद्यायै नमः ।
855.	Oṃ Śatrutroṭanakāriṇyai Namaḥ		ॐ शत्रुत्रोटनकारिण्यै नमः ।
856.	Oṃ Truṭitāyai Namaḥ		ॐ त्रुटितायै नमः ।
857.	Oṃ Truṭirūpāyai Namaḥ		ॐ त्रुटिरूपायै नमः ।
858.	Oṃ Truṭisandehakāriṇyai Namaḥ		ॐ त्रुटिसन्देहकारिण्यै नमः ।
859.	Oṃ Tarṣiṇyai Namaḥ		ॐ तर्षिण्यै नमः ।
860.	Oṃ Tṛtpariklāntāyai Namaḥ		ॐ तृत्परिक्लान्तायै नमः ।
861.	Oṃ Kṣutkṣāmāyai Namaḥ		ॐ क्षुत्क्षामायै नमः ।
862.	Oṃ Kṣutpariplutāyai Namaḥ		ॐ क्षुत्परिप्लुतायै नमः
863.	Oṃ Akṣiṇyai Namaḥ		ॐ अक्षिण्यै नमः ।

864.	Oṃ Takṣiṇyai Namaḥ		ॐ तक्षिण्यै नमः ।
865.	Oṃ Bhikṣāprārthinyai Namaḥ		ॐ भिक्षाप्रार्थिन्यै नमः ।
866.	Oṃ Śatrubhakṣiṇyai Namaḥ		ॐ शत्रुभक्षिण्यै नमः ।
867.	Oṃ Kāṅkṣiṇyai Namaḥ		ॐ काङ्क्षिण्यै नमः ।
868.	Oṃ Kuṭṭanyai Namaḥ		ॐ कुट्टन्यै नमः ।
869.	Oṃ Krūrāyai Namaḥ		ॐ क्रूरायै नमः ।
870.	Oṃ Kuṭṭanīveśmavāsinyai Namaḥ		ॐ कुट्टनीवेश्मवासिन्यै नमः ।
871.	Oṃ Kuṭṭanīkoṭisampūjyāyai Namaḥ		ॐ कुट्टनीकोटिसम्पूज्यायै नमः ।
872.	Oṃ Kuṭṭanīkulamārgiṇyai Namaḥ		ॐ कुट्टनीकुलमार्गिण्यै नमः ।
873.	Oṃ Kuṭṭanīkulasaṃrakṣyāyai Namaḥ		ॐ कुट्टनीकुलसंरक्ष्यायै नमः ।
874.	Oṃ Kuṭṭanīkularakṣiṇyai Namaḥ		ॐ कुट्टनीकुलरक्षिण्यै नमः ।
875.	Oṃ Kālapāśāvṛtāyai Namaḥ		ॐ कालपाशावृतायै नमः ।
876.	Oṃ Kanyāyai Namaḥ		ॐ कन्यायै नमः ।
877.	Oṃ Kumārīpūjanapriyāyai Namaḥ		ॐ कुमारीपूजनप्रियायै नमः ।
878.	Oṃ Kaumudyai Namaḥ		ॐ कौमुद्यै नमः ।
879.	Oṃ Kaumudīhṛṣṭāyai Namaḥ		ॐ कौमुदीहृष्टायै नमः ।
880.	Oṃ Karuṇādṛṣṭisaṃyutāyai Namaḥ		ॐ करुणादृष्टिसंयुतायै नमः ।
881.	Oṃ Kautukācāranipuṇāyai Namaḥ		ॐ कौतुकाचारनिपुणायै नमः ।
882.	Oṃ Kautukāgāravāsinyai Namaḥ		ॐ कौतुकागारवासिन्यै नमः ।
883.	Oṃ Kākapakṣadharāyai Namaḥ		ॐ काकपक्षधरायै नमः ।
884.	Oṃ Kākarakṣiṇyai Namaḥ		ॐ काकरक्षिण्यै नमः ।
885.	Oṃ Kākasaṃvṛtāyai Namaḥ		ॐ काकसंवृतायै नमः ।
886.	Oṃ Kākāṅkarathasaṃsthānāyai Namaḥ		ॐ काकाङ्करथसंस्थानायै नमः ।
887.	Oṃ Kākāṅkasyandanāsthitāyai Namaḥ		ॐ काकाङ्कस्यन्दना स्थितायै नमः ।
888.	Oṃ Kākinyai Namaḥ		ॐ काकिन्यै नमः ।
889.	Oṃ Kākadṛṣṭyai Namaḥ		ॐ काकदृष्ट्यै नमः ।

890.	Oṃ Kākabhakṣaṇadāyinyai Namaḥ	ॐ काकभक्षणदायिन्यै नमः ।
891.	Oṃ Kākamātre Namaḥ ।	ॐ काकमात्रे नमः ।
892.	Oṃ Kākayonyai Namaḥ ।	ॐ काकयोन्यै नमः ।
893.	Oṃ Kākamaṇḍalamaṇḍitāyai Namaḥ ।	ॐ काकमण्डलमण्डितायै नमः ।
894.	Oṃ Kākadarśanasaṃśīlāyai Namaḥ	ॐ काकदर्शनसंशीलायै नमः
895.	Oṃ Kākasaṅkīrṇamandirāyai Namaḥ ।	ॐ काकसङ्कीर्णमन्दिरायै नमः ।
896.	Oṃ Kākadhyānastha Dehādidhyānagamyāyai Namaḥ ।	ॐ काकध्यानस्थ देहादिध्यानगम्यायै नमः ।
897.	Oṃ Adhamāvṛtāyai Namaḥ ।	ॐ अधमावृतायै नमः ।
898.	Oṃ Dhaninyai Namaḥ ।	ॐ धनिन्यै नमः ।
899.	Oṃ Dhanasaṃsevyāyai Namaḥ ।	ॐ धनसंसेव्यायै नमः ।
900.	Oṃ Dhanacchedanakāriṇyai Namaḥ ।	ॐ धनच्छेदनकारिण्यै नमः ।
901.	Oṃ Dhundhurāyai Namaḥ ।	ॐ धुन्धुरायै नमः ।
902.	Oṃ Dhundhurākārāyai Namaḥ ।	ॐ धुन्धुराकारायै नमः ।
903.	Oṃ Dhūmralocanaghātinyai Namaḥ ।	ॐ धूम्रलोचनघातिन्यै नमः ।
904.	Oṃ Dhūṅkāriṇyai Namaḥ ।	ॐ धूङ्कारिण्यै नमः ।
905.	Oṃ Dhūmmantrapūjitāyai Namaḥ ।	ॐ धूम्मन्त्रपूजितायै नमः ।
906.	Oṃ Dharmanāśinyai Namaḥ ।	ॐ धर्मनाशिन्यै नमः ।
907.	Oṃ Dhūmravarṇinyai Namaḥ ।	ॐ धूम्रवर्णिन्यै नमः ।
908.	Oṃ Dhūmrākṣyai Namaḥ ।	ॐ धूम्राक्ष्यै नमः ।
909.	Oṃ Dhūmrākṣāsuraghātinyai Namaḥ ।	ॐ धूम्राक्षासुरघातिन्यै नमः ।
910.	Oṃ Dhūmbījajapasantuṣṭāyai Namaḥ ।	ॐ धूम्बीजजपसन्तुष्टायै नमः ।
911.	Oṃ Dhūmbījajapamānasāyai Namaḥ ।	ॐ धूम्बीजजपमानसायै नमः ।
912.	Oṃ Dhūmbījajapapūjārhāyai Namaḥ ।	ॐ धूम्बीजजपपूजाहर्यै नमः ।

913.	Oṃ Dhūmbījajapakāriṇyai Namaḥ |	ॐ धूम्बीजजपकारिण्यै नमः ।
914.	Oṃ Dhūmbījākarṣitāyai Namaḥ |	ॐ धूम्बीजाकर्षितायै नमः ।
915.	Oṃ Dhṛṣyāyai Namaḥ |	ॐ धृष्यायै नमः ।
916.	Oṃ Dharṣiṇyai Namaḥ |	ॐ धर्षिण्यै नमः ।
917.	Oṃ Dhṛṣṭamānasāyai Namaḥ |	ॐ धृष्टमानसायै नमः ।
918.	Oṃ Dhūlīprakṣepiṇyai Namaḥ |	ॐ धूलीप्रक्षेपिण्यै नमः ।
919.	Oṃ Dhūlīvyāpta Dhammilla Dhāriṇyai Namaḥ |	ॐ धूलीव्याप्त धम्मिल्ल धारिण्यै नमः ।
920.	Oṃ Dhūmbījajapamālāḍhyāyai Namaḥ |	ॐ धूम्बीजजपमालाढ्यायै नमः ।
921.	Oṃ Dhūmbījanindakāntakāyai Namaḥ |	ॐ धूम्बीजनिन्दकान्तकायै नमः ।
922.	Oṃ Dharmavidveṣiṇyai Namaḥ |	ॐ धर्मविद्वेषिण्यै नमः ।
923.	Oṃ Dharmarakṣiṇyai Namaḥ |	ॐ धर्मरक्षिण्यै नमः ।
924.	Oṃ Dharmatoṣitāyai Namaḥ |	ॐ धर्मतोषितायै नमः ।
925.	Oṃ Dhārāstambhakaryai Namaḥ |	ॐ धारास्तम्भकर्यै नमः ।
926.	Oṃ Dhūrtāyai Namaḥ |	ॐ धूर्तायै नमः ।
927.	Oṃ Dhārāvārivilāsinyai Namaḥ |	ॐ धारावारिविलासिन्यै नमः
928.	Oṃ Dhāndhīndhūndhaim Mantravarṇāyai Namaḥ |	ॐ धान्धीन्धून्धैम्मन्त्रवर्णायै नमः ।
929.	Oṃ Dhaundhaḥsvāhāsvarūpiṇyai Namaḥ |	ॐ धौन्धःस्वाहास्वरूपिण्यै नमः ।
930.	Oṃ Dharitrīpūjitāyai Namaḥ |	ॐ धरित्रीपूजितायै नमः ।
931.	Oṃ Dhūrvāyai Namaḥ |	ॐ धूर्वायै नमः ।
932.	Oṃ Dhānyacchedanakāriṇyai Namaḥ |	ॐ धान्यच्छेदनकारिण्यै नमः ।
933.	Oṃ Dhikkāriṇyai Namaḥ |	ॐ धिक्कारिण्यै नमः ।
934.	Oṃ Sudhīpūjyāyai Namaḥ |	ॐ सुधीपूज्यायै नमः ।
935.	Oṃ Dhāmodyānanivāsinyai Namaḥ	ॐ धामोद्याननिवासिन्यै नमः
936.	Oṃ Dhāmodyānapayodātryai Namaḥ |	ॐ धामोद्यानपयोदात्र्यै नमः ।

937.	Oṃ Dhāmadhūlīpradhūlitāyai Namaḥ		ॐ धामधूलीप्रधूलितायै नमः ।
938.	Oṃ Mahādhvanimatyai Namaḥ		ॐ महाध्वनिमत्यै नमः ।
939.	Oṃ Dhūpyadhūpāmoda Oraharṣiṇyai Namaḥ		ॐ धूप्यधूपामोदप्रहर्षिण्यै नमः ।
940.	Oṃ Dhūpadānamatiprītāyai Namaḥ	ॐ धूपदानमतिप्रीतायै नमः ।
941.	Oṃ Dhūpadānavinodinyai Namaḥ		ॐ धूपदानविनोदिन्यै नमः ।
942.	Oṃ Dhīvarīgaṇasampūjyāyai Namaḥ		ॐ धीवरीगणसम्पूज्यायै नमः ।
943.	Oṃ Dhīvarīvaradāyinyai Namaḥ		ॐ धीवरीवरदायिन्यै नमः ।
944.	Oṃ Dhīvarīgaṇamadhyasthāyai Namaḥ		ॐ धीवरीगणमध्यस्थायै नमः ।
945.	Oṃ Dhīvarīdhāmavāsinyai Namaḥ		ॐ धीवरीधामवासिन्यै नमः ।
946.	Oṃ Dhīvarīgaṇagoptryai Namaḥ		ॐ धीवरीगणगोप्त्र्यै नमः ।
947.	Oṃ Dhīvarīgaṇatoṣitāyai Namaḥ		ॐ धीवरीगणतोषितायै नमः ।
948.	Oṃ Dhīvarīdhanadātryai Namaḥ		ॐ धीवरीधनदात्र्यै नमः ।
949.	Oṃ Dhīvarīprāṇarakṣiṇyai Namaḥ		ॐ धीवरीप्राणरक्षिण्यै नमः ।
950.	Oṃ Dhātrīśāyai Namaḥ		ॐ धात्रीशायै नमः ।
951.	Oṃ Dhātṛrsampūjyāyai Namaḥ		ॐ धात्रृसम्पूज्यायै नमः ।
952.	Oṃ Dhātrīvakṣasamāśrayāyai Namaḥ		ॐ धात्रीवक्षसमाश्रयायै नमः ।
953.	Oṃ Dhātrīpūjanakartryai Namaḥ		ॐ धात्रीपूजनकर्त्र्यै नमः ।
954.	Oṃ Dhātrīropaṇakāriṇyai Namaḥ		ॐ धात्रीरोपणकारिण्यै नमः ।
955.	Oṃ Dhūmrapānaratāsaktāyai Namaḥ		ॐ धूम्रपानरतासक्तायै नमः ।
956.	Oṃ Dhūmrapānarateṣṭadāyai Namaḥ		ॐ धूम्रपानरतेष्टदायै नमः ।
957.	Oṃ Dhūmrapānakarānandāyai Namaḥ		ॐ धूम्रपानकरानन्दायै नमः ।
958.	Oṃ Dhūmravarṣaṇakāriṇyai Namaḥ		ॐ धूम्रवर्षणकारिण्यै नमः ।
959.	Oṃ Dhanyaśabdaśrutiprītāyai Namaḥ		ॐ धन्यशब्दश्रुतिप्रीतायै नमः ।

960.	Oṃ Dhundhukārījanacchidāyai Namaḥ	ॐ धुन्धुकारीजनच्छिदायै नमः ।
961.	Oṃ Dhundhukārīṣṭasandātryai Namaḥ	ॐ धुन्धुकारीष्टसन्दात्र्यै नमः ।
962.	Oṃ Dhundhukārisumuktidāyai Namaḥ	ॐ धुन्धुकारिसुमुक्तिदायै नमः ।
963.	Oṃ Dhundhukāryārādhyarūpāyai Namaḥ	ॐ धुन्धुकार्याराध्यरूपायै नमः ।
964.	Oṃ Dhundhukārimanaḥsthitāyai Namaḥ	ॐ धुन्धुकारिमनःस्थितायै नमः ।
965.	Oṃ Dhundhukārihitākāṅkṣāyai Namaḥ	ॐ धुन्धुकारिहिताकाङ्क्षायै नमः ।
966.	Oṃ Dhundhukārihitaiṣiṇyai Namaḥ	ॐ धुन्धुकारिहितैषिण्यै नमः ।
967.	Oṃ Dhindhimārāviṇyai Namaḥ	ॐ धिन्धिमाराविण्यै नमः ।
968.	Oṃ Dhyātṛdhyānagamyāyai Namaḥ	ॐ ध्यातृध्यानगम्यायै नमः ।
969.	Oṃ Dhanārthinyai Namaḥ	ॐ धनार्थिन्यै नमः ।
970.	Oṃ Dhoriṇīdhoraṇaprītāyai Namaḥ	ॐ धोरिणीधोरणप्रीतायै नमः
971.	Oṃ Dhāriṇyai Namaḥ	ॐ धारिण्यै नमः ।
972.	Oṃ Dhorarūpiṇyai Namaḥ	ॐ धोररूपिण्यै नमः ।
973.	Oṃ Dharitrīrakṣiṇyai Devyai Namaḥ	ॐ धरित्रीरक्षिण्यै देव्यै नमः ।
974.	Oṃ Dharāpralayakāriṇyai Namaḥ	ॐ धराप्रलयकारिण्यै नमः ।
975.	Oṃ Dharādharasutāyai Namaḥ	ॐ धराधरसुतायै नमः ।
976.	Oṃ Aśeṣadhārādharasamadyutyai Namaḥ	ॐ अशेषधाराधरसमद्युत्यै नमः ।
977.	Oṃ Dhanādhyakṣāyai Namaḥ	ॐ धनाध्यक्षायै नमः ।
978.	Oṃ Dhanaprāptyai Namaḥ	ॐ धनप्राप्त्यै नमः ।
979.	Oṃ Dhanadhānyavivardhinyai Namaḥ	ॐ धनधान्यविवर्धिन्यै नमः ।
980.	Oṃ Dhanākarṣaṇakartryai Namaḥ	ॐ धनाकर्षणकर्त्र्यै नमः ।
981.	Oṃ Dhanāharaṇakāriṇyai Namaḥ	ॐ धनाहरणकारिण्यै नमः ।
982.	Oṃ Dhanacchedanakartryai Namaḥ	ॐ धनच्छेदनकर्त्र्यै नमः ।

983.	Oṃ Dhanahīnāyai Namaḥ	ॐ धनहीनायै नमः ।
984.	Oṃ Dhanapriyāyai Namaḥ	ॐ धनप्रियायै नमः ।
985.	Oṃ Dhanasaṃvṛddhisampannāyai Namaḥ	ॐ धनसंवृद्धिसम्पन्नायै नमः ।
986.	Oṃ Dhanadānaparāyaṇāyai Namaḥ	ॐ धनदानपरायणायै नमः ।
987.	Oṃ Dhanahṛṣṭāyai Namaḥ	ॐ धनहृष्टायै नमः ।
988.	Oṃ Dhanapuṣṭāyai Namaḥ	ॐ धनपुष्टायै नमः ।
989.	Oṃ Dānādhyayanakāriṇyai Namaḥ	ॐ दानाध्ययनकारिण्यै नमः ।
990.	Oṃ Dhanarakṣāyai Namaḥ	ॐ धनरक्षायै नमः ।
991.	Oṃ Dhanaprāṇāyai Namaḥ	ॐ धनप्राणायै नमः ।
992.	Oṃ Sadā Dhanānandakaryai Namaḥ	ॐ सदा धनानन्दकर्यै नमः ।
993.	Oṃ Śatruhantryai Namaḥ	ॐ शत्रुहन्त्र्यै नमः ।
994.	Oṃ Śavārūḍhāyai Namaḥ	ॐ शवारूढायै नमः ।
995.	Oṃ Śatrusaṃhārakāriṇyai Namaḥ	ॐ शत्रुसंहारकारिण्यै नमः ।
996.	Oṃ Śatrupakṣakṣatiprītāyai Namaḥ	ॐ शत्रुपक्षक्षतिप्रीताये नमः ।
997.	Oṃ Śatrupakṣaniṣūdinyai Namaḥ	ॐ शत्रुपक्षनिषूदिन्यै नमः ।
998.	Oṃ Śatrugrīvācchidācchāyāyai Namaḥ	ॐ शत्रुग्रीवाच्छिदाच्छायायै नमः ।
999.	Oṃ Śatrupaddhatikhaṇḍinyai Namaḥ	ॐ शत्रुपद्धतिखण्डिन्यै नमः ।
1000	Oṃ Śatruprāṇaharāhāryāyai Namaḥ	ॐ शत्रुप्राणहराहायायै नमः ।
1001	Oṃ Śatrūnmūlanakāriṇyai Namaḥ	ॐ शत्रून्मूलनकारिण्यै नमः ।
1002	Oṃ Śatrukāryavihantryai Namaḥ	ॐ शत्रुकार्यविहन्त्र्यै नमः ।
1003	Oṃ Sāṅgaśatruvināśinyai Namaḥ	ॐ साङ्गशत्रुविनाशिन्यै नमः ।
1004	Oṃ Sāṅgaśatrukulacchetryai Namaḥ	ॐ साङ्गशत्रुकुलच्छेत्र्यै नमः ।
1005	Oṃ Śatrusadmapradāhinyai Namaḥ	ॐ शत्रुसद्मप्रदाहिन्यै नमः ।
1006	Oṃ Sāṅga Sāyudha Sarvārisarva Sampatti Nāśinyai Namaḥ	ॐ साङ्ग सायुध सर्वारिसर्व सम्पत्ति नाशिन्यै नमः ।

| 1007 | Oṃ Sāṅga Sāyudha Sarvāri Deha Geha Pradāhinyai Namaḥ | | ॐ साङ्ग सायुध सर्वारि देह गेह प्रदाहिन्यै नमः । |

Iti Śrī Dhūmāvatī Sahasranāmāvaliḥ Sampūrṇā |
इति श्रीधूमावती सहस्रनामावलिः सम्पूर्णा ।

*****

8. *Bagalāmukhī* – बगलामुखी

Śrī Bhagalāmukhī Devī

Adiparasakti, *Paradevata*, *Sarva Loka Jaganmata*, *Sri Devi* creates, preserves and destroys all the worlds. In addition, she performs the tasks of *Tirodhāna* and *Anugrahā* also, in accordance with one of the names in Sri Lalita Sahasranama *"Pancha Krutya Parayana"*. As a *Parabrahma Mahishi*, she, after creating lives, has taken many divine incarnations for the state and has been regularly doing *sishta* maintenance and evil discipline.

Among the various incarnations of Sriman Narayana described by Sri Vishnu Bhagavatam, ten avatars are prominent. Similarly, to protect the entire world, Sri Devi has manifested herself in ten different forms known as Dasha Maha Vidyas, as described in the previous chapter. Among those ten, Sri *Bhagalāmukhī* Devi Vidya is the eighth one.

This *Bhagalāmukhī Devi* shines in the *Anāhata chakra* in the heart of our body in 12 petalled lotus. Among the 10 incarnations of Sri Maha Vishnu, Sri *Bhagalāmukhī* Devi is compared to Koorma Avatar and Mars (Angaraka) among the Navagrahas.

Bhagalāmukhī has other names like *Pītāmbarā* or *Dhandanāthā*. People used to worship this *Devī*, mainly to win over the enemies and to win over others in debates. However, this *Devī* is capable of providing all the four wishes (beneficence, worldly substances, happiness and bliss). A book called *Śrī Bhagalāmukhī Rahasya* published by *Śrī Pītāmbara Pīṭa* in a place called Dadiyaa in Madhya Pradesh, India, clearly deals in detail about the worshipping methods of this *Devī* and its results with evidences.

Bhagalāmukhī Devī is the one who protected Lord *Parameshwara* from the demon *Basmāsura*. **She** also protected Lord *Nārāyaṇā*, who was in the form of a child in *Vadabadra*. **She** removes all the sorrows of her devotees. **She** is the remover of enemies.

The word *Bagalā* is the transformation from the Samskruta word *valkaa*. *Valkaa* means bridle. *Valka* transformed into *Vaklaa* and then to *Bagalaa*. Such a transformation has been seen in the words like *simha – himsa*, *pashyaka – kashyapa*. A bridle controls the mouth of a horse. Similarly worship of this *Devee* controls the mouth and other organs of an enemy.

Another interpretation translates her name as 'Kalyani'. In Kubjika Tantra there is a reference to yet another interpretation of the meaning of the name 'Bagala'. In the initial chapter of the text, there is a verse –
Bakare Baruni Devi Gakare Siddhida Smrita |

Lakare Prithivi Chaiba Chaitanya Prakrirtita ||

- '*Ba*', the first letter of the name – 'Bagala', means 'Baruni' or "She Who is filled with the intoxicating mood to vanquish the demon".
- '*Ga*', the second letter, means "She Who grants all kinds of divine powers or siddhis and successes to human beings".
- '*La*', the third letter, means "She Who is the foundation of all kinds of sustaining powers in the world like the earth and is Consciousness Herself".

The *tattva* of *Bhagalāmukhī Devī*;

Bagalāmukhī Dēvī is the ultimate enchantress. She can be called *Pītāmbarā, Śatrubuddhi Vināśinī, Brahmāstra Rūpiṇī, Brahmāstra Vidyā, Caṇḍī, Caṇḍikā, Durgā* and *Pīta Kālī*. Her consort is *Ēkavaktra Mahārudra Paramaśiva*. Her *Gaṇapati* is *Haridra Gaṇapati*[3]. She presides over the southern direction (*Dakshina*) and is associated with *Śrī Kūrma* incarnation of *Sri Vishnu*. She governs the planet Mars (*Maṅgala*). She appeared on a *vīrarātri*. Her origin or birth is celebrated in the month of *Vaishakha* during the Shukla Paksha Ashtami Tithi (8th day).

In *Śrī Vidyā* tradition, instead of *Dēvī Bhairavī*, it is *Dēvī Bagalāmukhī* who is *Śrīvidyā Navavarṇa Caṇḍī*. In the *Lalitōpākhyāna* of the *Brahmāṇḍa Purāṇa*, when *Bhaṇḍāsura* creates *Madhu, Kaiṭabha, Mahiṣāsura, Cikṣura, Cāmara, Dhūmralōcana, Caṇḍa, Muṇḍa, Raktabīja, Śumbha* and *Niśumbha, Dēvī Lalitā* becomes furious and makes a boisterous laughter of challenge which creates '*Durgā*'. It is indicated that this was *Dēvī Navarṇa Caṇḍī* and due to *Lalitā* is same as *Śrīvidyā*, it would make sense if this was *Śrīvidyā Navarṇa Caṇḍī* i.e., *Bagalāmukhī*.

According to the *Svatantra Tantra*, in *Satya* Yug, there was a storm named '*Vātakṣōbha*; that was devouring the universe. Upon seeing this, the gods were terrified and they ran to *Nārāyaṇa* for help. Upon analyzing the situation, *Nārāyaṇa* went to the *Haridra Sarōvara* and did *Ghēraṇḍa-yōga* for a thousand years. Then, *Dēvī Lalitā Mahā Tripura Sundarī* emerged from the lake upon being pleased by his tapa. She created *Bagalāmukhī* from her heart with the essence of *Viṣṇu's pītāmbara*. Hence, *Bagalāmukhī* became fond of the color yellow. Then, *Bagalā* stopped the storm with her *stambhana Sakti* and saved the universe from destruction.

According to the *Nārada Pāñcarātra*, there was a demon named *Madana* who pleased *Brahma* with penance and was rewarded with *Vāksiddhi*. He

---

[3] It is worth noting here that in all the *karmas* we used to make *Ganapati* with turmeric powder and start the pooja.

used his powers to create commotion in the universe and disturb all the gods. Annoyed by *Madanāsura*, they went to *Śrī Viṣṇu* once again. *Nārāyaṇa* went to the *Haridra Sarōvara* once again and prayed to *Dēvī*. This time, *Parāśaktī* left her sugarcane bow and flowery arrows and emerged as *Bhuvanēśvarī* instead of *Tripura Sundari*. Then, she recreated *Bagalāmukhī* from her heart with the essence of *Viṣṇu* again. *Bagalāmukhī* then waged war against *Madana* and used her enchanting powers to freeze *Madanāsura*. Then, she pulled his tongue out and chopped it with her club.

Though there are many *naadis* (pulses) in our body, the 101 *naadis* around the heart are considered as important –

"*Śadam Ca Ekā Ca Hrudyasya Nādyāḥ*" (*Kāṭaka Upanishat* 3-2-16).

Still important are the three viz., *Idaa*, *Pingala* and *Sushumnaa*. *Sushumnaa* is the one which moves in the mid of the spine at the back of our body. *Idaa* and *pingala* coil themselves around both the sides and join the *Sushumnaa* at the *Aagnaa chakra*. This is *Triveni sangama* (meeting of three – as meeting of three rivers Ganga, Yamuna and Saraswathi in Allahabad). *Idaa* is Ganga, *Pingala* – Yamuna and *Sushumnaa* is invisible Saraswathi. This is what is told in *Vedas* as –

"*Sitaa Sito Sarito Yatra Sangate*".

Worshiping male gods is called mantra. The method of worshiping female deities is called Vidya. Worshiping Sri Vidya, the unison of Shiva and Shakti. So, this also comes under Mantra group. Sri Vidya is said to be the best of all mantras.

That Devi is also known as Tripura Sundari, Raja Rajeshwari, Shodasee, Kamakshi, Lalita and so on. She is also an important Maha Vidya. She is glorified in many Shakta texts like Sri Lalitha Sahasranamam, Soundarya-lahari, etc. She is called Adi Para Shakti in the Lalithopakyanam of Brahmanda Purana.

According to the Srikula tradition in Shaktaism, *Bhagalāmukhī* is the Shakta's supreme deity of Hinduism and the principal deity of Sri Vidya. The Tripura Upanishad places her as the ultimate Shakti (energy, power) of the universe. She is described as the Supreme Consciousness ruling from above Brahma, Vishnu and Shiva.

May the Divine Mother guide us all in our every action and thought. And may She remove the veil of maya and bestow upon us the greatest gift of all, moksha (liberation).

*****

Form(s) of *Śrī Bhagalāmukhī Devī*

Usually Meditative Hymns (*Dhyana Shlokas*) about the Gods are figurative of the concerned God or Goddess.

The Meditation Hymn of *Śrī Bhagalāmukhī Devī* is;

सौवर्णासिनसंस्थितां त्रिनयनां पीतांशुकोल्लासिनीं

हेमाभांगरुचिं शशांकमुकुताम् सच्चंपक सरग्युताम् ।

हस्तैर्मुद्ररपाश वज्रत्ररसना: सम्बिभ्रतीम् भूशणैर्व्याप्ताङ्गीम्

बगालामुखीम् त्रिजगतां संस्तम्भिनीम् चिन्तयेत् ॥

Souvarṇāsanasamsthitām Trinayanām Pītāmśukollāsinīm
Hemābhāmgaruchim Śaśānkamukutām Sachchampaka Saragyutām
Hastairmudgarapāśa Vajstrarasanāḥ Sambibhratīm Bhūṣaṇairvyāptāngīm
Bagalāmukhīm Trijagatām Samstambhinīm Chintayet ||

There is a precious throne made of gold, amidst the milky ocean in a platform of gems in the house of jewels. *Bhagalāmukhī* is sitting on this throne. **She** is yellow in colour, dressed in yellow colour and wearing yellow-coloured jewels and garlands. **She** holds the elongated tongue of the enemy in one hand and the other hand is in a striking pose holding a maze. She wears a crescent moon on the head. Her hair is entangled. In the same way, as per *Yaamalaa tantra*, the meditation has been mentioned as with four hands and three eyes, sitting on a lotus. *Vedas* also worship this *Devee* as "*Hiranyavarnām Hariṇīm*" (*R.V.4.434.*). When the golden colour matures and its brightness reduces it becomes yellow in colour. The same case is the nature of all the other colours in this world – when the brightness reduces yellow colour adds to it. Similarly, when one's greatness is reduced *tantras* prescribe meditation of *Bhagalāmukhī*.

Two descriptions of the goddess are found in various texts – the *Dwi-Bhuja* (two-handed) and the *Chatur-bhuja* (four-handed). The *Dwi-Bhuja* depiction is the more common and is described as the '*Soumya*' or milder form. She holds a club in her right hand with which she beats a demon, while pulling his tongue out with her left hand. This image is sometimes interpreted as an exhibition of *stambana*, the power to stun or paralyse an enemy into silence. This is one of the boons for which Bagalamukhi's devotees worship her. Other Mahavidya goddesses are also said to represent similar powers useful for defeating enemies, to be invoked by their worshippers through various rituals.

Kinsley translates Bagalamukhi as "she who has the face of a crane". Bagalamukhi is rarely depicted with a crane-head or with cranes. Kinsley believes that the crane's behaviour of standing still to catch prey is reflective of the occult powers bestowed by the goddess.

In another text she is described as – Her skin tone is yellow. She has three eyes and wears a crescent moon on her hair. She wears yellow silks. She has two arms in which she holds a club/ mace and the tongue of Madanāsura. She is seated on a corpse (Śiva) who lies on a golden throne in the middle of the Haridra Sarōvara. Her vehicle is a crane named '*Balākā*'. In the morning, she is the crane-headed *Śvēta Bagalā*, at noon, she is four-handed *Pītāmbarā Bagalā*, and at night, she is simply *Bagalā*.

Goddess *Bhagalāmukhī* manifests in our body in the Nadi called *Sanginee*. The path which the Vedas say is the Pitruyana route is the form of this Goddess. This Devi Upasana is the Indrayoni Vidya.

Winning over enemies is the main use of this Upasana. That is why yellow colour is prescribed for all the items used for her worship. At the cost of duplication in this book, it is re-stressed – By saying `enemies' it should not be construed as external enemies of humans – it is desires, anger, etc., within everyone. Self-enlightenment and liberation can be achieved only when these internal enemies are destroyed. One can get wealth like Kubera, good position and power to win the world.

According to the Tantras, yellow colour is very suitable for winning the enemies. That is reason, the Gnanarnava Tantra text also prescribes that Sri Chakra can be put in turmeric liquid and worshiped with yellow-coloured flowers to attain sarva stampanam (halt everything).

This *Bhagalāmukhī* is worshiped as the Varahi named Dandanatha, the army commander[4] of Sri Lalita Parameshwari (Sri Tripura Sundari). Puranic legends say that Brahmastra is the mantra of this goddess. It is said that even the wind stops just by thinking of that astra.

This *Bhagalāmukhī* Devi regulates thinking. Kali is the destroyer of all. At the same time, *Bhagalāmukhī* is the one who restrains the action in order to be effective before the action and then leaves it.

One holds the breath and blocks it. But if he does this for a while and then leave it, isn't it a life-enhancing *pranayama*? Holding like this is called *'Stampanam'*. Goddess *Bhagalāmukhī*, the "stopper of speech". That is, she who stops the speech. She will make us think later. She is depicted holding a man's tongue with her left hand and ready to crush his thoughts with a mace (club) with her right hand.

'Valga' means *'Lagan'* (bits used to control horse). Valkamukhi is said to be Vakalamukhi who puts Lagan in the mouth (face) of the enemy and beats him to death. In vernacular *'Va'* and *'Bha'* are interchangeable. like Vangali – Bengali.

Temples for *Bhagalāmukhī* Devi –

Bhagalāmukhī temples are extremely rare. The *Bhagalāmukhī* Temple, Bankhandi is located on Kangra district of Himachal Pradesh, India. It is dedicated to the goddess Bagalamukhi. She is associated with the colour yellow. She is also named as *Peethambara*. She sits on golden throne having pillars decorated with various jewels and has three eyes, that symbolises that she can impart ultimate knowledge to the devotee. The temple is popular at the time of the Navaratri festival. It is one of three in India noted historically as having shrines to Bagalamukhi, the others being in Datia and Nalkheda, Madhya Pradesh. It was restored in 1815.

This Goddess should be meditated upon in the 12 petalled lotus at the Anahata Chakra in the heart of the human body. Let us all cry at her feet to be able to meditate her.

Kanchi Paramacharya would say – In all deities, many heads, hands, etc., are described. But does any deity said to have more than two legs? Nope. Why?

---

[4] Sri Lalita Parameshwari is the Empress. Matangi is her minister. Varahi is the army commander. In this world, these three Devis, grace the devotees respectively as Kanchi Kamakshi, Madurai Meenakshi and as Thiruvanaikoil Akhilendeshwari.

We only have two hands. All deities are told to have only two legs to enable us to cry holding the two legs of the deity. At least if we cry clasping the two feet of Ambika, she will turn her merciful eye on us!

*****

Śrī Bhagalāmukhī Devī Mantras

Śrī Bhagalāmukhī Vidyā

In Samskrutam, in general *Vidyā* means mantra. Vidya means knowledge. Here is a very powerful *Sri Bhagalāmukhī Devī Mantra*.

Oṃ Asya Śrī Bhagalāmukhī Mahā Mantrasya Nārada Riśiḥ ।
Bruhatī Chandaḥ । Śrī Bhagalāmukhī Devatā ।
Hrīm Bījam, Svāhā Śaktiḥ Bhagalāmukhī Kīlakam ।
Śrī Bhagalāmukhī Prasāda Siddhyarte Jape Viniyogaḥ ।

Oṃ Hrlīm Angushṭābhyām Namaḥ
Oṃ Bhagalāmukhīm Darjanībhyām Namaḥ
Oṃ Sarvadhusṭānām Madhymābhyām Namaḥ
Oṃ Vāśam, Mukham, Pādam Stampaya Anāmikābhyām Namaḥ
Oṃ Jihvām Kīlaya Bhudhim Vināśaya Hrlīm Kanishṭikābhyām Namaḥ
Oṃ Svāhā Karatala Karabrushṭābhyām Namaḥ

Oṃ Hrlīm Hrudayāya Namaḥ
Oṃ Bhagalāmukhīm Sirase Svāhā
Oṃ Sarvadhusṭānām Śikāyai Vashat
Oṃ Vāśam, Mukham, Pādam Stampaya Kavachāya Hūm
Oṃ Jihvām Kīlaya Bhudhim Vināśaya Hrlīm Netratrayāya Vouśaṭ
Oṃ Svāhā Astrāyaphaṭ
Bhūrbhuvasvaromiti Digbandhaḥ ।

Dhyānam

सौवर्णासनसंस्थितां त्रिनयनां पीतांशुकोल्लासिनीं
हेमाभांगरुचिं शशांकमुकुताम् सच्चंपक सरग्युताम्।
हस्तैर्मुद्ररपाश वज्रस्वरसना: सम्बिभ्रतीम् भूशणैर्व्याप्ताङ्गीम्
बगालामुखीम् त्रिजगतां संस्तम्भिनीम् चिन्तयेत् ॥

Souvarṇāsanasamsthitām Trinayanām Pītāmśukollāsinīm
Hemābhāmgaruchim Śaśānkamukutām Sachchampaka Saragyutām
Hastairmudgarapāśa Vajstrarasanāḥ Sambibhratīm Bhūśaṇairvyāptāngīm
Bagalāmukhīm Trijagatām Samstambhinīm Chintayet ।।

Lam Pritviyātmikāyai Gandham Samarpayāmi ।
Ham Ākashātmikāyai Puśpaiḥ Pūjayāmi ।

Yam Vaivātmikāyai Dhūpam Āgrāpayāmi |
Ram Vahniyātmikāyai Dhīpam Dharśayāmi |
Vam Amrutātmikāyai Amrutam Mahāneivedhyam Nivedayāmi |
Sam Sarvātmikāyai Sarvopahāra Pūjām Samarpayāmi ||

Bhagalāmukhī Mūla Mantras

Śrī Bhagalāmukhī Mahā Mantrāḥ (36 lettered) |

ॐ ह्रूलीं बगलामुखी सर्वदुष्टानां वाचं मुखं पदं स्तंबय स्तंबय जिह्वां कीलय कीलय बुद्धिं विनाशयविनाशय ह्रूलीं ॐ (स्वाहा) ||

Oṃ Hrlīm Bagalāmukhī Sarvadhuṣṭānām Vāsam, Mukham, Pādam Stampaya Stampaya Jihvām Kīlaya Bhudhim Vināśaya Vināśaya Hrlīm Oṃ (Svāhā) ||

Oṃ Hrlīm Hrudayāya Namaḥ
Oṃ Bhagalāmukhīm Sirase Svāhā
Oṃ Sarvadhuṣṭānām Śikāyai Vashat
Oṃ Vāsam, Mukham, Pādam Stampaya Kavachāya Hūm
Oṃ Jihvām Kīlaya Bhudhim Vināśaya Hrlīm Netratrayāya Vouśaṭ
Oṃ Svāhā Astrāyaphaṭ
Bhūrbhuvasvaromiti Digvimogaḥ |

Dhyānam

सौवर्णासनसंस्थितां त्रिनयनां पीतांशुकोल्लासिनीं
हेमाभांगरुचिं शशांकमुकुताम् सच्चंपक सरग्युताम्।
हस्तैर्मुद्ररपाश वज्र्त्ररसना: सम्बिभ्रतीम् भूशणैर्व्याप्ताङ्गीम्
बगालामुखीम् त्रिजगतां संस्तम्भिनीम् चिन्तयेत् ||

Souvarṇāsanasamsthitām Trinayanām Pītāmśukollāsinīm
Hemābhāmgaruchim Śaśānkamukutām Sachchampaka Saragyutām
Hastairmudgarapāśa Vajstrarasanāḥ Sambibhratīm Bhūśaṇairvyāptāngīm
Bagalāmukhīm Trijagatām Samstambhinīm Chintayet ||

Lam Pritviyātmikāyai Gandham Samarpayāmi |
Ham Ākashātmikāyai Puśpaiḥ Pūjayāmi |
Yam Vaivātmikāyai Dhūpam Āgrāpayāmi |
Ram Vahniyātmikāyai Dhīpam Dharśayāmi |
Vam Amrutātmikāyai Amrutam Mahāneivedhyam Nivedayāmi |
Sam Sarvātmikāyai Sarvopahāra Pūjām Samarpayāmi ||

One other famous mantra of *Śrī Bagalāmukhī Devī* is;

ॐ ह्रीं ऐं क्लीं श्री बगलानने मम रिपून नाशय नाशय ममैश्वर्याणि देहि देहि शीघ्रं मनोवान्छितं साधय साधय ह्रीं स्वाहा ।

Oṃ Hrīm Aim Klīm Śrī Bagalānane Mama Ripūn Nāśaya Nāśaya Mamaiśwaryāṇi Dehi Dehi Śīghram Manovānchitam Sādhaya Sādhaya Hrīm Swāhā |

Bagalāmukhī halts the enemies temporarily. Through this **she** prevents disgrace and loss to the worshippers. **She** does not kill the enemies. During the protection period halting for a short-while is **her** task. The flowing water is stopped for a while and turned towards the useful path. Similarly, the energy in our body is turned towards noble path and reaches all the gains by worshipping this, *Devee.*

This is called *hatayoga* or *raajayoga* – the path towards the same. Hence, those who want to progress in this path will worship this, *Devee.*

An important result of this worship is winning over the enemies. That is the reason yellow colour is prescribed.

The path of *tantras* is that yellow colour is most suitable to win over the enemies. That is the reason *Gnaanaarnava tantra* has prescribed to worship *Shree Chakra* with yellow articles and with yellow flowers – with this the worshipper can halt all the diseases.

Bagalāmukhī Worshipping process:

Rules of *Bhagalāmukhī* Sadhana – Devi should be treated as yellow in colour, yellow clothes should be worn, puja should be done with yellow flowers, japam should be done with turmeric garland, etc. Pranayama is one most important technique.

The important tools are – imagining *Devee* as yellow, wearing yellow dress, using yellow flowers, sitting on a yellow seat, using garland of turmeric for chanting and *pranayama.* There are *Ashtotra* and *Sahasranaamas* on this *Devee.* Before and after doing *Ashtotra* or *Sahasranaama archanas, Gayatri mantra* has to be chant.

Results of worshipping *Bhagalāmukhī*;

Important result is winning over the enemies. The other results are curtailing the inner enemies like desires, anger, etc., and the gain of

Samadhi. With the gain of *Samadhi* one can get self realisation and liberation. By the blessings of *Peetaambara Devee* one can get wealth like a Kubera, good position and energy to control the entire world.

This goddess is not as widely worshiped as other popular goddesses such as Kali and Durga, to name a few. However, if any tantric sadhak is asked about Devi Dhoomavati, we will hear a lot of praise for her being a goddess who is equally difficult to please and violent if not worshiped correctly. It can be noticed that the majority of Hindus are afraid of Dhoomavati Devi and other tantric goddesses. They don't even want any pictures of this goddess in their home. Tantric practitioners, on the other hand, worship her in order to gain siddhis and supernatural powers.

Only the most advanced tantric practitioners have access to the mantra's full potential (Sadhaks). There is no hard rule in normal recitation, but please do not chant the mantra with any unusual desire, as this can easily backfire.

There are numerous other mantras and stotrams dedicated to Devi *Bhagalāmukhī*. However, the most popular one and that can be chant by the average person without any extreme tantric rituals is discussed here. Tantric practitioners' worship *Bhagalāmukhī* for acquiring siddhis or supernatural powers.

One should be interested in the words of the teacher. The four – self, teacher, *mantra* and the God should be treated as same. One should not reprimand other religions. One should always think of himself as Lord *Shiva*. One should not rebuke ladies.

Shakta ideologies affirm – *Sri Devi* in the form of, *kundalini* energy has to be brought from *Mūlādhāra Chakra* to *Sahasrāra Chakra* through *Brahma Granti, Swādhiṣṭāna Chakra, Maṇipūraka Chakra, Vishnu Granti, Anāhata Chakra, Viśuddhi Chakra, Rudra Granti and Agjna Chakra.* At the *Sahasrāra Chakra,* in a *Sahasradala Padma* (1000 petalled lotus), the unison of *Shiva-Shakti* has to be inwardly looked (*antharmukha* – inwardly imagined) into and the devotee should be soaked in the rain of nectar (*Amruta Tara*).

Important results of worshipping *Śrī Bhagalāmukhī*;

With the blessings of this *Devee,* the worshipper gets the state of *Shiva.* He will get children, wealth and grains very early. With the blessings of *Shree Devee,* he becomes wealthy and becomes expert poet. Nothing is impossible to get through the worship of this *Devee.* After getting all the wealth, he gets the knowledge of *Vedantas* and hence the benefit of liberation through desireless meditation.

By worshipping this *Devee*, the devotee can obtain the art of speech, clear knowledge of *shastras*, wealth like Kubera, energy to win anything in this world and at last liberation.

Progress is the only in the life, if the grace of Devī is given to a devotee. Motivation comes naturally in the actions that are done. There is nothing he cannot achieve by her grace. She is interested in removing the sins of her devotees and showing him the right way. She lovingly bestows grace on those who are active, solid, and engaged in worship.

Let us all get initiated with these mantras from an appropriate guru and reap all the benefits.

*****

Śrī Bhagalāmukhī Devī Yantram

Sri Bhagalāmukhī Devi Yantra

When this yantra is looked at, it can be noticed that certain symbols are engraved or printed on it. The design on the yantra consists of Bindu that is carved inside the inverted triangle. The inverted triangle or trikona is surrounded by a hexagon or star shape known as shatkona which is encircled by a circle. The circle shape is surrounded by a shape of the lotus petals. The lotus petals can be seen in almost in all the yantras pertaining to Sri Devi, including Sri Chakra. The lotus petals are again within a circle, which is again surrounded by lotus petals, which have small petal carvings on them. The Bindu indicates the energy and its extreme concentration at the centre. It also indicates the center of cosmic radiation. Bounded by different surfaces such as a triangle, a hexagon, a circle, the Bindu represents the union with the force or creative energy ruling the Yantra. The lotus petals symbol is known as the *Padma* (lotus).

A lotus in the Yantra represents the unconditional force of the Supreme Absolute truth. The lotus serves as a divine seat for Devas. It also represents detachment. It grows in the mud but never touches even a tinge of mud, representing detachment to the external forces (material world) and maintaining the original nature of pure and divine. The circle also known as the chakra stands for rotation which is central to the functioning of the macrocosmic progression. At the same time, the circle signified perfection and the peaceful creative void of the *Vishudha Chakra*. In the series of the five fundamental elements, it represents the Air Element. The Hexagon also known as the Shatkona is an archetypal amalgamation of two triangles structured in all the *Yantra*. It characteristically signifies the divine unification of Shiva (male energy) and Shakti (Female energy) which is the cause of all creation and the triangle also known as the Trikona is the emblem of Shakti, the absolute female energy of the Divine. It completes the creation or manifestation of both, material as well as spiritual worlds. The triangle pointing down characterises the Yoni, which is the source of all creations. A triangle pointing downwards represents the Water Element, since water flows down. Water Element represents Shakti.

Bagalamukhi yantra is a spiritual device with specific geometric patterns that assist in bringing boons of the mighty goddess Bagalamukhi. The yantra bolsters financial and spiritual well-being and supports the all-round development of a person. This yantra works like magic for uplifting life and keeps all sorts of enemies and poor influences away.

This yantra is highly significant as it brings the pious blessings of mighty goddess Bagalamukhi in life. Devi Bagalamukhi is also known as Pitambari Maa; she is the powerful goddess who suspends the effect of negative energies and enemies. The commanding divinity Bagalamukhi is affiliated as a manifestation of Goddess Shakti and Parvati, which enhances the impact of Bagalamukhi yantra to significant margins.

This yantra is highly needed by those unravelling perpetual failures in life and having a bitter life stage. This yantra is magical for removing the evil effects of black magic and is renowned for keeping the hostile energies away. If one's life is troublesome because of evil powers or enemies, this yantra is highly effective.

Here are some of the notable benefits of worshipping the *Bagalamukhi yantra*;

- Bagalamukhi yantra eradicates the poor effect of terrible energies and opponents.
- The yantra brings an aura that assists in attaining success.
- The yantra also brings prosperity and abundance to life by loading it with economic boons.
- The yantra augments the daily life with peaceful and tranquility.
- It empowers with excellent financial stability and immense bliss in life.
- The yantra also assists in getting rid of the troublesome cycle of birth and death and leads towards salvation.

To get the maximum benefits the *Bagalamukhi yantra* can be used as detailed below;

- The yantra must be placed facing East or North direction and should be regularly cleaned with either rosewater or clean water.

- Light incense sticks in front of the *yantra* after putting four dots on its four surfaces using sandalwood or vermillion paste.
- It has to be ensured that this *mantra* is chant for 108 times to get the maximum benefit, while worshipping this *yantra*;

ॐ ह्रूलीं बगलामुखी सर्वदुष्टानां वाचं मुखं पदं स्तंबय स्तंबय जिह्वां कीलय कीलय बुद्धिं विनाशयविनाशय ह्रूलीं ॐ (स्वाहा) ॥

Oṃ Hrlīm Bagalāmukhī Sarvadhuṣṭānām Vāśam, Mukham, Pādam Stampaya Samaya Jihvām Kīlaya Bhudhim Vināśaya Vināśaya Hrlīm Oṃ (Svāhā) ॥

The *yantras* pertaining to most of the Gods are kept beneath or in front of the deities in temples. One *yantra* is a drawing of lines or circles or angles drawn in a prescribed measurements and ratios. There cannot be any deviation plus or minus. If a *mantra* is wrongly chant, it can result in negative impact or even end up with destruction. In the same manner, if there is an error in drawing of a *yantra*, it may end up in devastation.

In modern days, lot many worship *Śrī Chakra* in their houses. In general, this is very good. But many do it as a pride, some do it as a style and some with ignorance. But the customs are not strictly followed. Resultantly, they suffer for want of peace.

It is not enough if one wants to follow the bigger things. Exact rules prescribed by *Sastras* have to be clearly understood, absorbed and followed. These are time tested and handed over to us by our ancestors. It is our duty to stringently follow the same and get benefited. Definitely *Śrī Chakra* has been raised upto the sky by the *Sastras*. But the same *Sastras* have recommended lots of dos and don'ts, lots of processes. The approach that "I will do the pooja in my way" is not acceptable, the expected fruits will be missed. Sometimes that may result in negative angle.

One *yantra* is not a place of dwelling for the deity; It is the deity her/himself. It is not an alternative to the deity. It is not a representation – it the deity. It is all the more apt in the case of *Śrī Devī*.

The radiations of the Yantra will bring the devotee and the Goddess into direct contact. The energy will soothe the inner peace and will gift with beauty, happiness and prosperity. These power lines attract the amiability of the Goddess opening doors for harmony and success.

This Yantra is a great cosmic conductor of energy, an antenna of Nature, a powerful tool for harmony, prosperity, success, good health, yoga and meditation! Yantras consist of a series of geometric patterns. The eyes and mind concentrate at the center of the yantra to achieve higher levels of consciousness. Yantras are usually made out of copper.

Let us all choose an appropriate guru, get initiated and worship this yantra to exploit maximum benefits.

*****

Śrī Bhagalāmukhī Dhyānam

Or *Bagalāmukhī (Pītāmbarī) Dhyānam*

Madhye Sudhābdhimaṇimaṇḍaparatnavedī Siṃhāsanopari Gatāṃ

Parivītavarṇām |

Pītāmbarābharaṇamālyavibhūṣitāṅgīṃ

Devīṃ Namāmi Dhṛtamudgaravairijihvām || 1

Jihvāgramādāya Kareṇa Devīṃ Vāmena Śatrūnparipīḍayantīm |

Gadābhighātena Ca Dakṣiṇena Pītāmbarāḍhyāṃ Dvibhujāṃ Namāmi || 2

Sauvarṇāsanasaṃsthitāṃ Trinayanāṃ Pītāṃśukollāsinīṃ

Hemābhāṅgaruciṃ Śaśāṅkamukuṭāṃ Saccampakasragyutām |

Hastairmudgarapāśavajraraśanāḥ Sambibhratīṃ Bhūṣaṇaiḥ

Vyāptāṅgīṃ Bagalāmukhīṃ Trijagatāṃ Saṃstambhinīṃ Cintaye || 3

Iti Bagalāmukhī Athavā Pītāmbarī Dhyānam ||

बगलामुखी (पीताम्बरी) ध्यानम्

मध्ये सुधाब्धिमणिमण्डपरत्नवेदी सिंहासनोपरि गतां परिवीतवर्णाम् ।
पीताम्बराभरणमाल्यविभूषिताङ्गीं देवीं नमामि धृतमुद्गरवैरिजिह्वाम् ॥ १

जिह्वाग्रमादाय करेण देवीं वामेन शत्रून्परिपीडयन्तीम् ।
गदाभिघातेन च दक्षिणेन पीताम्बराढ्यां द्विभुजां नमामि ॥ २

सौवर्णासनसंस्थितां त्रिनयनां पीतांशुकोल्लासिनीं
हेमाभाङ्गरुचिं शशाङ्कमुकुटां सच्चम्पकस्रग्युताम् ।
हस्तैर्मुद्गरपाशवज्ररशनाः सम्बिभ्रतीं भूषणैः
व्याप्ताङ्गीं बगलामुखीं त्रिजगतां संस्तम्भिनीं चिन्तये ॥ ३

इति बगलामुखी अथवा पीताम्बरी ध्यानम् ॥

Śrī Bhagalāmukhī Kavacaṃ

Śrī Bagalāmukhī Śatruvināśaka Kavacam

Śrī Gaṇeśāya Namaḥ |　　　Śrī Pītāmbarāyai Namaḥ |

Śrī Devyuvāca -

Namaste Śambhave Tubhyaṃ Namaste Śaśiśekhara |
Tvatprasādācchrutaṃ Sarvamadhunā Kavacaṃ Vada || 1

Śrī Śiva Uvāca -

Śṛṇu Devi Pravakṣyāmi Kavacaṃ Paramādbhutam |
Yasya Smaraṇamātreṇa Ripoḥ Stambho Bhavet Kṣaṇāt || 2

Kavacasya Ca Deveśi Mahāmāyāprabhāvataḥ |
Paṅktiḥ Chandaḥ Samuddiṣṭaṃ Devatā Bagalāmukhī || 3

Dharmārthakāmamokṣeṣu Viniyogaḥ Prakīrtitaḥ |
Oṃkāro Me Śiraḥ Pātu Hrīṅkāro Vadane'vatu || 4

Bagalāmukhī Doryugmaṃ Kaṇṭhe Sarvadā'vatu |
Duṣṭānāṃ Pātu Hṛdayaṃ Vācaṃ Mukhaṃ Tataḥ Padam || 5

Udare Sarvadā Pātu Stambhayeti Sadā Mama |
Jihvāṃ Kīlaya Me Mātarbagalā Sarvasadā'vatu || 6

Buddhiṃ Vināśaya Pādau Tu Hlīṃ Oṃ Me Digvidikṣu Ca |
Svāhā Me Sarvadā Pātu Sarvatra Sarvasandhiṣu || 7

Iti Te Kathitaṃ Devi Kavacaṃ Paramādbhutam |
Yasya Smaraṇamātreṇa Sarvasthambho Bhavet Kṣaṇāt || 8

Yad Dhṛtvā Vividhā Daityā Vāsavena Hatāḥ Purā |
Yasya Prasādāt Siddho'haṃ Hariḥ Sattvaguṇānvitaḥ || 9

Vedhā Sṛṣṭiṃ Vitanute Kāmaḥ Sarvajagajjayī |
Likhitvā Dhārayedyastu Kaṇṭhe Vā Dakṣiṇe Bhuje || 10

Ṣaṭkarmasiddhīstasyāśu Mama Tulyo Bhaveddhruvam |

Ajñātvā Kavacaṃ Devi Tasya Mantro Na Sidhyati || 11

Iti Śrī Bagalāmukhī Śatruvināśaka Kavacaṃ Samāptam |

श्री बगलामुखी शत्रुविनाशक कवचम्

श्रीगणेशाय नमः ।   श्री पीताम्बरायै नमः ।

श्री देव्युवाच -

नमस्ते शाम्भवे तुभ्यं नमस्ते शशिशेखर ।
त्वत्प्रसादाच्छुतं सर्वमधुना कवचं वद ॥ १

श्री शिव उवाच -

शृणु देवि प्रवक्ष्यामि कवचं परमाद्भुतम् ।
यस्य स्मरणमात्रेण रिपोः स्तम्भो भवेत् क्षणात् ॥ २

कवचस्य च देवेशि महामायाप्रभावतः ।
पङ्क्तिः छन्दः समुद्दिष्टं देवता बगलामुखी ॥ ३

धर्मार्थिकाममोक्षेषु विनियोगः प्रकीर्तितः ।
ॐकारो मे शिरः पातु हीङ्कारो वदनेऽवतु ॥ ४

बगलामुखी दोर्युग्मं कण्ठे सर्वदाऽवतु ।
दुष्टानां पातु हृदयं वाचं मुखं ततः पदम् ॥ ५

उदरे सर्वदा पातु स्तम्भयेति सदा मम ।
जिह्वां कीलय मे मातर्बगला सर्वसदाऽवतु ॥ ६

बुद्धिं विनाशय पादौ तुह्लीं ॐ मे दिग्विदिक्षु च ।
स्वाहा मे सर्वदा पातु सर्वत्र सर्वसन्धिषु ॥ ७

इति ते कथितं देवि कवचं परमाद्भुतम् ।
यस्य स्मरणमात्रेण सर्वस्थम्भो भवेत् क्षणात् ॥ ८

यद् धृत्वा विविधा दैत्या वासवेन हताः पुरा ।
यस्य प्रसादात् सिद्धोऽहं हरिः सत्त्वगुणान्वितः ॥ ९

वेधा सृष्टिं वितनुते कामः सर्वजगज्जयी ।
लिखित्वा धारयेद्यस्तु कण्ठे वा दक्षिणे भुजे ॥ १०

षट्कर्मसिद्धीस्तस्याशु मम तुल्यो भवेद्ध्रुवम् ।
अज्ञात्वा कवचं देवि तस्य मन्त्रो न सिध्यति ॥ ११

इति श्री बगलामुखी शत्रु विनाशक कवचं समाप्तम् ।

*****

Śrī Brahmāstra Bhagalāmukhī Kavacaṃ

Śrī Gaṇeśāya Namaḥ | Śrī Bagalāyai Namaḥ |

Atha Brahmāstra Bagalā Kavacam |

Śrī Brahmovāca |

Viśveśa Dakṣiṇāmūrte Nigamāgamavit Prabho |
Mahyaṃ Purā Tvayā Dattā Vidyā Brahmāstrasaṃjñitā || 1

Tasya Me Kavacaṃ Brūhi Yenāhaṃ Siddhimāpnuyām ||

Bhavāmi Vajrakavacaṃ Brahmāstranyāsamātrataḥ || 2

Śrī Dakṣiṇāmūrtiruvāca |

Śṛṇu Brahman Paraṃ Guhya Brahmāstrakavacaṃ Śubham |
Yasyoccāraṇamātreṇa Bhaved Vai Sūryasannibhaḥ || 3

Sudarśanaṃ Mayā Dattaṃ Kṛpayā Viṣṇave Tathā |
Tadvat Brahmāstravidyāyāḥ Kavacaṃ Kavayāmyaham || 4

Aṣṭāviṃśatyastrahetumādyaṃ Brahmāstramuttamam |
Sarvatejomayaṃ Sarvaṃ Sāmarthyaṃ Vigrahaṃ Param || 5

Sarvaśatrukṣayakaraṃ Sarvadāridryanāśanam |
Sarvāpacchailarāśīnāmastrakam Kuliśopamam || 6

Na Tasya Śatravaścāpi Bhayaṃ Cauryabhayaṃ Jarā |
Narā Nāryaśca Rājendra Khagā Vyāghrādayo'pi Ca || 7

Taṃ Dṛṣṭvā Vaśamāyānti Kimanyat Sādhavo Janāḥ |
Yasya Dehe Nyased Dhīmān Kavacaṃ Bagalāmayam || 8

Sa Eva Puruṣo Loke Kevalaḥ Śaṅkaropamaḥ |
Na Deyaṃ Paraśiṣyāya Śaṭhāya Piśunāya Ca || 9

Dātavyaṃ Bhaktiyuktāya Gurudāsāya Dhīmate |
Kavacasya Ṛṣiḥ Śrīmān Dakṣiṇāmūrtireva Ca ǁ 10

Asyānuṣṭap Chandaḥ Syāt Śrībagalā Cāsya Devatā |
Bījaṃ Śrīvahnijāyā Ca Śaktiḥ Śrībagalāmukhī ǁ 11

Kīlakaṃ Viniyogaśca Svakārye Sarvasādhake |

Atha Dhyānam |

Śuddhasvarṇanibhāṃ Rāmāṃ Pītendukhaṇḍaśekharām |
Pītagandhānuliptāṅgīṃ Pītaratnavibhūṣaṇām ǁ 1

Pīnonnatakucāṃ Snigdhāṃ Pītalāṅgīṃ Supeśalām |
Trilocanāṃ Caturhastāṃ Gambhīrāṃ Madavihvalām ǁ 2

Vajrārirasanāpāśamudgaraṃ Dadhatīṃ Karaiḥ |
Mahāvyāghrāsanāṃ Devīṃ Sarvadevanamaskṛtām ǁ 3

Prasannāṃ Susmitāṃ Klinnāṃ Supītāṃ Pramadottamām |
Subhaktaduḥkhaharaṇe Dayārdrāṃ Dīnavatsalām ǁ 4

Evaṃ Dhyātvā Pareśāni Bagalākavacaṃ Smaret |

Atha Rakṣākavacam |

Bagalā Me Śiraḥ Pātuḥ Lalāṭaṃ Brahmasaṃstutā |
Bagalā Me Bhruvau Nityaṃ Karṇayoḥ Kleśahāriṇī ǁ 1

Trinetrā Cakṣuṣī Pātu Stambhinī Gaṇḍayostathā |
Mohinī Nāsikāṃ Pātu Śrīdevī Bagalāmukhī ǁ 2

Oṣṭhayordurdharā Pātu Sarvadanteṣu Cañcalā |
Siddhānnapūrṇā Jihvāyāṃ Jihvāgre Śāradāmbike ǁ 3

Akalmaṣā Mukhe Pātu Cibuke Bagalāmukhī |
Dhīrā Me Kaṇṭhadeśe Tu Kaṇṭhāgre Kālakarṣiṇī ǁ 4

Śuddhasvarṇanibhā Pātu Kaṇṭhamadhye Tathā'mbikā |
Kaṇṭhamūle Mahābhogā Skandhau Śatruvināśinī || 5

Bhujau Me Pātu Satataṃ Bagalā Susmitā Parā |
Bagalā Me Sadā Pātu Kūrpare Kamalodbhavā || 6

Bagalā'mbā Prakoṣṭhau Tu Maṇibandhe Mahābalā |
Bagalāśrīrhastayośca Kurukullā Karāṅgulim || 7

Nakheṣu Vajrahastā Ca Hṛdaye Brahmavādinī |
Stanau Me Mandagamanā Kukṣayoryoginī Tathā || 8

Udaraṃ Bagalā Mātā Nābhiṃ Brahmāstradevatā |
Puṣṭiṃ Mudgarahastā Ca Pātu No Devavanditā || 9

Pārśvayorhanumadvandyā Paśupāśavimocinī |
Karau Rāmapriyā Pātu Ūruyugmaṃ Maheśvarī || 10

Bhagamālā Tu Guhyaṃ Me Liṅgaṃ Kāmeśvarī Tathā |
Liṅgamūle Mahāklinnā Vṛṣaṇau Pātu Dūtikā || 11

Bagalā Jānunī Pātu Jānuyugmaṃ Ca Nityaśaḥ |
Jaṅghe Pātu Jagaddhātrī Gulphau Rāvaṇapūjitā || 12

Caraṇau Durjayā Pātu Pītāmbā Caraṇāṅgulīḥ |
Pādapṛṣṭhaṃ Padmahastā Pādādhaścakradhāriṇī || 13

Sarvāṅgaṃ Bagalā Devī Pātu Śrībagalāmukhī |
Brāhmī Me Pūrvataḥ Pātu Māheśī Vahnibhāgataḥ || 14

Kaumārī Dakṣiṇe Pātu Vaiṣṇavī Svargamārgataḥ |
Ūrdhvaṃ Pāśadharā Pātu Śatrujihvādharā Hyadhaḥ || 15

Raṇe Rājakule Vāde Mahāyoge Mahābhaye |
Bagalā Bhairavī Pātu Nityaṃ Klīṅkārarūpiṇī || 16

Phalaśrutiḥ |

Ityevaṃ Vajrakavacaṃ Mahābrahmāstrasaṃjñakam |
Trisandhyaṃ Yaḥ Paṭhed Dhīmān Sarvaiśvaryamavāpnuyāt ‖ 1

Na Tasya Śatravaḥ Ke'pi Sakhāyaḥ Sarva Eva Ca |
Balenākṛṣya Śatruṃ Syāt So'pi Mitratvamāpnuyāt ‖ 2

Śatrutve Marutā Tulyo Dhanena Dhanadopamaḥ |
Rūpeṇa Kāmatulyaḥ Syād Āyuṣā Śūladhṛksamaḥ ‖ 3

Sanakādisamo Dhairye Śriyā Viṣṇusamo Bhavet |
Tattulyo Vidyayā Brahman Yo Japet Kavacaṃ Naraḥ ‖ 4

Nārī Vāpi Prayatnena Vāñchitārthamavāpnuyāt |
Dvitīyā Sūryavāreṇa Yadā Bhavati Padmabhūḥ ‖ 5

Tasyāṃ Jātaṃ Śatāvṛtyā Śīghraṃ Pratyakṣamāpnuyāt |
Yātā Turīyaṃ Sandhyāyāṃ Bhūśayyāyāṃ Prayatnataḥ ‖ 6

Sarvān Śatrūn Kṣayaṃ Kṛtvā Vijayaṃ Prāpnuyān Naraḥ |
Dāridryān Mucyate Cā''śu Sthirā Lakṣmīrbhaved Gṛhe ‖ 7

Sarvān Kāmānavāpnoti Saviṣo Nirviṣo Bhavet |
Ṛṇaṃ Nirmocanaṃ Syād Vai Sahasrāvartanād Vidhe ‖ 8

Bhūtapretapiśācādipīḍā Tasya Na Jāyate |
Dyumaṇirbhrājate Yadvat Tadvat Syācchrīprabhāvataḥ ‖ 9

Sthirābhayā Bhavet Tasya Yaḥ Smared Bagalāmukhīm |
Jayadaṃ Bodhanaṃ Kāmamamukaṃ Dehi Me Śive ‖ 10

Japasyānte Smared Yo Vai So'bhīṣṭaphalamāpnuyāt |
Idaṃ Kavacamajñātvā Yo Japed Bagalāmukhīm ‖ 11

Na Sa Siddhimavāpnoti Sākṣād Vai Lokapūjitaḥ |
Tasmāt Sarvaprayatnena Kavacaṃ Brahmatejasam ‖ 12

Nityaṃ Padāmbujadhyānān Maheśānasamo Bhavet |

Iti Śrī Dakṣiṇāmūrti Saṃhitāyāṃ Brahmāstra Bagalāmukhī Kavacaṃ Samāptam |

श्री ब्रह्मास्त्र बगलामुखी कवचं

श्री गणेशाय नमः । श्री बगलायै नमः ।

अथ ब्रह्मास्त्रबगलाकवचम् ।

श्रीब्रह्मोवाच ।

विश्वेश दक्षिणामूर्ते निगमागमवित् प्रभो ।
मह्यं पुरा त्वयादत्ता विद्या ब्रह्मास्त्रसंज्ञिता ॥ १

तस्य मे कवचं ब्रूहि येनाहं सिद्धिमाप्नुयाम् ॥

भवामि वज्रकवचं ब्रह्मास्त्रन्यासमात्रतः ॥ २

श्री दक्षिणामूर्तिरुवाच ।

शृणु ब्रह्मन् परं गुह्य ब्रह्मास्त्रकवचं शुभम् ।
यस्योच्चारणमात्रेण भवेद् वै सूर्यसन्निभः ॥ ३

सुदर्शनं मया दत्तं कृपया विष्णवे तथा ।
तद्वत् ब्रह्मास्त्रविद्यायाः कवचं कवयाम्यहम् ॥ ४

अष्टाविंशत्यस्त्रहेतुमाद्यं ब्रह्मास्त्रमुत्तमम् ।
सर्वतेजोमयं सर्वं सामर्थ्यं विग्रहं परम् ॥ ५

सर्वशत्रुक्षयकरं सर्वदारिद्र्यनाशनम् ।
सर्वापच्छैलराशीनामस्त्रकं कुलिशोपमम् ॥ ६

न तस्य शत्रवश्चापि भयं चौर्यभयं जरा ।
नरा नार्यश्च राजेन्द्र खगा व्याघ्रादयोऽपि च ॥ ७

तं दृष्ट्वा वशमायान्ति किमन्यत् साधवो जनाः ।
यस्य देहे न्यसेद् धीमान् कवचं बगलामयम् ॥ ८

स एव पुरुषो लोके केवलः शङ्करोपमः ।
न देयं परशिष्याय शठाय पिशुनाय च ॥ ९

दातव्यं भक्तियुक्ताय गुरुदासाय धीमते ।
कवचस्य ऋषिः श्रीमान् दक्षिणामूर्तिरेव च ॥ १०

अस्यानुष्टप् छन्दः स्यात् श्रीबगला चास्य देवता ।
बीजं श्रीवह्निजाया च शक्तिः श्रीबगलामुखी ॥ ११

कीलकं विनियोगश्च स्वकार्ये सर्वसाधके ।

अथ ध्यानम् ।

शुद्धस्वर्णनिभां रामां पीतेन्दुखण्डशेखराम् ।
पीतगन्धानुलिप्ताङ्गीं पीतरत्नविभूषणाम् ॥ १

पीनोन्नतकुचां स्निग्धां पीतलाङ्गीं सुपेशलाम् ।
त्रिलोचनां चतुर्हस्तां गम्भीरां मदविह्वलाम् ॥ २

वज्रारिरसनापाशमुद्ररं दधतीं करैः ।
महाव्याघ्रासनां देवीं सर्वदेवनमस्कृताम् ॥ ३

प्रसन्नां सुस्मितां क्लिन्नां सुपीतां प्रमदोत्तमाम् ।
सुभक्तदुःखहरणे दयार्द्रां दीनवत्सलाम् ॥ ४

एवं ध्यात्वा परेशानि बगलाकवचं स्मरेत् ।

अथ रक्षा कवचम् ।

बगला मे शिरः पातुः ललाटं ब्रह्मसंस्तुता ।
बगला मे भ्रुवौ नित्यं कर्णयोः क्लेशहारिणी ॥ १

त्रिनेत्रा चक्षुषी पातु स्तम्भिनी गण्डयोस्तथा ।
मोहिनी नासिकां पातु श्रीदेवी बगलामुखी ॥ २

ओष्ठयोर्दुर्धरा पातु सर्वदन्तेषु चञ्चला ।
सिद्धान्नपूर्णा जिह्वायां जिह्वाग्रे शारदाम्बिके ॥ ३

अकल्मषा मुखे पातु चिबुके बगलामुखी ।
धीरा मे कण्ठदेशे तु कण्ठाग्रे कालकर्षिणी ॥ ४

शुद्धस्वर्णनिभा पातु कण्ठमध्ये तथाऽम्बिका ।
कण्ठमूले महाभोगा स्कन्धौ शत्रुविनाशिनी ॥ ५

भुजौ मे पातु सततं बगला सुस्मिता परा ।
बगला मे सदा पातु कूर्परे कमलोद्भवा ॥ ६

बगलाऽम्बा प्रकोष्ठौ तु मणिबन्धे महाबला ।
बगलाश्रीर्हस्तयोश्च कुरुकुल्ला कराङ्गुलिम् ॥ ७

नखेषु वज्रहस्ता च हृदये ब्रह्मवादिनी ।
स्तनौ मे मन्दगमना कुक्षयोर्योगिनी तथा ॥ ८

उदरं बगला माता नाभिं ब्रह्मास्त्रदेवता ।
पुष्टिं मुद्ररहस्ता च पातु नो देववन्दिता ॥ ९

पार्श्वयोर्हनुमद्वन्द्या पशुपाशविमोचिनी ।
करौ रामप्रिया पातु ऊरुयुग्मं महेश्वरी ॥ १०

भगमाला तु गुह्यं मे लिङ्गं कामेश्वरी तथा ।
लिङ्गमूले महाक्लिन्ना वृषणौ पातु दूतिका ॥ ११

बगला जानुनी पातु जानुयुग्मं च नित्यशः ।
जङ्घे पातु जगद्धात्री गुल्फौ रावणपूजिता ॥ १२

चरणौ दुर्जया पातु पीताम्बा चरणाङ्गुलीः ।
पादपृष्ठं पद्महस्ता पादाधश्चक्रधारिणी ॥ १३

सर्वाङ्गं बगला देवी पातु श्रीबगलामुखी ।
ब्राह्मी मे पूर्वतः पातु माहेशी वह्निभागतः ॥ १४

कौमारी दक्षिणे पातु वैष्णवी स्वर्गमार्गतः ।
ऊर्ध्वं पाशधरा पातु शत्रुजिह्वाधरा ह्यधः ॥ १५

रणे राजकुले वादे महायोगे महाभये ।
बगला भैरवी पातु नित्यं क्लीङ्काररूपिणी ॥ १६

फलश्रुतिः ।

इत्येवं वज्रकवचं महाब्रह्मास्त्रसंज्ञकम् ।
त्रिसन्ध्यं यः पठेद् धीमान् सर्वैश्वर्यमवाप्नुयात् ॥ १

न तस्य शत्रवः केऽपि सखायः सर्व एव च ।
बलेनाकृष्य शत्रुं स्यात् सोऽपि मित्रत्वमाप्नुयात् ॥ २

शत्रुत्वे मरुता तुल्यो धनेन धनदोपमः ।
रूपेण कामतुल्यः स्याद् आयुषा शूलधृक्समः ॥ ३

सनकादिसमो धैर्ये श्रिया विष्णुसमो भवेत् ।
तत्तुल्यो विद्यया ब्रह्मन् यो जपेत् कवचं नरः ॥ ४

नारी वापि प्रयत्नेन वाञ्छितार्थमवाप्नुयात् ।
द्वितीया सूर्यवारेण यदा भवति पद्मभूः ॥ ५

तस्यां जातं शतावृत्या शीघ्रं प्रत्यक्षमाप्नुयात् ।
याता तुरीयं सन्ध्यायां भूशय्यायां प्रयत्नतः ॥ ६

सर्वान् शत्रून् क्षयं कृत्वा विजयं प्राप्नुयान् नरः ।
दारिद्र्यान् मुच्यते चाऽऽशु स्थिरा लक्ष्मीर्भवेद् गृहे ॥ ७

सर्वान् कामानवाप्नोति सविषो निर्विषो भवेत् ।
ऋणं निर्मोचनं स्याद् वै सहस्रावर्तनाद् विधे ॥ ८

भूतप्रेतपिशाचादिपीडा तस्य न जायते ।
द्युमणिर्भ्राजिते यद्वत् तद्वत् स्याच्छ्रीप्रभावतः ॥ ९

स्थिराभया भवेत् तस्य यः स्मरेद् बगलामुखीम् ।
जयदं बोधनं काममममुकं देहि मे शिवे ॥ १०

जपस्यान्ते स्मरेद् यो वै सोऽभीष्टफलमाप्नुयात् ।
इदं कवचमज्ञात्वा यो जपेद् बगलामुखीम् ॥ ११

न स सिद्धिमवाप्नोति साक्षाद् वै लोकपूजितः ।
तस्मात् सर्वप्रयत्नेन कवचं ब्रह्मतेजसम् ॥ १२

नित्यं पदाम्बुजध्यानान् महेशानसमो भवेत् ।

इति श्री दक्षिणामूर्ति संहितायां ब्रह्मास्त्र बगलामुखी कवचं समाप्तम् ।

*****

Śrī Bhagalāmukhī Mālā Mantraḥ

|| Mūla Bagalāmukhī Mantraḥ ||

|| Oṃ Hrlīṃ Bagalāmukhīṃ Sarvaduṣṭānāṃ Vācaṃ Mukhaṃ Padaṃ Stambhaya Stambhaya Jihvāṃ Kīlaya Kīlaya Buddhiṃ Vināśaya Vināśaya Hrlīṃ Phaṭ ||

|| Atha Bagalāmukhī Mālā Mantraḥ ||

|| Oṃ Namo Bhagavati Oṃ Namo Vīrapratāpa Vijaya Bhagavati Bagalāmukhi Mama Sarvanindakānāṃ Sarvaduṣṭānāṃ Vācaṃ Mukhaṃ Padaṃ Stambhaya Stambhaya Brāhmīṃ Mudraya Mudraya Buddhiṃ Vināśaya Vināśaya Aparabuddhiṃ Kuru Kuru Ātmavirodhināṃ Śatruṇāṃ Śiro - Lalāṭa - Mukha - Netra - Karṇa Nāsikorū - Pada - Aṇureṇu - Dantoṣṭha - Jihvā - Tālu - Guhya - Guda - Kaṭi - Jānu Sarvāṅgeṣu Keśādipādaparyantaṃ Pādādi - Keśaparyantaṃ Stambhaya Stambhaya Kheṃ Khīṃ Māraya Māraya, Paramantra - Parayantra - Paratantrāṇi Chedaya Chedaya, Ātmamantrayantratantrāṇi Rakṣa Rakṣa, Grahaṃ Nivāraya Nivāraya Vyādhiṃ Vināśaya Vināśaya, Duḥkhaṃ Hara Hara Dāridrayaṃ Nivāraya Nivāraya Sarvamantrasvarūpiṇi, Sarvatantrasvarūpiṇi, Sarva Śilpaprayogasvarūpiṇi, Sarvatatvasvarūpiṇi, Duṣṭagraha - Bhūtagraha - Ākāśagraha - Pāṣāṇagraha - Sarvacāṇḍālagraha - Yakṣakinnarakimpuruṣagraha - Bhūtapretapiśācānāṃ Śākinī - Ḍākinīgrahāṇāṃ Pūrvadiśāṃ Bandhaya Bandhaya, Vārtāli Māṃ Rakṣa Rakṣa, Dakṣiṇadiśāṃ Bandhaya Bandhaya, Kirātavārtāli Māṃ Rakṣa Rakṣa, Paścimadiśāṃ Bandhaya Bandhaya, Svapnavārtāli Māṃ Rakṣa Rakṣa, Uttaradiśāṃ Bandhaya Bandhaya, Kāli Māṃ Rakṣa Rakṣa, Ūrdhva Diśaṃ Bandhaya Bandhaya Ugra Kāli Māṃ Rakṣa Rakṣa, Pātāladiśaṃ Bandhaya Bandhaya, Bagalāparameśvari Māṃ Rakṣa Rakṣa, Sakalarogān Vināśaya Vināśaya, Sarvaśatrupalāyanāya Pañcayojanamadhye Rājajanastrīvaśatāṃ Kuru Kuru, Śatrūn Daha Daha, Paca Paca, Stambhya Stambhya, Mohaya Mohaya, Ākarṣaya Ākarṣaya, Mama Śatrūn Uccāṭaya Uccāṭaya, Huṃ Phaṭ Svāhā ||

Iti Bagalāmukhī Mālā Mantraḥ |

बगलामुखी माला मन्त्रः

मूल बगलामुखीमन्त्रः ॥

॥ ॐ ह्रलीं बगलामुखीं सर्वदुष्टानां वाचं मुखं पदस्तम्भय स्तम्भय जिह्वां कीलय कीलय बुद्धिं विनाशय विनाशय ह्रलीं फट् ॥

अथ बगलामुखीमालामन्त्रः ॥

ॐ नमो भगवति ॐ नमो वीरप्रतापविजयभगवति बगलामुखि मम सर्वनिन्दकानां सर्वदुष्टानां वाचं मुखं पदं स्तम्भय स्तम्भय ब्राह्मीं मुद्रय मुद्रय बुद्धिं विनाशय विनाशय अपरबुद्धिं कुरु कुरु आत्मविरोधिनां शत्रुणां शिरो- ललाट - मुख - नेत्र - कर्ण नासिकोरू - पद - अणुरेणु-दन्तोष्ठ - जिह्वा - तालु - गुह्य-गुद- कटि - जानु सर्वाङ्गेषु केशादिपादपर्यन्तं पादादि - केशपर्यन्तं स्तम्भय स्तम्भय खें खीं मारय मारय, परमन्त्र - परयन्त्र - परतन्त्राणि छेदय छेदय, आत्ममन्त्रयन्त्रतन्त्राणि रक्ष रक्ष, ग्रहं निवारय निवारय व्याधिं विनाशय विनाशय, दुःखं हर हर दारिद्र्यं निवारय निवारय सर्वमन्त्रस्वरूपिणि, सर्वतन्त्रस्वरूपिणि, सर्व शिल्पप्रयोगस्वरूपिणि, सर्वतत्त्वस्वरूपिणि, दुष्टग्रह - भूतग्रह - आकाशग्रह - पाषाणग्रह - सर्वचाण्डालग्रह - यक्षकिन्नरकिम्पुरुषग्रह - भूतप्रेतपिशाचानां शाकिनी- डाकिनीग्रहाणां पूर्वदिशां बन्धय बन्धय वार्तालि मां रक्ष रक्ष, दक्षिणदिशां बन्धय बन्धय, किरातवार्तालि मां रक्ष रक्ष, पश्चिमदिशां बन्धय बन्धय, स्वप्नवार्तालि मां रक्ष रक्ष, उत्तरदिशां बन्धय बन्धय, कालि मां रक्ष रक्ष, ऊर्ध्व दिशं बन्धय बन्धय उग्र कालि मां रक्ष रक्ष पातालदिशं बन्धय बन्धय, बगलापरमेश्वरि मां रक्ष रक्ष, सकलरोगान् विनाशय विनाशय, सर्वशत्रुपलायनाय पञ्चयोजनमध्ये राजजनस्त्रीवशतां कुरु कुरु, शत्रून् दह दह, पच पच, स्तम्भय स्तम्भय, मोहय मोहय, आकर्षय आकर्षय, मम शत्रून् उच्चाटय उच्चाटय हुं फट् स्वाहा ॥

इति बगलामुखी माला मन्त्रः ।

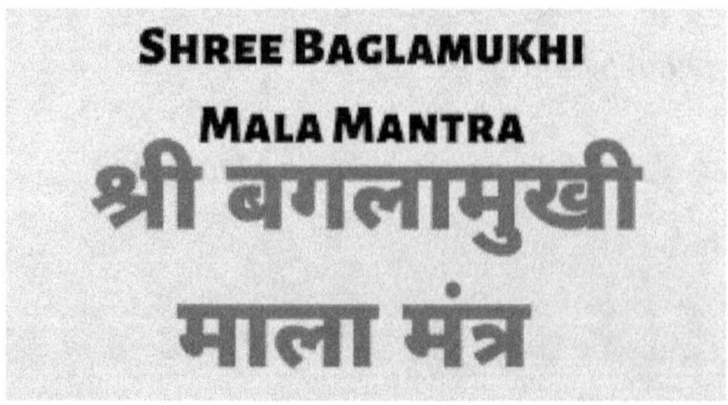

Śrī Bhagalāmukhī Stotram

Śrī Gaṇeśāya Namaḥ |

Calatkanakakuṇḍalollasitacārugaṇḍasthalīṃ
Lasatkanakacampakadyutimadindubimbānanāṃ |
Gadāhatavipakṣakāṃ Kalitalolajihvāṃcalāṃ
Smarāmi Bagalāmukhīṃ Vimukhavāṅmanasstambhinīṃ || 1

Pīyūṣodadhimadhyacāruviladraktotpale Maṇḍape
Satsiṃhāsanamaulipātitaripuṃ Pretāsanādhyāsinīm |
Svarṇābhāṃ Karapīḍitārirasanāṃ Bhrāmyadgadāṃ Vibhratīmitthaṃ
Dhyāyati Yānti Tasya Sahasā Sadyo'tha Sarvāpadaḥ || 2

Devi Tvaccaraṇāmbujārcanakṛte Yaḥ Pītapuṣpāñjalīnbhaktyā
Vāmakare Nidhāya Ca Manuṃ Mantrī Manojñākṣaram |
Pīṭhadhyānaparo'tha Kumbhakavaśādbījaṃ Smaretpārthivaṃ
Tasyāmitramukhasya Vāci Hṛdaye Jāḍyaṃ Bhavettatkṣaṇāt || 3

Vādī Mūkati Raṅkati Kṣitipatirvaiśvānaraḥ Śītati Krodhī
Śāmyati Durjanaḥ Sujanati Kṣiprānugaḥ Khañjati |
Garvī Kharvati Sarvavicca Jaḍati Tvanmantriṇā Yantritaḥ
Śrīrnitye Bagalāmukhi Pratidinaṃ Kalyāṇi Tubhyaṃ Namaḥ || 4

Mantrastāvadalaṃ Vipakṣadalane Stotraṃ Pavitraṃ Ca Te
Yantraṃ Vādiniyantraṇaṃ Trijagatāṃ Jaitraṃ Ca Citraṃ Ca Te |
Mātaḥ Śrībagaleti Nāma Lalitaṃ Yasyāsti Jantormukhe
Tvannāmagrahaṇena Saṃsadi Mukhe Stambho Bhavedvādinām || 5

Duṣṭastambhanamugravighnaśamanaṃ Dāridryavidrāvaṇaṃ
Bhūbhṛtsandamanaṃ Calanmṛgadṛśāṃ Cetaḥsamākarṣaṇam |
Saubhāgyaikaniketanaṃ Samadṛśaḥ Kāruṇyapūrṇekṣaṇam
Mṛtyormāraṇamāvirastu Purato Mātastvadīyaṃ Vapuḥ || 6

Mātarbhañjaya Madvipakṣavadanaṃ Jihvāṃ Ca Saṅkīlaya
Brāhmīṃ Mudraya Daityadevadhiṣaṇāmugrāṃ Gatiṃ Stambhaya |
Śatrūṃścūrṇaya Devi Tīkṣṇagadayā Gaurāṅgi Pītāmbare
Vighnaughaṃ Bagale Hara Praṇamatāṃ Kāruṇyapūrṇekṣaṇe || 7

Mātarbhairavi Bhadrakāli Vijaye Vārāhi Viśvāśraye

Śrīvidye Samaye Maheśi Bagale Kāmeśi Vāme Rame |

Mātaṅgi Tripure Parātparatare Svargāpavargaprade

Dāso'haṃ Śaraṇāgataḥ Karuṇayā Viśveśvari Trāhi Mām ‖ 8

Saṃrambhe Caurasaṅghe Praharaṇasamaye Bandhane Vyādhimadhye

Vidyāvāde Vivāde Prakupitanṛpatau Divyakāle Niśāyām |

Vaśye Vā Stambhane Vā Ripuvadhasamaye Nirjane Vā Vane Vā

Gacchaṃstiṣṭhaṃstrikālaṃ Yadi Paṭhati Śivaṃ Prāpnuyādāśu Dhīraḥ ‖ 9

Tvaṃ Vidyā Paramā Trilokajananī Vighnaughasaṃchedinī

Yoṣitkarṣaṇakāriṇī Janamanaḥsammohasandāyinī |

Stambhotsāraṇakāriṇī Paśumanaḥsammohasandāyinī

Jihvākīlanabhairavī Vijayate Brahmādimantro Yathā ‖ 10

Vidyā Lakṣmīrnityasaubhāgyamāyuḥ Putraiḥ Pautraiḥ Sarva Sāmrājya

Siddhiḥ |

Māno Bhogo Vaśyamārogyasaukhyaṃ Prāptaṃ Tattadbhūta

Le'sminnareṇa ‖ 11

Tvatkṛte Japasannāham Gaditaṃ Parameśvari |

Duṣṭānāṃ Nigrahārthāya Tadgṛhāṇa Namo'stu Te ‖ 12

Pītāmbarāṃ Ca Dvibhujāṃ Trinetrāṃ Gātrakomalām |

Śilāmudgarahastāṃ Ca Smare Tāṃ Bagalāmukhīm ‖ 13

Brahmāstramiti Vikhyātaṃ Triṣu Lokeṣu Viśrutam |

Gurubhaktāya Dātavyaṃ Na Deyaṃ Yasya Kasyacit ‖ 14

Nityaṃ Stotramidaṃ Pavitramiha Yo Devyāḥ Paṭhatyādarāddhṛtvā

Yantramidaṃ Tathaiva Samare Bāhau Kare Vā Gale |

Rājāno'pyarayo Madāndhakariṇaḥ Sarpā Mṛgendrādikāste

Vai Yānti Vimohitā Ripugaṇā Lakṣmīḥ Sthirā Siddhayaḥ ‖ 15

‖ Iti Śrī Rudrayāmale Tantre Śrī Bagalāmukhī Stotraṃ Samāptam ‖

श्रीबगला(वल्गा)मुखीस्तोत्रम्

श्रीगणेशाय नमः ।

चलत्कनककुण्डलोल्लसितचारुगण्डस्थलीं
लसत्कनकचम्पकद्युतिमदिन्दुबिम्बाननाम् ।
गदाहतविपक्षकां कलितलोलजिह्वांचलां
स्मरामि बगलामुखीं विमुखवाङ्मनस्स्तम्भिनीम् ॥ १

पीयूषोदधिमध्यचारुविलद्रक्तोत्पले मण्डपे
सत्सिंहासनमौलिपातितरिपुं प्रेतासनाध्यासिनीम् ।
स्वर्णाभां करपीडितारिरसनां भ्राम्यद्गदां विभ्रतीमित्थं
ध्यायति यान्ति तस्य सहसा सद्योऽथ सर्वापदः ॥ २

देवि त्वच्चरणाम्बुजार्चनकृते यः पीतपुष्पाञ्जलीन्भक्त्या
वामकरे निधाय च मनुं मन्त्री मनोज्ञाक्षरम् ।
पीठध्यानपरोऽथ कुम्भकवशाद्बीजं स्मरेत्पार्थिवं
तस्यामित्रमुखस्य वाचि हृदये जाड्यं भवेत्तत्क्षणात् ॥ ३

वादी मूकति रङ्कति क्षितिपतिर्वैश्वानरः शीतति क्रोधी
शाम्यति दुर्जनः सुजनति क्षिप्रानुगः खञ्जति ।
गर्वी खर्वति सर्वविच्च जडति त्वन्मन्त्रिणा यन्त्रितः
श्रीर्नित्ये बगलामुखि प्रतिदिनं कल्याणि तुभ्यं नमः ॥ ४

मन्त्रस्तावदलं विपक्षदलने स्तोत्रं पवित्रं च ते
यन्त्रं वादिनियन्त्रणं त्रिजगतां जैत्रं च चित्रं च ते ।
मातः श्रीबगलेति नाम ललितं यस्यास्ति जन्तोर्मुखे
त्वन्नामग्रहणेन संसदि मुखे स्तम्भो भवेद्वादिनाम् ॥ ५

दुष्टस्तम्भनमुग्रविघ्नशमनं दारिद्र्यविद्रावणं
भूभृत्सन्दमनं चलन्मृगदृशां चेतःसमाकर्षणम् ।
सौभाग्यैकनिकेतनं समदृशः कारुण्यपूर्णेक्षणम्
मृत्योर्मारणमाविरस्तु पुरतो मातस्त्वदीयं वपुः ॥ ६

मातर्भञ्जय मद्विपक्षवदनं जिह्वां च सङ्कीलय
ब्राह्मीं मुद्रय दैत्यदेवधिषणामुग्रां गतिं स्तंभय ।

शत्रूंश्चूर्णय देवि तीक्ष्णगदया गौराङ्गि पीताम्बरे
विघ्नौघं बगले हर प्रणमतां कारुण्यपूर्णेक्षणे ॥ ७

मातर्भैरवि भद्रकालि विजये वाराहि विश्वाश्रये
श्रीविद्ये समये महेशि बगले कामेशि वामे रमे ।
मातङ्गि त्रिपुरे परात्परतरे स्वर्गापवर्गप्रदे
दासोऽहं शरणागतः करुणया विश्वेश्वरि त्राहि माम् ॥ ८

संरम्भे चौरसङ्घे प्रहरणसमये बन्धने व्याधिमध्ये
विद्यावादे विवादे प्रकुपितनृपतौ दिव्यकाले निशायाम् ।
वश्ये वा स्तम्भने वा रिपुवधसमये निर्जने वा वने वा
गच्छंस्तिष्ठंस्त्रिकालं यदि पठति शिवं प्राप्नुयादाशु धीरः ॥ ९

त्वं विद्या परमा त्रिलोकजननी विघ्नौघसंछेदिनी
योषित्कर्षणकारिणी जनमनःसम्मोहसन्दायिनी ।
स्तम्भोत्सारणकारिणी पशुमनःसम्मोहसन्दायिनी
जिह्वाकीलनभैरवी विजयते ब्रह्मादिमन्त्रो यथा ॥ १०

विद्या लक्ष्मीर्नित्यसौभाग्यमायुः पुत्रैः पौत्रैः सर्वसाम्राज्यसिद्धिः ।
मानो भोगो वश्यमारोग्यसौख्यं प्राप्तं तत्तद्भूतलेऽस्मिन्नरेण ॥ ११

त्वत्कृते जपसन्नाहं गदितं परमेश्वरि ।
दुष्टानां निग्रहार्थाय तद्गृहाण नमोऽस्तु ते ॥ १२

पीताम्बरां च द्विभुजां त्रिनेत्रां गात्रकोमलाम् ।
शिलामुद्ररहस्तां च स्मरे तां बगलामुखीम् ॥ १३

ब्रह्मास्त्रमिति विख्यातं त्रिषु लोकेषु विश्रुतम् ।
गुरुभक्ताय दातव्यं न देयं यस्य कस्यचित् ॥ १४

नित्यं स्तोत्रमिदं पवित्रमिह यो देव्याः पठत्यादराद्भूत्वा
यन्त्रमिदं तथैव समरे बाहौ करे वा गले ।

राजानोऽप्यरयो मदान्धकरिणः सर्पा मृगेन्द्रादिकास्ते
वै यान्ति विमोहिता रिपुगणा लक्ष्मीः स्थिरा सिद्धयः ॥ १५

॥ इति श्रीरुद्रयामले तन्त्रे श्रीबगलामुखीस्तोत्रं समाप्तम् ॥

*****

Śrī Bagalāmukhī Stavarājaḥ

Vande Sakalasandehadāvapāvakamīśvaram |
Karuṇāvaruṇāvāsaṃ Bhaktakalpataruṃ Gurum ‖ 1

Ullasatpītavidyoti Vidyotita Tanutrayam |
Nigamāgamasarvasvamīḍe'haṃ Tanmahanmahaḥ ‖ 2

Oṃ Pūrvaṃ Sthiramāyāṃ Ca Bagalāmukhī Sarvataḥ |
Duṣṭānāṃ Vācamuccārya Mukhaṃ Padaṃ Tathoddharet ‖ 3

Stambhayeti Tato Jihvāṃ Kīlayeti Samuddharet |
Buddhiṃ Vināśayeti Padaṃ Sthiramāyāmanusmaret ‖ 4

Praṇavaṃ Vahnijāyā Cetyeva Paitāmbaro Manuḥ |
Pātu Māṃ Sarvadā Sarvaṃ Nigrahānugrahakṣamaḥ ‖ 5

Kaṇṭhaṃ Nārada Ṛṣiḥ Pātu Paṅktichando'vatānmukham |
Pītāmbarā Devatā Tu Hṛnmadhyamavatānmama ‖ 6

Halī Bījaṃ Stanayorme'vyāt Svāhā Śaktiśca Dantayoḥ |
Sa Kīlakaṃ Tathā Guhye Viniyogo'vatādvapuḥ ‖ 7

Ṣaḍ-Dīrghabhājā Bījena Vyāso'vyānme Karādikam |
Dvipañjapañca Nandeṣu Daśabhirmantravarṇakaiḥ ‖ 8

Ṣaḍaṅgakalpanā Pātu Ṣaḍaṅgāni Hyanukramāt |
Aiṃ Vidyātattvaṃ Klīṃ Māyātattvaṃ Sauśca Śivātmakam ‖ 9

Tattvatrayaṃ Saṃ Bījaṃ Ca Mūlaṃ Hṛtkaṇṭhaṃ Madhyagaḥ |
Sudhābdhau Hemabhūrūḍhacampakodyānamadhyataḥ ‖ 10

Gāruḍotpalanirvyūḍhasvarṇasiṃhāsanopari |
Svarṇapaṅkajasaṃviṣṭāṃ Trinetrāṃ Śaśiśekharām ‖ 11

Pītālaṅkāravasanāṃ Mallīcandanaśobhitām |
Savyābhāṃ Pañcaśākhāyāṃ Vajrajihvāṃ Ca Bibhratīm ‖ 12

Mudgaraṃ Nāgapāśaṃ Ca Dakṣiṇābhyāṃ Madālasām |

Bhaktārivigrahodyogapragalbhāṃ Bagalāmukhīm || 13

Dhyāyamānasya Me Pātu Śāstravodveṣaṇe Bhṛśam |

Bhūkalādaladikpatraṣaṭkoṇaṃ Tryastrabaindukam || 14

Yantraṃ Paitāmbaraṃ Pātu Sā Māṃ Pāyādavigrahā |

Ādhāraśaktimārabhya Jñānātmāntāstu Śaktayaḥ || 15

Pīṭhādyāḥ Pāntu Pīṭhe'traṃ Prathamaṃ Māṃ Ca Rakṣatu |

Śāntiśaṅkhaviśeṣātmaśaktibhūtāni Pāntu Mām || 16

Āvāhanādyāḥ Pañcāpi Mudrāśca Sumanojalaiḥ |

Trikoṇamadhyamārabhya Pūjitā Bagalāmukhī || 17

Krodhinī Stambhinī Cāpi Dhāriṇyaścāpi Madhyagāḥ |

Ojaḥ Pūṣādipīṭhāni Koṇāgreṣu Sthitāni Vai || 18

Trikoṇa Bāhyataḥ Siddhanāthādyā Guravastathā |

Siddhanāthaḥ Siddhānandanāthaḥ Siddhaparameṣṭhi Hi || 19

Nāthaḥ Siddhaḥ Śrīkaṇṭhaśca Nāthaḥ Siddhacatuṣṭayam |

Pātu Māmatha Ṣaṭkoṇe Subhagā Bhagarūpiṇī || 20

Bhagodayā Ca Bhaganipātinī Bhagamālinī |

Bhagavāhā Ca Māṃ Pātu Ṣaṭkoṇāgreṣu Ca Kramāt || 21

Tvagātmā Śoṇitātmā Ca Māṃsātmā Medasātmakaḥ |

Rūpātmā Paramātmā Ca Pātu Māṃ Sthiravigrahā || 22

Aṣṭapatreṣu Mūleṣu Brāhmī Māheśvarī Tathā |

Kaumārī Vaiṣṇavī Vārāhīndrāṇī Ca Tathā Punaḥ || 23

Cāmuṇḍā Ca Mahālakṣmīstatra Madhye Punarjayā |

Vijayā Ca Jayāmbā Ca Rājitā Jṛmbhiṇī Tathā || 24

Stambhinī Mohinī Vaśyā'karṣiṇyatha Tadagrake |

Asitāṅgo Ruruścaṇḍaḥ Kraudhonmattakapālinaḥ |

Bhīṣaṇāścāpi Saṃhāra Ete Rakṣantu Māṃ Sadā || 25

Tataḥ Ṣoḍaśapatreṣu Maṅgalā Stambhinī Tathā |

Jṛmbhiṇī Mohinī Vaśyā Jvālā Siṃhī Balāhakā || 26

Bhūdharā Kalmaṣā Dhātrī Kanyakā Kālakarṣiṇī |

Bhāntikā Mandagamanā Bhogasthā Bhāvaketi Ca || 27

Pātu Māmatha Bhūsadma Daśadikṣu Digīśvarāḥ |

Indro'nalo Yamo Rakṣo Varuṇo Mārutaḥ Śaśiḥ || 28

Īśo'nantaḥ Svayambhūśca Daśaite Pāntu Me Vapuḥ |

Vajraśaktirdaṇḍakhaḍgau Pāśāṅkuśagadāḥ Kramāt |

Śūlaṃ Cakraṃ Sarojaṃ Ca Tattacchastrāṇi Pāntu Mām || 29

Atha Ca Pūrvādi Caturdiśāsu Parataḥ Kramāt |

Pātu Vighneśabaṭukau Yoginī Kṣetrapālakaḥ || 30

Gurutrayaṃ Trirekhāsu Pātu Me Vapurañjasā |

Punaḥ Pītāmbarā Pātu Upacāraiḥ Prapūjitā || 31

Sāṅgāvaraṇaśaktiśca Jayaśrīḥ Pātu Sarvadā |

Valayaṃ Baṭukādibhyo Rakṣāṃ Kurvantu Me Sadā || 32

Śaktayaḥ Sādhakā Vīrāḥ Pātu Me Devatā Imāḥ |

Ityarcākramataḥ Proktaṃ Stotraṃ Paitāmbaraṃ Param || 33

Yaḥ Paṭhet Sakṛdapyetat So'rcāphalamavāpnuyāt |

Sarvathā Kārayet Kṣipraṃ Prapadyante Gadāturān || 34

Rājāno Rājapatnyaśca Paurajānapadāstathā |

Vaśagāstasya Jāyante Satataṃ Sevakā Iva || 35

Gurukalpāśca Vibudhā Mūkatāṃ Yānti Te'grataḥ |

Sthirā Bhavati Tadgehe Capalāpi Haripriyā || 36

Pītāmbarāṅgavasano Yadi Lakṣasaṅkhyaṃ

Paitāmbaraṃ Manumamuṃ Prajapennaro Yaḥ |

Hemī Sakṛnniyamavān Vidhinā Haridrā-

Mālāṃ Dadhadbhavati Tadvaśagā Trilokī || 37

Bhavāni Bagalāmukhi Tridaśakalpavalli Prabho

Kṛpājalanidhe Tava Caraṇadhūtabādhākhilaḥ |

Surāsuranarādikasakalabhaktabhāgyaprade

Tvadaṅghrisarasīruhadvayamahaṃ Tu Dhyāye Sadā || 38

Tvamasya Jagatāṃ Janisthitivināśabījaṃ Nija

Prakāśabahuladyutirbhavati Bhaktahṛnmadhyagā |

Trayīmanu Supūjitā Hariharādi Vṛndārakai-

Ranukṣaṇamanukṣaṇaṃ Mayi Śive Kṣaṇaṃ Vīkṣyatām || 39

Śive Tava Tanūmahaṃ Hariharādyagamyāṃ Parāṃ

Nikhilatāpapratyūhahṛdayābhāvayuktāṃ Smare |

Vidāraya Vicūrṇaya Glapaya Śoṣaya Stambhaya

Praṇodaya Virodhaya Pravilaya Prabaddhāriṇām || 40

Pārvati Kṛpālasanmayi Kaṭākṣapātaṃ Manā-

Ganākulatayā Kṣaṇaṃ Kṣipa Vipakṣasaṃkṣobhiṇi |

Yadīkṣaṇapathaṃ Gataḥ Sakṛdapi Prabhuḥ Kaścana

Sphuṭaṃ Mama Vaśaṃvado Bhavatu Tena Pītāmbare || 41

Oṃ Namo Bhagavate Mahārudrāya Huṃ Phaṭ Svāhā |

Iti Atharvaṇa Rahasyāntargataḥ Śrī Bagalāmukhī Stavarājaḥ Samāptaḥ |

श्री बगलामुखी स्तवराजः

वन्दे सकलसन्देहदावपावकमीश्वरम् ।
करुणावरुणावासं भक्तकल्पतरुं गुरुम् ॥ १

उल्लसत्पीतविद्योति विद्योतित तनुत्रयम् ।
निगमागमसर्वस्वमीडेऽहं तन्महन्महः ॥ २

ॐ पूर्वं स्थिरमायां च बगलामुखी सर्वतः ।
दुष्टानां वाचमुच्चार्य मुखं पदं तथोद्धरेत् ॥ ३

स्तम्भयेति ततो जिह्वां कीलयेति समुद्धरेत् ।
बुद्धिं विनाशयेति पदं स्थिरमायामनुस्मरेत् ॥ ४

प्रणवं वह्निजाया चेत्येव पैताम्बरो मनुः ।
पातु मां सर्वदा सर्वनिग्रहानुग्रहक्षमः ॥ ५

कण्ठं नारद ऋषिः पातु पङ्क्तिच्छन्दोऽवतान्मुखम् ।
पीताम्बरा देवता तु हृन्मध्यमवतान्मम ॥ ६

हली बीजं स्तनयोर्मेऽव्यात् स्वाहा शक्तिश्च दन्तयोः ।
स कीलकं तथा गुह्ये विनियोगोऽवताद्द्रुपुः ॥ ७

षड्-दीर्घभाजा बीजेन व्यासोऽव्यान्मे करादिकम् ।
द्विपञ्जपञ्च नन्देषु दशभिर्मन्त्रवर्णकैः ॥ ८

षडङ्गकल्पना पातु षडङ्गानि ह्यनुक्रमात् ।
ऐं विद्यातत्त्वं क्लीं मायातत्त्वं सौश्च शिवात्मकम् ॥ ९

तत्त्वत्रयं सं बीजं च मूलं हृत्कण्ठं मध्यगः ।
सुधाब्धौ हेमभूरूढचम्पकोद्यानमध्यतः ॥ १०

गारुडोत्पलनिर्व्यूढस्वर्णसिंहासनोपरि ।
स्वर्णपङ्कजसंविष्टां त्रिनेत्रां शशिशेखराम् ॥ ११

पीतालङ्कारवसनां मल्लीचन्दनशोभिताम् ।
सव्याभां पञ्चशाखायां वज्रजिह्वां च बिभ्रतीम् ॥ १२

मुद्ररं नागपाशं च दक्षिणाभ्यां मदालसाम् ।
भक्तारिविग्रहोद्योगप्रगल्भां बगलामुखीम् ॥ १३

ध्यायमानस्य मे पातु शास्त्रवोद्रेषणे भृशम् ।
भूकलादलदिक्पत्रषट्कोणं त्र्यस्त्रबैन्दुकम् ॥ १४

यन्त्रं पैताम्बरं पातु सा मां पायादविग्रहा ।
आधारशक्तिमारभ्य ज्ञानात्मान्तास्तु शक्तयः ॥ १५

पीठाद्याः पान्तु पीठेऽत्रं प्रथमं मां च रक्षतु ।
शान्तिशङ्खविशेषात्मशक्तिभूतानि पान्तु माम् ॥ १६

आवाहनाद्याः पञ्चापि मुद्राश्च सुमनोजलैः ।
त्रिकोणमध्यमारभ्य पूजिता बगलामुखी ॥ १७

क्रोधिनी स्तम्भिनी चापि धारिण्यश्चापि मध्यगाः ।
ओजः पूषादिपीठानि कोणाग्रेषु स्थितानि वै ॥ १८

त्रिकोण बाह्यतः सिद्धनाथाद्या गुरवस्तथा ।
सिद्धनाथः सिद्धानन्दनाथः सिद्धपरमेष्ठि हि ॥ १९

नाथः सिद्धः श्रीकण्ठश्च नाथः सिद्धचतुष्टयम् ।
पातु मामथ षट्कोणे सुभगा भगरूपिणी ॥ २०

भगोदया च भगनिपातिनी भगमालिनी ।
भगवाहा च मां पातु षट्कोणाग्रेषु च क्रमात् ॥ २१

त्वगात्मा शोणितात्मा च मांसात्मा मेदसात्मकः ।
रूपात्मा परमात्मा च पातु मां स्थिरविग्रहा ॥ २२

अष्टपत्रेषु मूलेषु ब्राह्मी माहेश्वरी तथा ।
कौमारी वैष्णवी वाराहीन्द्राणी च तथा पुनः ॥ २३

चामुण्डा च महालक्ष्मीस्तत्र मध्ये पुनर्जया ।
विजया च जयाम्बा च राजिता जृम्भिणी तथा ॥ २४

स्तम्भिनी मोहिनी वश्याऽऽकर्षिण्यथ तदग्रके ।
असिताङ्गो रुरुश्चण्डः क्रौधोन्मत्तकपालिनः ।
भीषणाश्चापि संहार एते रक्षन्तु मां सदा ॥ २५

ततः षोडशपत्रेषु मङ्गला स्तम्भिनी तथा ।
जृम्भिणी मोहिनी वश्या ज्वाला सिंही बलाहका ॥ २६

भूधरा कल्मषा धात्री कन्यका कालकर्षिणी ।
भान्तिका मन्दगमना भोगस्था भावकेति च ॥ २७

पातु मामथ भूसद्म दशदिक्षु दिगीश्वराः ।
इन्द्रोऽनलो यमो रक्षो वरुणो मारुतः शशिः ॥ २८

ईशोऽनन्तः स्वयम्भूश्च दशैते पान्तु मे वपुः ।

वज्रशक्तिर्दण्डखड्गौ पाशाङ्कुशगदाः क्रमात् ।

शूलं चक्रं सरोजं चतत्तच्छस्त्राणि पान्तु माम् ॥ २९

अथ च पूर्वादि चतुर्दिशासु परतः क्रमात् ।

पातु विघ्नेशबटुकौ योगिनी क्षेत्रपालकः ॥ ३०

गुरुत्रयं त्रिरेखासु पातु मे वपुरञ्जसा ।

पुनः पीताम्बरा पातु उपचारैः प्रपूजिता ॥ ३१

साङ्गावरणशक्तिश्च जयश्रीः पातु सर्वदा ।

वलयं बटुकादिभ्यो रक्षां कुर्वन्तु मे सदा ॥ ३२

शक्तयः साधका वीराः पातु मे देवता इमाः ।

इत्यर्चाक्रमतः प्रोक्तं स्तोत्रं पैताम्बरं परम् ॥ ३३

यः पठेत् सकृदप्येतत् सोऽर्चफलमवाप्नुयात् ।

सर्वथा कारयेत् क्षिप्रं प्रपद्यन्ते गदातुरान् ॥ ३४

राजानो राजपत्न्यश्च पौरजानपदास्तथा ।

वशगास्तस्य जायन्ते सततं सेवका इव ॥ ३५

गुरुकल्पाश्च विबुधा मूकतां यान्ति तेऽग्रतः ।

स्थिरा भवति तद्गेहे चपलापि हरिप्रिया ॥ ३६

पीताम्बराङ्गवसनो यदि लक्षसङ्ख्यं पैताम्बरं मनुममुं प्रजपेन्नरो यः ।

हेमी सकृन्नियमवान् विधिना हरिद्रा मालां दधद्भवति तद्वशगा त्रिलोकी ॥ ३७

भवानि बगलामुखि त्रिदशकल्पवल्लि प्रभो कृपाजलनिधे तव चरणधूतबाधाखिलः ।

सुरासुरनरादिकसकलभक्तभाग्यप्रदेत्वदङ्घ्रिसरसीरुहहृदयमहं तु ध्याये सदा ॥ ३८

त्वमस्य जगतां जनिस्थितिविनाशबीजं निजप्रकाशबहुलद्युतिर्भवति भक्तहृन्मध्यगा ।

त्रयीमनु सुपूजिता हरिहरादि वृन्दारकैरनुक्षणमनुक्षणं मयि शिवे क्षणं वीक्ष्यताम् ॥ ३९

शिवे तव तनूमहं हरिहराद्यगम्यां परां निखिलतापप्रत्यूहहृदयाभावयुक्तां स्मरे ।

विदारय विचूर्णय ग्लपय शोषय स्तम्भय प्रणोदय विरोधय प्रविलय

प्रबद्धारिणाम् ॥ ४०

पार्वति कृपालसन्मयि कटाक्षपातं मना गनाकुलतया क्षणं क्षिप विपक्षसंक्षोभिणि ।

यदीक्षणपथं गतः सकृदपि प्रभुः कश्चनस्फुटं मम वशंवदो भवतु तेन पीताम्बरे ॥ ४१

ॐ नमो भगवते महारुद्राय हुं फट् स्वाहा ।

इति अथर्वण रहस्यान्तर्गतः श्रीबगलामुखी स्तवराजः समाप्तः ।

श्री बगलामुखी-स्तवराज
(अथर्वण रहस्य से)

Shri Bagalamukhi StavaRaj

*****

Śrī Bhagalāmukhī Hṛdayam

Oṃ Asya Śrī Bagalāmukhī Hṛdayaya Stotrasya Nārada Ṛṣiḥ |

Anuṣṭup Chandaḥ | Śrībagalāmukhī Devatā |

Hlīṃ Bījam | Klīṃ Śaktiḥ | Aiṃ Kīlakam |
Śrī Bagalāmukhī Prasāda Siddhyarthe Śrī Bagalāmukhī Hṛdaya

Jape Viniyogaḥ ||

Ṛṣyādi Nyāsaḥ |

Oṃ Nāradarṣaye Namaḥ Śirasi |

Oṃ Anuṣṭup Chandase Namaḥ Mukhe |

Oṃ Śrībagalāmukhī Devatāyai Namaḥ Hṛdaye |

Oṃ Hlīṃ Bījāya Namaḥ Guhye | Oṃ Klīṃ Śaktayenamaḥ Pādayoḥ |

Oṃ Aiṃ Kīlakāya Namaḥ Sarvāṅge |

Atha Karanyāsaḥ |

Oṃ Hlīṃ Aṅguṣṭhābhyāṃ Namaḥ |

Oṃ Klīṃ Tarjanībhyāṃ Namaḥ |

Oṃ Aiṃ Madhyamābhyāṃ Namaḥ |

Oṃ Hlīṃ Anāmikābhyāṃ Namaḥ |

Oṃ Klīṃ Kaniṣṭhikābhyāṃ Namaḥ |

Oṃ Aiṃ Karatalakarapṛṣṭhābhyāṃ Namaḥ |

Atha Hṛdayādi Ṣaḍaṅga Nyāsaḥ |

Oṃ Hlīṃ Hṛdayāya Namaḥ | *Oṃ Klīṃ Śirase Svāhā |*

Oṃ Aiṃ Śikhāyai Vaṣaṭ | *Oṃ Hlīṃ Kavacāya Hum |*

Oṃ Klīṃ Netratrayāya Vauṣaṭ | Oṃ Aiṃ Astrāya Phaṭ |

Oṃ Hlīṃ Klīṃ Aiṃ Iti Digbandhaḥ ||

Dhyānam

Pītāmbarāṃ Pītamālyāṃ Pītābharaṇabhūṣitām |

Pītakañjapadadvandvāṃ Bagalāṃ Cintaye'niśam || Cintate'niśam

Pītaśaṅkhagadāhaste Pītacandanacarcite |

Bagale Me Varaṃ Dehi Śatrusaṅghavidāriṇī ||

Oṃ Hlīṃ Klīṃ Aiṃ Bagalāmukhyai Gadādhāriṇyai Pretāsanādhyāsinyai

Svāhā ||

(Iti Mantraṃ Japitvā Punaḥ Pūrvavaddhṛdayādi Ṣaḍaṅganyāsaṅkṛtvā Stotrampaṭhet ||)

This mantra can be chant for 11 21 51 or 108 times and the *Hṛdayaya Stotram* can be chant |

Atha Karanyāsaḥ |

Oṃ Hlīṃ Aṅguṣṭhābhyāṃ Namaḥ |

Oṃ Klīṃ Tarjanībhyāṃ Namaḥ |

Oṃ Aiṃ Madhyamābhyāṃ Namaḥ |

Oṃ Hlīṃ Anāmikābhyāṃ Namaḥ |

Oṃ Klīṃ Kaniṣṭhikābhyāṃ Namaḥ |

Oṃ Aiṃ Karatala Karapṛṣṭhābhyāṃ Namaḥ |

Atha Hṛdayādi Ṣaḍaṅga Nyāsaḥ |

Oṃ Hlīṃ Hṛdayāya Namaḥ |

Oṃ Klīṃ Śirase Svāhā |　　　*Oṃ Aiṃ Śikhāyai Vaṣaṭ |*

Oṃ Hlīṃ Kavacāya Hum |　　　*Oṃ Klīṃ Netratrayāya Vauṣaṭ |*

Oṃ Aiṃ Astrāya Phaṭ |　　　*Oṃ Hlīṃ Klīṃ Aiṃ Iti Digbandhaḥ ||*

Tadyathā ||

Bande'haṃ Bagalāṃ Devīṃ Pītabhūṣaṇabhūṣitām |

Tejorūpamayīṃ Devīṃ Pītatejassvarūpiṇīm || 1

Gadābhramaṇābhinnābhrāṃ Bhrukuṭībhīṣaṇānanām |

Bhīṣayantīṃ Bhīmaśatrūn Bhaje Bhaktasya Bhavyadām || 2

Pūrṇacandrasamānāsyāṃ Pītagandhānulepanām |

Pītāmbaraparīdhānāṃ Pavitrāmāśrayāmyaham || 3

Pālayantīmanupalaṃ Prasamīkṣyāvanītale |

Pītācāraratāṃ Bhaktāṃ Stāmbhavānīṃ Bhajāmyaham || 4

Pītapadmapadadvandvāṃ Campakāraṇyarūpiṇīm |

Pītāvataṃsāṃ Paramāṃ Vande Padmajavanditām || 5

Lasaccārusiñjatsumañjīrapādāṃ Calatsvarṇakarṇāvataṃsāñcitāsyām |

Valatpītacandrānanāṃ Candravandyāṃ Bhaje

Padmajādīḍyasatpādapadmām || 6

Supītābhayāmālayā Pūtamantraṃ Paraṃ Te Japanto Jayaṃ Sallabhante |

Raṇe Rāgaroṣāplutānāṃ Ripūṇāṃ Vivāde Balādvairakṛddhātamātaḥ || 7

Bharatpītabhāsvatprabhāhaskarābhāṃ Gadāgañjitāmitragarvāṃ

Gariṣṭhām |

Garīyo Guṇāgāragātrāṃ Guṇāḍhyāṃ Gaṇeśādigamyāṃ Śraye

Nirguṇāḍhyām || 8

Janā Ye Japantyugrabījaṃ Jagatsu Paraṃ Pratyahaṃ Te Smarantaḥ

Svarūpam |

Bhavedvādināṃ Vāṅmukhastambha Ādye Jayo Jāyate Jalpatāmāśu

Teṣām || 9

Tava Dhyānaniṣṭhā Pratiṣṭhātmaprajñāvatāṃ Pādapadmārcane

Premayuktāḥ |

Prasannā Nṛpāḥ Prākṛtāḥ Paṇḍitā Vā Purāṇādikā Dāsatulyā Bhavanti || 10

Namāmaste Mātaḥ Kanakakamanīyāṅghrijalajaṃ

Baladvidyudvarṇāṃ Ghanatimiravidhvaṃsakaraṇam |

Bhavābdhau Magnātmottaraṇakaraṇaṃ Sarvaśaraṇaṃ

Prapannānāṃ Mātarjagati Bagale Duḥkhadamanam || 11

Jvalajjyotsnāratnākaramaṇiviṣaktāṅkabhavanaṃ

Smarāmaste Dhāma Smaraharaharīndrendupramukhaiḥ |

Ahorātraṃ Prātaḥ Praṇayanavanīyaṃ Suviśadaṃ

Paraṃ Pītākāraṃ Paricitamaṇidvīpavasanam || 12

Vadāmaste Mātaḥ Śrutisukhakaraṃ Nāma Lalitaṃ

Lasanmātrāvarṇaṃ Jagati Bagaleti Pracaritam |

Calantastiṣṭhanto Vayamupaviśanto'pi Śayane
Bhajāmo Yacchreyo Divi Duravalabhyaṃ Diviṣadām || 13

Padārcāyāṃ Prītiḥ Pratidinamapūrvā Prabhavatu
Yathā Te Prāsannyaṃ Pratipalamapekṣyaṃ Praṇamatām |
Analpaṃ Tanmātarbhavati Bhṛtabhaktyā Bhavatu No
Diśātaḥ Sadbhaktiṃ Bhuvi Bhagavatāṃ Bhūri Bhavadām || 14

Mama Sakalaripūṇāṃ Vāṅmukhe Stambhayāśu
Bhagavati Ripujihvāṃ Kīlaya Prasthatulyām |
Vyavasitakhalabuddhiṃ Nāśayāśu Pragalbhāṃ
Mama Kuru Bahukāryaṃ Satkṛpe'mba Prasīda || 15

Vrajatu Mama Ripūṇāṃ Sadmani Pretasaṃsthā
Karadhṛtagadayā Tān Ghātayitvāśu Roṣāt |
Sadhanavasanadhānyaṃ Sadma Teṣāṃ Pradahya
Punarapi Bagalā Svasthānamāyātu Śīghram || 16

Karadhṛtaripu Jihvāpīḍana Vyagrahastāṃ
Punarapi Gadayā Tāṃstāḍayantīṃ Sutantrām |
Praṇatasuragaṇānāṃ Pālikāṃ Pītavastrāṃ
Bahubalabagalāntāṃ Pītavastrāṃ Namāmaḥ || 17

Hṛdayavacanakāyaiḥ Kurvatāṃ Bhaktipuñjaṃ
Prakaṭita Karuṇārdrāṃ Prīṇatījalpatīti |
Dhanamatha Bahudhānyaṃ Putrapautrādivṛddhiḥ
Sakalamapi Kimebhyo Deyamevaṃ Tvavaśyam || 18

Tava Caraṇasarojaṃ Sarvadā Sevyamānaṃ
Druhiṇahariharādyairdevavṛndaiḥ Śaraṇyam |
Mṛdulamapi Śaraṇaṃ Te Śarmadaṃ Sūrisevyaṃ
Vayamiha Karavāmo Mātaretad Vidheyam || 19

Bagalāhṛdayastotramidaṃ Bhaktisamanvitaḥ |
Paṭhed Yo Bagalā Tasya Prasannā Pāṭhato Bhavet || 20

Pītādhyānaparo Bhakto Yaḥ Śṛṇotyavikalpataḥ |
Niṣkalmaṣo Bhavenmarttyo Mṛto Mokṣamavāpnuyāt || 21

Āśvinasya Site Pakṣe Mahāṣṭamyāṁ Divāniśam |

Yastvidaṁ Paṭhate Premṇā Bagalāprītimeti Saḥ || 22

Devyālaye Paṭhan Marttyo Bagalāṁ Dhyāyatīśvarīm |

Pītavastrāvṛto Yastu Tasya Naśyanti Śatravaḥ || 23

Pītācārarato Nityaṁ Pītabhūṣāṁ Vicintayan |

Bagalāyāḥ Paṭhennityaṁ Hṛdayastotramuttamam || 24

Na Kiñcid Durllabhaṁ Tasya Dṛśyate Jagatītale |

Śatravo Glānimāyānti Tasya Darśanamātrataḥ || 25

Iti Siddheśvara Tantre Uttara Khaṇḍe Bagalāpaṭale Śrī Bagalā Hṛdaya

Stotraṁ Samāptam ||

श्री बगलामुखी हृदयम्

ॐ अस्य श्रीबगलामुखीहृदयस्य नारद ऋषिः ।
अनुष्टुप् छन्दः । श्रीबगलामुखी देवता ।
ह्रीं बीजम् । क्लीं शक्तिः । ऐं कीलकम् ।
श्रीबगलामुखीप्रसादसिद्ध्यर्थे श्रीबगलामुखीहृदयम् जपे विनियोगः ॥

ऋष्यादिन्यासः ।

ॐ नारदऋषये नमः शिरसि ।   ॐ अनुष्टुप् छन्दसे नमः मुखे ।
ॐ श्रीबगलामुखी देवतायै नमः हृदये ।
ॐ ह्रीं बीजाय नमः गुह्ये ।   ॐ क्लीं शक्तयेनमः पादयोः ।
ॐ ऐं कीलकाय नमः सर्वाङ्गे ।

अथ करन्यासः ।

ॐ ह्रीं अङ्गुष्ठाभ्यां नमः ।   ॐ क्लीं तर्जनीभ्यां नमः ।
ॐ ऐं मध्यमाभ्यां नमः ।   ॐ ह्रीं अनामिकाभ्यां नमः ।
ॐ क्लीं कनिष्ठिकाभ्यां नमः ।   ॐ ऐं करतलकरपृष्ठाभ्यां नमः ।

अथ हृदयादि षडङ्गन्यासः ।

ॐ ह्रीं हृदयाय नमः ।   ॐ क्लीं शिरसे स्वाहा ।
ॐ ऐं शिखायै वषट् ।   ॐ ह्रीं कवचाय हुम् ।

ॐ क्लीं नेत्रत्रयाय वौषट् । ॐ ऐं अस्त्राय फट् ।

ॐ ह्रीं क्लीं ऐं इति दिग्बन्धः ॥

पीताम्बरां पीतमाल्यां पीताभरणभूषिताम् ।
पीतकञ्जपदद्वन्द्वां बगलां चिन्तयेऽनिशम् ॥

इति ध्यात्वा सम्पूज्य ॥

पीतशङ्खगदाहस्ते पीतचन्दनचर्चिते ।
बगले मे वरं देहि शत्रुसङ्घविदारिणी ॥

इति सम्प्रार्थ्य ॥

ॐ ह्रीं क्लीं ऐं बगलामुख्यै गदाधारिण्यै प्रेतासनाध्यासिन्यै स्वाहा ॥

(इति मन्त्रं जपित्वा पुनः पूर्ववद्धृदयादि षडङ्गन्यासङ्कृत्वा स्तोत्रम्पठेत् ॥)

इस मन्त्रका जप ११ २१ ५१ या १०८ बार करें और पुनः न्यास करें ।

अथ करन्यासः ।

ॐ ह्रीं अङ्गुष्ठाभ्यां नमः । ॐ क्लीं तर्जनीभ्यां नमः ।
ॐ ऐं मध्यमाभ्यां नमः । ॐ ह्रीं अनामिकाभ्यां नमः ।
ॐ क्लीं कनिष्ठिकाभ्यां नमः । ॐ ऐं करतल करपृष्ठाभ्यां नमः ।

अथ हृदयादि षडङ्ग न्यासः ।

ॐ ह्रीं हृदयाय नमः । ॐ क्लीं शिरसे स्वाहा ।
ॐ ऐं शिखायै वषट् । ॐ ह्रीं कवचाय हुम् ।
ॐ क्लीं नेत्रत्रयाय वौषट् । ॐ ऐं अस्त्राय फट् ।
ॐ ह्रीं क्लीं ऐं इति दिग्बन्धः ॥

तद्यथा ॥

बन्देऽहं बगलां देवीं पीतभूषणभूषिताम् ।
तेजोरूपमयीं देवीं पीततेजस्स्वरूपिणीम् ॥ १

गदाभ्रमणाभिन्नाभ्रां भ्रुकुटीभीषणाननाम् ।
भीषयन्तीं भीमशत्रून् भजे भक्तस्य भव्यदाम् ॥ २

पूर्णचन्द्रसमानास्यां पीतगन्धानुलेपनाम् ।
पीताम्बरपरीधानां पवित्रामाश्रयाम्यहम् ॥ ३

पालयन्तीमनुपलं प्रसमीक्ष्यावनीतले ।
पीताचाररतां भक्तां स्ताम्भवानीं भजाम्यहम् ॥ ४

पीतपद्मपदद्वन्द्वां चम्पकारण्यरूपिणीम् ।
पीतावतंसां परमां वन्दे पद्मजवन्दिताम् ॥ ५

लसच्चारुसिञ्जत्सुमञ्जीरपादां चलत्स्वर्णकर्णावतंसाञ्चितास्याम् ।
वलत्पीतचन्द्राननां चन्द्रवन्द्यां भजे पद्मजादीड्यसत्पादपद्माम् ॥ ६

सुपीताभयामालया पूतमन्त्रं परं ते जपन्तो जयं सल्लभन्ते ।
रणे रागरोषाप्लुतानां रिपूणां विवादे बलाद्वैरकृद्धातमातः ॥ ७

भरत्पीतभास्वत्प्रभाहस्कराभां गदागञ्जितामित्रगर्वां गरिष्ठाम् ।
गरीयो गुणागारगात्रां गुणाढ्यां गणेशादिगम्यां श्रये निर्गुणाढ्याम् ॥ ८

जना ये जपन्त्युग्रबीजं जगत्सु परं प्रत्यहं ते स्मरन्तः स्वरूपम् ।
भवेद्वादिनां वाङ्मुखस्तम्भ आद्ये जयो जायते जल्पतामाशु तेषाम् ॥ ९

तव ध्याननिष्ठा प्रतिष्ठात्मप्रज्ञावतां पादपद्मार्चने प्रेमयुक्ताः ।
प्रसन्ना नृपाः प्राकृताः पण्डिता वा पुराणादिका दासतुल्या भवन्ति ॥ १०

नमामस्ते मातः कनककमनीयाङ्घ्रिजलजं बलद्विद्युद्वर्णां घनतिमिरविध्वंसकरणम् ।
भवाब्धौ मग्नात्मोत्तरणकरणं सर्वशरणं प्रपन्नानां मातर्जगति बगले दुःखदमनम् ॥ ११

ज्वलज्ज्योत्स्नारत्नाकरमणिविषक्ताङ्कभवनं स्मरामस्ते धाम स्मरहरहरीन्द्रेन्द्रप्रमुखैः ।
अहोरात्रं प्रातः प्रणयनवनीयं सुविशदंपरं पीताकारं परिचितमणिद्वीपवसनम् ॥ १२

वदामस्ते मातः श्रुतिसुखकरं नाम ललितंलसन्मात्रावर्णं जगति बगलेति प्रचरितम् ।
चलन्तस्तिष्ठन्तो वयमुपविशन्तोऽपि शयने भजामो यच्छ्रेयो दिवि दुर्लभ्यं
दिविषदाम् ॥ १३

पदार्चायां प्रीतिः प्रतिदिनमपूर्वा प्रभवतु यथा ते प्रासन्यं प्रतिपलमपेक्ष्यं प्रणमताम् ।
अनल्पं तन्मातर्भवति भृतभक्त्या भवतु नोदिशातः सद्भक्तिं भुवि भगवतां भूरि
भवदाम् ॥ १४

मम सकलरिपूणां वाङ्मुखे स्तम्भयाशु भगवति रिपुजिह्वां कीलय प्रस्थतुल्याम् ।
व्यवसितखलबुद्धिं नाशयाशु प्रगल्भांमम कुरु बहुकार्य सत्कृपेऽम्ब प्रसीद ॥ १५

व्रजतु मम रिपूणां सद्मनि प्रेतसंस्थाकरधृतगदया तान् घातयित्वाशु रोषात् ।
सधनवसनधान्यं सद्म तेषां प्रदह्यपुनरपि बगला स्वस्थानमायातु शीघ्रम् ॥ १६

करधृतरिपु जिह्वापीडन व्यग्रहस्तां पुनरपि गदया तांस्ताडयन्तीं सुतन्त्राम् ।
प्रणतसुरगणानां पालिकां पीतवस्त्रां बहुबलबगलान्तां पीतवस्त्रां नमामः ॥ १७

हृदयवचनकायैः कुर्वतां भक्तिपुञ्जं प्रकटित करुणार्द्रां प्रीणतीजल्पतीति ।
धनमथ बहुधान्यं पुत्रपौत्रादिवृद्धिःसकलमपि किमेभ्यो देयमेवं त्ववश्यम् ॥ १८

तव चरणसरोजं सर्वदा सेव्यमानं द्रुहिणहरिहराद्यैर्देववृन्दैः शरण्यम् ।
मृदुलमपि शरणं ते शर्मदं सूरिसेव्यंवयमिह करवामो मातरेतद् विधेयम् ॥ १९

बगलाहृदयस्तोत्रमिदं भक्तिसमन्वितः ।
पठेद् यो बगला तस्य प्रसन्ना पाठतो भवेत् ॥ २०

पीताध्यानपरो भक्तो यः शृणोत्यविकल्पतः ।
निष्कल्मषो भवेन्मर्त्यो मृतो मोक्षमवाप्नुयात् ॥ २१

आश्विनस्य सिते पक्षे महाष्टम्यां दिवानिशम् ।
यस्त्विदं पठते प्रेम्णा बगलाप्रीतिमेति सः ॥ २२

देव्यालये पठन् मर्त्यो बगलां ध्यायतीश्वरीम् ।
पीतवस्त्रावृतो यस्तु तस्य नश्यन्ति शत्रवः ॥ २३

पीताचाररतो नित्यं पीतभूषां विचिन्तयन् ।
बगलायाः पठेन्नित्यं हृदयस्तोत्रमुत्तमम् ॥ २४

न किञ्चिद् दुर्ल्लभं तस्य दृश्यते जगतीतले ।
शत्रवो ग्लानिमायान्ति तस्य दर्शनमात्रतः ॥ २५

इति सिद्धेश्वर तन्त्रे उत्तर खण्डे
बगला पटले श्री बगला हृदय
स्तोत्रं समाप्तम् ॥

*****

Śrī Bhagalāmukhī Aṣtotra Śata Nāma Stotram

Oṃ Brahmāstrarūpiṇī Devī Mātā Śrībagalāmukhī |
Cicchiktirjñānarūpā Ca Brahmānandapradāyinī || 1

Mahāvidyā Mahālakṣmī Śrīmattripurasundarī |
Bhuvaneśī Jaganmātā Pārvatī Sarvamaṅgalā || 2

Lalitā Bhairavī Śāntā Annapūrṇā Kuleśvarī |
Vārāhī Chīnnamastā Ca Tārā Kālī Sarasvatī || 3

Jagatpūjyā Mahāmāyā Kāmeśī Bhagamālinī |
Dakṣaputrī Śivāṅkasthā Śivarūpā Śivapriyā || 4

Sarvasampatkarī Devī Sarvaloka Vaśaṅkarī |
Vedavidyā Mahāpūjyā Bhaktādveṣī Bhayaṅkarī || 5

Stambharūpā Stambhinī Ca Duṣṭastambhanakāriṇī |
Bhaktapriyā Mahābhogā Śrīvidyā Lalitāmbikā || 6

Maināputrī Śivānandā Mātaṅgī Bhuvaneśvarī |
Nārasiṃhī Narendrā Ca Nṛpārādhyā Narottamā || 7

Nāginī Nāgaputrī Ca Nagarājasutā Umā |
Pītāmbā Pītapuṣpā Ca Pītavastrapriyā Śubhā || 8

Pītagandhapriyā Rāmā Pītaratnārcitā Śivā |
Arddhacandradharī Devī Gadāmudgaradhāriṇī || 9

Sāvitrī Tripadā Śuddhā Sadyorāga Vivardhinī |
Viṣṇurūpā Jaganmohā Brahmarūpā Haripriyā || 10

Rudrarūpā Rudraśaktiścinmayī Bhaktavatsalā |
Lokamātā Śivā Sandhyā Śivapūjanatatparā || 11

Dhanādhyakṣā Dhaneśī Ca Narmadā Dhanadā Dhanā |
Caṇḍadarpaharī Devī Śumbhāsuranibarhiṇī || 12

Rājarājeśvarī Devī Mahiṣāsuramardinī |

Madhūkaiṭabhahantrī Devī Raktabījavināśinī || 13

Dhūmrākṣadaityahantrī Ca Bhaṇḍāsura Vināśinī |

Reṇuputrī Mahāmāyā Bhrāmarī Bhramarāmbikā || 14

Jvālāmukhī Bhadrakālī Bagalā Śatrunāśinī |

Indrāṇī Indrapūjyā Ca Guhamātā Guṇeśvarī || 15

Vajrapāśadharā Devī Jhvāmudgaradhāriṇī |

Bhaktānandakarī Devī Bagalā Parameśvarī || 16

Aṣṭottaraśatam Nāmnām Bagalāyāstu Yaḥ Paṭhet |

Ripubādhāvinirmuktaḥ Lakṣmīsthairyamavāpnuyāt || 17

Bhūtapretapiśācāśca Grahapīḍānivāraṇam |

Rājāno Vaśamāyānti Sarvaiśvaryaṃ Ca Vindati || 18

Nānāvidyāṃ Ca Labhate Rājyaṃ Prāpnoti Niścitam |

Bhuktimuktimavāpnoti Sākṣāt Śivasamo Bhavet || 19

Phala-Śrutiḥ.

Aṣṭottara Śatan Nāmnām, Bagalāyāstu Yah Paṭhet |

Ripu Bādhā Vinirmuktaḥ, Lakśmīsthairyamavāpnuyāt || 1

Bhūta Preta Piśācāśca, Graha Pīḍa Nivāraṇam |

Rājāno Vaśamāyati, Sarvaiśvaryan Ca Vindati || 2

Nānā Vidyān Ca Labhate, Rājyam Prāpnoti Niśchitam |

Bhukti Muktimavāpnoti, Sakśāt Śiva Samo Bhavet || 3

|| Śrī Rudrayāmale Sarva Siddhi Prada Bagalāṣṭottara Śata Nāma Stotram

Sampūrṇam ||

श्री बगलाष्टोत्तर शतनाम स्तोत्रम्

ॐ ब्रह्मास्त्ररूपिणी देवी माता श्रीबगलामुखी ।
चिच्छक्तिर्ज्ञानरूपा च ब्रह्मानन्दप्रदायिनी ॥ १

महाविद्या महालक्ष्मी श्रीमत्त्रिपुरसुन्दरी ।
भुवनेशी जगन्माता पार्वती सर्वमङ्गला ॥ २

ललिता भैरवी शान्ता अन्नपूर्णा कुलेश्वरी ।
वाराही छीन्नमस्ता च तारा काली सरस्वती ॥ ३

जगत्पूज्या महामाया कामेशी भगमालिनी ।
दक्षपुत्री शिवाङ्कस्था शिवरूपा शिवप्रिया ॥ ४

सर्वसम्पत्करी देवी सर्वलोक वशङ्करी ।
वेदविद्या महापूज्या भक्ताद्वेषी भयङ्करी ॥ ५

स्तम्भरूपा स्तम्भिनी च दुष्टस्तम्भनकारिणी ।
भक्तप्रिया महाभोगा श्रीविद्या ललिताम्बिका ॥ ६

मैनापुत्री शिवानन्दा मातङ्गी भुवनेश्वरी ।
नारसिंही नरेन्द्रा च नृपाराध्या नरोत्तमा ॥ ७

नागिनी नागपुत्री च नगराजसुता उमा ।
पीताम्बा पीतपुष्पा च पीतवस्त्रप्रिया शुभा ॥ ८

पीतगन्धप्रिया रामा पीतरत्नार्चिता शिवा ।
अर्द्धचन्द्रधरी देवी गदामुद्ररधारिणी ॥ ९

सावित्री त्रिपदा शुद्धा सद्योराग विवर्धिनी ।
विष्णुरूपा जगन्मोहा ब्रह्मरूपा हरिप्रिया ॥ १०

रुद्ररूपा रुद्रशक्तिश्चिन्मयी भक्तवत्सला ।
लोकमाता शिवा सन्ध्या शिवपूजनतत्परा ॥ ११

धनाध्यक्षा धनेशी च नर्मदा धनदा धना ।
चण्डदर्पहरी देवी शुम्भासुरनिबर्हिणी ॥ १२

राजराजेश्वरी देवी महिषासुरमर्दिनी ।
मधूकैटभहन्त्री देवी रक्तबीजविनाशिनी ॥ १३

धूम्राक्षदैत्यहन्त्री च भण्डासुर विनाशिनी ।
रेणुपुत्री महामाया भ्रामरी भ्रमराम्बिका ॥ १४

ज्वालामुखी भद्रकाली बगला शत्रुनाशिनी ।
इन्द्राणी इन्द्रपूज्या च गुहमाता गुणेश्वरी ॥ १५

वज्रपाशधरा देवी झ्वामुद्ररधारिणी ।
भक्तानन्दकरी देवी बगला परमेश्वरी ॥ १६

अष्टोत्तरशतं नाम्नां बगलायास्तु यः पठेत् ।
रिपुबाधाविनिर्मुक्तः लक्ष्मीस्थैर्यमवाप्नुयात् ॥ १७

भूतप्रेतपिशाचाश्च ग्रहपीडानिवारणम् ।
राजानो वशमायान्ति सर्वैश्वर्य च विन्दति ॥ १८

नानाविद्यां च लभते राज्यं प्राप्नोति निश्चितम् ।
भुक्तिमुक्तिमवाप्नोति साक्षात् शिवसमो भवेत् ॥ १९

फल- श्रुतिः ॥

अष्टोत्तरशतं नाम्नां, बगलायास्तु यः पठेत् ।
रिपु-बाधा-विनिर्मुक्तः लक्ष्मीस्थैर्यमवाप्नुयात् ॥1

भूत-प्रेत-पिशाचाश्च, ग्रह-पीड़ा-निवारणम् ।
राजानो वशमायाति, सर्वैश्वर्य च विन्दति ॥ 2

नाना-विद्यां च लभते, राज्यं प्राप्नोति निश्चितम् ।
भुक्ति-मुक्तिमवाप्नोति, साक्षात्
शिव-समो भवेत् ॥ 3

॥ श्री रुद्रयामले सर्व सिद्धि प्रद
बगलाष्टोत्तर शत नाम स्तोत्रं
सम्पूर्णम् ॥

*****

Śrī Bhagalāmukhī Aṣtotra Śata Nāmāvaliḥ

108 Divine Names of *Śrī Bhagalāmukhī Devi.*

Śrī Bagalāṣṭottara Śata Nāmāvaliḥ | श्री बगलाष्टोत्तरशतनामावलिः |

#		
1.	*Śrī Brahmāstrarūpiṇīdevīmātā Śrī Bagalāmukhyai Namaḥ*		श्री ब्रह्मास्त्र रूपिणी देवी माताश्री बगलामुख्यै नमः	
2.	*Śrī Cicchaktyai Namaḥ*		श्री चिच्छक्त्यै नमः	
3.	*Śrī Jñānarūpāyai Namaḥ*		श्री ज्ञानरूपायै नमः	
4.	*Śrī Brahmānandapradāyinyai Namaḥ*		श्री ब्रह्मानन्दप्रदायिन्यै नमः	
5.	*Śrī Mahāvidyāyai Namaḥ*		श्री महाविद्यायै नमः	
6.	*Śrī Mahālakṣmyai Namaḥ*		श्री महालक्ष्म्यै नमः	
7.	*Śrī Mattripurasundaryai Namaḥ*		श्री मत्रिपुरसुन्दर्यै नमः	
8.	*Śrī Bhuvaneśyai Namaḥ*		श्री भुवनेश्यै नमः	
9.	*Śrī Jaganmātre Namaḥ*		श्री जगन्मात्रे नमः	
10	*Śrī Pārvatyai Namaḥ*		श्री पार्वत्यै नमः	
11	*Śrī Sarvamaṅgalāyai Namaḥ*		श्री सर्वमङ्गलायै नमः	
12	*Śrī Lalitāyai Namaḥ*		श्री ललितायै नमः	
13	*Śrī Bhairavyai Namaḥ*		श्री भैरव्यै नमः	
14	*Śrī Śāntāyai Namaḥ*		श्री शान्तायै नमः	
15	*Śrī Annapūrṇāyai Namaḥ*		श्री अन्नपूर्णायै नमः	
16	*Śrī Kuleśvaryai Namaḥ*		श्री कुलेश्वर्यै नमः	
17	*Śrī Vārāhyai Namaḥ*		श्री वाराह्यै नमः	
18	*Śrī Chinnamastāyai Namaḥ*		श्री छिन्नमस्तायै नमः	
19	*Śrī Tārāyai Namaḥ*		श्री तारायै नमः	
20	*Śrī Kālyai Namaḥ*		श्री काल्यै नमः	
21	*Śrī Sarasvatyai Namaḥ*		श्री सरस्वत्यै नमः	
22	*Śrī Jagatpūjyāyai Namaḥ*		श्री जगत्पूज्यायै नमः	
23	*Śrī Mahāmāyāyai Namaḥ*		श्री महामायायै नमः	

24	Śrī Kāmeśyai Namaḥ |	श्री कामेश्यै नमः ।
25	Śrī Bhagamālinyai Namaḥ |	श्री भगमालिन्यै नमः ।
26	Śrī Dakṣaputryai Namaḥ |	श्री दक्षपुत्र्यै नमः ।
27	Śrī Śivāṅkasthāyai Namaḥ |	श्री शिवाङ्कस्थायै नमः
28	Śrī Śivarūpāyai Namaḥ |	श्री शिवरूपायै नमः ।
29	Śrī Śivapriyāyai Namaḥ |	श्री शिवप्रियायै नमः ।
30	Śrī Sarvasampatkarīdevyai Namaḥ |	श्री सर्वसम्पत्करीदेव्यै नमः ।
31	Śrī Sarvalokavaśaṅkaryai Namaḥ	श्री सर्वलोकवशङ्कर्यै नमः ।
32	Śrī Vedavidyāyai Namaḥ |	श्री वेदविद्यायै नमः ।
33	Śrī Mahāpūjyāyai Namaḥ |	श्री महापूज्यायै नमः ।
34	Śrī Bhaktādveṣyai Namaḥ |	श्री भक्ताद्वेष्यै नमः ।
35	Śrī Bhayaṅkaryai Namaḥ |	श्री भयङ्कर्यै नमः ।
36	Śrī Stambharūpāyai Namaḥ |	श्री स्तम्भरूपायै नमः ।
37	Śrī Stambhinyai Namaḥ |	श्री स्तम्भिन्यै नमः ।
38	Śrī Duṣṭastambhanakāriṇyai Namaḥ |	श्री दुष्टस्तम्भनकारिण्यै नमः ।
39	Śrī Bhaktapriyāyai Namaḥ |	श्री भक्तप्रियायै नमः ।
40	Śrī Mahābhogāyai Namaḥ |	श्री महाभोगायै नमः ।
41	Śrī Śrī Vidyāyai Namaḥ |	श्री श्री विद्यायै नमः ।
42	Śrī Lalitāmbikāyai Namaḥ |	श्री ललिताम्बिकायै नमः
43	Śrī Menāputryai Namaḥ |	श्री मेनापुत्र्यै नमः ।
44	Śrī Śivānandāyai Namaḥ |	श्री शिवानन्दायै नमः ।
45	Śrī Mātaṅgyai Namaḥ |	श्री मातङ्ग्यै नमः ।
46	Śrī Bhuvaneśvaryai Namaḥ |	श्री भुवनेश्वर्यै नमः ।
47	Śrī Nārasiṃhyai Namaḥ |	श्री नारसिंह्यै नमः ।
48	Śrī Narendrāyai Namaḥ |	श्री नरेन्द्रायै नमः ।
49	Śrī Nṛpārādhyāyai Namaḥ |	श्री नृपाराध्यायै नमः ।
50	Śrī Narottamāyai Namaḥ |	श्री नरोत्तमायै नमः ।

51	*Śrī Nāginyai Namaḥ* ।	श्री नागिन्यै नमः ।
52	*Śrī Nāgaputryai Namaḥ* ।	श्री नागपुत्र्यै नमः ।
53	*Śrī Nagarājasutāyai Namaḥ* ।	श्री नगराजसुतायै नमः ।
54	*Śrī Umāyai Namaḥ* ।	श्री उमायै नमः ।
55	*Śrī Pītāmbarāyai Namaḥ* ।	श्री पीताम्बरायै नमः ।
56	*Śrī Pītapuṣpāyai Namaḥ* ।	श्री पीतपुष्पायै नमः ।
57	*Śrī Pītavastrapriyāyai Namaḥ* ।	श्री पीतवस्त्रप्रियायै नमः
58	*Śrī Śubhāyai Namaḥ* ।	श्री शुभायै नमः ।
59	*Śrī Pītagandhapriyāyai Namaḥ* ।	श्री पीतगन्धप्रियायै नमः
60	*Śrī Rāmāyai Namaḥ* ।	श्री रामायै नमः ।
61	*Śrī Pītaratnārcitāyai Namaḥ* ।	श्री पीतरत्नार्चितायै नमः
62	*Śrī Śivāyai Namaḥ* ।	श्री शिवायै नमः ।
63	*Śrī Arddhacandradharīdevyai Namaḥ* ।	श्री अर्द्धचन्द्रधरीदेव्यै नमः ।
64	*Śrī Gadāmudgaradhāriṇyai Namaḥ* ।	श्री गदामुद्गरधारिण्यै नमः
65	*Śrī Sāvitryai Namaḥ* ।	श्री सावित्र्यै नमः ।
66	*Śrī Tripadāyai Namaḥ* ।	श्री त्रिपदायै नमः ।
67	*Śrī Śuddhāyai Namaḥ* ।	श्री शुद्धायै नमः ।
68	*Śrī Sadyorāgavivarddhinyai Namaḥ* ।	श्री सद्योरागविवर्द्धिन्यै नमः ।
69	*Śrī Viṣṇurūpāyai Namaḥ* ।	श्री विष्णुरूपायै नमः ।
70	*Śrī Jaganmohāyai Namaḥ* ।	श्री जगन्मोहायै नमः ।
71	*Śrī Brahmarūpāyai Namaḥ* ।	श्री ब्रह्मरूपायै नमः ।
72	*Śrī Haripriyāyai Namaḥ* ।	श्री हरिप्रियायै नमः ।
73	*Śrī Rudrarūpāyai Namaḥ* ।	श्री रुद्ररूपायै नमः ।
74	*Śrī Rudraśaktyai Namaḥ* ।	श्री रुद्रशक्त्यै नमः ।
75	*Śrī Cinmayyai Namaḥ* ।	श्री चिन्मय्यै नमः ।
76	*Śrī Bhaktavatsalāyai Namaḥ* ।	श्री भक्तवत्सलायै नमः ।
77	*Śrī Lokamātāśivāyai Namaḥ* ।	श्री लोकमाताशिवायै नमः ।

78.	*Śrī Sandhyāyai Namaḥ* |	श्री सन्ध्यायै नमः ।
79.	*Śrī Śivapūjanatatparāyai Namaḥ*	श्री शिवपूजनतत्परायै नमः ।
80.	*Śrī Dhanādhyakṣāyai Namaḥ* |	श्री धनाध्यक्षायै नमः ।
81.	*Śrī Dhaneśyai Namaḥ* |	श्री धनेश्यै नमः ।
82.	*Śrī Dharmadāyai Namaḥ* |	श्री धर्मदायै नमः ।
83.	*Śrī Dhanadāyai Namaḥ* |	श्री धनदायै नमः ।
84.	*Śrī Dhanāyai Namaḥ* |	श्री धनायै नमः ।
85.	*Śrī Caṇḍadarpaharīdevyai Namaḥ* |	श्री चण्डदर्पहरीदेव्यै नमः
86.	*Śrī Śumbhāsuranivarhiṇyai Namaḥ* |	श्री शुम्भासुरनिवर्हिण्यै नमः ।
87.	*Śrī Rājarājeśvarīdevyai Namaḥ* |	श्री राजराजेश्वरीदेव्यै नमः
88.	*Śrī Mahiṣāsuramardinyai Namaḥ*	श्री महिषासुरमर्दिन्यै नमः
89.	*Śrī Madhukaiṭabhahantryai Namaḥ* |	श्री मधुकैटभहन्त्र्यै नमः ।
90.	*Śrī Raktabījavināśinyai Namaḥ* |	श्री रक्तबीजविनाशिन्यै नमः ।
91.	*Śrī Dhūmrākṣadaityahantryai Namaḥ* |	श्री धूम्राक्षदैत्यहन्त्र्यै नमः
92.	*Śrī Caṇḍāsuravināśinyai Namaḥ* |	श्री चण्डासुरविनाशिन्यै नमः ।
93.	*Śrī Reṇuputryai Namaḥ* |	श्री रेणुपुत्र्यै नमः ।
94.	*Śrī Mahāmāyāyai Namaḥ* |	श्री महामायायै नमः ।
95.	*Śrī Bhrāmaryai Namaḥ* |	श्री भ्रामर्यै नमः ।
96.	*Śrī Bhramarāmbikāyai Namaḥ* |	श्री भ्रमराम्बिकायै नमः ।
97.	*Śrī Jvālāmukhyai Namaḥ* |	श्री ज्वालामुख्यै नमः ।
98.	*Śrī Bhadrakālyai Namaḥ* |	श्री भद्रकाल्यै नमः ।
99.	*Śrī Śatrunāśinyai Namaḥ* |	श्री शत्रुनाशिन्यै नमः ।
100.	*Śrī Indrāṇyai Namaḥ* |	श्री इन्द्राण्यै नमः ।
101.	*Śrī Indrapūjyāyai Namaḥ* |	श्री इन्द्रपूज्यायै नमः ।
102.	*Śrī Guhamātre Namaḥ* |	श्री गुहमात्रे नमः ।
103.	*Śrī Guṇeśvaryai Namaḥ* |	श्री गुणेश्वर्यै नमः ।

104.	*Śrī Vajrapāśadharādevyai Namaḥ*	श्री वज्रपाशधरादेव्यै नमः ।
105.	*Śrī Jihvādhāriṇyai Namaḥ*	श्री जिह्वाधारिण्यै नमः ।
106.	*Śrī Mudgaradhāriṇyai Namaḥ*	श्री मुद्गरधारिण्यै नमः ।
107.	*Śrī Bhaktānandakarīdevyai Namaḥ*	श्री भक्तानन्दकरीदेव्यै नमः ।
108.	*Śrī Bagalāparameśvaryai Namaḥ*	श्री बगलापरमेश्वर्यै नमः ।

Śrī Rudrayāmale Sarva Siddhi Prada Bagalā'ṣṭottara Śata nāmāvaliḥ Samāptā ||

|| श्री रुद्रयामले सर्व सिद्धि प्रद बगला ष्टोत्तर शत नामावलिः समाप्ता ||

*****

Śrī Bhagalāmukhī Sahasranāma Stotram

Surālayapradhāne Tu Devadevaṃ Maheśvaram |
Śailādhirājatanayā Saṅgrahe Tamuvāca Ha || 1

Śrī Devyuvāca ||

Parameṣṭhinparandhāma Pradhāna Parameśvara |
Nāmnāṃ Sahasrambagalāmukhyādyā Brūhi Vallabha || 2

Śrī Īśvara Uvāca ||

Śṛṇu Devi Pravakṣyāmi Nāmadheyasahasrakam |
Parabrahmāstravidyāyāścaturvargaphalapradam || 3

Guhyādguhyatarandevi Sarvasiddhaikavanditam |
Atiguptataravidyā Sarvatantreṣu Gopitā || 4

Viśeṣataḥ Kaliyuge Mahāsiddhyaughadāyinī |
Gopanīyaṅgopanīyaṅgopanīyamprayatnataḥ || 5

Aprakāśyamidaṃ Satyaṃ Svayoniriva Suvrate |
Rodhinī Vighnasaṅghānāṃ Mohinī Parayoṣitām || 6

Stambhinī Rājasainyānāvādinī Paravādinām |
Purā Caikārṇave Ghore Kāle Paramabhairavaḥ || 7

Sundarīsahito Devaḥ Keśavaḥ Kleśanāśanaḥ |
Uragāsanamāsīno Yoganidrāmupāgamat || 8

Nidrākāle Ca Te Kāle Mayā Proktaḥ Sanātanaḥ |
Mahāstambhakarandevi Stotravā Śatanāmakam || 9

Sahasranāma Paramavada Devasya Kasyacit |

Śrī Bhagavānuvāca ||

Śṛṇu Śaṅkara Deveśa Paramātirahasyakam || 10

Ajoham̐ Yatprasādena Viṣṇuḥ Sarveśvareśvaraḥ |

Gopanīyamprayatnena Prakāśātsiddhihānikṛt || 11

Oṃ Asya Śrī Bagalāmukhī Sahasranāma stotramantrasya Bhagavān
Sadāśiva Ṛṣiḥ Anuṣṭupchandaś
Śrī Jagadvaśyakarī Bagalāmukhī Devatā
Sarvābhīṣṭasiddhyartthe Jape Viniyogaḥ ||

Atha Dhyānam ||

Pītāmbaraparīdhānāṃ Pīnonnatapayodharām |

Jaṭāmukuṭaśobhāḍhyāmpītabhūmisukhāsanām || 12

Śatrorjihvāṃ Mudgarañca Bibhratīmparamāṅkalām |

Sarvāgamapurāṇeṣu Vikhyātāmbhuvanatraye || 13

Sṛṣṭisthitivināśānāmādi Bhūtāmaheśvarīm |

Gopyā Sarvaprayatnena Śṛṇu Tāṅkathayāmi Te || 14

Jagadvidhvaṃsinīndevīmajarāmarakāriṇīm |

Tānnamāmi Mahāmāyāmahadaiścaryadāyinīm || 15

Atha Sahasranāma Stotram ||

Praṇavampūrvamuddhṛtya Sthiramāyāntato Vadet |

Bagalāmukhī Sarveti Duṣṭānāvācameva Ca || 16

Mukhampadaṃ Stambhayeti Jihvāṅkīlaya Buddhimat |

Vināśayeti Tārañca Sthiramāyāntato Vadet || 17

Vahnipriyāntato Mantraścaturvargaphalapradaḥ |

Brahmāstrambrahmavidyā Ca Brahmamātā Sanātanī || 18

Brahmeśī Brahmakaivalyabagalā Brahmacāriṇī |

Nityānandā Nityasiddhā Nityarūpā Nirāmayā || 19

Sandhāriṇī Mahāmāyā Kaṭākṣakṣemakāriṇī |

Kamalā Vimalā Nīlā Ratnakāntiguṇāśritā || 20

Kāmapriyā Kāmaratā Kāmakāmasvarūpiṇī |
Maṅgalā Vijayā Jāyā Sarvamaṅgalakāriṇī ‖ 21

Kāminī Kāminīkāmyā Kāmukā Kāmacāriṇī |
Kāmapriyā Kāmaratā Kāmākāmasvarūpiṇī ‖ 22

Kāmākhyā Kāmabījasthā Kāmapīṭhanivāsinī |
Kāmadā Kāmahā Kālī Kapālī Ca Karālikā ‖ 23

Kaṃsāriḥ Kamalā Kāmā Kailāseśvaravallabhā |
Kātyāyanī Keśavā Ca Karuṇā Kāmakelibhuk ‖ 24

Kriyākīrttiḥ Kṛttikā Ca Kāśikā Mathurā Śivā |
Kālākṣī Kālikā Kālī Dhavalānanasundarī ‖ 25

Khecarī Ca Khamūrttiśca Kṣudrā Kṣudrakṣudhāvarā |
Khaḍgahastā Khaḍgaratā Khaḍginī Kharparapriyā ‖ 26

Gaṅgā Gaurī Gāminī Ca Gītā Gotravivarddhinī |
Godharā Gokarā Godhā Gandharvapuravāsinī ‖ 27

Gandharvā Gandharvakalā Gopanī Garuḍāsanā |
Govindabhāvā Govindā Gāndhārī Gandhamādinī ‖ 28

Gaurāṅgī Gopikāmūrttirgopīgoṣṭhanivāsinī |
Gandhā Gajendragāmānyā Gadādharapriyā Grahā ‖ 29

Ghoraghorā Ghorarūpā Ghanaśroṇī Ghanaprabhā |
Daityendraprabalā Ghaṇṭāvādinī Ghoranissvanā ‖ 30

Ḍākinyumā Upendrā Ca Urvaśī Uragāsanā |
Uttamā Unnatā Unnā Uttamasthānavāsinī ‖ 31

Cāmuṇḍā Muṇḍitā Caṇḍī Caṇḍadarpahareti Ca |
Ugracaṇḍā Caṇḍacaṇḍā Caṇḍadaityavināśinī ‖ 32

Caṇḍarūpā Pracaṇḍā Ca Caṇḍācaṇḍaśarīriṇī |
Caturbhujā Pracaṇḍā Ca Carācaranivāsinī ‖ 33

Kṣatraprāyaśśirovāhā Chalā Chalatarā Chalī |

Kṣatrarūpā Kṣatradharā Kṣatriyakṣayakāriṇī || 34

Jayā Ca Jayadurgā Ca Jayantī Jayadā Parā |

Jāyinī Jayinī Jyotsnā Jaṭādharapriyā Jitā || 35

Jitendriyā Jitakrodhā Jayamānā Janeśvarī |

Jitamṛtyurjarātītā Jāhnavī Janakātmajā || 36

Jhaṅkārā Jhañjharī Jhaṇṭā Jhaṅkārī Jhakaśobhinī |

Jhakhā Jhameśā Jhaṅkārī Yonikalyāṇadāyinī || 37

Jhañjharā Jhamurī Jhārā Jharājharatarā Parā |

Jhañjhā Jhametā Jhaṅkārī Jhaṇākalyāṇadāyinī || 38

Īmanā Mānasī Cintyā Īmunā Śaṅkarapriyā |

Ṭaṅkārī Ṭiṭikā Ṭīkā Ṭaṅkinī Ca Ṭavargagā || 39

Ṭāpā Ṭopā Ṭaṭapatiṣṭamanī Ṭamanapriyā |

Ṭhakāradhāriṇī Ṭhīkā Ṭhaṅkarī Ṭhikarapriyā || 40

Ṭhekaṭhāsā Ṭhakaratī Ṭhāminī Ṭhamanapriyā |

Ḍārahā Ḍākinī Ḍārā Ḍāmarā Ḍamarapriyā || 41

Ḍakhinī Ḍaḍayuktā Ca Ḍamarūkaravallabhā |

Dhakkā Dhakkī Dhakkanādā Dholaśabdaprabodhinī || 42

Ḍhāminī Ḍhāmanaprītā Ḍhagatantraprakāśinī |

Anekarūpiṇī Ambā Aṇimāsiddhidāyinī || 43

Amantriṇī Aṇukarī Aṇumadbhānusaṃsthitā |

Tārā Tantrāvatī Tantratattvarūpā Tapasvinī || 44

Taraṅgiṇī Tattvaparā Tantrikā Tantravigrahā |

Taporūpā Tattvadātrī Tapaḥprītipradharṣiṇī || 45

Tantrā Yantrārccanaparā Talātalanivāsinī |

Talpadā Tvalpadā Kāmyā Sthirā Sthiratarā Sthitiḥ || 46

Sthāṇupriyā Sthaparā Sthitā Sthānapradāyinī |
Digambarā Dayārūpā Dāvāgni Damanīdamā || 47

Durgā Durgāparā Devī Duṣṭadaityavināśinī |
Damanapramadā Daityadayādānaparāyaṇā || 48

Durgārtināśinī Dāntā Dambhinī Dambhavarjitā |
Digambarapriyā Dambhā Daityadambhavidāriṇī || 49

Damanā Daśanasaundaryā Dānavendravināśinī |
Dayā Dharā Ca Damanī Darbhapatravilāsinī || 50

Dhariṇī Dhāriṇī Dhātrī Dharādharadharapriyā |
Dharādharasutā Devī Sudharmā Dharmacāriṇī || 51

Dharmajñā Dhavalā Dhūlā Dhanadā Dhanavarddhinī |
Dhīrā Dhīrā Dhīratarā Dhīrasiddhipradāyinī || 52

Dhanvantaridharādhīrā Dhyeyā Dhyānasvarūpiṇī |
Nārāyaṇī Nārasiṃhī Nityānandanarottamā || 53

Naktā Naktāvatī Nityā Nīlajīmūtasannibhā |
Nīlāṅgī Nīlavastrā Ca Nīlaparvatavāsinī || 54

Sunīlapuṣpakhacitā Nīlajambusamaprabhā |
Nityākhyā Ṣoḍaśī Vidyā Nityā Nityasukhāvahā || 55

Narmadā Nandanānandā Nandānandavivarddhinī |
Yaśodānandatanayā Nandanodyānavāsinī || 56

Nāgāntakā Nāgavṛddhā Nāgapatnī Ca Nāginī |
Namitāśeṣajanatā Namaskāravatī Namaḥ || 57

Pītāmbarā Pārvatī Ca Pītāmbaravibhūṣitā |
Pītamīlyāmbaradharā Pītābhā Piṅgamūrddhajā || 58

Pītapuṣpārccanaratā Pītapuṣpasamarccitā |
Paraprabhā Pitṛpatiḥ Parasainyavināśinī || 59

Paramā Paratantrā Ca Paramantrā Parātparā |
Parāvidyā Parāsiddhiḥ Parāsthānapradāyinī || 60

Puṣpā Puṣpavatī Nityā Puṣpamālāvibhūṣitā |
Purātanā Pūrvaparā Parasiddhipradāyinī || 61

Pītānitambinī Pītā Pīnonnatapayastanī |
Premāpramadhyamāśeṣā Padmapatravilāsinī || 62

Padmāvatī Padmanetrā Padmā Padmamukhī Parā |
Padmāsanā Padmapriyā Padmarāgasvarūpiṇī || 63

Pāvanī Pālikā Pātrī Paradā Varadā Śivā |
Pretasaṃsthā Parānandā Parabrahmasvarūpuṇī || 64

Jineśvarapriyā Devī Paśuraktaratapriyā |
Paśumāṃsapriyā Parṇā Parāmṛtaparāyaṇā || 65

Pāśīnī Pāśikā Cāpi Paśughnī Paśubhāṣiṇī |
Phullāravindavadanī Phullotpalaśarīriṇī || 66

Parānandapradā Vīṇāpaśupāśavināśinī |
Phūtkārā Phutparā Pheṇī Phullendīvaralocanā || 67

Phaṭmantrā Sphaṭikā Svāhā Sphoṭā Ca Phaṭsvarūpiṇī |
Sphāṭikā Ghuṭikā Ghorā Sphaṭikādrisvarūpiṇī || 68

Varāṅganā Varadharā Vārāhī Vāsukī Varā |
Bindusthā Bindunī Vāṇī Binducakranivāsinī || 69

Vidyādharī Viśālākṣī Kāśīvāsijanapriyā |
Vedavidyā Virūpākṣī Viśvayugbahurūpiṇī || 70

Brahmaśaktirviṣṇuśaktiḥ Pañcavaktrā Śivapriyā |
Vaikuṇṭhavāsinī Devī Vaikuṇṭhapadadāyinī || 71

Brahmarūpā Viṣṇurūpā Parabrahmamaheśvarī |
Bhavapriyā Bhavodbhāvā Bhavarūpā Bhavottamā || 72

Bhavapārā Bhavadhārā Bhāgyavatpriyakāriṇī |

Bhadrā Subhadrā Bhavadā Śumbhadaityavināśinī || 73

Bhavānī Bhairavī Bhīmā Bhadrakālī Subhadrikā |

Bhaginī Bhagarūpā Ca Bhagamānā Bhagottamā || 74

Bhagapriyā Bhagavatī Bhagavāsā Bhagākarā |

Bhagasṛṣṭā Bhāgyavatī Bhagarūpā Bhagāsinī || 75

Bhagaliṅgapriyā Devī Bhagaliṅgaparāyaṇā |

Bhagaliṅgasvarūpā Ca Bhagaliṅgavinodinī || 76

Bhagaliṅgaratā Devī Bhagaliṅganivāsinī |

Bhagamālā Bhagakalā Bhagādhārā Bhagāmbarā || 77

Bhagavegā Bhagābhūṣā Bhagendrā Bhāgyarūpiṇī |

Bhagaliṅgāṅgasambhogā Bhagaliṅgāsavāvahā || 78

Bhagaliṅgasamādhuryā Bhagaliṅganiveśitā |

Bhagaliṅgasupūjā Ca Bhagaliṅgasamanvitā || 79

Bhagaliṅgaviraktā Ca Bhagaliṅgasamāvṛtā |

Mādhavī Mādhavīmānyā Madhurā Madhumāninī || 80

Mandahāsā Mahāmāyā Mohinī Mahaduttamā |

Mahāmohā Mahāvidyā Mahāghorā Mahāsmṛtiḥ || 81

Manasvinī Mānavatī Modinī Madhurānanā |

Menikā Māninī Mānyā Maṇiratnavibhūṣaṇā || 82

Mallikā Maulikā Mālā Mālādharamadottamā |

Madanāsundarī Medhā Madhumattā Madhupriyā || 83

Mattahaṃsāsamonnāsā Mattasiṃhamahāsanī |

Mahendravallabhā Bhīmā Maulyañca Mithunātmajā || 84

Mahākālyā Mahākālī Mahābuddhirmahotkaṭā |

Māheśvarī Mahāmāyā Mahiṣāsuraghātinī || 85

Madhurākīrttimattā Ca Mattamātaṅgagāminī |

Madapriyā Māṃsaratā Mattayukkāmakāriṇī || 86

Maithunyavallabhā Devī Mahānandā Mahvotsavā |

Marīcirmāratirmāyā Manobuddhipradāyinī || 87

Mohā Mokṣā Mahālakṣmīrmahatpadapradāyinī |

Yamarūpā Ca Yamunā Jayantī Ca Jayapradā || 88

Yāmyā Yamavatī Yuddhā Yadoḥ Kulavivarddhinī |

Ramā Rāmā Rāmapatnī Ratnamālā Ratipriyā || 89

Ratnasiṃhāsanasthā Ca Ratnābharaṇamaṇḍitā |

Ramaṇī Ramaṇīyā Ca Ratyārasaparāyaṇā || 90

Ratānandā Ratavatī Radhūṇāṅkulavarddhinī |

Ramaṇāriparibhrājyā Raidhārādhikaratnajā || 91

Rāvī Rasasvarūpā Ca Rātrirājasukhāvahā |

Ṛtujā Ṛtudā Ṛddhā Ṛturūpā Ṛtupriyā || 92

Raktapriyā Raktavatī Raṅgiṇī Raktadantikā |

Lakṣmīrllajjā Latikā Ca Līlālagnānitākṣiṇī || 93

Līlā Līlāvatī Lomāharṣāhlādanapaṭṭikā |

Brahmasthitā Brahmarūpā Brahmaṇā Vedavanditā || 94

Brahmodbhavā Brahmakalā Brahmāṇī Brahmabodhinī |

Vedāṅganā Vedarūpā Vanitā Vinatā Vasā || 95

Bālā Ca Yuvatī Vṛddhā Brahmakarmaparāyaṇā |

Vindhyasthā Vindhyavāsī Ca Binduyugbindubhūṣaṇā || 96

Vidyāvatī Vedadhārī Vyāpikā Barhiṇī Kalā |

Vāmācārapriyā Vahnirvāmācāraparāyaṇā || 97

Vāmācāraratā Devī Vāmadevapriyottamā |

Buddhendriyā Vibuddhā Ca Buddhācaraṇamālinī || 98

Bandhamocanakartrī Ca Vāruṇā Varuṇālayā |

Śivā Śivapriyā Śuddhā Śuddhāṅgī Śuklavarṇikā || 99

Śuklapuṣpapriyā Śuklā Śivadharmaparāyaṇā |

Śuklasthā Śuklinī Śuklarūpaśuklapaśupriyā || 100

Śukrasthā Śukriṇī Śukrā Śukrarūpā Ca Śukrikā |

Ṣaṇmukhī Ca Ṣaḍaṅgā Ca Ṣaṭcakravinivāsinī || 101

Ṣaḍgranthiyuktā Ṣoḍhā Ca Ṣaṇmātā Ca Ṣaḍātmikā |

Ṣaḍaṅgayuvatī Devī Ṣaḍaṅgaprakṛtirvaśī || 102

Ṣaḍānanā Ṣaḍrasā Ca Ṣaṣṭhī Ṣaṣṭheśvarīpriyā |

Ṣaṅgavādā Ṣoḍaśī Ca Ṣoḍhānyāsasvarūpiṇī || 103

Ṣaṭcakrabhedanakarī Ṣaṭcakrasthasvarūpiṇī |

Ṣoḍaśasvararūpā Ca Ṣaṇmukhī Ṣaḍradānvitā || 104

Sanakādisvarūpā Ca Śivadharmaṣarāyaṇā |

Siddhā Saptasvarī Śuddhā Suramātā Svarottamā || 105

Siddhavidyā Sidhamātā Siddhā Siddhasvarūpiṇī |

Harā Haripriyā Hārā Hariṇī Hārayuk Tathā || 106

Harirūpā Haridhārā Hariṇākṣī Haripriyā |

Hetupriyā Heturatā Hitāhitasvarūpiṇī || 107

Kṣamā Kṣamāvatī Kṣītā Kṣudraghaṇṭāvibhūṣaṇā |

Kṣayaṅkarī Kṣitīśā Ca Kṣīṇamadhyasuśobhanā || 108

Ajānantā Aparṇā Ca Ahalyāśeṣaśāyinī |

Svāntargatā Ca Sādhūnāmantarānantarūpiṇī || 109

Arūpā Amalā Cārddhā Anantaguṇaśālinī |

Svavidyā Vidyakāvidyā Vidyā Cārvindalocanā || 110

Aparājitā Jātavedā Ajapā Amarāvatī |

Alpā Svalpā Analpādyā Aṇimāsiddhidāyinī || 111

Aṣṭasiddhipradā Devī Rūpalakṣaṇasaṃyutā |
Aravindamukhā Devī Bhogasaukhyapradāyinī || 112

Ādividyā Ādibhūtā Ādisiddhipradāyinī |
Sītkārarūpiṇī Devī Sarvāsanavibhūṣitā || 113

Indrapriyā Ca Indrāṇī Indraprasthanivāsinī |
Indrākṣī Indravajrā Ca Indramadyokṣaṇī Tathā || 114

Īlā Kāmanivāsā Ca Īśvarīśvaravallabhā |
Jananī Ceśvarī Dīnā Bhedāceśvarakarmakṛt || 115

Umā Kātyāyanī Ūrddhvā Mīnā Cottaravāsinī |
Umāpatipriyā Devī Śivā Coṅkārarūpiṇī || 116

Uragendraśiroratnā Uragoragavallabhā |
Udyānavāsinī Mālā Praśastamaṇibhūṣaṇā || 117

Urddhvadantottamāṅgī Ca Uttamā Cordhvakeśinī |
Umāsiddhipradā Yā Ca Uragāsanasaṃsthitā || 118

Ṛṣiputrī Ṛṣicchandā Ṛddhisiddhipradāyinī |
Utsavotsavasīmantā Kāmikā Ca Guṇānvitā || 119

Elā Ekāravidyā Ca Eṇīvidyādharā Tathā |
Oṅkāravalayopetā Oṅkāraparamā Kalā || 120

Oṃvadavadavāṇī Ca Oṅkārākṣaramaṇḍitā |
Aindrī Kuliśahastā Ca Oṃlokaparavāsinī || 121

Oṅkāramadhyabījā Ca Oṃnamorūpadhāriṇī |
Prabrahmasvarūpā Ca Aṃśukāṃśukavallabhā || 122

Oṅkārā Aḥphaḍmantrā Ca Akṣākṣaravibhūṣitā |
Amantrā Mantrarūpā Ca Padaśobhāsamanvitā || 123

Praṇavoṅkārarūpā Ca Praṇavoccārabhāk Punaḥ |
Hrīṅkārarūpā Hrīṃṅkārī Vāgbījākṣarabhūṣaṇā || 124

Hṛllekhā Siddhi Yogā Ca Hṛtpadmāsanasaṃsthitā |
Bījākhyā Netrahṛdayā Hrīmbījābhuvaneśvarī || 125

Klīṅkāmarājā Klinnā Ca Caturvargaphalapradā |
Klīṅklīṅklīṃrūpikā Devī Krīṅkrīṅkrīṃnāmadhāriṇī || 126

Kamalāśaktibījā Ca Pāśāṅkuśavibhūṣitā |
Śrīṃśrīṅkārā Mahāvidyā Śraddhā Śraddhāvatī Tathā || 127

Oṃ Aiṃ Klīṃhrīṃśrīmparā Ca Klīṅkārī Paramā Kalā |
Hrīṅklīṃśrīṅkārasvarūpā Sarvakarmaphalapradā || 128

Sarvāḍhyā Sarvadevī Ca Sarvasiddhipradā Tathā |
Sarvajñā Sarvaśaktiśca Vāgvibhūtipradāyinī || 129

Sarvamokṣapradā Devī Sarvabhogapradāyinī |
Guṇendravallabhā Vāmā Sarvaśaktipradāyinī || 130

Sarvānandamayī Caiva Sarvasiddhipradāyinī |
Sarvacakreśvarī Devī Sarvasiddheśvarī Tathā || 131

Sarvapriyaṅkarī Caiva Sarvasaukhyapradāyinī |
Sarvānandapradā Devī Brahmānandapradāyinī || 132

Manovāñchitadātrī Ca Manovṛddhisamanvitā |
Akārādikṣakārāntā Durgā Durgārttināśinī || 133

Padmanetrā Sunetrā Ca Svadhāsvāhāvaṣaṭkarī |
Svavargā Devavargā Ca Tavargā Ca Samanvitā || 134

Antassthā Veśmarūpā Ca Navadurgā Narottamā |
Tattvasiddhipradā Nīlā Tathā Nīlapatākinī || 135

Nityarūpā Niśākārī Stambhinī Mohinīti Ca |
Vaśaṅkarī Tathoccāṭī Unmādī Karṣiṇīti Ca || 136

Mātaṅgī Madhumattā Ca Aṇimā Laghimā Tathā |
Siddhā Mokṣapradā Nityā Nityānandapradāyinī || 137

Raktāṅgī Raktanetrā Ca Raktacandanabhūṣitā |
Svalpasiddhissukalpā Ca Divyacāraṇaśukrabhā || 138

Saṅkrāntissarvavidyā Ca Sasyavāsarabhūṣitā |
Prathamā Ca Dvitīyā Ca Tṛtīyā Ca Caturtthikā || 139

Pañcamī Caiva Ṣaṣṭhī Ca Viśuddhā Saptamī Tathā |
Aṣṭamī Navamī Caiva Daśamyekādaśī Tathā || 140

Dvādaśī Trayodaśī Ca Caturddaśyatha Pūrṇimā |
Āmāvasyā Tathā Pūrvā Uttarā Paripūrṇimā || 141

Khaḍginī Cakriṇī Ghorā Gadinī Śūlinī Tathā |
Bhuśuṇḍī Cāpinī Bāṇā Sarvāyudhavibhūṣaṇā || 142

Kuleśvarī Kulavatī Kulācāraparāyaṇā |
Kulakarmasuraktā Ca Kulācārapravarddhinī || 143

Kīrtiśśrīśca Ramā Rāmā Dharmāyai Satatannamaḥ |
Kṣamā Dhṛtiḥ Smṛtirmedhā Kalpavṛkṣanivāsinī || 144

Ugrā Ugraprabhā Gaurī Vedavidyāvibodhinī |
Sādhyā Siddhā Susiddhā Ca Viprarūpā Tathaiva Ca || 145

Kālī Karālī Kālyā Ca Kalādaityavināśinī |
Kaulinī Kālikī Caiva Ka-Ca-Ṭa-Ta-Pavarṇikā || 146

Jayinī Jayayuktā Ca Jayadā Jṛmbhinī Tathā |
Srāviṇī Drāviṇī Devī Bharuṇḍā Vindhyavāsinī || 147

Jyotirbhūtā Ca Jayadā Jvālāmālāsamākulā |
Bhinnā Bhinnaprakāśā Ca Vibhinnā Bhinnarūpiṇī || 148

Aśvinī Bharaṇī Caiva Nakṣatrasambhavānilā |
Kāśyapī Vinatā Khyātā Ditijāditireva Ca || 149

Kīrttiḥ Kāmapriyā Devī Kīrttyā Kīrtivivarddhinī |
Sadyomāṃsasamālabdhā Sadyaśchinnāsiśaṅkarā || 150

Dakṣiṇā Cottarā Pūrvā Paścimā Dik Tathaiva Ca |
Agninairṛtivāyavyā Īśānyādik Tathā Smṛtā || 151

Ūrdhvāṅgādhogatā Śvetā Kṛṣṇā Raktā Ca Pītakā |
Caturvargā Caturvarṇā Caturmātrātmikākṣarā || 152

Caturmukhī Caturvedā Caturvidyā Caturmukhā |
Caturgaṇā Caturmātā Caturvargaphalapradā || 153

Dhātrī Vidhātrī Mithunā Nārī Nāyakavāsinī |
Surāmudā Mudavatī Modinī Menakātmajā || 154

Ūrddhvakālī Siddhikālī Dakṣiṇākālikā Śivā |
Nīlyā Sarasvatī Sātvambagalā Chinnamastakā || 155

Sarveśvarī Siddhavidyā Parā Paramadevatā |
Hiṅgulā Hiṅgulāṅgī Ca Hiṅgulādharavāsinī || 156

Hiṅgulottamavarṇābhā Hiṅgulābharaṇā Ca Sā |
Jāgratī Ca Jaganmātā Jagadīśvaravallabhā || 157

Janārddanapriyā Devī Jayayuktā Jayapradā |
Jagadānandakarī Ca Jagadāhlādakāriṇī || 158

Jñānadānakarī Yajñā Jānakī Janakapriyā |
Jayantī Jayadā Nityā Jvaladagnisamaprabhā || 159

Vidyādharā Ca Bimboṣṭhī Kailāsacalavāsinī |
Vibhavā Vaḍavāgniśca Agnihotraphalapradā || 160

Mantrarūpā Parā Devī Tathaiva Gururūpiṇī |
Gayā Gaṅgā Gomatī Ca Prabhāsā Puṣkarāpi Ca || 161

Vindhyācalaratā Devī Vindhyācalanivāsinī |
Bahū Bahusundarī Ca Kaṁsāsuravināśinī || 162

Śūlinī Śūlahastā Ca Vajrā Vajraharāpi Ca |
Dūrgā Śivā Śāntikarī Brahmāṇī Brāhmaṇapriyā || 163

Sarvalokapraṇetrī Ca Sarvarogaharāpi Ca |
Maṅgalā Śobhanā Śuddhā Niṣkalā Paramā Kalā ǁ 164

Viśveśvarī Viśvamātā Lalitā Vasitānanā |
Sadāśivā Umā Kṣemā Caṇḍikā Caṇḍavikramā ǁ 165

Sarvadevamayī Devī Sarvāgamabhayāpahā |
Brahmeśaviṣṇunamitā Sarvakalyāṇakāriṇī ǁ 166

Yoginī Yogamātā Ca Yogīndrahṛdayasthitā |
Yogijāyā Yogavatī Yogīndrānandayoginī ǁ 167

Indrādinamitā Devī Īśvarī Ceśvarapriyā |
Viśuddhidā Bhayaharā Bhaktadveṣibhayaṅkarī ǁ 168

Bhavaveṣā Kāminī Ca Bharuṇḍā Bhayakāriṇī |
Balabhadrapriyākārā Saṃsārārṇavatāriṇī ǁ 169

Pañcabhūtā Sarvabhūtā Vibhūtirbhūtidhāriṇī |
Siṃhavāhā Mahāmohā Mohapāśavināśinī ǁ 170

Mandurā Madirā Mudrā Mudrāmudgaradhāriṇī |
Sāvitrī Ca Mahādevī Parapriyanināyikā ǁ 171

Yamadūtī Ca Piṅgākṣī Vaiṣṇavī Śaṅkarī Tathā |
Candrapriyā Candraratā Candanāraṇyavāsinī ǁ 172

Candanendrasamāyuktā Caṇḍadaityavināśinī |
Sarveśvarī Yakṣiṇī Ca Kirātī Rākṣasī Tathā ǁ 173

Mahābhogavatī Devī Mahāmokṣapradāyinī |
Viśvahantrī Viśvarūpā Viśvasaṃhārakāriṇī ǁ 174

Dhātrī Ca Sarvalokānāṃ Hitakāraṇakāminī |
Kamalā Sūkṣmadā Devī Dhātrī Haravināśinī ǁ 175

Surendrapūjitā Siddhā Mahātejovatīti Ca |
Parārūpavatī Devī Trailokyākarṣakāriṇī ǁ 176

Phala Śruti:

Iti Te Kathitandevi Pītānāma Sahasrakam |
Paṭhedvā Pāṭhayedvāpi Sarvasiddhirbhavetpriye || 177

Iti Me Viṣṇunā Proktaṃ Mahāstambhakaraṃ Param |
Prātaḥ Kāle Ca Madhyāhne Sandhyākāle Ca Pārvati || 178

Ekacittaḥ Paṭhedetatsarvasiddhirbhaviṣyati |
Ekavārampaṭhedyastu Sarvapāpakṣayo Bhavet || 179

Dvivāramprapaṭhedyastu Vighneśvarasamo Bhavet |
Trivārampaṭhanāddevi Sarvaṃ Siddhyati Sarvathā || 180

Stavasyāsya Prabhāveṇa Sākṣādbhavati Suvrate |
Mokṣārtthī Labhate Mokṣandhanārthī Labhate Dhanam || 181

Vidyārtthī Labhate Vidyāntarkavyākaraṇānvitām |
Mahitvavatsarāntācca Śatruhāniḥ Prajāyate || 182

Kṣoṇīpatirvaśastasya Smaraṇe Sadṛśo Bhavet |
Yaḥ Paṭhetsarvadā Bhaktyā Śreyastu Bhavati Priye || 183

Gaṇādhyakṣapratinidhiḥ Kavikāvyaparo Varaḥ |
Gopanīyamprayatnena Jananījāravatsadā || 184

Hetuyukto Bhavennityaṃ Śaktiyuktaḥ Sadā Bhavet |
Ya Idampaṭhate Nityaṃ Śivena Sadṛśo Bhavet || 185

Jīvandharmārtthabhogī Syānmṛto Mokṣapatirbhavet |
Satyaṃ Satyaṃ Mahādevi Satyaṃ Satyanna Saṃśayaḥ || 186

Stavasyāsya Prabhāveṇa Devena Saha Modate |
Sucittāśca Surāssarve Stavarājasya Kīrttanāt || 187

Pītāmbaraparīdhānā Pītagandhānulepanā |
Paramodayakīrttiḥ Syātparatassurasundari || 188

Iti Śrīutkaṭaśambare Nāgendraprayāṇatantre Ṣoḍaśasahasre

Viṣṇuśaṅkara Saṃvāde Bagalāmukhī Sahasranāma Stotraṃ Samāptam ॥

श्री बगलामुखी सहस्रनाम स्तोत्रम्

सुरालयप्रधाने तु देवदेवं महेश्वरम् ।शैलाधिराजतनया सङ्ग्रहे तमुवाच ह॥ १

श्री देव्युवाच

परमेष्ठिन्परन्धाम प्रधान परमेश्वर ।
नाम्नां सहस्रम्बगलामुख्याद्या ब्रूहि वल्लभ॥ २

ईश्वर उवाच

शृणु देवि प्रवक्ष्यामि नामधेयसहस्रकम् ।परब्रह्मास्त्रविद्यायाश्चतुर्वर्गफलप्रदम्॥ ३

गुह्यादु ह्यतरन्देवि सर्वसिद्धैकवन्दितम् ।अतिगुप्ततरविद्या सर्वतन्त्रेषु गोपिता॥ ४

विशेषतः कलियुगे महासिद्ध्यौघदायिनी ।
गोपनीयङ्गोपनीयङ्गोपनीयम्प्रयत्नतः॥ ५

अप्रकाश्यमिदं सत्यं स्वयोनिरिव सुव्रते ।
रोधिनी विघ्नसङ्घानां मोहिनी परयोषिताम्॥ ६

स्तम्भिनी राजसैन्यानावादिनी परवादिनाम् ।पुरा चैकार्णवे घोरे काले परमभैरवः॥ ७

सुन्दरीसहितो देवः केशवः क्लेशनाशनः ।उरगासनमासीनो योगनिद्रामुपागमत्॥ ८

निद्राकाले च ते काले मया प्रोक्तः सनातनः ।
महास्तम्भकरन्देवि स्तोत्रवा शतनामकम्॥ ९

सहस्रनाम परमवद देवस्य कस्यचित् ।

श्री भगवानुवाच ।

शृणु शङ्कर देवेश परमातिरहस्यकम्॥ १०

अजोहं यत्प्रसादेन विष्णुः सर्वेश्वरेश्वरः ।
गोपनीयम्प्रयत्नेन प्रकाशात्सिद्धिहानिकृत्॥ ११

ॐ अस्य श्री बगलामुखी सहस्रनाम स्तोत्र मन्त्रस्य भगवान्सदाशिव ऋषिः

अनुष्टुप्छन्दः श्री जगद्वश्यकरी बगलामुखी देवता
सर्वाभीष्टसिद्ध्यर्थे जपे विनियोगः ॥

अथ ध्यानम्

पीताम्बरपरीधानां पीनोन्नतपयोधराम् ।
जटामुकुटशोभाढ्याम्पीतभूमिसुखासनाम् ॥ १२

शत्रोर्जिह्वां मुद्रञ्च बिभ्रतीम्परमाङ्कलाम् ।
सर्वागमपुराणेषु विख्याताम्भुवनत्रये ॥ १३

सृष्टिस्थितिविनाशानामादि भूतामहेश्वरीम् ।
गोप्या सर्वप्रयत्नेन शृणु ताङ्कथयामि ते ॥ १४

जगद्विध्वंसिनीन्देवीमजरामरकारिणीम् ।
तान्नमामि महामायामहदैश्वर्यदायिनीम् ॥ १५

अथ सहस्रनाम स्तोत्रः

प्रणवम्पूर्वमुद्धृत्य स्थिरमायान्ततो वदेत् ।
बगलामुखी सर्वेति दुष्टानावाचमेव च ॥ १६

मुखम्पदं स्तम्भयेति जिह्वाङ्कीलय बुद्धिमत् ।
विनाशयेति तारञ्च स्थिरमायान्ततो वदेत् ॥ १७

वह्निप्रियान्ततो मन्त्रश्चतुर्वर्गफलप्रदः ।
ब्रह्मास्त्रम्ब्रह्मविद्या च ब्रह्ममाता सनातनी ॥ १८

ब्रह्मेशी ब्रह्मकैवल्यबगला ब्रह्मचारिणी ।
नित्यानन्दा नित्यसिद्धा नित्यरूपा निरामया ॥ १९

सन्धारिणी महामाया कटाक्षक्षेमकारिणी ।
कमला विमला नीला रत्नकान्तिगुणाश्रिता ॥ २०

कामप्रिया कामरता कामकामस्वरूपिणी ।
मङ्गला विजया जाया सर्वमङ्गलकारिणी ॥ २१

कामिनी कामिनीकाम्या कामुका कामचारिणी ।
कामप्रिया कामरता कामाकामस्वरूपिणी ॥ २२

कामाख्या कामबीजस्था कामपीठनिवासिनी ।
कामदा कामहा काली कपाली च करालिका ॥ २३

कंसारिः कमला कामा कैलासेश्वरवल्लभा ।
कात्यायनी केशवा च करुणा कामकेलिभुक् ॥ २४

क्रियाकीर्तिः कृत्तिका च काशिका मथुरा शिवा ।
कालाक्षी कालिका काली धवलाननसुन्दरी ॥ २५

खेचरी च खमूर्त्तिश्च क्षुद्रा क्षुद्रक्षुधावरा ।
खड्गहस्ता खड्गरता खड्गिनी खर्परप्रिया ॥ २६

गङ्गा गौरी गामिनी च गीता गोत्रविवर्द्धिनी ।
गोधरा गोकरा गोधा गन्धर्वपुरवासिनी ॥ २७

गन्धर्वा गन्धर्वकला गोपनी गरुडासना ।
गोविन्दभावा गोविन्दा गान्धारी गन्धमादिनी ॥ २८

गौराङ्गी गोपिकामूर्त्तिर्गोपीगोष्ठनिवासिनी ।
गन्धा गजेन्द्रगामान्या गदाधरप्रिया ग्रहा ॥ २९

घोरघोरा घोररूपा घनश्रोणी घनप्रभा ।
दैत्येन्द्रप्रबला घण्टावादिनी घोरनिस्स्वना ॥ ३०

डाकिन्युमा उपेन्द्रा च उर्वशी उरगासना ।
उत्तमा उन्नता उन्ना उत्तमस्थानवासिनी ॥ ३१

चामुण्डा मुण्डिताचण्डी चण्डदर्पहरेति च ।
उग्रचण्डा चण्डचण्डा चण्डदैत्यविनाशिनी ॥ ३२

चण्डरूपा प्रचण्डा च चण्डाचण्डशरीरिणी ।
चतुर्भुजा प्रचण्डा च चराचरनिवासिनी ॥ ३३

क्षत्रप्रायशिशेरोवाहा छला छलतरा छली ।
क्षत्ररूपा क्षत्रधरा क्षत्रियक्षयकारिणी ॥ ३४

जया च जयदुर्गा च जयन्ती जयदा परा ।
जायिनी जयिनी ज्योत्स्ना जटाधरप्रिया जिता ॥ ३५

जितेन्द्रिया जितक्रोधा जयमाना जनेश्वरी ।
जितमृत्युर्जरातीता जाह्नवी जनकात्मजा ॥ ३६

झङ्कारा झञ्झरी झण्टा झङ्कारी झकशोभिनी ।
झखा झमेशा झङ्कारी योनिकल्याणदायिनी ॥ ३७

झञ्झरा झमुरी झारा झराझरतरा परा ।
झञ्झा झमेता झङ्कारी झणाकल्याणदायिनी ॥ ३८

ईमना मानसी चिन्त्या ईमुना शङ्करप्रिया ।
टङ्कारी टिटिका टीका टङ्किनी च टवर्गगा ॥ ३९

टापा टोपा टटपतिष्ठमनी टमनप्रिया ।
ठकारधारिणी ठीका ठङ्करी ठिकरप्रिया ॥ ४०

ठेकठासा ठकरती ठामिनी ठमनप्रिया ।
डारहा डाकिनी डारा डामरा डमरप्रिया ॥ ४१

डखिनी डडयुक्ता च डमरूकरवल्लभा ।
ढक्का ढक्की ढक्कनादा ढोलशब्दप्रबोधिनी ॥ ४२

ढामिनी ढामनप्रीता ढगतन्त्रप्रकाशिनी ।
अनेकरूपिणी अम्बा अणिमासिद्धिदायिनी ॥ ४३

अमन्त्रिणी अणुकरी अणुमब्दानुसंस्थिता ।
तारा तन्त्रावती तन्त्रतत्त्वरूपा तपस्विनी ॥ ४४

तरङ्गिणी तत्त्वपरा तन्त्रिका तन्त्रविग्रहा ।
तपोरूपा तत्त्वदात्री तपःप्रीतिप्रधर्षिणी ॥ ४५

तन्त्रा यन्त्राच्चर्चनपरा तलातलनिवासिनी ।
तल्पदा त्वल्पदा काम्या स्थिरा स्थिरतरा स्थितिः ॥ ४६

स्थाणुप्रिया स्थपरा स्थिता स्थानप्रदायिनी ।
दिगम्बरा दयारूपा दावाग्नि दमनीदमा ॥ ४७

दुर्गा दुर्गापरा देवी दुष्टदैत्यविनाशिनी । दमनप्रमदा दैत्यदयादानपरायणा ॥ ४८

दुर्गार्तिनाशिनी दान्ता दम्भिनी दम्भवर्जिता ।
दिगम्बरप्रिया दम्भा दैत्यदम्भविदारिणी ॥ ४९

दमना दशनसौन्दर्या दानवेन्द्रविनाशिनी ।
दया धरा च दमनी दर्भपत्रविलासिनी ॥ ५०

धरिणी धारिणी धात्री धराधरधरप्रिया ।
धराधरसुता देवी सुधर्मा धर्मचारिणी ॥ ५१

धर्मज्ञा धवला धूला धनदा धनवर्द्धिनी ।
धीरा धीरा धीरतरा धीरसिद्धिप्रदायिनी ॥ ५२

धन्वन्तरिधराधीरा ध्येया ध्यानस्वरूपिणी ।
नारायणी नारसिंही नित्यानन्दनरोत्तमा ॥ ५३

नक्ता नक्तावती नित्या नीलजीमूतसन्निभा ।
नीलाङ्गी नीलवस्त्रा च नीलपर्वतवासिनी ॥ ५४

सुनीलपुष्पखचिता नीलजम्बुसमप्रभा ।
नित्याख्या षोडशी विद्या नित्या नित्यसुखावहा ॥ ५५

नर्मदा नन्दनानन्दा नन्दानन्दविवर्द्धिनी ।
यशोदानन्दतनया नन्दनोद्यानवासिनी ॥ ५६

नागान्तका नागवृद्धा नागपत्नी च नागिनी ।
नमिताशेषजनता नमस्कारवती नमः ॥ ५७

पीताम्बरा पार्वती च पीताम्बरविभूषिता ।
पीतमील्याम्बरधरा पीताभा पिङ्गमूर्द्धजा ॥ ५८

पीतपुष्पार्च्चनरता पीतपुष्पसमर्च्चिता ।
परप्रभा पितृपतिः परसैन्यविनाशिनी ॥ ५९

परमा परतन्त्रा च परमन्त्रा परात्परा ।
पराविद्या परासिद्धिः परास्थानप्रदायिनी ॥ ६०

पुष्पा पुष्पवती नित्या पुष्पमालाविभूषिता ।
पुरातना पूर्वपरा परसिद्धिप्रदायिनी ॥ ६१

पीतानितम्बिनी पीता पीनोन्नतपयस्तनी ।
प्रेमाप्रमध्यमाशेषा पद्मपत्रविलासिनी ॥ ६२

पद्मावती पद्मनेत्रा पद्मा पद्ममुखी परा ।
पद्मासना पद्मप्रिया पद्मरागस्वरूपिणी ॥ ६३

पावनी पालिका पात्री परदा वरदा शिवा ।
प्रेतसंस्था परानन्दा परब्रह्मस्वरूपुणी ॥ ६४

जिनेश्वरप्रिया देवी पशुरक्तरतप्रिया ।
पशुमांसप्रिया पर्णा परामृतपरायणा ॥ ६५

पाशीनी पाशिका चापि पशुघ्नी पशुभाषिणी ।
फुल्लारविन्दवदनी फुल्लोत्पलशरीरिणी ॥ ६६

परानन्दप्रदा वीणापशुपाशविनाशिनी ।
फूत्कारा फुत्परा फेणी फुल्लेन्दीवरलोचना ॥ ६७

फट्मन्त्रा स्फटिका स्वाहा स्फोटा च फट्स्वरूपिणी ।
स्फाटिका घुटिका घोरा स्फटिकाद्रिस्वरूपिणी ॥ ६८

वराङ्गना वरधरा वाराही वासुकी वरा ।
बिन्दुस्था बिन्दुनी वाणी बिन्दुचक्रनिवासिनी ॥ ६९

विद्याधरी विशालाक्षी काशीवासिजनप्रिया ।
वेदविद्या विरूपाक्षी विश्वयुग्बहुरूपिणी ॥ ७०

ब्रह्मशक्तिर्विष्णुशक्तिः पञ्चवक्त्रा शिवप्रिया ।
वैकुण्ठवासिनी देवी वैकुण्ठपददायिनी ॥ ७१

ब्रह्मरूपा विष्णुरूपा परब्रह्ममहेश्वरी ।
भवप्रिया भवोद्भवा भवरूपा भवोत्तमा ॥ ७२

भवपारा भवधारा भाग्यवत्प्रियकारिणी ।
भद्रा सुभद्रा भवदा शुम्भदैत्यविनाशिनी ॥ ७३

भवानी भैरवी भीमा भद्रकाली सुभद्रिका ।
भगिनी भगरूपा च भगमाना भगोत्तमा ॥ ७४

भगप्रिया भगवती भगवासा भगाकरा ।
भगसृष्टा भाग्यवती भगरूपा भगासिनी ॥ ७५

भगलिङ्गप्रिया देवी भगलिङ्गपरायणा ।
भगलिङ्गस्वरूपा च भगलिङ्गविनोदिनी ॥ ७६

भगलिङ्गरता देवी भगलिङ्गनिवासिनी ।
भगमाला भगकला भगाधारा भगाम्बरा ॥ ७७

भगवेगा भगाभूषा भगेन्द्रा भाग्यरूपिणी ।
भगलिङ्गाङ्गसम्भोगा भगलिङ्गासवावहा ॥ ७८

भगलिङ्गसमाधुर्या भगलिङ्गनिवेशिता ।
भगलिङ्गसुपूजा च भगलिङ्गसमन्विता ॥ ७९

भगलिङ्गविरक्ता च भगलिङ्गसमावृता ।
माधवी माधवीमान्या मधुरा मधुमानिनी ॥ ८०

मन्दहासा महामाया मोहिनी महदुत्तमा ।
महामोहा महाविद्या महाघोरा महास्मृतिः ॥ ८१

मनस्विनी मानवती मोदिनी मधुरानना ।
मेनिका मानिनी मान्या मणिरत्नविभूषणा ॥ ८२

मल्लिका मौलिका माला मालाधरमदोत्तमा ।
मदनासुन्दरी मेधा मधुमत्ता मधुप्रिया ॥ ८३

मत्तहंसासमोन्नासा मत्तसिंहमहासनी ।
महेन्द्रवल्लभा भीमा मौल्यञ्च मिथुनात्मजा ॥ ८४

महाकाल्या महाकाली महाबुद्धिर्महोत्कटा ।
माहेश्वरी महामाया महिषासुरघातिनी ॥ ८५

मधुराकीर्त्तिमत्ता च मत्तमातङ्गगामिनी ।
मदप्रिया मांसरता मत्तयुक्कामकारिणी ॥ ८६

मैथुन्यवल्लभा देवी महानन्दा महोत्सवा ।
मरीचिर्मारतिर्माया मनोबुद्धिप्रदायिनी ॥ ८७

मोहा मोक्षा महालक्ष्मीर्महत्पदप्रदायिनी ।
यमरूपा च यमुना जयन्ती च जयप्रदा ॥ ८८

याम्या यमवती युद्धा यदोः कुलविवर्द्धिनी ।
रमा रामा रामपत्नी रत्नमाला रतिप्रिया ॥ ८९

रत्नसिंहासनस्था च रत्नाभरणमण्डिता ।
रमणी रमणीया च रत्यारसपरायणा ॥ ९०

रतानन्दा रतवती रधूणाङ्कुलवर्द्धिनी ।
रमणारिपरिभ्राज्या रैधाराधिकरत्नजा ॥ ९१

रावी रसस्वरूपा च रात्रिराजसुखावहा ।
ऋतुजा ऋतुदा ऋद्धा ऋतुरूपा ऋतुप्रिया ॥ ९२

रक्तप्रिया रक्तवती रङ्गिणी रक्तदन्तिका ।
लक्ष्मीर्ल्लज्जा लतिका च लीलालग्नानिताक्षिणी ॥ ९३

लीला लीलावती लोमाहर्षाह्लादनपट्टिका ।
ब्रह्मस्थिता ब्रह्मरूपा ब्रह्मणा वेदवन्दिता ॥ ९४

ब्रह्मोद्भवा ब्रह्मकला ब्रह्माणी ब्रह्मबोधिनी ।
वेदाङ्गना वेदरूपा वनिता विनता वसा ॥ ९५

बाला च युवती वृद्धा ब्रह्मकर्मपरायणा ।
विन्ध्यस्था विन्ध्यवासी च बिन्दुयुग्बिन्दुभूषणा ॥ ९६

विद्यावती वेदधारी व्यापिका बर्हिणी कला ।
वामाचारप्रिया वह्निर्वामाचारपरायणा ॥ ९७

वामाचाररता देवी वामदेवप्रियोत्तमा ।
बुद्धेन्द्रिया विबुद्धा च बुद्धाचरणमालिनी ॥ ९८

बन्धमोचनकर्त्री च वारुणा वरुणालया ।
शिवा शिवप्रिया शुद्धा शुद्धाङ्गी शुक्लवर्णिका ॥ ९९

शुक्लपुष्पप्रिया शुक्ला शिवधर्मपरायणा ।
शुक्लस्था शुक्लिनी शुक्लरूपशुक्लपशुप्रिया ॥ १००

शुक्रस्था शुक्रिणी शुक्रा शुक्ररूपा च शुक्रिका ।
षण्मुखी च षडङ्गा च षट्चक्रविनिवासिनी ॥ १०१

षड्ग्रन्थियुक्ता षोढा च षण्माता च षडात्मिका ।
षडङ्गयुवती देवी षडङ्गप्रकृतिर्वशी ॥ १०२

षडानना षड्रसा च षष्ठी षष्ठेश्वरीप्रिया ।
षड्गवादा षोडशी च षोढान्यासस्वरूपिणी ॥ १०३

षट्चक्रभेदनकरी षट्चक्रस्थस्वरूपिणी ।
षोडशस्वरूपा च षण्मुखी षड्रदान्विता ॥ १०४

सनकादिस्वरूपा च शिवधर्मषरायणा ।
सिद्धा सप्तस्वरी शुद्धा सुरमाता स्वरोत्तमा ॥ १०५

सिद्धविद्या सिधमाता सिद्धा सिद्धस्वरूपिणी ।
हरा हरिप्रिया हारा हरिणी हारयुक् तथा ॥ १०६

हरिरूपा हरिधारा हरिणाक्षी हरिप्रिया ।
हेतुप्रिया हेतुरता हिताहितस्वरूपिणी ॥ १०७

क्षमा क्षमावती क्षीता क्षुद्रघण्टाविभूषणा ।
क्षयङ्करी क्षितीशा च क्षीणमध्यसुशोभना ॥ १०८

अजानन्ता अपर्णा च अहल्याशेषशायिनी ।
स्वान्तर्गता च साधूनामन्तरानन्तरूपिणी ॥ १०९

अरूपा अमला चार्द्रा अनन्तगुणशालिनी ।
स्वविद्या विद्यकाविद्या विद्या चार्विन्दलोचना ॥ ११०

अपराजिता जातवेदा अजपा अमरावती ।
अल्पा स्वल्पा अनल्पाद्या अणिमासिद्धिदायिनी ॥ १११

अष्टसिद्धिप्रदा देवी रूपलक्षणसंयुता ।
अरविन्दमुखा देवी भोगसौख्यप्रदायिनी ॥ ११२

आदिविद्या आदिभूता आदिसिद्धिप्रदायिनी ।
सीत्काररूपिणी देवी सर्वासनविभूषिता ॥ ११३

इन्द्रप्रिया च इन्द्राणी इन्द्रप्रस्थनिवासिनी ।
इन्द्राक्षी इन्द्रवज्रा च इन्द्रमद्योक्षणी तथा ॥ ११४

ईला कामनिवासा च ईश्वरीश्वरवल्लभा ।
जननी चेश्वरी दीना भेदाचेश्वरकर्मकृत् ॥ ११५

उमा कात्यायनी ऊर्द्ध्वा मीना चोत्तरवासिनी ।
उमापतिप्रिया देवी शिवा चोङ्कारूपिणी ॥ ११६

उरगेन्द्रशिरोरत्ना उरगोरगवल्लभा ।
उद्यानवासिनी माला प्रशस्तमणिभूषणा ॥ ११७

उर्द्ध्वदन्तोत्तमाङ्गी च उत्तमा चोर्ध्वकेशिनी ।
उमासिद्धिप्रदा या च उरगासनसंस्थिता ॥ ११८

ऋषिपुत्री ऋषिच्छन्दा ऋद्धिसिद्धिप्रदायिनी ।
उत्सवोत्सवसीमन्ता कामिका च गुणान्विता ॥ ११९

एला एकारविद्या च एणीविद्याधरा तथा ।
ओङ्कारवलयोपेता ओङ्कारपरमा कला ॥ १२०

ओंवदवदवाणी च ओङ्काराक्षरमण्डिता ।
ऐन्द्री कुलिशहस्ता च ओंलोकपरवासिनी ॥ १२१

ओङ्कारमध्यबीजा च ओंनमोरूपधारिणी ।
प्रब्रह्मस्वरूपा च अंशुकांशुकवल्लभा ॥ १२२

ओङ्कारा अःफड्मन्त्रा च अक्षाक्षरविभूषिता ।
अमन्त्रा मन्त्ररूपा च पदशोभासमन्विता ॥ १२३

प्रणवोङ्काररूपा च प्रणवोच्चारभाक् पुनः ।
हीङ्काररूपा हींङ्कारी वाग्बीजाक्षरभूषणा ॥ १२४

हल्लेखा सिद्धि योगा च हृत्पद्मासनसंस्थिता ।
बीजाख्या नेत्रहृदया हीम्बीजाभुवनेश्वरी ॥ १२५

क्लीङ्कामराजा क्लिन्ना च चतुर्वर्गफलप्रदा ।
क्लीङ्क्लीङ्क्लींरूपिका देवी क्रीङ्क्रीङ्क्रींनामधारिणी ॥ १२६

कमलाशक्तिबीजा च पाशाङ्कुशविभूषिता ।
श्रींश्रींङ्कारा महाविद्या श्रद्धा श्रद्धावती तथा ॥ १२७

ओं ऐं क्लीं ह्रीं श्रीम्परा च क्लीङ्कारी परमा कला ।
ह्रीङ्क्लीं श्रीङ्कारस्वरूपा सर्वकर्मफलप्रदा ॥ १२८

सर्वाद्या सर्वदेवी च सर्वसिद्धिप्रदा तथा ।
सर्वज्ञा सर्वशक्तिश्च वाग्विभूतिप्रदायिनी ॥ १२९

सर्वमोक्षप्रदा देवी सर्वभोगप्रदायिनी ।
गुणेन्द्रवल्लभा वामा सर्वशक्तिप्रदायिनी ॥ १३०

सर्वानन्दमयी चैव सर्वसिद्धिप्रदायिनी ।
सर्वचक्रेश्वरी देवी सर्वसिद्धेश्वरी तथा ॥ १३१

सर्वप्रियङ्करी चैव सर्वसौख्यप्रदायिनी ।
सर्वानन्दप्रदा देवी ब्रह्मानन्दप्रदायिनी ॥ १३२

मनोवाञ्छितदात्री च मनोवृद्धिसमन्विता ।
अकारादिक्षकारान्ता दुर्गा दुर्गार्त्तिनाशिनी ॥ १३३

पद्मनेत्रा सुनेत्रा च स्वधास्वाहावषट्करी ।
स्ववर्गा देववर्गा च तवर्गा च समन्विता ॥ १३४

अन्तस्था वेशमरूपा च नवदुर्गा नरोत्तमा ।
तत्त्वसिद्धिप्रदा नीला तथा नीलपताकिनी ॥ १३५

नित्यरूपा निशाकारी स्तम्भिनी मोहिनीति च ।
वशङ्करी तथोच्चाटी उन्मादी कर्षिणीति च ॥ १३६

मातङ्गी मधुमत्ता च अणिमा लघिमा तथा ।
सिद्धा मोक्षप्रदा नित्या नित्यानन्दप्रदायिनी ॥ १३७

रक्ताङ्गी रक्तनेत्रा च रक्तचन्दनभूषिता ।
स्वल्पसिद्धिस्सुकल्पा च दिव्यचारणशुक्रभा ॥ १३८

सङ्क्रान्तिस्सर्वविद्या च सस्यवासरभूषिता ।
प्रथमा च द्वितीया च तृतीया च चतुर्त्थिका ॥ १३९

पञ्चमी चैव षष्ठी च विशुद्धा सप्तमी तथा ।
अष्टमी नवमी चैव दशम्येकादशी तथा ॥ १४०

द्वादशी त्रयोदशी च चतुर्दश्यथ पूर्णिमा ।
आमावस्या तथा पूर्वा उत्तरा परिपूर्णिमा ॥ १४१

खड्गिनी चक्रिणी घोरा गदिनी शूलिनी तथा ।
भुशुण्डी चापिनी बाणा सर्वायुधविभूषणा ॥ १४२

कुलेश्वरी कुलवती कुलाचारपरायणा ।
कुलकर्मसुरक्ता च कुलाचारप्रवर्द्धिनी ॥ १४३

कीर्तिश्श्रीश्च रमा रामा धर्मायै सततन्नमः ।
क्षमा धृतिः स्मृतिर्मेधा कल्पवृक्षनिवासिनी ॥ १४४

उग्रा उग्रप्रभा गौरी वेदविद्याविबोधिनी ।
साध्या सिद्धा सुसिद्धा च विप्ररूपा तथैव च ॥ १४५

काली कराली काल्या च कलादैत्यविनाशिनी ।
कौलिनी कालिकी चैव क-च-ट-त-पवर्णिका ॥ १४६

जयिनी जययुक्ता च जयदा जृम्भिनी तथा ।
स्राविणी द्राविणी देवी भरुण्डा विन्ध्यवासिनी ॥ १४७

ज्योतिर्भूता च जयदा ज्वालामालासमाकुला ।
भिन्ना भिन्नप्रकाशा च विभिन्ना भिन्नरूपिणी ॥ १४८

अश्विनी भरणी चैव नक्षत्रसम्भवानिला ।
काश्यपी विनता ख्याता दितिजादितिरेव च ॥ १४९

कीर्तिः कामप्रिया देवी कीर्त्या कीर्तिविवर्द्धिनी ।
सद्योमांससमालब्धा सद्यश्छिन्नासिशङ्करा ॥ १५०

दक्षिणा चोत्तरा पूर्वा पश्चिमा दिक् तथैव च ।
अग्निनैर्ऋतिवायव्या ईशान्यादिक् तथा स्मृता ॥ १५१

ऊर्ध्वाङ्गाधोगता श्वेता कृष्णा रक्ता च पीतका ।
चतुर्वर्गा चतुर्वर्णा चतुर्मात्रात्मिकाक्षरा ॥ १५२

चतुर्मुखी चतुर्वेदा चतुर्विद्या चतुर्मुखा ।
चतुर्गणा चतुर्माता चतुर्वर्गफलप्रदा ॥ १५३

धात्री विधात्री मिथुना नारी नायकवासिनी ।
सुरामुदा मुदवती मोदिनी मेनकात्मजा ॥ १५४

ऊर्ध्वकाली सिद्धिकाली दक्षिणाकालिका शिवा ।
नील्या सरस्वती सात्वम्बगला छिन्नमस्तका ॥ १५५

सर्वेश्वरी सिद्धविद्या परा परमदेवता ।
हिङ्गुला हिङ्गुलाङ्गी च हिङ्गुलाधरवासिनी ॥ १५६

हिङ्गुलोत्तमवर्णाभा हिङ्गुलाभरणा च सा ।
जाग्रती च जगन्माता जगदीश्वरवल्लभा ॥ १५७

जनार्दनप्रिया देवी जययुक्ता जयप्रदा । जगदानन्दकरी च जगदाह्लादकारिणी ॥ १५८

ज्ञानदानकरी यज्ञा जानकी जनकप्रिया । जयन्ती जयदा नित्या ज्वलदग्निसमप्रभा ॥

विद्याधरा च बिम्बोष्ठी कैलासचलवासिनी ।
विभवा वडवाग्निश्च अग्निहोत्रफलप्रदा ॥ १६०

मन्त्ररूपा परा देवी तथैव गुरुरूपिणी ।
गया गङ्गा गोमती च प्रभासा पुष्करापि च ॥ १६१

विन्ध्याचलरता देवी विन्ध्याचलनिवासिनी ।
बहू बहुसुन्दरी च कंसासुरविनाशिनी ॥ १६२

शूलिनी शूलहस्ता च वज्रा वज्रहरापि च ।
दुर्गा शिवा शान्तिकरी ब्रह्माणी ब्राह्मणप्रिया ॥ १६३

सर्वलोकप्रणेत्री च सर्वरोगहरापि च ।
मङ्गला शोभना शुद्धा निष्कला परमा कला ॥ १६४

विश्वेश्वरी विश्वमाता ललिता वसितानना ।
सदाशिवा उमा क्षेमा चण्डिका चण्डविक्रमा ॥ १६५

सर्वदेवमयी देवी सर्वागमभयापहा ।
ब्रह्मेशविष्णुनमिता सर्वकल्याणकारिणी ॥ १६६

योगिनी योगमाता च योगीन्द्रहृदयस्थिता ।
योगिजाया योगवती योगीन्द्रानन्दयोगिनी ॥ १६७

इन्द्रादिनमिता देवी ईश्वरी चेश्वरप्रिया ।
विशुद्धिदा भयहरा भक्तद्वेषिभयङ्करी ॥ १६८

भववेषा कामिनी च भरुण्डा भयकारिणी ।
बलभद्रप्रियाकारा संसारार्णवतारिणी ॥ १६९

पञ्चभूता सर्वभूता विभूतिर्भूतिधारिणी ।
सिंहवाहा महामोहा मोहपाशविनाशिनी ॥ १७०

मन्दुरा मदिरा मुद्रा मुद्रामुद्रधारिणी ।
सावित्री च महादेवी परप्रियनिनायिका ॥ १७१

यमदूती च पिङ्गाक्षी वैष्णवी शङ्करी तथा ।
चन्द्रप्रिया चन्द्ररता चन्दनारण्यवासिनी ॥ १७२

चन्दनेन्द्रसमायुक्ता चण्डदैत्यविनाशिनी ।
सर्वेश्वरी यक्षिणी च किराती राक्षसी तथा ॥ १७३

महाभोगवती देवी महामोक्षप्रदायिनी ।
विश्वहन्त्री विश्वरूपा विश्वसंहारकारिणी ॥ १७४

धात्री च सर्वलोकानां हितकारणकामिनी ।
कमला सूक्ष्मदा देवी धात्री हरविनाशिनी ॥ १७५

सुरेन्द्रपूजिता सिद्धा महातेजोवतीति च ।
परारूपवती देवी त्रैलोक्याकर्षकारिणी ॥ १७६

फलश्रुति:

इति ते कथितन्देवि पीतानाम सहस्रकम् ।
पठेद्वा पाठयेद्वापि सर्वसिद्धिर्भवेत्प्रिये ॥ १७७

इति मे विष्णुना प्रोक्तं महास्तम्भकरं परम् ।
प्रातः काले च मध्याह्ने सन्ध्याकाले च पार्वति ॥ १७८

एकचित्तः पठेदेतत्सर्वसिद्धिर्भविष्यति । एकवारम्पठेद्यस्तु सर्वपापक्षयो भवेत् ॥ १७९

द्विवारम्प्रपठेद्यस्तु विघ्नेश्वरसमो भवेत् ।
त्रिवारम्पठनादेवि सर्व सिद्ध्यति सर्वथा ॥ १८०

स्तवस्यास्य प्रभावेण साक्षाद्भवति सुव्रते ।
मोक्षार्थी लभते मोक्षन्धनार्थी लभते धनम् ॥ १८१

विद्यार्थी लभते विद्यान्तर्कव्याकरणान्विताम् ।
महित्ववत्सरान्ताच्च शत्रुहानिः प्रजायते ॥ १८२

क्षोणीपतिर्वशस्तस्य स्मरणे सदृशो भवेत् ।
यः पठेत्सर्वदा भक्त्या श्रेयस्तु भवति प्रिये ॥ १८३

गणाध्यक्षप्रतिनिधिः कविकाव्यपरो वरः ।
गोपनीयम्प्रयत्नेन जननीजारवत्सदा ॥ १८४

हेतुयुक्तो भवेन्नित्यं शक्तियुक्तः सदा भवेत् ।
य इदम्पठते नित्यं शिवेन सदृशो भवेत् ॥ १८५

जीवन्धर्मार्त्थिभोगी स्यान्मृतो मोक्षपतिर्भवेत् ।
सत्यं सत्यं महादेवि सत्यं सत्यन्न संशयः ॥ १८६

स्तवस्यास्य प्रभावेण देवेन सह मोदते ।
सुचित्ताश्च सुरास्सर्वे स्तवराजस्य कीर्त्तनात् ॥ १८७

पीताम्बरपरीधाना पीतगन्धानुलेपना ।
परमोदयकीर्त्तिः स्यात्परतस्सुरसुन्दरि ॥ १८८

इति श्रीउत्कटशम्बरे नागेन्द्रप्रयाण तन्त्रे षोडश सहस्रे
विष्णु शङ्कर संवादे बगलामुखी सहस्र नामस्तोत्रं समाप्तम् ॥

*****

Śrī Bhagalāmukhī Sahasra Nāmāvaliḥ

1,000 divine names on *Śrī Bhagalāmukhī Devi.*

Dhyānam ||

Pītāmbaraparīdhānāṃ Pīnonnatapayodharām |

Jaṭāmukuṭaśobhāḍhyāmpītabhūmisukhāsanām || 1

Śatrorjihvāṃ Mudgarañca Bibhratīmparamāṅkalām |

Sarvāgamapurāṇeṣu Vikhyātāmbhuvanatraye || 2

Sṛṣṭisthitivināśānāmādi Bhūtāmaheśvarīm |

Gopyā Sarvaprayatnena Śṛṇu Tāṅkathayāmi Te || 3

Jagadvidhvaṃsinīndevīmajarāmarakāriṇīm |

Tānnamāmi Mahāmāyāmahadaiścaryadāyinīm || 4

श्रीबगलामुखी सहस्रनामावलिः

ध्यानम्

पीताम्बरपरीधानां पीनोन्नतपयोधराम् ।
जटामुकुटशोभाद्द्याम्पीतभूमिसुखासनाम् ॥ १

शत्रोर्जिह्वां मुद्ररञ्चबिभ्रतीम्परमाङ्कलाम् ।
सर्वागमपुराणेषु विख्याताम्भुवनत्रये ॥ २

सृष्टिस्थितिविनाशानामादि भूतामहेश्वरीम् ।
गोप्या सर्वप्रयत्नेन शृणु ताङ्कथयामि ते ॥ ३

जगद्विध्वंसिनीन्देवीमजरामरकारिणीम् ।
तान्नमामि महामायामहदैश्वर्यदायिनीम् ॥ ४

Atha Sahasra Nāmāvaliḥ - अथ सहस्रनामावलिः

1.	*Oṃ Brahmāstrāya Namaḥ* ǀ	ॐ ब्रह्मास्त्राय नमः ǀ
2.	*Oṃ Brahma Vidyāyai Namaḥ* ǀ	ॐ ब्रह्म विद्यायै नमः ǀ
3.	*Oṃ Brahma Mātre Namaḥ* ǀ	ॐ ब्रह्म मात्रे नमः ǀ
4.	*Oṃ Sanātanyai Namaḥ* ǀ	ॐ सनातन्यै नमः ǀ
5.	*Oṃ Brahmeśyai Namaḥ* ǀ	ॐ ब्रह्मेश्यै नमः ǀ
6.	*Oṃ Brahma Kaivalya Bagalāyai Namaḥ* ǀ	ॐ ब्रह्मकैवल्यबगलायै नमः ǀ
7.	*Oṃ Brahmacāriṇyai Namaḥ* ǀ	ॐ ब्रह्मचारिण्यै नमः ǀ
8.	*Oṃ Nityānandāyai Namaḥ* ǀ	ॐ नित्यानन्दायै नमः ǀ
9.	*Oṃ Nityasiddhāyai Namaḥ* ǀ	ॐ नित्यसिद्धायै नमः ǀ
10.	*Oṃ Nityarūpāyai Namaḥ* ǀ	ॐ नित्यरूपायै नमः ǀ
11.	*Oṃ Nirāmayāyai Namaḥ* ǀ	ॐ निरामयायै नमः ǀ
12.	*Oṃ Sandhāriṇyai Namaḥ* ǀ	ॐ सन्धारिण्यै नमः ǀ
13.	*Oṃ Mahāmāyāyai Namaḥ* ǀ	ॐ महामायायै नमः ǀ
14.	*Oṃ Kaṭākṣakṣemakāriṇyai Namaḥ* ǀ	ॐ कटाक्षक्षेमकारिण्यै नमः ǀ
15.	*Oṃ Kamalāyai Namaḥ* ǀ	ॐ कमलायै नमः ǀ
16.	*Oṃ Vimalāyai Namaḥ* ǀ	ॐ विमलायै नमः ǀ
17.	*Oṃ Nīlaratnakāntiguṇāśritāyai Namaḥ* ǀ	ॐ नीलरत्नकान्तिगुणाश्रितायै नमः ǀ
18.	*Oṃ Kāmapriyāyai Namaḥ* ǀ	ॐ कामप्रियायै नमः ǀ
19.	*Oṃ Kāmaratāyai Namaḥ* ǀ	ॐ कामरतायै नमः ǀ
20.	*Oṃ Kāmakāmasvarūpiṇyai Namaḥ* ǀ	ॐ कामकामस्वरूपिण्यै नमः ǀ
21.	*Oṃ Maṅgalāyai Namaḥ* ǀ	ॐ मङ्गलायै नमः ǀ
22.	*Oṃ Vijayāyai Namaḥ* ǀ	ॐ विजयायै नमः ǀ
23.	*Oṃ Jāyāyai Namaḥ* ǀ	ॐ जायायै नमः ǀ
24.	*Oṃ Sarvamaṅgalakāriṇyai Namaḥ* ǀ	ॐ सर्वमङ्गलकारिण्यै नमः ǀ
25.	*Oṃ Kāminyai Namaḥ* ǀ	ॐ कामिन्यै नमः ǀ

26.	Oṃ Kāminīkāmyāyai Namaḥ l	ॐ कामिनीकाम्यायै नमः l
27.	Oṃ Kāmukāyai Namaḥ l	ॐ कामुकायै नमः l
28.	Oṃ Kāmacāriṇyai Namaḥ l	ॐ कामचारिण्यै नमः l
29.	Oṃ Kāmapriyāyai Namaḥ l	ॐ कामप्रियायै नमः l
30.	Oṃ Kāmaratāyai Namaḥ l	ॐ कामरतायै नमः l
31.	Oṃ Kāmakāmasvarūpiṇyai Namaḥ l	ॐ कामकामस्वरूपिण्यै नमः l
32.	Oṃ Kāmākhyāyai Namaḥ l	ॐ कामाख्यायै नमः l
33.	Oṃ Kāmabījasthāyai Namaḥ l	ॐ कामबीजस्थायै नमः l
34.	Oṃ Kāmapīṭhanivāsinyai Namaḥ	ॐ कामपीठनिवासिन्यै नमः l
35.	Oṃ Kāmadāyai Namaḥ l	ॐ कामदायै नमः l
36.	Oṃ Kāmahāyai Namaḥ l	ॐ कामहायै नमः l
37.	Oṃ Kālyai Namaḥ l	ॐ काल्यै नमः l
38.	Oṃ Kapālyai Namaḥ l	ॐ कपाल्यै नमः l
39.	Oṃ Karālikāyai Namaḥ l	ॐ करालिकायै नमः l
40.	Oṃ Kaṃsāryai Namaḥ l	ॐ कंसार्यै नमः l
41.	Oṃ Kamalāyai Namaḥ l	ॐ कमलायै नमः l
42.	Oṃ Kāmāyai Namaḥ l	ॐ कामायै नमः l
43.	Oṃ Kailāseśvaravallabhāyai Namaḥ l	ॐ कैलासेश्वरवल्लभायै नमः l
44.	Oṃ Kātyāyanyai Namaḥ l	ॐ कात्यायन्यै नमः l
45.	Oṃ Keśavāyai Namaḥ l	ॐ केशवायै नमः l
46.	Oṃ Karuṇāyai Namaḥ l	ॐ करुणायै नमः l
47.	Oṃ Kāmakelibhuje Namaḥ l	ॐ कामकेलिभुजे नमः l
48.	Oṃ Kriyākīrtyai Namaḥ l	ॐ क्रियाकीर्त्यै नमः l
49.	Oṃ Kṛttikāyai Namaḥ l	ॐ कृत्तिकायै नमः l
50.	Oṃ Kāśikāyai Namaḥ l	ॐ काशिकायै नमः l
51.	Oṃ Mathurāyai Namaḥ l	ॐ मथुरायै नमः l
52.	Oṃ Śivāyai Namaḥ l	ॐ शिवायै नमः l
53.	Oṃ Kālākṣyai Namaḥ l	ॐ कालाक्ष्यै नमः l
54.	Oṃ Kālikāyai Namaḥ l	ॐ कालिकायै नमः l

55.	Oṃ Kālīdhavalānanasundaryai Namaḥ		ॐ कालीधवलाननसुन्दर्यै नमः ।
56.	Oṃ Khecaryai Namaḥ		ॐ खेचर्यै नमः ।
57.	Oṃ Khamūrtyai Namaḥ		ॐ खमूर्त्यै नमः ।
58.	Oṃ Kṣudrā Kṣudra Kṣudhā Varāyai Namaḥ		ॐ क्षुद्राक्षुद्रक्षुधावराये नमः
59.	Oṃ Khaḍgahastāyai Namaḥ		ॐ खड्गहस्तायै नमः ।
60.	Oṃ Khaḍgaratāyai Namaḥ		ॐ खड्गरताये नमः ।
61.	Oṃ Khaḍginyai Namaḥ		ॐ खड्गिन्यै नमः ।
62.	Oṃ Kharparapriyāyai Namaḥ		ॐ खर्परप्रियायै नमः ।
63.	Oṃ Gaṅgāyai Namaḥ		ॐ गङ्गायै नमः ।
64.	Oṃ Gauryai Namaḥ		ॐ गौर्यै नमः ।
65.	Oṃ Gāminyai Namaḥ		ॐ गामिन्यै नमः ।
66.	Oṃ Gītāyai Namaḥ		ॐ गीतायै नमः ।
67.	Oṃ Gotravivardhinyai Namaḥ		ॐ गोत्रविवर्धिन्यै नमः ।
68.	Oṃ Godharāyai Namaḥ		ॐ गोधराये नमः ।
69.	Oṃ Gokarāyai Namaḥ		ॐ गोकराये नमः ।
70.	Oṃ Godhāyai Namaḥ		ॐ गोधाये नमः ।
71.	Oṃ Gandharvapuravāsinyai Namaḥ		ॐ गन्धर्वपुरवासिन्यै नमः ।
72.	Oṃ Gandharvāyai Namaḥ		ॐ गन्धर्वायै नमः ।
73.	Oṃ Gandharva Kalāgopinyai Namaḥ		ॐ गन्धर्वकलागोपिन्यै नमः ।
74.	Oṃ Garuḍāsanāyai Namaḥ		ॐ गरुडासनाये नमः ।
75.	Oṃ Govindabhāvāyai Namaḥ		ॐ गोविन्दभावाये नमः ।
76.	Oṃ Govindāyai Namaḥ		ॐ गोविन्दाये नमः ।
77.	Oṃ Gāndhāryai Namaḥ		ॐ गान्धार्यै नमः ।
78.	Oṃ Gandhamādinyai Namaḥ		ॐ गन्धमादिन्यै नमः ।
79.	Oṃ Gaurāṅgyai Namaḥ		ॐ गौराङ्ग्यै नमः ।
80.	Oṃ Gopikāmūrtaye Namaḥ		ॐ गोपिकामूर्तये नमः ।
81.	Oṃ Gopīgoṣṭhanivāsinyai Namaḥ		ॐ गोपीगोष्ठनिवासिन्यै नमः ।

82.	*Oṃ Gandhāyai Namaḥ* |	ॐ गन्धायै नमः ।
83.	*Oṃ Gajendragāmānyāyai Namaḥ*	ॐ गजेन्द्रगामान्यायै नमः ।
84.	*Oṃ Gadādharapriyāgrahāyai Namaḥ* |	ॐ गदाधरप्रियाग्रहायै नमः ।
85.	*Oṃ Ghoraghorāyai Namaḥ* |	ॐ घोरघोरायै नमः ।
86.	*Oṃ Ghorarūpāyai Namaḥ* |	ॐ घोररूपायै नमः ।
87.	*Oṃ Ghanaśreṇyai Namaḥ* |	ॐ घनश्रेण्यै नमः ।
88.	*Oṃ Ghanaprabhāyai Namaḥ* |	ॐ घनप्रभायै नमः ।
89.	*Oṃ Daityendraprabalāyai Namaḥ* |	ॐ दैत्येन्द्रप्रबलायै नमः ।
90.	*Oṃ Ghaṇṭāvādinyai Namaḥ* |	ॐ घण्टावादिन्यै नमः ।
91.	*Oṃ Ghoraniḥsvanāyai Namaḥ* |	ॐ घोरनिःस्वनायै नमः ।
92.	*Oṃ Ḍākinyai Namaḥ* |	ॐ डाकिन्यै नमः ।
93.	*Oṃ Umāyai Namaḥ* |	ॐ उमायै नमः ।
94.	*Oṃ Upendrāyai Namaḥ* |	ॐ उपेन्द्रायै नमः ।
95.	*Oṃ Urvaśyai Namaḥ* |	ॐ उर्वश्यै नमः ।
96.	*Oṃ Uragāsanāyai Namaḥ* |	ॐ उरगासनायै नमः ।
97.	*Oṃ Uttamāyai Namaḥ* |	ॐ उत्तमायै नमः ।
98.	*Oṃ Unnatāyai Namaḥ* |	ॐ उन्नतायै नमः ।
99.	*Oṃ Unnāyai Namaḥ* |	ॐ उन्नायै नमः ।
100.	*Oṃ Uttamasthānavāsinyai Namaḥ* |	ॐ उत्तमस्थानवासिन्यै नमः ।
101.	*Oṃ Cāmuṇḍāyai Namaḥ* |	ॐ चामुण्डायै नमः ।
102.	*Oṃ Muṇḍitāyai Namaḥ* |	ॐ मुण्डितायै नमः ।
103.	*Oṃ Caṇḍyai Namaḥ* |	ॐ चण्ड्यै नमः ।
104.	*Oṃ Caṇḍadarpaharāyai Namaḥ* |	ॐ चण्डदर्पहरायै नमः ।
105.	*Oṃ Ugracaṇḍāyai Namaḥ* |	ॐ उग्रचण्डायै नमः ।
106.	*Oṃ Caṇḍacaṇḍāyai Namaḥ* |	ॐ चण्डचण्डायै नमः ।
107.	*Oṃ Caṇḍadaityavināśinyai Namaḥ* |	ॐ चण्डदैत्यविनाशिन्यै नमः ।
108.	*Oṃ Caṇḍarūpāyai Namaḥ* |	ॐ चण्डरूपायै नमः ।

109.	Oṃ Pracaṇḍāyai Namaḥ l	ॐ प्रचण्डायै नमः l
110.	Oṃ Caṇḍācaṇḍaśarīriṇyai Namaḥ l	ॐ चण्डाचण्डशरीरिण्यै नमः l
111.	Oṃ Caturbhujāyai Namaḥ l	ॐ चतुर्भुजायै नमः l
112.	Oṃ Pracaṇḍāyai Namaḥ l	ॐ प्रचण्डायै नमः l
113.	Oṃ Carācaranivāsinyai Namaḥ l	ॐ चराचरनिवासिन्यै नमः l
114.	Oṃ Chatraprāyaśirovāhāyai Namaḥ l	ॐ छत्रप्रायशिरोवाहायै नमः l
115.	Oṃ Chalācchalatarāyai Namaḥ l	ॐ छलाच्छलतरायै नमः l
116.	Oṃ Chalyai Namaḥ l	ॐ छल्यै नमः l
117.	Oṃ Kṣatrarūpāyai Namaḥ l	ॐ क्षत्ररूपायै नमः l
118.	Oṃ Kṣatradharāyai Namaḥ l	ॐ क्षत्रधरायै नमः l
119.	Oṃ Kṣatriyakṣayakāriṇyai Namaḥ l	ॐ क्षत्रियक्षयकारिण्यै नमः l
120.	Oṃ Jayāyai Namaḥ l	ॐ जयायै नमः l
121.	Oṃ Jayadurgāyai Namaḥ l	ॐ जयदुर्गायै नमः l
122.	Oṃ Jayantyai Namaḥ l	ॐ जयन्त्यै नमः l
123.	Oṃ Jayadāyai Namaḥ l	ॐ जयदायै नमः l
124.	Oṃ Parāyai Namaḥ l	ॐ परायै नमः l
125.	Oṃ Jāyinījayinyai Namaḥ l	ॐ जायिनीजयिन्यै नमः l
126.	Oṃ Jyotsnājaṭādharapriyāyai Namaḥ l	ॐ ज्योत्स्नाजटाधरप्रियायै नमः l
127.	Oṃ Ajitāyai Namaḥ l	ॐ अजितायै नमः l
128.	Oṃ Jitendriyāyai Namaḥ l	ॐ जितेन्द्रियायै नमः l
129.	Oṃ Jitakrodhāyai Namaḥ l	ॐ जितक्रोधायै नमः l
130.	Oṃ Jayamānāyai Namaḥ l	ॐ जयमानायै नमः l
131.	Oṃ Janeśvaryai Namaḥ l	ॐ जनेश्वर्यै नमः l
132.	Oṃ Jitamṛtyave Namaḥ l	ॐ जितमृत्यवे नमः l
133.	Oṃ Jarātītāyai Namaḥ l	ॐ जरातीतायै नमः l
134.	Oṃ Jāhnavyai Namaḥ l	ॐ जाह्नव्यै नमः l
135.	Oṃ Janakātmajāyai Namaḥ l	ॐ जनकात्मजायै नमः l

136.	Oṃ Jhaṅkārāyai Namaḥ		ॐ झङ्कारायै नमः ।
137.	Oṃ Jhañjharījhaṇṭāyai Namaḥ		ॐ झञ्झरीझण्टायै नमः ।
138.	Oṃ Jhaṅkārījhakaśobhinyai Namaḥ	ॐ झङ्कारीझकशोभिन्यै नमः
139.	Oṃ Jhakhājhameśāyai Namaḥ		ॐ झखाझमेशायै नमः ।
140.	Oṃ Jhaṅkārī Yonikalyāṇa Dāyinyai Namaḥ		ॐ झङ्कारीयोनिकल्याण दायिन्यै नमः ।
141.	Oṃ Jhañjharāyai Namaḥ		ॐ झञ्झरायै नमः ।
142.	Oṃ Jhamurījhārāyai Namaḥ		ॐ झमुरीझारायै नमः ।
143.	Oṃ Jharājharatarāyai Parāyai Namaḥ		ॐ झराझरतरायै परायै नमः ।
144.	Oṃ Jhañjhājhametāyai Namaḥ		ॐ झञ्झाझमेतायै नमः ।
145.	Oṃ Jhaṅkārī Jhaṇākalyāṇa Dāyinyai Namaḥ		ॐ झङ्कारीझणाकल्याण दायिन्यै नमः ।
146.	Oṃ Ñamunāmānasīcintyāyai Namaḥ		ॐ अमुनामानसीचिन्त्यायै नमः ।
147.	Oṃ Ñamunāśaṅkarapriyāyai Namaḥ	ॐ अमुनाशङ्करप्रियायै नमः ।
148.	Oṃ Ṭaṅkārīṭiṭikāyai Namaḥ		ॐ टङ्कारीटिटिकायै नमः ।
149.	Oṃ Ṭīkāṭaṅkinyai Namaḥ		ॐ टीकाटङ्किन्यै नमः ।
150.	Oṃ Ṭavargagāyai Namaḥ		ॐ टवर्गगायै नमः ।
151.	Oṃ Ṭāpāṭopāyai Namaḥ		ॐ टापाटोपायै नमः ।
152.	Oṃ Ṭaṭapataye Namaḥ		ॐ टटपतये नमः ।
153.	Oṃ Ṭamanyai Namaḥ		ॐ टमन्यै नमः ।
154.	Oṃ Ṭamanapriyāyai Namaḥ		ॐ टमनप्रियायै नमः ।
155.	Oṃ Ṭhakāradhāriṇyai Namaḥ		ॐ ठकारधारिण्यै नमः ।
156.	Oṃ Ṭhīkāṭhaṅkaryai Namaḥ		ॐ ठीकाठङ्कर्यै नमः ।
157.	Oṃ Ṭhikarapriyāyai Namaḥ		ॐ ठिकरप्रियायै नमः ।
158.	Oṃ Ṭhekaṭhāsāyai Namaḥ		ॐ ठेकठासायै नमः ।
159.	Oṃ Ṭhakaratīṭhāminyai Namaḥ		ॐ ठकरतीठामिन्यै नमः ।
160.	Oṃ Ṭhamanapriyāyai Namaḥ		ॐ ठमनप्रियायै नमः ।
161.	Oṃ Ḍārahāyai Namaḥ		ॐ डारहायै नमः ।
162.	Oṃ Ḍākinyai Namaḥ		ॐ डाकिन्यै नमः ।

163.	Oṃ Ḍārāḍāmarāyai Namaḥ ǀ	ॐ डाराडामराये नमः ǀ
164.	Oṃ Ḍamarapriyāyai Namaḥ ǀ	ॐ डमरप्रियायै नमः ǀ
165.	Oṃ Ḍakhinīḍaḍayuktāyai Namaḥ ǀ	ॐ डखिनीडडयुक्तायै नमः ǀ
166.	Oṃ Ḍamarūkaravallabhāyai Namaḥ	ॐ डमरूकरवल्लभायै नमः ǀ
167.	Oṃ Ḍhakkā Ḍhakkī Ḍhakkanādāyai Namaḥ ǀ	ॐ ढक्काढक्कीढक्कनादायै नमः ǀ
168.	Oṃ Ḍholaśabdaprabodhinyai Namaḥ ǀ	ॐ ढोलशब्दप्रबोधिन्यै नमः ǀ
169.	Oṃ Ḍhāminīḍhāmanaprītāyai Namaḥ ǀ	ॐ ढामिनीढामनप्रीतायै नमः ǀ
170.	Oṃ Ḍhagatantraprakāśinyai Namaḥ	ॐ ढगतन्त्रप्रकाशिन्यै नमः ǀ
171.	Oṃ Anekarūpiṇyai Namaḥ ǀ	ॐ अनेकरूपिण्यै नमः ǀ
172.	Oṃ Ambāyai Namaḥ ǀ	ॐ अम्बायै नमः ǀ
173.	Oṃ Aṇimāsiddhidāyinyai Namaḥ	ॐ अणिमासिद्धिदायिन्यै नमः
174.	Oṃ Amantriṇyai Namaḥ ǀ	ॐ अमन्त्रिण्यै नमः ǀ
175.	Oṃ Aṇukaryai Namaḥ ǀ	ॐ अणुकर्यै नमः ǀ
176.	Oṃ Aṇumadbhānusaṃsthitāyai Namaḥ ǀ	ॐ अणुमब्द्रानुसंस्थितायै नमः ǀ
177.	Oṃ Tārātantravatyai Namaḥ ǀ	ॐ तारातन्त्रवत्यै नमः ǀ
178.	Oṃ Tantratattvarūpāyai Namaḥ ǀ	ॐ तन्त्रतत्त्वरूपायै नमः ǀ
179.	Oṃ Tapasvinyai Namaḥ ǀ	ॐ तपस्विन्यै नमः ǀ
180.	Oṃ Taraṅgiṇyai Namaḥ ǀ	ॐ तरङ्गिण्यै नमः ǀ
181.	Oṃ Tattvaparāyai Namaḥ ǀ	ॐ तत्त्वपरायै नमः ǀ
182.	Oṃ Tantrikātantravigrahāyai Namaḥ ǀ	ॐ तन्त्रिकातन्त्रविग्रहायै नमः ǀ
183.	Oṃ Taporūpāyai Namaḥ ǀ	ॐ तपोरूपायै नमः ǀ
184.	Oṃ Tattvadātryai Namaḥ ǀ	ॐ तत्त्वदात्र्यै नमः ǀ
185.	Oṃ Tapaḥprītipradharṣiṇyai Namaḥ	ॐ तपःप्रीतिप्रधर्षिण्यै नमः ǀ
186.	Oṃ Tantrayantrārcanaparāyai Namaḥ ǀ	ॐ तन्त्रयन्त्रार्चनपरायै नमः ǀ
187.	Oṃ Talātalanivāsinyai Namḥ ǀ	ॐ तलातलनिवासिन्यै नमः ǀ

188.	Oṃ Talpadāyai Namaḥ l	ॐ तल्पदायै नमः l
189.	Oṃ Alpadāyai Namaḥ l	ॐ अल्पदायै नमः l
190.	Oṃ Kāmyāyai Namaḥ l	ॐ काम्यायै नमः l
191.	Oṃ Sthirāyai Namaḥ l	ॐ स्थिरायै नमः l
192.	Oṃ Sthiratarāyai Sthityai Namaḥ l	ॐ स्थिरतरायै स्थित्यै नमः l
193.	Oṃ Sthāṇupriyāyai Namaḥ l	ॐ स्थाणुप्रियायै नमः l
194.	Oṃ Sthāṇuparāyai Namaḥ l	ॐ स्थाणुपरायै नमः l
195.	Oṃ Sthitāsthānapradāyinyai Namaḥ	ॐ स्थितास्थानप्रदायिन्यै नमः
196.	Oṃ Digambarāyai Namaḥ l	ॐ दिगम्बरायै नमः l
197.	Oṃ Dayārūpāyai Namaḥ l	ॐ दयारूपायै नमः l
198.	Oṃ Dāvāgnidamanīdamāyai Namaḥ	ॐ दावाग्निदमनीदमायै नमः l
199.	Oṃ Durgāyai Namaḥ l	ॐ दुर्गायै नमः l
200.	Oṃ Durgaparādevyai Namaḥ l	ॐ दुर्गापरादेव्यै नमः l
201.	Oṃ Duṣṭadaityavināśinyai Namaḥ l	ॐ दुष्टदैत्यविनाशिन्यै नमः l
202.	Oṃ Damanapramadāyai Namaḥ	ॐ दमनप्रमदायै नमः l
203.	Oṃ Daitya Dayādāna Parāyaṇāyai Namaḥ l	ॐ दैत्यदयादानपरायणायै नमः l
204.	Oṃ Durgārtināśinyai Namaḥ l	ॐ दुर्गार्तिनाशिन्यै नमः l
205.	Oṃ Dāntāyai Namaḥ l	ॐ दान्तायै नमः l
206.	Oṃ Dambhinyai Namaḥ l	ॐ दम्भिन्यै नमः l
207.	Oṃ Dambhavarjitāyai Namaḥ l	ॐ दम्भवर्जितायै नमः l
208.	Oṃ Digambarapriyāyai Namaḥ l	ॐ दिगम्बरप्रियायै नमः l
209.	Oṃ Dambhāyai Namaḥ l	ॐ दम्भायै नमः l
210.	Oṃ Daityadambhavidāriṇyai Namaḥ	ॐ दैत्यदम्भविदारिण्यै नमः l
211.	Oṃ Damanāśanasaundaryāyai Namaḥ l	ॐ दमनाशनसौन्दर्यायै नमः l
212.	Oṃ Dānavendravināśinyai Namaḥ l	ॐ दानवेन्द्रविनाशिन्यै नमः l
213.	Oṃ Dayādharāyai Namaḥ l	ॐ दयाधरायै नमः l
214.	Oṃ Damanyai Namaḥ l	ॐ दमन्यै नमः l
215.	Oṃ Darbhapatravilāsinyai Namaḥ l	ॐ दर्भपत्रविलासिन्यै नमः l

216.	Oṃ Dharaṇīdhāriṇyai Namaḥ		ॐ धरणीधारिण्यै नमः ।
217.	Oṃ Dhātryai Namaḥ		ॐ धात्र्यै नमः ।
218.	Oṃ Dharādharadharapriyāyai Namaḥ		ॐ धराधरधरप्रियायै नमः ।
219.	Oṃ Dharādharasutāyai Devyai Namaḥ		ॐ धराधरसुतायै देव्यै नमः ।
220.	Oṃ Sudharmādharmacāriṇyai Namaḥ		ॐ सुधर्माधर्मचारिण्यै नमः ।
221.	Oṃ Dharmajñāyai Namaḥ		ॐ धर्मज्ञायै नमः ।
222.	Oṃ Dhavalādhūlāyai Namaḥ		ॐ धवलाधूलायै नमः ।
223.	Oṃ Dhanadāyai Namaḥ		ॐ धनदायै नमः ।
224.	Oṃ Dhanavardhinyai Namaḥ		ॐ धनवर्धिन्यै नमः ।
225.	Oṃ Dhīrāyai Namaḥ		ॐ धीरायै नमः ।
226.	Oṃ Adhīrāyai Namaḥ		ॐ अधीरायै नमः ।
227.	Oṃ Dhīratarāyai Namaḥ		ॐ धीरतरायै नमः ।
228.	Oṃ Dhīrasiddhipradāyinyai Namaḥ		ॐ धीरसिद्धिप्रदायिन्यै नमः ।
229.	Oṃ Dhanvantaridharādhīrāyai Namaḥ		ॐ धन्वन्तरिधराधीरायै नमः ।
230.	Oṃ Dhyeyadhyānasvarūpiṇyai Namaḥ		ॐ ध्येयध्यानस्वरूपिण्यै नमः ।
231.	Oṃ Nārāyaṇyai Namaḥ		ॐ नारायण्यै नमः ।
232.	Oṃ Nārasiṃhyai Namaḥ		ॐ नारसिंह्यै नमः ।
233.	Oṃ Nityānandanarottamāyai Namaḥ		ॐ नित्यानन्दनरोत्तमायै नमः ।
234.	Oṃ Naktānaktāvatyai Namaḥ		ॐ नक्तानक्तावत्यै नमः ।
235.	Oṃ Nityāyai Namaḥ		ॐ नित्यायै नमः ।
236.	Oṃ Nīlajīmūtasannibhāyai Namaḥ		ॐ नीलजीमूतसन्निभायै नमः
237.	Oṃ Nīlāṅgyai Namaḥ		ॐ नीलाङ्ग्यै नमः ।
238.	Oṃ Nīlavastrāyai Namaḥ		ॐ नीलवस्त्रायै नमः ।
239.	Oṃ Nīlaparvatavāsinyai Namaḥ		ॐ नीलपर्वतवासिन्यै नमः ।
240.	Oṃ Sunīlapuṣpakhacitāyai Namaḥ		ॐ सुनीलपुष्पखचितायै नमः ।

241.	*Oṃ Nīlajambūsamaprabhāyai Namaḥ ǀ*	ॐ नीलजम्बूसमप्रभायै नमः ǀ
242.	*Oṃ Nityākhyāyai Ṣoḍaśyai Namaḥ ǀ*	ॐ नित्याख्यायै षोडश्यै नमः ǀ
243.	*Oṃ Vidyāyai Nityāyai Namaḥ ǀ*	ॐ विद्यायै नित्यायै नमः ǀ
244.	*Oṃ Nityasukhāvahāyai Namaḥ ǀ*	ॐ नित्यसुखावहायै नमः ǀ
245.	*Oṃ Narmadāyai Namaḥ ǀ*	ॐ नर्मदायै नमः ǀ
246.	*Oṃ Nandanānandāyai Namaḥ ǀ*	ॐ नन्दनानन्दायै नमः ǀ
247.	*Oṃ Nandānanda Vivardhinyai Namaḥ ǀ*	ॐ नन्दानन्द विवर्धिन्यै नमः ǀ
248.	*Oṃ Yaśodānandatanayāyai Namaḥ*	ॐ यशोदानन्दतनयायै नमः ǀ
249.	*Oṃ Nandanodyānavāsinyai Namaḥ*	ॐ नन्दनोद्यानवासिन्यै नमः ǀ
250.	*Oṃ Nāgāntakāyai Namaḥ ǀ*	ॐ नागान्तकायै नमः ǀ
251.	*Oṃ Nāgavṛddhāyai Namaḥ ǀ*	ॐ नागवृद्धायै नमः ǀ
252.	*Oṃ Nāgapatnyai Namaḥ ǀ*	ॐ नागपत्न्यै नमः ǀ
253.	*Oṃ Nāginyai Namaḥ ǀ*	ॐ नागिन्यै नमः ǀ
254.	*Oṃ Namitāśeṣajanatāyai Namaḥ ǀ*	ॐ नमिताशेषजनतायै नमः ǀ
255.	*Oṃ Namaskāravatyai Namaḥ ǀ*	ॐ नमस्कारवत्यै नमः ǀ
256.	*Oṃ Namase Namaḥ ǀ*	ॐ नमसे नमः ǀ
257.	*Oṃ Pītāmbarāyai Namaḥ ǀ*	ॐ पीताम्बरायै नमः ǀ
258.	*Oṃ Pārvatyai Namaḥ ǀ*	ॐ पार्वत्यै नमः ǀ
259.	*Oṃ Pītāmbaravibhūṣitāyai Namaḥ ǀ*	ॐ पीताम्बरविभूषितायै नमः ǀ
260.	*Oṃ Pītamālyāmbaradharāyai Namaḥ ǀ*	ॐ पीतमाल्याम्बरधरायै नमः ǀ
261.	*Oṃ Pītābhāyai Namaḥ ǀ*	ॐ पीताभायै नमः ǀ
262.	*Oṃ Piṅgamūrdhajāyai Namaḥ ǀ*	ॐ पिङ्गमूर्धजायै नमः ǀ
263.	*Oṃ Pītapuṣpārcanaratāyai Namaḥ ǀ*	ॐ पीतपुष्पार्चनरतायै नमः ǀ
264.	*Oṃ Pītapuṣpasamarcitāyai Namaḥ ǀ*	ॐ पीतपुष्पसमर्चितायै नमः ǀ
265.	*Oṃ Paraprabhāyai Namaḥ ǀ*	ॐ परप्रभायै नमः ǀ
266.	*Oṃ Pitṛpataye Namaḥ ǀ*	ॐ पितृपतये नमः ǀ
267.	*Oṃ Parasainyavināśinyai Namaḥ*	ॐ परसैन्यविनाशिन्यै नमः ǀ
268.	*Oṃ Paramāyai Namaḥ ǀ*	ॐ परमायै नमः ǀ

269.	Oṃ Paratantrāyai Namaḥ		ॐ परतन्त्रायै नमः ।
270.	Oṃ Paramantrāyai Namaḥ		ॐ परमन्त्रायै नमः ।
271.	Oṃ Parātparāyai Namaḥ		ॐ परात्परायै नमः ।
272.	Oṃ Parāyai Vidyāyai Namaḥ		ॐ परायै विद्यायै नमः ।
273.	Oṃ Parāyai Siddhyai Namaḥ		ॐ परायै सिद्ध्यै नमः ।
274.	Oṃ Parāsthānapradāyinyai Namaḥ	ॐ परास्थानप्रदायिन्यै नमः ।
275.	Oṃ Puṣpāyai Namaḥ		ॐ पुष्पायै नमः ।
276.	Oṃ Nityaṃ Puṣpavatyai Namaḥ	ॐ नित्यं पुष्पवत्यै नमः ।
277.	Oṃ Puṣpamālāvibhūṣitāyai Namaḥ		ॐ पुष्पमालाविभूषितायै नमः
278.	Oṃ Purātanāyai Namaḥ		ॐ पुरातनायै नमः ।
279.	Oṃ Pūrvaparāyai Namaḥ		ॐ पूर्वपरायै नमः ।
280.	Oṃ Parasiddhipradāyinyai Namaḥ		ॐ परसिद्धिप्रदायिन्यै नमः ।
281.	Oṃ Pītānitambinyai Namaḥ	ॐ पीतानितम्बिन्यै नमः ।
282.	Oṃ Pītāpīnonnatapayasstanyai Namaḥ		ॐ पीतापीनोन्नतपयस्स्तन्यै नमः ।
283.	Oṃ Premāpramadhyamāśeṣāyai Namaḥ		ॐ प्रेमाप्रमध्यमाशेषायै नमः ।
284.	Oṃ Padmapatravilāsinyai Namaḥ		ॐ पद्मपत्रविलासिन्यै नमः ।
285.	Oṃ Padmāvatyai Namaḥ		ॐ पद्मावत्यै नमः ।
286.	Oṃ Padmanetrāyai Namaḥ		ॐ पद्मनेत्रायै नमः ।
287.	Oṃ Padmāyai Namaḥ		ॐ पद्मायै नमः ।
288.	Oṃ Padmamukhīparāyai Namaḥ		ॐ पद्ममुखीपरायै नमः ।
289.	Oṃ Padmāsanāyai Namaḥ		ॐ पद्मासनायै नमः ।
290.	Oṃ Padmapriyāyai Namaḥ		ॐ पद्मप्रियायै नमः ।
291.	Oṃ Padmarāgasvarūpiṇyai Namaḥ		ॐ पद्मरागस्वरूपिण्यै नमः ।
292.	Oṃ Pāvanyai Namaḥ		ॐ पावन्यै नमः ।
293.	Oṃ Pālikāyai Namaḥ		ॐ पालिकायै नमः ।
294.	Oṃ Pātryai Namaḥ		ॐ पात्र्यै नमः ।
295.	Oṃ Paradāyai Namaḥ		ॐ परदायै नमः ।
296.	Oṃ Avaradāyai Namaḥ		ॐ अवरदायै नमः ।

297.	Oṃ Śivāyai Namaḥ		ॐ शिवायै नमः ।
298.	Oṃ Pretasaṃsthāyai Namaḥ		ॐ प्रेतसंस्थायै नमः ।
299.	Oṃ Parānandāyai Namaḥ		ॐ परानन्दायै नमः ।
300.	Oṃ Parabrahmasvarūpiṇyai Namaḥ	ॐ परब्रह्मस्वरूपिण्यै नमः ।
301.	Oṃ Jineśvarapriyāyai Devyai Namaḥ	ॐ जिनेश्वरप्रियायै देव्यै नमः ।
302.	Oṃ Paśuraktaratapriyāyai Namaḥ		ॐ पशुरक्तरतप्रियायै नमः ।
303.	Oṃ Paśumāṃsapriyāyai Namaḥ	ॐ पशुमांसप्रियायै नमः
304.	Oṃ Aparṇāyai Namaḥ		ॐ अपर्णायै नमः ।
305.	Oṃ Parāmṛtaparāyaṇāyai Namaḥ		ॐ परामृतपरायणायै नमः ।
306.	Oṃ Pāśinyai Namaḥ		ॐ पाशिन्यै नमः ।
307.	Oṃ Pāśikāyai Namaḥ		ॐ पाशिकायै नमः ।
308.	Oṃ Paśughnyai Namaḥ		ॐ पशुघ्न्यै नमः ।
309.	Oṃ Paśubhāṣiṇyai Namaḥ		ॐ पशुभाषिण्यै नमः ।
310.	Oṃ Phullāravindavadanyai Namaḥ		ॐ फुल्लारविन्दवदन्यै नमः ।
311.	Oṃ Phullotpalaśarīriṇyai Namaḥ		ॐ फुल्लोत्पलशरीरिण्यै नमः
312.	Oṃ Parānandapradāyai Namaḥ	ॐ परानन्दप्रदायै नमः ।
313.	Oṃ Vīṇāyai Namaḥ		ॐ वीणायै नमः ।
314.	Oṃ Paśupāśavināśinyai Namaḥ		ॐ पशुपाशविनाशिन्यै नमः ।
315.	Oṃ Phūtkārāyai Namaḥ		ॐ फूत्कारायै नमः ।
316.	Oṃ Phūtparāyai Namaḥ		ॐ फूत्परायै नमः ।
317.	Oṃ Pheṇyai Namaḥ		ॐ फेण्यै नमः ।
318.	Oṃ Phullendīvaralocanāyai Namaḥ	ॐ फुल्लेन्दीवरलोचनायै नमः
319.	Oṃ Phaṭmantrāyai Namaḥ		ॐ फट्मन्त्रायै नमः ।
320.	Oṃ Sphaṭikāyai Namaḥ		ॐ स्फटिकायै नमः ।
321.	Oṃ Svāhāyai Namaḥ		ॐ स्वाहायै नमः ।
322.	Oṃ Sphoṭāyai Namaḥ		ॐ स्फोटायै नमः ।
323.	Oṃ Phaṭsvarūpiṇyai Namaḥ		ॐ फट्स्वरूपिण्यै नमः ।
324.	Oṃ Sphāṭikāghuṭikāyai Namaḥ		ॐ स्फाटिकाघुटिकायै नमः ।
325.	Oṃ Ghorāyai Namaḥ		ॐ घोरायै नमः ।

326.	Oṃ Sphaṭikādrisvarūpiṇyai Namaḥ		ॐ स्फटिकाद्रिस्वरूपिण्यै नमः
327.	Oṃ Varāṅganāyai Namaḥ		ॐ वराङ्गनायै नमः	
328.	Oṃ Varadharāyai Namaḥ		ॐ वरधरायै नमः	
329.	Oṃ Vārāhyai Namaḥ		ॐ वाराह्यै नमः	
330.	Oṃ Vāsukīvarāyai Namaḥ		ॐ वासुकीवरायै नमः	
331.	Oṃ Bindusthāyai Namaḥ		ॐ बिन्दुस्थायै नमः	
332.	Oṃ Bindunīvāṇyai Namaḥ		ॐ बिन्दुनीवाण्यै नमः	
333.	Oṃ Binducakranivāsinyai Namaḥ		ॐ बिन्दुचक्रनिवासिन्यै नमः	
334.	Oṃ Vidyādharyai Namaḥ		ॐ विद्याधर्यै नमः	
335.	Oṃ Viśālākṣyai Namaḥ		ॐ विशालाक्ष्यै नमः	
336.	Oṃ Kāśīvāsijanapriyāyai Namaḥ		ॐ काशीवासिजनप्रियायै नमः
337.	Oṃ Vedavidyāyai Namaḥ		ॐ वेदविद्यायै नमः	
338.	Oṃ Virūpākṣyai Namaḥ		ॐ विरूपाक्ष्यै नमः	
339.	Oṃ Viśvayuje Namaḥ		ॐ विश्वयुजे नमः	
340.	Oṃ Bahurūpiṇyai Namaḥ		ॐ बहुरूपिण्यै नमः	
341.	Oṃ Brahmaśaktyai Namaḥ		ॐ ब्रह्मशक्त्यै नमः	
342.	Oṃ Viṣṇuśaktyai Namaḥ		ॐ विष्णुशक्त्यै नमः	
343.	Oṃ Pañcavaktrāyai Namaḥ		ॐ पञ्चवक्त्रायै नमः	
344.	Oṃ Śivapriyāyai Namaḥ		ॐ शिवप्रियायै नमः	
345.	Oṃ Vaikuṇṭhavāsinyai Devyai Namaḥ		ॐ वैकुण्ठवासिन्यै देव्यै नमः	
346.	Oṃ Vaikuṇṭhapadadāyinyai Namaḥ	ॐ वैकुण्ठपददायिन्यै नमः	
347.	Oṃ Brahmarūpāyai Namaḥ		ॐ ब्रह्मरूपायै नमः	
348.	Oṃ Viṣṇurūpāyai Namaḥ		ॐ विष्णुरूपायै नमः	
349.	Oṃ Parabrahmamaheśvaryai Namaḥ		ॐ परब्रह्ममहेश्वर्यै नमः	
350.	Oṃ Bhavapriyāyai Namaḥ		ॐ भवप्रियायै नमः	
351.	Oṃ Bhavodbhāvāyai Namaḥ		ॐ भवोद्भावायै नमः	
352.	Oṃ Bhavarūpāyai Namaḥ		ॐ भवरूपायै नमः	
353.	Oṃ Bhavottamāyai Namaḥ		ॐ भवोत्तमायै नमः	
354.	Oṃ Bhavapārāyai Namaḥ		ॐ भवपारायै नमः	

355.	Oṃ Bhavādhārāyai Namaḥ ।	ॐ भवाधारायै नमः ।
356.	Oṃ Bhāgyavatpriyakāriṇyai Namaḥ	ॐ भाग्यवत्प्रियकारिण्यै नमः ।
357.	Oṃ Bhadrāyai Namaḥ ।	ॐ भद्रायै नमः ।
358.	Oṃ Subhadrāyai Namaḥ ।	ॐ सुभद्रायै नमः ।
359.	Oṃ Bhavadāyai Namaḥ ।	ॐ भवदायै नमः ।
360.	Oṃ Śumbhadaityavināśinyai Namaḥ	ॐ शुम्भदैत्यविनाशिन्यै नमः ।
361.	Oṃ Bhavānyai Namaḥ ।	ॐ भवान्यै नमः ।
362.	Oṃ Bhairavyai Namaḥ ।	ॐ भैरव्यै नमः ।
363.	Oṃ Bhīmāyai Namaḥ ।	ॐ भीमायै नमः ।
364.	Oṃ Bhadrakālyai Namaḥ ।	ॐ भद्रकाल्यै नमः ।
365.	Oṃ Subhadrikāyai Namaḥ ।	ॐ सुभद्रिकायै नमः ।
366.	Oṃ Bhaginyai Namaḥ ।	ॐ भगिन्यै नमः ।
367.	Oṃ Bhagarūpāyai Namaḥ ।	ॐ भगरूपायै नमः ।
368.	Oṃ Bhagamānāyai Namaḥ ।	ॐ भगमानायै नमः ।
369.	Oṃ Bhagottamāyai Namaḥ ।	ॐ भगोत्तमायै नमः ।
370.	Oṃ Bhagapriyāyai Namaḥ ।	ॐ भगप्रियायै नमः ।
371.	Oṃ Bhagavatyai Namaḥ ।	ॐ भगवत्यै नमः ।
372.	Oṃ Bhagavāsāyai Namaḥ ।	ॐ भगवासायै नमः ।
373.	Oṃ Bhagākarāyai Namaḥ ।	ॐ भगाकरायै नमः ।
374.	Oṃ Bhagasṛṣṭāyai Namaḥ ।	ॐ भगसृष्टायै नमः ।
375.	Oṃ Bhāgyavatyai Namaḥ ।	ॐ भाग्यवत्यै नमः ।
376.	Oṃ Bhagarūpāyai Namaḥ ।	ॐ भगरूपायै नमः ।
377.	Oṃ Bhagāsinyai Namaḥ ।	ॐ भगासिन्यै नमः ।
378.	Oṃ Bhagaliṅgapriyāyai Devyai Namaḥ ।	ॐ भगलिङ्गप्रियायै देव्यै नमः ।
379.	Oṃ Bhagaliṅgaparāyaṇāyai Namaḥ	ॐ भगलिङ्गपरायणायै नमः ।
380.	Oṃ Bhagaliṅgasvarūpāyai Namaḥ ।	ॐ भगलिङ्गस्वरूपायै नमः ।
381.	Oṃ Bhagaliṅgavinodinyai Namaḥ ।	ॐ भगलिङ्गविनोदिन्यै नमः ।
382.	Oṃ Bhagaliṅgaratāyai Devyai Namaḥ ।	ॐ भगलिङ्गरतायै देव्यै नमः ।

383.	Oṃ Bhagaliṅganivāsinyai Namaḥ		ॐ भगलिङ्गनिवासिन्यै नमः
384.	Oṃ Bhagamālāyai Namaḥ		ॐ भगमालायै नमः	
385.	Oṃ Bhagakalāyai Namaḥ		ॐ भगकलायै नमः	
386.	Oṃ Bhagādhārāyai Namaḥ		ॐ भगाधारायै नमः	
387.	Oṃ Bhagāmbarāyai Namaḥ		ॐ भगाम्बरायै नमः	
388.	Oṃ Bhagavegāyai Namaḥ		ॐ भगवेगायै नमः	
389.	Oṃ Bhagāpūṣāyai Namaḥ		ॐ भगापूषायै नमः	
390.	Oṃ Bhagendrāyai Namaḥ		ॐ भगेन्द्रायै नमः	
391.	Oṃ Bhāgyarūpiṇyai Namaḥ		ॐ भाग्यरूपिण्यै नमः	
392.	Oṃ Bhagaliṅgāṅgasambhogāyai Namaḥ		ॐ भगलिङ्गाङ्गसम्भोगायै नमः	
393.	Oṃ Bhagaliṅgāsavāvahāyai Namaḥ	ॐ भगलिङ्गासवावहायै नमः
394.	Oṃ Bhagaliṅgasamādhuryāyai Namaḥ		ॐ भगलिङ्गसमाधुर्यायै नमः	
395.	Oṃ Bhagaliṅganiveśitāyai Namaḥ		ॐ भगलिङ्गनिवेशितायै नमः
396.	Oṃ Bhagaliṅgasupūjāyai Namaḥ	ॐ भगलिङ्गसुपूजायै नमः	
397.	Oṃ Bhagaliṅgasamanvitāyai Namaḥ	ॐ भगलिङ्गसमन्वितायै नमः
398.	Oṃ Bhagaliṅgaviraktāyai Namaḥ		ॐ भगलिङ्गविरक्तायै नमः	
399.	Oṃ Bhagaliṅgasamāvṛtāyai Namaḥ	ॐ भगलिङ्गसमावृतायै नमः
400.	Oṃ Mādhavyai Namaḥ		ॐ माधव्यै नमः	
401.	Oṃ Mādhavīmānyāyai Namaḥ		ॐ माधवीमान्यायै नमः	
402.	Oṃ Madhurāyai Namaḥ		ॐ मधुरायै नमः	
403.	Oṃ Madhumāninyai Namaḥ		ॐ मधुमानिन्यै नमः	
404.	Oṃ Mandahāsāyai Namaḥ		ॐ मन्दहासायै नमः	
405.	Oṃ Mahāmāyāyai Namaḥ		ॐ महामायायै नमः	
406.	Oṃ Mohinyai Namaḥ		ॐ मोहिन्यै नमः	
407.	Oṃ Mahaduttamāyai Namaḥ		ॐ महदुत्तमायै नमः	
408.	Oṃ Mahāmohāyai Namaḥ		ॐ महामोहायै नमः	
409.	Oṃ Mahāvidyāyai Namaḥ		ॐ महाविद्यायै नमः	
410.	Oṃ Mahāghorāyai Namaḥ		ॐ महाघोरायै नमः	

411.	Oṃ Mahāsmṛtyai Namaḥ		ॐ महास्मृत्यै नमः ।
412.	Oṃ Manasvinyai Namaḥ		ॐ मनस्विन्यै नमः ।
413.	Oṃ Mānavatyai Namaḥ		ॐ मानवत्यै नमः ।
414.	Oṃ Modinyai Namaḥ		ॐ मोदिन्यै नमः ।
415.	Oṃ Madhurānanāyai Namaḥ		ॐ मधुराननायै नमः ।
416.	Oṃ Menakāyai Namaḥ		ॐ मेनकायै नमः ।
417.	Oṃ Māninīmānyāyai Namaḥ		ॐ मानिनीमान्यायै नमः ।
418.	Oṃ Maṇiratnavibhūṣaṇāyai Namaḥ	ॐ मणिरत्नविभूषणायै नमः ।
419.	Oṃ Mallikāmaulikāmālāyai Namaḥ		ॐ मल्लिकामौलिकामालायै नमः ।
420.	Oṃ Mālādharamadottamāyai Namaḥ		ॐ मालाधरमदोत्तमायै नमः ।
421.	Oṃ Madanāsundaryai Namaḥ		ॐ मदनासुन्दर्यै नमः ।
422.	Oṃ Medhāyai Namaḥ		ॐ मेधायै नमः ।
423.	Oṃ Madhumattāyai Namaḥ		ॐ मधुमत्तायै नमः ।
424.	Oṃ Madhupriyāyai Namaḥ		ॐ मधुप्रियायै नमः ।
425.	Oṃ Mattahaṃsīsamonnāsāyai Namaḥ		ॐ मत्तहंसीसमोन्नासायै नमः ।
426.	Oṃ Mattasiṃhamahāsanyai Namaḥ	ॐ मत्तसिंहमहासन्यै नमः ।
427.	Oṃ Mahendravallabhāyai Namaḥ		ॐ महेन्द्रवल्लभायै नमः ।
428.	Oṃ Bhīmāyai Namaḥ		ॐ भीमायै नमः ।
429.	Oṃ Maulyañcamithunātmajāyai Namaḥ		ॐ मौल्यञ्चमिथुनात्मजायै नमः ।
430.	Oṃ Mahākālyā Mahākālyai Namaḥ		ॐ महाकाल्या महाकाल्यै नमः ।
431.	Oṃ Mahābuddhaye Namaḥ	ॐ महाबुद्धये नमः ।
432.	Oṃ Mahotkaṭāyai Namaḥ		ॐ महोत्कटायै नमः ।
433.	Oṃ Māheśvaryai Namaḥ		ॐ माहेश्वर्यै नमः ।
434.	Oṃ Mahāmāyāyai Namaḥ		ॐ महामायायै नमः ।
435.	Oṃ Mahiṣāsuraghātinyai Namaḥ		ॐ महिषासुरघातिन्यै नमः ।

436.	Oṃ Madhurāyai Kīrtimattāyai Namaḥ ǀ	ॐ मधुरायै कीर्तिमत्तायै नमः ǀ
437.	Oṃ Mattamātaṅgagāminyai Namaḥ	ॐ मत्तमातङ्गगामिन्यै नमः ǀ
438.	Oṃ Madapriyāyai Namaḥ ǀ	ॐ मदप्रियायै नमः ǀ
439.	Oṃ Māṃsaratāyai Namaḥ ǀ	ॐ मांसरतायै नमः ǀ
440.	Oṃ Mattayukkāmakāriṇyai Namaḥ	ॐ मत्तयुक्कामकारिण्यै नमः ǀ
441.	Oṃ Maithunyavallabhāyai Devyai Namaḥ ǀ	ॐ मैथुन्यवल्लभायै देव्यै नमः ǀ
442.	Oṃ Mahānandāyai Namaḥ ǀ	ॐ महानन्दायै नमः ǀ
443.	Oṃ Mahotsavāyai Namaḥ ǀ	ॐ महोत्सवायै नमः ǀ
444.	Oṃ Marīcaye Namaḥ ǀ	ॐ मरीचये नमः ǀ
445.	Oṃ Māratyai Namaḥ ǀ	ॐ मारत्यै नमः ǀ
446.	Oṃ Māyāyai Namaḥ ǀ	ॐ मायायै नमः ǀ
447.	Oṃ Manobuddhipradāyinyai Namaḥ	ॐ मनोबुद्धिप्रदायिन्यै नमः ǀ
448.	Oṃ Mohāyai Namaḥ ǀ	ॐ मोहायै नमः ǀ
449.	Oṃ Mokṣāyai Namaḥ ǀ	ॐ मोक्षायै नमः ǀ
450.	Oṃ Mahālakṣmai Namaḥ ǀ	ॐ महालक्ष्मै नमः ǀ
451.	Oṃ Mahatpadapradāyinyai Namaḥ	ॐ महत्पदप्रदायिन्यै नमः ǀ
452.	Oṃ Yamarūpāyai Namaḥ ǀ	ॐ यमरूपायै नमः ǀ
453.	Oṃ Yamunāyai Namaḥ ǀ	ॐ यमुनायै नमः ǀ
454.	Oṃ Jayantyai Namaḥ ǀ	ॐ जयन्त्यै नमः ǀ
455.	Oṃ Jayapradāyai Namaḥ ǀ	ॐ जयप्रदायै नमः ǀ
456.	Oṃ Yāmyāyai Namaḥ ǀ	ॐ याम्यायै नमः ǀ
457.	Oṃ Yamavatyai Namaḥ ǀ	ॐ यमवत्यै नमः ǀ
458.	Oṃ Yuddhāyai Namaḥ ǀ	ॐ युद्धायै नमः ǀ
459.	Oṃ Yadoḥ Kulavivardhinyai Namaḥ	ॐ यदोः कुलविवर्धिन्यै नमः ǀ
460.	Oṃ Ramārāmāyai Namaḥ ǀ	ॐ रमारामायै नमः ǀ
461.	Oṃ Rāmapatnyai Namaḥ ǀ	ॐ रामपत्न्यै नमः ǀ
462.	Oṃ Ratnamālāratipriyāyai Namaḥ ǀ	ॐ रत्नमालारतिप्रियायै नमः ǀ
463.	Oṃ Ratnasiṃhāsanasthāyai Namaḥ	ॐ रत्नसिंहासनस्थायै नमः ǀ

464.	Oṃ Ratnābharaṇamaṇḍitāyai Namaḥ		ॐ रत्नाभरणमण्डितायै नमः।
465.	Oṃ Ramaṇyai Namaḥ		ॐ रमण्यै नमः।
466.	Oṃ Ramaṇīyāyai Namaḥ		ॐ रमणीयायै नमः।
467.	Oṃ Ratyārasaparāyaṇāyai Namaḥ		ॐ रत्यारसपरायणायै नमः।
468.	Oṃ Ratānandāyai Namaḥ		ॐ रतानन्दायै नमः।
469.	Oṃ Ratavatyai Namaḥ		ॐ रतवत्यै नमः।
470.	Oṃ Raghūṇāṃ Kulavardhinyai Namaḥ		ॐ रघूणां कुलवर्धिन्यै नमः
471.	Oṃ Ramaṇāriparibhrājyāyai Namaḥ		ॐ रमणारिपरिभ्राज्यायै नमः।
472.	Oṃ Raidhāyai Namaḥ		ॐ रैधायै नमः।
473.	Oṃ Rādhikaratnajāyai Namaḥ		ॐ राधिकरत्नजायै नमः।
474.	Oṃ Rāvīrasasvarūpāyai Namaḥ		ॐ रावीरसस्वरूपायै नमः।
475.	Oṃ Rātrirājasukhāvahāyai Namaḥ		ॐ रात्रिराजसुखावहायै नमः।
476.	Oṃ Ṛtujāyai Namaḥ		ॐ ऋतुजायै नमः।
477.	Oṃ Ṛtudāyai Namaḥ		ॐ ऋतुदायै नमः।
478.	Oṃ Ṛddhāyai Namaḥ		ॐ ऋद्धायै नमः।
479.	Oṃ Ṛturūpāyai Namaḥ		ॐ ऋतुरूपायै नमः।
480.	Oṃ Ṛtupriyāyai Namaḥ		ॐ ऋतुप्रियायै नमः।
481.	Oṃ Raktapriyāyai Namaḥ		ॐ रक्तप्रियायै नमः।
482.	Oṃ Raktavatyai Namaḥ		ॐ रक्तवत्यै नमः।
483.	Oṃ Raṅgiṇyai Namaḥ		ॐ रङ्गिण्यै नमः।
484.	Oṃ Raktadantikāyai Namaḥ		ॐ रक्तदन्तिकायै नमः।
485.	Oṃ Lakṣmyai Namaḥ		ॐ लक्ष्म्यै नमः।
486.	Oṃ Lajjāyai Namaḥ		ॐ लज्जायै नमः।
487.	Oṃ Latikāyai Namaḥ		ॐ लतिकायै नमः।
488.	Oṃ Līlālagnānitākṣiṇyai Namaḥ		ॐ लीलालग्नानिताक्षिण्यै नमः।
489.	Oṃ Līlāyai Namaḥ		ॐ लीलायै नमः।
490.	Oṃ Līlāvatyai Namaḥ		ॐ लीलावत्यै नमः।

491.	Oṃ Lomaharṣāhlādinapaṭṭikāyai Namaḥ |	ॐ लोमहर्षाह्लादिनपट्टिकायै नमः ।
492.	Oṃ Brahmasthitāyai Namaḥ |	ॐ ब्रह्मस्थितायै नमः ।
493.	Oṃ Brahmarūpāyai Namaḥ |	ॐ ब्रह्मरूपायै नमः ।
494.	Oṃ Brahmaṇā Vedavanditāyai Namaḥ |	ॐ ब्रह्मणा वेदवन्दितायै नमः ।
495.	Oṃ Brahmodbhavāyai Namaḥ |	ॐ ब्रह्मोद्भवायै नमः ।
496.	Oṃ Brahmakalāyai Namaḥ |	ॐ ब्रह्मकलायै नमः ।
497.	Oṃ Brahmāṇyai Namaḥ |	ॐ ब्रह्माण्यै नमः ।
498.	Oṃ Brahmabodhinyai Namaḥ |	ॐ ब्रह्मबोधिन्यै नमः ।
499.	Oṃ Vedāṅganāyai Namaḥ |	ॐ वेदाङ्गनायै नमः ।
500.	Oṃ Vedarūpāyai Namaḥ |	ॐ वेदरूपायै नमः ।
501.	Oṃ Vanitāyai Namaḥ |	ॐ वनितायै नमः ।
502.	Oṃ Vinatāvasāyai Namaḥ |	ॐ विनतावसायै नमः ।
503.	Oṃ Bālāyai Namaḥ |	ॐ बालायै नमः ।
504.	Oṃ Yuvatyai Namaḥ |	ॐ युवत्यै नमः ।
505.	Oṃ Vṛddhāyai Namaḥ |	ॐ वृद्धायै नमः ।
506.	Oṃ Brahmakarmaparāyaṇāyai Namaḥ |	ॐ ब्रह्मकर्मपरायणायै नमः ।
507.	Oṃ Vindhyasthāyai Namaḥ |	ॐ विन्ध्यस्थायै नमः ।
508.	Oṃ Vindhyavāsyai Namaḥ |	ॐ विन्ध्यवास्यै नमः ।
509.	Oṃ Binduyugbindubhūṣaṇāyai Namaḥ |	ॐ बिन्दुयुग्बिन्दुभूषणायै नमः ।
510.	Oṃ Vidyāvatyai Namaḥ |	ॐ विद्यावत्यै नमः ।
511.	Oṃ Vedadhāryai Namaḥ |	ॐ वेददार्यै नमः ।
512.	Oṃ Vyāpikāyai Namaḥ |	ॐ व्यापिकायै नमः ।
513.	Oṃ Barhiṇyai Kalāyai Namaḥ |	ॐ बर्हिण्यै कलायै नमः ।
514.	Oṃ Vāmācārapriyāyai Namaḥ |	ॐ वामाचारप्रियायै नमः ।
515.	Oṃ Vahnaye Namaḥ |	ॐ वह्नये नमः ।
516.	Oṃ Vāmācāraparāyaṇāyai Namaḥ |	ॐ वामाचारपरायणायै नमः ।
517.	Oṃ Vāmācāraratāyai Devyai Namaḥ	ॐ वामाचाररतायै देव्यै नमः ।

518.	Oṃ Vāmadevapriyottamāyai Namaḥ I	ॐ वामदेवप्रियोत्तमायै नमः I
519.	Oṃ Buddhendriyāyai Namaḥ I	ॐ बुद्धेन्द्रियायै नमः I
520.	Oṃ Vibuddhāyai Namaḥ I	ॐ विबुद्धायै नमः I
521.	Oṃ Buddhācaraṇamālinyai Namaḥ I	ॐ बुद्धाचरणमालिन्यै नमः I
522.	Oṃ Bandhamocanatartryai Namaḥ	ॐ बन्धमोचनतर्त्र्यै नमः I
523.	Oṃ Vāruṇāyai Namaḥ I	ॐ वारुणायै नमः I
524.	Oṃ Varuṇālayāyai Namaḥ I	ॐ वरुणालयायै नमः I
525.	Oṃ Śivāyai Namaḥ I	ॐ शिवायै नमः I
526.	Oṃ Śivapriyāyai Namaḥ I	ॐ शिवप्रियायै नमः I
527.	Oṃ Śuddhāyai Namaḥ I	ॐ शुद्धायै नमः I
528.	Oṃ Śuddhāṅgyai Namaḥ I	ॐ शुद्धाङ्ग्यै नमः I
529.	Oṃ Śuklavarṇikāyai Namaḥ I	ॐ शुक्लवर्णिकायै नमः I
530.	Oṃ Śuklapuṣpapriyāyai Namaḥ I	ॐ शुक्लपुष्पप्रियायै नमः I
531.	Oṃ Śuklāyai Namaḥ I	ॐ शुक्लायै नमः I
532.	Oṃ Śivadharmaparāyaṇāyai Namaḥ	ॐ शिवधर्मपरायणायै नमः I
533.	Oṃ Śuklasthāyai Namaḥ I	ॐ शुक्लस्थायै नमः I
534.	Oṃ Śuklinyai Namaḥ I	ॐ शुक्लिन्यै नमः I
535.	Oṃ Śuklarūpaśuklapaśupriyāyai Namaḥ I	ॐ शुक्लरूपशुक्लपशुप्रियायै नमः I
536.	Oṃ Śukrasthāyai Namaḥ I	ॐ शुक्रस्थायै नमः I
537.	Oṃ Śukriṇyai Namaḥ I	ॐ शुक्रिण्यै नमः I
538.	Oṃ Śukrāyai Namaḥ I	ॐ शुक्रायै नमः I
539.	Oṃ Śukrarūpāyai Namaḥ I	ॐ शुक्ररूपायै नमः I
540.	Oṃ Śukrikāyai Namaḥ I	ॐ शुक्रिकायै नमः I
541.	Oṃ Ṣaṇmukhyai Namaḥ I	ॐ षण्मुख्यै नमः I
542.	Oṃ Ṣaḍaṅgāyai Namaḥ I	ॐ षडङ्गायै नमः I
543.	Oṃ Ṣaṭcakravinivāsinyai Namaḥ	ॐ षट्चक्रविनिवासिन्यै नमः I
544.	Oṃ Ṣaḍgranthiyuktāyai Namaḥ I	ॐ षड्ग्रन्थियुक्तायै नमः I
545.	Oṃ Ṣoḍhāyai Namaḥ I	ॐ षोढायै नमः I

546.	Oṃ Ṣaṇmātre Namaḥ		ॐ षण्मात्रे नमः ।
547.	Oṃ Ṣaḍātmikāyai Namaḥ		ॐ षडात्मिकायै नमः ।
548.	Oṃ Ṣaḍaṅgayuvatyai Devyai Namaḥ	ॐ षडङ्गयुवत्यै देव्यै नमः ।
549.	Oṃ Ṣaḍaṅgaprakṛtyai Namaḥ		ॐ षडङ्गप्रकृत्यै नमः ।
550.	Oṃ Vaśyai Namaḥ		ॐ वश्यै नमः ।
551.	Oṃ Ṣaḍānanāyai Namaḥ		ॐ षडाननायै नमः ।
552.	Oṃ Ṣaḍrasāyai Namaḥ		ॐ षड्रसायै नमः ।
553.	Oṃ Ṣaṣṭhīṣaṣṭheśvarīpriyāyai Namaḥ		ॐ षष्ठीषष्ठेश्वरीप्रियायै नमः ।
554.	Oṃ Ṣaḍjavādāyai Namaḥ		ॐ षड्जवादायै नमः ।
555.	Oṃ Ṣoḍaśyai Namaḥ		ॐ षोडश्यै नमः ।
556.	Oṃ Ṣoḍhānyāsasvarūpiṇyai Namaḥ	ॐ षोढान्यासस्वरूपिण्यै नमः
557.	Oṃ Ṣaṭcakrabhedanakaryai Namaḥ	ॐ षट्चक्रभेदनकर्यै नमः ।
558.	Oṃ Ṣaṭcakrasthasvarūpiṇyai Namaḥ	ॐ षट्चक्रस्थस्वरूपिण्यै नमः
559.	Oṃ Ṣoḍaśasvararūpāyai Namaḥ	ॐ षोडशस्वररूपायै नमः ।
560.	Oṃ Ṣaṇmukhyai Namaḥ		ॐ षण्मुख्यै नमः ।
561.	Oṃ Ṣaṭpadānvitāyai Namaḥ	ॐ षट्पदान्वितायै नमः ।
562.	Oṃ Sanakādi Svarūpāyai Namaḥ	ॐ सनकादि स्वरूपायै नमः ।
563.	Oṃ Śivadharmaparāyaṇāyai Namaḥ	ॐ शिवधर्मपरायणायै नमः ।
564.	Oṃ Siddhasaptasvaryai Namaḥ		ॐ सिद्धसप्तस्वर्यै नमः ।
565.	Oṃ Śuddhāyai Namaḥ		ॐ शुद्धायै नमः ।
566.	Oṃ Suramātre Namaḥ		ॐ सुरमात्रे नमः ।
567.	Oṃ Surottamāyai Namaḥ		ॐ सुरोत्तमायै नमः ।
568.	Oṃ Siddhavidyāyai Namaḥ		ॐ सिद्धविद्यायै नमः ।
569.	Oṃ Siddhamātre Namaḥ		ॐ सिद्धमात्रे नमः ।
570.	Oṃ Siddhāsiddhasvarūpiṇyai Namaḥ		ॐ सिद्धासिद्धस्वरूपिण्यै नमः ।
571.	Oṃ Harāyai Namaḥ		ॐ हरायै नमः ।
572.	Oṃ Haripriyāharāyai Namaḥ		ॐ हरिप्रियाहारायै नमः ।
573.	Oṃ Hariṇīhārayuje Namaḥ		ॐ हरिणीहारयुजे नमः ।

574.	Oṃ Harirūpāyai Namaḥ l	ॐ हरिरूपायै नमः l
575.	Oṃ Haridharāyai Namaḥ l	ॐ हरिधरायै नमः l
576.	Oṃ Hariṇākṣyai Namaḥ l	ॐ हरिणाक्ष्यै नमः l
577.	Oṃ Haripriyāyai Namaḥ l	ॐ हरिप्रियायै नमः l
578.	Oṃ Hetupriyāyai Namaḥ l	ॐ हेतुप्रियायै नमः l
579.	Oṃ Heturatāyai Namaḥ l	ॐ हेतुरतायै नमः l
580.	Oṃ Hitāhitasvarūpiṇyai Namaḥ l	ॐ हिताहितस्वरूपिण्यै नमः l
581.	Oṃ Kṣamāyai Namaḥ l	ॐ क्षमायै नमः l
582.	Oṃ Kṣamāvatyai Namaḥ l	ॐ क्षमावत्यै नमः l
583.	Oṃ Kṣītāyai Namaḥ l	ॐ क्षीतायै नमः l
584.	Oṃ Kṣudraghaṇṭāvibhūṣaṇāyai Namaḥ l	ॐ क्षु द्रघण्टाविभूषणायै नमः
585.	Oṃ Kṣayaṅkaryai Namaḥ l	ॐ क्षयङ्कर्यै नमः l
586.	Oṃ Kṣitīśāyai Namaḥ l	ॐ क्षितीशायै नमः l
587.	Oṃ Kṣīṇamadhyasuśobhanāyai Namaḥ l	ॐ क्षीणमध्यसुशोभनायै नमः l
588.	Oṃ Ajāyai Namaḥ l	ॐ अजायै नमः l
589.	Oṃ Anantāyai Namaḥ l	ॐ अनन्तायै नमः l
590.	Oṃ Aparṇāyai Namaḥ l	ॐ अपर्णायै नमः l
591.	Oṃ Ahalyāśeṣaśāyinyai Namaḥ l	ॐ अहल्याशेषशायिन्यै नमः l
592.	Oṃ Svāntargatāyai Namaḥ l	ॐ स्वान्तर्गतायै नमः l
593.	Oṃ Sādhū Nāmantarā Nanda Rūpiṇyai Namaḥ l	ॐ साधूनामन्तरानन्दरूपिण्यै नमः l
594.	Oṃ Arūpāyai Namaḥ l	ॐ अरूपायै नमः l
595.	Oṃ Amalāyai Namaḥ l	ॐ अमलायै नमः l
596.	Oṃ Ardhāyai Namaḥ l	ॐ अर्धायै नमः l
597.	Oṃ Anantaguṇaśālinyai Namaḥ l	ॐ अनन्तगुणशालिन्यै नमः l
598.	Oṃ Svavidyāyai Namaḥ l	ॐ स्वविद्यायै नमः l
599.	Oṃ Vidyakāvidyāyai Namaḥ l	ॐ विद्यकाविद्यायै नमः l
600.	Oṃ Vidyāyai Namaḥ l	ॐ विद्यायै नमः l
601.	Oṃ Cārvindulocanāyai Namaḥ l	ॐ चार्विन्दुलोचनायै नमः l

602.	Oṃ Aparājitāyai Namaḥ ǀ	ॐ अपराजितायै नमः ǀ
603.	Oṃ Jātavedāyai Namaḥ ǀ	ॐ जातवेदायै नमः ǀ
604.	Oṃ Ajapāyai Namaḥ ǀ	ॐ अजपायै नमः ǀ
605.	Oṃ Amarāvatyai Namaḥ ǀ	ॐ अमरावत्यै नमः ǀ
606.	Oṃ Alpāyai Namaḥ ǀ	ॐ अल्पायै नमः ǀ
607.	Oṃ Svalpāyai Namaḥ ǀ	ॐ स्वल्पायै नमः ǀ
608.	Oṃ Analpādyāyai Namaḥ ǀ	ॐ अनल्पाद्यायै नमः ǀ
609.	Oṃ Aṇimāsiddhidāyinyai Namaḥ	ॐ अणिमासिद्धिदायिन्यै नमः
610.	Oṃ Aṣṭasiddhipradāyai Devyai Namaḥ ǀ	ॐ अष्टसिद्धिप्रदायै देव्यै नमः ǀ
611.	Oṃ Rūpalakṣaṇasaṃyutāyai Namaḥ	ॐ रूपलक्षणसंयुतायै नमः ǀ
612.	Oṃ Aravindamukhāyai Devyai Namaḥ ǀ	ॐ अरविन्दमुखायै देव्यै नमः ǀ
613.	Oṃ Bhogasaukhyapradāyinyai Namaḥ ǀ	ॐ भोगसौख्यप्रदायिन्यै नमः ǀ
614.	Oṃ Ādividyāyai Namaḥ ǀ	ॐ आदिविद्यायै नमः ǀ
615.	Oṃ Ādibhūtāyai Namaḥ ǀ	ॐ आदिभूतायै नमः ǀ
616.	Oṃ Ādisiddhipradāyinyai Namaḥ	ॐ आदिसिद्धिप्रदायिन्यै नमः
617.	Oṃ Sītkārarūpiṇyai Devyai Namaḥ ǀ	ॐ सीत्काररूपिण्यै देव्यै नमः
618.	Oṃ Sarvāsanavibhūṣitāyai Namaḥ ǀ	ॐ सर्वासनविभूषितायै नमः ǀ
619.	Oṃ Indrapriyāyai Namaḥ ǀ	ॐ इन्द्रप्रियायै नमः ǀ
620.	Oṃ Indrāṇyai Namaḥ ǀ	ॐ इन्द्राण्यै नमः ǀ
621.	Oṃ Indraprasthanivāsinyai Namaḥ ǀ	ॐ इन्द्रप्रस्थनिवासिन्यै नमः ǀ
622.	Oṃ Indrākṣyai Namaḥ ǀ	ॐ इन्द्राक्ष्यै नमः ǀ
623.	Oṃ Indravajrāyai Namaḥ ǀ	ॐ इन्द्रवज्रायै नमः ǀ
624.	Oṃ Indramadyokṣaṇyai Namaḥ ǀ	ॐ इन्द्रमद्योक्षण्यै नमः ǀ
625.	Oṃ Īlākāmanivāsāyai Namaḥ ǀ	ॐ ईलाकामनिवासायै नमः ǀ
626.	Oṃ Īśvaryai Namaḥ ǀ	ॐ ईश्वर्यै नमः ǀ
627.	Oṃ Īśvaravallabhāyai Namaḥ ǀ	ॐ ईश्वरवल्लभायै नमः ǀ
628.	Oṃ Jananyai Namaḥ ǀ	ॐ जनन्यै नमः ǀ

629.	Oṃ Īśvaryai Namaḥ ।	ॐ ईश्वर्यै नमः ।
630.	Oṃ Dīnābhedāyai Namaḥ ।	ॐ दीनाभेदायै नमः ।
631.	Oṃ Īśvarakarmakṛte Namaḥ ।	ॐ ईश्वरकर्मकृते नमः ।
632.	Oṃ Umāyai Namaḥ ।	ॐ उमायै नमः ।
633.	Oṃ Kātyāyanyai Namaḥ ।	ॐ कात्यायन्यै नमः ।
634.	Oṃ Ūrdhvāyai Namaḥ ।	ॐ ऊर्ध्वायै नमः ।
635.	Oṃ Mīnāyai Namaḥ ।	ॐ मीनायै नमः ।
636.	Oṃ Uttaravāsinyai Namaḥ ।	ॐ उत्तरवासिन्यै नमः ।
637.	Oṃ Umāpatipriyāyai Devyai Namaḥ	ॐ उमापतिप्रियायै देव्यै नमः ।
638.	Oṃ Śivāyai Namaḥ ।	ॐ शिवायै नमः ।
639.	Oṃ Oṅkārarūpiṇyai Namaḥ ।	ॐ ओङ्काररूपिण्यै नमः ।
640.	Oṃ Uragendraśiroratnāyai Namaḥ ।	ॐ उरगेन्द्रशिरोरत्नायै नमः ।
641.	Oṃ Uragāyai Namaḥ ।	ॐ उरगायै नमः ।
642.	Oṃ Uragavallabhāyai Namaḥ ।	ॐ उरगवल्लभायै नमः ।
643.	Oṃ Udyānavāsinyai Namaḥ ।	ॐ उद्यानवासिन्यै नमः ।
644.	Oṃ Mālāyai Namaḥ ।	ॐ मालायै नमः ।
645.	Oṃ Praśastamaṇibhūṣaṇāyai Namaḥ ।	ॐ प्रशस्तमणिभूषणायै नमः ।
646.	Oṃ Ūrdhvadantottamāṅgyai Namaḥ ।	ॐ ऊर्ध्वदन्तोत्तमाङ्ग्यै नमः ।
647.	Oṃ Uttamāyai Namaḥ ।	ॐ उत्तमायै नमः ।
648.	Oṃ Ūrdhvakeśinyai Namaḥ ।	ॐ ऊर्ध्वकेशिन्यै नमः ।
649.	Oṃ Umāsiddhipradāyai Namaḥ ।	ॐ उमासिद्धिप्रदायै नमः ।
650.	Oṃ Uragāsanasaṃsthitāyai Namaḥ	ॐ उरगासनसंस्थितायै नमः ।
651.	Oṃ Ṛṣiputryai Namaḥ ।	ॐ ऋषिपुत्र्यै नमः ।
652.	Oṃ Ṛṣicchandāyai Namaḥ ।	ॐ ऋषिच्छन्दायै नमः ।
653.	Oṃ Ṛddhisiddhipradāyinyai Namaḥ	ॐ ऋद्धिसिद्धिप्रदायिन्यै नमः ।
654.	Oṃ Utsavotsavasīmantāyai Namaḥ	ॐ उत्सवोत्सवसीमन्तायै नमः
655.	Oṃ Kāmikāyai Namaḥ ।	ॐ कामिकायै नमः ।
656.	Oṃ Guṇānvitāyai Namaḥ ।	ॐ गुणान्वितायै नमः ।
657.	Oṃ Elāyai Namaḥ ।	ॐ एलायै नमः ।

658.	Oṃ Ekāravidyāyai Namaḥ		ॐ एकारविद्यायै नमः ।
659.	Oṃ Eṇīvidyādharāyai Namaḥ		ॐ एणीविद्याधरायै नमः ।
660.	Oṃ Oṅkārāvalayopetāyai Namaḥ		ॐ ओङ्कारावलयोपेतायै नमः ।
661.	Oṃ Oṅkāraparamāyai Kalāyai Namaḥ		ॐ ओङ्कारपरमायै कलायै नमः ।
662.	Oṃ Vadavadavāṇyai Namaḥ		ॐ वदवदवाण्यै नमः ।
663.	Oṃ Oṅkārākṣaramaṇḍitāyai Namaḥ		ॐ ओङ्काराक्षरमण्डितायै नमः ।
664.	Oṃ Aindryai Namaḥ		ॐ ऐन्द्र्यै नमः ।
665.	Oṃ Kuliśahastāyai Namaḥ		ॐ कुलिशहस्तायै नमः ।
666.	Oṃ Lokaparavāsinyai Namaḥ		ॐ लोकपरवासिन्यै नमः ।
667.	Oṃ Oṅkāramadhyabījāyai Namaḥ		ॐ ओङ्कारमध्यबीजायै नमः
668.	Oṃ Namorūpadhāriṇyai Namaḥ		ॐ नमोरूपधारिण्यै नमः ।
669.	Oṃ Parabrahmasvarūpāyai Namaḥ		ॐ परब्रह्मस्वरूपायै नमः ।
670.	Oṃ Aṃśukāyai Namaḥ		ॐ अंशुकायै नमः ।
671.	Oṃ Aṃśukavallabhāyai Namaḥ		ॐ अंशुकवल्लभायै नमः ।
672.	Oṃ Oṅkārāyai Namaḥ		ॐ ओङ्कारायै नमः ।
673.	Oṃ Aḥphaḍmantrāyai Namaḥ		ॐ अःफड्मन्त्रायै नमः ।
674.	Oṃ Akṣākṣaravibhūṣitāyai Namaḥ		ॐ अक्षाक्षरविभूषितायै नमः ।
675.	Oṃ Amantrāyai Namaḥ		ॐ अमन्त्रायै नमः ।
676.	Oṃ Mantrarūpāyai Namaḥ		ॐ मन्त्ररूपायै नमः ।
677.	Oṃ Padaśobhāsamanvitāyai Namaḥ		ॐ पदशोभासमन्वितायै नमः ।
678.	Oṃ Praṇavoṅkārarūpāyai Namaḥ		ॐ प्रणवोङ्काररूपायै नमः ।
679.	Oṃ Praṇavoccārabhāje Namaḥ		ॐ प्रणवोच्चारभाजे नमः ।
680.	Oṃ Hrīṃkārarūpāyai Namaḥ		ॐ ह्रींकाररूपायै नमः ।
681.	Oṃ Hrīṃkāryai Namaḥ		ॐ ह्रींकार्यै नमः ।
682.	Oṃ Vāgbījākṣarabhūṣaṇāyai Namaḥ		ॐ वाग्बीजाक्षरभूषणायै नमः ।
683.	Oṃ Hṛllekhāsiddhiyogāyai Namaḥ		ॐ हल्लेखासिद्धियोगायै नमः

684.	Oṃ Hṛtpadmāsanasaṃsthitāyai Namaḥ		ॐ हृत्पद्मासनसंस्थितायै नमः ।
685.	Oṃ Bījākhyāyai Namaḥ		ॐ बीजाख्यायै नमः ।
686.	Oṃ Netrahṛdayāyai Namaḥ		ॐ नेत्रहृदयायै नमः ।
687.	Oṃ Hrīmbījāyai Namaḥ		ॐ ह्रीम्बीजायै नमः ।
688.	Oṃ Bhuvaneśvaryai Namaḥ		ॐ भुवनेश्वर्यै नमः ।
689.	Oṃ Klīṅkāmarājāyai Namaḥ		ॐ क्लीङ्कामराजायै नमः ।
690.	Oṃ Klinnāyai Namaḥ		ॐ क्लिन्नायै नमः ।
691.	Oṃ Caturvargaphalapradāyai Namaḥ		ॐ चतुर्वर्गफलप्रदायै नमः ।
692.	Oṃ Klīṅklīṅklīṃrūpikāyai Devyai Namaḥ		ॐ क्लीङ्क्लीङ्क्लींरूपिकायै देव्यै नमः ।
693.	Oṃ Krīṅkrīṅkrīnnāmadhāriṇyai Namaḥ		ॐ क्रीङ्क्रीङ्क्रीन्नामधारिण्यै नमः ।
694.	Oṃ Kamalāśaktibījāyai Namaḥ		ॐ कमलाशक्तिबीजायै नमः ।
695.	Oṃ Pāśāṅkuśavibhūṣitāyai Namaḥ		ॐ पाशाङ्कुशविभूषितायै नमः ।
696.	Oṃ Śrīṃśrīṃkārāyai Namaḥ		ॐ श्रीं श्रींकारायै नमः ।
697.	Oṃ Mahāvidyāyai Namaḥ		ॐ महाविद्यायै नमः ।
698.	Oṃ Śraddhāyai Namaḥ		ॐ श्रद्धायै नमः ।
699.	Oṃ Śraddhāvatyai Namaḥ		ॐ श्रद्धावत्यै नमः ।
700.	Oṃ Aiṅklīṃhrīṃśrīṃparāyai Namaḥ		ॐ ऐङ्क्लीं ह्रीं श्रीम्परायै नमः ।
701.	Oṃ Klīṅkāryai Namaḥ		ॐ क्लीङ्कार्यै नमः ।
702.	Oṃ Paramāyai Kalāyai Namaḥ		ॐ परमायै कलायै नमः ।
703.	Oṃ Hrīṃklīṃśrīṃkārasvarūpāyai Namaḥ		ॐ ह्रीं क्लीं श्रींकारस्वरूपायै नमः ।
704.	Oṃ Sarvakarmaphalapradāyai Namaḥ		ॐ सर्वकर्मफलप्रदायै नमः ।
705.	Oṃ Sarvādhyāyai Namaḥ		ॐ सर्वाद्यायै नमः ।
706.	Oṃ Sarvadevyai Namaḥ		ॐ सर्वदेव्यै नमः ।
707.	Oṃ Sarvasiddhipradāyai Namaḥ		ॐ सर्वसिद्धिप्रदायै नमः ।

708.	Oṃ Sarvajñāyai Namaḥ		ॐ सर्वज्ञायै नमः ।
709.	Oṃ Sarvaśaktyai Namaḥ		ॐ सर्वशक्त्यै नमः ।
710.	Oṃ Vāgvibhūtipradāyinyai Namaḥ		ॐ वाग्विभूतिप्रदायिन्यै नमः ।
711.	Oṃ Sarvamokṣapradāyai Devyai Namaḥ		ॐ सर्वमोक्षप्रदायै देव्यै नमः ।
712.	Oṃ Sarvabhogapradāyinyai Namaḥ	ॐ सर्वभोगप्रदायिन्यै नमः ।
713.	Oṃ Guṇendravallabhāyai Vāmāyai Namaḥ		ॐ गुणेन्द्रवल्लभायै वामायै नमः ।
714.	Oṃ Sarvaśaktipradāyinyai Namaḥ		ॐ सर्वशक्तिप्रदायिन्यै नमः ।
715.	Oṃ Sarvānandamayyai Namaḥ		ॐ सर्वानन्दमय्यै नमः ।
716.	Oṃ Sarvasiddhipradāyinyai Namaḥ	ॐ सर्वसिद्धिप्रदायिन्यै नमः ।
717.	Oṃ Sarvacakreśvaryai Devyai Namaḥ		ॐ सर्वचक्रेश्वर्यै देव्यै नमः ।
718.	Oṃ Sarvasiddheśvaryai Namaḥ		ॐ सर्वसिद्धेश्वर्यै नमः ।
719.	Oṃ Sarvapriyaṅkaryai Namaḥ		ॐ सर्वप्रियङ्कर्यै नमः ।
720.	Oṃ Sarvasaukhyapradāyinyai Namaḥ		ॐ सर्वसौख्यप्रदायिन्यै नमः ।
721.	Oṃ Sarvānandapradāyai Devyai Namaḥ		ॐ सर्वानन्दप्रदायै देव्यै नमः ।
722.	Oṃ Brahmānandapradāyinyai Namaḥ		ॐ ब्रह्मानन्दप्रदायिन्यै नमः ।
723.	Oṃ Manovāñchitadātryai Namaḥ		ॐ मनोवाञ्छितदात्र्यै नमः ।
724.	Oṃ Manobuddhisamanvitāyai Namaḥ		ॐ मनोबुद्धिसमन्वितायै नमः ।
725.	Oṃ Akārādikṣakārāntāyai Namaḥ		ॐ अकारादिक्षकारान्तायै नमः
726.	Oṃ Durgāyai Namaḥ		ॐ दुर्गायै नमः ।
727.	Oṃ Durgārtināśinyai Namaḥ		ॐ दुर्गार्तिनाशिन्यै नमः ।
728.	Oṃ Padmanetrāyai Namaḥ		ॐ पद्मनेत्रायै नमः ।
729.	Oṃ Sunetrāyai Namaḥ		ॐ सुनेत्रायै नमः ।
730.	Oṃ Svadhāsvāhāvaṣaṭkaryai Namaḥ	ॐ स्वधास्वाहावषट्कर्यै नमः
731.	Oṃ Svarvargāyai Namaḥ		ॐ स्वर्वर्गायै नमः ।
732.	Oṃ Devavargāyai Namaḥ		ॐ देववर्गायै नमः ।

733.	Oṃ Tavargāyai Namaḥ		ॐ तवर्गायै नमः ।
734.	Oṃ Samanvitāyai Namaḥ		ॐ समन्वितायै नमः ।
735.	Oṃ Antasthāyai Namaḥ		ॐ अन्तस्थायै नमः ।
736.	Oṃ Veśmarūpāyai Namaḥ		ॐ वेश्मरूपायै नमः ।
737.	Oṃ Navadurgāyai Namaḥ		ॐ नवदुर्गायै नमः ।
738.	Oṃ Narottamāyai Namaḥ		ॐ नरोत्तमायै नमः ।
739.	Oṃ Tattvasiddhipradāyai Namaḥ		ॐ तत्त्वसिद्धिप्रदायै नमः ।
740.	Oṃ Nīlāyai Namaḥ		ॐ नीलायै नमः ।
741.	Oṃ Nīlapatākinyai Namaḥ		ॐ नीलपताकिन्यै नमः ।
742.	Oṃ Nityarūpāyai Namaḥ		ॐ नित्यरूपायै नमः ।
743.	Oṃ Niśākāryai Namaḥ		ॐ निशाकार्यै नमः ।
744.	Oṃ Stambhinyai Namaḥ		ॐ स्तम्भिन्यै नमः ।
745.	Oṃ Mohinyai Namaḥ		ॐ मोहिन्यै नमः ।
746.	Oṃ Vaśaṅkaryai Namaḥ		ॐ वशङ्कर्यै नमः ।
747.	Oṃ Uccāṭyai Namaḥ		ॐ उच्चाट्यै नमः ।
748.	Oṃ Unmādyai Namaḥ		ॐ उन्माद्यै नमः ।
749.	Oṃ Karṣiṇyai Namaḥ		ॐ कर्षिण्यै नमः ।
750.	Oṃ Mātaṅgyai Namaḥ		ॐ मातङ्ग्यै नमः ।
751.	Oṃ Madhumattāyai Namaḥ		ॐ मधुमत्तायै नमः ।
752.	Oṃ Aṇimāyai Namaḥ		ॐ अणिमायै नमः ।
753.	Oṃ Laghimāyai Namaḥ		ॐ लघिमायै नमः ।
754.	Oṃ Siddhāyai Namaḥ		ॐ सिद्धायै नमः ।
755.	Oṃ Mokṣapradāyai Nityāyai Namaḥ	ॐ मोक्षप्रदायै नित्यायै नमः ।
756.	Oṃ Nityānandapradāyinyai Namaḥ	ॐ नित्यानन्दप्रदायिन्यै नमः ।
757.	Oṃ Raktāṅgyai Namaḥ		ॐ रक्ताङ्ग्यै नमः ।
758.	Oṃ Raktanetrāyai Namaḥ		ॐ रक्तनेत्रायै नमः ।
759.	Oṃ Raktacandanabhūṣitāyai Namaḥ		ॐ रक्तचन्दनभूषितायै नमः ।
760.	Oṃ Svalpasiddhyai Namaḥ		ॐ स्वल्पसिद्ध्यै नमः ।
761.	Oṃ Sukalpāyai Namaḥ		ॐ सुकल्पायै नमः ।

762.	Oṃ Divyacāraṇaśukrabhāyai Namaḥ	ॐ दिव्यचारणशुक्रभायै नमः ।
763.	Oṃ Saṅkrāntyai Namaḥ ।	ॐ सङ्क्रान्त्यै नमः ।
764.	Oṃ Sarvavidyāyai Namaḥ ।	ॐ सर्वविद्यायै नमः ।
765.	Oṃ Saptavāsarabhūṣitāyai Namaḥ ।	ॐ सप्तवासरभूषितायै नमः ।
766.	Oṃ Prathamāyai Namaḥ ।	ॐ प्रथमायै नमः ।
767.	Oṃ Dvitīyāyai Namaḥ ।	ॐ द्वितीयायै नमः ।
768.	Oṃ Tṛtīyāyai Namaḥ ।	ॐ तृतीयायै नमः ।
769.	Oṃ Caturthikāyai Namaḥ ।	ॐ चतुर्थिकायै नमः ।
770.	Oṃ Pañcamyai Namaḥ ।	ॐ पञ्चम्यै नमः ।
771.	Oṃ Ṣaṣṭhyai Namaḥ ।	ॐ षष्ठ्यै नमः ।
772.	Oṃ Viśuddhāyai Saptamyai Namaḥ	ॐ विशुद्धायै सप्तम्यै नमः ।
773.	Oṃ Aṣṭamyai Namaḥ ।	ॐ अष्टम्यै नमः ।
774.	Oṃ Navamyai Namaḥ ।	ॐ नवम्यै नमः ।
775.	Oṃ Daśamyai Namaḥ ।	ॐ दशम्यै नमः ।
776.	Oṃ Ekādaśyai Namaḥ ।	ॐ एकादश्यै नमः ।
777.	Oṃ Dvādaśyai Namaḥ ।	ॐ द्वादश्यै नमः ।
778.	Oṃ Trayodaśyai Namaḥ ।	ॐ त्रयोदश्यै नमः ।
779.	Oṃ Caturdaśyai Namaḥ ।	ॐ चतुर्दश्यै नमः ।
780.	Oṃ Pūrṇimāyai Namaḥ ।	ॐ पूर्णिमायै नमः ।
781.	Oṃ Amāvāsyāyai Namaḥ ।	ॐ अमावास्यायै नमः ।
782.	Oṃ Pūrvāyai Namaḥ ।	ॐ पूर्वायै नमः ।
783.	Oṃ Uttarāyai Namaḥ ।	ॐ उत्तरायै नमः ।
784.	Oṃ Paripūrṇimāyai Namaḥ ।	ॐ परिपूर्णिमायै नमः ।
785.	Oṃ Khaḍginyai Namaḥ ।	ॐ खड्गिन्यै नमः ।
786.	Oṃ Cakriṇyai Namaḥ ।	ॐ चक्रिण्यै नमः ।
787.	Oṃ Ghorāyai Namaḥ ।	ॐ घोरायै नमः ।
788.	Oṃ Gadinyai Namaḥ ।	ॐ गदिन्यै नमः ।
789.	Oṃ Śūlinyai Namaḥ ।	ॐ शूलिन्यै नमः ।
790.	Oṃ Bhuśuṇḍīcāpinyai Namaḥ ।	ॐ भुशुण्डीचापिन्यै नमः ।
791.	Oṃ Bāṇāyai Namaḥ ।	ॐ बाणायै नमः ।

792.	Oṃ Sarvāyudhavibhūṣaṇāyai Namaḥ l	ॐ सर्वायुधविभूषणायै नमः l
793.	Oṃ Kuleśvaryai Namaḥ l	ॐ कुलेश्वर्यै नमः l
794.	Oṃ Kulavatyai Namaḥ l	ॐ कुलवत्यै नमः l
795.	Oṃ Kulācāraparāyaṇāyai Namaḥ l	ॐ कुलाचारपरायणायै नमः l
796.	Oṃ Kulakarmasuraktāyai Namaḥ l	ॐ कुलकर्मसुरक्तायै नमः l
797.	Oṃ Kulācārapravardhinyai Namaḥ l	ॐ कुलाचारप्रवर्धिन्यै नमः l
798.	Oṃ Kīrtyai Namaḥ l	ॐ कीर्त्यै नमः l
799.	Oṃ Śriyai Namaḥ l	ॐ श्रियै नमः l
800.	Oṃ Ramāyai Namaḥ l	ॐ रमायै नमः l
801.	Oṃ Rāmāyai Namaḥ l	ॐ रामायै नमः l
802.	Oṃ Dharmāyai Satataṃ Namaḥ l	ॐ धर्मायै सततं नमः l
803.	Oṃ Kṣamāyai Namaḥ l	ॐ क्षमायै नमः l
804.	Oṃ Dhṛtyai Namaḥ l	ॐ धृत्यै नमः l
805.	Oṃ Smṛtyai Namaḥ l	ॐ स्मृत्यै नमः l
806.	Oṃ Medhāyai Namaḥ l	ॐ मेधायै नमः l
807.	Oṃ Kalpavṛkṣanivāsinyai Namaḥ	ॐ कल्पवृक्षनिवासिन्यै नमः l
808.	Oṃ Ugrāyai Namaḥ l	ॐ उग्रायै नमः l
809.	Oṃ Ugraprabhāyai Namaḥ l	ॐ उग्रप्रभायै नमः l
810.	Oṃ Gauryai Namaḥ l	ॐ गौर्यै नमः l
811.	Oṃ Vedavidyāvibodhinyai Namaḥ l	ॐ वेदविद्याविबोधिन्यै नमः l
812.	Oṃ Sādhyāyai Namaḥ l	ॐ साध्यायै नमः l
813.	Oṃ Siddhāyai Namaḥ l	ॐ सिद्धायै नमः l
814.	Oṃ Susiddhāyai Namaḥ l	ॐ सुसिद्धायै नमः l
815.	Oṃ Viprarūpāyai Namaḥ l	ॐ विप्ररूपायै नमः l
816.	Oṃ Kālyai Namaḥ l	ॐ काल्यै नमः l
817.	Oṃ Karālyai Namaḥ l	ॐ कराल्यै नमः l
818.	Oṃ Kālyāyai Kalāyai Namaḥ l	ॐ काल्यायै कलायै नमः l
819.	Oṃ Daityavināśinyai Namaḥ l	ॐ दैत्यविनाशिन्यै नमः l
820.	Oṃ Kaulinyai Namaḥ l	ॐ कौलिन्यै नमः l

821.	Oṃ Kālikyai Namaḥ		ॐ कालिक्यै नमः ।
822.	Oṃ Ka Ca Ṭa Ta Pa Varṇikāyai Namaḥ		ॐ क च ट त प वर्णिकायै नमः ।
823.	Oṃ Jayinyai Namaḥ		ॐ जयिन्यै नमः ।
824.	Oṃ Jayayuktāyai Namaḥ		ॐ जययुक्तायै नमः ।
825.	Oṃ Jayadāyai Namaḥ		ॐ जयदायै नमः ।
826.	Oṃ Jṛmbhiṇyai Namaḥ		ॐ जृम्भिण्यै नमः ।
827.	Oṃ Srāviṇyai Namaḥ		ॐ स्राविण्यै नमः ।
828.	Oṃ Drāviṇyai Devyai Namaḥ		ॐ द्राविण्यै देव्यै नमः ।
829.	Oṃ Bheruṇḍāyai Namaḥ		ॐ भेरुण्डायै नमः ।
830.	Oṃ Vindhyavāsinyai Namaḥ		ॐ विन्ध्यवासिन्यै नमः ।
831.	Oṃ Jyotirbhūtāyai Namaḥ		ॐ ज्योतिर्भूतायै नमः ।
832.	Oṃ Jayadāyai Namaḥ		ॐ जयदायै नमः ।
833.	Oṃ Jvālāmālāsamākulāyai Namaḥ		ॐ ज्वालामालासमाकुलायै नमः ।
834.	Oṃ Bhinnābhinnaprakāśāyai Namaḥ		ॐ भिन्नाभिन्नप्रकाशायै नमः ।
835.	Oṃ Vibhinnābhinnarūpiṇyai Namaḥ	ॐ विभिन्नाभिन्नरूपिण्यै नमः
836.	Oṃ Aśvinyai Namaḥ		ॐ अश्विन्यै नमः ।
837.	Oṃ Bharaṇyai Namaḥ		ॐ भरण्यै नमः ।
838.	Oṃ Nakṣatrasambhavānilāyai Namaḥ		ॐ नक्षत्रसम्भवानिलायै नमः ।
839.	Oṃ Kāśyapyai Namaḥ		ॐ काश्यप्यै नमः ।
840.	Oṃ Vinatākhyātāyai Namaḥ		ॐ विनताख्यातायै नमः ।
841.	Oṃ Ditijāyai Namaḥ		ॐ दितिजायै नमः ।
842.	Oṃ Adityai Namaḥ		ॐ अदित्यै नमः ।
843.	Oṃ Kīrtyai Namaḥ		ॐ कीर्त्यै नमः ।
844.	Oṃ Kāmapriyāyai Devyai Namaḥ	ॐ कामप्रियायै देव्यै नमः ।
845.	Oṃ Kīrtyākīrtivivardhinyai Namaḥ		ॐ कीर्त्याकीर्तिविवर्धिन्यै नमः
846.	Oṃ Sadyomāṃsasamālabdhāyai Namaḥ		ॐ सद्योमांससमालब्धायै नमः ।

847.	Oṃ Sadyaśchinnāsiśaṅkarāyai Namaḥ |	ॐ सद्यश्छिन्नासिशङ्करायै नमः ।
848.	Oṃ Dakṣiṇāyai Diśe Namaḥ |	ॐ दक्षिणायै दिशे नमः ।
849.	Oṃ Uttarāyai Diśe Namaḥ |	ॐ उत्तरायै दिशे नमः ।
850.	Oṃ Pūrvāyai Diśe Namaḥ |	ॐ पूर्वायै दिशे नमः ।
851.	Oṃ Paścimāyai Diśe Namaḥ |	ॐ पश्चिमायै दिशे नमः ।
852.	Oṃ Agni Nairṛti Vāyavy Eśānyādi Diśe Namaḥ |	ॐ अग्निनैरृति वायव्येशान्यादिदिशे नमः ।
853.	Oṃ Smṛtāyai Namaḥ |	ॐ स्मृतायै नमः ।
854.	Oṃ Ūrdhvāṅgādhogatāyai Namaḥ |	ॐ ऊर्ध्वाङ्गाधोगतायै नमः ।
855.	Oṃ Śvetāyai Namaḥ |	ॐ श्वेतायै नमः ।
856.	Oṃ Kṛṣṇāyai Namaḥ |	ॐ कृष्णायै नमः ।
857.	Oṃ Raktāyai Namaḥ |	ॐ रक्तायै नमः ।
858.	Oṃ Pītakāyai Namaḥ |	ॐ पीतकायै नमः ।
859.	Oṃ Caturvargāyai Namaḥ |	ॐ चतुर्वर्गायै नमः ।
860.	Oṃ Caturvarṇāyai Namaḥ |	ॐ चतुर्वर्णायै नमः ।
861.	Oṃ Caturmātrātmikākṣarāyai Namaḥ |	ॐ चतुर्मात्रात्मिकाक्षरायै नमः ।
862.	Oṃ Caturmukhyai Namaḥ |	ॐ चतुर्मुख्यै नमः ।
863.	Oṃ Caturvedāyai Namaḥ |	ॐ चतुर्वेदायै नमः ।
864.	Oṃ Caturvidyāyai Namaḥ |	ॐ चतुर्विद्यायै नमः ।
865.	Oṃ Caturmukhāyai Namaḥ |	ॐ चतुर्मुखायै नमः ।
866.	Oṃ Caturgaṇāyai Namaḥ |	ॐ चतुर्गणायै नमः ।
867.	Oṃ Caturmātre Namaḥ |	ॐ चतुर्मात्रि नमः ।
868.	Oṃ Caturvargaphalapradāyai Namaḥ |	ॐ चतुर्वर्गफलप्रदायै नमः ।
869.	Oṃ Dhātrīvidhātrīmithunāyai Namaḥ |	ॐ धात्रीविधात्रीमिथुनायै नमः ।
870.	Oṃ Nāryai Namaḥ |	ॐ नार्यै नमः ।
871.	Oṃ Nāyakavāsinyai Namaḥ |	ॐ नायकवासिन्यै नमः ।
872.	Oṃ Surāmudāmudavatyai Namaḥ |	ॐ सुरामुदामुदवत्यै नमः ।

873.	Oṃ Medinyai Namaḥ		ॐ मेदिन्यै नमः ।
874.	Oṃ Menakātmajāyai Namaḥ		ॐ मेनकात्मजायै नमः ।
875.	Oṃ Ūrdhvakālyai Namaḥ		ॐ ऊर्ध्वकाल्यै नमः ।
876.	Oṃ Siddhikālyai Namaḥ		ॐ सिद्धिकाल्यै नमः ।
877.	Oṃ Dakṣiṇākālikāyai Namaḥ		ॐ दक्षिणाकालिकायै नमः ।
878.	Oṃ Śivāyai Namaḥ		ॐ शिवायै नमः ।
879.	Oṃ Nīlāyai Sarasvatyai Namaḥ		ॐ नीलायै सरस्वत्यै नमः ।
880.	Oṃ Sā Tvaṃ Bagalāyai Namaḥ		ॐ सा त्वं बगलायै नमः ।
881.	Oṃ Chinnamastakāyai Namaḥ		ॐ छिन्नमस्तकायै नमः ।
882.	Oṃ Sarveśvaryai Namaḥ		ॐ सर्वेश्वर्यै नमः ।
883.	Oṃ Siddhavidyāyai Parāyai Namaḥ		ॐ सिद्धविद्यायै परायै नमः ।
884.	Oṃ Paramadevatāyai Namaḥ		ॐ परमदेवतायै नमः ।
885.	Oṃ Hiṅgulāyai Namaḥ		ॐ हिङ्गुलायै नमः ।
886.	Oṃ Hiṅgulāṅgyai Namaḥ		ॐ हिङ्गुलाङ्ग्यै नमः ।
887.	Oṃ Hiṅgulādharavāsinyai Namaḥ		ॐ हिङ्गुलाधरवासिन्यै नमः ।
888.	Oṃ Hiṅgulottamavarṇābhāyai Namaḥ		ॐ हिङ्गुलोत्तमवर्णाभायै नमः ।
889.	Oṃ Hiṅgulābharaṇāyai Namaḥ		ॐ हिङ्गुलाभरणायै नमः ।
890.	Oṃ Jāgratyai Namaḥ		ॐ जाग्रत्यै नमः ।
891.	Oṃ Jaganmātre Namaḥ		ॐ जगन्मात्रे नमः ।
892.	Oṃ Jagadīśvaravallabhāyai Namaḥ		ॐ जगदीश्वरवल्लभायै नमः ।
893.	Oṃ Janārdanapriyāyai Devyai Namaḥ		ॐ जनार्दनप्रियायै देव्यै नमः ।
894.	Oṃ Jayayuktāyai Namaḥ		ॐ जययुक्तायै नमः ।
895.	Oṃ Jayapradāyai Namaḥ		ॐ जयप्रदायै नमः ।
896.	Oṃ Jagadānandakāryai Namaḥ		ॐ जगदानन्दकार्यै नमः ।
897.	Oṃ Jagadāhlādikāriṇyai Namaḥ		ॐ जगदाह्लादिकारिण्यै नमः ।
898.	Oṃ Jñānadānakaryai Namaḥ		ॐ ज्ञानदानकर्यै नमः ।
899.	Oṃ Yajñāyai Namaḥ		ॐ यज्ञायै नमः ।
900.	Oṃ Jānakyai Namaḥ		ॐ जानक्यै नमः ।

901.	Oṃ Janakapriyāyai Namaḥ	ॐ जनकप्रियायै नमः ।
902.	Oṃ Jayantyai Namaḥ	ॐ जयन्त्यै नमः ।
903.	Oṃ Jayadāyai Nityāyai Namaḥ	ॐ जयदायै नित्यायै नमः ।
904.	Oṃ Jvaladagnisamaprabhāyai Namaḥ	ॐ ज्वलदग्निसमप्रभायै नमः ।
905.	Oṃ Vidyādharāyai Namaḥ	ॐ विद्याधरायै नमः ।
906.	Oṃ Bimboṣṭhyai Namaḥ	ॐ बिम्बोष्ठ्यै नमः ।
907.	Oṃ Kailāsācalavāsinyai Namaḥ	ॐ कैलासाचलवासिन्यै नमः ।
908.	Oṃ Vibhavāyai Namaḥ	ॐ विभवायै नमः ।
909.	Oṃ Vaḍavāgnaye Namaḥ	ॐ वडवाग्नये नमः ।
910.	Oṃ Agnihotraphalapradāyai Namaḥ	ॐ अग्निहोत्रफलप्रदायै नमः ।
911.	Oṃ Mantrarūpāyai Parāyai Devyai Namaḥ	ॐ मन्त्ररूपायै परायै देव्यै नमः ।
912.	Oṃ Gururūpiṇyai Namaḥ	ॐ गुरुरूपिण्यै नमः ।
913.	Oṃ Gayāyai Namaḥ	ॐ गयायै नमः ।
914.	Oṃ Gaṅgāyai Namaḥ	ॐ गङ्गायै नमः ।
915.	Oṃ Gomatyai Namaḥ	ॐ गोमत्यै नमः ।
916.	Oṃ Prabhāsāyai Namaḥ	ॐ प्रभासायै नमः ।
917.	Oṃ Puṣkarāyai Namaḥ	ॐ पुष्करायै नमः ।
918.	Oṃ Vindhyācalaratāyai Devyai Namaḥ	ॐ विन्ध्याचलरतायै देव्यै नमः ।
919.	Oṃ Vindhyācalanivāsinyai Namaḥ	ॐ विन्ध्याचलनिवासिन्यै नमः
920.	Oṃ Bahvai Namaḥ	ॐ बह्वै नमः ।
921.	Oṃ Bahusundaryai Namaḥ	ॐ बहुसुन्दर्यै नमः ।
922.	Oṃ Kaṃsāsuravināśinyai Namaḥ	ॐ कंसासुरविनाशिन्यै नमः ।
923.	Oṃ Śūlinyai Namaḥ	ॐ शूलिन्यै नमः ।
924.	Oṃ Śūlahastāyai Namaḥ	ॐ शूलहस्तायै नमः ।
925.	Oṃ Vajrāyai Namaḥ	ॐ वज्रायै नमः ।
926.	Oṃ Vajraharāyai Namaḥ	ॐ वज्रहरायै नमः ।
927.	Oṃ Durgāyai Namaḥ	ॐ दुर्गायै नमः ।
928.	Oṃ Śivāyai Namaḥ	ॐ शिवायै नमः ।

929.	Om Śāntikaryai Namaḥ		ॐ शान्तिकर्यै नमः ।
930.	Om Brahmāṇyai Namaḥ		ॐ ब्रह्माण्यै नमः ।
931.	Om Brāhmaṇapriyāyai Namaḥ		ॐ ब्राह्मणप्रियायै नमः ।
932.	Om Sarvalokapraṇetryai Namaḥ	ॐ सर्वलोकप्रणेत्र्यै नमः ।
933.	Om Sarvarogaharāyai Namaḥ		ॐ सर्वरोगहरायै नमः ।
934.	Om Maṅgalāyai Namaḥ		ॐ मङ्गलायै नमः ।
935.	Om Śobhanāyai Namaḥ		ॐ शोभनायै नमः ।
936.	Om Śuddhāyai Namaḥ		ॐ शुद्धायै नमः ।
937.	Om Niṣkalāyai Namaḥ		ॐ निष्कलायै नमः ।
938.	Om Paramāyai Kalāyai Namaḥ		ॐ परमायै कलायै नमः ।
939.	Om Viśveśvaryai Namaḥ		ॐ विश्वेश्वर्यै नमः ।
940.	Om Viśvamātre Namaḥ		ॐ विश्वमात्रे नमः ।
941.	Om Lalitāyai Vāsitānanāyai Namaḥ		ॐ ललितायै वासिताननायै नमः ।
942.	Om Sadāśivāyai Namaḥ		ॐ सदाशिवायै नमः ।
943.	Om Umāyai Kṣemāyai Namaḥ		ॐ उमायै क्षेमायै नमः ।
944.	Om Caṇḍikāyai Namaḥ		ॐ चण्डिकायै नमः ।
945.	Om Caṇḍavikramāyai Namaḥ		ॐ चण्डविक्रमायै नमः ।
946.	Om Sarvadevamayyai Devyai Namaḥ		ॐ सर्वदेवमय्यै देव्यै नमः ।
947.	Om Sarvāgamabhayāpahāyai Namaḥ		ॐ सर्वागमभयापहाये नमः ।
948.	Om Brahmeśaviṣṇunamitāyai Namaḥ		ॐ ब्रह्मेशविष्णुनमितायै नमः ।
949.	Om Sarvakalyāṇakāriṇyai Namaḥ		ॐ सर्वकल्याणकारिण्यै नमः ।
950.	Om Yoginīyogamātre Namaḥ		ॐ योगिनीयोगमात्रे नमः ।
951.	Om Yogīndrahṛdayasthitāyai Namaḥ	ॐ योगिन्द्रहृदयस्थितायै नमः
952.	Om Yogijāyāyai Namaḥ		ॐ योगिजायायै नमः ।
953.	Om Yogavatyai Namaḥ		ॐ योगवत्यै नमः ।
954.	Om Yogīndrānandayoginyai Namaḥ	ॐ योगीन्द्रानन्दयोगिन्यै नमः ।

955.	Om Indrādi Namitāyai Devyai Namaḥ		ॐ इन्द्रादि नमिताये देव्यै नमः ।
956.	Om Īśvaryai Namaḥ		ॐ ईश्वर्यै नमः ।
957.	Om Īśvarapriyāyai Namaḥ		ॐ ईश्वरप्रियायै नमः ।
958.	Om Viśuddhidāyai Namaḥ		ॐ विशुद्धिदायै नमः ।
959.	Om Bhayaharāyai Namaḥ		ॐ भयहरायै नमः ।
960.	Om Bhaktadveṣibhayaṅkaryai Namaḥ		ॐ भक्तद्वेषिभयङ्कर्यै नमः ।
961.	Om Bhavaveṣāyai Namaḥ		ॐ भववेषायै नमः ।
962.	Om Kāminyai Namaḥ		ॐ कामिन्यै नमः ।
963.	Om Bheruṇḍāyai Namaḥ		ॐ भेरुण्डायै नमः ।
964.	Om Bhavakāriṇyai Namaḥ		ॐ भवकारिण्यै नमः ।
965.	Om Balabhadrapriyākārāyai Namaḥ	ॐ बलभद्रप्रियाकारायै नमः ।
966.	Om Saṃsārārṇavatāriṇyai Namaḥ		ॐ संसारार्णवतारिण्यै नमः ।
967.	Om Pañcabhūtāyai Namaḥ		ॐ पञ्चभूतायै नमः ।
968.	Om Sarvabhūtāyai Namaḥ		ॐ सर्वभूतायै नमः ।
969.	Om Vibhūtyai Namaḥ		ॐ विभूत्यै नमः ।
970.	Om Bhūtidhāriṇyai Namaḥ		ॐ भूतिधारिण्यै नमः ।
971.	Om Siṃhavāhāyai Namaḥ		ॐ सिंहवाहायै नमः ।
972.	Om Mahāmohāyai Namaḥ		ॐ महामोहायै नमः ।
973.	Om Mohapāśavināśinyai Namaḥ	ॐ मोहपाशविनाशिन्यै नमः ।
974.	Om Mandurāyai Namaḥ		ॐ मन्दुरायै नमः ।
975.	Om Madirāyai Namaḥ		ॐ मदिरायै नमः ।
976.	Om Mudrāyai Namaḥ		ॐ मुद्रायै नमः ।
977.	Om Mudrāmudgaradhāriṇyai Namaḥ		ॐ मुद्रामुद्गरधारिण्यै नमः ।
978.	Om Sāvitryai Namaḥ		ॐ सावित्र्यै नमः ।
979.	Om Mahādevyai Namaḥ		ॐ महादेव्यै नमः ।
980.	Om Parapriyavināyikāyai Namaḥ	ॐ परप्रियविनायिकायै नमः ।
981.	Om Yamadūtyai Namaḥ		ॐ यमदूत्यै नमः ।
982.	Om Piṅgākṣyai Namaḥ		ॐ पिङ्गाक्ष्यै नमः ।

983.	Oṃ Vaiṣṇavyai Namaḥ		ॐ वैष्णव्यै नमः ।
984.	Oṃ Śaṅkaryai Namaḥ		ॐ शङ्कर्यै नमः ।
985.	Oṃ Candrapriyāyai Namaḥ		ॐ चन्द्रप्रियायै नमः ।
986.	Oṃ Candraratāyai Namaḥ		ॐ चन्द्रतायै नमः ।
987.	Oṃ Candanāraṇyavāsinyai Namaḥ		ॐ चन्दनारण्यवासिन्यै नमः
988.	Oṃ Candanendrasamāyuktāyai Namaḥ		ॐ चन्दनेन्द्रसमायुक्तायै नमः ।
989.	Oṃ Caṇḍadaityavināśinyai Namaḥ		ॐ चण्डदैत्यविनाशिन्यै नमः
990.	Oṃ Sarveśvaryai Namaḥ		ॐ सर्वेश्वर्यै नमः ।
991.	Oṃ Yakṣiṇyai Namaḥ		ॐ यक्षिण्यै नमः ।
992.	Oṃ Kirātyai Namaḥ		ॐ किरात्यै नमः ।
993.	Oṃ Rākṣasyai Namaḥ		ॐ राक्षस्यै नमः ।
994.	Oṃ Mahābhogavatyai Devyai Namaḥ		ॐ महाभोगवत्यै देव्यै नमः ।
995.	Oṃ Mahāmokṣapradāyinyai Namaḥ		ॐ महामोक्षप्रदायिन्यै नमः ।
996.	Oṃ Viśvahantryai Namaḥ		ॐ विश्वहन्त्र्यै नमः ।
997.	Oṃ Viśvarūpāyai Namaḥ		ॐ विश्वरूपायै नमः ।
998.	Oṃ Viśvasaṃhārakāriṇyai Namaḥ		ॐ विश्वसंहारकारिण्यै नमः ।
999.	Oṃ Sarvalokānāṃ Dhātryai Namaḥ		ॐ सर्वलोकानां धात्र्यै नमः ।
1000.	Oṃ Hitakāraṇakāminyai Namaḥ		ॐ हितकारणकामिन्यै नमः ।
1001.	Oṃ Kamalāyai Namaḥ		ॐ कमलायै नमः ।
1002.	Oṃ Sūkṣmadāyai Devyai Namaḥ		ॐ सूक्ष्मदायै देव्यै नमः ।
1003.	Oṃ Dhātryai Namaḥ		ॐ धात्र्यै नमः ।
1004.	Oṃ Haravināśinyai Namaḥ		ॐ हरविनाशिन्यै नमः ।
1005.	Oṃ Surendrapūjitāyai Namaḥ		ॐ सुरेन्द्रपूजितायै नमः ।
1006.	Oṃ Siddhāyai Namaḥ		ॐ सिद्धायै नमः ।
1007.	Oṃ Mahātejovatyai Namaḥ		ॐ महातेजोवत्यै नमः ।
1008.	Oṃ Parārūpavatyai Devyai Namaḥ		ॐ पराऱूपवत्यै देव्यै नमः ।
1009.	Oṃ Trailokyākarṣakāriṇyai Namaḥ		ॐ त्रैलोक्याकर्षकारिण्यै नमः।

Iti Śrī Bagalāmukhī Sahasranāmāvaliḥ Sampūrṇā ॥

इति श्रीबगलामुखी सहस्रनामावलिः सम्पूर्णा ॥

*****

9. *Mātangī* – मातंगी

Śrī Mātangī Devī

Adiparasakti, Paradevata, Sarva Loka Jaganmata, Sri Devi creates, preserves and destroys all the worlds. In addition, she performs the tasks of *Tirodhāna* and *Anugrahā* also, in accordance with one of the names in Sri Lalita Sahasranama *"Pancha Krutya Parayana"*. As a *Parabrahma Mahishi*, she, after creating lives, has taken many divine incarnations for the state and has been regularly doing *sishta* maintenance and evil discipline.

Among the various incarnations of Sriman Narayana described by Sri Vishnu Bhagavatam, ten avatars are prominent. Similarly, to protect the entire world, Sri Devi has manifested herself in ten different forms known as Dasha Maha Vidyas, as described in the previous chapter. Among those ten, Sri *Mātangī* Devi Vidya is the Nineth one.

The *Dhyana* verse of the seventh chapter of *Sri Devi Mahatmya*, particularly mentions about *Sri Matangi Devi*. Throughout that chapter, Ambigai is in the form of *Sri Matangi Devi* only.
   "Mātangīm Śankapātrām Maturamatumatām Citrakōtpāsi Pālām ||"

This *Mātangī Devi* shines in the *Viśuddhi chakra* in the neck of our body in 16 petalled lotus. Among the 10 incarnations of *Sri Maha Vishnu*, *Sri Mātangī Devi* is compared to *Sri Rama* incarnation and the Sun (*Surya*) among the Navagrahas.

Mātangī is a minister of *Śrī Lalitā Devī*, who is the amperes. In this world *Mātangī* Devi is in the form Madurai *Minakshi*. The important activity of ours in this world is speech. This is also called as sound or *vāg*. One of the important energies that support this activity is *Mātangī Devi*. This speech has four stages viz., *Parā, Paśyantī, Madhyamā* and *Vaikharī*[5]. It has already been seen that, out of these, *Tripura Bhairavī* is in the form of *Parā Vāg* and *Tārā Devī* in the form of *Paśyantī*. *Vaikharī vāg* is the last stage among these. The *Parā*, which is stationed in *Mūlādhāra*, becomes *Paśyantī* when it moves to *Maṇipūraka cakra*. Again, when it is move out it turns as *Vaikharī* in *Viśuddhi chakra* in neck. *Mātangī* is in this form of *Vaikharī*.

This *Mātangī Devī* is also called *Ucchiṣṭa Chāndālī, Rāja Mātangī* or *Śyāmalā*. *Śyāmalā* means black object. *Shastras* indicate the pure sound, at the moment when it indicates an object in this world, as black. Hence it is also called as *Chāndālī*. This stage is the last one in speech and hence indicated as the last caste as a simile.

---

[5] *Sri Lalita Devi* is in all these four forms as per *Sri Lalita Sahasranama*.

One of the tribes living in Yaazhpaanam in Sri Lanka is called Matangar. One of the sages borne in this tribe was called as *Matanga Muni*. In Ramayana, we have heard of Sabari, an old lady, waiting for Sri Rama and offered him fruits after tasting herself. This *Matanga Muni* was the guru of Sabari. His father was a *Sri Vidya Upasaka*. *Matanga Muni* got initiated into *Sri Vidya* from his father himself.

He did heavy penance on *Sri Devī*. **She** appeared before him and asked what is the boon he wants. But, Matangar said, that he is happy with the very sight (*darshan*) of *Devī* and he does not want any other boon. On the other hand, *Devī* insisted that it is **her** practice to offer boons to those who do penance on **her**. Hence, **she** has to give some boon to him. *Matangar* replied, in that case, give me the fortune of having yourself as my daughter. He remembered his friend Himavan got *Parvati* herself as his daughter. Matangar also wanted a similar fortune. *Devī* also agreed. Thus, born *Shyamala Devī* to the parents *Matangar* and *Siddhimati*. Being daughter of *Matangar*, she is also called as *Mātangī*. Being an incarnation of *Shyamala*, she is also called as *Raja Shyamala* or *Raja Mātangī*. In Samskrutam, *Shyama* means a mix of blue and green colours. In North India this *Devī* is called as *Shyama*.

In *Shakta* worship, we have 7 forms of *Devī* called *Sapta Mata*-s. *Shyamala* is one among them. Others being – *Brāhmee, Maheshwaree, Koumāree, Indrāṇee, Chāmuṇḍee* and *Vārāhee*. *Mātangī* alias *Shyāmala Devī* appears both in the list of *Sapta Mata*-s and *Dasha Maha Vidya* as well.

Kalidasa's Shyamala Daṇḍakam goes this way; –
    Mātā Maragata Shyāmā Mātangī Madashālinee ----
    Mātanga Kanyām Manasā Smarāmi.

His other works like *Raghuvamsam, Kumara Sambavam, Mega Santesham,* etc., are very famous. *Kalidasa* was so innocent and ignorant, but he became the greatest poet in Samskrutam. All these are possible only because of the blessings of *Mātangī*. The idol worshipped by *Kalidasa* can still be seen at Ujjain. There are two *Sahasranama*-s about this *Devī* – *Shyamala Sahasranama* and *Raja Mātangī Sahasranama*.

A story goes in *Mahabharata* written by Veda *Vyasa* – *Devī* incarnated as a daughter of the sage called *Matanga*, who is a *chandaala*, a low caste person. Hence her name *Chandaalee*. *Mati* means mind. *Matam* means thought. *Matanga* means the status of explaining the thought. When it explains the sound, it becomes *Mātangī*. This is the tattva of *Mātangī*. Even when this transforms to many states, the base form as *Paraa vaag* in the *Moolaadhaara* energy does not get destructed. That is eternal. That always remains as residue. That is the reason **she** is called as *Uchchishta Chaandaalee* or *Shyaamalaa* since, **she** acts as a guide to reach the residual *Paraa vaag* and since **she** is in the circumstance to indicate the original objects of this world.

There is one more story about the incarnation of *Mātangī Devī* – this story is mentioned in the *Tiruvenkaadu Stalapuraanam*.

During one of the dissolution periods, *Brahma* in the form of an elephant was on a meditation on *Lord Shiva*. At that time, a son was born from the minds of *Brahma*. He is *Matangar* (*Matanga* means elephant). Brahma ordered Matangar to perform penance. Since it was the dissolution period, the entire universe was flooded. Sage Narada came to him and suggested that even during dissolution period the Tiruvenkadu is not flooded and he can go and do penance at that place. Matangar was happy and started his penance at Tiruvenkadu. *Manmata* (Cupid) tried to disturb his penance. *Lord Shiva* burnt him into ashes through his third eye. Lord *Vishnu* disguising as *Mohini*, a beautiful lady appeared before Matangar. He requested Vishnu to stay at Tiruvenkadu as Mohini and Vishnu also accepted. Being happy about the penance of Matangar, Lord Ganesha visited him and offered eight *siddhis* (*ashta siddhis*). At last Lord Shiva also appeared before Matangar and blessed.

As per the request of Matangar, Shyamala *Devī* incarnated as a baby girl in a Bloom (*Neelotbala*) flower, in the Matanga Pond in the early mornings of a Friday of *Aashada* month (Jul-Aug). Matangar brought this girl and grew her. Still there is one *Matangaashramam* (hermitage of Matangar) 3 KMs from Tiruvenkaadu village.

Abhiraami Bhattar in his *Abhiraami Antaati*, 50th and 70th songs have sung about *Mātangī*;

Varahi Shoolini Matangi En -----------	50
Vannamumaki Matangarkula --------	70

Mātangī Devī originated from the sugar-cane bow of *Maha Tripura Sundari*. *Mātangī Devī* is in the role of a minister to *Raja Rajeshvari* called as *Tripura Sundari*. Hence, **she** is also called as *Mantrinee*. Only if the minister is satiated one can get the influence of the king. Similarly, *tantras* say, if one reaches out to *Mātangī*, he can easily get the blessings of *Lalita Parameshvaree*. There is nothing which cannot be acted by *Mātangī*. One can get through *Mātangī's* blessings – the art of speech to get anything at any point of time, energy, the capability of attracting others to self, un-fearful status, tension-free state of mind, the capacity to complete the tasks taken without any obstruction, the foreseeing capacity of anticipating the contingencies and avoiding it in advance, etc.

Mātangī has two aides viz., *Vāgvādinī* and *Nakulī*. *Vāgvādinī Devī* energy makes us speak well. With the blessings of this *Devī*, the worshipper will speak lot of golden words. Only with compassion of this *Devī*, one can explain the complicated *shastras* even to a lay man un-tiresomely. The task of *Nakulī* is to curtail the speech capacity of defendants. By controlling others speech and to win we need *Vāgvādinī Devī's* blessings. To speak sweetly and clearly, thousand times better than others we need *Nakulī's* compassion.

Mātangī Jayanti is celebrated on the *Tritiya Tithi* (the third day) of Shukla Paksha (bright lunar fortnight) in the month of Vaishakha.

Kula Kunta means *Moolaadhaara*. The energy residing here moves to *Sasarara* through *kula marga* (path) called *sushumna*. At that time, it is transformed to the sound form which can be recognised by us and this form is called sound or *Vaikharee*. Since this sound, at this moment, leaves any form or race, it is called *na-kula* (without family). This energy is called *nakulī*.

If our speech is sweet, it is called music. The spine where *sushumna nadi* (pulse) resides is also called as *Veena Dandam*. Hence *Mātangī Devī* is also praised as *Sangita Matruka*. A sweet speech will remind us a parrot. *Devī* holds it in **her** hand.

Sri Lalita Sahasranama says –

Geya Chakra Rathārūḍa Mantriṇī Parisevitā   and again
Mantrinyambā Viracita Vishanga Vadha Toshitā

Shyamala Devī won the demon *Vishangan* in the battle, brother of *Bandasura*, by sitting in the chariot called *Geya Chakra*.

Lalita Upakyanam praises *Shyamala Devī* as – *Sangita Yogini, Shyama, Shyamala, Mantrini, Mantrinayaki, Sashivesani, Pradaneshi, Shukapriya, Veenapati, Priyacapriya* and so on.

Vedas consider *Ganapati* as *Brahmanaspati*, who is the minister of *Indra – Brihaspati*. Similarly, *Mātangī* acts as a minister for *Lalita Parameshvaree*. The names of both seem to be similar as *Ucchishta Chaṇḍalee* and *Ucchishta Ganapati*.
During the *Makara* month (Jan-Feb), *Śyāmalā Navaratri* is being celebrated by *Shakta* devotees.

Though there are many *naadis* (pulses) in our body, the 101 *naadis* around the heart are considered as important –

"*Śadam Ca Ekā Ca Hrudyasya Nādyāḥ*" (*Kāṭaka Upanishat* 3-2-16).

Still important are the three viz., *Idaa*, *Pingala* and *Sushumnaa*. *Sushumnaa* is the one which moves in the mid of the spine at the back of our body. *Idaa* and *pingala* coil themselves around both the sides and join the *Sushumnaa* at the *Aagnaa chakra*. This is *Triveni sangama* (meeting of three – as meeting of three rivers Ganga, Yamuna and Saraswathi in Allahabad). *Idaa* is Ganga, *Pingala* – Yamuna and *Sushumnaa* is invisible Saraswathi. This is what is told in *Vedas* as –

"*Sitā Sito Sarito Yatra Sangate*".

Worshiping male gods is called mantra. The method of worshiping female deities is called Vidya. Worshiping Sri Vidya, the unison of Shiva and Shakti. So, this also comes under Mantra group. Sri Vidya is said to be the best of all mantras.

That Devi is also known as Tripura Sundari, Raja Rajeshwari, Shodasee, Kamakshi, Lalita and so on. She is also an important Maha Vidya. She is glorified in many Shakta texts like Sri Lalitha Sahasranamam, Soundarya-lahari, etc. She is called Adi Para Shakti in the Lalithopakyanam of Brahmanda Purana.

According to the Srikula tradition in Shaktaism, *Mātangī* is the Shakta's supreme deity of Hinduism and the principal deity of Sri Vidya. The Tripura Upanishad places her as the ultimate Shakti (energy, power) of the universe. She is described as the Supreme Consciousness ruling from above Brahma, Vishnu and Shiva.

May the Divine Mother guide us all in our every action and thought. And may She remove the veil of maya and bestow upon us the greatest gift of all, moksha (liberation).

Form(s) of *Śrī Mātangī Devī*

Usually Meditative Hymns (*Dhyana Shlokas*) about the Gods are figurative of the concerned God or Goddess.

The Meditation Hymn of *Śrī Mātangī Devī* is;

मातङ्गीं भूषिताङ्गीं विविध मनिधरामिन्दु सूर्याक्षियुग्मां
स्विद्यद्वक्त्रां कदम्ब प्रसवपरिलसद्वेणुकामात्र वीणाम् ।
बिम्बोष्ठीं रक्तवस्त्रां म्रुगमदतिलकामिन्दु रेखावतंसां
कर्णोद्यच्छङ्ख पत्रां कठिनकुचभराक्रान्त मध्यां नमामि ॥

Mātangīm Bhūṣitāngīm Vividha Manidharāmindu Sūryākśiyugmām
Svidmadvaktrām Kadamba Prasavaparilasadvenukāmātra Vīnām |
Bimboṣṭhīm Raktavastrām Mrugamadatilakāmindu Rekhāvatamsām
Karṇodyacchankha Patrām Kaṭhinakuchabharākrānta Madhyām

Namāmi ॥

Mātangī Devī has eight hands and has Veena, Parrot, Book and a Lotus flower and sits on a lotus flower. An idol in such a form can be seen in the Kamakshi temple at Kancheepuram.

Sri *Mātangī* Devi is seated on Ratna Simhasana with emerald complexion and three eyes with a crescent moon on her head. She carries weapons like knife, pasam, ankusam and shield in her four hands.
Mātangī is described as jewel green in color. Uchchhishta-Matangini carries a noose, sword, goad, and club, her other well-known form, Raja-

Matangi, plays the veena and is often pictured with a parrot. She 64 arts personified Goddess.

She is considered to be the Tantric form of Saraswati, the goddess of music and learning. Matangi governs speech, music, knowledge and the arts. Her worship is prescribed to acquire supernatural powers, especially gaining control over enemies, attracting people to oneself, acquiring mastery over the arts and gaining supreme knowledge.

Lord Shiva is also known as Matanga. His Shakti (consort) is called Matangi. Her complexion is dark and possess a Moon on her forehead. The three eyed Goddess is seated on the crown decorated with jewels. Her luster is like a blue lotus and is the destroyer of the demons like forest fire. In each of her four hands, she has a noose, a mace, an axe and a hook. She is a destroyer of the demons by enchanting them first with her beauty and fulfiller of every desire of her devotees.

The Dhyana mantra of the Bruhat Tantrasara describes Uchchhishta-Matangini, one of the most popular forms of the goddess. Matangi is seated on a corpse and wears red garments, red jewelry and a garland of gunja seeds. The goddess is described as a young, sixteen-year-old maiden with fully developed breasts. She carries a skull bowl and a sword in her two hands, and is offered leftovers.

The Dhyana mantras in the Tantrasara describe Matangi as blue in colour. The crescent moon adorns her forehead. She has three eyes and a smiling face. She wears jewelry and is seated on a jeweled throne. In her four arms, she carries a noose, a sword, a goad, and a club. Her waist is slim and her breasts well-developed.

The Dhyana Mantra of Raja-Matangi from the Purashcharyarnava describes Matangi as green in colour with the crescent moon upon her forehead. She has long hair, a smiling expression and intoxicated eyes, and wears a garland of kadamba flowers and various ornaments. She perspires a little around the face, which renders her even more beautiful. Below her navel are three horizontal folds of skin and a thin vertical line of fine hair. Seated on an altar and flanked by two parrots, she represents the 64 arts. The Sarada Tilaka, adds to this description that Raja-Matangi plays the veena, wears conch-shell earrings and flower garlands, and has flower paintings adorning her forehead. She is also depicted wearing a garland of white lotus (here lotus signifies multi-colored world creation), similar to the iconography of goddess Saraswati, with whom she is associated with.

According to Kalidasa's Shyamala Dandakam, Matangi plays a ruby-studded veena and speaks sweetly. The Dhyana Mantra describes her to be four-armed, with a dark emerald complexion, full breasts anointed with red Kumkum powder, and a crescent moon on her forehead. She carries a noose, a goad, a sugarcane bows and flower arrows, which the goddess Tripura Sundari is often described to hold. She is also described to love the parrot and is embodied in the nectar of song.

The green complexion is associated with deep knowledge and is also the colour of Budha, the presiding deity of the planet Mercury who governs intelligence. Matangi is often depicted with a parrot in her hands, representing speech. The veena symbolizes her association with music.

One who worships *Matangi Devi* will soon become the best in the world. He will make the whole world by himself. Matangi is *Sarva Shankari*. Through *Nathobasana* and knowledge of Shastras, one can attain immense wealth, good fame and liberation.

Devotees of Matangi Devi should not disrespect the music or the singers. No one should go up in the middle of a good concert.

Temples for *Mātangī* Devi –

Mātangī temples are somewhat famous and a lot more when compared to other Dasha Maha Vidyas.

Matangi along with the other Maha vidyas finds place in the Kamakya Temple complex, the most important Shaktipeeth for Tantra worship. While other Maha vidyas are worshipped in individual temples, Matangi and Kamala find place in the main Kamakya shrine along with Kamakya, in the form of a *'yoni'*.

Goddess Meenakshi of Madurai is also considered as none other than Raja Matangi. Here, she is seen as two-handed and standing, holding a parrot.

The Modh community of Gujarat worship Matangi as Modheshwari, patron deity of the Modh community. Here, Matangi is seen in a Durga-like form sitting over a lion.

Other than the above, Rajrappa Chinna Masta shrine also has a temple dedicated to Matangi and the other Maha vidyas. There are several temples in South India where Matangi is venerated as Shyamala or Mantrinee, the Prime minister of Goddess Lalita in Srikula tradition.

This Goddess should be meditated upon in the 16 petalled lotus at the *Viśuddhi Chakra* in the neck of the human body. Let us all cry at her feet to be able to meditate her.

Kanchi Paramacharya would say – In all deities, many heads, hands, etc., are described. But does any deity said to have more than two legs? Nope. Why?

We only have two hands. All deities are told to have only two legs to enable us to cry holding the two legs of the deity. At least if we cry clasping the two feet of Ambika, she will turn her merciful eye on us!

*****

Śrī Mātangī Devī Mantras

Śrī Mātangī Vidyā

In Samskrutam, in general *Vidyā* means mantra. Vidya means knowledge. Here is a very powerful *Sri Mātangī Devī Mantra*.

Oṃ Asya Śrī Mātangī Mahā Mantrasya Matanga Riśiḥ |
Amita Chandaḥ | Śrī Mātangī Devatā |
Im Bījam, Hroum Śaktiḥ, Śrīm Kīlakam |
Śrī Mātangī Prasāda Siddhyarte Jape Viniyogaḥ |

Oṃ Namo Mātangīśvari Sarvajana Manohārinī Angushṭābhyām Namaḥ
Oṃ Sarvajana Mukharanjanī Klīm Sarvarāja Vaśankarī Sarva Strī Puruṣa
Vaśankarī Darjanībhyām Namaḥ
Oṃ Sarvadhuṣṭa Mruga Vaśankarī Sarva Satva Vaśankarī Madhymābhyām
Namaḥ

Oṃ Trailokyamme Anāmikābhyām Namaḥ
Oṃ Vaśamānāya Kaniṣṭikābhyām Namaḥ
Oṃ Svāhā Karatala Karabrushṭābhyām Namaḥ

Oṃ Namo Mātangīśvari Sarvajana Manohārinī Hrudayāya Namaḥ
Oṃ Sarvajana Mukharanjanī Klīm Sarvarāja Vaśankarī Sarva Strī Puruṣa
Vaśankarī Sirase Svāhā
Oṃ Sarvadhuṣṭa Mruga Vaśankarī Sarva Satva Vaśankarī Śikāyai Vashat
Oṃ Trailokyamme Kavachāya Hūm
Oṃ Vaśamānāya Netratrayāya Vouśaṭ
Oṃ Svāhā Astrāyaphaṭ
Bhūrbhuvasvaromiti Digbandhaḥ |

Dhyānam

मातङ्गीं भूषिताङ्गीं विविध मनिधरामिन्दु सूर्याक्षियुग्मां
स्विद्यद्वक्त्रां कदम्ब प्रसवपरिलसद्वेणुकामात्र वीणाम् ।
बिम्बोष्ठीं रक्तवस्त्रां म्रुगमदतिलकामिन्दु रेखावतंसां
कर्णोद्यच्छङ्ख पत्रां कठिनकुचभराक्रान्त मध्यां नमामि ॥

Mātangīm Bhūṣitāngīm Vividha Manidharāmindu Sūryākṣiyugmām
Svidmadvaktrām Kadamba Prasavaparilasadvenukāmātra Vīnām |
Bimboṣṭhīm Raktavastrām Mrugamadatilakāmindu Rekhāvatamsām

Karṇodyacchankha Patrām Kaṭhinakuchabharākrānta Madhyām

Namāmi ||

Lam Pritviyātmikāyai Gandham Samarpayāmi |
Ham Ākashātmikāyai Puśpaiḥ Pūjayāmi |
Yam Vaivātmikāyai Dhūpam Āgrāpayāmi |
Ram Vahniyātmikāyai Dhīpam Dharśayāmi |
Vam Amrutātmikāyai Amrutam Mahāneivedhyam Nivedayāmi |
Sam Sarvātmikāyai Sarvopahāra Pūjām Samarpayāmi ||

Mātangī Mūla Mantras

Śrī Mātangī Mahā Mantrāḥ || (A little bit long mantra)

ॐ ऐं ह्रीं श्रीं ऐं क्लीं सौ: ॐ नमो भगवति श्री मातंगीश्वरि सर्वजन मनोहरि सर्वमुख रञ्जनि क्लीं ह्रीं श्रीं सर्वराज वशङ्करि सर्व स्त्री पुरुष वशङ्करि सर्व दुष्ट मृग वशङ्करि सर्व सत्व वशङ्करि सर्व लोक वशङ्करि त्रैलोक्यं मे वशमानय स्वाहा सौ: क्लीं ऐं श्रीं ह्रीं ऐं (स्वाहा) ||

Om Aim Hrīm Śrīm Aim Klīm Souḥ Om Namo Bhagavati Śrī Mātangīśwari Sarvajana Manohari Sarvamukha Ranjani Klīm Hrīm Śrīm Sarvaraaja Vaśankari Sarva Strī Puruṣa Vaśankari Sarva Duṣṭa Mruga Vaśankari Sarva Satva Vaśankari Sarva Loka Vaśankari Trailokyam Me Vaśamānaya Svāhā Souḥ Klīm Aim Śrīm Hrīm Aim (Svāhā) ||

Oṃ Namo Mātangīśvari Sarvajana Manohārinī Hrudayāya Namaḥ
Oṃ Sarvajana Mukharanjanī Klīm Sarvarāja Vaśankarī Sarva Strī Puruṣa

Vaśankarī Sirase Svāhā

Oṃ Sarvadhuṣṭa Mruga Vaśankarī Sarva Satva Vaśankarī Śikāyai Vashat
Oṃ Trailokyamme Kavachāya Hūm
Oṃ Vaśamānāya Netratrayāya Vouśaṭ
Oṃ Svāhā Astrāyaphaṭ
Bhūrbhuvasvaromiti Digvimogaḥ |

Dhyānam

मातङ्गीं भूषिताङ्गीं विविध मनिधरामिन्दु सूर्याक्षियुग्मां
स्विद्यद्वक्त्रां कदम्ब प्रसवपरिलसद्वेणुकामात्र वीणाम् ।
बिम्बोष्ठीं रक्तवस्त्रां म्रुगमदतिलकामिन्दु रेखावतंसां
कर्णोद्यच्छङ्ख पत्रां कठिनकुचभराक्रान्त मध्यां नमामि ॥

Mātangīm Bhūṣitāngīm Vividha Manidharāmindu Sūryākṣiyugmām
Svidmadvaktrām Kadamba Prasavaparilasadvenukāmātra Vīnām |
Bimboṣṭhīm Raktavastrām Mrugamadatilakāmindu Rekhāvatamsām
Karṇodyacchankha Patrām Kaṭhinakuchabharākrānta Madhyām

Namāmi ||

Lam Pritviyātmikāyai Gandham Samarpayāmi |
Ham Ākashātmikāyai Puśpaiḥ Pūjayāmi |
Yam Vaivātmikāyai Dhūpam Āgrāpayāmi |
Ram Vahniyātmikāyai Dhīpam Dharśayāmi |
Vam Amrutātmikāyai Amrutam Mahāneivedhyam Nivedayāmi |
Sam Sarvātmikāyai Sarvopahāra Pūjām Samarpayāmi ||

Some more important mantras with respect to *Mātangī Devī*;

1. *Aṣṭākśar Mātangī Mantra* (8 Syllables Mantra)

कामिनी रञ्जिनी स्वाहा || – *Kāmini Ranjini Svāhā ||*

2. *Daśakśar Mātangī Mantra* (10 Syllables Mantra)

ॐ ह्रीं क्लीं हूं मातंग्यै फट् स्वाहा ||

Oṃ Hrīm Klīm Hum Mātangyai Phat Svāhā ||

Mātangī's Daśākṣarī Mantra (10 syllabled mantra) has 7 words and 10 *akṣaras*. It takes the energy of the 7th *bhāva* (feelings of partnership) to the 10th house of career/ karma. *Matanga* is an elephant. Hence, it brings auspicious energy to one's work, as well as fame and good name. It suppresses the negative aspects of the Sun, which are ego and controlling nature. It supports vitality, speech and *dhī* (wisdom). *Mātangī mantras* cleanse the shadow from the solar power and heal shame. This *mantra* particularly removes the shame that is holding one back from career success.

3. *Mātangī Gāyatri Mantra*;

ॐ शुक्रप्रियायै च विद्महे श्रीकामेश्वर्यै च धीमहि तन्नः श्यामा प्रचोदयात् ||

Oṃ Śukrapriyāyai Ca Vidmahe Śrīkāmeśvaryai Ca Dhīmahi Tannaḥ Śyāmā

Prachodayāt ||

4. *Mātangī Mūla Mantra*;

ॐ ह्रीं ऐं भगवती मतंगेश्वरी श्रीं स्वाहा ||

Oṃ Hrīm Aim Bhagawati Mātangeśwari Śrīm Svāhā ||

This *Mātangī Mūla Mantra* is to attain everything positive one desire to have in life for a comfortable as well as luxurious survival.

Significance of Maa Matangi Mantra;

- Maa Matangi's Mantra helps fulfilling all the desires and wishes.
- One has, all the desires and wishes that are endless also gets fulfilled by regular chanting of Maa Matangi's Mantra.
- For wisdom and knowledge
- For the power of listening and grasping speech
- For improvement of attraction powers
- For skills to achieve worldly goals.

Matangi mantra chanting procedure;

- Wear white dhoti/saree and sit on a white mat facing East.
- Spread a white cloth over a wooden plank and on it place the Matangi Yantra or Sarva Karya Siddhi Yantra.
- Light a ghee lamp and chant the Moola Mantra for 40 minutes continuously or 11 mala.
- Offering blue and black thread to Matangi during puja and later wearing it on right hand will help in overcoming all kinds of scandals and bad name.
- This mudra can be practiced as often as required, for at least four minutes at a time. For maximum benefits, Matangi mudra can be practiced at least three times per day.

Only the most advanced tantric practitioners have access to the mantra's full potential (Sadhaks). There is no hard rule in normal recitation, but please do not chant the mantra with any unusual desire, as this can easily backfire.

There are numerous other mantras and stotrams dedicated to Devi *Mātangī*. However, the most popular one and that can be chant by the average person without any extreme tantric rituals is discussed here. Tantric practitioners' worship *Mātangī* for acquiring siddhis or supernatural powers.

One should be interested in the words of the teacher. The four – self, teacher, *mantra* and the God should be treated as same. One should not reprimand other religions. One should always think of himself as Lord *Shiva*. One should not rebuke ladies.

Shakta ideologies affirm – *Sri Devi* in the form of, *kundalini* energy has to be brought from *Mūlādhāra Chakra* to *Sahasrāra Chakra* through *Brahma Granti, Swādhiṣṭāna Chakra, Maṇipūraka Chakra, Vishnu Granti, Anāhata Chakra, Viśuddhi Chakra, Rudra Granti and Agjna Chakra*. At the *Sahasrāra Chakra*, in a *Sahasradala Padma* (1000 petalled lotus), the unison of *Shiva-Shakti* has to be inwardly looked (*antharmukha* – inwardly imagined) into and the devotee should be soaked in the rain of nectar (*Amruta Tara*).

Progress is the only in the life, if the grace of Devī is given to a devotee. Motivation comes naturally in the actions that are done. There is nothing he cannot achieve by her grace. She is interested in removing the sins of her devotees and showing him the right way. She lovingly bestows grace on those who are active, solid, and engaged in worship.

Let us all get initiated with these mantras from an appropriate guru and reap all the benefits.

*****

Śrī Mātangī Devī Yantram

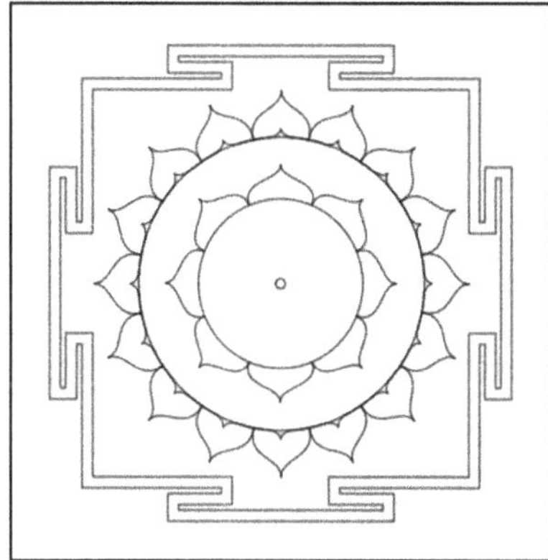

The structure of this yantra is like this – a Bindu or a dot in the middle, encircled, surrounded by 8 lotus petals, encircled again surrounded by 18 lotus petals. All these shapes are within 2 lined Bhoopuram. Almost every yantra, especially pertaining to various forms of Sri Devi, will have lotus petals.

A lotus in the Yantra represents the unconditional force of the Supreme Absolute truth. The lotus serves as a divine seat for Devas. It also represents detachment. It grows in the mud but never touches even a tinge of mud, representing detachment to the external forces (material world) and maintaining the original nature of pure and divine. The circle also known as the chakra stands for rotation which is central to the functioning of the macrocosmic progression. At the same time, the circle signified perfection and the peaceful creative void of the *Vishudha Chakra*.

Matangi Yantra contains the seed mantra of the goddess Matangi that blesses the worshippers with great powers, speech, harmonious family life and the peace of mind.

Matangi is herself described as the leftover or residue, symbolizing the Divine Self that is left over after all things perish. As the patron of left-over food offerings, she embodies inauspiciousness and the forbidden transgression of social norms. Matangi is often described as an outcaste and impure.

Significance of Matangi Yantra;

Worshipping Matangi Yantra is great for students, teachers, lecturers, actors, writers, poets, designers, artists, researchers, musicians, singers, performers, dancers, and those in artistic or creative fields. Goddess

Matangi is associated with pollution, inauspiciousness and the edge of Hindu society, which is represented in her most well-known form, known as Ucchishta-Chandalini or Uchchhishta-Matangini. She controls planet Mercury who rules intelligence. Matangi Yantra is good for getting wisdom and knowledge. It also relates to the power of listening and grasping speech and changing it back to knowledge and thought.

Here are some of the notable benefits of worshipping the *Mātangī yantra*;

- For the blessings of Maa Matangi.
- For the power of listening and grasping speech.
- For the improvements in music and art.
- For wisdom and knowledge.
- For skills to achieve worldly goals.
- For improvement of attraction powers.
- It can keep the negative energy away from your house.
- It destroys sins and past karma by Antahkarna Shuddhi.
- It is the most powerful Yantra for dhyana/ meditation and spiritual attainments.
- Helps in attaining mental peace and stability.
- Give liberation and devotional service.
- Promotes spiritual growth.
- Prevents mental & physical diseases.
- Prevents accidents and injury.
- Protects from death, accidents and theft.
- For freedom from diseases.
- Worshippers get relief from diseases, difficulties and dangers
- Boosts immunity and bestows longevity.
- Protects from ailments and improves health.

To get the maximum benefits the ***Mātangī*** *yantra* can be used as detailed below;

- Devotees can do Abhishek of Yantra once or twice a week as per convenience. Bath Yantra with rose-water or pure water. Possibly bathing the yantra with Gandaki river water/ gangajal is very special.
- Offer all abhisheka liquid one by one – Panchgavya (Water, Milk, Curd, Ghee, Honey) and any one Fruit Juice (Coconut water, Sugarcane Juice, Pomegranate Juice)
- Now wipe off yantra with a clean cloth and place it on pedestal
- First of all, place the yantra on a metal plate
- Sit facing east direction

- Apply tika of sandal paste on the yantra and place one Tulsi leaf on the yantra so the Tulsi rests on the yantra nicely
- Chant mantra of God/ goddess
- Show Dhoop/ Agarbatti to Yantra
- Offer some sweet, fruits and other eatable to the yantra
- One can convey one's wish aloud in front of the Yantra and pray.

Mātangī yantra is a spiritual device with specific geometric patterns that assist in bringing boons of the mighty goddess *Mātangī*. The yantra bolsters financial and spiritual well-being and supports the all-round development of a person. This yantra works like magic for uplifting life and keeps all sorts of enemies and poor influences away.

This yantra is highly significant as it brings the pious blessings of mighty goddess *Mātangī* in life. she is the powerful goddess who suspends the effect of negative energies and enemies. The commanding divinity *Mātangī* is affiliated as a manifestation of Goddess Shakti and Parvati, which enhances the impact of Bagalamukhi yantra to significant margins.

The *yantras* pertaining to most of the Gods are kept beneath or in front of the deities in temples. One *yantra* is a drawing of lines or circles or angles drawn in a prescribed measurements and ratios. There cannot be any deviation plus or minus. If a *mantra* is wrongly chant, it can result in negative impact or even end up with destruction. In the same manner, if there is an error in drawing of a *yantra*, it may end up in devastation.

In modern days, lot many worship *Śrī Chakra* in their houses. In general, this is very good. But many do it as a pride, some do it as a style and some with ignorance. But the customs are not strictly followed. Resultantly, they suffer for want of peace.

It is not enough if one wants to follow the bigger things. Exact rules prescribed by *Sastras* have to be clearly understood, absorbed and followed. These are time tested and handed over to us by our ancestors. It is our duty to stringently follow the same and get benefited. Definitely *Śrī Chakra* has been raised upto the sky by the *Sastras*. But the same *Sastras* have recommended lots of dos and don'ts, lots of processes. The approach that "I will do the pooja in my way" is not acceptable, the expected fruits will be missed. Sometimes that may result in negative angle.

One *yantra* is not a place of dwelling for the deity; It is the deity her/ himself. It is not an alternative to the deity. It is not a representation – it the deity. It is all the more apt in the case of *Śrī Devī*.

The radiations of the Yantra will bring the devotee and the Goddess into direct contact. The energy will soothe the inner peace and will gift with beauty, happiness and prosperity. These power lines attract the amiability of the Goddess opening doors for harmony and success.

This Yantra is a great cosmic conductor of energy, an antenna of Nature, a powerful tool for harmony, prosperity, success, good health, yoga and meditation! Yantras consist of a series of geometric patterns. The eyes and mind concentrate at the center of the yantra to achieve higher levels of consciousness. Yantras are usually made out of copper.

Let us all choose an appropriate guru, get initiated and worship this yantra to exploit maximum benefits.

*****

Śrī Mātaṅgī Dhyānam

Tālīdalenārpitakarṇabhūṣām Mādhvīmadodghūrṇitanetrapadmām |

Ghanastanīṃ Śambhuvadhūṃ Namāmi |

Taḍillatākāntimanarghyabhūṣām ‖ 1

Ghanaśyāmalāṅgīṃ Sthitāṃ Ratnapīṭhe

Śukasyoditaṃ Śṛṇvatīṃ Raktavastrām |

Surāpānamattāṃ Sarojasthitāṃ Śrīṃ

Bhaje Vallakīṃ Vādayantīṃ Mataṅgīm ‖ 2

Māṇikyābharaṇānvitāṃ Smitamukhīṃ Nīlotpalābhāṃ Varāṃ

Ramyālaktaka Liptapādakamalāṃ Netratrayollāsinīm |

Vīṇāvādanatatparāṃ Suranutāṃ Kīracchadaśyāmalāṃ

Mataṅgīṃ Śaśiśekharāmanubhaje Tāmbūlapūrṇānanām ‖ 3

Śyāmāṅgīṃ Śaśiśekharāṃ Trinayanāṃ Vedaiḥ Karairbibhratīṃ

Pāśaṃ Kheṭamathāṅkuśaṃ Dṛḍhamasiṃ Nāśāya Bhaktadviṣām |

Ratnālaṅkaraṇaprabhojvalatanuṃ Bhāsvatkirīṭāṃ Śubhāṃ

Mataṅgīṃ Manasā Smarāmi Sadayāṃ Sarvārthasiddhipradām ‖ 4

Devīṃ Ṣoḍaśavārṣikīṃ Śavagatāṃ Mādhvīrasāghūrṇitāṃ

Śyāmāṅgīmaruṇāmbarāṃ Pṛthukucāṃ Guñjāvalīśobhitām |

Hastābhyāṃ Dadhatīṃ Kapālamamalaṃ Tīkṣṇāṃ Tathā Kartrikāṃ

Dhyāyenmānasapaṅkaje Bhagavatīmucchiṣṭacāṇḍālinīm ‖ 5

Iti Śrī Mātaṅgī Dhyānam ‖

श्री मातङ्गी ध्यानम्

तालीदलेनार्पितकर्णभूषां माध्वीमदोद्धूर्णितनेत्रपद्माम्।
घनस्तनीं शम्भुवधूं नमामि। तडिल्लताकान्तिमनर्घ्यभूषाम् ॥ १

घनश्यामलाङ्गीं स्थितां रत्नपीठे शुकस्योदितं शृण्वतीं रक्तवस्त्राम्।
सुरापानमत्तां सरोजस्थितां श्रींभजे वल्लकीं वादयन्तीं मतङ्गीम् ॥ २

माणिक्याभरणान्वितां स्मितमुखीं नीलोत्पलाभां वरां
रम्यालक्तक लिप्तपादकमलां नेत्रत्रयोल्लासिनीम्।

वीणावादनतत्परां सुरनुतां कीरच्छदश्यामलां
मातङ्गीं शशिशेखरामनुभजे ताम्बूलपूर्णाननाम् ॥ ३

श्यामाङ्गीं शशिशेखरां त्रिनयनां वेदैः करैर्बिभ्रतीं
पाशं खेटमथाङ्कुशं दृढमसिं नाशाय भक्तद्विषाम्।
रत्नालङ्करणप्रभोज्ज्वलतनुं भास्वत्किरीटां शुभां
मातङ्गीं मनसा स्मरामि सदयां सर्वार्थसिद्धिप्रदाम् ॥ ४

देवीं षोडशवार्षिकीं शवगतां माध्वीरसाघूर्णितां
श्यामाङ्गीमरुणाम्बरां पृथुकुचां गुञ्जावलीशोभिताम्।
हस्ताभ्यां दधतीं कपालममलं तीक्ष्णां तथा कर्त्रिकां
ध्यायेन्मानसपङ्कजे भगवतीमुच्छिष्टचाण्डालिनीम् ॥ ५

इति श्री मातङ्गीध्यानम् ॥

*****

Śrī Mātaṅgī Kavacaṃ

*Asya Śrīmātaṅgīkavacamantrasya Mahāyogīśvararṣiḥ
Anuṣṭup Chandaḥ Śrīrājamātaṅgīśvarī
Śrīmātaṅgī Prasāda Siddhyarthe Jape Viniyogaḥ ‖*

*Nīlotpalapratīkāśāmañjanādrisamaprabhām |
Vīṇāhastāṃ Gānaratāṃ Madhupātraṃ Ca Bibhratīm ‖ 1*

*Sarvālaṅkārasaṃyuktāṃ Śyāmalāṃ Madaśālinīm |
Namāmi Rājamātaṅgīṃ Bhaktānāmiṣṭadāyinīm ‖ 2*

*Evaṃ Dhyātvā Japennityaṃ Kavacaṃ Sarvakāmadam |
Śikhāṃ Me Śyāmalā Pātu Mātaṅgī Me Śiro'vatu ‖ 3*

*Lalāṭaṃ Pātu Caṇḍālī Bhruvau Me Madaśālinī |
Karṇau Me Pātu Mātaṅgī Śaṅkhau Kuṇḍalaśobhitā ‖ 4*

*Netre Me Pātu Raktākṣī Nāsikāṃ Pātu Me Śivā |
Gaṇḍau Me Pātu Deveśī Oṣṭhau Bimbaphalādharā ‖ 5*

*Jihvāṃ Me Pātu Vāgīśī Dantān Kalyāṇakāriṇī |
Pātu Me Rājamātaṅgī Vadanaṃ Sarvasiddhidā ‖ 6*

*Kaṇṭhaṃ Me Pātu Hṛdyāṅgī Vīṇāhastā Karau Mama |
Hṛdayaṃ Pātu Me Lakṣmīrnābhiṃ Me Viśavanāyikā ‖ 7*

*Mama Pārśvadvayaṃ Pātu Sūkṣmamadhyā Maheśvarī |
Śukaśyāmā Kaṭiṃ Pātu Guhyaṃ Me Lokamohinī ‖ 8*

*Ūrū Me Pātu Bhadrāṅgī Jānunī Pātu Śāṅkarī |
Jaṅghādvayaṃ Me Lokeśī Pādau Me Parameśvarī ‖ 9*

*Prāgādidikṣu Māṃ Pātu Sarvaiśvaryapradāyinī |
Romāṇi Pātu Me Kṛṣṇā Bhāryāṃ Me Bhavavallabhā ‖ 10*

*Śaṅkarī Sarvataḥ Pātu Mama Sarvavaśaṅkarī |
Mahālakṣmīrmama Dhanaṃ Viśvamātā Sutān Mama ‖ 11*

Śrīmātaṅgīśvarī Nityaṃ Māṃ Pātu Jagadīśvarī |

Mātaṅgī Kavacaṃ Nityaṃ Ya Etatprapaṭhennaraḥ || 12

Sukhitvaṃ Sakalān Lokān Dāsībhūtānkarotyasau |

Prāpnoti Mahatīṃ Kāntiṃ Bhavetkāma Śataprabhaḥ || 13

Labhate Mahatīṃ Lakṣmīṃ Trailokye Cāpi Durlabhām |

Aṇimādyaṣṭasiddhaṃ Yaṃ Sañcaratyeṣa Mānavaḥ || 14

Sarvavidyānidhirayaṃ Bhavedvāgīśvareśvaraḥ |

Brahmarākṣasavetālabhūtapreta Piśācakaiḥ || 15

Jvalanvahniriva Śasyairveśyate Bhūtapūrvakaiḥ |

Paramaṃ Yogamāpnoti Divyajñānaṃ Samaśnute || 16

Putrān Pautrānavāpnoti Śrīrvidyākānti Saṃyutān |

Tadbhāryā Durbhagā Cāpi Kāntyā Ratisamābhavet || 17

Sarvān Kāmānavāpnoti Mahābhogāṃśca Durlabhān |

Bhuktimante Samāpnoti Sākṣātparaśivo Bhavet || 18

Iti Śrī Mahā''gamarahasye Dattātreya Vāmadeva Saṃvāde
Saptama Paricchede Śrī Mātaṅgī Kavacam Sampūrṇam |

श्री मातङ्गी कवचम्

अस्य श्रीमातङ्गीकवचमन्त्रस्य महायोगीश्वरऋषिः
अनुष्टुप् छन्दः श्रीराजमातङ्गीश्वरीदेवता:
श्री मातङ्गी प्रसाद सिद्ध्यर्थे जपे विनियोगः ॥

नीलोत्पलप्रतीकाशामञ्जनाद्रिसमप्रभाम् ।
वीणाहस्तां गानरतां मधुपात्रं च बिभ्रतीम् ॥ १

सर्वालङ्कारसंयुक्तां श्यामलां मदशालिनीम्
नमामि राजमातङ्गीं भक्तानामिष्टदायिनीम् ॥ २

एवं ध्यात्वा जपेन्नित्यं कवचं सर्वकामदम्
शिखां मे श्यामला पातु मातङ्गी मे शिरोऽवतु ॥ ३

ललाटं पातु चण्डाली भ्रुवौ मे मदशालिनी।
कर्णौ मे पातु मातङ्गी शङ्खौ कुण्डलशोभिता ॥ ४

नेत्रे मे पातु रक्ताक्षी नासिकां पातु मे शिवा।
गण्डौ मे पातु देवेशी ओष्ठौ बिम्बफलाधरा ॥ ५

जिह्वां मे पातु वागीशी दन्तान् कल्याणकारिणी।
पातु मे राजमातङ्गी वदनं सर्वसिद्धिदा ॥ ६

कण्ठं मे पातु ह्रद्याङ्गी वीणाहस्ता करौ मम।
हृदयं पातु मे लक्ष्मीर्नाभिं मे विशवनायिका ॥ ७

मम पार्श्वद्वयं पातु सूक्ष्ममध्या महेश्वरी।
शुकश्यामा कटिं पातु गुह्यं मे लोकमोहिनी ॥ ८

ऊरू मे पातु भद्राङ्गी जानुनी पातु शाङ्करी।
जङ्घाद्वयं मे लोकेशी पादौ मे परमेश्वरी ॥ ९

प्रागादिदिक्षु मां पातु सर्वैश्वर्यप्रदायिनी।
रोमाणि पातु मे कृष्णा भार्यां मे भववल्लभा ॥ १०

शङ्करी सर्वतः पातु मम सर्ववशङ्करी।
महालक्ष्मीर्मम धनं विश्वमाता सुतान् मम ॥ ११

श्रीमातङ्गीश्वरी नित्यं मां पातु जगदीश्वरी।
मातङ्गी कवचं नित्यं य एतत्प्रपठेन्नरः ॥ १२

सुखित्वं सकलान् लोकान् दासीभूतान्करोत्यसौ
प्राप्नोति महतीं कान्तिं भवेत्काम शतप्रभः ॥ १३

लभते महतीं लक्ष्मीं त्रैलोक्ये चापि दुर्लभाम् ।
अणिमाद्यष्टसिद्धं यं सञ्चरत्येष मानवः ॥ १४

सर्वविद्यानिधिरयं भवेद्वागीश्वरेश्वरः।
ब्रह्मराक्षसवेतालभूतप्रेत पिशाचकैः ॥ १५

ज्वलन्वह्निरिव शस्यैर्वेश्यते भूतपूर्वकैः।
परमं योगमाप्नोति दिव्यज्ञानं समश्नुते ॥ १६

पुत्रान् पौत्रानवाप्नोति श्रीर्विद्याकान्ति संयुतान्।
तद्द्वार्या दुर्भगा चापि कान्त्या रतिसमाभवेत् ॥ १७

सर्वान् कामानवाप्नोति महाभोगां श्च दुर्लभान्। महाभोगान् सुदुर्लभान्
भुक्तिमन्ते समाप्नोति साक्षात्परशिवो भवेत् ॥ १८

इति श्री महाऽऽगमरहस्ये दत्तात्रेय वामदेव संवादे सप्तम परिच्छेदे श्री मातङ्गी
कवचम् सम्पूर्णम्।

*****

Śrī Mātangī Sumukhī Kavacam

Śrī Gaṇeśāya Namaḥ | Śrī Pārvatyuvāca |

Devadeva Mahādeva Sṛṣṭisaṃhārakāraka |
Mātaṅgyāḥ Kavacaṃ Brūhi Yadi Sneho'sti Te Mayi || 1

Śrī Śiva Uvāca |

Atyantagopanaṃ Guhyaṃ Kavacaṃ Sarvakāmadam |
Tava Prītyā Mayā''khyātaṃ Nānyeṣu Kathyate Śubhe || 2

Śapathaṃ Kuru Me Devi Yadi Kiñcitprakāśase |
Anayā Sadṛśī Vidyā Na Bhūtā Na Bhaviṣyati || 3

Śavāsanāṃ Raktavastrāṃ Yuvatīṃ Sarvasiddhidām |
Evaṃ Dhyātvā Mahādevīṃ Paṭhetkavacamuttamam || 4

Ucchiṣṭaṃ Rakṣatu Śiraḥ Śikhāṃ Caṇḍālinī Tataḥ |
Sumukhī Kavacaṃ Rakṣeddevī Rakṣatu Cakṣuṣī || 5

Mahāpiśācinī Pāyānnāsikāṃ Hrīṃ Sadā'vatu |
Ṭhaḥ Pātu Kaṇṭhadeśaṃ Me Ṭhaḥ Pātu Hṛdayaṃ Tathā || 6

Ṭho Bhujau Bāhumūle Ca Sadā Rakṣatu Caṇḍikā |
Aiṃ Ca Rakṣatu Pādau Me Sauḥ Kukṣiṃ Sarvataḥ Śivā || 7

Aiṃ Hrīṃ Kaṭideśaṃ Ca Āṃ Hrīṃ Sandhiṣu Sarvadā |
Jyeṣṭhamātaṅgyaṅgulirme Aṅgulyagre Namāmi Ca || 8

Ucchiṣṭacāṇḍāli Māṃ Pātu Trailokyasya Vaśaṅkarī |
Śive Svāhā Śarīraṃ Me Sarvasaubhāgyadāyinī || 9

Ucchiṣṭacāṇḍāli Mātaṅgi Sarvavaśaṅkari Namaḥ |
Svāhā Stanadvayaṃ Pātu Sarvaśatruvināśinī || 10

Atyantagopanaṃ Devi Devairapi Sudurlabham |
Bhraṣṭebhyaḥ Sādhakebhyo'pi Draṣṭavyaṃ Na Kadācana || 11

Dattena Siddhihāniḥ Syātsarvathā Na Prakāśyatām |

Ucchiṣṭena Baliṃ Datvā Śanau Vā Maṅgale Niśi || 12

Rajasvalābhagaṃ Spṛṣṭvā Japenmantraṃ Ca Sādhakaḥ |

Rajasvalāyā Vastreṇa Homaṃ Kuryātsadā Sudhīḥ || 13

Siddhavidyā Ito Nāsti Niyamo Nāsti Kaścana |

Aṣṭasahasraṃ Japenmantraṃ Daśāṃśaṃ Havanādikam || 14

Bhūrjapatre Likhitvā Ca Raktasūtreṇa Veṣṭayet |

Prāṇapratiṣṭhāmantreṇa Jīvanyāsaṃ Samācaret || 15

Svarṇamadhye Tu Saṃsthāpya Dhārayeddakṣiṇe Kare |

Sarvasiddhirbhavettasya Acirātputravānbhavet || 16

Strībhirvāmakare Dhāryaṃ Bahuputrā Bhavettadā |

Vandyā Vā Kākavandyā Vā Mṛtavatsā Ca Sāṅganā || 17

Jīvadvatsā Bhavetsāpi Samṛddhirbhavati Dhruvam |

Śaktipūjāṃ Sadā Kuryācchivābaliṃ Pradāpayet || 18

Idaṃ Kavacamajñātvā Mātaṅgī Yo Japetsadā |

Tasya Siddhirna Bhavati Puraścaraṇalakṣataḥ || 19

|| Iti Śrī Rudra Yāmale Tantre Mātaṅgī Sumukhī Kavacaṃ Samāptam ||

श्री मातङ्गी सुमुखी कवचम्

श्री गणेशाय नमः | श्री पार्वत्युवाच |

देवदेव महादेव सृष्टिसंहारकारक।

मातङ्ग्याः कवचं ब्रूहि यदि स्नेहोऽस्ति ते मयि || १

श्री शिव उवाच |

अत्यन्तगोपनं गुह्यां कवचं सर्वकामदम्।

तव प्रीत्या मयाऽऽख्यातं नान्येषु कथ्यते शुभे || २

शपथं कुरु मे देवि यदि किञ्चित्प्रकाशसे।

अनया सदृशी विद्या न भूता न भविष्यति || ३

शवासनां रक्तवस्त्रां युवतीं सर्वसिद्धिदाम्।
एवं ध्यात्वा महादेवीं पठेत्कवचमुत्तमम् ॥ ४

उच्छिष्टं रक्षतु शिरः शिखां चण्डालिनी ततः।
सुमुखी कवचं रक्षेद्देवी रक्षतु चक्षुषी ॥ ५

महापिशाचिनी पायान्नासिकां ह्रीं सदाऽवतु।
ठः पातु कण्ठदेशं मे ठः पातु हृदयं तथा ॥ ६

ठो भुजौ बाहुमूले च सदा रक्षतु चण्डिका।
ऐं च रक्षतु पादौ मे सौः कुक्षिं सर्वतः शिवा ॥ ७

ऐं ह्रीं कटिदेशं च आं ह्रीं सन्धिषु सर्वदा।
ज्येष्ठमातङ्ग्यङ्गुलिर्मे अङ्गुल्यग्रे नमामि च ॥ ८

उच्छिष्टचाण्डालि मां पातु त्रैलोक्यस्य वशङ्करी।
शिवे स्वाहा शरीरं मे सर्वसौभाग्यदायिनी ॥ ९

उच्छिष्टचाण्डालि मातङ्गि सर्ववशङ्करि नमः।
स्वाहा स्तनद्वयं पातु सर्वशत्रुविनाशिनी ॥ १०

अत्यन्तगोपनं देवि देवैरपि सुदुर्लभम्।
भ्रष्टेभ्यः साधकेभ्योऽपि द्रष्टव्यं न कदाचन ॥ ११

दत्तेन सिद्धिहानिः स्यात्सर्वथा न प्रकाश्यताम्।
उच्छिष्टेन बलिं दत्त्वा शनौ वा मङ्गले निशि ॥ १२

रजस्वलाभगं स्पृष्ट्वा जपेन्मन्त्रं च साधकः।
रजस्वलाया वस्त्रेण होमं कुर्यात्सदा सुधीः ॥ १३

सिद्धविद्या इतो नास्ति नियमो नास्ति कश्चन।
अष्टसहस्रं जपेन्मन्त्रं दशांशं हवनादिकम् ॥ १४

भूर्जपत्रे लिखित्वा च रक्तसूत्रेण वेष्टयेत्।
प्राणप्रतिष्ठामन्त्रेण जीवन्यासं समाचरेत् ॥ १५

स्वर्णमध्ये तु संस्थाप्य धारयेद्दक्षिणे करे।
सर्वसिद्धिर्भवेत्तस्य अचिरात्पुत्रवान्भवेत् ॥ १६

स्त्रीभिर्वामकरे धार्यं बहुपुत्रा भवेत्तदा।
वन्ध्या वा काकवन्ध्या वा मृतवत्सा च साङ्गना ॥ १७

जीवद्वत्सा भवेत्सापि समृद्धिर्भवति ध्रुवम्।
शक्तिपूजां सदा कुर्याच्छिवाबलिं प्रदापयेत् ॥ १८

इदं कवचमज्ञात्वा मातङ्गी यो जपेत्सदा।
तस्य सिद्धिर्न भवति पुरश्चरणलक्षतः ॥ १९

॥ इति श्रीरुद्रयामले तन्त्रे मातङ्गीसुमुखीकवचं समाप्तम् ॥

*****

Śrī Mātangī Stutiḥ

Mātaṅgīṃ Navayāvakārdra Caraṇāmullāsi Kṛṣṇāṃśukāṃ
Vīṇāpustaka Dhāriṇīṃ Natakucāṃ Muktāpravālāvalim |
Śyāmāṅgīṃ Śaśiśaṅkhakuṇḍaladharāṃ Dantaprabhāsusmitāṃ
Ākarṇālaka-Veṇi-Kañja-Nayanāṃ Dhyāyecchuka Śyāmalām || 1

Karpūra Śobhi Karṇābharaṇābhirāmāṃ Māṇikyabhūṣāṃ

Sumukhāravindām |

Hālāmadāghūrṇita Locanābhāṃ Bālāṃ Bhaje Bālatamāla Nīlām || 2

Kastūrī Tilakābhirāma Racitā Karpūra Tāṭaṅkinī
Bālā Nīlaviśālacāruvadanā Prālambidhammillakā |
Hārodañcita Pīvarastanataṭī Hālāmadollāsinī
Śyāmā Kācana Mohinī Vijayate Cañcatprapañcīkṛtā || 3

Aṃśe Veṇīṃ Cikurakusumāṃ Cūlikāṃ Nīlacelāṃ
Muktābhūṣāṅkarayugalatāṃ Vallakīṃ Vādayantīm |
Mādhvīmattāṃ Madhukara Ninadāṃ Śyāmalāṃ Komalāṅgīṃ
Mātaṅgīṃ Tāṃ Sakalaphaladāṃ Santataṃ Bhāvayāmi || 4

Vīṇā Pustaka Dhāriṇīṃ Smitamukhīṃ Tālīdalākalpita
Sphāyatkuṇḍalabhūṣaṇāṃ Kuvalayaśyāmāṃ Kuraṅgīdṛśīm |
Uttuṅgastanakumbhayugma Vilasatkāśmīrapatrāvalīṃ
Mātaṅgīṃ Padakairavaṃ Navacaraccandrātapatrāmbhaje || 5

Dhyāyehaṃ Ratnapīṭheśukakularaṇitaṃ Śṛṇvatīṃ Śyāmalāṅgīṃ
Nyastaikāghriṃ Saroje Śaśiśakaladharāṃ Vallakīṃvādayantīm |
Kalhnārābaddhamālāṃ Niyamitavilasaccūlikāṃ Raktavastrāṃ
Mātaṅgīṃ Śaṅkhapātrāṃ Madhumadavivaśāṃ Citrakodbhāsibhālām || 6

Ārādhyamānāścaraṇāṃ Pibantobrahmādayo Viśruta Kīrtimāpuḥ |
Anyeparaṃ Vāgvibhavaṃ Munīndrā Parāṃśriyaṃ Bhaktibhareṇa

Cānye || 7

Namāmi Devīṃ Navacandramauliṃ Mātaṅginīṃ Candrakalāvataṃsām |
Āmnāya Vākyaiḥ Pratipādanārthe Prabodhayantīṃ Śukamādareṇa || 8

Mātaṅgalīlā Gamane'pi Bhaktyā Śiñjānamañjīramiṣādbhajanti |

Mātastvadīyaṃ Caraṇāravindamakṛtrimāṇāṃ Vacasāṃ Niricchāḥ | 9

Parādhikāśiñjitanūpurābhyāṃ Kṛtāgamāṃ Padavīṃ Tāṃ Padābhyām |

Āsphoṭayantīṃ Karavallakīṃ Tāṃ Mātaṅginīṃ Maddhṛdaye Bhajāmi || 10

Nīlāṃśukābaddhanitambabimbāṃ Nālīdalenānatakarṇabhūṣām |

Madhye Madāghūrṇita Netrapadmāṃ Mātaṅginīṃ Śambhuvadhūṃ

Namāmi || 11

Nīlotpalānāṃ Śriyamāvahantīṃ Kāñcyā Kaṭākṣaikaśubhāṃ Karāṇām |

Kadamba Mālāṅkitakeśapāśāṃ Mātaṅgakanyāṃ Hṛdibhāvayāmi || 12

Stutyānayā Śaṅkaradharmapatnīṃ Mātaṅginīṃ Vāgadhidevatāṃ Tām |

Svargaṃgatiṃ Bhaktajanā Manuṣyāḥ Parāṃ Śriyaṃ Bhakti Bhareṇa

Cānye || 13

Kucakumbha Taṭanyasta Maṇivīṇāmadālasām |

Śyāmāṃ Vāmāṅka Vinyasta Mālikāṃ Bālikāmbhaje || 14

Abdhauyāti Sarojacāmaramaruddodhūyamānālakā
Cūlīcumbita Cārucampaka Dalāgaurī Madollāsinī |
Nālī Bāla Palāśa Karṇavilasatkallola Kālicchaṭā
Kālī Sācalakanyakā Vijayate Maccitta Padmāsanā || 15

Vīṇānartita Pāṇi Paṅkajayugāmāśoṇabimbādharāṃ
Veṇī Baddha Kadamba Puṣpa Kalikāmeṇī Vilolekṣaṇām |
Śroṇī Lamba Virājamāna Sujapā Śoṇāmbarālaṅkṛtāṃ
Eṇāṅkārka Vibhūṣaṇāṃ Kalayatāṃ Bhillīṃ Purandhrīmbhaje || 16

Tamāla Śyāmāṅgīmatimadhura Saṅgīta Niratāṃ
Kṛpāpūrṇāpāṅgīṃ Kucabhara Natāṅgīṃ Smitamukhīm |
Bhramadbhrūbhaṅge Te Vividha Kusumaistairivayutāṃ
Bhaje'haṃ Mātaṅgīṃ Madaparavaśāṅgīmanudinam || 17

Sukaśyāmāṃ Śyāmāṃ Śukaraṇita Kallola Niratāṃ
Vipañcī Sañcārāruṇa Karasarojāṃ Bhagavatīm |
Madāsaktāmuktā Phalaguṇitahārastanataṭāṃ
Kṛpāvāsāmīśāmatirucirahāsāṃ Bhajaśivām || 18

Raktāravinda Makaranda Rasānulepāṃ

Pānapramatta Calitāli Kulālakāntām |

Vīṇāmanoharaninādavinodaśīlāṃ

Vāṇīṃ Bhaje Śukanibhāṃ Madhupāna Lolām || 19

Saṅgīta Nāda Rasapānaghanārdradehāṃ

Netrāravinda Karuṇāmṛtavāhinīṃ Tām |

Raktāravinda Viniveśitavāmapādāṃ

Śyāmāṃ Mataṅgatanayāṃ Manasā Smarāmi || 20

Kastūrikā Śyāmala Komalāṅgīṃ Kādambarīpānamadālasāṅgīm |

Vāmastanāliṅgitaratnavīṇāṃ Mātaṅgakanyāṃ Manasāsmarāmi || 21

Smaretprathama Puṣpiṇīṃ Rudhirabindu Nīlāmbarāṃ

Gṛhītamadhupātrikāṃ Madavighūrṇa Netrojvalām |

Ghanastanabharānatāṃ Galita Cūlikāṃ Śyāmalāṃ

Karasphurita Vallakīṃ Vimalaśaṅkha Tāṭaṅkinīm || 22

Māṇikyavīṇāmupalālayantīṃ Madālasāṃ Mañjula Vāgvilāsām |

Māhendra Nīlotpala Komalāṅgīṃ Mātaṅga Kanyāṃ Manasāsmarāmi ||23

Kuvalaya Dalanīlāṅgīṃ Kuvalaya Cārucañcalāpāṅgīm |

Kuvalaya Samottamāṅgīṃ Kuvalaya Cūlīṃ Namāmi Mātaṅgīm || 24

Śyāmā Kuvalayaśyāmā Nāmakalādhāma Bhāgasthā |

Madhupānaratāratāpāyādvāṇī Vīṇāvinodaviśrāntā || 25

Tamālapatrāñcitanīlagātrīṃ Tālīdalenārpita Karṇapatrām |

Saptasvarālāpaviśeṣatantrīṃ Bālāmbhaje Bhavyamataṅgaputrīm || 26

Nityānupātrārpitasatkalābhāṃ Nīlāmbarodbhāsinitambabimbām |

Bhaktoparinyastakṛpāvalambāṃ Bālāṃ Bhaje Bhavyaguṇāṃ

Madambām || 27

Śivatanubhavasaṅgaṃ Śivacūlī Lola Cañcalotsaṅgam |

Kalimala Tanumaṅgaṃ Kalaye Mātaṅgakanyakāpāṅgam || 28

Kalādhīśottaṃsāṃ Karakalita Vīṇāhitarasāṃ

Kalindāpatyābhāṃ Karakalita Hṛdayāṃ Raktavasanām |

Purāṇīṃ Kalyāṇīṃ Puramathanapuṇyodayakalā-
Madhīrākṣīṃ Vande Bahukusumasannaddhakabarīm ‖ 29

Kalodañcadveṇīṃ Kanakadalatāṭaṅkamahitāṃ
Stanābhyāmānamrāṃ Taruṇamihirāṃ Raktavasanām ǀ
Mahākalyāṇīṃ Tanmadhumadabharāṃ Tāmranayanāṃ
Tamālaśyāmāṃ Nastavakayatu Saukhyānisatatam ‖ 30

Karāñcitavipañcikāṃ Kalitacandracūḍāmaṇiṃ
Kapolavilasanmahākanakapatra Tāṭaṅkinīm ǀ
Tapaḥ Phalamihāśritāṃ Taruṇabhāsaraktāmbarāṃ
Tamāladalamecakāṃ Taruṇalocanāmāśraye ‖ 31

Mātā Marakataśyāmā Mātaṅgī Madhuśālinī ǀ
Kaṭākṣayatu Kalyāṇī Kadambavanavāsinī ‖ 32

Jagadānandakalaṅkakaṇṭhamālā Kabarī Veṣṭana Kāṅkṣaṇīya Guñjā ǀ
Kurutāṃ Duritādvimokṣaṇam Me Tuhinā Bhillikuṭumbinī Bhavānī ‖ 33

Vāme Vismṛtaśālinī Stanataṭe Vinyasta Vīṇāmukhaṃ
Tantrītāla Virāviṇīmasakalairāsphālayantī Nakhaiḥ ǀ
Ardhonmīlita Locanaṃ Savilasadgrīvaṃ Mukhaṃvibhratī
Śyāmā Kācana Mohinī Vijayate Mātaṅgakanyāmayi ‖ 34

Pratiṣṭhā Payodhara Prasāra Karapaṅkajaṃ Balabhidaḥ ǀ
Kadamba Vanamālikaṃ Śaśikalā Samudbhāsitam ‖ 35

Mataṅga Kulanandinī Manasi Me Muhujṛmbhatām ǀ
Samasta Sukhadāyinī Taruṇapatra Tāṭaṅkinī ‖ 36

Lākṣārāga Kapolapallavaratāmāpīna Tuṅgastanīṃ
Karpūrojvalacāruśaṅkhavalayāṃ Kāśmīraraktāṃśukām ǀ
Tantrītālasapāṭalāṃ Gulidalāṃ Vandāmahe Mātaraṃ
Mātaṅgīṃ Madamantharāṃ Marakataśyāmāṃ Manohāriṇīm ‖ 37

Srastaṃ Ketakidāmabhirvalayitaṃ Dhammillamābibhratī
Tālīpatra Puṭāntaraiḥ Samanataistāṭaṅkinī Mauktikaiḥ ǀ
Bhāle Kalpataroḥ Prasūnavilasadṛṣṭvaiva Sammohinī
Kāñcī Dāmavatī Vijayate Vīṇāsavādānanā ‖ 38

Mātaṅgīṁ Bhūṣitāṅgīṁ Madhumadamuditāṁ Ghūrṇamānākṣiyugmāṁ
Svidyadvaktrāṁ Kadamba Pravilasadveṇikāmatta Vīṇām |
Bimboṣṭhīṁ Raktavastrāṁ Mṛgamada Tilakāmindurekhāvataṁsāṁ
Karṇodyacchaṅkhapatrāṁ Karakalitaśukāṁ Naumi Tuṅgastanīṁ Tām || 39

Unmīlidyāvakādyānniviḍamadabharodvignabhālālakāśāṁ
Ratnagaiveyahārāṅgada Kaṭilasatsūtra Mañjīraghoṣām |
Āniyārthānabhīṣṭān Smitamadhuradṛśā Sādhikaṁ Tarpayantīṁ
Dhyāyeddevīṁ Śukābhāṁśukamakhilakalārūpamasyāścapārśve || 40

Veṇīmūla Vilāsitendu Śakalāṁ Vīṇāninādapriyāṁ
Kṣoṇīpāla Surendra Pannagagaṇai Rārādhitāṅghridvayām |
Eṇīcañcalalocanāṁ Suvadanāṁ Vāṇīṁ Purāṇojvalāṁ
Śroṇībhārabharālasāmanimiṣāṁ Paśyāmi Viśveśvarīm || 41

Kucakalaśaniṣaṇṇavīṇāṁ Kalamadhuradhvani Kampitottamāṅgīm |
Marakatamaṇibhāgamecakābhāṁmadamavirodhamanasvinīmupāse ||42

Tālīdalollasitakomalakarṇapālīṁ Phālāntarācikurāmatinīlaveṇīm |
Vakṣojapīṭhanihitojvalacāruvīṇāṁ Śyāmāṁ Namāmi Madirāruṇa
Netrayugmām || 43

Madhyebaddhamayūkhapicchanikarāṁ Śyāmāṁprabālādharāṁ
Bhṛṅgīvādanatatparāṁ Sunayanāṁ Mūrdhālakairbarbarām |
Guñjāhāradharāṁ Samunnatakucāṁ Candrānanāṁ Śāmbhavīṁ
Bhillī Veṣadharāṁ Namāmi Śabarī Tāmekavīrāṁ Parām || 44

Lasatguñjāhāra Stanabhara Samunmadhyalaṭikā
Mudañcatsvedāmbhaḥ Kṣaṇagaṇita Phenodgama Rucim |
Śivaṁ Śāntaṁ Pātrapravaṇamṛgayākārakaraṇaṁ
Śivāmambajñātiṁ Caraṇamahamanvemiśaraṇam || 45

Naṭadaguñjā Pañjābharaṇakiraṇāṁ Raktavasanāṁ
Japākarṇābhūṣāṁ Śikhivarakṣakalāpāmbaravatīm |
Nadajjhallī Vallīnavakisalayaistāṁ Parivṛtāṁ
Navāmohārūḍhāṁ Kuṭilakabarīṁ Mohaśabarīm || 46

Gale Guñjā Puñjāvali Mapi Ca Karṇe Śikhiśikhāṁ
Śiro Raṅge Nṛtyatkanakadala Dūba Mañjuladalam |

Dhanurvāme Cāpe Śaramaparapāṇau Nidadhatīṃ
Nitambe Barhāliṃ Kuṭilakabarīṃ Naumi Śabarīṃ || 47

Vīṇāvādana Nirataṃ Tallīlā Baddhagīta Vāmakucam |
Śyāmala Komala Gātraṃ Pāṭalanayanaṃ Paraṃ Bhajedhāma || 48

Aṅkita Pāṇicatuṣṭyamaṅkuśapāśekṣu Cāpaśakalam |
Śaṅkara Jitetyamitraṃ Paṅkajanetraṃ Paraṃ Bhajedhāma || 49

Karakalita Kesārālānukāreyaṃ Kucakalaśā Jayate Jagatām |
Mātāmātaṅgī Maṅgesvāyatanā || 50

Mudākarakadamba Kānane Kanakamaṣṭapātrasthite
Lasanmaṇimayāsane Sahacarībhirārādhitām |
Lasatkanakakaṅkaṇāṃ Rajatamañjumañjīrakāṃ
Jagajjanavimohinīṃ Japavidhau Smaredambikām || 51

Akṛśā Kucayorvilagne Vipulaṃ Vakṣasi Vistṛtaṃ Nitambe |
Aruṇādharamāvirastucitte Karuṇāśāli Kapāli Bhāgadheyam || 52

Vīṇātāla Vinodagīta Niratāṃ Nīlāṃśukollāsinīm |
Bimboṣṭhīṃ Navayāvakārdra Caraṇāmākīrṇa Keśojvalām || 53

Hṛdyāveśita Śaṅkhakuṇḍaladharāṃ Māṇikyabhūṣojvalāṃ
Mātaṅgīṃ Praṇato'smi Susmitamukhāṃ Devīṃśukaśyāmalām || 54

Divyahālāmadonmattāṃ Divyabhūṣaṇabhūṣitām |
Divyagandharvakanyābhissamārādhitapādukām || 55

Divyasiṃhāsanāsīnāṃ Śukavīṇālasatkarām |
Saṅgīta Mātṛkāṃ Vande Varadāṃ Susmitānanām || 56

Stutiṣu Navadeva Devi Vividha Kavi Vilohitamatirbhavati |
Nihitamatiryadyapi Māmapetacetībhavati Stotuṃ Vilobhayati || 57

Sādhyākṣaragarbhita Pañcanava Ityakṣarātmike Jaganmātaḥ |
Bhagavati Mātaṅgeśvari Namastubhyaṃ Mahādevi || 58

Ityumā Sāhacaryā Bhagavān Mātaṅgarṣipraṇītā Iyaṃ Stutiḥ Samāptā |

श्री मातङ्गी स्तुतिः

मातङ्गीं नवयावकार्द्र चरणामुल्लासि कृष्णांशुकां
वीणापुस्तक धारिणीं नतकुचां मुक्ताप्रवालावलिम्।
श्यामाङ्गीं शशिशङ्खकुण्डलधरां दन्तप्रभासुस्मितां
आकर्णालक-वेणि-कज्ज-नयनां ध्यायेच्छुक श्यामलाम्॥ १

कर्पूर शोभि कर्णाभरणाभिरामां माणिक्यभूषां सुमुखारविन्दाम्
हालामदाघूर्णित लोचनाभां बालां भजे बालतमाल नीलाम्॥ २

कस्तूरी तिलकाभिराम रचिता कर्पूर ताटङ्किनी
बाला नीलविशालचारुवदना प्रालम्बिधम्मिल्लका।
हारोदञ्चित पीवरस्तनतटी हालामदोल्लासिनी
श्यामा काचन मोहिनी विजयते चञ्चत्प्रपञ्चीकृता॥ ३

अंशे वेणीं चिकुरकुसुमां चूलिकां नीलचेलां
मुक्ताभूषाङ्करयुगलतां वल्लकीं वादयन्तीम्।
माध्वीमत्तां मधुकर निनदां श्यामलां कोमलाङ्गीं
मातङ्गीं तां सकलफलदां सन्ततं भावयामि॥ ४

वीणा पुस्तक धारिणीं स्मितमुखीं तालीदलाकल्पित
स्फायत्कुण्डलभूषणां कुवलयश्यामां कुरङ्गीदृशीम्।
उत्तुङ्गस्तनकुम्भयुग्म विलसत्काश्मीरपत्रावलीं
मातङ्गीं पदकैरवं नवचरच्चन्द्रातपत्राम्भजे॥ ५

ध्यायेहं रत्नपीठेशुककुलरणितं शृण्वतीं श्यामलाङ्गीं
न्यस्तैकाघ्रि सरोजे शशिशकलधरां वल्लकींवादयन्तीम्।
कल्ह्वाराबद्धमालां नियमितविलसच्चूलिकां रक्तवस्त्रां
मातङ्गीं शङ्खपात्रां मधुमदविवशां चित्रकोद्भासिभालाम्॥ ६

आराध्यमानाश्ररणां पिबन्तोब्रह्मादयो विश्रुत कीर्तिमापुः।
अन्येपरं वाग्विभवं मुनीन्द्रा परांश्रियं भक्तिभरेण चान्ये॥ ७

नमामि देवीं नवचन्द्रमौलिं मातङ्गिनीं चन्द्रकलावतंसाम्।
आम्नाय वाक्यैः प्रतिपादनार्थे प्रबोधयन्तीं शुकमादरेण॥ ८

मातङ्गलीला गमनेऽपि भक्त्या शिञ्जानमञ्जीरमिषाद्‌व्रजन्ति।
मातस्त्वदीयं चरणारविन्दमकृत्रिमाणां वचसां निरिच्छाः। ९

पराधिकाशिञ्जितनूपुराभ्यां कृतागमां पदवीं तां पदाभ्याम्‌।
आस्फोटयन्तीं करवल्लकीं तां मातङ्गिनीं मद्धृदये भजामि ॥ १०

नीलांशुकाबद्धनितम्बबिम्बां नालीदलेनानतकर्णभूषाम्‌।
मध्ये मदाघूर्णित नेत्रपद्मां मातङ्गिनीं शम्भुवधूं नमामि ॥ ११

नीलोत्पलानां श्रियमावहन्तीं काञ्च्या कटाक्षैकशुभां कराणाम्‌।
कदम्ब मालाङ्कितकेशपाशां मातङ्गकन्यां हृदिभावयामि ॥ १२

स्तुत्यानया शङ्करधर्मपत्नीं मातङ्गिनीं वागधिदेवतां ताम्‌।
स्वर्गगतिं भक्तजना मनुष्याः परां श्रियं भक्ति भरेण चान्ये ॥ १३

कुचकुम्भ तटन्यस्त मणिवीणामदालसाम्‌।
श्यामां वामाङ्क विन्यस्त मालिकां बालिकाम्भजे ॥ १४

अब्धौयाति सरोजचामरमरुद्धूयमानालका
चूलीचुम्बित चारुचम्पक दलागौरी मदोल्लासिनी।
नाली बाल पलाश कर्णविलसत्कल्लोल कालिच्छटा
काली साचलकन्यका विजयते मच्चित्त पद्मासना ॥ १५

वीणानर्तित पाणि पङ्कजयुगामाशोणबिम्बाधरां
वेणी बद्ध कदम्ब पुष्प कलिकामेणी विलोलेक्षणाम्‌।
श्रोणी लम्ब विराजमान सुजपा शोणाम्बरालङ्कृतां
एणाङ्काकर्क विभूषणां कलयतां भिल्लीं पुरन्ध्रीम्भजे ॥ १६

तमाल श्यामाङ्गीमतिमधुर सङ्गीत निरतां
कृपापूर्णापाङ्गीं कुचभर नताङ्गीं स्मितमुखीम्‌।
भ्रमद्भ्रूभङ्गे ते विविध कुसुमैस्तैरिवयुतां
भजेऽहं मातङ्गीं मदपरवशाङ्गीमनुदिनम्‌ ॥ १७

सुकश्यामां श्यामां शुकरणित कल्लोल निरतां
विपञ्ची सञ्चारारुण करसरोजां भगवतीम्‌।
मदासक्तामुक्ता फलगुणितहारस्तनतटां
कृपावासामीशामतिरुचिरहासां भजशिवाम्‌ ॥ १८

रक्तारविन्द मकरन्द रसानुलेपां पानप्रमत्त चलितालि कुलालकान्ताम् ।
वीणामनोहरनिनादविनोदशीलां वाणीं भजे शुकनिभां मधुपान लोलाम् ॥ १९

सङ्गीत नाद रसपानघनार्द्रदेहां नेत्रारविन्द करुणामृतवाहिनीं ताम् ।
रक्तारविन्द विनिवेशितवामपादां श्यामां मतङ्गतनयां मनसास्मरामि ॥ २०

कस्तूरिका श्यामल कोमलाङ्गीं कादम्बरीपानमदालसाङ्गीम् ।
वामस्तनालिङ्गितरत्नवीणां मातङ्गकन्यां मनसास्मरामि ॥ २१

स्मरेत्प्रथम पुष्पिणीं रुधिरबिन्दु नीलाम्बरां गृहीतमधुपात्रिकां मदविघूर्ण नेत्रोज्वलाम् ।
घनस्तनभरानतां गलित चूलिकां श्यामलां करस्फुरित वल्लकीं विमलशङ्ख
                                        ताटङ्किनीम् ॥ २२

माणिक्यवीणामुपलालयन्तीं मदालसां मञ्जुल वाग्विलासाम् ।
माहेन्द्र नीलोत्पल कोमलाङ्गीं मातङ्ग कन्यां मनसास्मरामि ॥ २३

कुवलय दलनीलाङ्गीं कुवलय चारुचञ्चलापाङ्गीम् ।
कुवलय समोत्तमाङ्गीं कुवलय चूलीं नमामि मातङ्गीम् ॥ २४

श्यामा कुवलयश्यामा नामकलाधाम भागस्था ।
मधुपानरतारतापायाद्ब्राणी वीणाविनोदविश्रान्ता ॥ २५

तमालपत्राञ्चितनीलगात्रीं तालीदलेनार्पित कर्णपत्राम् ।
सप्तस्वरालापविशेषतन्त्रीं बालाम्भजे भव्यमतङ्गपुत्रीम् ॥ २६

नित्यानुपात्रार्पितसत्कलाभां नीलाम्बरोद्भासिनितम्बबिम्बाम् ।
भक्तोपरिन्यस्तकृपावलम्बां बालां भजे भव्यगुणां मदम्बाम् ॥ २७

शिवतनुभवसङ्गं शिवचूली लोल चञ्चलोत्सङ्गम् ।
कलिमल तनुमङ्गं कलये मातङ्गकन्यकापाङ्गम् ॥ २८

कलाधीशोत्तंसां करकलित वीणाहितरसां
कलिन्दापत्याभां करकलित हृदयां रक्तवसनाम् ।
पुराणीं कल्याणीं पुरमथनपुण्योदयकलामधीराक्षीं वन्दे बहुकुसुमसन्नद्धकबरीम् ॥ २९

कलोदञ्चद्वेणीं कनकदलताटङ्कमहितां स्तनाभ्यामानम्रां तरुणमिहिरां रक्तवसनाम् ।
महाकल्याणीं तन्मधुमदभरां ताम्रनयनांतमालश्यामां नस्तवकयतु
                                        सौख्यानिसततम् ॥ ३०

कराञ्चितविपञ्चिकां कलितचन्द्रचूडामणिं
कपोलविलसन्महाकनकपत्र ताटङ्किनीम् ।
तपः फलमिहाश्रितां तरुणभासरक्ताम्बरां
तमालदलमेचकां तरुणलोचनामाश्रये ॥ ३१

माता मरकतश्यामा मातङ्गी मधुशालिनी ।
कटाक्षयतु कल्याणी कदम्बवनवासिनी ॥ ३२

जगदानन्दकलङ्ककण्ठमाला कबरी वेष्टन काङ्क्षणीय गुञ्जा ।
कुरुतां दुरिताद्रिमोक्षणं मे तुहिना भिल्लिकुटुम्बिनी भवानी ॥ ३३

वामे विस्मृतशालिनी स्तनतटे विन्यस्त वीणामुखं
तन्त्रीताल विराविणीमसकलैरास्फालयन्ती नखैः ।
अर्धोन्मीलित लोचनं सविलसद्ग्रीवं मुखंविभ्रती
श्यामा काचन मोहिनी विजयते मातङ्गकन्यामयि ॥ ३४

प्रतिष्ठा पयोधर प्रसार करपङ्कजं बलभिदः ।
कदम्ब वनमालिकं शशिकला समुद्धासितम् ॥ ३५

मतङ्ग कुलनन्दिनी मनसि मे मुहुजृम्भताम् ।
समस्त सुखदायिनी तरुणपत्र ताटङ्किनी ॥ ३६

लाक्षाराग कपोलपल्लवरतामापीन तुङ्गस्तनीं
कर्पूरोज्ज्वलचारुशङ्खवलयां काश्मीररक्तांशुकाम् ।
तन्त्रीतालसपाटलां गुलिदलां वन्दामहे मातरं
मातङ्गीं मदमन्थरां मरकतश्यामां मनोहारिणीम् ॥ ३७

स्रस्तं केतकिदामभिर्वलयितं धम्मिल्लमाबिभ्रती
तालीपत्र पुटान्तरैः समनतैस्ताटङ्किनी मौक्तिकैः ।
भाले कल्पतरोः प्रसूनविलसदृष्ट्वैव सम्मोहिनी
काञ्ची दामवती विजयते वीणासवादानना ॥ ३८

मातङ्गीं भूषिताङ्गीं मधुमदमुदितां घूर्णमानाक्षियुग्मां
स्विद्यद्वक्त्रां कदम्ब प्रविलसद्वेणिकामत्त वीणाम् ।
बिम्बोष्ठीं रक्तवस्त्रां मृगमद तिलकामिन्दुरेखावतंसां
कर्णोद्यच्छङ्खपत्रां करकलितशुकां नौमि तुङ्गस्तनीं ताम् ॥ ३९

उन्मीलिद्यावकाद्यान्निविडमदभरोद्धिग्नभालालकाशां
रत्नगैवेयहाराङ्गद कटिलसत्सूत्र मञ्जीरघोषाम्।
आनीयार्थानभीष्टान् स्मितमधुरदृशा साधिकं तर्पयन्तीं
ध्यायेद्देवीं शुकाभां शुकमखिलकलारूपमस्याश्चपार्श्वे ॥ ४०

वेणीमूल विलासितेन्दु शकलां वीणानिनादप्रियां
क्षोणीपाल सुरेन्द्र पन्नगगणै राराधिताङ्घ्रिद्वयाम्।
एणीचञ्चललोचनां सुवदनां वाणीं पुराणोज्वलां
श्रोणीभारभरालसामनिमिषां पश्यामि विश्वेश्वरीम् ॥ ४१

कुचकलशनिषण्णवीणां कलमधुरध्वनि कम्पितोत्तमाङ्गीम्।
मरकतमणिभागमेचकाभां मदमविरोधमनस्विनीमुपासे ॥ ४२

तालीदलोल्लसितकोमलकर्णपालीं फालान्तराचिकुरामतिनीलवेणीम्।
वक्षोजपीठनिहितोज्वलचारुवीणां श्यामां नमामि मदिरारुणनेत्रयुग्माम् ॥ ४३

मध्येबद्धमयूखपिच्छनिकरां श्यामाम्प्रबालाधरां
भृङ्गीवादनतत्परां सुनयनां मूर्धालकैर्बर्बराम्।
गुञ्जाहारधरां समुन्नतकुचां चन्द्राननां शाम्भवीं
भिल्ली वेषधरां नमामि शबरी तामेकवीरां पराम् ॥ ४४

लसतगुञ्जाहार स्तनभर समुन्मध्यलतिका
मुदञ्चत्स्वेदाम्भः क्षणगणित फेनोद्गम रुचिम्।
शिवं शान्तं पात्रप्रवणमृगयाकारकरणं
शिवामम्बज्ञातिं चरणमहमन्वेमिशरणम् ॥ ४५

नटदगुञ्जा पञ्जाभरणकिरणां रक्तवसनां
जपाकर्णाभूषां शिखिवरक्षकलापाम्बरवतीम्।
नदज्झल्ली वल्लीनवकिसलयैस्तां परिवृतां
नवामोहारूढां कुटिलकबरीं मोहशबरीम् ॥ ४६

गले गुञ्जा पुञ्जावलि मपि च कर्णे शिखिशिखां
शिरो रङ्गे नृत्यत्कनकदल दूब मञ्जुलदलम्।
धनुर्वामे चापे शरमपरपाणौ निदधतीं
नितम्बे बर्हालिं कुटिलकबरीं नौमि शबरीम् ॥ ४७

वीणावादन निरतं तल्लीला बद्धगीत वामकुचम्।
श्यामल कोमल गात्रं पाटलनयनं परं भजेधाम ॥ ४८

अङ्कित पाणिचतुष्ट्यमङ्कुशपाशेक्षु चापशकलम्।
शङ्कर जितेत्यमित्रं पङ्कजनेत्रं परं भजेधाम ॥ ४९

करकलित केसारालानुकारेयं कुचकलशा जयते जगताम्।
मातामातङ्गी मङ्गेस्वायतना ॥ ५०

मुदाकरकदम्ब कानने कनकमष्टपात्रस्थिते
लसन्मणिमयासने सहचरीभिराराधिताम्।
लसत्कनककङ्कणां रजतमञ्जुमञ्जीरकां
जगज्जनविमोहिनीं जपविधौ स्मरेदम्बिकाम् ॥ ५१

अकृशा कुचयोर्विलग्ने विपुलं वक्षसि विस्तृतं नितम्बे।
अरुणाधरमाविरस्तुचित्ते करुणाशालि कपालि भागधेयम् ॥ ५२

वीणाताल विनोदगीत निरतां नीलांशुकोल्लासिनीम्।
बिम्बोष्ठीं नवयावकार्द्रं चरणामाकीर्ण केशोज्ज्वलाम् ॥ ५३

हृद्यावेशित शङ्खकुण्डलधरां माणिक्यभूषोज्ज्वलां
मातङ्गीं प्रणतोऽस्मि सुस्मितमुखां देवींशुकश्यामलाम् ॥ ५४

दिव्यहालामदोन्मत्तां दिव्यभूषणभूषिताम्।
दिव्यगन्धर्वकन्याभिस्समाराधितपादुकाम् ॥ ५५

दिव्यसिंहासनासीनां शुकवीणालसत्कराम्।
सङ्गीत मातृकां वन्दे वरदां सुस्मिताननाम् ॥ ५६

स्तुतिषु नवदेव देवि विविध कवि विलोहितमतिर्भवति।
निहितमतिर्यद्यपि मामपेतचेतीभवति स्तोतुं विलोभयति ॥ ५७

साध्याक्षरगर्भित पञ्चनव इत्यक्षरात्मिके जगन्मातः।
भगवति मातङ्गेश्वरि नमस्तुभ्यं महांदेवि ॥ ५८

इत्युमा साहचर्या भगवान्मातङ्गऋषिप्रणीता इयं स्तुतिः समाप्ता।

*****

Śrī Mātangī Stotram

Mātaṅgīṃ Madhupānamattanayanāṃ Mātaṅga Sañcāriṇīṃ
Kumbhīkumbhavivṛttapīvarakucāṃ Kumbhādipātrāñcitām |
Dhyāye'haṃ Madhumāraṇaikasahajāṃ Dhyātussuputrapradāṃ
Śarvāṇīṃ Surasiddhasādhyavanitā Saṃsevitā Pādukām || 1

Mātaṅgī Mahiṣādirākṣasakṛtadhvāntaikadīpo Maṇiḥ
Manvādistuta Mantrarājavilasatsadbhakta Cintāmaṇiḥ |
Śrīmatkaulikadānahāsyaracanā Cāturya Rākāmaṇiḥ
Devitvaṃ Hṛdaye Vasādyamahime Madbhāgya Rakṣāmaṇiḥ || 2

Jayadevi Viśālākṣi Jaya Sarveśvari Jaya |
Jayāñjanagiriprakhye Mahādeva Priyaṅkari || 3

Mahāviśveśa Dayite Jaya Brahmādi Pūjite |
Puṣpāñjaliṃ Pradāsyāmi Gṛhāṇa Kulanāyike || 4

Jayamātarmahākṛṣṇe Jaya Nīlotpalaprabhe |
Manohāri Namaste'stu Namastubhyaṃ Vaśaṅkari || 5

Jaya Saubhāgyade Nṝṇāṃ Lokamohini Te Namaḥ |
Sarvaiśvaryaprade Puṃsāṃ Sarvavidyāprade Namaḥ || 6

Sarvāpadāṃ Nāśakarīṃ Sarvadāridryanāśinīm |
Namo Mātaṅgatanaye Namaścāṇḍāli Kāmade || 7

Nīlāmbare Namastubhyaṃ Nīlālakasamanvite |
Namastubhyaṃ Mahāvāṇi Mahālakṣmi Namo'stute || 8

Mahāmātaṅgi Pādābjaṃ Tava Nityaṃ Namāmyaham |
Etaduktaṃ Mahādevyā Mātaṅgayāḥ Stotramuttamam || 9

Sarvakāmapradaṃ Nityaṃ Yaḥ Paṭhenmānavottamaḥ |
Vimuktassakalaiḥ Pāpaiḥ Samagraṃ Puṇyamaśnute || 10

Rājāno Dāsatāṃ Yānti Nāryo Dāsītvamāpnuyuḥ |
Dāsībhūtaṃ Jagatsarvaṃ Śīghraṃ Tasya Bhaved Dhruvam || 11

Mahākavībhavedvāgbhiḥ Sākṣād Vāgīśvaro Bhavet |

Acalāṃ Śriyamāpnoti Aṇimādyaṣṭakaṃ Labhet || 12

Labhenmanorathān Sarvān Trailokye Nāpi Durlabhān |

Ante Śivatvamāpnoti Nātra Kāryā Vicāraṇā || 13

Śrī Raja Mātaṅagī Pādukārpaṇamastu |

Iti Śrī Mātaṅgī Stotraṃ Sampūrṇam |

श्री मातङ्गी स्तोत्रम्

मातङ्गीं मधुपानमत्तनयनां मातङ्ग सञ्चारिणीं
कुम्भीकुम्भविवृत्तपीवरकुचां कुम्भादिपात्राञ्चिताम्।
ध्यायेऽहं मधुमारणैकसहजां ध्यातुस्सुपुत्रप्रदां
शर्वाणीं सुरसिद्धसाध्यवनिता संसेविता पादुकाम् ॥ १

मातङ्गीं महिषादिराक्षसकृतध्वान्तैकदीपो मणिः
मन्वादिस्तुत मन्त्रराजविलसत्सद्रक्त चिन्तामणिः।
श्रीमत्कौलिकदानहास्यरचना चातुर्य राकामणिः
देवित्वं हृदये वसाद्यमहिमे मद्भाग्य रक्षामणिः ॥ २

जयदेवि विशालाक्षि जय सर्वेश्वरि जय ।
जयाञ्जनगिरिप्रख्ये महादेव प्रियङ्करि ॥ ३

महाविश्वेश दयिते जय ब्रह्मादि पूजिते ।
पुष्पाञ्जलिं प्रदास्यामि गृहाण कुलनायिके ॥ ४

जयमातर्महाकृष्णे जय नीलोत्पलप्रभे ।
मनोहारि नमस्तेऽस्तु नमस्तुभ्यं वशङ्करि ॥ ५

जय सौभाग्यदे नृणां लोकमोहिनि ते नमः ।
सर्वैश्वर्यप्रदे पुंसां सर्वविद्याप्रदे नमः ॥ ६

सर्वापदां नाशकरीं सर्वदारिद्र्यनाशिनीम्।
नमो मातङ्गतनये नमश्चाण्डालि कामदे ॥ ७

नीलाम्बरे नमस्तुभ्यं नीलालकसमन्विते।
नमस्तुभ्यं महावाणि महालक्ष्मि नमोऽस्तुते ॥ ८

महामातङ्गि पादाब्जं तव नित्यं नमाम्यहम्।
एतदुक्तं महादेव्या मातङ्गयाः स्तोत्रमुत्तमम् ॥ ९

सर्वकामप्रदं नित्यं यः पठेन्मानवोत्तमः।
विमुक्तस्सकलैः पापैः समग्रं पुण्यमश्रुते ॥ १०

राजानो दासतां यान्ति नार्यो दासीत्वमाप्नुयुः।
दासीभूतं जगत्सर्वं शीघ्रं तस्य भवेद् ध्रुवम् ॥ ११

महाकवीभवेद्वाग्भिः साक्षाद् वागीश्वरो भवेत् ।
अचलां श्रियमाप्नोति अणिमाद्यष्टकं लभेत् ॥ १२

लभेन्मनोरथान् सर्वान् त्रैलोक्ये नापि दुर्लभान् ।
अन्ते शिवत्वमाप्नोति नात्र कार्या विचारणा ॥ १३

श्री राज मातङ्गी पादुकार्पणमस्तु ।

इति श्री मातङ्गी स्तोत्रं संपूर्णम्।

Matangi
Stotram

*****

Śrī Mātangī Hṛdayam

Śrī Gaṇeśāya Namaḥ ‖   *Śrī Umā Maheśvarābhyāṃ Namaḥ* ‖

Atha Śrī Mātaṅgī Hṛdaya Prārambhaḥ ‖

Ekadā Kautukāviṣṭā Bhairavaṃ Bhūtasevitam |
Bhairavī Paripapraccha Sarvabhūtahite Ratā ‖ 1

Śrī Bhairavyuvāca |

Bhagavansarvadharmajña Bhūtavātsalyabhāvana |
Ahaṃ Tu Vettumicchāmi Sarvabhūtopakāram ‖ 2

Kena Mantreṇa Japtena Stotreṇa Paṭhitena Ca |
Sarvathā Śreyasāṃ Prāptirbhūtānāṃ Bhūtimicchatām ‖ 3

Śrī Bhairava Uvāca |

Śṛṇu Devi Tava Snehātprāyo Gopyamapi Priye |
Kathayiṣyāmi Tatsarvaṃ Sukhasampatkaraṃ Śubham ‖ 4

Paṭhatāṃ Śṛṇvatāṃ Nityaṃ Sarvasampattidāyakam |
Vidyaiśvaryasukhāvāptimaṅgalapradamuttamam ‖ 5

Mātaṃgyā Hṛdayaṃ Stotra Duḥkhadāridryabhañjanam |
Maṅgalaṃ Maṅgalānāṃ Ca Hyasti Sarvasukhapradam ‖ 6

‖ *Viniyogaḥ* ‖

Oṃ Asya Śrīmātaṅgīhṛdayastotramantrasya Dakṣiṇāmūrtirṛṣiḥ |
Virāṭ Chandaḥ | *Mātaṅgī Devatā* | *Hrīṃ Bījam* | *Hūṃ Śaktiḥ* |
Klīṃ Kīlakam | *Sarvavāñchitārthasiddhaye Pāṭhe Viniyogaḥ* ‖

Ṛṣyādinyāsaḥ |

Dakṣiṇāmūrtiṛṣaye Namaḥ Śirasi |
Virāṭchandase Namaḥ Mukhe |

Mātaṅgīdevatāyai Namaḥ Hṛdi | *Hrīṃ Bījāya Namaḥ Guhye |*
Hūṃ Śaktaye Namaḥ Pādayoḥ | *Klīṃ Kīlakāya Namaḥ Nābhau |*
Viniyogāya Namaḥ Sarvāṅge ||

Hṛdayādi Ṣaḍaṅga Nyāsaḥ |

Oṃ Hrīṃ Hṛdayāya Namaḥ | *Oṃ Klīṃ Śirase Svāhā |*
Oṃ Hūṃ Śikhāyai Vaṣaṭ | *Oṃ Hrīṃ Netratrayāya Vauṣaṭ |*
Oṃ Klīṃ Kavacāya Hum | *Oṃ Hūṃ Astrāya Phaṭ ||*

Karanyāsaḥ |

Oṃ Hrīṃ Aṅguṣṭhābhyāṃ Namaḥ |
Oṃ Klīṃ Tarjanībhyāṃ Namaḥ |
Oṃ Hūṃ Madhyamābhyāṃ Namaḥ |
Oṃ Hrīṃ Anāmikābhyāṃ Namaḥ |
Oṃ Klīṃ Kaniṣṭhikābhyāṃ Namaḥ |
Oṃ Hūṃ Karatalakarapṛṣṭhābhyāṃ Namaḥ ||

|| Atha Dhyānam ||

Oṃ Śyāmāṃ Śubhrāṃśubhālāṃ Trikamalanayanāṃ Ratnasiṃhā
                               Sanasthāṃ
Bhaktābhīṣṭapradātrīṃ Suranikarakarāsevyakañjāṃghriyugmām |
Nīlāmbhojāṃśukāntiṃ Niśicaranikarāraṇyadāvāgnirūpāṃ
Pāśaṃ Khaḍgaṃ Caturbhirvarakamalakaraiḥ Kheṭakaṃ Cāṅkuśaṃ Ca
(Mātaṅgīmāvahantīmabhimataphaladāṃ Modinīṃ Cintayāmi) || 7

Namaste Mātaṃgyai Mṛdumuditatanvai Tanumatāṃ
Paraśreyodāyai Kamalacaraṇadhyānamanasām |
Sadā Saṃsevyāyai Sadasi Vibudhairdivyadhiṣaṇai-
Rdayārdrāyai Devyai Duritadalanoddaṇḍamanase || 8

Paraṃ Mātaste Yo Japati Manumavyagrahṛdayaḥ
Kavitvaṃ Kalpānāṃ Kalayati Sukalpaḥ Pratipadam |
Api Prāyo Ramyāmṛtamayapadā Tasya Lalitā
Naṭīṃmanyā Vāṇī Naṭati Rasanāyāṃ Capalitā || 9

Tava Dhyāyanto Ye Vapuranujapanti Pravalitaṃ
Sadā Mantraṃ Mātarnahi Bhavati Teṣāṃ Paribhavaḥ |
Kadambānāṃ Mālāḥ Śirasi Tava Yuñjanti Sadaye
Bhavanti Prāyaste Yuvatijanayūthasvavaśagāḥ || 10

Sarojaiḥ Sāhasraiḥ Sarasijapadadvandvamapi Ye
Sahasraṃ Nāmoktvā Tadapi Tava Ṅe'ntaṃ Manumitam |
Pṛthaṅnāmnāṃ Tenāyutakalitamarcanti Khalu Te
Sadā Devavrātapraṇamitapadāmbhojayugalāḥ || 11

Tava Prītyai Mātarddadati Balimādhāya Balinā
Samatsyaṃ Māṃsaṃ Vā Surucirasitaṃ Rājarucitam |
Supuṇyā Ye Svāntastavacaraṇamodaikarasikā
Aho Bhāgyaṃ Teṣāṃ Tribhuvanamalaṃ Vaśyamakhilam || 12

Lasallolaśrotrābharaṇakiraṇakrāntikalitaṃ
Mitasmityāpannapratibhitamamannaṃ Vikaritam |
Mukhāmbhojaṃ Mātastava Pariluṭhadbhrūmadhukaraṃ
Ramā Ye Dhyāyanti Tyajati Na Hi Teṣāṃ Subhavanam || 13

Paraḥ Śrīmātaṃgyā Jayati Hṛdayākhyaḥ Sumanasām-
Ayaṃ Sevyaḥ Sudyo'bhimataphaladaśvātilalitaḥ |
Narā Ye Śṛṇvanti Stavamapi Paṭhantīmamaniśaṃ
Na Teṣāṃ Duḥprāpyaṃ Jagati Yadalabhyaṃ Diviṣadām || 14

Dhanārthī Dhanamāpnoti Dārārthī Sundarīṃ Priyām |
Sutārthī Labhate Putraṃ Stavasyāsya Prakīrttanāt || 15

Vidyārthī Labhate Vidyāṃ Vividhāṃ Vibhavapradām |
Jayārthī Paṭhanādasya Jayaṃ Prāpnoti Niścitam || 16

Naṣṭarājyo Labhedrājyaṃ Sarvasampatsamāśritam |
Kuberasamasampattiḥ Sa Bhavedhṛdayaṃ Paṭhan || 17

Kimatra Bahunoktena Yadyadicchati Mānavaḥ |
Mātaṅgī Hṛdayastotrapāṭhāttatsarvamāpnuyāt || 18

Iti Śrī Dakṣiṇāmūrti Saṃhitāyāṃ Śrī Mātaṅgī Hṛdaya Stotraṃ Samāptam |
Śrī Mantramahārṇave Madhyakhaṇḍe Mātaṅgītantre Dvadaśarataṅgaḥ |

श्री मातङ्गीहृदयम्

श्री गणेशाय नमः ॥　　　श्री उमा महेश्वराभ्यां नमः ॥

अथ श्री मातङ्गी हृदय प्रारम्भः ॥

एकदा कौतुकाविष्टा भैरवं भूतसेवितम् ।
भैरवी परिपप्रच्छ सर्वभूतहिते रता ॥ १

श्री भैरव्युवाच ।

भगवन्सर्वधर्मज्ञ भूतवात्सल्यभावन ।
अहं तु वेत्तुमिच्छामि सर्वभूतोपकारम् ॥ २

केन मन्त्रेण जप्तेन स्तोत्रेण पठितेन च ।
सर्वथा श्रेयसां प्राप्तिर्भूतानां भूतिमिच्छताम् ॥ ३

श्री भैरव उवाच ।

शृणु देवि तव स्नेहात्प्रायो गोप्यमपि प्रिये ।
कथयिष्यामि तत्सर्वं सुखसम्पत्करं शुभम् ॥ ४

पठतां शृण्वतां नित्यं सर्वसम्पत्तिदायकम् ।
विद्यैश्वर्यसुखावाप्तिमङ्गलप्रदमुत्तमम् ॥ ५

मातंग्या हृदयं स्तोत्र दुःखदारिद्र्यभञ्जनम् ।
मङ्गलं मङ्गलानां च ह्यस्ति सर्वसुखप्रदम् ॥ ६

॥ विनियोगः ॥

ॐ अस्य श्रीमातङ्गीहृदयस्तोत्रमन्त्रस्य दक्षिणामूर्तिर्ऋषिः ।
विराट् छन्दः । मातङ्गी देवता । ह्रीं बीजम् । हूं शक्तिः । क्लीं कीलकम् ।
सर्ववाञ्छितार्थसिद्धये पाठे विनियोगः ॥

ऋष्यादि न्यासः ।

दक्षिणामूर्तिऋषये नमः शिरसि ।　　विराट्छन्दसे नमः मुखे ।
मातङ्गीदेवतायै नमः हृदि ।　　ह्रीं बीजाय नमः गुह्ये ।
हूं शक्तये नमः पादयोः ।　　क्लीं कीलकाय नमः नाभौ ।
विनियोगाय नमः सर्वाङ्गे ।

हृदयादि षडङ्ग न्यासः ।

ॐ ह्रीं हृदयाय नमः ।　　　ॐ क्लीं शिरसे स्वाहा ।

ॐ हूं शिखायै वषट् ।　　　ॐ ह्रीं नेत्रत्रयाय वौषट् ।

ॐ क्लीं कवचाय हुम् ।　　　ॐ हूं अस्त्राय फट् ।

करन्यासः ।

ॐ ह्रीं अङ्गुष्ठाभ्यां नमः ।　　　ॐ क्लीं तर्जनीभ्यां नमः ।

ॐ हूं मध्यमाभ्यां नमः ।　　　ॐ ह्रीं अनामिकाभ्यां नमः ।

ॐ क्लीं कनिष्ठिकाभ्यां नमः ।　　　ॐ हूं करतलकरपृष्ठाभ्यां नमः ।

॥ अथ ध्यानम् ॥

ॐ श्यामां शुभ्रांशुभालां त्रिकमलनयनां रत्नसिंहासनस्थां
भक्ताभीष्टप्रदात्रीं सुरनिकरकरासेव्यकञ्जाङ्घ्रियुग्माम्।
नीलाम्भोजांशुकान्तिं निशिचरनिकरारण्यदावाग्निरूपां
पाशं खड्गं चतुर्भिर्वरकमलकरैः खेटकं चाङ्कुशं च
(मातङ्गीमावहन्तीमभिमतफलदां मोदिनीं चिन्तयामि) ॥ ७

नमस्ते मातंग्यै मृदुमुदिततन्वै तनुमतां
परश्रेयोदायै कमलचरणध्यानमनसाम् ।
सदा संसेव्यायै सदसि विबुधैर्दिव्यधिषणै -
र्दयार्द्रायै देव्यै दुरितदलनोद्दण्डमनसे ॥ ८

परं मातस्ते यो जपति मनुमव्यग्रहृदयः
कवित्वं कल्पानां कलयति सुकल्पः प्रतिपदम् ।
अपि प्रायो रम्यामृतमयपदा तस्य ललिता
नटींमन्या वाणी नटति रसनायां चपलिता ॥ ९

तव ध्यायन्तो ये वपुरनुजपन्ति प्रवलितं
सदा मन्त्रं मातर्नहि भवति तेषां परिभवः ।
कदम्बानां मालाः शिरसि तव युञ्जन्ति सदये
भवन्ति प्रायस्ते युवतिजनयूथस्ववशगाः ॥ १०

सरोजैः साहस्रैः सरसिजपदद्वन्द्वमपि ये
सहस्रं नामोक्त्वा तदपि तव डेऽन्तं मनुमितम्।

पृथङ्ङाम्नां तेनायुतकलितमर्चन्ति खलु ते
सदा देवव्रातप्रणमितपदाम्भोजयुगलाः ॥ ११

तव प्रीत्यै मातर्ददति बलिमाधाय बलिना
समत्स्यं मांसं वा सुरुचिरसितं राजरुचितम् ।
सुपुण्या ये स्वान्तस्तवचरणमोदैकरसिका
अहो भाग्यं तेषां त्रिभुवनमलं वश्यमखिलम् ॥ १२

लसल्लोलश्रोत्राभरणकिरणक्रान्तिकलितं
मितस्मित्यापन्नप्रतिभितममन्नं विकरितम् ।
मुखाम्भोजं मातस्तव परिलुठद्भ्रूमधुकरं
रमा ये ध्यायन्ति त्यजति न हि तेषां सुभवनम् ॥ १३

परः श्रीमातंग्या जयति हृदयाख्यः सुमनसाम्
अयं सेव्यः सुद्योऽभिमतफलदश्चातिललितः ।
नरा ये शृण्वन्ति स्तवमपि पठन्तीममनिशं
न तेषां दुःप्राप्यं जगति यदलभ्यं दिविषदाम् ॥ १४

धनार्थी धनमाप्नोति दारार्थी सुन्दरीं प्रियाम् ।
सुतार्थी लभते पुत्रं स्तवस्यास्य प्रकीर्त्तनात् ॥ १५

विद्यार्थी लभते विद्यां विविधां विभवप्रदाम् ।
जयार्थी पठनादस्य जयं प्राप्नोति निश्चितम् ॥ १६

नष्टराज्यो लभेद्राज्यं सर्वसम्पत्समाश्रितम् ।
कुबेरसमसम्पत्तिः स भवेध्दृदयं पठन् ॥ १७

किमत्र बहुनोक्तेन यद्यदिच्छति मानवः ।
मातङ्गी हृदयस्तोत्रपाठात्तत्सर्वमाप्नुयात् ॥ १८

इति श्री दक्षिणामूर्ति संहितायां श्री
   मातङ्गी हृदय स्तोत्रं समाप्तम् ।
   श्री मन्त्र महार्णवे मध्यखण्डे
   मातङ्गी तन्त्रे द्वदशरतङ्गः ।

   *****

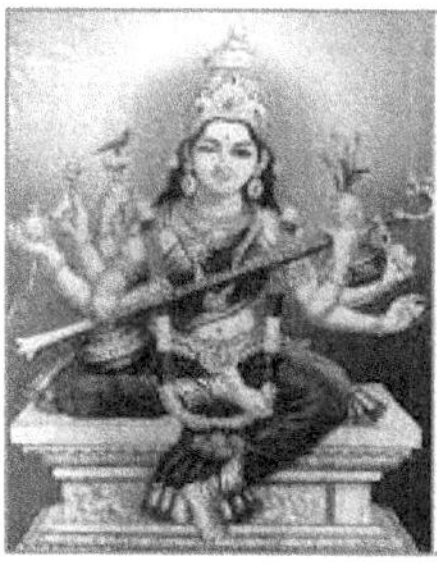

Śrī Mātangī Aṣtotra Śata Nāma Stotram

Śrī Bhairavyuvāca –

Bhagavan Śrōtumicchāmi Mātaṅgyāśśatanāmakam |

Yadguhyaṁ Sarvatantrēṣu Na Kēnāpi Prakāśitam || 1

Śrī Bhairava Uvāca –

Śṛṇu Dēvi Pravakṣyāmi Rahasyātirahasyakam |

Nākhyēyaṁ Yatra Kutrāpi Paṭhanīyaṁ Parātparam || 2

Yasyaikavārapaṭhanātsarvē Vighnā Upadravāḥ |

Naśyanti Tatkṣaṇāddēvi Vahninā Tūlarāśivat || 3

Prasannā Jāyatē Dēvī Mātaṅgī Cāsya Pāṭhataḥ |

Sahasranāmapaṭhanē Yatphalaṁ Parikīrtitam |

Tatkōṭiguṇitaṁ Dēvī Nāmāṣṭaśatakaṁ Śubham || 4

Asya Śrī Mātaṅgī Śatanāmnāṁ Bhagavān Mataṅga Ṛṣiḥ |

Anuṣṭupchandaḥ | Śrī Mātaṅgī Dēvatā |

Śrī Mātaṅgī Prītayē Japē Viniyōgaḥ |

Ōṁ Mahāmattamātaṅginī Siddhirūpā Tathā Yōginī Bhadrakālī Ramā Ca |

Bhavānī Bhayaprītidā Bhūtiyuktā Bhavārādhitā Bhūtisampatkarī Ca || 1

Janādhīśamātā Dhanāgāradṛṣṭi Rdhanēśārcitā Dhīravāsī Varāṅgī |

Prakṛṣṭā Prabhārūpiṇī Kāmarūpā Prahṛṣṭā Mahākīrtidā Karṇanālī || 2

Karālī Bhagā Ghōrarūpā Bhagāṅgī Bhagākhyā Bhagaprītidā Bhīmarūpā |

Bhavānī Mahākauśikī Kōśapūrṇā Kiśōrī Kiśōrapriyā Nandaīhā || 3

Mahākāraṇā:'Kāraṇā Karmaśīlā Kapālī Prasiddhā Mahāsiddhakhaṇḍā |

Makārapriyā Mānarūpā Mahēśī Mahōllāsinī Lāsyalīlālayāṅgī || 4

Kṣamā Kṣēmaśīlā Kṣapākāriṇī Cā:'Kṣayaprītidā Bhūtiyuktā Bhavānī |

Bhavārādhitā Bhūtisatyātmikā Ca Prabhōdbhāsitā Bhānubhāsvatkarā

Ca || 5

Dharādhīśamātā Dhanāgāradṛṣṭi Rdhanēśārcitā Dhīvarā Dhīvarāṅgī |

Prakṛṣṭā Prabhārūpiṇī Prāṇarūpā Prakṛṣṭasvarūpā Svarūpapriyā Ca || 6

Calatkuṇḍalā Kāminī Kāntayuktā Kapālā:'Calā Kālakōddhāriṇī Ca |

Kadambapriyā Kōṭarī Kōṭadēhā Kramā Kīrtidā Karṇarūpā Ca Lakṣmīḥ || 7

Kṣamāṅgī Kṣayaprēmarūpā Kṣapā Ca Kṣayākṣā Kṣayākhyā Kṣayāprāntarā

Ca |

Kṣavatkāminī Kṣāriṇī Kṣīrapūṣā Śivāṅgī Ca Śākambharī Śākadēhā || 8

Mahāśākayajñā Phalaprāśakā Ca Śakāhvā:'Śakāhvā Śakākhyā Śakā Ca |

Śakākṣāntarōṣā Surōṣā Surēkhā Mahāśēṣayajñōpavītapriyā Ca || 9

Jayantī Jayā Jāgratī Yōgyarūpā Jayāṅgā Japadhyānasantuṣṭasañjñā |

Jayaprāṇarūpā Jayasvarṇadēhā Jayajvālinī Yāminī Yāmyarūpā || 10

Jaganmātṛrūpā Jagadrakṣaṇā Ca Svadhāvauṣaḍantā Vilambā:'Vilambā |

Ṣaḍaṅgā Mahālambarūpā:'Sihastā Padāhāriṇī Hāriṇī Hāriṇī Ca || 11

Mahāmaṅgalā Maṅgalaprēmakīrti Rniśumbhakṣidā Śumbhadarpāpahā

Ca |

Tathānandabījādimuktisvarūpā Tathā Caṇḍamuṇḍāpadā Mukhya

Caṇḍā || 12

Pracaṇḍā:'Pracaṇḍā Mahācaṇḍavēgā Calaccāmarā Cāmarācandrakīrtiḥ |

Sucāmīkarā Citrabhūṣōjjvalāṅgī Susaṅgītagītā Ca Pāyādapāyāt || 13

Iti Tē Kathitaṁ Dēvi Nāmnāmaṣṭōttaraṁ Śatam |

Phala Śrutiḥ

Gōpyaṁ Ca Sarvatantrēṣu Gōpanīyaṁ Ca Sarvadā || 14

Ētasya Satatābhyāsātsākṣāddēvō Mahēśvaraḥ |

Trisandhyaṁ Ca Mahābhaktyā Paṭhanīyaṁ Sukhōdayam || 15

Na Tasya Duṣkaraṁ Kiñcijjāyatē Sparśataḥ Kṣaṇāt |

Svakṛtaṁ Yattadēvāptaṁ Tasmādāvartayētsadā || 16

Sadaiva Sannidhau Tasya Dēvī Vasati Sādaram |

Ayōgā Yē Ta Ēvāgrē Suyōgāśca Bhavanti Vai || 17

Ta Ēvamitrabhūtāśca Bhavanti Tatprasādataḥ |

Viṣāṇi Nōpasarpanti Vyādhayō Na Spṛśanti Tān || 18

Lūtāvisphōṭakāssarvē Śamayanti Ca Tatkṣaṇāt |

Jarāpalitanirmuktaḥ Kalpajīvī Bhavēnnaraḥ || 19

Api Kiṁ Bahunōktēna Sānnidhyaṁ Phalamāpnuyāt |

Yāvanmayā Purā Prōktaṁ Phalaṁ Sāhasranāmakam |

Tatsarvaṁ Labhatē Martyō Mahāmāyāprasādataḥ || 20

Iti Śrī Rudrayāmalē Śrī Mātaṅgī Śatanāma Stōtram |

श्री मातंगी अष्टोत्तर शतनाम स्तोत्रम्

श्रीभैरव्युवाच –

भगवञ्छ्रोतुमिच्छामि मातङ्ग्याः शतनामकम् ।
यद्ब्रह्मां सर्वतन्त्रेषु केनापि न प्रकाशितम् ॥ १

भैरव उवाच –

श्रृणु देवि प्रवक्ष्यामि रहस्यातिरहस्यकम् ।
नाख्येयं यत्र कुत्रापि पठनीयं परात्परम् ॥ २

यस्यैकवारपठनात्सर्वे विघ्ना उपद्रवाः ।
नश्यन्ति तत्क्षणाद्देवि वह्निना तूलराशिवत् ॥ ३

प्रसन्ना जायते देवी मातङ्गी चास्य पाठतः ।
सहस्रनामपठने यत्फलं परिकीर्तितम् ।
तत्कोटिगुणितं देवीनामाष्टशतकं शुभम् ॥ ४

अस्य श्री मातङ्गी शतनाम स्तोत्रस्य भगवान्मतङ्ग ऋषिः ।
अनुष्टुप् छन्दः । मातङ्गी देवता । मातङ्गी प्रीतये जपे विनियोगः ।

महामत्तमातङ्गिनी सिद्धिरूपा तथा योगिनी भद्रकाली रमा च ।
भवानी भवप्रीतिदा भूतियुक्ता भवाराधिता भूतिसम्पत्करी च ॥ १

धनाधीशमाता धनागारदृष्टिर्धनेशार्चिता धीरवापीवराङ्गी ।
प्रकृष्टप्रभारूपिणी कामरूपप्रहृष्टा महाकीर्तिदा कर्णनाली ॥ २

कराली भगा घोररूपा भगाङ्गी भगाह्वा भगप्रीतिदा भीमरूपा ।
भवानी महाकौशिकी कोशपूर्णा किशोरीकिशोरप्रियानन्द ईहा ॥ ३

महाकारणाकारणा कर्मशीला कपालिप्रसिद्धा महासिद्खण्डा ।
मकारप्रिया मानरूपा महेशी महोल्लासिनीलास्यलीलालयाङ्गी ॥ ४

क्षमाक्षेमशीला क्षपाकारिणी चाक्षयप्रीतिदा भूतियुक्ता भवानी ।
भवाराधिता भूतिसत्यात्मिका च प्रभोद्धासिता भानुभास्वत्करा च ॥ ५

धराधीशमाता धरागारदृष्टिर्धरेशार्चिता धीवराधीवराङ्गी ।
प्रकृष्टप्रभारूपिणी प्राणरूपप्रकृष्टस्वरूपा स्वरूपप्रिया च ॥ ६

चलत्कुण्डला कामिनी कान्तयुक्ता कपालाचला कालकोद्धारिणी च ।
कदम्बप्रिया कोटरीकोटदेहा क्रमा कीर्तिदा कर्णरूपा च काक्ष्मीः ॥ ७

क्षमाङ्गी क्षयप्रेमरूपा क्षपा च क्षयाक्षा क्षयाह्वा क्षयप्रान्तरा च ।
क्षवत्कामिनी क्षारिणी क्षीरपूर्णा शिवाङ्गी च शाकम्भरी शाकदेहा ॥ ८

महाशाकयज्ञा फलप्राशका च शकाह्वा शकाह्वाशकाख्या शका च ।
शकाक्षान्तरोषा सुरोषा सुरेखा महाशेषयज्ञोपवीतप्रिया च ॥ ९

जयन्ती जया जाग्रतीयोग्यरूपा जयाङ्गा जपध्यानसन्तुष्टसंज्ञा ।
जयप्राणरूपा जयस्वर्णदेहा जयज्वालिनी यामिनी याम्यरूपा ॥ १०

जगन्मातृरूपा जगद्रक्षणा च स्वधावौषडन्ता विलम्बाविलम्बा ।
षडङ्गा महालम्बरूपासिहस्ता पदाहारिणीहारिणी हारिणी च ॥ ११

महामङ्गला मङ्गलप्रेमकीर्तिर्निशुम्भच्छिदा शुम्भदर्पत्वहा च ।
तथाऽऽनन्दबीजादिमुक्तस्वरूपा तथा चण्डमुण्डापदामुख्यचण्डा ॥ १२

प्रचण्डाप्रचण्डा महाचण्डवेगा चलच्चामरा चामराचन्द्रकीर्तिः ।
सुचामीकराचित्रभूषोज्ज्वलाङ्गी सुसङ्गीतगीता च पायादपायात् ॥ १३

इति ते कथितं देवि नाम्नामष्टोत्तरं शतम् ।

फलश्रुति:

गोप्यञ्च सर्वतन्त्रेषु गोपनीयञ्च सर्वदा ॥ १४

एतस्य सतताभ्यासात्साक्षाद्देवो महेश्वरः ।
त्रिसन्ध्यञ्च महाभक्त्या पठनीयं सुखोदयम् ॥ १५

न तस्य दुष्करं किञ्चिज्जायते स्पर्शतः क्षणात् ।
स्वकृतं यत्तदेवाग्रं तस्मादावर्तयेत्सदा ॥ १६

सदैव सन्निधौ तस्य देवी वसति सादरम् ।
अयोगा ये तवैवाग्रे सुयोगाश्च भवन्ति वै ॥ १७

त एवमित्रभूताश्च भवन्ति तत्प्रसादतः ।
विषाणि नोपसर्पन्ति व्याधयो न स्पृशन्ति तान् ॥ १८

लूताविस्फोटकास्सर्वे शमं यान्ति च तत्क्षणात् ।
जरापलितनिर्मुक्तः कल्पजीवी भवेन्नरः ॥ १९

अपि किं बहुनोक्तेन सान्निध्यं फलमाप्नुयात् ।
यावन्मया पुरा प्रोक्तं फलं साहस्रनामकम् ।
तत्सर्वं लभते मर्त्यो महामायाप्रसादतः ॥ २०

इति श्री मातंगी अष्टोत्तर शतनाम स्तोत्रम् सम्पूर्णम् ॥

*****

Śrī Mātaṅgī Aṣtotra Śata Nāmāvaliḥ

108 Divine Names of *Śrī Mātaṅgī Devi.*

Śrī Mātaṅgī Aṣṭottara Śata Nāmāvaliḥ
श्री मातङ्गी अष्टोत्तरशतनामावलिः

1.	Oṃ Mahāmata Mātaṅginī Siddhi Rūpāyai Namaḥ l	ॐ महामत्तमातङ्गिनी सिद्धिरूपायै नमः l
2.	Oṃ Yoginyai Namaḥ l	ॐ योगिन्यै नमः l
3.	Oṃ Bhadrakālyai Namaḥ l	ॐ भद्रकाल्यै नमः l
4.	Oṃ Ramāyai Namaḥ l	ॐ रमायै नमः l
5.	Oṃ Bhavānyai Namaḥ l	ॐ भवान्यै नमः l
6.	Oṃ Bhavaprītidāyai Namaḥ l	ॐ भवप्रीतिदायै नमः l
7.	Oṃ Bhūtiyuktāyai Namaḥ l	ॐ भूतियुक्तायै नमः l
8.	Oṃ Bhavārādhitāyai Namaḥ l	ॐ भवाराधितायै नमः l
9.	Oṃ Bhūtisampatkaryai Namaḥ l	ॐ भूतिसम्पत्कर्यै नमः l
10.	Oṃ Dhanādhīśamātre Namaḥ l	ॐ धनाधीशमात्रे नमः l
11.	Oṃ Dhanāgāradṛṣtyai Namaḥ l	ॐ धनागारदृष्ट्यै नमः l
12.	Oṃ Dhaneśārcitāyai Namaḥ l	ॐ धनेशार्चितायै नमः l
13.	Oṃ Dhīravāpīvarāṅgyai Namaḥ l	ॐ धीरवापीवराङ्ग्यै नमः l
14.	Oṃ Prakṛṣtaprabhārūpiṇyai Namaḥ l	ॐ प्रकृष्टप्रभारूपिण्यै नमः l
15.	Oṃ Kāmarūpaprahṛṣṭāyai Namaḥ	ॐ कामरूपप्रहृष्टायै नमः l
16.	Oṃ Mahākīrtidāyai Namaḥ l	ॐ महाकीर्तिदायै नमः l
17.	Oṃ Karṇanālyai Namaḥ l	ॐ कर्णनाल्यै नमः l
18.	Oṃ Karālībhagāyai Ghorarūpāyai Namaḥ l	ॐ करालीभगायै घोररूपायै नमः l
19.	Oṃ Bhagāṅgyai Namaḥ l	ॐ भगाङ्ग्यै नमः l
20.	Oṃ Bhagāhvāyai Namaḥ l	ॐ भगाह्वायै नमः l
21.	Oṃ Bhagaprītidāyai Namaḥ l	ॐ भगप्रीतिदायै नमः l
22.	Oṃ Bhīmarūpāyai Namaḥ l	ॐ भीमरूपायै नमः l

23.	Oṃ Bhavānyai Namaḥ ǀ	ॐ भवान्यै नमः ǀ
24.	Oṃ Mahākauśikyai Namaḥ ǀ	ॐ महाकौशिक्यै नमः ǀ
25.	Oṃ Kośapūrṇāyai Namaḥ ǀ	ॐ कोशपूर्णायै नमः ǀ
26.	Oṃ Kiśorīkiśorapriyānandehāyai Namaḥ ǀ	ॐ किशोरीकिशोरप्रियानन्देहायै नमः ǀ
27.	Oṃ Mahākāraṇākāraṇāyai Namaḥ	ॐ महाकारणाकारणायै नमः ǀ
28.	Oṃ Karmaśīlāyai Namaḥ ǀ	ॐ कर्मशीलायै नमः ǀ
29.	Oṃ Kapāliprasiddhāyai Namaḥ ǀ	ॐ कपालिप्रसिद्धायै नमः ǀ
30.	Oṃ Mahāsiddhakhaṇḍāyai Namaḥ	ॐ महासिद्धखण्डायै नमः ǀ
31.	Oṃ Makārapriyāyai Namaḥ ǀ	ॐ मकारप्रियायै नमः ǀ
32.	Oṃ Mānarūpāyai Namaḥ ǀ	ॐ मानरूपायै नमः ǀ
33.	Oṃ Maheśyai Namaḥ ǀ	ॐ महेश्यै नमः ǀ
34.	Oṃ Mahollāsinīlāsyalīlālayāṅgyai Namaḥ ǀ	ॐ महोल्लासिनी लास्य लीलालयाङ्ग्यै नमः ǀ
35.	Oṃ Kṣamākṣemaśīlāyai Namaḥ ǀ	ॐ क्षमाक्षेमशीलायै नमः ǀ
36.	Oṃ Kṣapākāriṇyai Namaḥ ǀ	ॐ क्षपाकारिण्यै नमः ǀ
37.	Oṃ Akṣayaprītidāyai Namaḥ ǀ	ॐ अक्षयप्रीतिदायै नमः ǀ
38.	Oṃ Bhūtiyuktāyai Namaḥ ǀ	ॐ भूतियुक्तायै नमः ǀ
39.	Oṃ Bhavānyai Namaḥ ǀ	ॐ भवान्यै नमः ǀ
40.	Oṃ Bhavārādhitāyai Namaḥ ǀ	ॐ भवाराधितायै नमः ǀ
41.	Oṃ Bhūtisatyātmikāyai Namaḥ ǀ	ॐ भूतिसत्यात्मिकायै नमः ǀ
42.	Oṃ Prabhodbhāsitāyai Namaḥ ǀ	ॐ प्रभोद्भासितायै नमः ǀ
43.	Oṃ Bhānubhāsvatkarāyai Namaḥ ǀ	ॐ भानुभास्वत्करायै नमः ǀ
44.	Oṃ Dharādhīśamātre Namaḥ ǀ	ॐ धराधीशमात्रे नमः ǀ
45.	Oṃ Dharāgāradṛṣṭyai Namaḥ ǀ	ॐ धरागारदृष्ट्यै नमः ǀ
46.	Oṃ Dhareśārcitāyai Namaḥ ǀ	ॐ धरेशार्चितायै नमः ǀ
47.	Oṃ Dhīvarādhīvarāṅgyai Namaḥ ǀ	ॐ धीवराधीवराङ्ग्यै नमः ǀ
48.	Oṃ Prakṛṣṭaprabhārūpiṇyai Namaḥ ǀ	ॐ प्रकृष्टप्रभारूपिण्यै नमः ǀ

49.	Oṃ Prāṇarūpaprakṛṣṭasvarūpāyai Namaḥ		ॐ प्राणरूपप्रकृष्टस्वरूपायै नमः ।
50.	Oṃ Svarūpapriyāyai Namaḥ		ॐ स्वरूपप्रियायै नमः ।
51.	Oṃ Calatkuṇḍalākāminyai Namaḥ	ॐ चलत्कुण्डलाकामिन्यै नमः ।
52.	Oṃ Kāntayuktāyai Namaḥ		ॐ कान्तयुक्तायै नमः ।
53.	Oṃ Kapālācalāyai Namaḥ		ॐ कपालाचलायै नमः ।
54.	Oṃ Kālakoddhāriṇyai Namaḥ		ॐ कालकोद्धारिण्यै नमः ।
55.	Oṃ Kadambapriyāyai Namaḥ		ॐ कदम्बप्रियायै नमः ।
56.	Oṃ Koṭarīkoṭadehāyai Namaḥ		ॐ कोटरीकोटदेहायै नमः ।
57.	Oṃ Kramāyai Namaḥ		ॐ क्रमायै नमः ।
58.	Oṃ Kīrtidāyai Namaḥ		ॐ कीर्तिदायै नमः ।
59.	Oṃ Karṇarūpāyai Namaḥ		ॐ कर्णरूपायै नमः ।
60.	Oṃ Kākṣmyai Namaḥ		ॐ काक्ष्म्यै नमः ।
61.	Oṃ Kṣamāṅgyai Namaḥ		ॐ क्षमाङ्ग्यै नमः ।
62.	Oṃ Kṣayapremarūpāyai Namaḥ		ॐ क्षयप्रेमरूपायै नमः ।
63.	Oṃ Kṣapāyai Namaḥ		ॐ क्षपायै नमः ।
64.	Oṃ Kṣayākṣāyai Namaḥ		ॐ क्षयाक्षायै नमः ।
65.	Oṃ Kṣayāhvāyai Namaḥ		ॐ क्षयाह्वायै नमः ।
66.	Oṃ Kṣayaprāntarāyai Namaḥ		ॐ क्षयप्रान्तरायै नमः ।
67.	Oṃ Kṣavatkāminyai Namaḥ		ॐ क्षवत्कामिन्यै नमः ।
68.	Oṃ Kṣāriṇīkṣīrapūrṇāyai Namaḥ		ॐ क्षारिणीक्षीरपूर्णायै नमः ।
69.	Oṃ Śivāṅgyai Namaḥ		ॐ शिवाङ्ग्यै नमः ।
70.	Oṃ Śākambharyai Namaḥ		ॐ शाकम्भर्यै नमः ।
71.	Oṃ Mahāśākayajñāyai Namaḥ		ॐ महाशाकयज्ञायै नमः ।
72.	Oṃ Phalaprāśakāyai Namaḥ		ॐ फलप्राशकायै नमः ।
73.	Oṃ Śakāhvāyai Namaḥ		ॐ शकाह्वायै नमः ।
74.	Oṃ Śakāhvāśakākhyāyai Namaḥ		ॐ शकाह्वाशकाख्यायै नमः ।
75.	Oṃ Śakāyai Namaḥ		ॐ शकायै नमः ।
76.	Oṃ Śakākṣāntaroṣāyai Namaḥ		ॐ शकाक्षान्तरोषायै नमः ।
77.	Oṃ Suroṣāyai Namaḥ		ॐ सुरोषायै नमः ।

78.	Oṃ Surekhāyai Namaḥ ǀ	ॐ सुरेखायै नमः।
79.	Oṃ Mahāśeṣayajñopavītapriyāyai Namaḥ ǀ	ॐ महाशेषयज्ञोपवीतप्रियायै नमः।
80.	Oṃ Jayantyai Namaḥ ǀ	ॐ जयन्त्यै नमः।
81.	Oṃ Jayāyai Namaḥ ǀ	ॐ जयायै नमः।
82.	Oṃ Jāgratīyogyarūpāyai Namaḥ ǀ	ॐ जाग्रतीयोग्यरूपायै नमः।
83.	Oṃ Jayāṅgāyai Namaḥ ǀ	ॐ जयाङ्गायै नमः।
84.	Oṃ Japadhyānasantuṣṭasaṃjñāyai Namaḥ ǀ	ॐ जपध्यानसन्तुष्टसंज्ञायै नमः।
85.	Oṃ Jayaprāṇarūpāyai Namaḥ ǀ	ॐ जयप्राणरूपायै नमः।
86.	Oṃ Jayasvarṇadehāyai Namaḥ ǀ	ॐ जयस्वर्णदेहायै नमः।
87.	Oṃ Jayajvālinīyāminyai Namaḥ ǀ	ॐ जयज्वालिनीयामिन्यै नमः।
88.	Oṃ Yāmyarūpāyai Namaḥ ǀ	ॐ याम्यरूपायै नमः।
89.	Oṃ Jaganmātṛrūpāyai Namaḥ ǀ	ॐ जगन्मातृरूपायै नमः।
90.	Oṃ Jagadrakṣaṇāyai Namaḥ ǀ	ॐ जगद्रक्षणायै नमः।
91.	Oṃ Svadhāvauṣaḍantāyai Namaḥ	ॐ स्वधावौषडन्तायै नमः।
92.	Oṃ Vilambāvilambāyai Namaḥ ǀ	ॐ विलम्बाविलम्बायै नमः।
93.	Oṃ Ṣaḍaṅgāyai Namaḥ ǀ	ॐ षडङ्गायै नमः।
94.	Oṃ Mahālambarūpāsihastāyai Namaḥ ǀ	ॐ महालम्बरूपासिहस्तायै नमः।
95.	Oṃ Padāhāriṇīhāriṇyai Namaḥ ǀ	ॐ पदाहारिणीहारिण्यै नमः।
96.	Oṃ Hāriṇyai Namaḥ ǀ	ॐ हारिण्यै नमः।
97.	Oṃ Mahāmaṅgalāyai Namaḥ ǀ	ॐ महामङ्गलायै नमः।
98.	Oṃ Maṅgalapremakīrtyai Namaḥ ǀ	ॐ मङ्गलप्रेमकीर्त्यै नमः।
99.	Oṃ Niśumbhacchidāyai Namaḥ ǀ	ॐ निशुम्भच्छिदायै नमः।
100	Oṃ Śumbhadarpatvahāyai Namaḥ	ॐ शुम्भदर्पत्वहायै नमः।
101	Oṃ Ānandabījādimuktasvarūpāyai Namaḥ ǀ	ॐ आनन्दबीजादिमुक्तस्वरूपायै नमः
102	Oṃ Caṇḍamuṇḍā Padāmukhyacaṇḍāyai Namaḥ ǀ	ॐ चण्डमुण्डापदामुख्यचण्डायै नमः।
103	Oṃ Pracaṇḍāpracaṇḍāyai Namaḥ	ॐ प्रचण्डाप्रचण्डायै नमः।

104	Oṃ Mahācaṇḍavegāyai Namaḥ		ॐ महाचण्डवेगायै नमः ।
105	Oṃ Calaccāmarāyai Namaḥ		ॐ चलच्चामरायै नमः ।
106	Oṃ Cāmarācandrakīrtaye Namaḥ		ॐ चामराचन्द्रकीर्तये नमः ।
107	Oṃ Sucāmīkarā Citrabhūṣojjvalāṅgyai Namaḥ		ॐ सुचामीकरा चित्रभूषोज्ज्वलाङ्ग्यै नमः ।
108	Oṃ Susaṅgītagītāyai Namaḥ		ॐ सुसङ्गीतगीतायै नमः ।

Iti Śrī Mātaṅgyaṣṭottara Śata Nāmāvaliḥ Sampūrṇā ॥

इति श्री मातङ्ग्यष्टोत्तर शतनामावलिः सम्पूर्णा ॥

*****

Śrī Mātangī Sahasranāma Stotram

Dhyānam

*Mātangīm Bhūṣitāngīm Vividha Manidharāmindu Sūryākṣiyugmām
Svidmadvaktrām Kadamba Prasavaparilasadvenukāmātra Vīnām |
Bimboṣṭhīm Raktavastrām Mrugamadatilakāmindu Rekhāvatamsām
Karṇodyacchankha Patrām Kaṭhinakuchabharākrānta Madhyām*

Namāmi ||

Īśvara Uvāca |

*Śṛṇu Devi Pravakṣyāmi Sāmpratantattvataḥ Param |
Nāmnāṃ Sahasramparamaṃ Sumukhyāḥ Siddhaye Hitam || 1*

*Sahasranāmapāṭhī Yaḥ Sarvatra Vijayī Bhavet |
Parābhavo Na Tasyāsti Sabhāyāvvā Mahāraṇe || 2*

*Yathā Tuṣṭā Bhaveddevī Sumukhī Cāsya Pāṭhataḥ |
Tathā Bhavati Deveśi Sādhakaḥ Śiva Eva Saḥ || 3*

*Aśvamedhasahasrāṇi Vājapeyasya Koṭayaḥ |
Sakṛtpāṭhena Jāyante Prasannā Sumukhī Bhavet || 4*

*Matango'sya Ṛṣiśchando'nuṣṭubdevī Samīritā |
Sumukhī Viniyogaḥ Syātsarvasampattihetave || 5*

*Evandhyātvā Paṭhedetadyadīcchetsiddhimātmanaḥ |
Devīṃ Ṣoḍaśavārṣikīṃ Śavagatāmmādhvīrasāghūrṇitāṃ
Śyāmāngīmaruṇāmbarāmpṛthukucāngguñjāvalīśobhitām |
Hastābhyāndadhatīnkapālamamalantīkṣṇāntathā
Karttrikāndhyāyenmānasapankaje Bhagavatīmucchiṣṭacāṇḍālinīm || 6*

Atha Mātangī Sahasranāma Stotram

*Oṃ Sumukhī Śemuṣīsevyā Surasā Śaśiśekharā |
Samānāsyā Sādhanī Ca Samastasurasanmukhī || 7*

*Sarvasampattijananī Sammadā Sindhusevinī |
Śambhusīmantinī Saumyā Samārādhyā Sudhārasā || 8*

Sāraṅgā Savalī Velālāvaṇyavanamālinī |
Vanajākṣī Vanacarī Vanī Vanavinodinī || 9

Veginī Vegadā Vegā Bagalasthā Balādhikā |
Kālī Kālapriyā Kelī Kamalā Kālakāminī || 10

Kamalā Kamalasthā Ca Kamalasthākalāvatī |
Kulīnā Kuṭilā Kāntā Kokilā Kalabhāṣiṇī || 11

Kīrākelikarā Kālī Kapālinyapi Kālikā |
Keśinī Ca Kuśāvarttā Kauśāmbhī Keśavapriyā || 12

Kālī Kāśī Mahākālasaṅkāśā Keśadāyinī |
Kuṇḍalā Ca Kulasthā Ca Kuṇḍalāṅgadamaṇḍitā || 13

Kuṇḍapadmā Kumudinī Kumudaprītivarddhinī |
Kuṇḍapriyā Kuṇḍaruciḥ Kuraṅganayanā Kulā || 14

Kundabimbālinadanī Kusumbhakusumākarā |
Kāñcī Kanakaśobhāḍhyā Kvaṇatkiṅkiṇikākaṭiḥ || 15

Kaṭhorakaraṇā Kāṣṭhā Kaumudī Kaṇḍavatyapi |
Kaparddinī Kapaṭinī Kaṭhinī Kalakaṇḍinī || 16

Kīrahastā Kumārī Ca Kurūḍhakusumapriyā |
Kuñjarasthā Kujaratā Kumbhī Kumbhastanī Kalā || 17

Kumbhīkāṅgā Karabhorūḥ Kadalī Kuśaśāyinī |
Kupitā Koṭarasthā Ca Kaṅkālī Kandalālayā || 18

Kapālavāsinī Keśī Kampamānaśiroruhā |
Kadambarī Kadambasthā Kuṅkumapremadhāriṇī || 19

Kuṭumbinī Kṛpāyuktā Kratuḥ Kratukarapriyā |
Kātyāyanī Kṛttikā Ca Kārttikī Kuśavarttinī || 20

Kāmapatnī Kāmadātrī Kāmeśī Kāmavanditā |
Kāmarūpā Kāmaratiḥ Kāmākhyā Jñānamohinī || 21

Khaḍginī Khecarī Khañjā Khañjarīṭekṣaṇā Khagā |

Kharagā Kharanādā Ca Kharasthā Khelanapriyā || 22

Kharāṁśuḥ Khelanī Khaṭvākharākhaṭvāṅgadhāriṇī |

Kharakhaṇḍinyapi Khyātiḥ Khaṇḍitā Khaṇḍanapriyā || 23

Khaṇḍapriyā Khaṇḍakhādyā Khaṇḍhasindhuśca Khaṇḍinī |

Gaṅgā Godāvarī Gaurī Gotamyapi Ca Gautamī || 24

Gaṅgā Gayā Gaganagā Gāruḍī Garuḍadhvajā |

Gītā Gītapriyā Geyā Guṇaprītirggururgirī |

Gaurgaurī Gaṇḍasadanā Gokulā Goḥpratāriṇī |

Goptā Govindinī Gūḍhā Gūḍhavigrastaguñjinī || 25

Gajagā Gopinī Gopī Gokṣājayapriyā Gaṇā |

Giribhūpāladuhitā Gogā Gokulavāsinī || 26

Ghanastanī Ghanarucirgghanorugghananissvanā |

Ghuṅkāriṇī Ghukṣakarī Ghūghūkaparivāritā || 27

Ghaṇṭānādapriyā Ghaṇṭā Ghoṭā Ghoṭakavāhinī |

Ghorarūpā Ca Ghorā Ca Ghṛtaprītirgghṛtāñjanī || 28

Ghṛtācī Ghṛtavṛṣṭiśca Ghaṇṭā Ghaṭaghaṭāvṛtā |

Ghaṭasthā Ghaṭanā Ghātakarī Ghātanivāriṇī || 29

Cañcarīkī Cakorī Ca Ca Cāmuṇḍā Cīradhāriṇī |

Cāturī Capalā Cañcuścitā Cintāmaṇisthitā || 30

Cāturvarṇyamayī Cañcuścorācāryā Camatkṛtiḥ |

Cakravartivadhūścitrā Cakrāṅgī Cakramodinī || 31

Cetaścarī Cittavṛttiścetanā Cetanapriyā |

Cāpinī Campakaprītiścaṇḍā Caṇḍālavāsinī || 32

Cirañjīvinī Taccintā Ciñcāmūlanivāsinī |

Chūrikā Chatramadhyasthā Chindā Chindakarī Chidā || 33

Chucchundarī Chalaprītiśchucchundaranibhasvanā |
Chalinī Chatradā Chinnā Chiṇṭicchedakarī Chaṭā || 34

Chadminī Chāndasī Chāyā Charū Chandākarītyapi |
Jayadā Jayadā Jātī Jāyinī Jāmalā Jatuḥ || 35

Jambūpriyā Jīvanasthā Jaṅgamā Jaṅgamapriyā |
Javāpuṣpapriyā Japyā Jagajjīvā Jagajjaniḥ || 36

Jagajjantupradhānā Ca Jagajjīvaparājavā |
Jātipriyā Jīvanasthā Jīmūtasadṛśīruciḥ || 37

Janyā Janahitā Jāyā Janmabhūrjjambhasī Jabhūḥ |
Jayadā Jagadāvāsā Jāyinī Jvarakṛcchrajit || 38

Japā Ca Japatī Japyā Japāhā Jāyinī Janā |
Jālandharamayījānurjjālaukā Jāpyabhūṣaṇā || 39

Jagajjīvamayījīvā Jaratkārurjjanapriyā |
Jagatī Jananiratā Jagacchobhākarī Javā || 40

Jagatītrāṇakṛjjaṅghā Jātīphalavinodinī |
Jātīpuṣpapriyā Jvālā Jātīhā Jātirūpiṇī || 41

Jīmūtavāhanarucirjjīmūtā Jīrṇavastrakṛt |
Jīrṇavastradharā Jīrṇā Jvalatī Jālanāśinī || 42

Jagatkṣobhakarī Jātirjjagatkṣobhavināśinī |
Janāpavādā Jīvā Ca Jananīgṛhavāsinī || 43

Janānurāgā Jānusthā Jalavāsā Jalārttikṛt |
Jalajā Jalavelā Ca Jalacakranivāsinī || 44

Jalamuktā Jalārohā Jalajā Jalajekṣaṇā |
Jalapriyā Jalaukā Ca Jalāṃśobhavatī Tathā || 45

Jalavisphūrjjitavapurjjvalatpāvakaśobhinī |
Jhiñjhā Jhillamayī Jhiñjhājhaṇatkārakarī Jayā || 46

Jhañjhī Jhampakarī Jhampā Jhampatrāsanivāriṇī |
Ṭaṅkārasthā Ṭaṅkakarī Ṭaṅkārakaraṇāṃhasā || 47

Ṭaṅkārottakṛtaṣṭhīvā Ḍiṇḍīravasanāvṛtā |
Ḍākinī Ḍāmirī Caiva Ḍiṇḍimadhvaninādinī || 48

Ḍakāranissvanarucistapinī Tāpinī Tathā |
Taruṇī Tundilā Tundā Tāmasī Ca Tamaḥ Priyā || 49

Tāmrā Tāmravatī Tantustundilā Tulasambhavā |
Tulākoṭisuvegā Ca Tulyakāmā Tulāśrayā || 50

Tudinī Tuninī Tumbā Tulyakālā Tulāśrayā |
Tumulā Tulajā Tulyā Tulādānakarī Tathā || 51

Tulyavegā Tulyagatistulākoṭininādinī |
Tāmroṣṭhā Tāmraparṇī Ca Tamaḥsaṅkṣobhakāriṇī || 52

Tvaritā Jvarahā Tīrā Tārakeśī Tamālinī |
Tamodānavatī Tāmatālasthānavatī Tamī |
Tāmasī Ca Tamisrā Ca Tīvrā Tīvraparākramā |
Taṭasthā Tilatailāktā Taruṇī Tapanadyutiḥ || 53

Tilottamā Ca Tilakṛttārakādhīśaśekharā |
Tilapuṣpapriyā Tārā Tārakeśī Kuṭumbinī || 54

Sthāṇupatnī Sthirakarī Sthūlasampadvivarddhinī |
Sthitiḥ Sthairyasthaviṣṭhā Ca Sthapatiḥ Sthūlavigrahā || 55

Sthūlasthalavatī Sthālī Sthalasaṅgavivarddhinī |
Daṇḍinī Dantinī Dāmā Daridrā Dīnavatsalā || 56

Devā Devavadhūrddityā Dāminī Devabhūṣaṇā |
Dayā Damavatī Dīnavatsalā Dāḍimastanī || 57

Devamūrttikarā Daityādāriṇī Devatānatā |
Dolākrīḍā Dayāluśca Dampatī Devatāmayī || 58

Daśādīpasthitā Doṣādoṣahā Doṣakāriṇī |

Durgā Durgārtiśamanī Durgamyā Durgavāsinī |

Durgandhanāśinī Dussthā Duḥkhapraśamakāriṇī |

Durggandhā Dundubhīdhvāntā Dūrasthā Dūravāsinī || 59

Daradāmaradātrī Ca Durvvyādhadayitā Damī |

Dhurandharā Dhurīṇā Ca Dhaureyī Dhanadāyinī || 60

Dhīrāravā Dharitrī Ca Dharmadā Dhīramānasā |

Dhanurddharā Ca Dhamanī Dhamanīdhūrttavigrahā || 61

Dhūmravarṇā Dhūmrapānā Dhūmalā Dhūmamodinī |

Nandinī Nandinīnandā Nandinīinandabālikā || 62

Navīnā Narmadā Narmanemirnniyamanissvanā |

Nirmalā Nigamādhārā Nimnagā Nagnakāminī || 63

Nīlā Niratnā Nirvāṇā Nirllobhā Nirguṇā Natiḥ |

Nīlagrīvā Nirīhā Ca Nirañjanajamānavā || 64

Nirguṇḍikā Ca Nirguṇḍā Nirnnāsā Nāsikābhidhā |

Patākinī Patākā Ca Patraprītiḥ Payasvinī || 65

Pīnā Pīnastanī Patnī Pavanāśī Niśāmayī |

Parāparaparākālī Pārakṛtyabhujapriyā || 66

Pavanasthā Ca Pavanā Pavanaprītivarddhinī |

Paśuvṛddhikarī Puṣpī Poṣakā Puṣṭivarddhinī || 67

Puṣpiṇī Pustakakarā Pūrṇimātalavāsinī |

Peśī Pāśakarī Pāśā Pāṃśuhā Pāṃśulā Paśuḥ || 68

Paṭuḥ Parāśā Paraśudhāriṇī Pāśinī Tathā |

Pāpaghnī Patipatnī Ca Patitā Patitāpatī || 69

Piśācī Ca Piśācaghnī Piśitāśanatoṣiṇī |

Pānadā Pānapātrī Ca Pānadānakarodyatā || 70

Peyāprasiddhā Pīyūṣā Pūrṇā Pūrṇamanorathā |

Pataṅgābhā Pataṅgā Ca Paunaḥpunyapibāparā ‖ 71

Paṅkilā Paṅkamagnā Ca Pānīyā Pañjarasthitā |

Pañcamī Pañcayajñā Ca Pañcatā Pañcamāpriyā ‖ 72

Picumandā Puṇḍarīkā Pikī Piṅgalalocanā |

Priyaṅgumañjarī Piṇḍī Paṇḍitā Pāṇḍuraprabhā ‖ 73

Pretāsanā Priyālasthā Pāṇḍughnī Pīnasāpahā |

Phalinī Phaladātrī Ca Phalaśrīḥ Phalabhūṣaṇā ‖ 74

Phūtkārakāriṇī Raphārī Phullā Phullāmbujānanā |

Sphuliṅgahā Sphītamatiḥ Sphītakīrttikarī Tathā ‖ 75

Bālamāyā Balārātirbbalinī Balavarddhinī |

Veṇuvādyā Vanacarī Virañcijanayatyapi ‖ 76

Vidyāpradā Mahāvidyā Bodhinī Bodhadāyinī |

Buddhamātā Ca Buddhā Ca Vanamālāvatī Varā ‖ 77

Varadā Vāruṇī Vīṇā Vīṇāvādanatatparā |

Vinodinī Vinodasthā Vaiṣṇavī Viṣṇuvallabhā ‖ 78

Vaidyā Vaidyacikitsā Ca Vivaśā Viśvaviśrutā |

Vidyaughavihvalā Velā Vittadā Vigatajvarā ‖ 79

Virāvā Vivarīkārā Bimboṣṭhī Bimbavatsalā |

Vindhyasthā Paravandyā Ca Vīrasthānavarā Ca Vit ‖ 80

Vedāntavedyā Vijayā Vijayāvijayapradā |

Virogī Vandinī Vandhyā Vandyabandhanivāriṇī ‖ 81

Bhaginī Bhagamālā Ca Bhavānī Bhavanāśinī |

Bhīmā Bhīmānanā Bhīmābhaṅgurā Bhīmadarśanā ‖ 82

Bhillī Bhilladharā Bhīrurbbharuṇḍābhī Bhayāvahā |

Bhagasarpiṇyapi Bhagā Bhagarūpā Bhagālayā ‖ 83

Bhagāsanā Bhavābhogā Bherījhaṅkārarañjitā |

Bhīṣaṇā Bhīṣaṇārāvā Vabhagatyahibhūṣaṇā || 84

Bhāradvājā Bhogadātrī Bhūtighnī Bhūtibhūṣaṇā |

Bhūmidābhūmidātrī Ca Bhūpatirbbharadāyinī || 85

Bhramarī Bhrāmarī Bhālā Bhūpālakulasaṃsthitā |

Mātā Manoharā Māyā Māninī Mohinī Mahī || 86

Mahālakṣmīrmadakṣībā Madirā Madirālayā |

Madoddhatā Mataṅgasthā Mādhavī Madhumarddinī || 87

Modā Modakarī Medhā Medhyāmadhyādhipasthitā |

Madyapā Māṃsalobhasthā Modinī Maithunodyatā || 88

Mūrddhāvatī Mahāmāyā Māyā Mahimamandirā |

Mahāmālā Mahāvidyā Mahāmārī Maheśvarī || 89

Mahādevavadhūmānyā Mathurā Merumaṇḍitā |

Medasvinī Milindākṣī Mahiṣāsuramarddinī || 90

Maṇḍalasthā Bhagasthā Ca Madirārāgagarvitā |

Mokṣadā Muṇḍamālā Ca Mālā Mālāvilāsinī || 91

Mātaṅginī Ca Mātaṅgī Mātaṅgatanayāpi Ca |

Madhusravā Madhurasā Bandhūkakusumapriyā || 92

Yāminī Yāminīnāthabhūṣā Yāvakarañjitā |

Yavāṅkurapriyā Yāmā Yavanī Yavanārdinī || 93

Yamaghnī Yamakalpā Ca Yajamānasvarūpiṇī |

Yajñā Yajñayajuryakṣī Yaśoniḥ Kampakākāriṇī || 94

Yakṣiṇī Yakṣajananī Yaśodāyāsadhāriṇī |

Yaśassūtrapradā Yāmā Yajñakarmakarītyapi || 95

Yaśasvinī Yakārasthā Bhūyastambhanivāsinī |

Rañjitā Rājapatnī Ca Ramā Rekhā Ravī Raṇā || 96

Rajovatī Rajaścitrā Rañjanī Rajanīpatiḥ |

Rogiṇī Rajanī Rājñā Rājyadā Rājyavarddhinī || 97

Rājanvatī Rājanītistathā Rajatavāsinī |

Ramaṇīramaṇīyā Ca Rāmā Rāmāvatī Ratiḥ |

Reto Ratī Ratotsāhā Rogaghnī Rogakāriṇī |

Raṅgā Raṅgavatī Rāgā Rāgā Rāgajñā Rāgakṛddayā || 98

Rāmikā Rajakī Revā Rajanī Raṅgalocanā |

Raktacarmadharā Raṅgī Raṅgasthā Raṅgavāhinī || 99

Ramā Rambhāphalaprītī Rambhorū Rāghavapriyā |

Raṅgā Raṅgāṅgamadhurā Rodasī Ca Mahāravā || 100

Rodhakṛdrogahantrī Ca Rūpabhṛdrogasrāviṇī |

Bandī Vandistutā Bandhurbandhūkakusumādharā || 101

Vanditā Vandyamānā Ca Vaidrāvī Vedavidvidhā |

Vikopā Vikapālā Ca Viṅkasthā Viṅkavatsalā || 102

Vedairvilagnalagnā Ca Vidhiviṅkakarī Vidhā |

Śaṅkhinī Śaṅkhavalayā Śaṅkhamālāvatī Śamī || 103

Śaṅkhapātrā Śinī Śaṅkhasvanaśaṅkhagalā Śaśī |

Śabarī Śambarī Śambhuḥ Śambhukeśā Śarāsinī || 104

Śavā Śyenavatī Śyāmā Śyāmāṅgī Śyāmalocanā |

Śmaśānasthā Śmaśānā Ca Śmaśānasthānabhūṣaṇā || 105

Samadā Samahantrī Ca Śaṅkhinī Śaṅkharoṣarā |

Śāntiśśāntipradā Śeṣā Śeṣākhyā Śeṣaśāyinī || 106

Śemuṣī Śoṣiṇī Śeṣā Śauryā Śauryaśarā Śarī |

Śāpadā Śāpahā Śāpāśāpapanthā Sadāśivā || 107

Śṛṅgiṇī Śṛṅgipalabhuk Śaṅkarī Śāṅkarī Śivā |

Śavasthā Śavabhuk Śāntā Śavakarṇā Śavodarī || 108

Śāvinī Śavaśiṃśāśrīḥ Śavā Ca Śamaśāyinī |
Śavakuṇḍalinī Śaivāśīkarā Śiśirāśinā || 109

Śavakāñcī Śavaśrīkā Śabamālā Śavākṛtiḥ |
Savantī Saṅkucā Śaktiśśantanuśśavadāyinī || 110

Sindhussarasvatī Sindhussundarī Sundarānanā |
Sādhuḥ Siddhipradātrī Ca Siddhā Siddhasarasvatī || 111

Santatissampadā Saṃvacchaṅkisampattidāyinī |
Sapatnī Sarasā Sārā Sārasvatakarī Sudhā || 112

Surāsamāṃsāśanā Ca Samārādhyā Samastadā |
Samadhīssāmadā Sīmā Sammohā Samadarśanā || 113

Sāmatissāmadhā Sīmā Sāvitrī Savidhā Satī |
Savanā Savanāsārā Savarā Sāvarā Samī || 114

Simarā Satatā Sādhvī Sadhrīcī Sasahāyinī |
Haṃsī Haṃsagatihaṃsī Haṃsojjvalanicolayuk || 115

Halinī Hālinī Hālā Halaśrīrharavallabhā |
Halā Halavatī Hyeṣā Helā Harṣavivarddhinī || 116

Hantirhantā Hayāhāhāhatāhantātikāriṇī |
Haṅkārī Haṅkṛtirhaṅkā Hīhīhāhāhitāhitā || 117

Hītirhemapradā Hārārāviṇī Harirasammatā |
Horā Hotrī Holikā Ca Homā Homahavirhaviḥ || 118

Hariṇī Hariṇīnetrā Himācalanivāsinī |
Lambodarī Lambakarṇā Lambikā Lambavigrahā || 119

Līlā Līlāvatī Lolā Lalanā Lalitā Latā |
Lalāmalocanā Lobhyā Lolākṣī Satkulālayā || 120

Lapatnī Lapatī Lampā Lopāmudrā Lalantikā |
Latikā Laṅghinī Laṅghā Lālimā Laghumadhyamā || 121

Laghīyasī Laghūdaryā Lūtā Lūtāvināśinī |

Lomaśā Lomalambī Ca Lulantī Ca Lulumpatī || 122

Lulāyasthā Balaharī Laṅkāpurapurandarā |

Lakṣmīrllakṣmīpradā Labhyā Lākṣākṣī Lulitaprabhā || 123

Kṣaṇā Kṣaṇakṣukṣukṣiṇī Kṣamākṣāntiḥ Kṣamāvatī |

Kṣāmā Kṣāmodarī Kṣemyā Kṣaumabhṛtkṣatriyāṅgaṇā || 124

Kṣayā Kṣāyākarī Kṣīrā Kṣīradā Kṣīrasāgarā |

Kṣemaṅkarī Kṣayakarī Kṣayakṛtkṣaṇadā Kṣatiḥ || 125

Kṣudrikā Kṣudrikākṣudrā Kṣutkṣamā Kṣīṇapātakā |

Phala Śrutiḥ

Mātuḥ Sahasranāmedam Sumukhyāssiddhidāyakam || 126

Yaḥ Paṭhetprayato Nityam Sa Eva Syānmaheśvaraḥ |

Anācārātpaṭhennityandaridro Dhanavānbhavet || 127

Mūkassyādvākpatirdevi Rogī Nirogatāvvrajet |

Putrārtthī Putramāpnoti Triṣu Lokeṣu Viśrutam || 128

Vandhyāpi Sūyate Putravviduṣassadṛśaṅguroḥ |

Satyañca Bahudhā Bhūyādgāvaśca Bahudugdhadāḥ || 129

Rājānaḥ Pādanamrāssyustasya Hāsā Iva Sphuṭāḥ |

Arayassaṅkṣayayyānti Mānasā Saṁsmṛtā Api || 130

Darśanādeva Jāyante Narā Nāryo'pi Tadvaśāḥ |

Karttā Harttā Svayavīro Jāyate Nātra Saṁśayaḥ || 131

Yayyaṅkāmayate Kāmantantamāpnoti Niścitam |

Duritanna Ca Tasyāsti Nāsti Śokaḥ Kathañcana || 132

Catuṣpathe'rddharātre Ca Yaḥ Paṭhetsādhakottamaḥ |

Ekākī Nirbbhayo Vīro Daśāvarttastavottamam || 133

Manasā Cintitaṅkāryaṃ Tasya Siddhirnna Saṃśayaḥ |
Vinā Sahasranāmnāyyo Japenmantraṅkadācana ‖ 134

Na Siddhirjjāyate Tasya Mantraṅkalpaśatairapi |
Kujavāre Śmaśāne Vā Madhyāhne Yo Japetsadā ‖ 135

Kṛtakṛtyassa Jāyeta Karttā Harttā Nṛṇāmiha |
Rogārtto'rddhaniśāyāyyaḥ Paṭhedāsanasaṃsthitaḥ ‖ 136

Sadyo Nīrogatāmeti Yadi Syānnirbbhayastadā |
Arddharātre Śmaśāne Vā Śanivāre Japenmanum |
Aṣṭottarasahasrantu Daśavārañjapettataḥ |
Sahasranāma Caitaddhi Tadā Yāti Svayaṃ Śivā ‖ 137

Mahāpavanarūpeṇa Ghoragomāyunādinī |
Tato Yadi Na Bhītiḥ Syāttadā Dehītivāgbhavet ‖ 138

Tadā Paśubalindadyātsvayaṃ Gṛhṇāti Caṇḍikā |
Yatheṣṭañca Varandattvā Prayāti Sumukhī Śivā ‖ 139

Rocanāgurukastūrīkarppūraiśca Sacandanaiḥ |
Kuṅkumena Dine Śreṣṭhe Likhitvā Bhūrjjapatrake ‖ 140

Śubhanakṣatrayoge Ca Kṛtamārutasakriyaḥ |
Kṛtvā Sampātanavidhindhārayeddakṣiṇe Kare ‖ 141

Sahasranāma Svarṇasthaṅkaṇṭhe Vā Vijitendriyaḥ |
Tadāyampraṇamenmantrī Kruddhassa Mriyate Naraḥ ‖ 142

Duṣṭaśvāpadajantūnānna Bhīḥ Kutrāpi Jāyate |
Bālakānāmiyaṃ Rakṣā Garbbhiṇīnāmapi Priye ‖ 143

Mohanastambhanākarṣa-Māraṇoccāṭanāni Ca |
Yantradhāraṇato Nūnañjāyante Sādhakasya Tu ‖ 144

Nīlavastre Vilikhite Dhvajāyāyyadi Tiṣṭhati |
Tadā Naṣṭā Bhavatyeva Pracaṇḍāpyarivāhinī ‖ 145

Etajjaptammahābhasma Lalāṭe Yadi Dhārayet |

Tadvilokana Eva Syuḥ Prāṇinastasya Kiṅkarāḥ || 146

Rājapatnyo'pi Vivaśāḥ Kimanyāḥ Purayoṣitaḥ |

Etajjaptampibettoyammāsena Syānmahākaviḥ || 147

Paṇḍitaśca Mahāvādī Jāyate Nātra Saṃśayaḥ |

Ayutañca Paṭhetstotrampuraścaraṇasiddhaye || 148

Daśāṃśaṅkamalairhutvā Trimadhvāktairvidhānataḥ |

Svayamāyāti Kamalā Vāṇyā Saha Tadālaye || 149

Mantro Niḥkīlatāmeti Sumukhī Sumukhī Bhavet |

Anantañca Bhavetpuṇyamapuṇyañca Kṣayavvrajet || 150

Puṣkarādiṣu Tīrttheṣu Snānato Yatphalambhavet |

Tatphalallabhate Jantuḥ Sumukhyāḥ Stotrapāṭhataḥ || 151

Etaduktaṃ Rahasyante Svasarvasvavvarānane |

Na Prakāśyantvayā Devi Yadi Siddhiñca Vindasi || 152

Prakāśanādasiddhissyātkupitā Sumukhī Bhavet |

Nātaḥ Parataro Loke Siddhidaḥ Prāṇināmiha || 153

Vande Śrīsumukhīmprasannavadanāmpūrṇendubimbānanāṃ

Sindūrāṅkitamastakāmmadhumadollolāñca Muktāvalīm |

Śyāmāṅkañjalikākarāṅkaragatañcādhyāpayantīṃ

Śukaṅguñjāpuñjavibhūṣaṇāṃ Sakaruṇāmāmuktaveṇīlatām || 154

Iti Śrī Nandyāvartta Tantre Uttarakhaṇḍe Mātaṅgī Sahasranāma Stotraṃ

Sampūrṇam ||

श्री मातङ्गी सहस्रनाम स्तोत्रम्

ध्यानम्

मातङ्गीं भूषिताङ्गीं विविध मनिधरामिन्दु सूर्याक्षियुग्मां
स्विद्यद्वक्त्रां कदम्ब प्रसवपरिलसद्वेणुकामात्र वीणाम् ।
बिम्बोष्ठीं रक्तवस्त्रां म्रुगमदतिलकामिन्दु रेखावतंसां
कर्णोद्यच्छङ्ख पत्रां कठिनकुचभराक्रान्त मध्यां नमामि ॥

ईश्वर उवाच ।

शृणु देवि प्रवक्ष्यामि साम्प्रतन्तत्त्वतः परम् ।
नाम्नां सहस्रम्परमं सुमुख्याः सिद्धये हितम् ॥1

सहस्रनामपाठी यः सर्वत्र विजयी भवेत् ।
पराभवो न तस्यास्ति सभायाव्वा महारणे ॥ 2

यथा तुष्टा भवेद्देवी सुमुखी चास्य पाठतः ।
तथा भवति देवेशि साधकः शिव एव सः ॥ 3

अश्वमेधसहस्राणि वाजपेयस्य कोटयः ।
सकृत्पाठेन जायन्ते प्रसन्ना सुमुखी भवेत् ॥4

मतङ्गोऽस्य ऋषिश्छन्दोऽनुष्टुब्देवी समीरिता ।
सुमुखी विनियोगः स्यात्सर्वसम्पत्तिहेतवे ॥5

एवन्ध्यात्वा पठेदेतद्यदीच्छेत्सिद्धिमात्मनः ।
देवीं षोडशवार्षिकीं शवगताम्माध्वीरसाघूर्णितां
श्यामाङ्गीमरुणाम्बराम्पृथुकुचाङ्गुञ्जावलीशोभिताम् ।
हस्ताभ्यान्दधतीङ्कपालममलन्तीक्ष्णान्तथा
कर्त्रिकान्ध्यायेन्मानसपङ्कजे भगवतीमुच्छिष्टचाण्डालिनीम् ॥6

अथ मातङ्गी सहस्रनाम स्तोत्रम् ॥

ॐ सुमुखी शेमुषीसेव्या सुरसा शशिशेखरा ।
समानास्या साधनी च समस्तसुरसन्मुखी ॥7

सर्वसम्पत्तिजननी सम्मदा सिन्धुसेविनी ।
शम्भुसीमन्तिनी सौम्या समाराध्या सुधारसा ॥ 8

सारङ्गा सवली वेलालावण्यवनमालिनी ।
वनजाक्षी वनचरी वनी वनविनोदिनी ॥ 9

वेगिनी वेगदा वेगा बगलस्था बलाधिका ।
काली कालप्रिया केली कमला कालकामिनी ॥ 10

कमला कमलस्था च कमलस्थाकलावती ।
कुलीना कुटिला कान्ता कोकिला कलभाषिणी ॥ 11

कीराकेलिकरा काली कपालिन्यपि कालिका ।
केशिनी च कुशावर्त्ता कौशाम्भी केशवप्रिया ॥ 12

काली काशी महाकालसङ्काशा केशदायिनी ।
कुण्डला च कुलस्था च कुण्डलाङ्गदमण्डिता ॥ 13

कुण्डपद्या कुमुदिनी कुमुदप्रीतिवर्द्धिनी ।
कुण्डप्रिया कुण्डरुचिः कुरङ्गनयना कुला ॥ 14

कुन्दबिम्बालिनदनी कुसुम्भकुसुमाकरा ।
काञ्ची कनकशोभाढ्या क्वणत्किङ्किणिकाकटिः ॥ 15

कठोरकरणा काष्ठा कौमुदी कण्डवत्यपि ।
कपर्दिनी कपटिनी कठिनी कलकण्डिनी ॥ 16

कीरहस्ता कुमारी च कुरूढकुसुमप्रिया ।
कुञ्जरस्था कुजरता कुम्भी कुम्भस्तनी कला ॥ 17

कुम्भीकाङ्गा करभोरूः कदली कुशशायिनी ।
कुपिता कोटरस्था च कङ्काली कन्दलालया ॥ 18

कपालवासिनी केशी कम्पमानशिरोरुहा ।
कदम्बरी कदम्बस्था कुङ्कुमप्रेमधारिणी ॥ 19

कुटुम्बिनी कृपायुक्ता ऋतुः ऋतुकरप्रिया ।
कात्यायनी कृत्तिका च कार्त्तिकी कुशवर्त्तिनी ॥ 20

कामपत्नी कामदात्री कामेशी कामवन्दिता ।
कामरूपा कामरतिः कामाख्या ज्ञानमोहिनी ॥ 21

खड्गिनी खेचरी खञ्जा खञ्जरीटेक्षणा खगा ।
खरगा खरनादा च खरस्था खेलनप्रिया ॥ 22

खरांशुः खेलनी खट्वाखराखट्वाङ्गधारिणी।
खरखण्डिन्यपि ख्यातिः खण्डिता खण्डनप्रिया ॥ 23

खण्डप्रिया खण्डखाद्या खण्डसिन्धुश्च खण्डिनी ।
गङ्गा गोदावरी गौरी गोतम्यपि च गौतमी ॥ 24

गङ्गा गया गगनगा गारुडी गरुडध्वजा ।
गीता गीतप्रिया गेया गुणप्रीतिर्गुरुर्गिरी ।
गौगौरी गण्डसदना गोकुला गोःप्रतारिणी ।
गोप्ता गोविन्दिनी गूढा गूढविग्रस्तगुञ्जिनी ॥25

गजगा गोपिनी गोपी गोक्षाजयप्रिया गणा ।
गिरिभूपालदुहिता गोगा गोकुलवासिनी ॥ 26

घनस्तनी घनरुचिर्घनोरुर्घननिस्स्वना ।
घुङ्कारिणी घुक्षकरी घूघूकपरिवारिता ॥27

घण्टानादप्रिया घण्टा घोटा घोटकवाहिनी ।
घोररूपा च घोरा च घृतप्रीतिर्घृताञ्जनी ॥ 28

घृताची घृतवृष्टिश्च घण्टा घटघटावृता ।
घटस्था घटना घातकरी घातनिवारिणी ॥ 29

चञ्चरीकी चकोरी च च चामुण्डा चीरधारिणी ।
चातुरी चपला चञ्चुश्रिता चिन्तामणिस्थिता ॥ 30

चातुर्वर्ण्यमयी चञ्चुश्चोराचार्या चमत्कृतिः ।
चक्रवर्तिवधूश्चित्रा चक्राङ्गी चक्रमोदिनी ॥ 31

चेतश्वरी चित्तवृत्तिश्चेतना चेतनप्रिया ।
चापिनी चम्पकप्रीतिश्चण्डा चण्डालवासिनी ॥ 32

चिरञ्जीविनी तच्चिन्ता चिञ्चामूलनिवासिनी ।
छूरिका छत्रमध्यस्था छिन्दा छिन्दकरी छिदा ॥ 33

छुच्छुन्दरी छलप्रीतिश्छुच्छुन्दरनिभस्वना ।
छलिनी छत्रदा छिन्ना छिण्टिच्छेदकरी छटा ॥ 34

छद्मिनी छान्दसी छाया छरू छन्दाकरीत्यपि ।
जयदा जयदा जाती जायिनी जामला जतुः ॥ 35

जम्बूप्रिया जीवनस्था जङ्गमा जङ्गमप्रिया ।
जवापुष्पप्रिया जप्या जगज्जीवा जगज्जनिः ॥ 36

जगज्जन्तुप्रधाना च जगज्जीवपराजवा ।
जातिप्रिया जीवनस्था जीमूतसदृशीरुचिः ॥ 37

जन्या जनहिता जाया जन्मभूर्ज्जम्भसी जभूः ।
जयदा जगदावासा जायिनी ज्वरकृच्छ्रजित् ॥ 38

जपा च जपती जप्या जपाहा जायिनी जना ।
जालन्धरमयीजानुर्ज्जलौका जाप्यभूषणा ॥39

जगज्जीवमयीजीवा जरत्कारुर्ज्जनप्रिया ।
जगती जननिरता जगच्छोभाकरी जवा ॥ 40

जगतीत्राणकृज्जङ्घा जातीफलविनोदिनी ।
जातीपुष्पप्रिया ज्वाला जातिहा जातिरूपिणी ॥ 41

जीमूतवाहनरुचिर्ज्जीमूता जीर्णवस्त्रकृत् ।
जीर्णवस्त्रधरा जीर्णा ज्वलती जालनाशिनी ॥ 42

जगत्क्षोभकरी जातिर्ज्जगत्क्षोभविनाशिनी ।
जनापवादा जीवा च जननीगृहवासिनी ॥ 43

जनानुरागा जानुस्था जलवासा जलार्त्तिकृत् ।
जलजा जलवेला च जलचक्रनिवासिनी ॥ 44

जलमुक्ता जलारोहा जलजा जलजेक्षणा ।
जलप्रिया जलौका च जलांशोभवती तथा ॥ 45

जलविस्फूर्जितवपुज्ज्वलत्पावकशोभिनी ।
झिञ्झा झिल्लमयी झिञ्झाझणत्कारकरी जया ॥ 46

झञ्झी झम्पूकरी झम्पा झम्पत्रासनिवारिणी ।
टङ्कारास्था टङ्ककरी टङ्कारकरणांहसा ॥47

टङ्कारोद्दृकृतष्ठीवा डिण्डीरवसनावृता ।
डाकिनी डामिरी चैव डिण्डिमध्वनिनादिनी ॥ 48

डकारनिस्स्वनरुचिस्तपिनी तापिनी तथा ।
तरुणी तुन्दिला तुन्दा तामसी च तमः प्रिया ॥ 49

ताम्रा ताम्रवती तन्तुस्तुन्दिला तुलसम्भवा ।
तुलाकोटिसुवेगा च तुल्यकामा तुलाश्रया ॥50

तुदिनी तुनिनी तुम्बा तुल्यकाला तुलाश्रया ।
तुमुला तुलजा तुल्या तुलादानकरी तथा ॥51

तुल्यवेगा तुल्यगतिस्तुलाकोटिनिनादिनी ।
ताम्रोष्ठा ताम्रपर्णी च तमःसङ्क्षोभकारिणी ॥ 52

त्वरिता ज्वरहा तीरा तारकेशी तमालिनी ।
तमोदानवती तामतालस्थानवती तमी ।
तामसी च तमिस्रा च तीव्रा तीव्रपराक्रमा ।
तटस्था तिलतैलाक्ता तरुणी तपनद्युतिः ॥ 53

तिलोत्तमा च तिलकृत्तारकाधीशशेखरा ।
तिलपुष्पप्रिया तारा तारकेशी कुटुम्बिनी ॥54

स्थाणुपत्नी स्थिरकरी स्थूलसम्पद्विवर्द्धिनी ।
स्थितिः स्थैर्यस्थविष्ठा च स्थपतिः स्थूलविग्रहा ॥ 55

स्थूलस्थलवती स्थाली स्थलसङ्गविविर्द्धिनी ।
दण्डिनी दन्तिनी दामा दरिद्रा दीनवत्सला ॥ 56

देवा देववधूर्द्दित्या दामिनी देवभूषणा ।
दया दमवती दीनवत्सला दाडिमस्तनी ॥ 57

देवमूर्त्तिकरा दैत्यादारिणी देवतानता ।
दोलाक्रीडा दयालुश्च दम्पती देवतामयी ॥ 58

दशादीपस्थिता दोषादोषहा दोषकारिणी ।
दुर्गा दुर्गार्तिशमनी दुर्गम्या दुर्गावासिनी ।
दुर्गन्धनाशिनी दुस्स्था दुःखप्रशमकारिणी ।
दुर्गन्धा दुन्दुभीध्वान्ता दूस्था दूर्वासिनी ॥   59

दरदामरदात्री च दुर्व्याधिदयिता दमी ।
धुरन्धरा धुरीणा च धौरेयी धनदायिनी ॥ 60

धीरारवा धरित्री च धर्मदा धीरमानसा ।
धनुर्द्धरा च धमनी धमनीधूर्त्तविग्रहा ॥ 61

धूम्रवर्णा धूम्रपाना धूमला धूममोदिनी ।
नन्दिनी नन्दिनीनन्दा नन्दिनीइनन्दबालिका ॥ 62

नवीना नर्मदा नर्मनेमिर्निर्नियमनिस्स्वना ।
निर्मला निगमाधारा निम्नगा नग्नकामिनी ॥ 63

नीला निरत्ना निर्वाणा निल्लोंभा निर्गुणा नतिः ।
नीलग्रीवा निरीहा च निरञ्जनजमानवा ॥ 64

निर्गुण्डिका च निर्गुण्डा निन्नार्सा नासिकाभिधा ।
पताकिनी पताका च पत्रप्रीतिः पयस्विनी ॥ 65

पीना पीनस्तनी पत्नी पवनाशी निशामयी ।
परापरपराकाली पारकृत्यभुजप्रिया ॥ 66

पवनस्था च पवना पवनप्रीतिवर्द्धिनी ।
पशुवृद्धिकरी पुष्पी पोषका पुष्टिवर्द्धिनी ॥ 67

पुष्पिर्णी पुस्तैककरा पूर्णिमातलवासिनी ।
पेशी पाशकरी पाशा पांशुहा पांशुला पशुः ॥68

पटुः पराशा परशुधारिणी पाशिनी तथा ।
पापघ्नी पतिपत्नी च पतिता पतितापती ॥ 69

पिशाची च पिशाचघ्नी पिशिताशनतोषिणी ।
पानदा पानपात्री च पानदानकरोद्यता ॥ 70

पेयाप्रसिद्धा पीयूषा पूर्णा पूर्णमनोरथा ।
पतङ्गाभा पतङ्गा च पौनःपुन्यपिबापरा ॥ 71

पङ्किला पङ्कमग्ना च पानीया पञ्जरस्थिता ।
पञ्चमी पञ्चयज्ञा च पञ्चता पञ्चमाप्रिया ॥ 72

पिचुमन्दा पुण्डरीका पिकी पिङ्गललोचना ।
प्रियङ्गुमञ्जरी पिण्डी पण्डिता पाण्डुरप्रभा ॥73

प्रेतासना प्रियालस्था पाण्डुघ्नी पीनसापहा ।
फलिनी फलदात्री च फलश्रीः फलभूषणा ॥ 74

फूत्कारकारिणी रफारी फुल्ला फुल्लाम्बुजानना ।
स्फुलिङ्गहा स्फीतमतिः स्फीतकीर्त्तिकरी तथा ॥ 75

बालमाया बलारातिर्ब्बलिनी बलवर्द्धिनी ।
वेणुवाद्या वनचरी विरञ्चिजनयत्यपि ॥ 76

विद्याप्रदा महाविद्या बोधिनी बोधदायिनी ।
बुद्धमाता च बुद्धा च वनमालावती वरा ॥77

वरदा वारुणी वीणा वीणावादनतत्परा ।
विनोदिनी विनोदस्था वैष्णवी विष्णुवल्लभा ॥ 78

वैद्या वैद्यचिकित्सा च विवशा विश्वविश्रुता ।
विद्यौघविह्वला वेला वित्तदा विगतज्वरा ॥ 79

विरावा विवरीकारा बिम्बोष्ठी बिम्बवत्सला ।
विन्ध्यस्था परवन्द्या च वीरस्थानवरा च वित् ॥ 80

वेदान्तवेद्या विजया विजयाविजयप्रदा ।
विरोगी वन्दिनी वन्ध्या वन्द्यबन्धनिवारिणी ॥ 81

भगिनी भगमाला च भवानी भवनाशिनी ।
भीमा भीमानना भीमाभङ्गुरा भीमदर्शना ॥ 82

भिल्ली भिल्लधरा भीरुर्भरुण्डाभी भयावहा ।
भगसर्पिण्यपि भगा भगरूपा भगालया ॥ 83

भगासना भवाभोगा भेरीझङ्काररञ्जिता ।
भीषणा भीषणारावा वभगत्यहिभूषणा ॥ 84

भारद्वाजा भोगदात्री भूतिघ्नी भूतिभूषणा ।
भूमिदाभूमिदात्री च भूपतिर्भरदायिनी ॥85

भ्रमरी भ्रामरी भाला भूपालकुलसंस्थिता ।
माता मनोहरा माया मानिनी मोहिनी मही ॥ 86

महालक्ष्मीर्मदक्षीबा मदिरा मदिरालया ।
मदोद्धता मतङ्गस्था माधवी मधुमर्दिनी ॥87

मोदा मोदकरी मेधा मेध्यामध्याधिपस्थिता ।
मद्यपा मांसलोभस्था मोदिनी मैथुनोद्यता ॥ 88

मूर्द्धावती महामाया माया महिममन्दिरा ।
महामाला महाविद्या महामारी महेश्वरी ॥ 89

महादेववधूमान्या मथुरा मेरुमण्डिता ।
मेदस्विनी मिलिन्दाक्षी महिषासुरमर्दिनी ॥ 90

मण्डलस्था भगस्था च मदिरारागगर्विता ।
मोक्षदा मुण्डमाला च माला मालाविलासिनी ॥ 91

मातङ्गिनी च मातङ्गी मातङ्गतनयापि च ।
मधुस्रवा मधुरसा बन्धूककुसुमप्रिया ॥92

यामिनी यामिनीनाथभूषा यावकरञ्जिता ।
यवाङ्कुरप्रिया यामा यवनी यवनार्दिनी ॥ 93

यमघ्नी यमकल्पा च यजमानस्वरूपिणी ।
यज्ञा यज्ञयजुर्यक्षी यशोनिः कम्पकाकारिणी ॥ 94

यक्षिणी यक्षजननी यशोदायासधारिणी ।
यशस्सूत्रप्रदा यामा यज्ञकर्मकरीत्यपि ॥ 95

यशस्विनी यकारस्था भूयस्तम्भनिवासिनी ।
रञ्जिता राजपत्नी च रमा रेखा रवी रणा ॥ 96

रजोवती रजश्चित्रा रञ्जनी रजनीपतिः ।
रोगिणी रजनी राज्ञा राज्यदा राज्यवर्द्धिनी ॥ 97

राजन्वती राजनीतिस्तथा रजतवासिनी ।
रमणीरमणीया च रामा रामावती रतिः ।
रेतो रती रतोत्साहा रोगघ्नी रोगकारिणी ।
रङ्गा रङ्गवती रागा रागा रागज्ञा रागकृद्धया ॥ 98

रामिका रजकी रेवा रजनी रङ्गलोचना ।
रक्तचर्मधरा रङ्गी रङ्गस्था रङ्गवाहिनी ॥ 99

रमा रम्भाफलप्रीती रम्भोरू राघवप्रिया ।
रङ्गा रङ्गाङ्गमधुरा रोदसी च महारवा ॥ 100

रोधकृद्रोगहन्त्री च रूपभृद्रोगस्राविणी ।
बन्दी वन्दिस्तुता बन्धुर्बन्धूककुसुमाधरा ॥101

वन्दिता वन्द्यमाना च वैद्रावी वेदविद्विधा ।
विकोपा विकपाला च विङ्कस्था विङ्कवत्सला ॥ 102

वेदैर्विलग्नलग्ना च विधिविङ्ककरी विधा ।
शङ्खिनी शङ्खवलया शङ्खमालावती शमी ॥ 103

शङ्खपात्रा शिनी शङ्खस्वनशङ्खगला शशी ।
शबरी शम्बरी शम्भुः शम्भुकेशा शरासिनी ॥104

शवा श्येनवती श्यामा श्यामाङ्गी श्यामलोचना ।
श्मशानस्था श्मशाना च श्मशानस्थानभूषणा ॥ 105

शमदा शमहन्त्री च शङ्खिनी शङ्खरोषिरा ।
शान्तिश्शान्तिप्रदा शेषा शेषाख्या शेषशायिनी ॥ 106

शेमुषी शोषिणी शेषा शौर्या शौर्यशिरा शरी ।
शापिदा शापहा शापाशापपन्था सदाशिवा ॥ 107

शृङ्गिणी शृङ्गिपलभुक् शङ्करी शाङ्करी शिवा ।
शवस्था शवभुक् शान्ता शवकर्णा शवोदरी ॥ 108

शाविनी शवशिंशाश्रीः शवा च शमशायिनी ।
शवकुण्डलिनी शैवाशीकरा शिशिराशिना ॥ 109

शवकाञ्ची शवश्रीका शबमाला शवाकृतिः ।
सवन्ती सङ्कुचा शक्तिश्शन्तनुश्शवदायिनी ॥ 110

सिन्धुस्सरस्वती सिन्धुस्सुन्दरी सुन्दरानना ।
साधुः सिद्धिप्रदात्री च सिद्धा सिद्धसरस्वती ॥ 111

सन्ततिस्सम्पदा संवच्छङ्किसम्पत्तिदायिनी ।
सपत्नी सरसा सारा सारस्वतकरी सुधा ॥ 112

सुरासमांसाशना च समाराध्या समस्तदा ।
समधीस्सामदा सीमा सम्मोहा समदर्शना ॥ 113

सामतिस्सामधा सीमा सावित्री सविधा सती ।
सवना सवनासारा सवरा सावरा समी ॥ 114

सिमरा सतता साध्वी सध्रीची ससहायिनी ।
हंसी हंसगतिहंसी हंसोज्ज्वलनिचोलयुक् ॥115

हलिनी हालिनी हाला हलश्रीहरवल्लभा ।
हला हलवती ह्येषा हेला हर्षविवर्द्धिनी ॥ 116

हन्तिर्हन्ता हयाहाहाहताहन्तातिकारिणी ।
हङ्कारी हङ्कृतिर्हङ्का हीहीहाहाहिताहिता ॥ 117

हीतिर्हेमप्रदा हारारविणी हरिरसम्मता ।
होरा होत्री होलिका च होमा होमहविर्हविः ॥ 118

हरिणी हरिणीनेत्रा हिमाचलनिवासिनी ।
लम्बोदरी लम्बकर्णा लम्बिका लम्बविग्रहा ॥ 119

लीला लीलावती लोला ललना ललिता लता ।
ललामलोचना लोभ्या लोलाक्षी सत्कुलालया ॥ 120

लपत्नी लपती लम्पा लोपामुद्रा ललन्तिका ।
लतिका लङ्घिनी लङ्घा लालिमा लघुमध्यमा ॥ 121

लघीयसी लघूदर्या लूता लूताविनाशिनी ।
लोमशा लोमलम्बी च लुलन्ती च लुलुम्पती ॥122

लुलायस्था बलहरी लङ्कापुरपुरन्दरा ।
लक्ष्मील्लक्ष्मीप्रदा लभ्या लाक्षाक्षी लुलितप्रभा ॥ 123

क्षणा क्षणक्षु क्षु क्षिणी क्षमाक्षान्तिः क्षमावती ।
क्षामा क्षामोदरी क्षेम्या क्षौमभृत्क्षत्रियाङ्गणा ॥ 124

क्षया क्षायाकरी क्षीरा क्षीरदा क्षीरसागरा ।
क्षेमङ्करी क्षयकरी क्षयकृत्क्षणदा क्षतिः ॥ 125

क्षु द्रिका क्षुद्रिकाक्षु द्रा क्षु त्क्षमा क्षीणपातका ।

फलश्रुतिः ।

मातुः सहस्रनामेदं सुमुख्यास्सिद्धिदायकम् ॥126

यः पठेत्प्रयतो नित्यं स एव स्यान्महेश्वरः ।
अनाचारात्पठेन्नित्यन्दरिद्रो धनवान्भवेत् ॥ 127

मूकस्स्याद्वाक्पतिर्देवि रोगी नीरोगताव्व्रजेत् ।
पुत्रार्थी पुत्रमाप्नोति त्रिषु लोकेषु विश्रुतम् ॥128

वन्ध्यापि सूयते पुत्रव्विदुषस्सदृशङ्गुरोः ।
सत्यञ्च बहुधा भूयाद्द्रावश्च बहुदुग्धदाः ॥ 129

राजानः पादनम्रास्स्युस्तस्य हासा इव स्फुटाः ।
अरयस्सङ्क्षयय्यान्ति मानसा संस्मृता अपि ॥ 130

दर्शनादेव जायन्ते नरा नार्योऽपि तद्दशाः ।
कर्त्ता हर्त्ता स्वयंवीरो जायते नात्र संशयः ॥ 131

यय्यङ्कामयते कामन्तन्तमाप्नोति निश्चितम् ।
दुरितन्न च तस्यास्ति नास्ति शोकः कथञ्चन ॥ 132

चतुष्पथेऽर्द्धरात्रे च यः पठेत्साधकोत्तमः ।
एकाकी निर्भयो वीरो दशावर्त्तस्तवोत्तमम् ॥ 133

मनसा चिन्तितङ्कार्यं तस्य सिद्धिर्न संशयः ।
विना सहस्रनाम्नाय्यो जपेन्मन्त्रङ्कदाचन ॥ 134

न सिद्धिर्ज्जायते तस्य मन्त्रङ्कल्पशतैरपि ।
कुजवारे श्मशाने वा मध्याह्ने यो जपेत्सदा ॥ 135

कृतकृत्यस्स जायेत कर्त्ता हर्त्ता नृणामिह ।
रोगार्त्तोऽर्द्धनिशायाय्यः पठेदासनसंस्थितः ॥ 136

सद्यो नीरोगतामेति यदि स्यान्निर्भयस्तदा ।
अर्द्धरात्रे श्मशाने वा शनिवारे जपेन्मनुम् ।
अष्टोत्तरसहस्रन्तु दशवारञ्जपेत्ततः ।
सहस्रनाम चैतद्धि तदा याति स्वयं शिवा ॥ 137

महापवनरूपेण घोरगोमायुनादिनी ।
ततो यदि न भीतिः स्यात्तदा देहीतिवाग्भवेत् ॥ 138

तदा पशुबलिन्दद्यात्स्वयं गृह्णाति चण्डिका ।
यथेष्टञ्च वरन्दत्त्वा प्रयाति सुमुखी शिवा ॥ 139

रोचनागुरुकस्तूरीकप्पूरैश्च सचन्दनैः ।
कुङ्कुमेन दिने श्रेष्ठे लिखित्वा भूर्ज्जपत्रके ॥ 140

शुभनक्षत्रयोगे च कृतमारुतसक्रियः ।
कृत्वा सम्पातनविधिन्धारयेद्दक्षिणे करे ॥ 141

सहस्रनाम स्वर्णस्थङ्कण्ठे वा विजितेन्द्रियः ।
तदायम्प्रणमेन्मन्त्री क्रुद्धस्स प्रियते नरः ॥ 142

दुष्टश्वापदजन्तूनान्न भीः कुत्रापि जायते ।
बालकानामियं रक्षा गर्भिणीनामपि प्रिये ॥ 143

मोहनस्तम्भनाकर्ष-मारणोच्चाटनानि च ।
यन्त्रधारणतो नूनञ्जायन्ते साधकस्य तु ॥ 144

नीलवस्त्रे विलिखिते ध्वजायाय्यदि तिष्ठति ।
तदा नष्टा भवत्येव प्रचण्डाप्यरिवाहिनी ॥ 145

एतज्जप्मम्महाभस्म ललाटे यदि धारयेत् ।
तद्विलोकन एव स्युः प्राणिनस्तस्य किङ्कराः ॥ 146

राजपत्न्योऽपि विवशाः किमन्याः पुरयोषितः ।
एतज्जप्मम्पिबेत्तोयम्मासेन स्यान्महाकविः ॥ 147

पण्डितश्च महावादी जायते नात्र संशयः ।
अयुतञ्च पठेत्स्तोत्रम्पुरश्चरणसिद्धये ॥148

दशांशङ्ककमलैर्हुत्वा त्रिमध्वाक्तैर्विधानतः ।
स्वयमायाति कमला वाण्या सह तदालये ॥ 149

मन्त्रो निःकीलतामेति सुमुखी सुमुखी भवेत् ।
अनन्तञ्च भवेत्पुण्यमपुण्यञ्च क्षयव्व्रजेत् ॥ 150

पुष्करादिषु तीर्थेषु स्नानतो यत्फलम्भवेत् ।
तत्फलल्लभते जन्तुः सुमुख्याः स्तोत्रपाठतः ॥151

एतदुक्तं रहस्यन्ते स्वसर्वस्वव्वरानने ।
न प्रकाशयन्त्वया देवि यदि सिद्धिञ्च विन्दसि ॥ 152

प्रकाशनादसिद्धिस्स्यात्कुपिता सुमुखी भवेत् ।
नातः परतरो लोके सिद्धिदः प्राणिनामिह ॥ 153

वन्दे श्रीसुमुखीम्प्रसन्नवदनाम्पूर्णेन्दुबिम्बाननां
सिन्दूराङ्कितमस्तकाम्मधुमदोल्लोलाञ्च मुक्तावलीम् ।
श्यामाङ्कञ्जलिकाकराङ्करगतञ्चाध्यापयन्तीं
शुकङ्गुञ्जापुञ्जविभूषणां सकरुणामामुक्तवेणीलताम् ॥154

इति श्री नन्द्यावर्त्त तन्त्रे उत्तर खण्डे मातङ्ग्गी सहस्र नाम स्तोत्रं सम्पूर्णम् ॥

Śrī Mātaṅgī Sahasra Nāmāvaliḥ

1,000 divine names on *Śrī Mātaṅgī Devi.*

Dhyānam ||

Mātaṅgīm Bhūṣitāṅgīm Vividha Manidharāmindu Sūryākṣiyugmām
Svidmadvaktrām Kadamba Prasavaparilasadvenukāmātra Vīnām |
Bimboṣṭhīm Raktavastrām Mrugamadatilakāmindu Rekhāvatamsām
Karṇodyacchankha Patrām Kaṭhinakuchabharākrānta Madhyām

Namāmi ||

ध्यानम्

मातङ्गीं भूषिताङ्गीं विविध मनिधरामिन्दु सूर्याक्षि युग्मां
स्विद्मद्वक्त्रां कदम्ब प्रसव परिलसद्वेणुकामात्र वीणाम् ।
बिम्बोष्ठीं रक्तवस्त्रां म्रुगमदतिलकामिन्दु रेखावतंसां
कर्णोद्यच्छङ्ख पत्रां कठिनकुचभराक्रान्त मध्यां नमामि ॥

Śrī Mātaṅgī Sahasranāmāvaliḥ || श्री मातङ्गी सहस्रनामावलिः

1.	*Oṃ Sumukhyai Namaḥ |*	ॐ सुमुख्यै नमः	
2.	*Oṃ Śemuṣyai Namaḥ |*	ॐ शेमुष्यै नमः ।
3.	*Oṃ Sevyāyai Namaḥ |*	ॐ सेव्यायै नमः ।
4.	*Oṃ Surasāyai Namaḥ |*	ॐ सुरसायै नमः ।
5.	*Oṃ Śaśiśekharāyai Namaḥ |*	ॐ शशिशेखरायै नमः ।
6.	*Oṃ Samānāsyāyai Namaḥ |*	ॐ समानास्यायै नमः ।
7.	*Oṃ Sādhanyai Namaḥ |*	ॐ साधन्यै नमः ।
8.	*Oṃ Samastasurasanmukhyai Namaḥ |*	ॐ समस्तसुरसन्मुख्यै नमः
9.	*Oṃ Sarvasampattijananyai Namaḥ*	ॐ सर्वसम्पत्तिजनन्यै नमः ।
10.	*Oṃ Sampadāyai Namaḥ |*	ॐ सम्पदायै नमः ।
11.	*Oṃ Sindhusevinyai Namaḥ |*	ॐ सिन्धुसेविन्यै नमः ।
12.	*Oṃ Śambhusīmantinyai Namaḥ |*	ॐ शम्भुसीमन्तिन्यै नमः ।
13.	*Oṃ Saumyāyai Namaḥ |*	ॐ सौम्यायै नमः ।
14.	*Oṃ Samārādhyāyai Namaḥ |*	ॐ समाराध्यायै नमः ।

15.	Oṃ Sudhārasāyai Namaḥ I	ॐ सुधारसायै नमः I
16.	Oṃ Sāraṅgāyai Namaḥ I	ॐ सारङ्गायै नमः I
17.	Oṃ Savalyai Namaḥ I	ॐ सवल्यै नमः I
18.	Oṃ Velāyai Namaḥ I	ॐ वेलायै नमः I
19.	Oṃ Lāvaṇyavanamālinyai Namaḥ I	ॐ लावण्यवनमालिन्यै नमः I
20.	Oṃ Vanajākṣyai Namaḥ I	ॐ वनजाक्ष्यै नमः I
21.	Oṃ Vanacaryai Namaḥ I	ॐ वनचर्यै नमः I
22.	Oṃ Vanyai Namaḥ I	ॐ वन्यै नमः I
23.	Oṃ Vanavinodinyai Namaḥ I	ॐ वनविनोदिन्यै नमः I
24.	Oṃ Veginyai Namaḥ I	ॐ वेगिन्यै नमः I
25.	Oṃ Vegadāyai Namaḥ I	ॐ वेगदायै नमः I
26.	Oṃ Vegāyai Namaḥ I	ॐ वेगायै नमः I
27.	Oṃ Bagalasthāyai Namaḥ I	ॐ बगलस्थायै नमः I
28.	Oṃ Balādhikāyai Namaḥ I	ॐ बलाधिकायै नमः I
29.	Oṃ Kālyai Namaḥ I	ॐ काल्यै नमः I
30.	Oṃ Kālapriyāyai Namaḥ I	ॐ कालप्रियायै नमः I
31.	Oṃ Kelyai Namaḥ I	ॐ केल्यै नमः I
32.	Oṃ Kamalāyai Namaḥ I	ॐ कमलायै नमः I
33.	Oṃ Kālakāminyai Namaḥ I	ॐ कालकामिन्यै नमः I
34.	Oṃ Kamalāyai Namaḥ I	ॐ कमलायै नमः I
35.	Oṃ Kamalasthāyai Namaḥ I	ॐ कमलस्थायै नमः I
36.	Oṃ Kamalasthāyai Namaḥ I	ॐ कमलस्थायै नमः I
37.	Oṃ Kamalasthāyai Kalāvatyai Namaḥ I	ॐ कमलस्थायै कलावत्यै नमः I
38.	Oṃ Kulīnāyai Namaḥ I	ॐ कुलीनायै नमः I
39.	Oṃ Kuṭilāyai Namaḥ I	ॐ कुटिलायै नमः I
40.	Oṃ Kāntāyai Namaḥ I	ॐ कान्तायै नमः I
41.	Oṃ Kokilāyai Namaḥ I	ॐ कोकिलायै नमः I
42.	Oṃ Kalabhāṣiṇyai Namaḥ I	ॐ कलभाषिण्यै नमः I
43.	Oṃ Kīrāyai Namaḥ I	ॐ कीरायै नमः I

44.	Oṃ Kelikarāyai Namaḥ ।	ॐ केलिकरायै नमः ।
45.	Oṃ Kālyai Namaḥ ।	ॐ काल्यै नमः ।
46.	Oṃ Kapālinyai Namaḥ ।	ॐ कपालिन्यै नमः ।
47.	Oṃ Kālikāyai Namaḥ ।	ॐ कालिकायै नमः ।
48.	Oṃ Keśinyai Namaḥ ।	ॐ केशिन्यै नमः ।
49.	Oṃ Kuśāvarttāyai Namaḥ ।	ॐ कुशावत्तायै नमः ।
50.	Oṃ Kauśāmbhyai Namaḥ ।	ॐ कौशाम्भ्यै नमः ।
51.	Oṃ Keśavapriyāyai Namaḥ ।	ॐ केशवप्रियायै नमः ।
52.	Oṃ Kālyai Namaḥ ।	ॐ काल्यै नमः ।
53.	Oṃ Kāśyai Namaḥ ।	ॐ काश्यै नमः ।
54.	Oṃ Mahākālasaṅkāśāyai Namaḥ	ॐ महाकालसङ्काशायै नमः ।
55.	Oṃ Keśadāyinyai Namaḥ ।	ॐ केशदायिन्यै नमः ।
56.	Oṃ Kuṇḍalāyai Namaḥ ।	ॐ कुण्डलायै नमः ।
57.	Oṃ Kulasthāyai Namaḥ ।	ॐ कुलस्थायै नमः ।
58.	Oṃ Kuṇḍalāṅgadamaṇḍitāyai Namaḥ ।	ॐ कुण्डलाङ्गदमण्डितायै नमः ।
59.	Oṃ Kuṇḍapadmāyai Namaḥ ।	ॐ कुण्डपद्मायै नमः ।
60.	Oṃ Kumudinyai Namaḥ ।	ॐ कुमुदिन्यै नमः ।
61.	Oṃ Kumudaprītivardhinyai Namaḥ	ॐ कुमुदप्रीतिवर्धिन्यै नमः ।
62.	Oṃ Kuṇḍapriyāyai Namaḥ ।	ॐ कुण्डप्रियायै नमः ।
63.	Oṃ Kuṇḍarucyai Namaḥ ।	ॐ कुण्डरुच्यै नमः ।
64.	Oṃ Kuraṅganayanāyai Namaḥ ।	ॐ कुरङ्गनयनायै नमः ।
65.	Oṃ Kulāyai Namaḥ ।	ॐ कुलायै नमः ।
66.	Oṃ Kundabimbālinadinyai Namaḥ	ॐ कुन्दबिम्बालिनदिन्यै नमः ।
67.	Oṃ Kusumbhakusumākarāyai Namaḥ ।	ॐ कुसुम्भकुसुमाकरायै नमः ।
68.	Oṃ Kāñcyai Namaḥ ।	ॐ काञ्च्यै नमः ।
69.	Oṃ Kanakaśobhāḍhyāyai Namaḥ ।	ॐ कनकशोभाढ्यायै नमः ।
70.	Oṃ Kvaṇatkiṅkiṇikākaṭyai Namaḥ ।	ॐ क्वणत्किङ्किणिकाकट्यै नमः ।
71.	Oṃ Kaṭhorakaraṇāyai Namaḥ ।	ॐ कठोरकरणायै नमः ।

72.	Oṃ Kāṣṭhāyai Namaḥ l	ॐ काष्ठायै नमः l
73.	Oṃ Kaumudyai Namaḥ l	ॐ कौमुद्यै नमः l
74.	Oṃ Kaṇṭhavatyai Namaḥ l	ॐ कण्ठवत्यै नमः l
75.	Oṃ Kapardinyai Namaḥ l	ॐ कपर्दिन्यै नमः l
76.	Oṃ Kapaṭinyai Namaḥ l	ॐ कपटिन्यै नमः l
77.	Oṃ Kaṭhinyai Namaḥ l	ॐ कठिन्यै नमः l
78.	Oṃ Kalakaṇṭhinyai Namaḥ l	ॐ कलकण्ठिन्यै नमः l
79.	Oṃ Karihastāyai Namaḥ l	ॐ करिहस्तायै नमः l
80.	Oṃ Kumāryai Namaḥ l	ॐ कुमार्यै नमः l
81.	Oṃ Kurūḍhakusumapriyāyai Namaḥ l	ॐ कुरूढकुसुमप्रियायै नमः l
82.	Oṃ Kuñjarasthāyai Namaḥ l	ॐ कुञ्जरस्थायै नमः l
83.	Oṃ Kuñjaratāyai Namaḥ l	ॐ कुञ्जरतायै नमः l
84.	Oṃ Kumbhyai Namaḥ l	ॐ कुम्भ्यै नमः l
85.	Oṃ Kumbhastanyai Namaḥ l	ॐ कुम्भस्तन्यै नमः l
86.	Oṃ Kalāyai Namaḥ l	ॐ कलायै नमः l
87.	Oṃ Kumbhīkāṅgāyai Namaḥ l	ॐ कुम्भीकाङ्गायै नमः l
88.	Oṃ Karabhorvai Namaḥ l	ॐ करभोर्वै नमः l
89.	Oṃ Kadalīkuśaśāyinyai Namaḥ l	ॐ कदलीकुशशायिन्यै नमः l
90.	Oṃ Kupitāyai Namaḥ l	ॐ कुपितायै नमः l
91.	Oṃ Koṭarasthāyai Namaḥ l	ॐ कोटरस्थायै नमः l
92.	Oṃ Kaṅkālyai Namaḥ l	ॐ कङ्काल्यै नमः l
93.	Oṃ Kandalālayāyai Namaḥ l	ॐ कन्दलालयायै नमः l
94.	Oṃ Kapālavasinyai Namaḥ l	ॐ कपालवसिन्यै नमः l
95.	Oṃ Keśyai Namaḥ l	ॐ केश्यै नमः l
96.	Oṃ Kampamānaśiroruhāyai Namaḥ l	ॐ कम्पमानशिरोरुहायै नमः l
97.	Oṃ Kādambaryai Namaḥ l	ॐ कादम्बर्यै नमः l
98.	Oṃ Kadambasthāyai Namaḥ l	ॐ कदम्बस्थायै नमः l

99.	Oṃ Kuṅkumapremadhāriṇyai Namaḥ		ॐ कुङ्कुमप्रेमधारिण्यै नमः ।
100.	Oṃ Kuṭumbinyai Namaḥ		ॐ कुटुम्बिन्यै नमः ।
101.	Oṃ Kṛpāyuktāyai Namaḥ		ॐ कृपायुक्तायै नमः ।
102.	Oṃ Kratave Namaḥ		ॐ क्रतवे नमः ।
103.	Oṃ Kratukarapriyāyai Namaḥ		ॐ क्रतुकरप्रियायै नमः ।
104.	Oṃ Kātyāyanyai Namaḥ		ॐ कात्यायन्यै नमः ।
105.	Oṃ Kṛttikāyai Namaḥ		ॐ कृत्तिकायै नमः ।
106.	Oṃ Kārtikyai Namaḥ		ॐ कार्तिक्यै नमः ।
107.	Oṃ Kuśavartinyai Namaḥ		ॐ कुशवर्तिन्यै नमः ।
108.	Oṃ Kāmapatnyai Namaḥ		ॐ कामपत्न्यै नमः ।
109.	Oṃ Kāmadātryai Namaḥ		ॐ कामदात्र्यै नमः ।
110.	Oṃ Kāmeśyai Namaḥ		ॐ कामेश्यै नमः ।
111.	Oṃ Kāmavanditāyai Namaḥ		ॐ कामवन्दितायै नमः ।
112.	Oṃ Kāmarūpāyai Namaḥ		ॐ कामरूपायै नमः ।
113.	Oṃ Kāmaratyai Namaḥ		ॐ कामरत्यै नमः ।
114.	Oṃ Kāmākhyāyai Namaḥ		ॐ कामाख्यायै नमः ।
115.	Oṃ Jñānamohinyai Namaḥ		ॐ ज्ञानमोहिन्यै नमः ।
116.	Oṃ Khaḍginyai Namaḥ		ॐ खड्गिन्यै नमः ।
117.	Oṃ Khecaryai Namaḥ		ॐ खेचर्यै नमः ।
118.	Oṃ Khañjāyai Namaḥ		ॐ खञ्जायै नमः ।
119.	Oṃ Khañjarīṭekṣaṇāyai Namaḥ		ॐ खञ्जरीटेक्षणायै नमः ।
120.	Oṃ Khagāyai Namaḥ		ॐ खगायै नमः ।
121.	Oṃ Kharagāyai Namaḥ		ॐ खरगायै नमः ।
122.	Oṃ Kharanādāyai Namaḥ		ॐ खरनादायै नमः ।
123.	Oṃ Kharasthāyai Namaḥ		ॐ खरस्थायै नमः ।
124.	Oṃ Khelanapriyāyai Namaḥ		ॐ खेलनप्रियायै नमः ।
125.	Oṃ Kharāṃśave Namaḥ		ॐ खरांशवे नमः ।
126.	Oṃ Khelanyai Namaḥ		ॐ खेलन्यै नमः ।
127.	Oṃ Khaṭvāyai Namaḥ		ॐ खट्वायै नमः ।

128.	Oṃ Kharāyai Namaḥ ।	ॐ खरायै नमः ।
129.	Oṃ Khaṭvāṅgadhāriṇyai Namaḥ	ॐ खट्वाङ्गधारिण्यै नमः ।
130.	Oṃ Kharakhaṇḍinyai Namaḥ	ॐ खरखण्डिन्यै नमः ।
131.	Oṃ Khyātyai Namaḥ	ॐ ख्यात्यै नमः ।
132.	Oṃ Khaṇḍitāyai Namaḥ	ॐ खण्डितायै नमः ।
133.	Oṃ Khaṇḍanapriyāyai Namaḥ ।	ॐ खण्डनप्रियायै नमः ।
134.	Oṃ Khaṇḍapriyāyai Namaḥ ।	ॐ खण्डप्रियायै नमः ।
135.	Oṃ Khaṇḍakhādyāyai Namaḥ ।	ॐ खण्डखाद्यायै नमः ।
136.	Oṃ Khaṇḍasindhave Namaḥ ।	ॐ खण्डसिन्धवे नमः ।
137.	Oṃ Khaṇḍinyai Namaḥ ।	ॐ खण्डिन्यै नमः ।
138.	Oṃ Gaṅgāyai Namaḥ ।	ॐ गङ्गायै नमः ।
139.	Oṃ Godāvaryai Namaḥ ।	ॐ गोदावर्यै नमः ।
140.	Oṃ Gauryai Namaḥ ।	ॐ गौर्यै नमः ।
141.	Oṃ Gotamyai Namaḥ ।	ॐ गोतम्यै नमः ।
142.	Oṃ Gautamyai Namaḥ ।	ॐ गौतम्यै नमः ।
143.	Oṃ Gaṅgāyai Namaḥ ।	ॐ गङ्गायै नमः ।
144.	Oṃ Gayāyai Namaḥ ।	ॐ गयायै नमः ।
145.	Oṃ Gaganagāyai Namaḥ ।	ॐ गगनगायै नमः ।
146.	Oṃ Gāruḍyai Namaḥ ।	ॐ गारुड्यै नमः ।
147.	Oṃ Garuḍadhvajāyai Namaḥ ।	ॐ गरुडध्वजायै नमः ।
148.	Oṃ Gītāyai Namaḥ ।	ॐ गीतायै नमः ।
149.	Oṃ Gītapriyāyai Namaḥ ।	ॐ गीतप्रियायै नमः ।
150.	Oṃ Geyāyai Namaḥ ।	ॐ गेयायै नमः ।
151.	Oṃ Guṇaprītyai Namaḥ ।	ॐ गुणप्रीत्यै नमः ।
152.	Oṃ Gurave Namaḥ ।	ॐ गुरवे नमः ।
153.	Oṃ Giryai Namaḥ ।	ॐ गिर्यै नमः ।
154.	Oṃ Gave Namaḥ ।	ॐ गवे नमः ।
155.	Oṃ Gauryai Namaḥ ।	ॐ गौर्यै नमः ।
156.	Oṃ Gaṇḍasadanāyai Namaḥ ।	ॐ गण्डसदनायै नमः ।
157.	Oṃ Gokulāyai Namaḥ ।	ॐ गोकुलायै नमः ।

158.	Oṃ Gopratāriṇyai Namaḥ		ॐ गोप्रतारिण्यै नमः ।
159.	Oṃ Goptryai Namaḥ		ॐ गोप्त्र्यै नमः ।
160.	Oṃ Govindinyai Namaḥ		ॐ गोविन्दिन्यै नमः ।
161.	Oṃ Gūḍhāyai Namaḥ		ॐ गूढायै नमः ।
162.	Oṃ Gūḍhavigrastaguñjinyai Namaḥ		ॐ गूढविग्रस्तगुञ्जिन्यै नमः
163.	Oṃ Gajagāyai Namaḥ		ॐ गजगायै नमः ।
164.	Oṃ Gopinyai Namaḥ		ॐ गोपिन्यै नमः ।
165.	Oṃ Gopyai Namaḥ		ॐ गोप्यै नमः ।
166.	Oṃ Gokṣāyai Namaḥ		ॐ गोक्षायै नमः ।
167.	Oṃ Jayapriyāyai Namaḥ		ॐ जयप्रियायै नमः ।
168.	Oṃ Gaṇāyai Namaḥ		ॐ गणायै नमः ।
169.	Oṃ Giribhūpāladuhitāyai Namaḥ		ॐ गिरिभूपालदुहितायै नमः ।
170.	Oṃ Gogāyai Namaḥ		ॐ गोगायै नमः ।
171.	Oṃ Gokulavāsinyai Namaḥ		ॐ गोकुलवासिन्यै नमः ।
172.	Oṃ Ghanastanyai Namaḥ		ॐ घनस्तन्यै नमः ।
173.	Oṃ Ghanarucyai Namaḥ		ॐ घनरुच्यै नमः ।
174.	Oṃ Ghanorave Namaḥ		ॐ घनोरवे नमः ।
175.	Oṃ Ghananisvanāyai Namaḥ		ॐ घननिस्वनायै नमः ।
176.	Oṃ Ghuṅkāriṇyai Namaḥ		ॐ घुङ्कारिण्यै नमः ।
177.	Oṃ Ghukṣakaryai Namaḥ		ॐ घुक्षकर्यै नमः ।
178.	Oṃ Ghūghūkaparivāritāyai Namaḥ		ॐ घूघूकपरिवारितायै नमः
179.	Oṃ Ghaṇṭānādapriyāyai Namaḥ		ॐ घण्टानादप्रियायै नमः ।
180.	Oṃ Ghaṇṭāyai Namaḥ		ॐ घण्टायै नमः ।
181.	Oṃ Ghoṭāyai Namaḥ		ॐ घोटायै नमः ।
182.	Oṃ Ghoṭakavāhinyai Namaḥ		ॐ घोटकवाहिन्यै नमः ।
183.	Oṃ Ghorarūpāyai Namaḥ		ॐ घोररूपायै नमः ।
184.	Oṃ Ghorāyai Namaḥ		ॐ घोरायै नमः ।
185.	Oṃ Ghṛtaprītyai Namaḥ		ॐ घृतप्रीत्यै नमः ।
186.	Oṃ Ghṛtāñjanyai Namaḥ		ॐ घृताञ्जन्यै नमः ।

187.	Oṃ Ghṛtācyai Namaḥ ।	ॐ घृताच्यै नमः ।
188.	Oṃ Ghṛtavṛṣṭyai Namaḥ ।	ॐ घृतवृष्ट्यै नमः ।
189.	Oṃ Ghaṇṭāyai Namaḥ ।	ॐ घण्टायै नमः ।
190.	Oṃ Ghaṭaghaṭāvṛtāyai Namaḥ ।	ॐ घटघटावृताये नमः ।
191.	Oṃ Ghaṭasthāyai Namaḥ ।	ॐ घटस्थायै नमः ।
192.	Oṃ Ghaṭanāyai Namaḥ ।	ॐ घटनायै नमः ।
193.	Oṃ Ghātakaryai Namaḥ ।	ॐ घातकर्यै नमः ।
194.	Oṃ Ghātanivāriṇyai Namaḥ ।	ॐ घातनिवारिण्यै नमः ।
195.	Oṃ Cañcarīkyai Namaḥ ।	ॐ चञ्चरीक्यै नमः ।
196.	Oṃ Cakoryai Namaḥ ।	ॐ चकोर्यै नमः ।
197.	Oṃ Cāmuṇḍāyai Namaḥ ।	ॐ चामुण्डायै नमः ।
198.	Oṃ Cīradhāriṇyai Namaḥ ।	ॐ चीरधारिण्यै नमः ।
199.	Oṃ Cāturyai Namaḥ ।	ॐ चातुर्यै नमः ।
200.	Oṃ Capalāyai Namaḥ ।	ॐ चपलायै नमः ।
201.	Oṃ Cañcave Namaḥ ।	ॐ चञ्चवे नमः ।
202.	Oṃ Citāyai Namaḥ ।	ॐ चितायै नमः ।
203.	Oṃ Cintāmaṇisthitāyai Namaḥ ।	ॐ चिन्तामणिस्थितायै नमः ।
204.	Oṃ Cāturvarṇyamayyai Namaḥ ।	ॐ चातुर्वर्ण्यमय्यै नमः ।
205.	Oṃ Cañcave Namaḥ ।	ॐ चञ्चवे नमः ।
206.	Oṃ Corācāryyāyai Namaḥ ।	ॐ चोराचार्य्यायै नमः ।
207.	Oṃ Camatkṛtyai Namaḥ ।	ॐ चमत्कृत्यै नमः ।
208.	Oṃ Cakravartivadhvai Namaḥ ।	ॐ चक्रवर्तिवध्वै नमः ।
209.	Oṃ Citrāyai Namaḥ ।	ॐ चित्रायै नमः ।
210.	Oṃ Cakrāṅgyai Namaḥ ।	ॐ चक्राङ्ग्यै नमः ।
211.	Oṃ Cakramodinyai Namaḥ ।	ॐ चक्रमोदिन्यै नमः ।
212.	Oṃ Cetaścaryai Namaḥ ।	ॐ चेतश्चर्यै नमः ।
213.	Oṃ Cittavṛtyai Namaḥ ।	ॐ चित्तवृत्यै नमः ।
214.	Oṃ Cetanāyai Namaḥ ।	ॐ चेतनायै नमः ।
215.	Oṃ Cetanapriyāyai Namaḥ ।	ॐ चेतनप्रियायै नमः ।
216.	Oṃ Cāpinyai Namaḥ ।	ॐ चापिन्यै नमः ।

217.	Oṃ Campakaprītyai Namaḥ l	ॐ चम्पकप्रीत्यै नमः l
218.	Oṃ Caṇḍāyai Namaḥ l	ॐ चण्डायै नमः l
219.	Oṃ Caṇḍālavāsinyai Namaḥ l	ॐ चण्डालवासिन्यै नमः l
220.	Oṃ Cirañjīvinyai Namaḥ l	ॐ चिरञ्जीविन्यै नमः l
221.	Oṃ Taccintāttāyai Namaḥ l	ॐ तच्चिन्तात्तायै नमः l
222.	Oṃ Ciñcāmūlanivāsinyai Namaḥ	ॐ चिञ्चामूलनिवासिन्यै नमः
223.	Oṃ Churikāyai Namaḥ l	ॐ छुरिकायै नमः l
224.	Oṃ Chatramadhyasthāyai Namaḥ	ॐ छत्रमध्यस्थायै नमः l
225.	Oṃ Chindāyai Namaḥ l	ॐ छिन्दायै नमः l
226.	Oṃ Chindākaryai Namaḥ l	ॐ छिन्दाकर्यै नमः l
227.	Oṃ Chidāyai Namaḥ l	ॐ छिदायै नमः l
228.	Oṃ Chucchundaryai Namaḥ l	ॐ छुच्छुन्दर्यै नमः l
229.	Oṃ Chalaprītyai Namaḥ l	ॐ छलप्रीत्यै नमः l
230.	Oṃ Chucchundaranibhasvanāyai Namaḥ l	ॐ छुच्छुन्दरनिभस्वनायै नमः l
231.	Oṃ Chalinyai Namaḥ l	ॐ छलिन्यै नमः l
232.	Oṃ Chatradāyai Namaḥ l	ॐ छत्रदायै नमः l
233.	Oṃ Chinnāyai Namaḥ l	ॐ छिन्नायै नमः l
234.	Oṃ Chiṇṭicchedakaryai Namaḥ l	ॐ छिण्टिच्छेदकर्यै नमः l
235.	Oṃ Chaṭāyai Namaḥ l	ॐ छटायै नमः l
236.	Oṃ Chadminyai Namaḥ l	ॐ छद्मिन्यै नमः l
237.	Oṃ Chāndasyai Namaḥ l	ॐ छान्दस्यै नमः l
238.	Oṃ Chāyāyai Namaḥ l	ॐ छायायै नमः l
239.	Oṃ Charvai Namaḥ l	ॐ छर्वै नमः l
240.	Oṃ Chandākaryai Namaḥ l	ॐ छन्दाकर्यै नमः l
241.	Oṃ Jayadāyai Namaḥ l	ॐ जयदायै नमः l
242.	Oṃ Jayadāyai Namaḥ l	ॐ जयदायै नमः l
243.	Oṃ Jātyai Namaḥ l	ॐ जात्यै नमः l
244.	Oṃ Jāyinyai Namaḥ l	ॐ जायिन्यै नमः l
245.	Oṃ Jāmalāyai Namaḥ l	ॐ जामलायै नमः l

246.	Oṃ Jatvai Namaḥ		ॐ जत्वै नमः ।
247.	Oṃ Jambūpriyāyai Namaḥ		ॐ जम्बूप्रियायै नमः ।
248.	Oṃ Jīvanasthāyai Namaḥ		ॐ जीवनस्थायै नमः ।
249.	Oṃ Jaṅgamāyai Namaḥ		ॐ जङ्गमायै नमः ।
250.	Oṃ Jaṅgamapriyāyai Namaḥ		ॐ जङ्गमप्रियायै नमः ।
251.	Oṃ Japāpuṣpapriyāyai Namaḥ		ॐ जपापुष्पप्रियायै नमः ।
252.	Oṃ Japyāyai Namaḥ		ॐ जप्यायै नमः ।
253.	Oṃ Jagajjīvāyai Namaḥ		ॐ जगज्जीवायै नमः ।
254.	Oṃ Jagajjanyai Namaḥ		ॐ जगज्जन्यै नमः ।
255.	Oṃ Jagate Namaḥ		ॐ जगते नमः ।
256.	Oṃ Jantupradhānāyai Namaḥ		ॐ जन्तुप्रधानायै नमः ।
257.	Oṃ Jagajjīvaparāyai Namaḥ		ॐ जगज्जीवपरायै नमः ।
258.	Oṃ Japāyai Namaḥ		ॐ जपायै नमः ।
259.	Oṃ Jātipriyāyai Namaḥ		ॐ जातिप्रियायै नमः ।
260.	Oṃ Jīvanasthāyai Namaḥ		ॐ जीवनस्थायै नमः ।
261.	Oṃ Jīmūtasadṛśīrucyai Namaḥ		ॐ जीमूतसदृशीरुच्यै नमः ।
262.	Oṃ Janyāyai Namaḥ		ॐ जन्यायै नमः ।
263.	Oṃ Janahitāyai Namaḥ		ॐ जनहितायै नमः ।
264.	Oṃ Jāyāyai Namaḥ		ॐ जायायै नमः ।
265.	Oṃ Janmabhuve Namaḥ		ॐ जन्मभुवे नमः ।
266.	Oṃ Jambhasyai Namaḥ		ॐ जम्भस्यै नमः ।
267.	Oṃ Jabhuve Namaḥ		ॐ जभुवे नमः ।
268.	Oṃ Jayadāyai Namaḥ		ॐ जयदायै नमः ।
269.	Oṃ Jagadāvāsāyai Namaḥ		ॐ जगदावासायै नमः ।
270.	Oṃ Jāyinyai Namaḥ		ॐ जायिन्यै नमः ।
271.	Oṃ Jvarakṛcchrajite Namaḥ		ॐ ज्वरकृच्छ्रजिते नमः ।
272.	Oṃ Japāyai Namaḥ		ॐ जपायै नमः ।
273.	Oṃ Japatyai Namaḥ		ॐ जपत्यै नमः ।
274.	Oṃ Japyāyai Namaḥ		ॐ जप्यायै नमः ।
275.	Oṃ Japārhāyai Namaḥ		ॐ जपार्हायै नमः ।

276.	Oṃ Jāyinyai Namaḥ		ॐ जायिन्यै नमः ।
277.	Oṃ Janāyai Namaḥ		ॐ जनायै नमः ।
278.	Jālandharamayījānave	जालन्धरमयीजानवे
279.	Oṃ Jalaukāyai Namaḥ		ॐ जलौकायै नमः ।
280.	Oṃ Jāpyabhūṣaṇāyai Namaḥ		ॐ जाप्यभूषणायै नमः ।
281.	Oṃ Jagajjīvamayyai Namaḥ		ॐ जगज्जीवमय्यै नमः ।
282.	Oṃ Jīvāyai Namaḥ		ॐ जीवायै नमः ।
283.	Oṃ Jaratkārave Namaḥ		ॐ जरत्कारवे नमः ।
284.	Oṃ Janapriyāyai Namaḥ		ॐ जनप्रियायै नमः ।
285.	Oṃ Jagatyai Namaḥ		ॐ जगत्यै नमः ।
286.	Oṃ Jananiratāyai Namaḥ		ॐ जननिरतायै नमः ।
287.	Oṃ Jagacchobhākaryai Namaḥ		ॐ जगच्छोभाकर्यै नमः ।
288.	Oṃ Javāyai Namaḥ		ॐ जवायै नमः ।
289.	Oṃ Jagatītrāṇakṛjjaṅghāyai Namaḥ		ॐ जगतीत्राणकृज्जङ्घायै नमः ।
290.	Oṃ Jātīphalavinodinyai Namaḥ		ॐ जातीफलविनोदिन्यै नमः ।
291.	Oṃ Jātīpuṣpapriyāyai Namaḥ		ॐ जातीपुष्पप्रियायै नमः ।
292.	Oṃ Jvālāyai Namaḥ		ॐ ज्वालायै नमः ।
293.	Oṃ Jātihāyai Namaḥ		ॐ जातिहायै नमः ।
294.	Oṃ Jātirūpiṇyai Namaḥ		ॐ जातिरूपिण्यै नमः ।
295.	Oṃ Jīmūtavāhanarucyai Namaḥ	ॐ जीमूतवाहनरुच्यै नमः ।
296.	Oṃ Jīmūtāyai Namaḥ		ॐ जीमूतायै नमः ।
297.	Oṃ Jīrṇavastrakṛte Namaḥ		ॐ जीर्णवस्त्रकृते नमः ।
298.	Oṃ Jīrṇavastradharāyai Namaḥ	ॐ जीर्णवस्त्रधरायै नमः ।
299.	Oṃ Jīrṇāyai Namaḥ		ॐ जीर्णायै नमः ।
300.	Oṃ Jvalatyai Namaḥ		ॐ ज्वलत्यै नमः ।
301.	Oṃ Jālanāśinyai Namaḥ		ॐ जालनाशिन्यै नमः ।
302.	Oṃ Jagatkṣobhakaryai Namaḥ		ॐ जगत्क्षोभकर्यै नमः ।
303.	Oṃ Jātyai Namaḥ		ॐ जात्यै नमः ।
304.	Oṃ Jagatkṣobhavināśinyai Namaḥ	ॐ जगत्क्षोभविनाशिन्यै नमः ।

305.	Oṃ Janāpavādāyai Namaḥ ।	ॐ जनापवादायै नमः ।
306.	Oṃ Jīvāyai Namaḥ ।	ॐ जीवायै नमः ।
307.	Oṃ Jananīgṛhavāsinyai Namaḥ ।	ॐ जननीगृहवासिन्यै नमः ।
308.	Oṃ Janānurāgāyai Namaḥ ।	ॐ जनानुरागायै नमः ।
309.	Oṃ Jānusthāyai Namaḥ ।	ॐ जानुस्थायै नमः ।
310.	Oṃ Jalavāsāyai Namaḥ ।	ॐ जलवासायै नमः ।
311.	Oṃ Jalārtikṛte Namaḥ ।	ॐ जलार्तिकृते नमः ।
312.	Oṃ Jalajāyai Namaḥ ।	ॐ जलजायै नमः ।
313.	Oṃ Jalavelāyai Namaḥ ।	ॐ जलवेलायै नमः ।
314.	Oṃ Jalacakranivāsinyai Namaḥ ।	ॐ जलचक्रनिवासिन्यै नमः ।
315.	Oṃ Jalamuktāyai Namaḥ ।	ॐ जलमुक्तायै नमः ।
316.	Oṃ Jalārohāyai Namaḥ ।	ॐ जलारोहायै नमः ।
317.	Oṃ Jalajāyai Namaḥ ।	ॐ जलजायै नमः ।
318.	Oṃ Jalajekṣaṇāyai Namaḥ ।	ॐ जलजेक्षणायै नमः ।
319.	Oṃ Jalapriyāyai Namaḥ ।	ॐ जलप्रियायै नमः ।
320.	Oṃ Jalaukāyai Namaḥ ।	ॐ जलौकायै नमः ।
321.	Oṃ Jalaśobhāvatyai Namaḥ ।	ॐ जलशोभावत्यै नमः ।
322.	Oṃ Jalavisphūrjitavapuṣe Namaḥ	ॐ जलविस्फूर्जितवपुषे नमः ।
323.	Oṃ Jvalatpāvakaśobhinyai Namaḥ	ॐ ज्वलत्पावकशोभिन्यै नमः ।
324.	Oṃ Jhiñjhāyai Namaḥ ।	ॐ झिञ्झायै नमः ।
325.	Oṃ Jhillamayyai Namaḥ ।	ॐ झिल्लमय्यै नमः ।
326.	Oṃ Jhiñjhāyai Namaḥ ।	ॐ झिञ्झायै नमः ।
327.	Oṃ Jhaṇatkārakaryai Namaḥ ।	ॐ झणत्कारकर्यै नमः ।
328.	Oṃ Jayāyai Namaḥ ।	ॐ जयायै नमः ।
329.	Oṃ Jhañjhyai Namaḥ ।	ॐ झञ्झ्यै नमः ।
330.	Oṃ Jhampakaryai Namaḥ ।	ॐ झम्पकर्यै नमः ।
331.	Oṃ Jhampāyai Namaḥ ।	ॐ झम्पायै नमः ।
332.	Oṃ Jhampatrāsanivāriṇyai Namaḥ	ॐ झम्पत्रासनिवारिण्यै नमः ।
333.	Oṃ Ṭaṅkārasthāyai Namaḥ ।	ॐ टङ्कारस्थायै नमः ।
334.	Oṃ Ṭaṅkakaryai Namaḥ ।	ॐ टङ्ककर्यै नमः ।

335.	Oṃ Ṭaṅkārakaraṇāṃhasāyai Namaḥ		ॐ टङ्कारकरणां हसायै नमः ।
336.	Oṃ Ṭaṅkārottakṛtasthīvāyai Namaḥ		ॐ टङ्कारोट्टकृतष्ठीवायै नमः ।
337.	Oṃ Ḍiṇḍīravasanāvṛtāyai Namaḥ	ॐ डिण्डीरवसनावृतायै नमः ।
338.	Oṃ Ḍākinyai Namaḥ		ॐ डाकिन्यै नमः ।
339.	Oṃ Ḍāmiryai Namaḥ		ॐ डामिर्यै नमः ।
340.	Oṃ Ḍiṇḍimadhvaninādinyai Namaḥ		ॐ डिण्डिमध्वनिनादिन्यै नमः ।
341.	Oṃ Ḍakāranissvanarucaye Namaḥ	ॐ डकारनिस्स्वनरुचये नमः ।
342.	Oṃ Tapinyai Namaḥ		ॐ तपिन्यै नमः ।
343.	Oṃ Tāpinyai Namaḥ		ॐ तापिन्यै नमः ।
344.	Oṃ Taruṇyai Namaḥ		ॐ तरुण्यै नमः ।
345.	Oṃ Tundilāyai Namaḥ		ॐ तुन्दिलायै नमः ।
346.	Oṃ Tundāyai Namaḥ		ॐ तुन्दायै नमः ।
347.	Oṃ Tāmasyai Namaḥ		ॐ तामस्यै नमः ।
348.	Oṃ Tamaḥpriyāyai Namaḥ		ॐ तमःप्रियायै नमः ।
349.	Oṃ Tāmrāyai Namaḥ		ॐ ताम्रायै नमः ।
350.	Oṃ Tāmravatyai Namaḥ		ॐ ताम्रवत्यै नमः ।
351.	Oṃ Tantave Namaḥ		ॐ तन्तवे नमः ।
352.	Oṃ Tundilāyai Namaḥ		ॐ तुन्दिलायै नमः ।
353.	Oṃ Tulasambhavāyai Namaḥ		ॐ तुलसम्भवायै नमः ।
354.	Oṃ Tulākoṭisuvegāyai Namaḥ		ॐ तुलाकोटिसुवेगायै नमः ।
355.	Oṃ Tulyakāmāyai Namaḥ		ॐ तुल्यकामायै नमः ।
356.	Oṃ Tulāśrayāyai Namaḥ		ॐ तुलाश्रयायै नमः ।
357.	Oṃ Tudinyai Namaḥ		ॐ तुदिन्यै नमः ।
358.	Oṃ Tuninyai Namaḥ		ॐ तुनिन्यै नमः ।
359.	Oṃ Tumbāyai Namaḥ		ॐ तुम्बायै नमः ।
360.	Oṃ Tulyakālāyai Namaḥ		ॐ तुल्यकालायै नमः ।
361.	Oṃ Tulāśrayāyai Namaḥ		ॐ तुलाश्रयायै नमः ।
362.	Oṃ Tumulāyai Namaḥ		ॐ तुमुलायै नमः ।

363.	Oṃ Tulajāyai Namaḥ		ॐ तुलजायै नमः ।
364.	Oṃ Tulyāyai Namaḥ		ॐ तुल्यायै नमः ।
365.	Oṃ Tulādānakaryai Namaḥ		ॐ तुलादानकर्यै नमः ।
366.	Oṃ Tulyavegāyai Namaḥ		ॐ तुल्यवेगायै नमः ।
367.	Oṃ Tulyagatyai Namaḥ		ॐ तुल्यगत्यै नमः ।
368.	Oṃ Tulākoṭininādinyai Namaḥ		ॐ तुलाकोटिनिनादिन्यै नमः ।
369.	Oṃ Tāmroṣṭhāyai Namaḥ		ॐ ताम्रोष्ठायै नमः ।
370.	Oṃ Tāmraparṇyai Namaḥ		ॐ ताम्रपर्ण्यै नमः ।
371.	Oṃ Tamaḥsaṅkṣobhakāriṇyai Namaḥ		ॐ तमःसङ्क्षोभकारिण्यै नमः ।
372.	Oṃ Tvaritāyai Namaḥ		ॐ त्वरितायै नमः ।
373.	Oṃ Tvarahāyai Namaḥ		ॐ त्वरहायै नमः ।
374.	Oṃ Tīrāyai Namaḥ		ॐ तीरायै नमः ।
375.	Oṃ Tārakeśyai Namaḥ		ॐ तारकेश्यै नमः ।
376.	Oṃ Tamālinyai Namaḥ		ॐ तमालिन्यै नमः ।
377.	Oṃ Tamodānavatyai Namaḥ		ॐ तमोदानवत्यै नमः ।
378.	Oṃ Tāmratālasthānavatyai Namaḥ		ॐ ताम्रतालस्थानवत्यै नमः ।
379.	Oṃ Tamyai Namaḥ		ॐ तम्यै नमः ।
380.	Oṃ Tāmasyai Namaḥ		ॐ तामस्यै नमः ।
381.	Oṃ Tamisrāyai Namaḥ		ॐ तमिस्रायै नमः ।
382.	Oṃ Tīvrāyai Namaḥ		ॐ तीव्रायै नमः ।
383.	Oṃ Tīvraparākramāyai Namaḥ		ॐ तीव्रपराक्रमायै नमः ।
384.	Oṃ Taṭasthāyai Namaḥ		ॐ तटस्थायै नमः ।
385.	Oṃ Tilatailāktāyai Namaḥ		ॐ तिलतैलाक्तायै नमः ।
386.	Oṃ Taruṇyai Namaḥ		ॐ तरुण्यै नमः ।
387.	Oṃ Tapanadyutyai Namaḥ		ॐ तपनद्युत्यै नमः ।
388.	Oṃ Tilottamāyai Namaḥ		ॐ तिलोत्तमायै नमः ।
389.	Oṃ Tilakṛte Namaḥ		ॐ तिलकृते नमः ।
390.	Oṃ Tārakādhīśaśekharāyai Namaḥ		ॐ तारकाधीशशेखरायै नमः ।

391.	Oṃ Tilapuṣpapriyāyai Namaḥ		ॐ तिलपुष्पप्रियायै नमः ।
392.	Oṃ Tārāyai Namaḥ		ॐ तारायै नमः ।
393.	Oṃ Tārakeśakuṭumbinyai Namaḥ	ॐ तारकेशकुटुम्बिन्यै नमः ।
394.	Oṃ Sthāṇupatnyai Namaḥ		ॐ स्थाणुपत्न्यै नमः ।
395.	Oṃ Sthirakaryai Namaḥ		ॐ स्थिरकर्यै नमः ।
396.	Oṃ Sthūlasampadvivardhinyai Namaḥ		ॐ स्थूलसम्पद्विवर्धिन्यै नमः ।
397.	Oṃ Sthityai Namaḥ		ॐ स्थित्यै नमः ।
398.	Oṃ Sthairyasthaviṣṭhāyai Namaḥ	ॐ स्थैर्यस्थविष्ठायै नमः ।
399.	Oṃ Sthapatyai Namaḥ		ॐ स्थपत्यै नमः ।
400.	Oṃ Sthūlavigrahāyai Namaḥ		ॐ स्थूलविग्रहायै नमः ।
401.	Oṃ Sthūlasthalavatyai Namaḥ		ॐ स्थूलस्थलवत्यै नमः ।
402.	Oṃ Sthālyai Namaḥ		ॐ स्थाल्यै नमः ।
403.	Oṃ Sthalasaṅgavivardhinyai Namaḥ		ॐ स्थलसङ्गविवर्धिन्यै नमः ।
404.	Oṃ Daṇḍinyai Namaḥ		ॐ दण्डिन्यै नमः ।
405.	Oṃ Dantinyai Namaḥ		ॐ दन्तिन्यै नमः ।
406.	Oṃ Dāmāyai Namaḥ		ॐ दामायै नमः ।
407.	Oṃ Daridrāyai Namaḥ		ॐ दरिद्रायै नमः ।
408.	Oṃ Dīnavatsalāyai Namaḥ		ॐ दीनवत्सलायै नमः ।
409.	Oṃ Devāyai Namaḥ		ॐ देवायै नमः ।
410.	Oṃ Devavadhvai Namaḥ		ॐ देववध्वै नमः ।
411.	Oṃ Dityāyai Namaḥ		ॐ दित्यायै नमः ।
412.	Oṃ Dāminyai Namaḥ		ॐ दामिन्यै नमः ।
413.	Oṃ Devabhūṣaṇāyai Namaḥ		ॐ देवभूषणायै नमः ।
414.	Oṃ Dayāyai Namaḥ		ॐ दयायै नमः ।
415.	Oṃ Damavatyai Namaḥ		ॐ दमवत्यै नमः ।
416.	Oṃ Dīnavatsalāyai Namaḥ		ॐ दीनवत्सलायै नमः ।
417.	Oṃ Dāḍimastanyai Namaḥ		ॐ दाडिमस्तन्यै नमः ।
418.	Oṃ Devamūrtikarāyai Namaḥ		ॐ देवमूर्तिकरायै नमः ।
419.	Oṃ Daityāyai Namaḥ		ॐ दैत्यायै नमः ।

420.	Oṃ Dāriṇyai Namaḥ l	ॐ दारिण्यै नमः l
421.	Oṃ Devatānatāyai Namaḥ l	ॐ देवतानतायै नमः l
422.	Oṃ Dolākrīḍāyai Namaḥ l	ॐ दोलाक्रीडायै नमः l
423.	Oṃ Dayālave Namaḥ l	ॐ दयालवे नमः l
424.	Oṃ Dampatībhyāṃ Namaḥ l	ॐ दम्पतीभ्यां नमः l
425.	Oṃ Devatāmayyai Namaḥ l	ॐ देवतामय्यै नमः l
426.	Oṃ Daśādīpasthitāyai Namaḥ l	ॐ दशादीपस्थितायै नमः l
427.	Oṃ Doṣādoṣahāyai Namaḥ l	ॐ दोषादोषहायै नमः l
428.	Oṃ Doṣakāriṇyai Namaḥ l	ॐ दोषकारिण्यै नमः l
429.	Oṃ Durgāyai Namaḥ l	ॐ दुर्गायै नमः l
430.	Oṃ Durgārtiśamanyai Namaḥ l	ॐ दुर्गार्तिशमन्यै नमः l
431.	Oṃ Durgamyāyai Namaḥ l	ॐ दुर्गम्यायै नमः l
432.	Oṃ Durgavāsinyai Namaḥ l	ॐ दुर्गवासिन्यै नमः l
433.	Oṃ Durgandhanāśinyai Namaḥ l	ॐ दुर्गन्धनाशिन्यै नमः l
434.	Oṃ Dussthāyai Namaḥ l	ॐ दुस्स्थायै नमः l
435.	Oṃ Duḥkhapraśamakāriṇyai Namaḥ l	ॐ दुःखप्रशमकारिण्यै नमः l
436.	Oṃ Durgandhāyai Namaḥ l	ॐ दुर्गन्धायै नमः l
437.	Oṃ Dundubhīdhvāntāyai Namaḥ	ॐ दुन्दुभीध्वान्तायै नमः l
438.	Oṃ Dūrasthāyai Namaḥ l	ॐ दूरस्थायै नमः l
439.	Oṃ Dūravāsinyai Namaḥ l	ॐ दूरवासिन्यै नमः l
440.	Oṃ Daradāyai Namaḥ l	ॐ दरदायै नमः l
441.	Oṃ Daradātryai Namaḥ l	ॐ दरदात्र्यै नमः l
442.	Oṃ Durvyādhadayitāyai Namaḥ	ॐ दुर्व्याधदयितायै नमः l
443.	Oṃ Damyai Namaḥ l	ॐ दम्यै नमः l
444.	Oṃ Dhurandharāyai Namaḥ l	ॐ धुरन्धरायै नमः l
445.	Oṃ Dhurīṇāyai Namaḥ l	ॐ धुरीणायै नमः l
446.	Oṃ Dhaureyyai Namaḥ l	ॐ धौरेय्यै नमः l
447.	Oṃ Dhanadāyinyai Namaḥ l	ॐ धनदायिन्यै नमः l
448.	Oṃ Dhīrāravāyai Namaḥ l	ॐ धीरारवायै नमः l

449.	Oṃ Dharitryai Namaḥ		ॐ धरित्र्यै नमः ।
450.	Oṃ Dharmadāyai Namaḥ		ॐ धर्मदायै नमः ।
451.	Oṃ Dhīramānasāyai Namaḥ		ॐ धीरमानसायै नमः ।
452.	Oṃ Dhanurdharāyai Namaḥ		ॐ धनुर्धरायै नमः ।
453.	Oṃ Dhamanyai Namaḥ		ॐ धमन्यै नमः ।
454.	Oṃ Dhamanīdhūrtavigrahāyai Namaḥ		ॐ धमनीधूर्तविग्रहायै नमः ।
455.	Oṃ Dhūmravarṇāyai Namaḥ		ॐ धूम्रवर्णायै नमः ।
456.	Oṃ Dhūmrapānāyai Namaḥ		ॐ धूम्रपानायै नमः ।
457.	Oṃ Dhūmalāyai Namaḥ		ॐ धूमलायै नमः ।
458.	Oṃ Dhūmamodinyai Namaḥ		ॐ धूममोदिन्यै नमः ।
459.	Oṃ Nandinyai Namaḥ		ॐ नन्दिन्यै नमः ।
460.	Oṃ Nandinīnandāyai Namaḥ		ॐ नन्दिनीनन्दायै नमः ।
461.	Oṃ Nandinīnandabālikāyai Namaḥ		ॐ नन्दिनीनन्दबालिकायै नमः ।
462.	Oṃ Navīnāyai Namaḥ		ॐ नवीनायै नमः ।
463.	Oṃ Narmadāyai Namaḥ		ॐ नर्मदायै नमः ।
464.	Oṃ Narmanemaye Namaḥ		ॐ नर्मनेमये नमः ।
465.	Oṃ Niyamaniḥsvanāyai Namaḥ		ॐ नियमनिःस्वनायै नमः ।
466.	Oṃ Nirmalāyai Namaḥ		ॐ निर्मलायै नमः ।
467.	Oṃ Nigamādhārāyai Namaḥ		ॐ निगमाधारायै नमः ।
468.	Oṃ Nimnagāyai Namaḥ		ॐ निम्नगायै नमः ।
469.	Oṃ Nagnakāminyai Namaḥ		ॐ नग्नकामिन्यै नमः ।
470.	Oṃ Nīlāyai Namaḥ		ॐ नीलायै नमः ।
471.	Oṃ Niratnāyai Namaḥ		ॐ निरत्नायै नमः ।
472.	Oṃ Nirvāṇāyai Namaḥ		ॐ निर्वाणायै नमः ।
473.	Oṃ Nirlobhāyai Namaḥ		ॐ निर्लोभायै नमः ।
474.	Oṃ Nirguṇāyai Namaḥ		ॐ निर्गुणायै नमः ।
475.	Oṃ Natyai Namaḥ		ॐ नत्यै नमः ।
476.	Oṃ Nīlagrīvāyai Namaḥ		ॐ नीलग्रीवायै नमः ।

477.	Oṃ Nirīhāyai Namaḥ ǀ	ॐ निरीहायै नमः ǀ
478.	Oṃ Nirañjanajanāyai Namaḥ ǀ	ॐ निरञ्जनजनायै नमः ǀ
479.	Oṃ Navāyai Namaḥ ǀ	ॐ नवायै नमः ǀ
480.	Oṃ Nirguṇḍikāyai Namaḥ ǀ	ॐ निर्गुण्डिकायै नमः ǀ
481.	Oṃ Nirguṇḍāyai Namaḥ ǀ	ॐ निर्गुण्डायै नमः ǀ
482.	Oṃ Nirnāsāyai Namaḥ ǀ	ॐ निर्नासायै नमः ǀ
483.	Oṃ Nāsikābhidhāyai Namaḥ ǀ	ॐ नासिकाभिधायै नमः ǀ
484.	Oṃ Patākinyai Namaḥ ǀ	ॐ पताकिन्यै नमः ǀ
485.	Oṃ Patākāyai Namaḥ ǀ	ॐ पताकायै नमः ǀ
486.	Oṃ Patraprītyai Namaḥ ǀ	ॐ पत्रप्रीत्यै नमः ǀ
487.	Oṃ Payasvinyai Namaḥ ǀ	ॐ पयस्विन्यै नमः ǀ
488.	Oṃ Pīnāyai Namaḥ ǀ	ॐ पीनायै नमः ǀ
489.	Oṃ Pīnastanyai Namaḥ ǀ	ॐ पीनस्तन्यै नमः ǀ
490.	Oṃ Patnyai Namaḥ ǀ	ॐ पत्न्यै नमः ǀ
491.	Oṃ Pavanāśyai Namaḥ ǀ	ॐ पवनाश्यै नमः ǀ
492.	Oṃ Niśāmayyai Namaḥ ǀ	ॐ निशामय्यै नमः ǀ
493.	Oṃ Parāyai Namaḥ ǀ	ॐ परायै नमः ǀ
494.	Oṃ Paraparāyai Kālyai Namaḥ ǀ	ॐ परपरायै काल्यै नमः ǀ
495.	Oṃ Pārakṛtyabhujapriyāyai Namaḥ ǀ	ॐ पारकृत्यभुजप्रियायै नमः ǀ
496.	Oṃ Pavanasthāyai Namaḥ ǀ	ॐ पवनस्थायै नमः ǀ
497.	Oṃ Pavanāyai Namaḥ ǀ	ॐ पवनायै नमः ǀ
498.	Oṃ Pavanaprītivardhinyai Namaḥ	ॐ पवनप्रीतिवर्धिन्यै नमः ǀ
499.	Oṃ Paśuvṛddhikaryai Namaḥ ǀ	ॐ पशुवृद्धिकर्यै नमः ǀ
500.	Oṃ Puṣpapoṣakāyai Namaḥ ǀ	ॐ पुष्पपोषकायै नमः ǀ
501.	Oṃ Puṣṭivardhinyai Namaḥ ǀ	ॐ पुष्टिवर्धिन्यै नमः ǀ
502.	Oṃ Puṣpiṇyai Namaḥ ǀ	ॐ पुष्पिण्यै नमः ǀ
503.	Oṃ Pustakakarāyai Namaḥ ǀ	ॐ पुस्तककरायै नमः ǀ
504.	Oṃ Pūrṇimātalavāsinyai Namaḥ	ॐ पूर्णिमातलवासिन्यै नमः ǀ
505.	Oṃ Peśyai Namaḥ ǀ	ॐ पेश्यै नमः ǀ

506.	Om Pāśakaryai Namaḥ ।	ॐ पाशकर्यै नमः ।
507.	Om Pāśāyai Namaḥ ।	ॐ पाशायै नमः ।
508.	Om Pāṃsuhāyai Namaḥ ।	ॐ पांशुहायै नमः ।
509.	Om Pāṃsulāyai Namaḥ ।	ॐ पांशुलायै नमः ।
510.	Om Paśave Namaḥ ।	ॐ पशवे नमः ।
511.	Om Paṭvai Namaḥ ।	ॐ पट्वै नमः ।
512.	Om Parāśāyai Namaḥ ।	ॐ पराशायै नमः ।
513.	Om Paraśudhāriṇyai Namaḥ ।	ॐ परशुधारिण्यै नमः ।
514.	Om Pāśinyai Namaḥ ।	ॐ पाशिन्यै नमः ।
515.	Om Pāpaghnyai Namaḥ ।	ॐ पापघ्न्यै नमः ।
516.	Om Patipatnyai Namaḥ ।	ॐ पतिपत्न्यै नमः ।
517.	Om Patitāyai Namaḥ ।	ॐ पतितायै नमः ।
518.	Om Patitāpinyai Namaḥ ।	ॐ पतितापिन्यै नमः ।
519.	Om Piśācyai Namaḥ ।	ॐ पिशाच्यै नमः ।
520.	Om Piśācaghnyai Namaḥ ।	ॐ पिशाचघ्न्यै नमः ।
521.	Om Piśitāśanatoṣiṇyai Namaḥ ।	ॐ पिशिताशनतोषिण्यै नमः ।
522.	Om Pānadāyai Namaḥ ।	ॐ पानदायै नमः ।
523.	Om Pānapātryai Namaḥ ।	ॐ पानपात्र्यै नमः ।
524.	Om Pānadānakarodyatāyai Namaḥ ।	ॐ पानदानकरोद्यतायै नमः ।
525.	Om Peyāyai Namaḥ ।	ॐ पेयायै नमः ।
526.	Om Prasiddhāyai Namaḥ ।	ॐ प्रसिद्धायै नमः ।
527.	Om Pīyūṣāyai Namaḥ ।	ॐ पीयूषायै नमः ।
528.	Om Pūrṇāyai Namaḥ ।	ॐ पूर्णायै नमः ।
529.	Om Pūrṇamanorathāyai Namaḥ	ॐ पूर्णमनोरथायै नमः ।
530.	Om Pataṅgābhāyai Namaḥ ।	ॐ पतङ्गाभायै नमः ।
531.	Om Pataṅgāyai Namaḥ ।	ॐ पतङ्गायै नमः ।
532.	Om Paunaḥpunyapibāparāyai Namaḥ ।	ॐ पौनःपुन्यपिबापरायै नमः ।
533.	Om Paṅkilāyai Namaḥ ।	ॐ पङ्किलायै नमः ।
534.	Om Paṅkamagnāyai Namaḥ ।	ॐ पङ्कमग्नायै नमः ।

535.	Oṃ Pānīyāyai Namaḥ ।	ॐ पानीयायै नमः ।
536.	Oṃ Pañjarasthitāyai Namaḥ ।	ॐ पञ्जरस्थितायै नमः ।
537.	Oṃ Pañcamyai Namaḥ ।	ॐ पञ्चम्यै नमः ।
538.	Oṃ Pañcayajñāyai Namaḥ ।	ॐ पञ्चयज्ञायै नमः ।
539.	Oṃ Pañcatāyai Namaḥ ।	ॐ पञ्चतायै नमः ।
540.	Oṃ Pañcamapriyāyai Namaḥ ।	ॐ पञ्चमप्रियायै नमः ।
541.	Oṃ Picumandāyai Namaḥ ।	ॐ पिचुमन्दायै नमः ।
542.	Oṃ Puṇḍarīkāyai Namaḥ ।	ॐ पुण्डरीकायै नमः ।
543.	Oṃ Pikyai Namaḥ ।	ॐ पिक्यै नमः ।
544.	Oṃ Piṅgalalocanāyai Namaḥ ।	ॐ पिङ्गललोचनायै नमः ।
545.	Oṃ Priyaṅgumañjaryai Namaḥ ।	ॐ प्रियङ्गुमञ्जर्यै नमः ।
546.	Oṃ Piṇḍyai Namaḥ ।	ॐ पिण्ड्यै नमः ।
547.	Oṃ Paṇḍitāyai Namaḥ ।	ॐ पण्डितायै नमः ।
548.	Oṃ Pāṇḍuraprabhāyai Namaḥ ।	ॐ पाण्डुरप्रभायै नमः ।
549.	Oṃ Pretāsanāyai Namaḥ ।	ॐ प्रेतासनायै नमः ।
550.	Oṃ Priyālasthāyai Namaḥ ।	ॐ प्रियालस्थायै नमः ।
551.	Oṃ Pāṇḍughnyai Namaḥ ।	ॐ पाण्डुघ्न्यै नमः ।
552.	Oṃ Pīnasāpahāyai Namaḥ ।	ॐ पीनसापहायै नमः ।
553.	Oṃ Phalinyai Namaḥ ।	ॐ फलिन्यै नमः ।
554.	Oṃ Phaladātryai Namaḥ ।	ॐ फलदात्र्यै नमः ।
555.	Oṃ Phalaśriye Namaḥ ।	ॐ फलश्रिये नमः ।
556.	Oṃ Phalabhūṣaṇāyai Namaḥ ।	ॐ फलभूषणायै नमः ।
557.	Oṃ Phūtkārakāriṇyai Namaḥ ।	ॐ फूत्कारकारिण्यै नमः ।
558.	Oṃ Sphāryai Namaḥ ।	ॐ स्फार्यै नमः ।
559.	Oṃ Phullāyai Namaḥ ।	ॐ फुल्लायै नमः ।
560.	Oṃ Phullāmbujānanāyai Namaḥ ।	ॐ फुल्लाम्बुजाननायै नमः ।
561.	Oṃ Sphuliṅgahāyai Namaḥ ।	ॐ स्फुलिङ्गहायै नमः ।
562.	Oṃ Sphītamatyai Namaḥ ।	ॐ स्फीतमत्यै नमः ।
563.	Oṃ Sphītakīrtikaryai Namaḥ ।	ॐ स्फीतकीर्तिकर्यै नमः ।
564.	Oṃ Bālamāyāyai Namaḥ ।	ॐ बालमायायै नमः ।

565.	Oṃ Balārātyai Namaḥ		ॐ बलारात्यै नमः ।
566.	Oṃ Balinyai Namaḥ		ॐ बलिन्यै नमः ।
567.	Oṃ Balavardhinyai Namaḥ		ॐ बलवर्धिन्यै नमः ।
568.	Oṃ Veṇuvādyāyai Namaḥ		ॐ वेणुवाद्यायै नमः ।
569.	Oṃ Vanacaryai Namaḥ		ॐ वनचर्यै नमः ।
570.	Oṃ Viriñcijanayitryai Namaḥ		ॐ विरिञ्चिजनयित्र्यै नमः ।
571.	Oṃ Vidyāpradāyai Namaḥ		ॐ विद्याप्रदायै नमः ।
572.	Oṃ Mahāvidyāyai Namaḥ		ॐ महाविद्यायै नमः ।
573.	Oṃ Bodhinyai Namaḥ		ॐ बोधिन्यै नमः ।
574.	Oṃ Bodhadāyinyai Namaḥ		ॐ बोधदायिन्यै नमः ।
575.	Oṃ Buddhamātre Namaḥ		ॐ बुद्धमात्रे नमः ।
576.	Oṃ Buddhāyai Namaḥ		ॐ बुद्धायै नमः ।
577.	Oṃ Vanamālāvatyai Namaḥ		ॐ वनमालावत्यै नमः ।
578.	Oṃ Varāyai Namaḥ		ॐ वरायै नमः ।
579.	Oṃ Varadāyai Namaḥ		ॐ वरदायै नमः ।
580.	Oṃ Vāruṇyai Namaḥ		ॐ वारुण्यै नमः ।
581.	Oṃ Vīṇāyai Namaḥ		ॐ वीणायै नमः ।
582.	Oṃ Vīṇāvādanatatparāyai Namaḥ	ॐ वीणावादनतत्परायै नमः ।
583.	Oṃ Vinodinyai Namaḥ		ॐ विनोदिन्यै नमः ।
584.	Oṃ Vinodasthāyai Namaḥ		ॐ विनोदस्थायै नमः ।
585.	Oṃ Vaiṣṇavyai Namaḥ		ॐ वैष्णव्यै नमः ।
586.	Oṃ Viṣṇuvallabhāyai Namaḥ		ॐ विष्णुवल्लभायै नमः ।
587.	Oṃ Vaidyāyai Namaḥ		ॐ वैद्यायै नमः ।
588.	Oṃ Vaidyacikitsāyai Namaḥ		ॐ वैद्यचिकित्सायै नमः ।
589.	Oṃ Vivaśāyai Namaḥ		ॐ विवशायै नमः ।
590.	Oṃ Viśvaviśrutāyai Namaḥ		ॐ विश्वविश्रुतायै नमः ।
591.	Oṃ Vidyaughavihvalāyai Namaḥ	ॐ विद्यौघविह्वलायै नमः ।
592.	Oṃ Velāyai Namaḥ		ॐ वेलायै नमः ।
593.	Oṃ Vittadāyai Namaḥ		ॐ वित्तदायै नमः ।
594.	Oṃ Vigatajvarāyai Namaḥ		ॐ विगतज्वरायै नमः ।

595.	Oṃ Virāvāyai Namaḥ		ॐ विरावायै नमः ।
596.	Oṃ Vivarīkārāyai Namaḥ		ॐ विवरीकारायै नमः ।
597.	Oṃ Bimboṣṭhyai Namaḥ		ॐ बिम्बोष्ट्यै नमः ।
598.	Oṃ Bimbavatsalāyai Namaḥ		ॐ बिम्बवत्सलायै नमः ।
599.	Oṃ Vindhyasthāyai Namaḥ		ॐ विन्ध्यस्थायै नमः ।
600.	Oṃ Varavandyāyai Namaḥ		ॐ वरवन्द्यायै नमः ।
601.	Oṃ Vīrasthānavarāyai Namaḥ		ॐ वीरस्थानवरायै नमः ।
602.	Oṃ Vide Namaḥ		ॐ विदे नमः ।
603.	Oṃ Vedāntavedyāyai Namaḥ		ॐ वेदान्तवेद्यायै नमः ।
604.	Oṃ Vijayāyai Namaḥ		ॐ विजयायै नमः ।
605.	Oṃ Vijayāvijayapradāyai Namaḥ	ॐ विजयाविजयप्रदायै नमः ।
606.	Oṃ Virogyai Namaḥ		ॐ विरोग्यै नमः ।
607.	Oṃ Vandinyai Namaḥ		ॐ वन्दिन्यै नमः ।
608.	Oṃ Vandhyāyai Namaḥ		ॐ वन्ध्यायै नमः ।
609.	Oṃ Vandyāyai Namaḥ		ॐ वन्द्यायै नमः ।
610.	Oṃ Bandhanivāriṇyai Namaḥ		ॐ बन्धनिवारिण्यै नमः ।
611.	Oṃ Bhaginyai Namaḥ		ॐ भगिन्यै नमः ।
612.	Oṃ Bhagamālāyai Namaḥ		ॐ भगमालायै नमः ।
613.	Oṃ Bhavānyai Namaḥ		ॐ भवान्यै नमः ।
614.	Oṃ Bhavanāśinyai Namaḥ		ॐ भवनाशिन्यै नमः ।
615.	Oṃ Bhīmāyai Namaḥ		ॐ भीमायै नमः ।
616.	Oṃ Bhīmānanāyai Namaḥ		ॐ भीमाननायै नमः ।
617.	Oṃ Bhīmābhaṅgurāyai Namaḥ		ॐ भीमाभङ्गुरायै नमः ।
618.	Oṃ Bhīmadarśanāyai Namaḥ		ॐ भीमदर्शनायै नमः ।
619.	Oṃ Bhillyai Namaḥ		ॐ भिल्ल्यै नमः ।
620.	Oṃ Bhilladharāyai Namaḥ		ॐ भिल्लधरायै नमः ।
621.	Oṃ Bhīrave Namaḥ		ॐ भीरवे नमः ।
622.	Oṃ Bheruṇḍāyai Namaḥ		ॐ भेरुण्डायै नमः ।
623.	Oṃ Bhiye Namaḥ		ॐ भिये नमः ।
624.	Oṃ Bhayāvahāyai Namaḥ		ॐ भयावहायै नमः ।

625.	Oṃ Bhagasarpiṇyai Namaḥ ǀ	ॐ भगसर्पिण्यै नमः ǀ
626.	Oṃ Bhagāyai Namaḥ ǀ	ॐ भगायै नमः ǀ
627.	Oṃ Bhagarūpāyai Namaḥ ǀ	ॐ भगरूपायै नमः ǀ
628.	Oṃ Bhagālayāyai Namaḥ ǀ	ॐ भगालयायै नमः ǀ
629.	Oṃ Bhagāsanāyai Namaḥ ǀ	ॐ भगासनायै नमः ǀ
630.	Oṃ Bhavābhogāyai Namaḥ ǀ	ॐ भवाभोगायै नमः ǀ
631.	Oṃ Bherījhaṅkārarañjitāyai Namaḥ ǀ	ॐ भेरीझङ्काररञ्जितायै नमः ǀ
632.	Oṃ Bhīṣaṇāyai Namaḥ ǀ	ॐ भीषणायै नमः ǀ
633.	Oṃ Bhīṣaṇārāvāyai Namaḥ ǀ	ॐ भीषणारावायै नमः ǀ
634.	Oṃ Bhagavatyai Namaḥ ǀ	ॐ भगवत्यै नमः ǀ
635.	Oṃ Ahibhūṣaṇāyai Namaḥ ǀ	ॐ अहिभूषणायै नमः ǀ
636.	Oṃ Bhāradvājāyai Namaḥ ǀ	ॐ भारद्वाजायै नमः ǀ
637.	Oṃ Bhogadātryai Namaḥ ǀ	ॐ भोगदात्र्यै नमः ǀ
638.	Oṃ Bhūtighnyai Namaḥ ǀ	ॐ भूतिघ्न्यै नमः ǀ
639.	Oṃ Bhūtibhūṣaṇāyai Namaḥ ǀ	ॐ भूतिभूषणायै नमः ǀ
640.	Oṃ Bhūmidāyai Namaḥ ǀ	ॐ भूमिदायै नमः ǀ
641.	Oṃ Bhūmidātryai Namaḥ ǀ	ॐ भूमिदात्र्यै नमः ǀ
642.	Oṃ Bhūpataye Namaḥ ǀ	ॐ भूपतये नमः ǀ
643.	Oṃ Bharadāyinyai Namaḥ ǀ	ॐ भरदायिन्यै नमः ǀ
644.	Oṃ Bhramaryai Namaḥ ǀ	ॐ भ्रमर्यै नमः ǀ
645.	Oṃ Bhrāmaryai Namaḥ ǀ	ॐ भ्रामर्यै नमः ǀ
646.	Oṃ Bhālāyai Namaḥ ǀ	ॐ भालायै नमः ǀ
647.	Oṃ Bhūpālakulasaṃsthitāyai Namaḥ ǀ	ॐ भूपालकुलसंस्थितायै नमः ǀ
648.	Oṃ Mātre Namaḥ ǀ	ॐ मात्रे नमः ǀ
649.	Oṃ Manoharyai Namaḥ ǀ	ॐ मनोहर्यै नमः ǀ
650.	Oṃ Māyāyai Namaḥ ǀ	ॐ मायायै नमः ǀ
651.	Oṃ Māninyai Namaḥ ǀ	ॐ मानिन्यै नमः ǀ
652.	Oṃ Mohinyai Namaḥ ǀ	ॐ मोहिन्यै नमः ǀ

653.	Oṃ Mahyai Namaḥ l	ॐ मह्यै नमः l
654.	Oṃ Mahālakṣmyai Namaḥ l	ॐ महालक्ष्म्यै नमः l
655.	Oṃ Madakṣībāyai Namaḥ l	ॐ मदक्षीबायै नमः l
656.	Oṃ Madirāyai Namaḥ l	ॐ मदिरायै नमः l
657.	Oṃ Madirālayāyai Namaḥ l	ॐ मदिरालयायै नमः l
658.	Oṃ Madoddhatāyai Namaḥ l	ॐ मदोद्धतायै नमः l
659.	Oṃ Mataṅgasthāyai Namaḥ l	ॐ मतङ्गस्थायै नमः l
660.	Oṃ Mādhavyai Namaḥ l	ॐ माधव्यै नमः l
661.	Oṃ Madhumardinyai Namaḥ l	ॐ मधुमर्दिन्यै नमः l
662.	Oṃ Modāyai Namaḥ l	ॐ मोदायै नमः l
663.	Oṃ Modakaryai Namaḥ l	ॐ मोदकर्यै नमः l
664.	Oṃ Medhāyai Namaḥ l	ॐ मेधायै नमः l
665.	Oṃ Medhyāyai Namaḥ l	ॐ मेध्यायै नमः l
666.	Oṃ Madhyādhipasthitāyai Namaḥ	ॐ मध्याधिपस्थितायै नमः l
667.	Oṃ Madyapāyai Namaḥ l	ॐ मद्यपायै नमः l
668.	Oṃ Māṃsalobhasthāyai Namaḥ	ॐ मांसलोभस्थायै नमः l
669.	Oṃ Modinyai Namaḥ l	ॐ मोदिन्यै नमः l
670.	Oṃ Maithunodyatāyai Namaḥ l	ॐ मैथुनोद्यतायै नमः l
671.	Oṃ Mūrdhāvatyai Namaḥ l	ॐ मूर्धावत्यै नमः l
672.	Oṃ Mahāmāyāyai Namaḥ l	ॐ महामायायै नमः l
673.	Oṃ Māyāyai Namaḥ l	ॐ मायायै नमः l
674.	Oṃ Mahimamandirāyai Namaḥ l	ॐ महिममन्दिरायै नमः l
675.	Oṃ Mahāmālāyai Namaḥ l	ॐ महामालायै नमः l
676.	Oṃ Mahāvidyāyai Namaḥ l	ॐ महाविद्यायै नमः l
677.	Oṃ Mahāmāryai Namaḥ l	ॐ महामार्यै नमः l
678.	Oṃ Maheśvaryai Namaḥ l	ॐ महेश्वर्यै नमः l
679.	Oṃ Mahādevavadhvai Namaḥ l	ॐ महादेववध्वै नमः l
680.	Oṃ Mānyāyai Namaḥ l	ॐ मान्यायै नमः l
681.	Oṃ Mathurāyai Namaḥ l	ॐ मथुरायै नमः l
682.	Oṃ Merumaṇḍitāyai Namaḥ l	ॐ मेरुमण्डितायै नमः l

683.	Oṃ Medasvinyai Namaḥ		ॐ मेदस्विन्यै नमः ।
684.	Oṃ Milindākṣyai Namaḥ		ॐ मिलिन्दाक्ष्यै नमः ।
685.	Oṃ Mahiṣāsuramardinyai Namaḥ	ॐ महिषासुरमर्दिन्यै नमः ।
686.	Oṃ Maṇḍalasthāyai Namaḥ		ॐ मण्डलस्थायै नमः ।
687.	Oṃ Bhagasthāyai Namaḥ		ॐ भगस्थायै नमः ।
688.	Oṃ Madirārāgagarvitāyai Namaḥ	ॐ मदिरारागगर्विताये नमः ।
689.	Oṃ Mokṣadāyai Namaḥ		ॐ मोक्षदायै नमः ।
690.	Oṃ Muṇḍamālāyai Namaḥ		ॐ मुण्डमालायै नमः ।
691.	Oṃ Mālāyai Namaḥ		ॐ मालायै नमः ।
692.	Oṃ Mālāvilāsinyai Namaḥ		ॐ मालाविलासिन्यै नमः ।
693.	Oṃ Mātaṅginyai Namaḥ		ॐ मातङ्गिन्यै नमः ।
694.	Oṃ Mātaṅgyai Namaḥ		ॐ मातङ्ग्यै नमः ।
695.	Oṃ Mātaṅgatanayāyai Namaḥ		ॐ मातङ्गतनयायै नमः ।
696.	Oṃ Madhusravāyai Namaḥ		ॐ मधुस्रवायै नमः ।
697.	Oṃ Madhurasāyai Namaḥ		ॐ मधुरसायै नमः ।
698.	Oṃ Bandhūkakusumapriyāyai Namaḥ		ॐ बन्धूककुसुमप्रियायै नमः
699.	Oṃ Yāminyai Namaḥ		ॐ यामिन्यै नमः ।
700.	Oṃ Yāminīnāthabhūṣāyai Namaḥ	ॐ यामिनीनाथभूषायै नमः ।
701.	Oṃ Yāvakarañjitāyai Namaḥ		ॐ यावकरञ्जितायै नमः ।
702.	Oṃ Yavāṅkurapriyāyai Namaḥ		ॐ यवाङ्कुरप्रियायै नमः ।
703.	Oṃ Yāmāyai Namaḥ		ॐ यामायै नमः ।
704.	Oṃ Yavanyai Namaḥ		ॐ यवन्यै नमः ।
705.	Oṃ Yavanārdinyai Namaḥ		ॐ यवनार्दिन्यै नमः ।
706.	Oṃ Yamaghnyai Namaḥ		ॐ यमघ्न्यै नमः ।
707.	Oṃ Yamakalpāyai Namaḥ		ॐ यमकल्पायै नमः ।
708.	Oṃ Yajamānasvarūpiṇyai Namaḥ	ॐ यजमानस्वरूपिण्यै नमः ।
709.	Oṃ Yajñāyai Namaḥ		ॐ यज्ञायै नमः ।
710.	Oṃ Yajñayajuṣe Namaḥ		ॐ यज्ञयजुषे नमः ।
711.	Oṃ Yakṣyai Namaḥ		ॐ यक्ष्यै नमः ।

712.	Oṃ Yaśoniṣkampakāriṇyai Namaḥ	ॐ यशोनिष्कम्पकारिण्यै नमः ।
713.	Oṃ Yakṣiṇyai Namaḥ ।	ॐ यक्षिण्यै नमः ।
714.	Oṃ Yakṣajananyai Namaḥ ।	ॐ यक्षजनन्यै नमः ।
715.	Oṃ Yaśodāyai Namaḥ ।	ॐ यशोदायै नमः ।
716.	Oṃ Yāsadhāriṇyai Namaḥ ।	ॐ यासधारिण्यै नमः ।
717.	Oṃ Yaśassūtrapradāyai Namaḥ ।	ॐ यशस्सूत्रप्रदायै नमः ।
718.	Oṃ Yāmāyai Namaḥ ।	ॐ यामायै नमः ।
719.	Oṃ Yajñakarmakaryai Namaḥ ।	ॐ यज्ञकर्मकर्यै नमः ।
720.	Oṃ Yaśasvinyai Namaḥ ।	ॐ यशस्विन्यै नमः ।
721.	Oṃ Yakārasthāyai Namaḥ ।	ॐ यकारस्थायै नमः ।
722.	Oṃ Yūpastambhanivāsinyai Namaḥ ।	ॐ यूपस्तम्भनिवासिन्यै नमः ।
723.	Oṃ Rañjitāyai Namaḥ ।	ॐ रञ्जितायै नमः ।
724.	Oṃ Rājapatnyai Namaḥ ।	ॐ राजपत्न्यै नमः ।
725.	Oṃ Ramāyai Namaḥ ।	ॐ रमायै नमः ।
726.	Oṃ Rekhāyai Namaḥ ।	ॐ रेखायै नमः ।
727.	Oṃ Ravīraṇāyai Namaḥ ।	ॐ रवीरणायै नमः ।
728.	Oṃ Rajovatyai Namaḥ ।	ॐ रजोवत्यै नमः ।
729.	Oṃ Rajaścitrāyai Namaḥ ।	ॐ रजश्चित्रायै नमः ।
730.	Oṃ Rañjanyai Namaḥ ।	ॐ रञ्जन्यै नमः ।
731.	Oṃ Rajanīpatyai Namaḥ ।	ॐ रजनीपत्यै नमः ।
732.	Oṃ Rogiṇyai Namaḥ ।	ॐ रोगिण्यै नमः ।
733.	Oṃ Rajanyai Namaḥ ।	ॐ रजन्यै नमः ।
734.	Oṃ Rājñyai Namaḥ ।	ॐ राज्ञ्यै नमः ।
735.	Oṃ Rājyadāyai Namaḥ ।	ॐ राज्यदायै नमः ।
736.	Oṃ Rājyavardhinyai Namaḥ ।	ॐ राज्यवर्धिन्यै नमः ।
737.	Oṃ Rājanvatyai Namaḥ ।	ॐ राजन्वत्यै नमः ।
738.	Oṃ Rājanītyai Namaḥ ।	ॐ राजनीत्यै नमः ।
739.	Oṃ Rajatavāsinyai Namaḥ ।	ॐ रजतवासिन्यै नमः ।
740.	Oṃ Ramaṇyai Namaḥ ।	ॐ रमण्यै नमः ।

741.	Oṃ Ramaṇīyāyai Namaḥ	ॐ रमणीयायै नमः ।
742.	Oṃ Rāmāyai Namaḥ	ॐ रामायै नमः ।
743.	Oṃ Rāmāvatyai Ratyai Namaḥ	ॐ रामावत्यै रत्यै नमः ।
744.	Oṃ Retoratyai Namaḥ	ॐ रेतोरत्यै नमः ।
745.	Oṃ Ratotsāhāyai Namaḥ	ॐ रतोत्साहायै नमः ।
746.	Oṃ Rogaghnyai Namaḥ	ॐ रोगघ्न्यै नमः ।
747.	Oṃ Rogakāriṇyai Namaḥ	ॐ रोगकारिण्यै नमः ।
748.	Oṃ Raṅgāyai Namaḥ	ॐ रङ्गायै नमः ।
749.	Oṃ Raṅgavatyai Namaḥ	ॐ रङ्गवत्यै नमः ।
750.	Oṃ Rāgāyai Namaḥ	ॐ रागायै नमः ।
751.	Oṃ Rāgajñāyai Namaḥ	ॐ रागज्ञायै नमः ।
752.	Oṃ Rāgakṛddayāyai Namaḥ	ॐ रागकृद्दयायै नमः ।
753.	Oṃ Rāmikāyai Namaḥ	ॐ रामिकायै नमः ।
754.	Oṃ Rajakyai Namaḥ	ॐ रजक्यै नमः ।
755.	Oṃ Revāyai Namaḥ	ॐ रेवायै नमः ।
756.	Oṃ Rajanyai Namaḥ	ॐ रजन्यै नमः ।
757.	Oṃ Raṅgalocanāyai Namaḥ	ॐ रङ्गलोचनायै नमः ।
758.	Oṃ Raktacarmadharāyai Namaḥ	ॐ रक्तचर्मधरायै नमः ।
759.	Oṃ Raṅgyai Namaḥ	ॐ रङ्ग्यै नमः ।
760.	Oṃ Raṅgasthāyai Namaḥ	ॐ रङ्गस्थायै नमः ।
761.	Oṃ Raṅgavāhinyai Namaḥ	ॐ रङ्गवाहिन्यै नमः ।
762.	Oṃ Rāmāyai Namaḥ	ॐ रमायै नमः ।
763.	Oṃ Rambhāphalaprītyai Namaḥ	ॐ रम्भाफलप्रीत्यै नमः ।
764.	Oṃ Rambhorave Namaḥ	ॐ रम्भोरवे नमः ।
765.	Oṃ Rāghavapriyāyai Namaḥ	ॐ राघवप्रियायै नमः ।
766.	Oṃ Raṅgāyai Namaḥ	ॐ रङ्गायै नमः ।
767.	Oṃ Raṅgāṅgamadhurāyai Namaḥ	ॐ रङ्गाङ्गमधुरायै नमः ।
768.	Oṃ Rodasyai Namaḥ	ॐ रोदस्यै नमः ।
769.	Oṃ Mahāravāyai Namaḥ	ॐ महारवायै नमः ।
770.	Oṃ Rodhakṛte Namaḥ	ॐ रोधकृते नमः ।

771.	Oṃ Rogahantryai Namaḥ		ॐ रोगहन्त्र्यै नमः ।
772.	Oṃ Rūpabhṛte Namaḥ		ॐ रूपभृते नमः ।
773.	Oṃ Rogasrāviṇyai Namaḥ		ॐ रोगस्राविण्यै नमः ।
774.	Oṃ Vandyai Namaḥ		ॐ वन्द्यै नमः ।
775.	Oṃ Vandistutāyai Namaḥ		ॐ वन्दिस्तुतायै नमः ।
776.	Oṃ Bandhave Namaḥ		ॐ बन्धवे नमः ।
777.	Oṃ Bandhūkakusumādharāyai Namaḥ		ॐ बन्धूककुसुमाधरायै नमः
778.	Oṃ Vanditāyai Namaḥ		ॐ वन्दितायै नमः ।
779.	Oṃ Vandyamānāyai Namaḥ		ॐ वन्द्यमानायै नमः ।
780.	Oṃ Vaidrāvyai Namaḥ		ॐ वैद्राव्यै नमः ।
781.	Oṃ Vedavide Namaḥ		ॐ वेदविदे नमः ।
782.	Oṃ Vidhāyai Namaḥ		ॐ विधायै नमः ।
783.	Oṃ Vikopāyai Namaḥ		ॐ विकोपायै नमः ।
784.	Oṃ Vikapālāyai Namaḥ		ॐ विकपालायै नमः ।
785.	Oṃ Viṅkasthāyai Namaḥ		ॐ विङ्कस्थायै नमः ।
786.	Oṃ Viṅkavatsalāyai Namaḥ		ॐ विङ्कवत्सलायै नमः ।
787.	Oṃ Vedyai Namaḥ		ॐ वेद्यै नमः ।
788.	Oṃ Valagnalagnāyai Namaḥ		ॐ वलग्नलग्नायै नमः ।
789.	Oṃ Vidhiviṅkakarīvidhāyai Namaḥ		ॐ विधिविङ्ककरीविधायै नमः ।
790.	Oṃ Śaṅkhinyai Namaḥ		ॐ शङ्खिन्यै नमः ।
791.	Oṃ Śaṅkhavalayāyai Namaḥ		ॐ शङ्खवलयायै नमः ।
792.	Oṃ Śaṅkhamālāvatyai Namaḥ		ॐ शङ्खमालावत्यै नमः ।
793.	Oṃ Śamyai Namaḥ		ॐ शम्यै नमः ।
794.	Oṃ Śaṅkhapātrāśinyai Namaḥ		ॐ शङ्खपात्राशिन्यै नमः ।
795.	Oṃ Śaṅkhasvanāyai Namaḥ		ॐ शङ्खस्वनायै नमः ।
796.	Oṃ Śaṅkhagalāyai Namaḥ		ॐ शङ्खगलायै नमः ।
797.	Oṃ Śasyai Namaḥ		ॐ शश्यै नमः ।
798.	Oṃ Śabaryai Namaḥ		ॐ शबर्यै नमः ।

799.	Oṃ Śambaryai Namaḥ		ॐ शम्बर्यै नमः	
800.	Oṃ Śambhvai Namaḥ		ॐ शम्भ्वै नमः	
801.	Oṃ Śambhukeśāyai Namaḥ		ॐ शम्भुकेशायै नमः	
802.	Oṃ Śarāsinyai Namaḥ		ॐ शरासिन्यै नमः	
803.	Oṃ Śavāyai Namaḥ		ॐ शवायै नमः	
804.	Oṃ Śyenavatyai Namaḥ		ॐ श्येनवत्यै नमः	
805.	Oṃ Śyāmāyai Namaḥ		ॐ श्यामायै नमः	
806.	Oṃ Śyāmāṅgyai Namaḥ		ॐ श्यामाङ्ग्यै नमः	
807.	Oṃ Śyāmalocanāyai Namaḥ		ॐ श्यामलोचनायै नमः	
808.	Oṃ Śmaśānasthāyai Namaḥ		ॐ श्मशानस्थायै नमः	
809.	Oṃ Śmaśānāyai Namaḥ		ॐ श्मशानायै नमः	
810.	Oṃ Śmaśānasthānabhūṣaṇāyai Namaḥ		ॐ श्मशानस्थानभूषणायै नमः	
811.	Oṃ Śamadāyai Namaḥ		ॐ शमदायै नमः	
812.	Oṃ Śamahantryai Namaḥ		ॐ शमहन्त्र्यै नमः	
813.	Oṃ Śaṅkhinyai Namaḥ		ॐ शङ्खिन्यै नमः	
814.	Oṃ Śaṅkharoṣaṇāyai Namaḥ		ॐ शङ्खरोषणायै नमः	
815.	Oṃ Śāntyai Namaḥ		ॐ शान्त्यै नमः	
816.	Oṃ Śāntipradāyai Namaḥ		ॐ शान्तिप्रदायै नमः	
817.	Oṃ Śeṣāśeṣākhyāyai Namaḥ		ॐ शेषाशेषाख्यायै नमः	
818.	Oṃ Śeṣaśāyinyai Namaḥ		ॐ शेषशायिन्यै नमः	
819.	Oṃ Śemuṣyai Namaḥ		ॐ शेमुष्यै नमः	
820.	Oṃ Śoṣiṇyai Namaḥ		ॐ शोषिण्यै नमः	
821.	Oṃ Śeṣāyai Namaḥ		ॐ शेषायै नमः	
822.	Oṃ Śauryāyai Namaḥ		ॐ शौर्यायै नमः	
823.	Oṃ Śauryaśarāyai Namaḥ		ॐ शौर्यशरायै नमः	
824.	Oṃ Śaryai Namaḥ		ॐ शर्यै नमः	
825.	Oṃ Śāpadāyai Namaḥ		ॐ शापदायै नमः	
826.	Oṃ Śāpahāyai Namaḥ		ॐ शापहायै नमः	
827.	Oṃ Śāpāyai Namaḥ		ॐ शापायै नमः	

828.	Oṃ Śāpapathe Namaḥ ।	ॐ शापपथे नमः ।
829.	Oṃ Sadāśivāyai Namaḥ ।	ॐ सदाशिवायै नमः ।
830.	Oṃ Śṛṅgiṇyai Namaḥ ।	ॐ शृङ्गिण्यै नमः ।
831.	Oṃ Śṛṅgipalabhuje Namaḥ ।	ॐ शृङ्गिपलभुजे नमः ।
832.	Oṃ Śaṅkaryai Namaḥ ।	ॐ शङ्कर्यै नमः ।
833.	Oṃ Śāṅkaryai Namaḥ ।	ॐ शाङ्कर्यै नमः ।
834.	Oṃ Śivāyai Namaḥ ।	ॐ शिवायै नमः ।
835.	Oṃ Śavasthāyai Namaḥ ।	ॐ शवस्थायै नमः ।
836.	Oṃ Śavabhuje Namaḥ ।	ॐ शवभुजे नमः ।
837.	Oṃ Śāntāyai Namaḥ ।	ॐ शान्तायै नमः ।
838.	Oṃ Śavakarṇāyai Namaḥ ।	ॐ शवकर्णायै नमः ।
839.	Oṃ Śavodaryai Namaḥ ।	ॐ शवोदर्यै नमः ।
840.	Oṃ Śāvinyai Namaḥ ।	ॐ शाविन्यै नमः ।
841.	Oṃ Śavaśiṃśāyai Namaḥ ।	ॐ शवशिंशायै नमः ।
842.	Oṃ Śriyai Namaḥ ।	ॐ श्रियै नमः ।
843.	Oṃ Śavāyai Namaḥ ।	ॐ शवायै नमः ।
844.	Oṃ Śavaśāyinyai Namaḥ ।	ॐ शवशायिन्यै नमः ।
845.	Oṃ Śavakuṇḍalinyai Namaḥ ।	ॐ शवकुण्डलिन्यै नमः ।
846.	Oṃ Śaivāyai Namaḥ ।	ॐ शैवायै नमः ।
847.	Oṃ Śīkarāyai Namaḥ ।	ॐ शीकरायै नमः ।
848.	Oṃ Śiśirāśinyai Namaḥ ।	ॐ शिशिराशिन्यै नमः ।
849.	Oṃ Śavakāñcyai Namaḥ ।	ॐ शवकाञ्च्यै नमः ।
850.	Oṃ Śavaśrīkāyai Namaḥ ।	ॐ शवश्रीकायै नमः ।
851.	Oṃ Śavamālāyai Namaḥ ।	ॐ शवमालायै नमः ।
852.	Oṃ Śavākṛtyai Namaḥ ।	ॐ शवाकृत्यै नमः ।
853.	Oṃ Sravantyai Namaḥ ।	ॐ स्रवन्त्यै नमः ।
854.	Oṃ Saṅkucāyai Namaḥ ।	ॐ सङ्कुचायै नमः ।
855.	Oṃ Śaktyai Namaḥ ।	ॐ शक्त्यै नमः ।
856.	Oṃ Śantanvai Namaḥ ।	ॐ शन्तन्वै नमः ।
857.	Oṃ Śavadāyinyai Namaḥ ।	ॐ शवदायिन्यै नमः ।

858.	Oṃ Sindhave Namaḥ		ॐ सिन्धवे नमः ।
859.	Oṃ Sarasvatyai Namaḥ		ॐ सरस्वत्यै नमः ।
860.	Oṃ Sindhusundaryai Namaḥ		ॐ सिन्धुसुन्दर्यै नमः ।
861.	Oṃ Sundarānanāyai Namaḥ		ॐ सुन्दराननायै नमः ।
862.	Oṃ Sādhave Namaḥ		ॐ साधवे नमः ।
863.	Oṃ Siddhipradātryai Namaḥ		ॐ सिद्धिप्रदात्र्यै नमः ।
864.	Oṃ Siddhāyai Namaḥ		ॐ सिद्धायै नमः ।
865.	Oṃ Siddhasarasvatyai Namaḥ		ॐ सिद्धसरस्वत्यै नमः ।
866.	Oṃ Santatyai Namaḥ		ॐ सन्तत्यै नमः ।
867.	Oṃ Sampadāyai Namaḥ		ॐ सम्पदायै नमः ।
868.	Oṃ Saṃvicchaṅki Sampattidāyinyai Namaḥ		ॐ संविच्छङ्किसम्पत्तिदायिन्यै नमः
869.	Oṃ Sapatnyai Namaḥ		ॐ सपत्न्यै नमः ।
870.	Oṃ Sarasāyai Namaḥ		ॐ सरसायै नमः ।
871.	Oṃ Sārāyai Namaḥ		ॐ सारायै नमः ।
872.	Oṃ Sārasvatakaryai Namaḥ		ॐ सारस्वतकर्यै नमः ।
873.	Oṃ Sudhāyai Namaḥ		ॐ सुधायै नमः ।
874.	Oṃ Surāsamāṃsāśanāyai Namaḥ	ॐ सुरासमांसाशनायै नमः ।
875.	Oṃ Samārādhyāyai Namaḥ		ॐ समाराध्यायै नमः ।
876.	Oṃ Samastadāyai Namaḥ		ॐ समस्तदायै नमः ।
877.	Oṃ Samadhiyai Namaḥ		ॐ समधियै नमः ।
878.	Oṃ Sāmadāyai Namaḥ		ॐ सामदायै नमः ।
879.	Oṃ Sīmāyai Namaḥ		ॐ सीमायै नमः ।
880.	Oṃ Sammohāyai Namaḥ		ॐ सम्मोहायै नमः ।
881.	Oṃ Samadarśanāyai Namaḥ		ॐ समदर्शनायै नमः ।
882.	Oṃ Sāmatyai Namaḥ		ॐ सामत्यै नमः ।
883.	Oṃ Sāmadhāyai Namaḥ		ॐ सामधायै नमः ।
884.	Oṃ Sīmāyai Namaḥ		ॐ सीमायै नमः ।
885.	Oṃ Sāvitryai Namaḥ		ॐ सावित्र्यै नमः ।
886.	Oṃ Savidhāyai Namaḥ		ॐ सविधायै नमः ।

887.	Oṃ Satyai Namaḥ		ॐ सत्यै नमः ।
888.	Oṃ Savanāyai Namaḥ		ॐ सवनायै नमः ।
889.	Oṃ Savanāsārāyai Namaḥ		ॐ सवनासारायै नमः ।
890.	Oṃ Savarāyai Namaḥ		ॐ सवरायै नमः ।
891.	Oṃ Sāvarāyai Namaḥ		ॐ सावरायै नमः ।
892.	Oṃ Samyai Namaḥ		ॐ सम्यै नमः ।
893.	Oṃ Simarāyai Namaḥ		ॐ सिमरायै नमः ।
894.	Oṃ Satatāyai Namaḥ		ॐ सततायै नमः ।
895.	Oṃ Sādhvyai Namaḥ		ॐ साध्व्यै नमः ।
896.	Oṃ Sadhrīcyai Namaḥ		ॐ सध्रीच्यै नमः ।
897.	Oṃ Sasahāyinyai Namaḥ		ॐ ससहायिन्यै नमः ।
898.	Oṃ Haṃsyai Namaḥ		ॐ हंस्यै नमः ।
899.	Oṃ Haṃsagatyai Namaḥ		ॐ हंसगत्यै नमः ।
900.	Oṃ Haṃsyai Namaḥ		ॐ हंस्यै नमः ।
901.	Haṃsojjvalanicolayuje	हंसोज्ज्वलनिचोलयुजे
902.	Oṃ Halinyai Namaḥ		ॐ हलिन्यै नमः ।
903.	Oṃ Hālinyai Namaḥ		ॐ हालिन्यै नमः ।
904.	Oṃ Hālāyai Namaḥ		ॐ हालायै नमः ।
905.	Oṃ Halaśriyai Namaḥ		ॐ हलश्रियै नमः ।
906.	Oṃ Haravallabhāyai Namaḥ		ॐ हरवल्लभायै नमः ।
907.	Oṃ Halāyai Namaḥ		ॐ हलायै नमः ।
908.	Oṃ Halavatyai Namaḥ		ॐ हलवत्यै नमः ।
909.	Oṃ Hreṣāyai Namaḥ		ॐ हेषायै नमः ।
910.	Oṃ Helāyai Namaḥ		ॐ हेलायै नमः ।
911.	Oṃ Harṣavivardhinyai Namaḥ		ॐ हर्षविवर्धिन्यै नमः ।
912.	Oṃ Hantyai Namaḥ		ॐ हन्त्यै नमः ।
913.	Oṃ Hantāyai Namaḥ		ॐ हन्तायै नमः ।
914.	Oṃ Hayāyai Namaḥ		ॐ हयायै नमः ।
915.	Oṃ Hāhāhitāyai Namaḥ		ॐ हाहाहितायै नमः ।
916.	Oṃ Ahantātikāriṇyai Namaḥ		ॐ अहन्तातिकारिण्यै नमः ।

917.	Oṃ Haṅkāryai Namaḥ		ॐ हङ्कार्यै नमः	
918.	Oṃ Haṅkṛtyai Namaḥ		ॐ हङ्कृत्यै नमः	
919.	Oṃ Haṅkāyai Namaḥ		ॐ हङ्काये नमः	
920.	Oṃ Hīhīhāhāhitāyai Namaḥ		ॐ हीहीहाहाहिताये नमः	
921.	Oṃ Hitāyai Namaḥ		ॐ हिताये नमः	
922.	Oṃ Hītyai Namaḥ		ॐ हीत्यै नमः	
923.	Oṃ Hemapradāyai Namaḥ		ॐ हेमप्रदाये नमः	
924.	Oṃ Hārārāviṇyai Namaḥ		ॐ हाराराविण्यै नमः	
925.	Oṃ Harisammatāyai Namaḥ		ॐ हरिसम्मताये नमः	
926.	Oṃ Horāyai Namaḥ		ॐ होराये नमः	
927.	Oṃ Hotryai Namaḥ		ॐ होत्र्यै नमः	
928.	Oṃ Holikāyai Namaḥ		ॐ होलिकाये नमः	
929.	Oṃ Homāyai Namaḥ		ॐ होमाये नमः	
930.	Oṃ Homahaviṣe Namaḥ		ॐ होमहविषे नमः	
931.	Oṃ Havyai Namaḥ		ॐ हव्यै नमः	
932.	Oṃ Hariṇyai Namaḥ		ॐ हरिण्यै नमः	
933.	Oṃ Hariṇīnetrāyai Namaḥ		ॐ हरिणीनेत्राये नमः	
934.	Oṃ Himācalanivāsinyai Namaḥ		ॐ हिमाचलनिवासिन्यै नमः	
935.	Oṃ Lambodaryai Namaḥ		ॐ लम्बोदर्यै नमः	
936.	Oṃ Lambakarṇāyai Namaḥ		ॐ लम्बकर्णाये नमः	
937.	Oṃ Lambikāyai Namaḥ		ॐ लम्बिकाये नमः	
938.	Oṃ Lambavigrahāyai Namaḥ		ॐ लम्बविग्रहाये नमः	
939.	Oṃ Līlāyai Namaḥ		ॐ लीलाये नमः	
940.	Oṃ Līlāvatyai Namaḥ		ॐ लीलावत्यै नमः	
941.	Oṃ Lolāyai Namaḥ		ॐ लोलाये नमः	
942.	Oṃ Lalanāyai Namaḥ		ॐ ललनाये नमः	
943.	Oṃ Lalitāyai Namaḥ		ॐ ललिताये नमः	
944.	Oṃ Latāyai Namaḥ		ॐ लताये नमः	
945.	Oṃ Lalāmalocanāyai Namaḥ		ॐ ललामलोचनाये नमः	
946.	Oṃ Lobhyāyai Namaḥ		ॐ लोभ्याये नमः	

947.	Oṃ Lolākṣyai Namaḥ ǀ	ॐ लोलाक्ष्यै नमः ǀ
948.	Oṃ Lakulāyai Namaḥ ǀ	ॐ लकुलायै नमः ǀ
949.	Oṃ Layāyai Namaḥ ǀ	ॐ लयायै नमः ǀ
950.	Oṃ Lapantyai Namaḥ ǀ	ॐ लपन्त्यै नमः ǀ
951.	Oṃ Lapatyai Namaḥ ǀ	ॐ लपत्यै नमः ǀ
952.	Oṃ Lampāyai Namaḥ ǀ	ॐ लम्पायै नमः ǀ
953.	Oṃ Lopāmudrāyai Namaḥ ǀ	ॐ लोपामुद्रायै नमः ǀ
954.	Oṃ Lalantikāyai Namaḥ ǀ	ॐ ललन्तिकायै नमः ǀ
955.	Oṃ Latikāyai Namaḥ ǀ	ॐ लतिकायै नमः ǀ
956.	Oṃ Laṅghinyai Namaḥ ǀ	ॐ लङ्घिन्यै नमः ǀ
957.	Oṃ Laṅghāyai Namaḥ ǀ	ॐ लङ्घायै नमः ǀ
958.	Oṃ Lālimāyai Namaḥ ǀ	ॐ लालिमायै नमः ǀ
959.	Oṃ Laghumadhyamāyai Namaḥ	ॐ लघुमध्यमायै नमः ǀ
960.	Oṃ Laghīyasyai Namaḥ ǀ	ॐ लघीयस्यै नमः ǀ
961.	Oṃ Laghūdaryāyai Namaḥ ǀ	ॐ लघूदर्यायै नमः ǀ
962.	Oṃ Lūtāyai Namaḥ ǀ	ॐ लूतायै नमः ǀ
963.	Oṃ Lūtāvināśinyai Namaḥ ǀ	ॐ लूताविनाशिन्यै नमः ǀ
964.	Oṃ Lomaśāyai Namaḥ ǀ	ॐ लोमशायै नमः ǀ
965.	Oṃ Lomalambyai Namaḥ ǀ	ॐ लोमलम्ब्यै नमः ǀ
966.	Oṃ Lulantyai Namaḥ ǀ	ॐ लुलन्त्यै नमः ǀ
967.	Oṃ Lulumpatyai Namaḥ ǀ	ॐ लुलुम्पत्यै नमः ǀ
968.	Oṃ Lulāyasthāyai Namaḥ ǀ	ॐ लुलायस्थायै नमः ǀ
969.	Oṃ Laharyai Namaḥ ǀ	ॐ लहर्यै नमः ǀ
970.	Oṃ Laṅkāpurapurandarāyai Namaḥ ǀ	ॐ लङ्कापुरपुरन्दरायै नमः ǀ
971.	Oṃ Lakṣmyai Namaḥ ǀ	ॐ लक्ष्म्यै नमः ǀ
972.	Oṃ Lakṣmīpradāyai Namaḥ ǀ	ॐ लक्ष्मीप्रदायै नमः ǀ
973.	Oṃ Labhyāyai Namaḥ ǀ	ॐ लभ्यायै नमः ǀ
974.	Oṃ Lākṣākṣyai Namaḥ ǀ	ॐ लाक्षाक्ष्यै नमः ǀ
975.	Oṃ Lulitaprabhāyai Namaḥ ǀ	ॐ लुलितप्रभायै नमः ǀ

976.	Oṃ Kṣaṇāyai Namaḥ		ॐ क्षणायै नमः ।
977.	Oṃ Kṣaṇakṣute Namaḥ		ॐ क्षणक्षुते नमः ।
978.	Oṃ Kṣutkṣīṇāyai Namaḥ		ॐ क्षुत्क्षीणायै नमः ।
979.	Oṃ Kṣamāyai Namaḥ		ॐ क्षमायै नमः ।
980.	Oṃ Kṣāntyai Namaḥ		ॐ क्षान्त्यै नमः ।
981.	Oṃ Kṣamāvatyai Namaḥ		ॐ क्षमावत्यै नमः ।
982.	Oṃ Kṣāmāyai Namaḥ		ॐ क्षामायै नमः ।
983.	Oṃ Kṣāmodaryai Namaḥ		ॐ क्षामोदर्यै नमः ।
984.	Oṃ Kṣemyāyai Namaḥ		ॐ क्षेम्यायै नमः ।
985.	Oṃ Kṣaumabhṛte Namaḥ		ॐ क्षौमभृते नमः ।
986.	Oṃ Kṣatriyāṅganāyai Namaḥ		ॐ क्षत्रियाङ्गनायै नमः ।
987.	Oṃ Kṣayāyai Namaḥ		ॐ क्षयायै नमः ।
988.	Oṃ Kṣayakaryai Namaḥ		ॐ क्षयकर्यै नमः ।
989.	Oṃ Kṣīrāyai Namaḥ		ॐ क्षीरायै नमः ।
990.	Oṃ Kṣīradāyai Namaḥ		ॐ क्षीरदायै नमः ।
991.	Oṃ Kṣīrasāgarāyai Namaḥ		ॐ क्षीरसागरायै नमः ।
992.	Oṃ Kṣemaṅkaryai Namaḥ		ॐ क्षेमङ्कर्यै नमः ।
993.	Oṃ Kṣayakaryai Namaḥ		ॐ क्षयकर्यै नमः ।
994.	Oṃ Kṣayakṛte Namaḥ		ॐ क्षयकृते नमः ।
995.	Oṃ Kṣaṇadāyai Namaḥ		ॐ क्षणदायै नमः ।
996.	Oṃ Kṣatyai Namaḥ		ॐ क्षत्यै नमः ।
997.	Oṃ Kṣudrikāyai Namaḥ		ॐ क्षुद्रिकायै नमः ।
998.	Oṃ Kṣudrikākṣudrāyai Namaḥ		ॐ क्षुद्रिकाक्षुद्रायै नमः
999.	Oṃ Kṣutkṣamāyai Namaḥ		ॐ क्षुत्क्षमायै नमः ।
1000.	Oṃ Kṣīṇapātakāyai Namaḥ		ॐ क्षीणपातकायै नमः ।

Iti Śrī Mātaṅgī Sahasranāmāvaliḥ Sampūrṇā ॥

इति श्री मातङ्गी सहस्रनामावलिः सम्पूर्णा ॥

*****

10. Ṣodaśī – षोडशी

Śrī Kamalātmikā Devī

This name is differently mentioned in various schools. In particular, Kamalatmika is also called as *Ṣodaśī*. These are further being discussed in the relevant places.

Adiparasakti, Paradevata, Sarva Loka Jaganmata, Sri Devi creates, preserves and destroys all the worlds. In addition, she performs the tasks of *Tirodhāna* and *Anugrahā* also, in accordance with one of the names in Sri Lalita Sahasranama *"Pancha Krutya Parayana"*. As a *Parabrahma Mahishi*, she, after creating lives, has taken many divine incarnations for the state and has been regularly doing *sishta* maintenance and evil discipline.

Among the various incarnations of Sriman Narayana described by Sri Vishnu Bhagavatam, ten avatars are prominent. Similarly, to protect the entire world, Sri Devi has manifested herself in ten different forms known as Dasha Maha Vidyas, as described in the previous chapter. Among those ten, Sri *Kamalātmikā* Devi Vidya is the Tenth and last one.

Don't we feel an excitement in the mind and a glow on the face when the name *Kamalatmika* is pronounced, instead of saying the names of Dasha Maha Vidya Devis like, Bhadra Kali, Bhairavi, Chinna Masta, Dhumavati and so on?

This *Kamalātmikā Devī* shines in the *Anāhata chakra* in the heart of our body in 12 petalled lotus alongwith other *Devis*. Among the 10 incarnations of *Sri Maha Vishnu, Sri Kamalātmikā Devī* is compared to *Sri Buddha* incarnation and the Sukran (*Venus*) among the Navagrahas.

This is the last *Vidya* among the ten. This is also called as *Sri Vidya*. The *Vidya* of *Tripura Sundari* is called as *Panchadhaśākṣarī*. It has 15 letters. If one more letter is added to *Panchadhaśī* it becomes *Ṣodaṣī Vidya*. This is *Kamalatmika*.

As soon as this name is uttered, it becomes clear that she is Mahalakshmi. In Sri Devi Mahatmyam, Madhyama Charitham (Chapters 2 to 4) is dedicated to Sri Mahalakshmi Devi.

The manifestation of the beauty and bliss of the divine is called 'Kamalatmika'. She appeared in *Ksheerasagara* (Ocean of Milk) which represents life. Born with nectar with nectar-mind. Indu (Moon)'s sister. She is revered as the lotus of pleasure that has sprouted from the ocean of life. She is located in Lotus in the ocean. She is the goddess who holds two lotuses in her hands, representing softness, prosperity, beauty, purity and auspiciousness.

Four elephants always bathe this blonde beauty, revealing her inner beauty. *'Kamalatmika'* is the one who has incorporated the aspect of *'Saraswati'* in eradicating not only poverty but also poverty of knowledge. She gave rise to the first incarnation of Lord Vishnu, who came as a fish (*Matsyavataram*) living in the water.

By the grace of this Goddess Kamalatmika, one can attain unrivaled wealth in the world, beauty in body, position and advancement in the spiritual field. Kamalatmika is the deity who has been worshiped by all since Vedic times throughout their life. Everyone in this world seek **her** compassion. In Shaktism, she is represented as the Devi in the fullness of her graceful aspect.

'Lotus' or Kamalātmikā, also known as *Kamalālayā* (the one who dwells in lotuses) is considered to be the Tantric characterisation of the goddess of prosperity, Lakshmi. In the city of Tiruvarur, in Tamilnadu, 'Kamala' is the main deity in the temple of "Sri Thiagarajar". The temple and its tank are equal in size and the biggest one. That tank is called as *Kamalālayām.* The chariot of this temple is very famous and the biggest one in the world. Some years it has taken weeks to come back to its position after procession during yearly festival.

The status before the creation of this world is called the status of *Dhoomavati.* After the creation, when it stabilises, it is called as the status of *Kamalatmika.* The beauty in every field of this globe is only due to **her**. The 15 *Rigs* in *Rig Veda* (*Sri sookta*) describe **her** in detail. This *sookta* is part of *Veda* used by every worshipper of *Devi*. With the compassion of this *Devi* the devotee becomes expert in all fields. She is very fond of bestowing boons to her devotees.

There are *Ashtotra* and *Sahasranamas* available on this *Devi*. Sri Muthusamy Deekshitar also has sung *Navavarna* songs (9 songs) on Kamala Devi, each one beginning as '*Kamalamba*'.

With the blessings of this *Kamalatmika Devi* the devotee can get unlimited wealth in this world, charisma in the body, position and progress in the field of spiritualism. Right from the ages of *Vedas*, the god worshiped by everyone throughout their life is *Kamalatmika.*

While Lakshmi is portrayed as a loving wife to Narayana and is often depicted as massaging his feet in her submissive role, Kamala is rendered more independent in her role, more candidly performing her duties as the goddess who ushers in bliss and prosperity. While she is still deemed as the beloved of Vishnu, she is less performative of her marital and domestic obligations to him. She is also depicted to be a more fearsome goddess who is to be reckoned in her own right, some of her epithets in Tantric traditions including Bhima (terrible), Kalaratri (black night), and Tamasi (darkness), indicating that she is not reliant on him for his preservation and can fight evil with her own powers. In her Mahavidya context, she is also rarely associated with incarnations of Lakshmi such as Sita and Rukmini, though she is identified as two of the Saptamatrikas who are also forms associated with Vishnu, Varahi, and Vaishnavi.

Let Kamalā protect us by her wonderful side-glances that delight the heart of Visňu.

Though there are many *naadis* (pulses) in our body, the 101 *naadis* around the heart are considered as important –
"*Śadam Ca Ekā Ca Hrudyasya Nādyāḥ*" (*Kāṭaka Upanishat* 3-2-16).

Still important are the three viz., *Idaa*, *Pingala* and *Sushumnaa*. *Sushumnaa* is the one which moves in the mid of the spine at the back of our body. *Idaa* and *pingala* coil themselves around both the sides and join the *Sushumnaa* at the *Aagnaa chakra*. This is *Triveni sangama* (meeting of three – as meeting of three rivers Ganga, Yamuna and Saraswathi in Allahabad). *Idaa* is Ganga, *Pingala* – Yamuna and *Sushumnaa* is invisible Saraswathi. This is what is told in *Vedas* as –
"*Sitaa Sito Sarito Yatra Sangate*".

Worshiping male gods is called mantra. The method of worshiping female deities is called Vidya. Worshiping Sri Vidya, the unison of Shiva and Shakti. So, this also comes under Mantra group. Sri Vidya is said to be the best of all mantras.

That Devi is also known as Tripura Sundari, Raja Rajeshwari, Shodasee, Kamakshi, Lalita and so on. She is also an important Maha Vidya. She is glorified in many Shakta texts like Sri Lalitha Sahasranamam, Soundarya-lahari, etc. She is called Adi Para Shakti in the Lalithopakyanam of Brahmanda Purana.

According to the Srikula tradition in Shaktaism, *Kamalātmikā* is the Shakta's supreme deity of Hinduism and the principal deity of Sri Vidya. The Tripura Upanishad places her as the ultimate Shakti (energy, power) of the universe. She is described as the Supreme Consciousness ruling from above Brahma, Vishnu and Shiva.

May the Divine Mother guide us all in our every action and thought. And may She remove the veil of maya and bestow upon us the greatest gift of all, moksha (liberation).

*****

Form(s) of *Śrī Kamalātmikā Devī*

Usually Meditative Hymns (*Dhyana Shlokas*) about the Gods are figurative of the concerned God or Goddess.

The Meditation Hymn of *Śrī Kamalātmikā Devī* is;

कान्त्या कांचनसन्निभां हिमगिरिप्रख्यैश्चतुर्भिर्गजै: ।

हस्तोक्षिप्त हिरण्मयामृत घटैरासिच्यमानां श्रियम् ॥

बिभ्राणांवरमब्ज युग्ममभयं हस्तै:किरीटोज्वलां ।

क्षौमाबध्दनिदंभबिम्ब लसिताम् वन्देरविन्दस्तिताम् ॥

Kāntyā Kāmchanasannibhām Himagiriprakhyaiśchaturbhirgajaiḥ |

Hastokśipta Hiranmayāmruta Ghatairāsichyamānām Śriyam ||

Bibhrānāmvaramabja Yugmamabhayam Hastaiḥ Kireetojvalām |

Kśou Mābadhdanidambhabimba Lasitām Vanderavindastitām ||

The meditation of *Kamalātmikā* has been mentioned in *Shāradhā Tilaka* and *Tantra Sastra*.

Kamalātmikā Devī is in *Mahalakshmi* form only. She also shows herself as *Saraswati*, who is in-charge of knowledge. *Devī* sits on an eight petalled lotus flower with a smiling face, holding one lotus flower in each **her** two hands. The remaining two hands show the signet of fearlessness. **She** shines auspiciously in a gold colour. **She** wears white silk dress and a crown of precious stones. Let us pay obeisance to her who is seated on a lotus in a lotus posture.

Four elephants on four sides, bathe her with nectar from golden pots. **She** is so beautiful with a smile and shines like a rising Sun. Eight *shaktis* fan her from the eight directions. They are *Vimalā, Udkarśinī, Gnānā, Kriyā, Yogā, Brahmā, Satyā* and *Eeśānā*.

'*Āpa*' means water. Water indicates the creation of this world. Our parents are also called as '*Appa*' and '*Amma*'. This is what is mentioned in *Vedas*, as the world originated from water (*Tai. Up.* 2.1). The same message is mentioned in *tantras* as *Kamalādevī* is being bathed in lotus which originated in water. Hence, it is beyond doubt that if anyone worships this *Devi*, he will definitely get the energy of creating everything. The elephants bathing the *Devi* remind us wisdom, energy, creativity and thinking.

Lotus has a special capacity among the flowers – i.e., adaptation to the light of Sun. When Sun rises in the East it blooms and turns in the same way as Sun moves. It closes itself, once Sun sets. Hence this shows us how to get energy from Sun by being Sun's friend. That is the reason *Devi* is sits on a Lotus flower, holding Lotus flowers and makes clear the capacity of wisdom.

She is seated on a lotus, has a smiling face and with her four hands holds two lotuses and makes the signs of giving favours and granting assurance. Her complexion is like the brightness of lightning. Her breasts are firm and heavy and are decorated with garlands of pearls.

She is resplendent like the rising sun and wears a bright moon disc on her fore-head. She is adorned with a crown and necklace of jewels. She is bent down due to the weight of her large breasts and in her hands, she holds two lotuses and two bunches of rice shoots. She has three lotus-like eyes. She wears the Gausṭuba gem and has a smiling face.

The fact that Kamala is associated with elephants has two connotations; Firstly, elephants are harbingers of clouds and rain in Hinduism, thus indicating fertility; Secondly, as a powerful creature, it represents royal authority and divinity. Her relationship with the lotus suggests that she exists in a state of refinement that transcends the material world, and yet is rooted in it.

When the grace of this Goddess departs from any object/man, that object/man becomes useless and a source of hatred.

The inner knowledge of poets and sculptors are all only due to the compassion of this *Devi*.

By the grace of this Goddess Kamalatmika one can attain unrivaled wealth in the world, beauty in body, position and progress in the spiritual field. Sri Kamalatmika Devi is the deity who is worshiped by all since Vedic times.

Temples for *Kamalātmikā* Devi –

Kamalatmika Devi Temples are very few in India. To mention them here;

1. Chikkaladinni – It is a small village at Hukkeri Taluk in Belgaum district of Karnataka State. Shri Kamala Devi Temple is here. Chikkaladinni is 35kms from Belgaum and 35kms from Hukkeri.
2. Dandi Pada – It is a small village near Palghar in Thane District of Maharashtra State. Kamala Devi Mandir is here near Maha Lakshmi Temple. This temple is 8kms from Palghar and 94kms from Thane.
3. Thiruvarur – It is the district headquarter city in Tamil Nadu State. Sri Kamalambika Temple is here in Thiruvarur Thyagarajar Temple at Thanjai Salai. This temple is just 1.5km from Bus station. 42kms from Kumbakonam and 25kms from Nagapattinam.
4. Challamambapuram (Anjuru) – It is a small village near Sri Kalahasti in Chittoor district of Andhra Pradesh State. Sri Kamala Kannemma Temple is here on a bank of big pond. This temple is just 1.5kms away from Anjuru bus stop. Challamambapuram is 15kms from Sri Kalahasti and 55 kms from Tirupati.

This Goddess should be meditated upon in the 12 petalled lotus at the *Anāhata Chakra* in the heart of the human body. Let us all cry at her feet to be able to meditate her.

Kanchi Paramacharya would say – In all deities, many heads, hands, etc., are described. But does any deity said to have more than two legs? Nope. Why?

We only have two hands. All deities are told to have only two legs to enable us to cry holding the two legs of the deity. At least if we cry clasping the two feet of Ambika, she will turn her merciful eye on us!

*****

Śrī Kamalātmikā Devī Mantras

Śrī Kamalātmikā Vidyā

In Samskrutam, in general *Vidyā* means mantra. Vidya means knowledge. Here is a very powerful *Srī Kamalātmikā Devī Mantra*.

Oṃ Asya Śrī Kamalātmikā Mahā Mantrasya Brugu Riśiḥ ।
Niśrut Chandaḥ । Śrī Kamalātmikā Devatā ।
Im Bījam, Hroum Śaktiḥ, Śrīm Kīlakam ।
Śrī Kamalātmikā Prasāda Siddhyarte Jape Viniyogaḥ ।

Oṃ Śrām Angushṭābhyām Namaḥ
Oṃ Śrīm Darjanībhyām Namaḥ
Oṃ Śrūm Madhymābhyām Namaḥ
Oṃ Śraim Anāmikābhyām Namaḥ
Oṃ Śroum Kaniṣṭikābhyām Namaḥ
Oṃ Śraḥ Karatala Karabrushṭābhyām Namaḥ

Oṃ Śrām Hrudayāya Namaḥ
Oṃ Śrīm Sirase Svāhā
Oṃ Śrūm Śikāyai Vashat
Oṃ Śraim Kavachāya Hūm
Oṃ Śroum Vouśaṭ
Oṃ Śraḥ Astrāyaphaṭ
Bhūrbhuvasvaromiti Digbandhaḥ ।

Dhyānam

कान्त्या कांचनसन्निभां हिमगिरिप्रख्यैश्चतुर्भिर्गजै: ।
हस्तोक्षिप्त हिरण्मयामृत घटैरासिच्यमानां श्रियम् ॥
बिभ्राणां वरमब्ज युग्ममभयं हस्तै:किरीटोज्वलां ।
क्षौमाबध्दनिदं भबिम्ब लसिताम् वन्देरविन्दस्तिताम् ॥

Kāntyā Kāmchanasannibhām Himagiriprakhyaiśchaturbhirgajaiḥ ।

Hastokśipta Hiranmayāmruta Ghatairāsichyamānām Śriyam ॥
Bibhrānāmvaramabja Yugmamabhayam Hastaiḥ Kireetojvalām ।

Kśou Mābadhdanidambhabimba Lasitām Vanderavindastitām ॥

Lam Pritviyātmikāyai Gandham Samarpayāmi ।
Ham Ākashātmikāyai Puśpaiḥ Pūjayāmi ।

Yam Vaivātmikāyai Dhūpam Āgrāpayāmi |
Ram Vahniyātmikāyai Dhīpam Dharśayāmi |
Vam Amrutātmikāyai Amrutam Mahāneivedhyam Nivedayāmi |
Sam Sarvātmikāyai Sarvopahāra Pūjām Samarpayāmi ||

Kamalātmikā Mūla Mantras

Śrī Kamalātmikā Mahā Mantrāḥ ||

ॐ ऐं ह्रीं श्रीं क्लीं ह्सौ: जगत्प्रसूत्यै नम: (स्वाहा) |

Om Aim Hrīm Śrīm Klīm Hsouḥ Jagatprasūtyai Namaḥ (Svāhā) ||

Oṃ Śrām Hrudayāya Namaḥ
Oṃ Śrīm Sirase Svāhā
Oṃ Śrūm Śikāyai Vashat
Oṃ Śraim Kavachāya Hūm
Oṃ Śroum Vouśaṭ
Oṃ Śraḥ Astrāyaphaṭ
Bhūrbhuvasvaromiti Digvimogaḥ |

Dhyānam

कान्त्या कांचनसन्निभां हिमगिरिप्रख्यैश्चतुर्भिर्गजै: ।
हस्तोक्षिप्त हिरण्मयामृत घटैरासिच्यमानां श्रियम् ॥
बिभ्राणां वरमब्ज युग्ममभयं हस्तै: किरीटोज्वलां ।
क्षौमाबध्दनिदंभबिम्ब लसिताम् वन्देरविन्दस्तिताम् ॥

Kāntyā Kāmchanasannibhām Himagiriprakhyaiśchaturbhirgajaiḥ |

Hastokśipta Hiranmayāmruta Ghatairāsichyamānām Śriyam ||

Bibhrānāmvaramabja Yugmamabhayam Hastaiḥ Kireetojvalām |

Kśou Mābadhdanidambhabimba Lasitām Vanderavindastitām ||

Lam Pritviyātmikāyai Gandham Samarpayāmi |
Ham Ākashātmikāyai Puśpaiḥ Pūjayāmi |
Yam Vaivātmikāyai Dhūpam Āgrāpayāmi |
Ram Vahniyātmikāyai Dhīpam Dharśayāmi |
Vam Amrutātmikāyai Amrutam Mahāneivedhyam Nivedayāmi |
Sam Sarvātmikāyai Sarvopahāra Pūjām Samarpayāmi ||

Other important mantras on this Devi;

1. *Ekākṣar Kamalā Mantra* (1 Syllable Mantra) – श्रीं॥ *Śrīm*॥

2. *Dvyākṣar Samrajya Lakśmi Mantra* (2 Syllables Mantra) –
स्त्क्ल्रीं हं॥ *Śklrīm Ham*॥

3. *Tryakṣar Samrajya Lakśmi Mantra* (3 Syllables Mantra) –
श्रीं क्लीं श्रीं॥ *Śrīm Klīm Śrīm*॥

4. *Chaturakṣar Kamala Mantra* (4 Syllables Mantra) –
ऐं श्रीं ह्रीं क्लीं॥ *Aim Śrīm Hrīm Klīm*॥

5. *Panchākṣar Kamala Mantra* (5 Syllables Mantra) –
श्रीं क्लीं श्रीं नमः॥ *Śrīm Klīm Śrīm Namaḥ*॥

6. *Navākṣar Siddha Lakśmi Mantra* (9 Syllables Mantra) –
ॐ ह्रीं हूं हां ग्रें क्षों क्रों नमः॥ *Oṃ Hrīm Hūm Hām Grem Kśom Krom Namaḥ*॥

7. *Dashakṣari Kamala Mantra* (10 Syllables Mantra) –
नमः कमलवासिन्यै स्वाहा॥ *Namaḥ Kamalavāsinyai Svāhā*॥

8. *Siddhalakṣmī Mantra* – ॐ श्रीं ह्रीं क्लीं श्रीं सिद्धलक्ष्मयै नमः॥

Oṃ Śrīṃ Hrīṃ Klīṃ Śrīṃ Siddhalakṣmyai Namaḥ॥

Two more simple mantras;

9. ॐ श्रीं ह्रीं क्लीं कमले कमलालये प्रसीद प्रसीद श्रीं ह्रीं श्रीं महालक्ष्मयै नमः॥
Oṃ Śrīṃ Hrīṃ Klīṃ Kamale Kamalālaye Prasīda Prasīda Śrīṃ Hrīṃ Śrīṃ
Mahālakṣmyai Namaḥ॥

10. ॐ ऐं ह्रीं श्रीं क्लीं सौं जगत्प्रसूत्यै नमः॥

Oṃ Aiṃ Hrīṃ Śrīṃ Klīṃ Sauṃ Jagatprasūtyai Namaḥ॥

There are other mantras as well, with some modifications and rearrangements of *bījākṣara*-s.

Results of worshipping *Kamalātmikā*;

Chanting the Kamala Mantras with utmost faith and unmatchable devotion can fulfill all the desires and help gain material wealth. She bestows her blessings upon all her devotees and eradicates the odds of poverty, loss of money, debt, etc. from their lives.

The worship of Kamala Devi frees from debts, poverty, tension, disease, problems, and dangers. Brings to the devotee nourishment, support, abundance of worldly wealth, love and bliss.

Sadhana of Kamala is considered ideal for eternal happiness, mental and spiritual satisfaction and overall prosperity. Kamala Devi is said to bring possessions, both in terms of spiritual power as well as material assets.

Only the most advanced tantric practitioners have access to the mantra's full potential (Sadhaks). There is no hard rule in normal recitation, but please do not chant the mantra with any unusual desire, as this can easily backfire.

There are numerous other mantras and stotrams dedicated to Devi *Kamalātmikā*. However, the most popular one and that can be chant by the average person without any extreme tantric rituals is discussed here. Tantric practitioners' worship *Kamalātmikā* for acquiring siddhis or supernatural powers.

One should be interested in the words of the teacher. The four – self, teacher, *mantra* and the God should be treated as same. One should not reprimand other religions. One should always think of himself as Lord *Shiva*. One should not rebuke ladies.

Shakta ideologies affirm – *Sri Devi* in the form of, *kundalini* energy has to be brought from *Mūlādhāra Chakra* to *Sahasrāra Chakra* through *Brahma Granti, Swādhiṣṭāna Chakra, Maṇipūraka Chakra, Vishnu Granti, Anāhata Chakra, Viśuddhi Chakra, Rudra Granti and Agjna Chakra*. At the *Sahasrāra Chakra*, in a *Sahasradala Padma* (1000 petalled lotus), the unison of *Shiva-Shakti* has to be inwardly looked (*antharmukha* – inwardly imagined) into and the devotee should be soaked in the rain of nectar (*Amruta Tara*).

There is nothing he cannot achieve by her grace. She is interested in removing the sins of her devotees and showing him the right way. She lovingly bestows grace on those who are active, solid, and engaged in worship.

Let us all get initiated with these mantras from an appropriate guru and reap all the benefits.

*****

Śrī Kamalātmikā Devī Yantram

As discussed in detail above, this **Kamalātmikā** yantra also has a Bindu in the center encircled and has 8 lotus petals around. Again, a *shatkonam*, within a circle which has 8 lotus petals around. At last, we have 2 lined *Bhoopuram*.

Kamalātmikā yantra is a spiritual device with specific geometric patterns that assist in bringing boons of the mighty goddess **Kamalātmikā**. The yantra bolsters financial and spiritual well-being and supports the all-round development of a person. This yantra works like magic for uplifting life and keeps all sorts of enemies and poor influences away.

This yantra is highly significant as it brings the pious blessings of mighty goddess **Kamalātmikā** in life. she is the powerful goddess who suspends the effect of negative energies and enemies. The commanding divinity **Kamalātmikā** is affiliated as a manifestation of Goddess Shakti and Parvati, which enhances the impact of Bagalamukhi yantra to significant margins.

This yantra is highly needed by those unravelling perpetual failures in life and having a bitter life stage. This yantra is magical for removing the evil effects of black magic and is renowned for keeping the hostile energies away. If one's life is troublesome because of evil powers or enemies, this yantra is highly effective.

Here are some of the notable benefits of worshipping the **Kamalātmikā** *yantra;*

- ***Kamalātmikā*** yantra eradicates the poor effect of terrible energies and opponents.
- The yantra brings an aura that assists in attaining success.
- The yantra also brings prosperity and abundance to life by loading it with economic boons.
- The yantra augments the daily life with peaceful and tranquility.
- It empowers with excellent financial stability and immense bliss in life.
- The yantra also assists in getting rid of the troublesome cycle of birth and death and leads towards salvation.

To get the maximum benefits the ***Kamalātmikā*** *yantra* can be used as detailed below;

- The yantra must be placed facing East or North direction and should be regularly cleaned with either rosewater or clean water.
- Light incense sticks in front of the *yantra* after putting four dots on its four surfaces using sandalwood or vermillion paste.
- It has to be ensured that this *mantra* is chant for 108 times to get the maximum benefit, while worshipping this *yantra*;

The *yantras* pertaining to most of the Gods are kept beneath or in front of the deities in temples. One *yantra* is a drawing of lines or circles or angles drawn in a prescribed measurements and ratios. There cannot be any deviation plus or minus. If a *mantra* is wrongly chant, it can result in negative impact or even end up with destruction. In the same manner, if there is an error in drawing of a *yantra*, it may end up in devastation.

In modern days, lot many worship *Śrī Chakra* in their houses. In general, this is very good. But many do it as a pride, some do it as a style and some with ignorance. But the customs are not strictly followed. Resultantly, they suffer for want of peace.

It is not enough if one wants to follow the bigger things. Exact rules prescribed by *Sastras* have to be clearly understood, absorbed and followed. These are time tested and handed over to us by our ancestors. It is our duty to stringently follow the same and get benefited. Definitely *Śrī Chakra* has been raised upto the sky by the *Sastras*. But the same *Sastras* have recommended lots of dos and don'ts, lots of processes. The approach that "I will do the pooja in my way" is not acceptable, the expected fruits will be missed. Sometimes that may result in negative angle.

One *yantra* is not a place of dwelling for the deity; It is the deity her/himself. It is not an alternative to the deity. It is not a representation – it the deity. It is all the more apt in the case of *Śrī Devī*.

The radiations of the Yantra will bring the devotee and the Goddess into direct contact. The energy will soothe the inner peace and will gift with beauty, happiness and prosperity. These power lines attract the amiability of the Goddess opening doors for harmony and success.

This Yantra is a great cosmic conductor of energy, an antenna of Nature, a powerful tool for harmony, prosperity, success, good health, yoga and meditation! Yantras consist of a series of geometric patterns. The eyes and mind concentrate at the center of the yantra to achieve higher levels of consciousness. Yantras are usually made out of copper.

Let us all choose an appropriate guru, get initiated and worship this yantra to exploit maximum benefits.

*****

Śrī Kamalātmikā Dhyānam

Kāntyā Kāñcanasannibhāṃ Himagiriprakhyaiścaturbhirgajaiḥ
Hastotkṣiptahiraṇmayāmṛtaghaṭairāsicyamānāṃ Śriyam |
Bibhrāṇāṃ Varamabjayugmamabhayaṃ Hastaiḥ Kirīṭojjvalāṃ
Kṣaumābaddha Nitambabimbalalitāṃ Vande'ravindasthitām || 1

Māṇikyapratimaprabhāṃ Himanibhaistuṅgaiścaturbhirgajaiḥ
Hastāgrāhitaratnakumbhasalilairāsicyamānāṃ Mudā |
Hastābjairvaradānamambujayugābhītīrdadhānāṃ Hareḥ
Kāntāṃ Kāṅkṣitapārijātalatikāṃ Vande Sarojāsanām || 2

Āsīnā Sarasīruhesmitamukhī Hastāmbujairbibhratī
Dānaṃ Padmayugābhaye Ca Vapuṣā Saudāminīsannibhā |
Muktāhāravirājamānapṛthulottuṅgastanodbhāsinī
Pāyādvaḥ Kamalā Kaṭākṣavibhavairānandayantī Harim || 3

Sindūrāruṇakāntimabjavasatiṃ Saundaryavārānnidhiṃ
Koṭīrāṅgadahārakuṇḍalakaṭīsūtrādibhirbhūṣitām |
Hastābjairvasupatramabjayugalādarśau Vahantīṃ Parāṃ
Āvītāṃ Paricārikābhiraniśaṃ Seve Priyāṃ Śārṅgiṇaḥ || 4

Bālārkadyutimindukhaṇḍavilasatkoṭīrahārojjvalāṃ
Ratnākalpavibhūṣitāṃ Kucanatāṃ Śāleḥ Karairmañjarīm |
Padmaṃ Kaustubharatnamapyaviratam Sambibhratīṃ Sasmitāṃ
Phullāmbhojavilocanatrayayutāṃ Vande Parāṃ Devatām || 5

Iti Śrī Kamalātmikā Dhyānam ||

श्री कमलात्मिका ध्यानम्

कान्त्या काञ्चनसन्निभां हिमगिरिप्रख्यैश्चतुर्भिर्गजैः
हस्तोत्क्षिप्तहिरण्मयामृतघटैरासिच्यमानां श्रियम् ।
बिभ्राणां वरमब्जयुग्ममभयं हस्तैः किरीटोज्ज्वलां
क्षौमाबद्ध नितम्बबिम्बललितां वन्देऽरविन्दस्थिताम् ॥ १

माणिक्यप्रतिमप्रभां हिमनिभैस्तुङ्गैश्चतुर्भिर्गजैः
हस्ताग्राहितरत्नकुम्भसलिलैरासिच्यमानां मुदा ।

हस्ताब्जैर्वरदानमम्बुजयुगाभीतीर्दधानां हरेः
कान्तां काङ्क्षितपारिजातलतिकां वन्दे सरोजासनाम् ॥ २

आसीना सरसीरुहेस्मितमुखी हस्ताम्बुजैर्बिभ्रती
दानं पद्मयुगाभये च वपुषा सौदामिनीसन्निभा ।
मुक्ताहारविराजमानपृथुलोत्तुङ्गस्तनोद्धासिनी
पायाद्वः कमला कटाक्षविभवैरानन्दयन्ती हरिम् ॥ ३

सिन्दूरारुणकान्तिमब्जवसतिं सौन्दर्यवारान्निधिं
कोटीराङ्गदहारकुण्डलकटीसूत्रादिभिर्भूषिताम् ।
हस्ताब्जैर्वसुपत्रमब्जयुगलादशौं वहन्तीं परां
आवीतां परिचारिकाभिरनिशं सेवे प्रियां शार्ङ्गिणः ॥ ४

बालार्कद्युतिमिन्दुखण्डविलसत्कोटीरहारोज्ज्वलां
रत्नाकल्पविभूषितां कुचनतां शालेः कैर्मञ्जरीम् ।
पद्मं कौस्तुभरत्नमप्यविरतं सम्बिभ्रतीं सस्मितां
फुल्लाम्भोजविलोचनत्रययुतां वन्दे परां देवताम् ॥ ५

इति श्री कमलात्मिका ध्यानम् ॥

*****

Śrī Kamalātmikā Kavacaṃ

Śrī Gaṇeśāya Namaḥ |

Oṃ Asyāścaturakṣarāviṣṇuvanitāyāḥ Kavacasya Śrībhagavān Śiva Ṛṣīḥ |
Anuṣṭupchandaḥ | Vāgbhavā Devatā | Vāgbhavaṃ Bījam | Lajjā Śaktiḥ |
Ramā Kīlakam | Kāmabījātmakaṃ Kavacam |
Mama Sukavitvapāṇḍityasamṛddhisiddhaye Pāṭhe Viniyogaḥ |

Aiṅkāro Mastake Pātu Vāgbhavāṃ Sarvasiddhidā |
Hrīṃ Pātu Cakṣuṣormadhye Cakṣuryugme Ca Śāṅkarī || 1

Jihvāyāṃ Mukhavṛtte Ca Karṇayordantayornasi |
Oṣṭhādhāre Dantapaṅktau Tālumūle Hanau Punaḥ || 2

Pātu Māṃ Viṣṇuvanitā Lakṣmīḥ Śrīvarṇarūpiṇī |
Karṇayugme Bhujadvandve Stanadvandve Ca Pārvatī || 3

Hṛdaye Maṇibandhe Ca Grīvāyāṃ Pārśvaryodvayoḥ |
Pṛṣṭhadeśe Tathā Guhye Vāme Ca Dakṣiṇe Tathā || 4

Upasthe Ca Nitambe Ca Nābhau Jaṃghādvaye Punaḥ |
Jānucakre Padadvandve Ghuṭike'ṅgulimūlake || 5

Svadhā Tu Prāṇaśaktyāṃ Vā Sīmanyāṃ Mastake Tathā |
Sarvāṅge Pātu Kāmeśī Mahādevī Samunnatiḥ || 6

Puṣṭiḥ Pātu Mahāmāyā Utkṛṣṭiḥ Sarvadā'vatu |
Ṛddhiḥ Pātu Sadā Devī Sarvatra Śambhuvallabhā || 7

Vāgbhavā Sarvadā Pātu Pātu Māṃ Haragehinī |
Ramā Pātu Mahādevī Pātu Māyā Svarāṭ Svayam || 8

Sarvāṅge Pātu Māṃ Lakṣmīrviṣṇumāyā Sureśvarī |
Vijayā Pātu Bhavane Jayā Pātu Sadā Mama || 9

Śivadūtī Sadā Pātu Sundarī Pātu Sarvadā |
Bhairavī Pātu Sarvatra Bheruṇḍā Sarvadā'vatu || 10

Tvaritā Pātu Māṃ Nityamugratārā Sadā'vatu |

Pātu Māṃ Kālikā Nityaṃ Kālarātriḥ Sadā'vatu ‖ 11

Navadurgāḥ Sadā Pātu Kāmākhyā Sarvadā'vatu |

Yoginyaḥ Sarvadā Pātu Mudrāḥ Pātu Sadā Sama ‖ 12

Mātrāḥ Pātu Sadā Devyaścakrasthā Yoginī Gaṇāḥ |

Sarvatra Sarvakāryeṣu Sarvakarmasu Sarvadā ‖ 13

Pātu Māṃ Devadevī Ca Lakṣmīḥ Sarvasamṛddhidā ‖

‖ Iti Viśvasāra Tantre Śrī Kamalātmikā Kavacaṃ Sampūrṇam ‖

श्री कमलात्मिका कवचम्

श्री गणेशाय नमः |

ॐ अस्याश्चतुरक्षराविष्णुवनितायाः कवचस्य श्रीभगवान् शिव ऋषीः |
अनुष्टुप्छन्दः | वाग्भवा देवता | वाग्भवं बीजम् | लज्जा शक्तिः |
रमा कीलकम् | कामबीजात्मकं कवचम् |
मम सुकवित्वपाण्डित्यसमृद्धिसिद्धये पाठे विनियोगः |

ऐङ्कारो मस्तके पातु वाग्भवां सर्वसिद्धिदा |
ह्रीं पातु चक्षुषोर्मध्ये चक्षुर्युग्मे च शाङ्करी ‖ १

जिह्वायां मुखवृत्ते च कर्णयोर्दन्तयोर्नसि |
ओष्ठाधारे दन्तपङ्क्तौ तालुमूले हनौ पुनः ‖ २
पातु मां विष्णुवनिता लक्ष्मीः श्रीवर्णरूपिणी |
कर्णयुग्मे भुजद्वन्द्वे स्तनद्वन्द्वे च पार्वती ‖ ३

हृदये मणिबन्धे च ग्रीवायां पार्श्वयोर्द्वयोः |
पृष्ठदेशे तथा गुह्ये वामे च दक्षिणे तथा ‖ ४

उपस्थे च नितम्बे च नाभौ जंघाद्वये पुनः |
जानुचक्रे पदद्वन्द्वे घुटिकेऽङ्गुलिमूलके ‖ ५

स्वधा तु प्राणशक्त्यां वा सीमन्यां मस्तके तथा |
सर्वाङ्गे पातु कामेशी महादेवी समुन्नतिः ‖ ६

पुष्टिः पातु महामाया उत्कृष्टिः सर्वदाऽवतु ।
ऋद्धिः पातु सदा देवी सर्वत्र शम्भुवल्लभा ॥ ७

वाग्भवा सर्वदा पातु पातु मां हरगेहिनी ।
रमा पातु महादेवी पातु माया स्वराट् स्वयम् ॥ ८

सर्वाङ्गे पातु मां लक्ष्मीर्विष्णुमाया सुरेश्वरी ।
विजया पातु भवने जया पातु सदा मम ॥ ९

शिवदूती सदा पातु सुन्दरी पातु सर्वदा ।
भैरवी पातु सर्वत्र भेरुण्डा सर्वदाऽवतु ॥ १०

त्वरिता पातु मां नित्यमुग्रतारा सदाऽवतु ।
पातु मां कालिका नित्यं कालरात्रिः सदाऽवतु ॥ ११

नवदुर्गाः सदा पातु कामाख्या सर्वदाऽवतु ।
योगिन्यः सर्वदा पातु मुद्राः पातु सदा सम ॥ १२

मात्राः पातु सदा देव्यश्चक्रस्था योगिनी गणाः ।
सर्वत्र सर्वकार्येषु सर्वकर्मसु सर्वदा ॥ १३

पातु मां देवदेवी च लक्ष्मीः सर्वसमृद्धिदा ॥

॥ इति विश्वसार तन्त्रे श्रीकमलात्मिका कवचं सम्पूर्णम् ॥

*****

Śrī Kamalātmikā Khaḍgamālā Stotram

Sri Kamaladmika Chakra/Yantra has 12 *Aavaranas*. The names of the goddesses in each *aavarana* are mentioned in this *Khadkamala Stotra*. In this *Devi Aavarana Pooja* one should worship these Goddesses in each of these *Aavaranas* and enter the next *Aavarana*.

Asya Śrī Kamalātmikā Khaḍgamālā Stotra Mahā Mantrasya

Bhṛgudakṣabrahma Ṛṣayaḥ | Nānāchandāṃsi |

Śrīkamalātmikā Devatā | Śrīṃ Bījam | Aiṃ Śaktiḥ | Hrīṃ Kīlakam |

Akhaṇḍa Aiśvaryaṃ Āyurārogyaprāptyarthe Jape Viniyogaḥ ||

Dhyānam

Kāntyā Kāñcanasannibhāṃ Himagiriprakhyaiścaturbhirgajaiḥ
    Hastotkṣiptahiraṇmayāmṛtaghaṭairāsicyamānāṃ Śriyam |
Bibhrāṇāṃ Varamabjayugmamabhayaṃ Hastaiḥ Kirīṭojjvalāṃ
    Kṣaumābaddha Nitambabimbalalitāṃ Vande'ravindasthitām ||

Oṃ Kamalātmikāyai Namaḥ |

Vāsudevamayi, Saṅkarṣaṇamayi, Pradyumnamayi, Aniruddhamayi, Śrīdharamayi, Hṛṣīkeśamayi, Vaikuṇṭhamayi, Viśvarūpamayi, Prathamāvaraṇa Rūpiṇi Sarvamāṅgalyapradacakrasvāmini Anantasameta Śrīkamalātmikā || 1

Salilamayi, Guggulamayi, Kuruṇṭakamayi, Śaṅkhanidhimayi, Vasudhāmayi, Padmanidhimayi, Vasumatimayi, Jahnusutāmayi, Sūryasutāmayi, Dvitīyāvaraṇarūpiṇi Sarvadhanapradacakrasvāmini Anantasameta Śrīkamalātmikā || 2

Balākamayi, Vimalāmayī, Kamalāmayi, Vanamālikāmayi, Vibhīṣikāmayi, Mālikāmayi, Śāṅkarīmayi, Vasumālikāmayi Tṛtīyāvaraṇarūpiṇi Sarvaśaktipradacakrasvāmini Anantasameta Śrīkamalātmikā || 3

Bhāratīmayi, Pārvatīmayi, Cāndrīmayi, Śacīmayi, Damakamayi, Umāmayi, Śrīmayi, Sarasvatīmayi, Durgāmayi, Dharaṇīmayi, Gāyatrimayi, Devīmayi, Uṣāmayi, Caturthāvaraṇarūpiṇi Sarvasiddhipradacakrasvāmini Anantasameta Śrīkamalātmikā || 4

Anurāga Mahālakṣmī Bāṇamayi, Saṃvāda Mahālakṣmī Bāṇamayi, Vijayā Mahālakṣmī Bāṇamayi, Vallabhā Mahālakṣmī Bāṇamayi, Madā Mahālakṣmī Bāṇamayi, Harṣā Mahālakṣmī Bāṇamayi, Balā Mahālakṣmī Bāṇamayi, Tejā Mahālakṣmī Bāṇamayi, Pañcamāvaraṇarūpiṇi Sarvasaṃkṣobhaṇacakrasvāmini Anantasameta Śrīkamalātmikā || 5

Brāhmimayi, Maheśvarīmayi, Kaumārīmayi, Vaiṣṇavīmayi, Vārāhīmayi, Indrāṇīmayi, Cāmuṇḍāmayi, Mahālakṣmīmayi, Ṣaṣṭāvaraṇarūpiṇi Sarvasaubhāgyadāyakacakrasvāmini Anantasameta Śrīkamalātmikā || 6

Airāvatamayi, Puṇḍarīkamayi, Vāmanamayi, Kumudamayi, Añjanamayi, Puṣpadantamayi, Sārvabhaumamayi, Supratīkamayi, Saptamāvaraṇarūpiṇi Sarvāśāparipūraka cakrasvāmini Anantasameta Śrīkamalātmikā || 7

Sūryaṃyi, Somamayi, Bhaumamayi, Budhamayi, Bṛhaspatimayi, Śukramayi, Śaneścaramayi, Rāhumayi, Ketumayi, Aṣṭamāvaraṇarūpiṇi Sarvarogaharacakrasvāmini Anantasameta Śrīkamalātmikā || 8

Laṃ Pṛthvīmayi, Raṃ Agnimayi, Haṃ Ākāśamayi, Vaṃ Udakamayi, Yaṃ Vāyumayi Navamāvaraṇarūpiṇi Sarvānandamayicakrasvāmini Anantasameta Śrīkamalātmikā || 9

Nivṛtimayi, Pratiṣṭhāmayi, Vidyāmayi, Śāntimayi, Daśamāvaraṇarūpiṇi Sarvaśāpaharacakrasvāmini Anantasameta Śrīkamalātmikā || 10

Gāyatrīsahita Brahmamayi, Sāvitrīsahita Viṣṇumayi, Sarasvatīsahita Rudramayi, Lakṣmī Sameta Kuberamayi, Ratisahita Kāmamayi, Puṣṭisahita Vijñarājamayi, Śaṅkhanidhisahita Vasudhāmayi, Padmanidhisahita Vasumatimayi, Gāyātryādisahita Kamalātmikā, Divaughugururūpiṇi Sidhdaughagururūpiṇi Mānavaughagururūpiṇi, Śrīgururūpiṇi, Paramagururūpiṇi Parameṣṭhigururūpiṇi, Parāparagururūpiṇi, Aṇimāsiddhe, Laghimāsiddhe, Mahimāsiddhe, Īśitvasiddhe, Vaśitvasiddhe, Prākāmyasiddhe, Bhuktisiddhe, Icchāsiddhe, Prāptisiddhe, Sarvakāmasiddhe, Ekādaśāvaraṇarūpiṇi Sarvārthasādhakacakrasvāmini Anantasameta Śrīkamalātmikā || 11

Varābhayamayi, Vaṭukamayi, Yoginīmayi, Kṣetrapālamayi, Gaṇapatimayi, Aṣṭavasumayi, Dvādaśādityamayi, Ekādaśarudramayi, Sarvabhūtamayi, Śuti-Smṛtī-Dhṛti-Śraddhā-Medhāmayi, Vajrasahita Indramayi, Śaktisahita Agnimayi, Daṇḍasahita Yamamayi, Khaḍgasahita Nirṛtimayi, Pāśasahita Varuṇamayi, Aṅkuśasahita Vāyumayi, Gadāsahita Somamayi,

Śūlasahita Īśānamayi, Padmasahita Brahmamayi, Cakrasahita Anantamayi, Dvādaśāvaraṇarūpiṇi Tryailokyamohanacakrasvāmini Anantasameta Sadāśivabhairavasevita Śrīkamalātmikā Namaste Namaste Namaste Namaḥ ॥ 12

Iti Śrī Kamalātmikā Khaḍgamālā Stotram Sampūrṇam ।

श्री कमलात्मिका खड्गमाला स्तोत्रम्

अस्य श्री कमलात्मिका खड्गमाला स्तोत्र महामन्त्रस्य भृगुदक्षब्रह्मऋषयः । नानाछन्दांसि । श्रीकमलात्मिका देवता । श्रीं बीजम् । ऐं शक्तिः । ह्रीं कीलकम् । अखण्ड ऐश्वर्य आयुरारोग्यप्राप्त्यर्थे जपे विनियोगः ॥

ध्यानं

कान्त्या काञ्चनसन्निभां हिमगिरिप्रख्यैश्चतुर्भिर्गजैः
हस्तोत्क्षिप्तहिरण्मयामृतघटैरासिच्यमानां श्रियम् ।
बिभ्राणां वरमब्जयुग्ममभयं हस्तैः किरीटोज्ज्वलां
क्षौमाबद्ध नितम्बबिम्बललितां वन्देऽरविन्दस्थिताम् ॥

ॐ कमलात्मिकायै नमः ।

वासुदेवमयि, सङ्कर्षणमयि, प्रद्युम्नमयि, अनिरुद्धमयि, श्रीधरमयि, हृषीकेशमयि, वैकुण्ठमयि, विश्वरूपमयि, प्रथमावरणरूपिणि सर्वमाङ्गल्यप्रदचक्रस्वामिनि अनन्तसमेत श्रीकमलात्मिका ॥ १

सलिलमयि, गुग्गुलमयि, कुरुण्टकमयि, शङ्खनिधिमयि, वसुधामयि, पद्मनिधिमयि, वसुमतिमयि, जह्नुसुतामयि, सूर्यसुतामयि, द्वितीयावरण रूपिणि सर्वधनप्रदचक्रस्वामिनि अनन्तसमेत श्री कमलात्मिका ॥ २

बलाकमयि, विमलामयी, कमलामयि, वनमालिकामयि, विभीषिकामयि, मालिकामयि, शाङ्करीमयि, वसुमालिकामयि तृतीयावरणरूपिणि सर्वशक्तिप्रदचक्रस्वामिनि अनन्तसमेत श्रीकमलात्मिका ॥ ३

भारतीमयि, पार्वतीमयि, चान्द्रीमयि, शचीमयि, दमकमयि, उमामयि, श्रीमयि, सरस्वतीमयि, दुर्गामयि, धरणीमयि, गायत्रिमयि, देवीमयि, उषामयि, चतुर्थावरणरूपिणि सर्वसिद्धिप्रदचक्रस्वामिनि अनन्तसमेत श्री कमलात्मिका ॥ ४

अनुराग महालक्ष्मी बाणमयि, संवाद महालक्ष्मी बाणमयि, विजया महालक्ष्मी बाणमयि, वल्लभा महालक्ष्मी बाणमयि, मदा महालक्ष्मी बाणमयि, हर्षा महालक्ष्मी बाणमयि, बला महालक्ष्मी बाणमयि, तेजा महालक्ष्मी बाणमयि, पञ्चमावरणरूपिणि सर्वसंक्षोभणचक्रस्वामिनि अनन्तसमेत श्रीकमलात्मिका ॥ ५

ब्राह्मिमयि, महेश्वरीमयि, कौमारीमयि, वैष्णवीमयि, वाराहीमयि, इन्द्राणीमयि, चामुण्डामयि, महालक्ष्मीमयि, षष्ठावरणरूपिणि सर्वसौभाग्यदायकचक्रस्वामिनि अनन्तसमेत श्रीकमलात्मिका ॥ ६

ऐरावतमयि, पुण्डरीकमयि, वामनमयि, कुमुदमयि, अञ्जनमयि, पुष्पदन्तमयि, सार्वभौममयि, सुप्रतीकमयि, सप्तमावरणरूपिणि सर्वाशापरिपूरकचक्रस्वामिनि अनन्तसमेत श्रीकमलात्मिका ॥ ७

सूर्यंयि, सोममयि, भौममयि, बुधमयि, बृहस्पतिमयि, शुक्रमयि, शनेश्वरमयि, राहुमयि, केतुमयि, अष्टमावरणरूपिणि सर्वरोगहरचक्रस्वामिनि अनन्तसमेत श्रीकमलात्मिका ॥ ८

लं पृथ्वीमयि, रं अग्निमयि, हं आकाशमयि, वं उदकमयि, यं वायुमयि नवमावरणरूपिणि सर्वानन्दमयिचक्रस्वामिनि अनन्तसमेत श्रीकमलात्मिका ॥ ९

निवृतिमयि, प्रतिष्ठामयि, विद्यामयि, शान्तिमयि, दशमावरणरूपिणि सर्वशापहरचक्रस्वामिनि अनन्तसमेत श्रीकमलात्मिका ॥ १०

गायत्रीसहित ब्रह्ममयि, सावित्रीसहित विष्णुमयि, सरस्वतीसहित रुद्रमयि, लक्ष्मी समेत कुबेरमयि, रतिसहित काममयि, पुष्टिसहित विघ्नराजमयि, शङ्खनिधिसहित वसुधामयि, पद्मनिधिसहित वसुमतिमयि, गायात्र्यादिसहित कमलात्मिका, दिवौघुगुरूरूपिणि सिध्दौघगुरूरूपिणि मानवौघगुरूरूपिणि, श्रीगुरूरूपिणि, परमगुरु रूपिणि परमेष्ठिगुरूरूपिणि, परापरगुरूरूपिणि, अणिमासिद्धे, लघिमासिद्धे, महिमासिद्धे, ईशित्वसिद्धे, वशित्वसिद्धे, प्राकाम्यसिद्धे, भुक्तिसिद्धे, इच्छासिद्धे, प्राप्तिसिद्धे, सर्वकामसिद्धे, एकादशावरणरूपिणि सर्वार्थसाधकचक्रस्वामिनि अनन्तसमेत श्रीकमलात्मिका ॥ ११

वराभयमयि, वटुकमयि, योगिनीमयि, क्षेत्रपालमयि, गणपतिमयि,
अष्टवसुमयि, द्वादशादित्यमयि, एकादशरुद्रमयि, सर्वभूतमयि,
शुति-स्मृती-धृति-श्रद्धा-मेधामयि, वज्रसहित इन्द्रमयि,
शक्तिसहित अग्निमयि, दण्डसहित यममयि, खड्गसहित निरृतिमयि,
पाशसहित वरुणमयि, अङ्कुशसहित वायुमयि, गदासहित सोममयि,
शूलसहित ईशानमयि, पद्मसहित ब्रह्ममयि, चक्रसहित अनन्तमयि,
द्वादशावरणरूपिणि त्रैलोक्यमोहनचक्रस्वामिनि अनन्तसमेत
सदाशिवभैरवसेवित श्रीकमलात्मिका नमस्ते नमस्ते नमस्ते नमः ॥ १२

इति श्री कमलात्मिका खड्गमाला स्तोत्रं सम्पूर्णम् ।

*****

Śrī Kamalātmikā Stotram

This stotra is also known as *Śrī Kamalāmbikāṣṭakam* since it has 8 verses.

Bandhūkadyutimindubimbavadanāṃ Vṛndārakairvanditāṃ
    Mandārādi Samarcitāṃ Madhumatīṃ Mandasmitāṃ Sundarīm |
Bandhacchedanakāriṇīṃ Trinayanāṃ Bhogāpavargapradāṃ
    Vande'haṃ Kamalāmbikāmanudinaṃ Vāñchānukūlāṃ Śivām || 1

Śrīkāmeśvarapīṭhamadhyanilayāṃ Śrīrājarājeśvarīṃ
    Śrīvāṇīparisevitāṅghriyugalāṃ Śrīmatkṛpāsāgarām |
Śokāpadbhayamocinīṃ Sukavitānandaikasandāyinīṃ
    Vande'haṃ Kamalāmbikāmanudinaṃ Vāñchānukūlāṃ Śivām || 2

Māyā Mohavināśinīṃ Muniganairārādhitāṃ Tanmayīṃ
    Śreyaḥsañcayadāyinīṃ Guṇamayīṃ Vāyvādi Bhūtāṃ Satām |
Prātaḥkālasamānaśobhamakuṭāṃ Sāmādi Vedaistutāṃ
    Vande'haṃ Kamalāmbikāmanudinaṃ Vāñchānukūlāṃ Śivām || 3

Bālāṃ Bhaktajanaughacittanilayāṃ Bālenducūḍāmbarāṃ
    Sālokyādi Caturvidhārthaphaladāṃ Nīlotpalākṣīmajām |
Kālāripriyanāyikāṃ Kalimalapradhvaṃsinīṃ Kaulinīṃ
    Vande'haṃ Kamalāmbikāmanudinaṃ Vāñchānukūlāṃ Śivām || 4

Ānandāmṛtasindhumadhyanilayāmajñānamūlāpahāṃ
    Jñānānandavivardhinīṃ Vijayadāṃ Mīnekṣaṇāṃ Mohinīm |
Jñānānandaparāṃ Gaṇeśajananīṃ Gandharvasampūjitāṃ
    Vande'haṃ Kamalāmbikāmanudinaṃ Vāñchānukūlāṃ Śivām || 5

Ṣaṭcakropari Nādabindunilayāṃ Sarveśvarīṃ Sarvagāṃ
    Ṣaṭśāstrāgamavedaveditaguṇāṃ Ṣaṭkoṇasaṃvāsinīm |
Ṣaṭkālena Samarccitātmavibhavāṃ Ṣaḍvargasañchedinīṃ
    Vande'haṃ Kamalāmbikāmanudinaṃ Vāñchānukūlāṃ Śivām || 6

Yogānandakarīṃ Jagatsukhakarīṃ Yogīndracittālayāṃ
    Ekāmīśasukhapradāṃ Dvijanutāmekāntasañcāriṇīm |
Vāgīśāṃ Vidhiviṣṇuśambhuvaradāṃ Viśveśvarīṃ Vaiṇikīṃ
    Vande'haṃ Kamalāmbikāmanudinaṃ Vāñchānukūlāṃ Śivām || 7

Bodhānandamayīṃ Budhairabhinutāṃ Modapradāmambikāṃ
    Śrīmadvedapurīṣadāsavinutāṃ Hrīṅkārasandhālayām |

Bhedābhedavivarjitāṃ Bahuvidhāṃ Vedāntacūḍāmaṇiṃ
    Vande'haṃ Kamalāmbikāmanudinaṃ Vāñchānukūlāṃ Śivām || 8

Itthaṃ Śrīkamalāmbikāpriyakaraṃ Stotraṃ Paṭhedyassadā
    Putraśrīpradamaṣṭasiddhiphaladaṃ Cintāvināśāspadam |
Eti Brahmapadaṃ Nijaṃ Nirupamaṃ Niṣkalmaṣaṃ Niṣkalaṃ
    Yogīndrairapi Durlabhaṃ Punarayaṃ Cintāvināśaṃ Param || 9

Iti Śrī Kamalāmbikā Stotraṃ Sampūrṇam |

श्री कमलाम्बिकास्तोत्रम्

बन्धूकद्युतिमिन्दुबिम्बवदनां वृन्दारकैर्वन्दितां
    मन्दारादि समर्चितां मधुमतीं मन्दस्मितां सुन्दरीम् ।
बन्धच्छेदनकारिणीं त्रिनयनां भोगापवर्गप्रदां
    वन्देऽहं कमलाम्बिकामनुदिनं वाञ्छानुकूलां शिवाम् ॥ १

श्रीकामेश्वरपीठमध्यनिलयां श्रीराजराजेश्वरीं
    श्रीवाणीपरिसेविताङ्घ्रियुगलां श्रीमत्कृपासागराम् ।
शोकापद्द्वयमोचिनीं सुकवितानन्दैकसन्दायिनीं
    वन्देऽहं कमलाम्बिकामनुदिनं वाञ्छानुकूलां शिवाम् ॥ २

माया मोहविनाशिनीं मुनिगणैराराधितां तन्मयीं
    श्रेयःसञ्चयदायिनीं गुणमयीं वाय्वादि भूतां सताम् ।
प्रातःकालसमानशोभमकुटां सामादि वेदैस्तुतां
    वन्देऽहं कमलाम्बिकामनुदिनं वाञ्छानुकूलां शिवाम् ॥ ३

बालां भक्तजनौघचित्तनिलयां बालेन्दुचूडाम्बरां
    सालोक्यादि चतुर्विधार्थफलदां नीलोत्पलाक्षीमजाम् ।
कालारिप्रियनायिकां कलिमलप्रध्वंसिनीं कौलिनीं
    वन्देऽहं कमलाम्बिकामनुदिनं वाञ्छानुकूलां शिवाम् ॥ ४

आनन्दामृतसिन्धुमध्यनिलयामज्ञानमूलापहां
    ज्ञानानन्दविवर्धिनीं विजयदां मीनेक्षणां मोहिनीम् ।
ज्ञानानन्दपरां गणेशजननीं गन्धर्वसम्पूजितां
    वन्देऽहं कमलाम्बिकामनुदिनं वाञ्छानुकूलां शिवाम् ॥ ५

षट्चक्रोपरि नादबिन्दुनिलयां सर्वेश्वरीं सर्वगां
     षट्शास्त्रागमवेदवेदितगुणां षट्कोणसंवासिनीम् ।
षट्कालेन समर्च्चितात्मविभवां षड्वर्गसञ्छेदिनीं
     वन्देऽहं कमलाम्बिकामनुदिनं वाञ्छानुकूलां शिवाम् ॥ ६

योगानन्दकरीं जगत्सुखकरीं योगीन्द्रचित्तालयां
     एकामीशसुखप्रदां द्विजनुतामेकान्तसञ्चारिणीम् ।
वागीशां विधिविष्णुशम्भुवरदां विश्वेश्वरीं वैनिकीं
     वन्देऽहं कमलाम्बिकामनुदिनं वाञ्छानुकूलां शिवाम् ॥ ७

बोधानन्दमयीं बुधैरभिनुतां मोदप्रदामम्बिकां
     श्रीमद्वेदपुरीशदासविनुतां ह्रीङ्कारसन्धालयाम् ।
भेदाभेदविवर्जितां बहुविधां वेदान्तचूडामणिं
     वन्देऽहं कमलाम्बिकामनुदिनं वाञ्छानुकूलां शिवाम् ॥ ८

इत्थं श्रीकमलाम्बिकाप्रियकरं स्तोत्रं पठेद्यस्सदा
     पुत्रश्रीप्रदमष्टसिद्धिफलदं चिन्ताविनाशास्पदम् ।
एति ब्रह्मपदं निजं निरुपमं निष्कल्मषं निष्कलं
     योगीन्द्रैरपि दुर्लभं पुनरयं चिन्ताविनाशं परम् ॥ ९

इति श्री कमलाम्बिका स्तोत्रं सम्पूर्णम् ।

*****

Śrī Kamalātmikā Pañcataśākṣarī stōtram

Panchadaśakṣari means 15 lettered. *Sri Lalita Trishati* (300 Divine Names) has 20 Names for each letter in *Panchadaśakṣari mantra*. In the similar fashion, the disciples of Thiruvaiyaru *Sri Thiagaraja Swami* have written this stotra with 15 letters. In 8 slokas, *Dhyana* verses have also been written as *Dhyanashtakam.*

Oṁ Śrīrāmajayam | Oṁ Sadguruśrītyāgarājasvāmine Namo Namaḥ |

Oṁ Mantradevyai Ca Vidmahe | Mātṛkāyai Ca Dhīmahi |
Tannaḥ Śivā Pracodayāt ||

Dhyānāṣṭakam |

Saṅgītasadgurusvāmityāgabrahmasukīrtitām |
Gurukīrtanasānandāṃ Vande Śrīkamalālayām || 1

Śrīdīkṣitakṛtāścaryanavāvaraṇakīrtanām |
Kīrtanāpūjyavāgdevīṃ Vande Śrīkamalāmbikām || 2

Kamanīyātilāvaṇyāṃ Kamanīyamṛdusvarām |
Kalasusvaragānīyāṃ Vande Śrīkamalāmbikām || 3

Nādopāsanasuprītāṃ Nādavidyātidevatām |
Nādasusvaravāgarthāṃ Vande Śrīkamalāmbikām || 4

Vīṇāsaṅgītalolāṃ Ca Kalavīṇāsvarasvarām |
Vīṇālayāṃ Svarāhlādāṃ Vande Śrīkamalāmbikām || 5

Saṅgītasusvarāṃ Vācāṃ Saptasvarasunṛtyakām |
Svaravidyārthisaṃśrāyāṃ Vande Śrīkamalāmbikām || 6

Saptasvaraparāniṣṭhāṃ Saptasvarasuvigrahām |
Saptasvarasupuṣpārcāṃ Vande Śrīkamalāmbikām || 7

Kaṃdadhāṃ Kamalāmbāṃ Śrīkādividyopacāritām |
Hādisādītimantrārthāṃ Vande Mantrasvarūpiṇīm || 8

Atha Stotram |

Kalyāṇī Kalagīrvāṇī Kāmbhojakaruṇekṣaṇā |
Kalyāṇasuvasantaśrīḥ Kīravāṇīsukhasvarā || 1

Ekaniṣṭhābhinidhyātā Ekākṣarī Suśaṅkarī |
Ekabrahmasvarūpā Ca Ekaśabdasvarālayā || 2

Īśavāmasupārśvā Ca Īśvarī Jagadīśvarī |
Īśvarānugrahāpūrṇā Īśasannutapūraṇī || 3

Lakṣaṇānvitapādāṅkā Śubhalakṣaṇalakṣitā |
Laganīyā Lasadrāgā Lalitā Lalitāmbikā || 4

Hrīṃkāramantrasadrūpā Hrīṃkāramantramodinī |
Hrīṃkāraśabdasārādhyā Hrīṃkāraśabdanādinī || 5

Hasitotpalasaundaryā Haṃsānandaprakāśinī |
Haṃsanādasusaṅgītā Haṃsaguhyaprasādinī || 6

Saṅgītasusvarārādhyā Saṅgītavaradāyinī |
Saṅgītasvarasānnidhyā Saṅgītasvarabhūṣaṇī || 7

Karābjadhṛtavīṇā Ca Karavīṇāsvarālayā |
Svarājitasuvīṇā Ca Karavīṇālayasvarā || 8

Harikedāragaulā Ca Haripriyasahodarī |
Harinārāyaṇī Gaurī Harikāmbhojapādabhā || 9

Lasacchaviprabhārūpā Labdhavarṇā Layālayā |
Lālityamṛduvāṇī Ca Lalitasvaramādhurī || 10

Hrīṃkārasvarasampūrṇā Hrīṃkāradhyānabhāsurā |
Hrīṃkāramantraguhyārthā Hrīṃkārabījaguptakā || 11

Sakalārthapradā Mātā Sakalāgamacāriṇī |
Sakalādharasa~Llāsyā Sakalāghapraṇāśinī || 12

Kalāmayī Kalārādhyā Kamalālayavaibhavā |
Kalasusvaramādhuryā Kalagānaprasādinī || 13

Layaśuddhisugārādhyā Layarāgarasākṛtiḥ |
Lasatsumukhalāvaṇyā Layārāmā Layāramā || 14

Hrīṃkāralayarāgā Ca Hrīṃkāraprīṇinī Satī |
Hrīṃkāramantrapāvitryā Hrīṃkārajapagocarā || 15

Śrīmmantrapūjitādhyātā Śrīrāgasundarī Dharī |
Śrīrāgasusvarāgītā Śrīrāgavāgvilāsinī || 16

Śrīśca Sarasvatīrūpā Śrīpañcadaśamantriṇī |
Śrīṣoḍaśākṣarīpūjyā Mantraprakāśinī Parā || 17

Sarvānandamayī Vidyā Sarvānandapradāyinī |
Sarvānandasucakrābhā Sarvānandasumaṅgalā || 18

Śrīcakradevatāyai Ca Śrīpurāyai Sumaṅgalam |
Rasamerusuvāsinyai Sadrasāyai Sumaṅgalam || 19

Maṅgalaṃ Mantravarṇāyai Śrīrāgiṇyai Sumaṅgalam |
Maṅgalaṃ Mūkavāgdāyai Kādambaryai Sumaṅgalam || 20

Tyāgarājagurusvāmiśiṣyāpuṣpākṛtastutiḥ |
Ambāprītā Guruprāeryā Ambāpādasamarpitā || 21

Amba Nānyopayuktāhaṃ Tvadbhaktikīrtanaṃ Vinā |
Etatsadbhaktinaivedyaṃ Svīkuruṣva Madambike || 22

Nyūnānicchidrasarvāṇi Kṣamasva Paradevate |
Sadā Tvāṃ Saṃśritāhaṃ Me Kṣipraṃ Prasīda Sāttviki || 23

Kādividyāṃ Na Jānāmi Hādisādiṃ Ca Nāmbike |
Jānāmi Tvaṃ Madambeti Jānāmi Tvat Padāśrayam || 24

Śabdāvaraṇadustāpaṃ Hara Me Parameśvari |

Śeṣajīvanaparyantaṃ Praśāntyāvārayāmbike || 25

Karmānubandhajālādvimocanaṃ Kuru Pāvani |

Śubhottuṅge Namastubhyaṃ Jñānaṃ Dehi Sunādakam || 26

Maṅgalaṃ Te Madamba Śrīrmayā Saha Sadā Vasa |

Maṅgalaitatsuvāgdevi Kuru Mokṣasumaṅgalam || 27

Maṅgalaṃ Nādamātaste Maṅgalaṃ Kamalāmbike |

Maṅgalaṃ Jñānasaubhāgye Mokṣade Śubhamaṅgalam || 28

Kaṃdāyai Kamalāmbāyai Kalagāyai Sumaṅgalam |

Kalahaṃsasvarūpiṇyai Kalyāṇyai Śubhamaṅgalam ||

Iti Sadguruśrītyāgarājasvāminaḥ Śiṣyayā Bhaktayā Puṣpayā Kṛtaṃ

Śrī Kamalāmbā Pañcadaśākṣarīstotraṃ Gurau Samarpitam |

श्री कमलाम्बा पञ्चदशाक्षरी स्तोत्रम्

ॐ श्रीरामजयम् ।

ॐ सद्गुरु श्री त्यागराज स्वामिने नमो नमः ।

ॐ मन्त्रदेव्यै च विद्महे । मातृकायै च धीमहि ।
तन्नः शिवा प्रचोदयात् ॥

ध्यानाष्टकम् ।

सङ्गीतसद्गुरुस्वामित्यागब्रह्मसुकीर्तिताम् ।
गुरुकीर्तनसानन्दां वन्दे श्रीकमलालयाम् ॥ १

श्रीदीक्षितकृताश्चर्यनवावरणकीर्तनाम् ।
कीर्तनापूज्यवाग्देवीं वन्दे श्रीकमलाम्बिकाम् ॥ २

कमनीयातिलावण्यां कमनीयमृदुस्वराम् ।
कलसुस्वरगानीयां वन्दे श्रीकमलाम्बिकाम् ॥ ३

नादोपासनसुप्रीतां नादविद्यातिदेवताम् ।
नादसुस्वरवागर्थां वन्दे श्रीकमलाम्बिकाम् ॥ ४

वीणासङ्गीतलोलां च कलवीणास्वरस्वराम् ।
वीणालयां स्वराह्लादां वन्दे श्रीकमलाम्बिकाम् ॥ ५

सङ्गीतसुस्वरां वाचां सप्तस्वरसुनृत्यकाम् ।
स्वरविद्यार्थिसंश्रायां वन्दे श्रीकमलाम्बिकाम् ॥ ६

सप्तस्वरपरानिष्ठां सप्तस्वरसुविग्रहाम् ।
सप्तस्वरसुपुष्पार्चां वन्दे श्रीकमलाम्बिकाम् ॥ ७

कंदधां कमलाम्बां श्रीकादिविद्योपचारिताम् ।
हादिसादीतिमन्त्रार्थां वन्दे मन्त्रस्वरूपिणीम् ॥ ८

अथ स्तोत्रम् ।

कल्याणी कलगीर्वाणी काम्भोजकरुणेक्षणा ।
कल्याणसुवसन्तश्रीः कीरवाणीसुखस्वरा ॥ १

एकनिष्ठाभिनिध्याता एकाक्षरी सुशङ्करी ।
एकब्रह्मस्वरूपा च एकशब्दस्वरालया ॥ २

ईशवामसुपार्श्वा च ईश्वरी जगदीश्वरी । ईश्वरानुग्रहापूर्णा ईशसन्नुतपूरणी ॥ ३

लक्षणान्वितपादाङ्का शुभलक्षणलक्षिता ।
लगनीया लसद्रागा ललिता ललिताम्बिका ॥ ४

ह्रींकारमन्त्रसद्रूपा ह्रींकारमन्त्रमोदिनी ।
ह्रींकारशब्दसाराध्या ह्रींकारशब्दनादिनी ॥ ५

हसितोत्पलसौन्दर्या हंसानन्दप्रकाशिनी । हंसनादसुसङ्गीता हंसगुह्यप्रसादिनी ॥ ६

सङ्गीतसुस्वराराध्या सङ्गीतवरदायिनी ।
सङ्गीतस्वरसान्निध्या सङ्गीतस्वरभूषणी ॥ ७

कराब्जधृतवीणा च करवीणास्वरालया ।
स्वराजितसुवीणा च करवीणालयस्वरा ॥ ८

हरिकेदारगौला च हरिप्रियसहोदरी । हरिनारायणी गौरी हरिकाम्भोजपादभा ॥ ९

लसच्छविप्रभारूपा लब्धवर्णा लयालया ।
लालित्यमृदुवाणी च ललितस्वरमाधुरी ॥ १०

ह्रींकारस्वरसम्पूर्णा ह्रींकारध्यानभासुरा ।
ह्रींकारमन्त्रगुह्यार्था ह्रींकारबीजगुप्तिका ॥ ११

सकलार्थप्रदा माता सकलागमचारिणी ।
सकलाधरसँल्लास्या सकलाघप्रणाशिनी ॥ १२

कलामयी कलाराध्या कमलालयवैभवा ।
कलसुस्वरमाधुर्या कलगानप्रसादिनी ॥ १३

लयशुद्धिसुगाराध्या लयरागरसाकृतिः ।
लसत्सुमुखलावण्या लयारामा लयारमा ॥ १४

ह्रींकारलयरागा च ह्रींकारप्रीणिनी सती ।
ह्रींकारमन्त्रपावित्र्या ह्रींकारजपगोचरा ॥ १५

श्रीमन्त्रपूजिताध्याता श्रीरागसुन्दरी धरी ।
श्रीरागसुस्वरागीता श्रीरागवाग्विलासिनी ॥ १६

श्रीश्च सरस्वतीरूपा श्रीपञ्चदशमन्त्रिणी ।
श्रीषोडशाक्षरीपूज्या मन्त्रप्रकाशिनी परा ॥ १७

सर्वानन्दमयी विद्या सर्वानन्दप्रदायिनी ।
सर्वानन्दसुचक्राभा सर्वानन्दसुमङ्गला ॥ १८

श्रीचक्रदेवतायै च श्रीपुरायै सुमङ्गलम् ।
रसमेरुसुवासिन्यै सद्रसायै सुमङ्गलम् ॥ १९

मङ्गलं मन्त्रवर्णायै श्रीरागिण्यै सुमङ्गलम् ।
मङ्गलं मूकवाग्दायै कादम्बयै सुमङ्गलम् ॥ २०

त्यागराजगुरुस्वामिशिष्यापुष्पाकृतस्तुतिः ।
अम्बाप्रीता गुरुप्रेर्या अम्बापादसमर्पिता ॥ २१

अम्ब नान्योपयुक्ताहं त्वद्भक्तिकीर्तनं विना ।
एतत्सद्भक्तिनैवेद्यं स्वीकुरुष्व मदम्बिके ॥ २२

न्यूनानिच्छिद्रसर्वाणि क्षमस्व परदेवते ।
सदा त्वां संश्रिताहं मे क्षिप्रं प्रसीद सात्त्विकि ॥ २३

कादिविद्यां न जानामि हादिसादिं च नाम्बिके ।
जानामि त्वं मदम्बेति जानामि त्वत् पदाश्रयम् ॥ २४

शब्दावरणदुस्तापं हर मे परमेश्वरि ।
शेषजीवनपर्यन्तं प्रशान्त्यावारयाम्बिके ॥ २५

कर्मानुबन्धजालाद्विमोचनं कुरु पावनि ।
शुभोत्तुङ्गे नमस्तुभ्यं ज्ञानं देहि सुनादकम् ॥ २६

मङ्गलं ते मदम्ब श्रीर्मया सह सदा वस ।
मङ्गलैतत्सुवाग्देवि कुरु मोक्षसुमङ्गलम् ॥ २७

मङ्गलं नादमातस्ते मङ्गलं कमलाम्बिके ।
मङ्गलं ज्ञानसौभाग्ये मोक्षदे शुभमङ्गलम् ॥ २८

कंदायै कमलाम्बायै कलगायै सुमङ्गलम् ।
कलहंसस्वरूपिण्यै कल्याण्यै शुभमङ्गलम् ॥

इति सद्गु श्री त्यागराज स्वामिनः शिष्यया भक्तया पुष्पया कृतं श्रीकमलाम्बा
पञ्चदशाक्षरी ।

*****

Śrī Kamalātmikā Upaniṣat

*Atha Lokān Paryaṭansanatkumāroha Vaidehaḥ Puṇyacittāṁllokānatītya
Vaiṣṇavandhāma Divyagaṇopetaṃ Vidrumavedikā
Maṇimuktāgaṇārccitamprāpa |*

*Tatrāpaśyanmahāmāyāṃ Parārddhyavastrībharaṇottarīyāṃ
Paryaṅkasthāṃ Pāre Carantīmādidevaṃ Bhagavantaṃ
Parameśvarandṛṣṭvā Ca Tāṅgadgadavākpraphullaromā
Stotumupacakrame ||*

*Vācaṃme Diśatu Śrīrdevī Mano Me Diśatu Vaiṣṇavī |
Ojastejo Balandākṣyambuddhervaibhavamastu Me ||*

*Tvatprasādādbhagavati Prajñānaṃ Me Dhruvaṃ Bhavet |
Śanno Diśatu Śrīrdaivī Mahāmāyā Vaiṣṇavīśaktirādyā
Yāmāsādya Svayamādidevo Bhagavānparāvarajñastridhāsambhinno
Lokāṃstrīnsṛjatyavatyatti Ca |
Yadbhrūvikṣepabalamāpanno Hyabjayonistaditare Cāmarā Mukhyāḥ
Sṛṣṭicakrapraṇetārassambabhūvuḥ ||*

*Yā Vai Varadā Svopāyā Suprasannā
Sukhayati Sahasrapuruṣān Ye Lokāḥ Santatamānamanti Śirasā Hṛadaye
Na Ca Tāmekāṁllokapūjyānna Te Durgatiṁyyānti Bhūtāḥ |*

*Atha Mahatyā Saṃvṛddhyā Sāmrājyena Putraiḥ Pautrairanvito
Bhūmipṛṣṭhe Śataṃ Samāsta Ijyābhiriṣṭvā Devān Pitṝn Manuṣyānatha
Bhūridakṣiṇābhistvatprasādānmahānto Gacchanti
Vaiṣṇavaṁllokamapunarbhavāya Ye Rājarṣayo Brahmarṣayastepi
Cāsatkṛttvāṃ Prāgasanta Eva Sukhamāmananti Nānyaḥ Panthā
Vidyate'yanāya Kimpunarihādidevo Bhagavān Nārāyaṇa
Stvāmādhidevākhilaṅkaroti Kiṃvarṇaye Tvāṃ Sahasrakṛtvo Namaste Ya
Imā Ṛcaḥ Paṭhanti Prātarutthāya Bhūridānateṣāṅkiñcidiha
Yāvaśiṣṭaṃyyadaiśvaryandurllabhamprāṇināṃ Hi |*

Iti Kamalātmikopaniṣat Samāptā ||

कमलात्मिकोपनिषत्

अथ लोकान् पर्यटन्सनत्कुमारोह वैदेहः पुण्यचित्ताँल्लोकानतीत्य
वैष्णवन्धाम दिव्यगणोपेतं विद्रुमवेदिकामणिमुक्तागणाच्चिर्चतम्प्राप ।

तत्रापश्यन्महामायां परार्द्ध्यवस्त्रीभरणोत्तरीयां पर्यङ्कस्थां पारे
चरन्तीमादिदेवं भगवन्तं परमेश्वरन्दृष्ट्वा च
ताङ्गद्द्रदवाक्प्रफुल्लरोमा स्तोतुमुपचक्रमे ॥

वाचं मे दिशतु श्रीर्देवी मनो मे दिशतु वैष्णवी ।
ओजस्तेजो बलन्दाक्ष्यम्बुद्धेर्वैभवमस्तु मे ॥

त्वत्प्रसादाद्भगवति प्रज्ञानं मे ध्रुवं भवेत् ।
शन्नो दिशतु श्रीर्देवी महामाया वैष्णवीशक्तिराद्या यामासाद्य स्वयमादिदेवो
भगवान्परावरज्ञस्त्रिधासम्भिन्नो लोकांस्त्रीन्सृजत्यवत्यत्ति च ।
यद्भ्रूविक्षेपबलमापन्नो ह्यब्जयोनिस्तदितरे चामरा मुख्याः
सृष्टि चक्र प्रणेतारस्सम्बभूवुः ॥

या वै वरदा स्वोपाया सुप्रसन्ना सुखयति सहस्रपुरुषान् ये लोकाः सन्ततमानमन्ति
शिरसा ह्अदये न च तामेकाँल्लोकपूज्यान्न ते दुर्गतिंय्यान्ति भूताः ।
अथ महत्या संवृद्ध्या साम्राज्येन पुत्रैः पौत्रैरन्वितो भूमिपृष्ठे
शतं समास्त इज्याभिरिष्ट्वा देवान् पितॄन् मनुष्यानथ
भूरिदक्षिणाभिस्त्वत्प्रसादान्महान्तो गच्छन्ति
वैष्णवँल्लोकमपुनर्भवाय ये राजर्षयो ब्रह्मर्षयस्तेपि
चासत्कृत्त्वां प्रागसन्त एव सुखमामनन्ति नान्यः पन्था
विद्यतेऽयनाय किम्पुनरिहादिदेवो भगवान्नारायण
स्वामाधिदेवा खिलङ्करोति किंवर्णये त्वां
सहस्रकृत्वो नमस्ते य इमा ऋचः पठन्ति प्रातरुत्थाय
भूरिदानतेषाङ्किञ्चिदिह यावशि
ष्ट्य्यदैश्वर्यन्दुल्लभम्प्राणिनां हि ।

    इति कमलात्मिकोपनिषत्समाप्ता ॥

            *****

Śrī Kamalātmikā Stavaḥ

Since this Stotra has 8 Verses and hence this is also called as *Śrī Kamalāmbikāṣṭakam.*

Kamalālayataṭaśobhitavimalālayavilasat
    Kamalāpati-Kamalāsana-Kamalārcitavibhavam |
Kamalāṅghrika-Kamalānana-Kamalāmbika-Vilasat
    Kamalābhidhamahamāntarakamale Mama Kalaye || 1

Yajanapara-Manujavara-Śivavadanajārcitāṃ
    Bhajanapara-Sanakamukha-Munihṛdayasaṃsthitām |
Ajajanaka-Hayavadana-Harihayasupūjitāṃ
    Bhaja Hṛdaya Ravijalaja Guruvaradaśaṅkarīm || 2

Īśānakoṇe Kamalālayasya Śrītyāgarājasya Tu Vāyukoṇe |
Īśānadṛṣṭiḥ Kamalāmbikāyāḥ Yā Bhāti Sā Śrīramṛtā Satāṃ Hi || 3

Madambikā Hṛtkamalāntarasthā Cidambikā Śrīkamalālayasthā |
Anantasaukhyaṃ Kamalāsanasthā Tanotu Devī Kamalāmbikā Me || 4

Anindhanaṃ Samedhite Nirantaraṃ Hṛdantare
    Cidāśuśukṣaṇau Mahāvimoharātrināśake |
Avācyavaibhave Pare Vicitramāvikāsite
    Juhomyahaṃ Dharādimaṃ Śivāntatattvamambike || 5

Akṣaratrayarūpiṇīmakhilākṣavṛttivināśinīṃ
    Ṛkṣarājasubhāvitāmamṛtākṣarāṅghriyugāṃ Bhaje |
Akṣarāsanasaṃsthitāmajaśikṣakebhamukhapriyāṃ
    Cikṣurādivināśinīṃ Varalakṣaṇāṃ Kamalāmbikām || 6

Makāravarjaṃ Tava Vāmanetrabindvāḍhyamādye Kamaleti Nāma |
Śrīkāmarajākhyavarārṇarūpaṃ Bhajanti Sādhyāḥ Svakabodhasiddhaye ||7

Svareśa Candrāhvayaśītabījatrayāḍhyamādhe Kamaleti Nāma |
Makāravarjaṃ Tava Mūlavidyāṃ Vidyotayatyeva Gurusvarūpe || 8
Śāntasvarūpā Vimalaprakāśā Tvamātmarūpā Ca Guhāntarasthā |
Mātaścidānandatanurvibhāsi Tvamambike'nantasukhapradātri || 9

Anantasūtragrathitā Suvarṇamālātimādhuryavacassumāḍhyā |

Gurusvarūpā Kamalāmbikā Yā Tadaṅghripadmaṃ Samalaṅkarotu ‖

‖ Iti Śrīmac Cidānandanāthākhya Sadguru Pādābjāmṛtapāyinā

Anantānandanāthena Racitaḥ Śrī Kamalāmbikāstavaḥ Sampūrṇaḥ ‖

श्रीकमलाम्बिकास्तवः

अथवा श्रीकमलाम्बिकाष्टकम्

कमलालयतटशोभितविमलालयविलसत्

　　कमलापति-कमलासन-कमलार्चितविभवम् ।

कमलाङ्घ्रिक-कमलानन-कमलाम्बिक-विलसत्

　　कमलाभिधमहमान्तरकमले मम कलये ‖ १

यजनपर-मनुजवर-शिववदनजार्चितां

　　भजनपर-सनकमुख-मुनिहृदयसंस्थिताम् ।

अजजनक-हयवदन-हरिहयसुपूजितां

　　भज हृदय रविजलज गुरुवरदशाङ्करीम् ‖ २

ईशानकोणे कमलालयस्य श्रीत्यागराजस्य तु वायुकोणे ।

ईशानदृष्टिः कमलाम्बिकायाः या भाति सा श्रीरमृता सतां हि ‖ ३

मदम्बिका हृत्कमलान्तरस्था चिदम्बिका श्रीकमलालयस्था ।

अनन्तसौख्यं कमलासनस्था तनोतु देवी कमलाम्बिका मे ‖ ४

अनिन्धनं समेधिते निरन्तरं हृदन्तरे

　　चिदाशुशुक्षणौ महाविमोहरात्रिनाशके ।

अवाच्यवैभवे परे विचित्रमाविकासिते

　　जुहोम्यहं धरादिमं शिवान्ततत्त्वमम्बिके ‖ ५

अक्षरत्रयरूपिणीमखिलाक्षवृत्तिविनाशिनीं

　　ऋक्षराजसुभाविताममृताक्षराङ्घ्रियुगां भजे ।

अक्षरासनसंस्थितामजशिक्षकेभमुखप्रियां

　　चिक्षुरादिविनाशिनीं वरलक्षणां कमलाम्बिकाम् ‖ ६

मकारवर्जं तव वामनेत्रबिन्द्वाद्यमाद्ये कमलेति नाम ।
श्रीकामरजाख्यवराण्रूपं भजन्ति साध्याः स्वकबोधसिद्धये ॥ ७

स्वरेश चन्द्राह्वयशीतबीजत्रयाद्यमाधे कमलेति नाम ।
मकारवर्जं तव मूलविद्यां विद्योतयत्येव गुरुस्वरूपे ॥ ८

शान्तस्वरूपा विमलप्रकाशा त्वमात्मरूपा च गुहान्तरस्था ।
मातश्चिदानन्दतनुर्विभासि त्वमम्बिकेऽनन्तसुखप्रदात्रि ॥ ९

अनन्तसूत्रग्रथिता सुवर्णमालातिमाधुर्यवचस्सुमाद्या ।
गुरुस्वरूपा कमलाम्बिका या तदङ्घ्रिपद्मं समलङ्करोतु ॥

इति श्रीमच्चिदानन्दनाथाख्य सद्गुरूपादाब्जामृतपायिना　अनन्तानन्दनाथेन रचितः श्री
कमलाम्बिकास्तवः सम्पूर्णः ॥

*****

Śrī Kamalātmikā Aṣtotra Śata Nāma Stotram

Śrī Śiva Uvāca |

Śatamaṣṭottaraṃ Nāmnāṃ Kamalāyā Varānane |
Pravakṣyāmyatiguhyaṃ Hi Na Kadāpi Prakāśayet || 1

Mahāmāyā Mahālakṣmīrmahāvāṇī Maheśvarī |
Mahādevī Mahārātrirmahiṣāsuramardi Nī || 2

Kālarātriḥ Kuhūḥ Pūrṇā Nandā''dyā Bhadrikā Niśā |
Jayā Riktā Mahāśaktirdevamātā Kṛśodarī || 3

Śacīndrāṇī Śakranutā Śaṅkarapriyavallabhā |
Mahāvarāhajananī Madanonmathinī Mahī || 4

Vaikuṇṭhanātharamaṇī Viṣṇuvakṣaḥsthalasthitā |
Viśveśvarī Viśvamātā Varadā'bhayadā Śivā || 5

Śūlinī Cakriṇī Mā Ca Pāśinī Śaṅkhadhāriṇī |
Gadinī Muṇḍamālā Ca Kamalā Karuṇālayā || 6

Padmākṣadhāriṇī Hyambā Mahāviṣṇupriyaṅkarī |
Golokanātharamaṇī Golokeśvarapūjitā || 7

Gayā Gaṅgā Ca Yamunā Gomatī Garuḍāsanā |
Gaṇḍakī Sarayūstāpī Revā Caiva Payasvinī || 8

Narmadā Caiva Kāverī Kedārasthalavāsinī |
Kiśorī Keśavanutā Mahendraparivanditā || 9

Brahmādidevanirmāṇakāriṇī Vedapūjitā |
Koṭibrahmāṇḍamadhyasthā Koṭibrahmāṇḍakāriṇī || 10

Śrutirūpā Śrutikarī Śrutismṛtiparāyaṇā |
Indirā Sindhutanayā Mātaṅgī Lokamātṛkā || 11

Trilokajananī Tantrā Tantramantrasvarūpiṇī |
Taruṇī Ca Tamohantrī Maṅgalā Maṅgalāyanā || 12

Madhukaiṭabhamathanī Śumbhāsuravināśinī |

Niśumbhādi Harā Mātā Hariśaṅkarapūjitā || 13

Sarvadevamayī Sarvā Śaraṇāgatapālinī |

Śaraṇyā Śambhuvanitā Sindhutīranivāsinī || 14

Gandharvagānarasikā Gītā Govindavallabhā |

Trailokyapālinī Tattvarūpā Tāruṇyapūritā || 15

Candrāvalī Candramukhī Candrikā Candrapūjitā |

Candrā Śaśāṅkabhaginī Gītavādyaparāyaṇā || 16

Sṛṣṭirūpā Sṛṣṭikarī Sṛṣṭisamhārakāriṇī |

Iti Te Kathitam Devi Ramānāmaśatāṣṭakam || 17

Trisandhyam Prayato Bhūtvā Paṭhedetatsamāhitaḥ |

Yam Yam Kāmayate Kāmam Tam Tam Prāpnotyasamśayam || 18

Imam Stavam Yaḥ Paṭhatīha Martyo Vaikuṇṭhapatnyāḥ Parasādareṇa |

Dhanādhipādyaiḥ Parivanditaḥ Syāt Prayāsyati Śrīpadamantakāle || 19

Iti Śrī Kamalāṣṭottara Śatanāmastotram Sampūrṇam ||

श्री कमलाष्टोत्तर शतनामस्तोत्रम्

श्री शिव उवाच।

शतमष्टोत्तरं नाम्नां कमलाया वरानने।
प्रवक्ष्याम्यतिगुह्यं हि न कदापि प्रकाशयेत्॥ १

महामाया महालक्ष्मीर्महावाणी महेश्वरी।
महादेवी महारात्रिर्महिषासुरमर्दि नी॥ २

कालरात्रिः कुहूः पूर्णा नन्दाऽद्या भद्रिका निशा।
जया रिक्ता महाशक्तिर्देवमाता कृशोदरी॥ ३

शचीन्द्राणी शक्रनुता शङ्करप्रियवल्लभा।
महावराहजननी मदनोन्मथिनी मही॥ ४

वैकुण्ठनाथरमणी विष्णुवक्षःस्थलस्थिता ।
विश्वेश्वरी विश्वमाता वरदाऽभयदा शिवा ॥ ५

शूलिनी चक्रिणी मा च पाशिनी शङ्खधारिणी ।
गदिनी मुण्डमाला च कमला करुणालया ॥ ६

पद्माक्षधारिणी ह्याम्बा महाविष्णुप्रियङ्करी ।
गोलोकनाथरमणी गोलोकेश्वरपूजिता ॥ ७

गया गङ्गा च यमुना गोमती गरुडासना ।
गण्डकी सरयूस्तापी रेवा चैव पयस्विनी ॥ ८

नर्मदा चैव कावेरी केदारस्थलवासिनी ।
किशोरी केशवनुता महेन्द्रपरिवन्दिता ॥ ९

ब्रह्मादिदेवनिर्माणकारिणी वेदपूजिता ।
कोटिब्रह्माण्डमध्यस्था कोटिब्रह्माण्डकारिणी ॥ १०

श्रुतिरूपा श्रुतिकरी श्रुतिस्मृतिपरायणा ।
इन्दिरा सिन्धुतनया मातङ्गी लोकमातृका ॥ ११

त्रिलोकजननी तन्त्रा तन्त्रमन्त्रस्वरूपिणी ।
तरुणी च तमोहन्त्री मङ्गला मङ्गलायना ॥ १२

मधुकैटभमथनी शुम्भासुरविनाशिनी ।
निशुम्भादि हरा माता हरिशङ्करपूजिता ॥ १३

सर्वदेवमयी सर्वा शरणागतपालिनी ।
शरण्या शम्भुवनिता सिन्धुतीरनिवासिनी ॥ १४

गन्धर्वगानरसिका गीता गोविन्दवल्लभा ।
त्रैलोक्यपालिनी तत्त्वरूपा तारुण्यपूरिता ॥ १५

चन्द्रावली चन्द्रमुखी चन्द्रिका चन्द्रपूजिता ।
चन्द्रा शशाङ्कभगिनी गीतवाद्यपरायणा ॥ १६

सृष्टिरूपा सृष्टिकरी सृष्टिसंहारकारिणी ।
इति ते कथितं देवि रमानामशताष्टकम् ॥ १७

त्रिसन्ध्यं प्रयतो भूत्वा पठेदेतत्समाहितः ।
यं यं कामयते कामं तं तं प्राप्नोत्यसंशयम् ॥ १८

इमं स्तवं यः पठतीह मर्त्यो वैकुण्ठपत्न्याः परसादरेण ।
धनाधिपाद्यैः परिवन्दितः स्यात् प्रयास्यति श्रीपदमन्तकाले ॥ १९

इति श्री कमलाष्टोत्तर शतनामस्तोत्रं सम्पूर्णम् ॥

*****

Śrī Kamalātmikā Aṣtotra Śata Nāmāvaliḥ

108 Divine Names of *Śrī Kamalātmikā Devi*.

Śrī Kamalāṣṭottara Śatanāmāvalī श्री कमलाष्टोत्तर शतनामावली

1.	*Śrī Mahāmāyāyai Namaḥ* ।	श्री महामायायै नमः ।
2.	*Śrī Mahālakṣmyai Namaḥ* ।	श्री महालक्ष्यै नमः ।
3.	*Śrī Mahāvāṇyai Namaḥ* ।	श्री महावाण्यै नमः ।
4.	*Śrī Maheśvaryai Namaḥ* ।	श्री महेश्वर्यै नमः ।
5.	*Śrī Mahādevyai Namaḥ* ।	श्री महादेव्यै नमः ।
6.	*Śrī Mahārātryai Namaḥ* ।	श्री महारात्र्यै नमः ।
7.	*Śrī Mahiṣāsuramardinyai Namaḥ*	श्री महिषासुरमर्दिन्यै नमः ।
8.	*Śrī Kālarātryai Namaḥ* ।	श्री कालरात्र्यै नमः ।
9.	*Śrī Kuhavai Namaḥ* ।	श्री कुहवै नमः ।
10.	*Śrī Pūrṇāyai Namaḥ* ।	श्री पूर्णायै नमः ।
11.	*Ānandāyai Namaḥ* ।	आनन्दायै नमः ।
12.	*Śrī Ādyāyai Namaḥ* ।	श्री आद्यायै नमः ।
13.	*Śrī Bhadrikāyai Namaḥ* ।	श्री भद्रिकायै नमः ।
14.	*Śrī Niśāyai Namaḥ* ।	श्री निशायै नमः ।
15.	*Śrī Jayāyai Namaḥ* ।	श्री जयायै नमः ।
16.	*Śrī Riktāyai Namaḥ* ।	श्री रिक्तायै नमः ।
17.	*Śrī Mahāśaktyai Namaḥ* ।	श्री महाशक्त्यै नमः ।
18.	*Śrī Devamātre Namaḥ* ।	श्री देवमात्रे नमः ।
19.	*Śrī Kṛśodaryai Namaḥ* ।	श्री कृशोदर्यै नमः ।
20.	*Śrī Śacyai Namaḥ* ।	श्री शच्यै नमः ।
21.	*Śrī Indrāṇyai Namaḥ* ।	श्री इन्द्राण्यै नमः ।
22.	*Śrī Śakranutāyai Namaḥ* ।	श्री शक्रनुतायै नमः ।
23.	*Śrī Śaṅkarapriyavallabhāyai Namaḥ* ।	श्री शङ्करप्रियवल्लभायै नमः ।
24.	*Śrī Mahāvarāhajananyai Namaḥ*	श्री महावराहजनन्यै नमः ।
25.	*Śrī Madanonmathinyai Namaḥ* ।	श्री मदनोन्मथिन्यै नमः ।

26.	*Śrī Mahyai Namaḥ*	श्री महौ नमः ।
27.	*Śrī Vaikuṇṭhanātharamaṇyai Namaḥ*	श्री वैकुण्ठनाथरमण्यै नमः ।
28.	*Śrī Viṣṇuvakṣasthalasthitāyai Namaḥ*	श्री विष्णुवक्षस्थलस्थितायै नमः ।
29.	*Śrī Viśveśvaryai Namaḥ*	श्री विश्वेश्वर्यै नमः ।
30.	*Śrī Viśvamātre Namaḥ*	श्री विश्वमात्रे नमः ।
31.	*Śrī Varadāyai Namaḥ*	श्री वरदायै नमः ।
32.	*Śrī Abhayadāyai Namaḥ*	श्री अभयदायै नमः ।
33.	*Śrī Śivāyai Namaḥ*	श्री शिवायै नमः ।
34.	*Śrī Śūlinyai Namaḥ*	श्री शूलिन्यै नमः ।
35.	*Śrī Cakriṇyai Namaḥ*	श्री चक्रिण्यै नमः ।
36.	*Śrī Padmāyai Namaḥ*	श्री पद्मायै नमः ।
37.	*Śrī Pāśinyai Namaḥ*	श्री पाशिन्यै नमः ।
38.	*Śrī Śaṅkhadhāriṇyai Namaḥ*	श्री शङ्खधारिण्यै नमः ।
39.	*Śrī Gadinyai Namaḥ*	श्री गदिन्यै नमः ।
40.	*Śrī Mūṇḍamālāyai Namaḥ*	श्री मूण्डमालायै नमः ।
41.	*Śrī Kamalāyai Namaḥ*	श्री कमलायै नमः ।
42.	*Śrī Karuṇālayāyai Namaḥ*	श्री करुणालयायै नमः ।
43.	*Śrī Padmākṣadhāriṇyai Namaḥ*	श्री पद्माक्षधारिण्यै नमः ।
44.	*Śrī Ambāyai Namaḥ*	श्री अम्बायै नमः ।
45.	*Śrī Mahāviṣṇupriyaṅkaryai Namaḥ*	श्री महाविष्णुप्रियङ्कर्यै नमः ।
46.	*Śrī Golokanātharamaṇyai Namaḥ*	श्री गोलोकनाथरमण्यै नमः ।
47.	*Śrī Golokeśvarapūjitāyai Namaḥ*	श्री गोलोकेश्वरपूजितायै नमः ।
48.	*Śrī Gayāyai Namaḥ*	श्री गयायै नमः ।
49.	*Śrī Gaṅgāyai Namaḥ*	श्री गङ्गायै नमः ।
50.	*Śrī Yamunāyai Namaḥ*	श्री यमुनायै नमः ।
51.	*Śrī Gomatyai Namaḥ*	श्री गोमत्यै नमः ।
52.	*Śrī Garuḍāsanāyai Namaḥ*	श्री गरुडासनायै नमः ।
53.	*Śrī Gaṇḍakyai Namaḥ*	श्री गण्डक्यै नमः ।

54.	Śrī Sarayvai Namaḥ I	श्री सरय्वै नमः I
55.	Śrī Tāpyai Namaḥ I	श्री ताप्यै नमः I
56.	Śrī Revāyai Namaḥ I	श्री रेवायै नमः I
57.	Śrī Payasvinyai Namaḥ I	श्री पयस्विन्यै नमः I
58.	Śrī Narmadāyai Namaḥ I	श्री नर्मदायै नमः I
59.	Śrī Kāveryai Namaḥ I	श्री कावेर्यै नमः I
60.	Śrī Kodārasthalavāsinyai Namaḥ I	श्री कोदारस्थलवासिन्यै नमः I
61.	Śrī Kiśoryai Namaḥ I	श्री किशोर्यै नमः I
62.	Śrī Keśavanutāyai Namaḥ I	श्री केशवनुतायै नमः I
63.	Śrī Mahendraparivanditāyai Namaḥ I	श्री महेन्द्रपरिवन्दितायै नमः I
64.	Śrī Brahmādi Deva Nirmāṇa Kāriṇyai Namaḥ I	श्री ब्रह्मादिदेवनिर्माणिकारिण्यै नमः I
65.	Śrī Devapūjitāyai Namaḥ I	श्री देवपूजितायै नमः I
66.	Śrī Koṭi Brahmāṇḍa Madhyasthāyai Namaḥ I	श्री कोटिब्रह्माण्डमध्यस्थायै नमः I
67.	Śrī Koṭibrahmāṇḍakāriṇyai Namaḥ	श्री कोटिब्रह्माण्डकारिण्यै नमः I
68.	Śrī Śrutirūpāyai Namaḥ I	श्री श्रुतिरूपायै नमः I
69.	Śrī Śrutikaryyai Namaḥ I	श्री श्रुतिकर्य्यै नमः I
70.	Śrī Śrutismṛtiparāyaṇāyai Namaḥ I	श्री श्रुतिस्मृतिपरायणायै नमः I
71.	Śrī Indirāyai Namaḥ I	श्री इन्दिरायै नमः I
72.	Śrī Sindhutanayāyai Namaḥ I	श्री सिन्धुतनयायै नमः I
73.	Śrī Mātaṅgyai Namaḥ I	श्री मातङ्ग्यै नमः I
74.	Śrī Lokamātṛkāyai Namaḥ I	श्री लोकमातृकायै नमः I
75.	Śrī Trilokajananyai Namaḥ I	श्री त्रिलोकजनन्यै नमः I
76.	Śrī Tantrāyai Namaḥ I	श्री तन्त्रायै नमः I
77.	Śrī Tantramantrasvarūpiṇyai Namaḥ I	श्री तन्त्रमन्त्रस्वरूपिण्यै नमः I
78.	Śrī Taruṇyai Namaḥ I	श्री तरुण्यै नमः I
79.	Śrī Tamohantryai Namaḥ I	श्री तमोहन्त्र्यै नमः I
80.	Śrī Maṅgalāyai Namaḥ I	श्री मङ्गलायै नमः I

81.	Śrī Maṅgalāyanāyai Namaḥ		श्री मङ्गलायनायै नमः	
82.	Śrī Madhukaiṭabhamathinyai Namaḥ		श्री मधुकैटभमथिन्यै नमः	
83.	Śrī Śumbhāsuravināśinyai Namaḥ		श्री शुम्भासुरविनाशिन्यै नमः	
84.	Śrī Niśumbhādiharāyai Namaḥ		श्री निशुम्भादिहराये नमः	
85.	Śrī Mātre Namaḥ		श्री मात्रे नमः	
86.	Śrī Haripūjitāyai Namaḥ		श्री हरिपूजितायै नमः	
87.	Śrī Śaṅkarapūjitāyai Namaḥ		श्री शङ्करपूजितायै नमः	
88.	Śrī Sarvadevamayyai Namaḥ		श्री सर्वदेवमय्यै नमः	
89.	Śrī Sarvāyai Namaḥ		श्री सर्वायै नमः	
90.	Śrī Śaraṇāgatapālinyai Namaḥ		श्री शरणागतपालिन्यै नमः	
91.	Śrī Śaraṇyāyai Namaḥ		श्री शरण्यायै नमः	
92.	Śrī Śambhuvanitāyai Namaḥ		श्री शम्भुवनितायै नमः	
93.	Śrī Sindhutīranivāsinyai Namaḥ		श्री सिन्धुतीरनिवासिन्यै नमः	
94.	Śrī Gandhārvagānarasikāyai Namaḥ		श्री गन्धार्वगानरसिकायै नमः	
95.	Śrī Gītāyai Namaḥ		श्री गीतायै नमः	
96.	Śrī Govindavallabhāyai Namaḥ		श्री गोविन्दवल्लभायै नमः	
97.	Śrī Trailokyapālinyai Namaḥ		श्री त्रैलोक्यपालिन्यै नमः	
98.	Śrī Tattvarūpatāruṇyapūritāyai Namaḥ		श्री तत्त्वरूपतारुण्यपूरितायै नमः	
99.	Śrī Candrāvalyai Namaḥ		श्री चन्द्रावल्यै नमः	
100.	Śrī Candramukhyai Namaḥ		श्री चन्द्रमुख्यै नमः	
101.	Śrī Candrikāyai Namaḥ		श्री चन्द्रिकायै नमः	
102.	Śrī Candrapūjitāyai Namaḥ		श्री चन्द्रपूजितायै नमः	
103.	Śrī Candrāyai Namaḥ		श्री चन्द्रायै नमः	
104.	Śrī Śaśāṅkabhaginyai Namaḥ		श्री शशाङ्कभगिन्यै नमः	
105.	Śrī Gītavādyaparāyaṇyai Namaḥ		श्री गीतवाद्यपरायण्यै नमः	
106.	Śrī Sṛṣṭirūpāyai Namaḥ		श्री सृष्टिरूपायै नमः	
107.	Śrī Sṛṣṭikaryai Namaḥ		श्री सृष्टिकर्यै नमः	
108.	Śrī Sṛṣṭisamhārakāriṇyai Namaḥ		श्री सृष्टिसंहारकारिण्यै नमः	

Śrī Kamalāṣṭottara Śatanāmāvalī Samāptā |

श्री कमलाष्टोत्तर शतनामावली समाप्ता ॥

*****

Śrī Kamalā Triśatī

Usually, when it is said as *Triśatī*, it will be 300 divine names on a particular God or Goddess. In this case, it is 300 verses on *Śrī Kamalā*. This is a different feature.

Gaṅgādharamakhiviracitā |

Paramābharaṇaṃ Viṣṇorvakṣasi Sā Sāgarendravaraputrī |

Yā Mūrtirmatī Kāle Kṣamā Janānāṃ Kṛtāparādhānām || 1

Sā Naḥ Śreyo Dadyāt Kamalā Kamalāsanādijananīṃ Yām |

Saṃprāpya Sahacarīṃ Hariravati Jagantyanākulaṃ Satatam || 2

Nityaśreyodāne Khyātā Yā Harigṛhasya Sarvasvam |

Śrutimaulistutavibhavā Sā Bhātu Puraḥ Sadāsmākam || 3

Viṣṇukrīḍālolā Vikhyātā Dīnarakṣaṇe Lakṣmīḥ |

Jananī Naḥ Sphuratu Sadā Tena Vayaṃ Kila Kṛtārthāḥ Smaḥ || 4

Nirvāṇāṅkurajananī Kāle Sā Sārvabhaumapadadogdhrī |

Nirasatimohasamūhā Mama Daivatamādṛtaṃ Gurubhiḥ || 5

Viṣṇorvakṣasi Lasitā Śītamayūkhasya Sodarī Kamalā |

Kamalāyatanayanā Naḥ Pātu Sadā Pāparāśibhyaḥ || 6

Kavipariṣadā Ca Vedaiḥ Nityaṃ Stutanijamahodayā Kamalā |

Manasi Mama Saṃnidhattāṃ Tvamitānandāya Lokanāthena || 7

Dugdhodadhitanayā Sā Duritanihantrī Kṛtapraṇāmānām |

Ānandapadavidhātrī Patyā Sākaṃ Pade Pade Loke || 8

Manmathajananī Sā Māmavatu Sarojā(Kṣa)Gehinī Kamalā |

Yāmārādhya Budhendrā Viśanti Paramaṃ Tu Tat Padaṃ Viṣṇoḥ || 9

Satsūktikṛtividhātrī Namatāmambā Trilokyāstu |

Nityaprasādabhūmnā Rakṣati Māmādarāt Kamalā || 10

Mama Sūktirañjalipuṭaḥ Praṇatiścānekasaṃkhyākā |
Kutukāt Kṣīrodasutāmamitānandāya Gāhate Kamalām || 11

Yā Pāramārthyasaraṇiḥ Sā Kamalā Niścitā Vedaiḥ |
Saiṣā Hi Jaganmātā Saṃsṛtitāpāpahantrī Ca || 12

Mandasmitamadhurānanamamandasaṃtoṣadāyi Bhajatāṃ Tat |
Kamalārūpaṃ Tejo Vibhātu Nityaṃ Madīyahṛtkamale || 13

Kāle Kṣapayati Kamalā Kaṭākṣadhāṭyā Hi Māmakaṃ Duritam |
Ata Evāśritarakṣaṇadīkṣetyevaṃ Jano Vadati || 14

Navanavaharmyavidhātrī Nākikirīṭārcitā Ca Sā Devī |
Jyotirmaṇḍalalasitā Munihṛdayābjāsanā Ca Sadgatidā || 15

Saṃvīkṣya Jaladhitanayāṃ Bhūyo Bhūyaḥ Praṇamya Bhaktagaṇaḥ |
Nirasitaduritaughaḥ San Stauti Mudā Mokṣasiddhaye Kamalām || 16

Rākāniśīva Devyāṃ Dṛṣṭāyāṃ Bhaktagaṇavāṇī |
Bhajate Jalanidhiśailīṃ Sāṅgopāṅgaṃ Kṛtānandā || 17

Durgatibhītyā Khinnaḥ So'haṃ Śaraṇaṃ Bhajāmi Tāṃ Kamalām |
Śaraṇārthināṃ Hi Rakṣākṛditi Khyātā Hi Yā Loke || 18

Na Hi Kalayate Hṛdante Mandāraṃ Kāmadhenuṃ Vā |
Yaḥ Sevate Mukundapriyāṃ Śriyaṃ Nityabhāvena || 19

Kaiṭabhamardanamahiṣīṃ Mamāñjalirgāhatāṃ Kāle |
Na Hi Nāthanīyamatra Kṣamātale Sā Prasannāstu || 20

Saṃtāpapīḍitaṃ Māmavatu Sadā Śrīrharipriyā Mātā |
Rakṣitavāyasamukhyā Kṛpānidhiḥ Puṇyakṛddṛśyā || 21

Na Hi Kevalaṃ Praṇāmaiḥ Stutyā Bhaktyā Samārādhyā |
Satyena Dharmanivahairbhāvena Ca Kamalagehinī Kamalā || 22

Kadācitkaviloke'pyakṣīṇānandadāyinī Kamalā |
Rakṣatu Kaṭākṣakalikāṅkūrairbhaktānihādarataḥ || 23

Kalipāpaglapitānāṃ Muramardanadivyagehinī Lakṣmīḥ |
Rājati Śaraṇaṃ Paramaṃ Vaśīkṛteśā Ca Vibudhagaṇasevyā || 24

Nityollasadurumālā Vakṣasi Kamalā Harerbhāti |
Nijatanubhāsā Dyotitakaustubhamaṇirambudhestanayā || 25

Mātarmaṅgaladāyinyamarendravadhūsamarcitāṅghriyuge |
Māṃ Pāhyapāyanivahāt Saṃtatamakalakṣamāmūrte || 26

Yadi Kalitā Copekṣā Naśyet Kila Tāvakī Mahatī |
Kīrtirato'mba Kaṭākṣaiḥ Pariṣiñca Mudā Muhuḥ Śītaiḥ || 27

Dhanadhānyasutādirucigrastaṃ Māṃ Pāhi Kamale Tvam |
Tenorjitakīrtiḥ Syā Mātastvaṃ Sarvarakṣiṇī Khyātā || 28

Tava Pādāmbujayugaladhyānaṃ Mātarmadīyamaghamāśu |
Kabalīkaroti Kāle Tenāhaṃ Siddhasaṃkalpaḥ || 29

Añjalikalikā Hi Kṛtā Yadi Tasyai Muranihantṛdayitāyai |
Rasanāgre Khelanabhāk Tasya Tu Puṃso Girāṃ Devī || 30

Mātastava Mūrtiriyaṃ Sudhāmayī Niścitā Nipuṇaiḥ |
Yat Taddarśanabhūmnā Nirastatāpā Budhā Bhavantyacirāt || 31

Kalitajagattrayarakṣābharāṇi Mayi Devi Saṃvidhehi Mudā |
Tvadvīkṣaṇāni Kamale Tenāhaṃ Siddhasaṃkalpaḥ || 32

Varade Murāridayite Jayanti Te Vīkṣaṇāni Yāni Divi |
Saṃprāpya Tāni Maghavā Vijitārirdevasaṃghavandyaśca || 33

Mohāndhakārabhāskaramamba Kaṭākṣaṃ Vidhehi Mayi Kamale |
Yenāptajñānakalāḥ Stuvanti Vibudhāstvadīyasadasi Kalam || 34

Kāmakrodhādimahāsattvanirāsaṃ Kṛpāsārāt |
Kuru Mātarmama Saṃsṛtibhītiṃ Ca Nirākuru Tvamevārāt || 35

Mūḍhānāmapi Hṛdyāṃ Kavitāṃ Dātuṃ Yadīyaparicaryā |
Prabhavati Kāle Sā Hi Śrīrambā Naḥ Prasannāstu || 36

Divyakṣetreṣu Budhā Dinakaramadhye Ca Vedamaulau Ca |
Yatsthānamiti Vadanti Śrīreṣā Bhāti Saṃśritaharirhi || 37

Nijalīlākrāntaharī Rakṣati Kamalā Kaṭākṣadhāṭyā Naḥ |
Śaraṇārthinaśca Kāle Vihagoragapaśumukhānurvyām || 38

Samarāṅgaṇeṣu Jayadā Tridaśānāṃ Maulibhirmānyā |
Āpadi Rakṣaṇadakṣā Sā Kamalā Naḥ Prasannāstu || 39

Nityānandāsanabhāḍ Navanidhivandyā Ca Sāgarendrasutā |
Vilasati Mādhavavakṣasi Pālitalokatrayā Ca Jananī Naḥ || 40

Muninutanijaparipāṭī Vāgdhāṭī Dānalolupā Bhajatām |
Śikṣitaripujanakoṭī Vilasati Dhṛtaśātakumbhamayaśāṭī || 41

Nikhilāgamavedyapadā Nityaṃ Sadbhiḥ Samārādhyā |
Saṃsṛtipāśanihantrī Yā Tasyai Cāñjaliḥ Kriyate || 42

Bhūyāṃsi Namāṃsi Mayā Bhaktena Kṛtāni Kamalajāṅghriyuge |
Nityaṃ Lagantu Tena Hi Sarvā Rājanti Saṃpado Mānyāḥ || 43

Nityaṃ Nirmalarūpe Barade Vārāśikanyake Mātaḥ |
Sadgaṇarakṣaṇadīkṣe Pāhīti Vadantamāśu Māṃ Pāhi || 44

Bhuvanajanani Tvamārāt Kṛtarakṣaṇasaṃtatiḥ Kṣamāmūrte |
Prativastu Rame Kalitasvarūpaśaktyā Hi Rājase Jagati || 45

Jaya Jaya Kalaśābdhisute Jaya Jaya Harivallabhe Rame Mātaḥ |
Prātariti Vibudhavaryāḥ Paṭhanti Nāmāni Te Hi Me Guravaḥ || 46

Netrarucivijitaśāradapadme Padme Namastubhyam |
Tena Vayaṃ Gatavipadaḥ Sā Muktiḥ Karagatā Kalitā || 47

Satataṃ Baddhāñjalipuṭamupāsmahe Tacchubhapradaṃ Tejaḥ |
Yat Kamalodaranilayaṃ Kamalākṣaprītivīcikāpūram || 48

Sphuratu Mama Vacasi Kamale Tvadīyavaibhavasudhādhārā |
Nityaṃ Vyaktiṃ Prāptā Dhutanutajanakhedajālakā Mahatī || 49

Kamale Tava Nutiviṣaye Buddhirjātā Hi Me Sahasā |
Tena Mama Bhāgadheyaṃ Pariṇatamityeva Nityasaṃtuṣṭaḥ || 50

Kavitārasaparimalitaṃ Karoti Vadanaṃ Natānāṃ Yā |
Stotuṃ Tāṃ Me Hyārāt Sā Devī Suprasannāstu || 51

Harigṛhiṇi Tāvakaṃ Nutarūpaṃ Ye Bhuvi Nije Hṛdambhoje |
Dhyāyanti Teṣu Vibudhā Api Kalpakakusumamarpayanti Mudā || 52

Nānāvaradānakalālolupahṛdaye Hṛdambhujasthe Mām |
Rakṣāpāyāt Sahasā Kuru Bhaktaṃ Doṣahīnaṃ Ca || 53

Nijaghanakeśarucā Jitanīlāmbudhare Śaśāṅkasahajanman |
Padme Tvadīyarūpaṃ Manoharaṃ Bhātu Me Hṛdaye || 54

Ghanakuṅkumalasitāṅgaṃ Muktāhārādibhūṣitaṃ Madhuram |
Mandasmitamadhurāsyaṃ Sūryenduvilocanaṃ Ca Budhamānyam || 55

Nibiḍakucakumbhayugalaṃ Nijadṛgjitahariṇaśābakākṣiyugam |
Līlāgatijitakalabhaṃ Madhuvairimanoharaṃ Ca Suramānyam || 56

Diśi Diśi Vistṛtasaṃpadvilāsamadhuraṃ Ca Kundadantāli |
Madanajanakaṃ Ca Viṣṇoḥ Sarvasvaṃ Sarvadānacaṇam || 57

Kuladaivatamasmākaṃ Saṃvidrūpaṃ Natārtihararūpam |
Nānādurgatiharaṇakṣamamamarīsevitaṃ Sakalam || 58

Pañcadaśavarṇamānaṃ Payojavaktraṃ Pitāmahasamarcyam |
Jagadavanajāgarūkaṃ Hariharasaṃmānyavaibhavaṃ Kimapi || 59

Karuṇāpūritanayanaṃ Paramānandapradaṃ Ca Pariśuddham |
Āgamagaṇasaṃvedyaṃ Kośagṛhaṃ Sarvasaṃpadāṃ Nityam || 60

Mātastāvakapādāmbujayugalaṃ Saṃtataṃ Sphuratu |
Tenāhaṃ Tava Rūpaṃ Drakṣyāmyānandasiddhaye Sakalam || 61

Devyā Kaṭākṣitāḥ Kila Puruṣā Vā Yoṣitaḥ Paśavaḥ |
Mānyante Surasaṃsadi Kalpakakusumaiḥ Kṛtārhaṇāḥ Kāle || 62

Sumanovāñchādāne Kṛtāvadhānaṃ Dhanaṃ Viṣṇoḥ |

Dhiṣaṇājāḍyādiharaṃ Yadvīkṣaṇamāmananti Jagati Budhāḥ || 63

Antarapi Bahirudāraṃ Tava Rūpaṃ Mantradevatopāsyam |

Janani Sphuratu Sadā Naḥ Sammānyaṃ Śreyase Kāle || 64

Muraripupuṇyaśreṇīparipākaṃ Tāvakaṃ Rūpam |

Kamale Janani Viśuddhaṃ Dadyācchreyo Muhurbhajatām || 65

Puṇyaśreṇī Kamalā Sā Jananī Bhaktamānase Sthitibhāk |

Tejastatibhirmohitabhuvanā Bhuvanādhināthagṛhiṇīyam || 66

Jalanidhikanyārūpaṃ Harimānyaṃ Sarvasaṃpadāṃ Hetuḥ |

Cirakṛtasukṛtaviśeṣānnayanayuge Bhāti Sarvasya || 67

Jalanidhitapaḥphalaṃ Yanmunijanahṛdayābjanityakṛtanṛttam |

Karuṇālolāpāṅgaṃ Tat Tejo Bhātu Niḥsamaṃ Vadane || 68

Śamitanataduritasaṃghā Haraye Nijanetrakalpitānaṅgā |

Kṛtasuraśātravabhaṅgā Sā Devī Maṅgalaistuṅgā || 69

Nikhilāgamasiddhāntaṃ Hariśuddhāntaṃ Sadā Naumi |

Tenaiva Sarvasiddhiḥ Śāstreṣu Viniścitā Vibudhaiḥ || 70

Kṛṣṇakṛtavividhalīlaṃ Tava Rūpaṃ Mātarādarānmānyam |

Sphuratu Vilocanayugale Nityaṃ Saṃpatsamṛddhyai Naḥ || 71

Karuṇākaṭākṣalaharī Kāmāyāstu Prakāmakṛtarakṣā |

Lakṣmyā Mādhavamānyā Satsukhadāne Diśi Khyātā || 72

Apavargasiddhaye Tvāmambāmambhojalocanāṃ Lakṣmīm |

Avalambe Haridayite Padmāsanamukhasurendrakṛtapūjām || 73

Tāvakakaṭākṣalaharīṃ Nidhehi Mayi Devi Kamale Tvam |

Tena Manorathasidhhirbhuvi Parame Dhāmani Pracurā || 74

Tvāmādareṇa Satataṃ Vīkṣemahi Mātarabjakṛtavāsām |

Viṣṇorvakṣonilayāmakṣayasukhasiddhaye Loke || 75

Sā Naḥ Sidhyatu Siddhyai Devānāṃ Vāṅmamano'tītā |
Harigṛhiṇī Hariṇākṣī Pālitalokatrayā Ca Jananīyam || 76

Sakalacarācaracinmayarūpaṃ Yasyā Hi Devatopāsyam |
Sā Dadatu Maṅgalaṃ Me Nityojjvalamādarājjananī || 77

Śītamayūkhasahodari Tāṃ Tvāmambāṃ Hi Śīlaye Nityam |
Nirasitavairigaṇo'haṃ Haricaraṇanyastarakṣaśca || 78

Dikṣi Vidikṣu Kṛtaśrīḥ Sā Me Jananī Nadīśatanayeyam |
Hariṇā Sākaṃ Bhajatu Prākāśyaṃ Hṛdi Satāṃ Samṛddhyai Naḥ || 79

Vārinidhivaṃśasampad Divyā Kāciddharermānyā |
Arcanti Yāṃ Tu Munayo Yogārambhe Tathānte Ca || 80

Dhṛtasumamadhupakrīḍāsthānāyitakeśabhārāyai |
Nama Uktirastu Mātre Vāgjitapīyūṣadhārāyai || 81

Saṃdehe Siddhānte Vāde Vā Samarabhūmibhāge Vā |
Yā Rājati Bahurūpā Sā Devī Viṣṇuvallabhā Khyātā || 82

Pratiphalatu Me Sadā Tanmunimānasapeṭikāratnam |
Viṣṇorvakṣobhūṣaṇamādṛtanirgatijanāvanaṃ Tejaḥ || 83

Bālakuraṅgavilocanadhāṭīrakṣitasurādi Manujānām |
Nayanayugāsevyaṃ Tad Bhātīha Dharātale Tejaḥ || 84

Mādhavadṛkṣāphalyaṃ Bhaktāvalidṛśyakāmadhenukalā |
Lakṣmīrūpaṃ Tejo Vibhātu Mama Mānase Vacasi || 85

Harisarasakrīḍārthaṃ Yā Vidhṛtānekarūpikā Mātā |
Sā Gehabhūṣaṇam Naḥ Sphuratu Sadā Nityasampūjyā || 86

Dvāravatīpurabhāge Maithilanagare Ca Yatkathāsāraḥ |
Sā Devī Jaladhisutā Viharaṇabhāṅ Māmake Manasi || 87

Jalanidhitapomahimne Devyai Paramātmanaḥ Śriyai Satatam |
Bhūyāṃsi Namāṃsi Punaḥ Sarvā Naḥ Sampadaḥ Santu || 88

Paramauṣadhaṃ Hi Saṃsṛtivyādheryat Kīrtitaṃ Nipuṇaiḥ |
Tadahaṃ Bhajāmi Satataṃ Lakṣmīrūpaṃ Sadānandam || 89

Daśarathasutakodaṇḍaprabhāvasākṣātkṛte Kṛtānandā |
Sītārūpā Māte Jajñe Yajñakṣitau Hi Sā Siddhyai || 90

Munijanamānasanilaye Kamale Te Caraṇapaṅkajaṃ Śirasi |
Avataṃsayannudāraṃ Viśāmi Devaiḥ Sudharmāṃ Vā || 91

Dhanamadamedurasevāṃ Tyaktavāhaṃ Te Padāmbhojam |
Śaraṇaṃ Yāmi Pumarthasphūrtikalāyai Bhṛśaṃ Dīnaḥ || 92

Na Ghaṭaya Kutsitasevāṃ Duṣṭairvā Saṃgamaṃ Mātaḥ |
Kuru Māṃ Dāsaṃ Saṃsṛtipāpaṃ Ca Hara Śīghram || 93

Mayi Namati Viṣṇukānte Tavāgratastāpabhārārte |
Mātaḥ Sahasā Sumukhī Bhava Bāle Doṣanilaye Ca || 94

Hanta Kadā Vā Mātastava Locanasecanaṃ Bhavenmayi Bhoḥ |
Ītthaṃ Prātaḥ Stuvatāṃ Tvameva Rakṣākarī Niyatam || 95

Saṃsārarogaśāntipradametallocanaṃ Mātaḥ |
Tāvatkamahamupāse Divyauṣadhamāśu Sāgarendrasute || 96

Saṃsṛtirogārtānāṃ Tava Nāmasmaraṇamatra Dharaṇitale |
Pūjāpradakṣiṇādikamāryā Mukhyauṣadhaṃ Vadanti Kila || 97

Mātarvinā Dharaṇyāṃ Sukṛtānāṃ Khaṇḍamiha Jantuḥ |
Dhyānaṃ Vā Na Hi Labhate Praṇatiṃ Vā Sampadāṃ Jananīm || 98

Guruvarakaṭākṣavibhavād Devi Tvāṅghripraṇāmadhutapāpaḥ |
Tava Ca Harerdāsaḥ San Viśāmi Deveśa Mānitāṃ Ca Sabhām || 99

Muraharanetramahotsavatāruṇyaśrīrnirastanataśatruḥ |
Lalitalikucābhakucabharayugalā Dṛgvijitahariṇasaṃdohā || 100

Kāruṇyapūrṇanayanā Kalikalmaṣahāriṇī Ca Sā Kamalā |
Mukhajitaśāradakamalā Vaktrāmbhoje Sadā Sphuratu Mātā || 101

Tāvakakaṭākṣasecanavibhavāṃ Nirdhūtaduritasaṃghā Hi |
Paramaṃ Sukhaṃ Labhante Pare Tu Loke Ca Sūribhiḥ Sārdham || 102

Tava Pādapadmavisṛmarakāntijharīṃ Manasi Kalayaṃstu |
Nirasitanarakādibhayo Virājate Nākisadasi Suravandyaḥ || 103

Hanta Sahasreṣvatha Vā Śateṣu Sukṛtī Pumān Mātaḥ |
Tāvakapādapayoruhavarivasyāṃ Kalayate Sakalam || 104

Janani Taraṅgaya Nayane Mayi Dīne Te Dayāsnigdhe |
Tena Vayaṃ Tu Kṛtārthā Nātaḥ Paramastiḥ Naḥ Prārthyam || 105

Tāvakakṛpāvaśādiha Nānāyogādināśitabhayā Ye |
Teṣāṃ Smaraṇamapi Drāk Śriyāvahaṃ Nityamākalaye || 106

Naiva Prāyaścittaṃ Duritānāṃ Māmakānāṃ Hi |
Tvāmeva Yāmi Śaraṇaṃ Tasmāllakṣmi Kṣamādhāre || 107

Muravairimānyacarite Mātastvāmakhilalokasāmrājye |
Paśyanti Divi Surendrā Munayastattvārthinaśca Nityakalām || 108

Svīyapadaprāptyai Nanu Vibudheśā Jaladhikanyake Mātaḥ |
Ārādhya Divyakusumaistava Pādābjaṃ Paraṃ Tuṣṭāḥ || 109

Sṛṣṭisthityādau Hariramba Tavāpāṅgavīkṣaṇādaravān |
Jagadetadavati Kāle Tvaṃ Ca Harirnaḥ Kramāt Pitarau || 110

Rājyasukhalābhasaṃpatprāptyai Kṣitipāśca Ye Ca Viprādyāḥ |
Gāṅgajalairapi Kusumairvarivasyāṃ Te Krameṇa Kalayanti || 111

Saṃtyaktakāmatadanujaḍambhāsūyādayo Narāḥ Kamale |
Ārādhya Tvāṃ Ca Hariṃ Kāle Caikāsanasthitāṃ Dhanyāḥ || 112

Jananī Kadā Punīte Mama Locanamārgamādarādeṣā |
Ye Kila Vadanti Dhanyāsteṣāṃ Darśanamahaṃ Kalaye || 113

Karadhṛtalīlāpadmā Padmā Padmākṣagehinī Nayane |
Siñcati Sakalaśreyaḥprāptyai Nirvyājakāruṇyā || 114

Nānāvidhavidyānāṃ Līlāsadanaṃ Sarojanilayeyam |
Kavikulavacaḥpayojadyumaṇirucirbhāti Naḥ Puraṭ || 115

Atasīkusumadyutibhāṅ Nākigaṇairvandyapādapadmayugā |
Sarasijanilayā Sā Me Prasīdatu Kṣipramādarāt Siddhyai || 116

Jagadīśavallabhe Tvayi Vinyastabharaḥ Pumān Sahasā |
Tīrtvā Nākisthānaṃ Viśati Paraṃ Vaiṣṇavaṃ Surairmānyam || 117

Mātarjñānavikāsaṃ Kāraya Karuṇāvalokanairmadhuraiḥ |
Tenāhaṃ Dhanyatamo Bhaveyamāryāvṛte Sadasi || 118

Harivakṣasi Maṇidīpaprakāśavatyānyā Mātrā |
Nityaṃ Vayamiha Dāsāḥ Śriyā Sanāthā Mudā Paraṃ Naumaḥ || 119

Vidrāvayatu Sarojāsane Tvadīyā Kaṭākṣadhāṭī Naḥ |
Ajñānāṅkuramudrāṃ Punarapi Saṃsārabhītidāṃ Sahasā || 120

Tāvakakaṭākṣasūryodaye Madīyaṃ Hṛdambhojam |
Bhajate Vikāsamacirāt Tamovināśaśca Niścito Vibudhaiḥ || 121

Lakṣmīkaṭākṣalaharī Lakṣmīṃ Pakṣmalayati Kramānnamatām |
Pādapayoruhasevā Paraṃ Padaṃ Citsukhollāsam || 122

Cidrūpā Paramā Sā Kamalekṣaṇanāyikā Mude Bhajatām |
Yatpraṇayakopakāle Jagadīśaḥ Kiṃkaro Bhavati || 123

Kācana Devī Viharatu Mama Citte Saṃtataṃ Siddhyai |
Yāpatyaṃ Kalaśābdherurageśayasatkalatraṃ Ca || 124

Aṣṭasu Mahiṣīṣvekā Kamalā Mukhyā Hi Nirdiṣṭā |
Anayaiva Sarvajagatāmudayādistanyate Kāle || 125

Kaivalyānandakalākandamahaṃ Saṃtataṃ Vande |
Tattu Mukundakalatraṃ Cintitaphaladānadīkṣitaṃ Kimapi || 126

Īkṣe Kamalāmenāmambāmambhojalocanāṃ Satatam |
Mandasmitamadhurāsyāṃ Nityaṃ Cājñātakopamukhadoṣām || 127

Aṅkitamādhavavakṣaḥsthalā Sarojekṣaṇā Ca Harikāntā |

Kabalayati Mānasaṃ Me Dayāprasārādibhirnityam || 128

Bhūtyai Mama Bhavatu Drāgajñānadhvaṃsinī Namatām |

Nāthānurūparūpā Śrutyanteḍyā Daśāvatāreṣu || 129

Sakalajanarakṣaṇeśu Praṇihitanayanā Trilokamātā Naḥ |

Puṣṇāti Maṅgalānāṃ Nikaraṃ Sevākrameṇa || 130

Padmāsanajananī Māṃ Pātu Mudā Sundarāpāṅgaiḥ |

Sarvaiśvaryanidānaṃ Yāmāhurvaidikā Dīptām || 131

Nānālaṃkāravatī Munimānasavāsinī Hareḥ Patnī |

Trailokyavinutavibhavā Māṃ Pāyādāpadāṃ Nicayāt || 132

Vidrāvayatu Bhayaṃ Naḥ Sā Kamalā Viṣṇuvallabhā Mātā |

Abdhiḥ Saṃkṣubhito'bhūt Yadarthamāryeṇa Rāmeṇa || 133

Bhūyo Yadarthamindraḥ Suratarukusumārthinā Ca Kṛṣṇena |

Hatagarvo'jani Yuddhe Sā Nityaṃ Śreyase Bhūyāt || 134

Tvāmārādhya Janā Api Dhanahīnāḥ Saudhamadhyatalabhājaḥ |

Nānādeśavanīpakajanastutā Bhānti Nityameva Rame || 135

Saṃsṛtitāpo Na Bhavati Punarapi Yatpādapaṅkajaṃ Namatām |

Sā Mayi Kalitadayā Syādambā Viṣṇoḥ Kalatramanurūpam || 136

Jananīkaṭākṣabhājāmiha Martyānāṃ Surāstu Kiṃkaratām |

Ripavo Giritaṭavāsaṃ Bhajanti Veśmāni Siddhayaḥ Sarvāḥ || 137

Smaraṇādvā Bhajanādvā Yasyāḥ Pādāmbujasya Bhuvi Dhanyāḥ |

Hanta Ramante Stamberamanivahāvṛtagṛhāṅgaṇe Manujāḥ || 138

Cirakṛtasukṛtaniṣevyā Sā Devī Viṣṇuvallabhā Khyātā |

Yasyāḥ Prasādabhūmnā Jātāḥ Paśvādayo Vadānyā Hi || 139

Amba Madhurān Kaṭākṣān Tāpaharān Vikira Mayi Kṛpājaladhe |

Ye Vinyastāḥ Karivaramārutimukhabhaktavaryeṣu || 140

Amṛtalaharīva Madhurā Jaladhararucirā Natārtiharaśīlā |
Sarvaśreyodātrī Kācid Devī Sadā Vibhātu Hṛdi || 141

Gītācāryapurandhrī Tvadīyanāmaprabhāvakalanādyaiḥ |
Yamabhayavārtā Dūre Harisāṃnidhyaṃ Kuto Na Syāt || 142

Jalanidhitanaye Kānte Viṣṇoruṣṇāṃśucandranayane Te |
Caturānanādayastu Khyātā Bālāḥ Śrutau Coktāḥ || 143

Manasijavairaṃ Gātraṃ Vāṇī Saudhārasī Ca Yadbhajatām |
Ślādhyā Saṃpat Sajjanasamāgamaścāśu Sidhyanti || 144

Saphalayatu Netrayugalaṃ Hatanataduritā Ca Sā Parā Devī |
Jalanidhikanyā Mānyā Patyavatārānukūlanijacaritā || 145

Nityaṃ Smarāmi Devīṃ Namatāṃ Sarvārthadāyinīṃ Kamalām |
Yāmāhurbhavanigaladhvaṃsanadīkṣāṃ Ca || 146
Sakalajagadaghanivāraṇasaṃkalpāṃ Madhujito Dayitām |
Jīvātumeva Kalaye Mokṣārthijanasya Bhūmisutām || 147

Mandānāmapi Dayayā Tamonirāsaṃ Vitanvantī |
Sarvatra Bhāti Kamalā Tanuriva Viṣṇornirastāghā || 148

Bālamarālīgatyai Surapurakanyādimahitakalagītyai |
Viracitanānānītyai Ceto Me Spṛhayate Bahulakīrtyai || 149

Abhilaṣitadānakuśalā Vāgdevīvanditā Ca Sā Kamalā |
Nityaṃ Mānasapadme Saṃcāraṃ Kalayate Muhuḥ Kutukāt || 150

Muramathananayanapaṅkajavilāsakalikā Sureśamukhasevyā |
Bhūtamayī Sāvitrī Gayatrī Sarvadevatā Jayati || 151

Sā Hi Parā Vidyā Me Lakṣmīrakṣobhaṇīyakīrtikalā |
Hṛdyāṃ Vidyāṃ Dayādadya Śreyaḥparaṃparāsiddhyai || 152

Kāmajananī Hi Lakṣmīḥ Nānālīlādibhirnijaṃ Nātham |
Mohayati Viṣṇumacirāt Prakṛtīnāṃ Kṣemasiddhyartham || 153

Manasijasāmrājyakalānidānamāryābhivanditaṃ Kimapi |
Lakṣmīrūpaṃ Tejo Vilasati Mama Manasi Viṣṇusaṃkrāntam || 154

Viṣṇumanorathapātraṃ Saṃtaptasvarṇakāmyanijagātram |
Āśritajalanidhigotraṃ Rakṣitanatabāhujacchātram || 155

Kavikulajihvālolaṃ Muramardanakalitaramyabahulīlam |
Nirasitanataduṣkālaṃ Vande Tejaḥ Sadālinutaśīlam || 156

Ādimapuruṣapurandhrīmambāmambhojalocanāṃ Vande |
Yāṃ Natvā Gatatāpāstyaktvā Dehaṃ Viśanti Paramapadam || 157

Lakṣmyā Harirapi Bhāti Prakṛtikṣemāya Dīkṣitāyāsau |
Mama Locanayoḥ Purato Lasatu Gabhīraṃ Kriyāsiddhyai || 158

Janani Kadā Vā Neṣyāmyahamārādarcitatvadīyapadaḥ |
Nimiṣamiva Hanta Divasan Dṛṣṭvā Tvāmādareṇa Kalyāṇīm || 159

Saṃpūrṇayauvanojjvaladehāṃ Yāṃ Vīkṣya Śaurirapi |
Kusumaśaraviddhacetāḥ Kiṃkarabhāvaṃ Svayaṃ Prāptaḥ || 160

Anunayaśīlastadanu Praṇayakrodhādinā Bhītaḥ |
Ādimapuruṣaḥ So'yaṃ Sā Lakṣmīrna Śriyai Bhavatu || 161

Maṇikuṇḍalalasitāsyaṃ Kṛpākaraṃ Kimapi Kuṅkumacchāyam |
Hariṇā Kṛtasaṃcāraṃ Tejo Me Bhātu Sarvadā Siddhyai || 162

Sāmrājyamaṅgalaśrīḥ Śrīreṣā Puṣkarākṣasya |
Gandharvakanyakādyairgaṅgātīreṣu Gītakīrtirhi || 163

Kavitābhāgyavidhātrī Parimalasaṃkrāntamadhupagaṇakeśā |
Mama Nayanayoḥ Kadā Vā Sā Devī Kalitasaṃnidhānakalā || 164

Kīrtiḥ Svayaṃ Vṛṇīte Vāgdevī Cāpi Vijayalakṣmīśca |
Taṃ Naramacirālloke Yo Lakṣmīpādabhaktastu || 165

Sanmitraṃ Pāṇḍityaṃ Saddārāḥ Satsutādyāśca |
Jāyante Tasya Bhuvi Śrībhakto Yaśca Nirdiṣṭaḥ || 166

Paramācāryairvinutāṃ Tāmambāmādarānnaumi |

Paramaiśvaryaṃ Viṣṇorapi Yā Vedeṣu Nirdiṣṭā || 167

Kavikulasūktiśreṇīśravaṇānandollasadvataṃsasumā |

Sā Devī Mama Hṛdaye Kṛtasāṃnidhyā Virājate Paramā || 168

Tāpārtāstu Taṭākaṃ Yathā Bhajante Ramāṃ Devīm |

Saṃsṛtitaptāḥ Sarve Yānti Hi Śaraṇaṃ Śaraṇyāṃ Tām || 169

Sarvajñatvaṃ Ślādhyaṃ Dharādhipatyaṃ Rame Devi |

Yadyat Prārthyaṃ Dayayā Tad Diśa Mokṣaṃ Ca Me Janani || 170

Vidyutamacañcalāṃ Tvāṃ Kṛṣṇe Meghe Payodhivarakanye |

Nityamavaimi Śreyaḥsidhya Mātaḥ Prasanne Naḥ || 171

Tvāmamba Saṃtataruciṃ Kṛṣṇo Meghaḥ Samāsādya |

Sadvartmani Varṣati Kila Kāṅkṣādhikamādareṇa Vārdhisute || 172

Amba Tvameva Kāle Mukundamapi Darśayantīha |

Śreyaḥsiddhyai Namatāṃ Bhāsi Hṛdi Śrutiśiraḥsu Salloke || 173

Vinamadamareśasudatīkacasumamakarandadhārayā Snigdham |

Tava Pādapadmametat Kadā Nu Mama Mūrdhni Bhūṣaṇam Janani || 174

Apavargasaukhyade Te Dayāprasāraḥ Kathaṃ Varṇyaḥ |

Yāmavalambya Hi Yaṣṭiṃ Na Patati Saṃsārapaṅkile Mārge || 175

Sūkṣmāt Sūkṣmataraṃ Te Rūpaṃ Paśyanti Yogino Hṛdaye |

Tāṃ Tvāmahaṃ Kadā Vā Drakṣye'laṃkāramaṇḍitāṃ Mātaḥ || 176

Cirataratapasā Kliṣṭe Yogihṛdi Sthānabhāg Ramā Devī |

Darśanamacirād Dayayā Dadāti Yogādihīnānām || 177

Tīraṃ Saṃsṛtijaladheḥ Pūraṃ Kamalākṣalocanaprīteḥ |

Sāraṃ Nigamāntānāṃ Dūraṃ Durjanataterhi Tattejaḥ || 178

Lakṣmīrūpaṃ Tejo Mamāvirastu Śriyai Nityam |

Yannityadharmadārān Viṣṇoramitaujasaḥ Prāhuḥ || 179

Jaladhisute Tvaṃ Jananī Sa Vāsudevaḥ Pitā Ca Naḥ Kathitaḥ |
Śaraṇaṃ Yuvāṃ Prapannā Nāto Durgatiparisphūrtiḥ || 180

Harinīlaratnabhāsā Prakaśitātmā Samudravarakanyā |
Maṅgalamātanuteyaṃ Kaṭākṣakalikāprasāraistu || 181

Maccittamattavāraṇabandhanamadhunā Tvadīyapādayuge |
Kalayāmi Rame Mātarmāṃ Rakṣa Kṣiprameva Saṃsṛtitaḥ || 182

Mocaya Saṃsṛtibandhaṃ Kaṭākṣakalikāṅkurai Rame Mātaḥ |
Nātaḥ Paramarthyamiha Kṣamātale Tvaṃ Dayāmūrtiḥ || 183

Mañjulakavitāsaṃtatibījāṅkuradāyisārasālokā |
Janani Tavāpāṅgaśrīḥ Jayati Jagattrāṇakalitadīkṣeyam || 184

Amba Tavāpāṅgaśrīrapāṅgakelīśatāni Janayantī |
Murahanturhṛdi Jayati Vrīḍāmadamohakāmasārakarī || 185

Baddhamapi Cittametad Yamaniyamādyaiḥ Pariṣkāraiḥ |
Dhāvati Balād Rame Tava Pādābjaṃ Yāmi Śaraṇamaham || 186

Mattagajamānyagamanā Madhurālāpā Ca Mānyacaritā Sā |
Mandasmeramukhābjā Kamalā Me Hṛdayasārase Lasatu || 187

Śāstrasmaraṇavihīnaṃ Pāpinamenaṃ Janaṃ Ramā Devī |
Dayayā Rakṣati Kāle Tasyāstena Prathā Mahatī || 188

Mukhavijitacandramaṇḍalamidamambhoruhavilocanaṃ Tejaḥ |
Dhyāne Jape Ca Sudṛśāṃ Cakāsti Hṛdaye Kaviśvarāṇāṃ Ca || 189

Amba Vivekavidūraṃ Janamenaṃ Śiśiralocanaprasaraiḥ |
Śiśiraya Kṛpayā Devi Tvameva Mātā Hi Lokasya || 190

Kopadupekṣase Yadi Mātarme Rakṣakaḥ Kaḥ Syāt |
Mayi Dīne Ko Lābhastava Tu Dayāyāḥ Prasāriṇyāḥ || 191

Bhavacaṇḍakiraṇataptaḥ Śrānto'haṃ Jñānavāridūrasthaḥ |
Śiśirāmaṅghricchāyāṃ Tava Mātaryāmi Śaraṇamārāttu || 192

Mātaraśokollāsaṃ Prakaṭaya Tava Komalakaṭākṣaiḥ |
Yairdīnā Narapatayaḥ Kalitā Vāraṇaśatāvṛte Gehe || 193

Jayati Rame Tava Mahatī Kṛpājharī Sarvasaṃmānyā |
Kṣemaṃkarī Yadeṣā Pratikalpaṃ Sarvajagatāṃ Ca || 194

Ajñānakūpakuhare Patitaṃ Māṃ Pāhi Kamale Tvam |
Nagare Vā Grāme Vā Vanamadhye Dikṣu Rakṣiṇī Tvamasi || 195

Tava Caraṇau Śaraṇamiti Bruvannahaṃ Mātarabdhitanaye Tvam |
Hariṇā Sahitā Dayayā Prāhyavilambena Dīnaṃ Mām || 196

Parisaranatavibudhālīkirīṭamaṇikāntivallarīvisaraiḥ |
Kṛtanīrājanavidhi Te Mama Tu Śirobhūṣaṇaṃ Hi Padayugalam || 197

Mama Hṛdayapaṅkajavanīvikāsahetau Dinādhipāyetām |
Tava Tu Kaṭākṣaprasaraḥ Dīpāyetāṃ Tamonirākaraṇe || 198

Yāvaccharaṇaṃ Yāti Kṣititanaye Tvāṃ Hi Janturiha Mūḍhaḥ |
Tāvat Tasya Tu Rasanāṅgaṇe Tu Vāṇī Samākalitanṛttā || 199

Paṅkajanilaye Tāvakacaraṇaṃ Śaraṇaṃ Samākalaye |
Tena Hi Sarvakṛtānāṃ Bhaviṣyatāṃ Hānireva Duritānām || 200

Śrutyantasevitaṃ Te Caraṇasarojaṃ Praṇamya Kila Jantuḥ |
Chatrollasitaśirāḥ San Vanīpakān Dānavāriṇā Siñcan || 201

Viṣvaksenamukhādyaiḥ Sevitamamba Tvadīyapādayugam |
Avataṃsayanti Santaḥ Kalitāpapraśamanāyāstu || 202

Dugdhodadhitanaye Tvāṃ Diśāgajendrāḥ Suvarṇaghaṭatoyaiḥ |
Maṇimaṇṭapamadhyatale Samabhyaṣiñcan Hariprītyai || 203

Diggajapuṣpakarakumbhairabhiṣiktāṃ Tvāṃ Hariḥ Prītyā |
Udavahadārānmunigaṇamadhye Sarvaśriyo Mūlam || 204

Jātaparākramakalikā Diśi Diśi Kiṃnarasugītanijayaśasaḥ |
Dhanyā Bhānti Hi Manujāḥ Yadvīkṣālavaviśeṣataḥ Kāle || 205

Namadamarīkacabharasumamarandadhārābhiṣiktaṃ Te |
Padakamalayugalametacchreyaḥsphūrtyai Sadā Bhavatu || 206

Rāgadveṣādihataṃ Māmava Kamale Hareḥ Kānte |
Darśaya Dayayā Kāle Hyapavargasthānamārgaṃ Ca || 207

Na Hi Jāne Varṇayituṃ Parame Sthane Tvadīyavibhavamaham |
Munayaśca Surā Vedā Yato Nivṛttāḥ Kṣamātanaye || 208

Manujāḥ Kaṭākṣitāḥ Kila Tathāmbayā Medinīputryā |
Satsutakalatrasahitāḥ Surabhiṃ Kālena Nirviśānti Mudā || 209

Jaladhīśakanyakā Sā Lasatu Puro'smākamādarakṛtaśrīḥ |
Yatpraṇamanājjanānāṃ Kavitonmeṣaḥ Sadīḍite Bhāti || 210

Dūrikarotu Duritaṃ Tvadbhaktirmāmakaṃ Kamale |
Ahamapi Sureśasevye Tava Sadasi Viśāmi Kīrtigānaparaḥ || 211

Paramajñānavidhātrī Tava Pādapayojabhaktirasmākam |
Kiṃ Vāśāsyamato'nyat Samudratanaye Harerjāye || 212

Amba Kadā Vā Lapsye Madīyapāpāpanodāya |
Tava Pādakamalasevāmabjabhavādyaistu Saṃprārthyām || 213

Mandānāmapi Mañjulakavitvarasadāyinī Jananī |
Kāpi Karuṇāmayī Sā Lasatu Purastāt Sadāsmākam || 214

Sakalakavilokavinute Kamale Kamalākṣi Vallabhe Viṣṇoḥ |
Tvannāmāni Hi Kalaye Vane Jale Śatrupīḍāyām || 215

Divi Vā Bhuvi Dikṣu Jale Vahnau Vā Sarvataḥ Kamale |
Jantūnāṃ Kila Rakṣā Tvadadhīnā Kīrtyate Vibudhaiḥ || 216

Kuśalavidhaye Tadastu Trivikramāsevyaramyanijakeli |
Kabalitapadanatadainyaṃ Taruṇāmbujalocanaṃ Tejaḥ || 217

Jananī Suvarṇavṛṣṭipradāyinī Bhāti Viṣṇuvakṣaḥsthā |
Kamalā Kalitakṣemā Prakṛtīnāṃ Śītalāpāṅgaiḥ || 218

Jagatāmādimajananī Lasati Kaverātmajāpuline |

Kṣetreṣūttamajuṣṭeṣvayonijā Lokarakṣāyai ‖ 219

Kucaśobhājitaviṣṇuḥ Kuṅkumapaṅkāṅkitā Kamalā |

Kāñcyāṃ Rājati Kāñcīmaṇigaṇanīrājitāṅghriyugā ‖ 220

Mandārakusumamadaharamandasmitamadhuravadanapaṅkaruhā |

Hṛdyatamanityayauvanamaṇḍitagātrī Virājate Kamalā ‖ 221

Kaṃsaripugehinī Sā Haṃsagatirhaṃsamānyanijacaritā |

Saṃsāratāpahāniṃ Kalayatu Kāle Ramāsmākam ‖ 222

Manasijajananī Jananī Cāsmākamihādarāt Kāle |

Śītalalolāpāṅgaistaraṅgayati Śreyasāṃ Sariṇam ‖ 223

Tava Mandahāsakalikāṃ Bhaje Bhujaṅge Śayānaṃ Tam |

Yā Kalayati Gatakopaṃ Bālānāṃ Naḥ Kṛtāparādhānām ‖ 224

Sā Sādhayedabhīṣṭaṃ Kamalā Śrīrviṣṇuvakṣaḥsthā |

Yasyāḥ Padavinyāsaḥ Śrutimauliṣu Tanyate Mahālakṣmyāḥ ‖ 225

Śāntirasanityaśevadhimambāṃ Seve Manorathāvāptyai |

Yāmārādhya Sureśāḥ Svapadaṃ Prāpurhi Tādṛkṣam ‖ 226

Dhāturapi Vedavacasāṃ Dūre Yatsthānamāmananti Budhāḥ |

Sāstu Mude Śrīreṣā Muramardanasatkalatramamitaujaḥ ‖ 227

Bhavaduḥkharāśijaladherhaṭhāt Taritrīṃ Paraṃ Vidmaḥ |

Tāmambāṃ Kamalasthāṃ Murārivakṣomaṇipradīpāṃ Ca ‖ 228

Munisārvabhaumavarṇitamahācaritraṃ Hareḥ Kalatraṃ Tat |

Pathi Maṅgalāya Bhavatu Prasthānajuṣāṃ Kṛpādhāram ‖ 229

Khaṇḍitavairigaṇeyaṃ Maṇḍitabhaktā Sutādyaiśca |

Bhāsurakīrtirjayati Kṣoṇīsuravandyacaraṇābjā ‖ 230

Natapālini Māṃ Pāhi Trijagadvandye Nidhehi Mayi Dayayā |

Tāvakakaṭākṣalaharīḥ Śaktimaye Sakalasiddhīnām ‖ 231

Bhavasāgaraṃ Titīrṣustava Caraṇābjaṃ Mahāseyum |
Mātaḥ Kadā Nu Lapsye Ghanatāpormyādipīḍito Dīnaḥ || 232

Kavivāgvāsantīnāṃ Vasantalakṣmīrmurāridayitā Naḥ |
Paramāṃ Mudaṃ Vidhatte Kāle Kāle Mahābhūtyai || 233

Suraharaparatantraṃ Tad Gatatandraṃ Vastu Nistulamupāse |
Tenaivāhaṃ Dhanyo Madvaṃśyā Nirasitātmatāpabharāḥ || 234

Tṛṣṇāṃ Śamayati Devī Rāghavadayitā Natālisuravallī |
Ityāryavaco Dhairyaṃ Janayati Kāle Dharāputri || 235

Raghupatidayite Mātaḥ Kākāsurarakṣaṇādinā Loke |
Tāvakakaruṇāmahimā Prathitaḥ Kila Bhūtidāyī Naḥ || 236

Pracurataduritapālīsamāvṛtānāṃ Kalau Hi Taptānām |
Tāvakadayā Hi Mātaḥ Śaraṇaṃ Varamiti Satāṃ Gaṇaḥ Stauti || 237

Atyantaśītalāṃ Tāṃ Kaṭākṣadhāṭīmupāse'ham |
Tena Mama Tridaśānāṃ Na Ko'pi Bhedo Dharātanaye || 238

Yaiḥ Sevā Saṃkalitā Tava Pādābje Dharātanaye |
Teṣāmajñānajharī Yāti Hi Vilayaṃ Kṣaṇenaiva || 239

Jñānāravindavilasanamacirādasya Stutau Hi Kavivaryāḥ |
Saṃpad Divyā Ca Tathā Vibudhāvalimānanīyātra || 240

Mātastava Pādābjaṃ Yasya Lalāṭe Kṛtorunijakānti |
Tatpādapadmamacirād Vimānagā Devatā Vahati || 241

Ājñāvaśena Devyā Lasanti Divi Devatāmānyāḥ |
Indrādyāḥ Sa Ca Dhātā Dikpālāścāpi Gandharvāḥ || 242

Kaivalyānandakalādātrīṃ Kamalāmaharniśaṃ Naumi |
Tenaiva Janma Saphalaṃ Tīrthādiniṣevaṇādyacca || 243

Yacca Haripādapaṅkeruhaparicaraṇādinā Loke |
Tat Sarvamāśu Ghaṭayati Sahasā Mandasya Me Mātā || 244

Nānāśrutyantakalāparimalaparivāhavāsitaṃ Mātaḥ |

Tava Caraṇakamalayugalaṃ Mamāvataṃsaḥ Kṣaṇaṃ Bhātu || 245

Natadevanagaranārīdhammillalasatsumālikṛtanādāḥ |

Prātarmurajavilāsaṃ Kalayanti Bhṛśaṃ Tavāgrato Bhṛṅgāḥ || 246

Pāpapraśamanadīkṣākalādhurīṇāḥ Payojanilaye Te |

Māṃ Ca Pavitrīkuryuḥ Pādaparāgāḥ Kṛpāvaśataḥ || 247

Hanta Kadā Vā Lapsye Tavāṅghriśuśrūṣaṇāsaktim |

Sahajānandaṃ Tena Hi Padaṃ Kramāt Prāpyamādiṣṭam || 248

Nalinīvilāsarucirāṃ Mayi Devi Tvatkaṭākṣalaharīṃ Hi |

Kāle Nidhehi Dayayā Sphītā Te Kīrtirādṛtā Sarvaiḥ || 249

Vinihataduritastomā Kāpi Madīye Hṛdambhoje |

Lasatu Paradevatākhyā Mādhavanetrapriyaṃkarī Kalikā || 250

Pañcāyudhagurumantraṃ Kalanūpuraninadamādarāt Kamale |

Kalayati Ramādhavagṛhaṃ Yātuṃ Kāle Tvayi Pravṛttāyām || 251

Natanākilokavanitālalāṭasindūraśoṇakāntibhṛtoḥ |

Kalaye Namāṃsi Kamale Tava Pādapayojayornityam || 252

Kamalasuṣumānivāsasthānakaṭākṣaṃ Cirāya Kṛtarakṣam |

Rakṣogaṇabhītikaraṃ Tejo Bhāti Prakāmamiha Manasi || 253

Jyotsneva Śiśirapātā Kaṭākṣadhāṭī Tvadīyā Hi |

Amba Mukunda Kurute || 254

Tāpahararasavivarṣamadhṛtakutukā Kāpi Nīlanalinaruciḥ |

Kādambinī Purastadāstāṃ Naḥ Saṃtataṃ Jananī || 255

Saphalayatu Netrayugalaṃ Māmakametat Tvadīyarūpamaho |

Yat Kamalanetrasucaritapacelimaṃ Vaidikī Śrutirbrūte || 256

Mādhavanetrapayojāmṛtalaharī Bhāti Tāvakaṃ Rūpam |

Amba Yuvāmādyau Naḥ Pitarau Vane Sukhāvāptyai || 257

Sarasakavitādisampadvilasanamārāduśānti Kavivaryāḥ |

Yatprīṇanena Sā Me Bhavatu Vibhūtyai Hi Sā Kamalā || 258

Manasijajayādikāryaṃ Yadapāṅgalavānnṛṇāṃ Bhavati |

Tatpadamānandakalaṃ Sevyaṃ Ca Bhaje Ramāṃ Jananīm || 259

Śithilatatamaḥsamūhā Bhaktānāṃ Sā Ramā Devī |

Janayati Dhairyaṃ Ca Hareḥ Kāle Yā Sarvadā Sevyā || 260

Yadbhrūvilāsavaśataḥ Śaktaḥ Sṛṣṭyādikaṃ Kartum |

Harirapi Loke Khyātaḥ Sā Naḥ Śaraṇaṃ Jaganmātā || 261

Nayanayugalīṃ Kadā Me Siñcati Evyāḥ Paraṃ Rūpam |

Yadbhajanānna Hi Loke Dṛṣṭaṃ Ślādhyaṃ Paraṃ Vastu || 262

Sucaritaphalaṃ Tvadīyaṃ Rūpaṃ Naḥ Kalitabhaktīnām |

Ata Eva Māmakānāṃ Pāpānāṃ Viratirūrjitā Kamale || 263

Sukṛtivibhavādupāsyā Kamalā Sā Sarvakalyāṇā |

Harivakṣasi Kṛtavāsā Rakṣati Lokānahorātram || 264

Saṃvidrūpā Hi Hareḥ Kuṭumbinī Bhāti Bhaktahṛdayeṣu |

Sarvaśreyaḥprāptyai Yāṃ Vidurāryā Ramāṃ Kamalām || 265

Viṣayalaharīpraśāntyai Kamalāpādāmbujaṃ Naumi |

Pūrvaṃ Śukādisudhiyo Yaddhyānād Galitaśatrubhayāḥ || 266

Lalitagamanaṃ Tvadīyaṃ Kalanūpuranādapūritaṃ Mātaḥ |

Naumi Padāmbujayugalaṃ Bhavatāpanirāsanāyādya || 267

Viralīkaroti Tāpaṃ Kamalāyā Mandahāsajharī |

Yatsevaneṣu Samuditakautukarasanirbharo Harirjayati || 268

Pratiphalatu Saṃtataṃ Me Purato Mātastvadīyarūpamidam |

Yaddarśanarasabhūmnā Harirapi Nānāsvarūpabhāk Kāle || 269

Amba Tava Caraṇasevāṃ Saṃtatamahamādarāt Kalaye |

Tena Mama Janma Saphalaṃ Tridaśānāmiva Munīndrāṇām || 270

Durvāragarvadurmatidurarthanirasanakalānipuṇāḥ |
Tava Caraṇasevayaiva Hi Kamale Mātarbudhā Jagati || 271

Ānadameti Mātastava Nāmoccāraṇena Sindhubhave |
Saṃprāptatvadrūpaṃ Mama Mānasamāttayogakalam || 272

Tava Dṛṣṭipātavibhavāt Sarve Loke Vidhūtatāpabharāḥ |
Yānti Mudā Tridaśaiḥ Saha Vibhānamāruhya Mātaraho || 273

Ko Vā Na Śrayati Budhaḥ Śreyo'rthī Tāmimāṃ Kamalām |
Yāṃ Pannagārivāhanasadgarmiṇīmarcayanti Suranāthāḥ || 274

Tāmaravindanivāsāmambāṃ Śaraṇārthināṃ Kalitarakṣām |
Bahurūpeṣvaghanicayeṣvapi Niścityātmano Dhairyam || 275

Karuṇāpravāhajharyā Gatapaṅka Bhūtalaṃ Mātaḥ |
Satvāṅkurādilasitaṃ Jayati Payorāśikakanyake Kamale || 276

Vidhiśivavāsavamukhyairvandyapadābje Namastubhyam |
Mātarviṣṇordayite Sarvajñatvaṃ Ca Me Kalaya || 277

Paradevate Prasīda Prasīda Harivallabhe Mātaḥ |
Tvāmāhuḥ Śrutayaḥ Kila Kalyāṇaguṇākarāṃ Nityām || 278

Kṣantavyamamba Māmakamagharāśiṃ Kṣapaya Vīkṣaṇataḥ |
Satvonmeṣaṃ Dehi Priye Harerdāsamapi Kuru Mām || 279

Vāñchitasiddhirna Syād Yadi Pādābje Kṛtapraṇāmānām |
Hānistvadīyayaśasāmiti Keciddhairyavantaśca || 280

Sadasadanugrahadakṣāṃ Tvāṃ Mātaḥ Saṃtataṃ Naumi |
Grahapīḍā Naiva Bhavedyamapīḍā Dūrataḥ Kāle || 281

Vidyāḥ Kalāśca Kāle Kṛpayā Kalaya Prasīdāśu |
Mātastvameva Jagatāṃ Sarveṣāṃ Rakṣaṇaṃ Tvayā Kriyate || 282

Ucheṣvapi Nīceṣu Prakāśate Tulyameva Tava Rūpam |
Etad Dṛṣṭvā Dhairyaṃ Ghanāgaso'pyamba Jāyate Nanu Me || 283

Kā Śaṅkā Tava Vaibhavajālaṃ Vaktuṃ Digantare Mātaḥ |

Varahārālaṃkārāṃ Sevante Tvāṃ Haritpatayaḥ || 284

Kamalāyāśca Harerapi Saṃdṛśyaṃ Divyadāṃpatyam |

Tāveva Naḥ Patī Kila Janmāntarapuṇyaparipākāt || 285

Sarvāsāmupaniṣadāṃ Vidyānāṃ Tvaṃparaṃ Sthānam |

Alpadhiyo Vayamete Tvatstotre Bhoḥ Kathaṃ Śaktāḥ || 286

Sāṣṭāṅgapraṇatiriyaṃ Prakalpitā Mātaradya Tava Caraṇe |

Tenāhaṃ Hi Kṛtārthaḥ Kiṃ Prārthyaṃ Vastvataḥ Kamale || 287

Stotramidaṃhi Mayā Te Caraṇāmbhoje Samarpitaṃ Bhaktyā |

Tava Ca Gurorapi Vīkṣā Tatra Nidānaṃ Paraṃ Nānyat || 288

Dehānte Nanu Mātarmokṣaṃ Tridaśaiḥ Samaṃ Dehi |

Ahamapi Sāma Paṭhan San Tvāṃ Ca Hariṃ Yāmi Śaraṇārthī || 289

Śukavāṇīmiva Mātarnirarthakāṃ Madvacobhaṅgīm |

Ārācchṛṇoṣi Dayayā Tadeva Cottamapadavyaktyai || 290

Vidyāṃ Kalāṃ Variṣṭhāṃ Amba Tvāṃ Saṃtataṃ Vande |

Yā Vyākaroṣi Kāle Vidvadbhirvedatattvādi || 291

Vaiduṣyaṃ Vāṇyāḥ Satsaṃpajjharyo Yadīyavīkṣaṇataḥ |

Sidhyantyapi Devānāṃ Sā Naḥ Śaraṇaṃ Ramā Devī || 292

Vipulaṃ Śriyo Vilāsaṃ Śraddhāṃ Bhaktyādikaṃ Dehi |

Amba Prasīda Kāle Tava Pādābjaikasevināmiha Naḥ || 293

Kecit Prāñcaḥ Kamalāṃ Prāpya Hi Śaraṇaṃ Vipatkāle |

Jhaṭiti Vidhūnitatāpāḥ Sā Me Devī Prasannāstu || 294

Marakatakāntimanoharamūrtiḥ Saiṣā Ramā Devī |

Pāti Sakalāni Kāle Jaganti Karuṇāvalokādyaiḥ || 295

Bhāgīrathīva Vāṇī Tava Nutirūpā Virājate Paramā |

Iha Mātaryadbhajanaṃ Sarveṣāṃ Sarvasaṃpadāṃ Hetuḥ || 296

Kalaśapayodadhitanaye Haripriye Lakṣmi Mātarambeti |

Tava Nāmāni Japan San Tvaddāso'haṃ Tu Muktaye Siddhaḥ || 297

Nikhilacarācararakṣāṃ Vitanvatī Viṣṇuvallabhā Kamalā |

Mama Kuladaivatameṣā Jayati Sadārādhyamānyapādakamalā || 298

Sarvajannutavibhave Saṃtatamapi Vāñchitaprade Devi |

Amba Tvameva Śaraṇaṃ Tenāhaṃ Prāptasarvakāryārthaḥ || 299

Kamale Kathaṃ Nu Varṇyastava Mahimā Nigamamauligaṇavedyaḥ |

Iti Niścitya Padābjaṃ Tava Vande Mokṣakāmo'ham || 300

Tvāmamba Bāliśo'haṃ Tvacamatkārairgirāṃ Gumbhaiḥ |

Ayathāyathakramaṃ Hi Stuvannapi Prāptajanmasāphalyaḥ || 301

Iti Śrī Kamala Triśatī Samāptā |

श्री कमला त्रिशती

गङ्गाधरमखिविरचिता ।

परमाभरणं विष्णोर्वक्षसि सा सागरेन्द्रवरपुत्री ।
या मूर्तिर्मती काले क्षमा जनानां कृतापराधानाम् ॥ १

सा नः श्रेयो दद्यात् कमला कमलासनादिजननीं याम् ।
संप्राप्य सहचरीं हरिरवति जगन्त्यनाकुलं सततम् ॥ २

नित्यश्रेयोदाने ख्याता या हरिगृहस्य सर्वस्वम् ।
श्रुतिमौलिस्तुतविभवा सा भातु पुरः सदास्माकम् ॥ ३

विष्णुक्रीडालोला विख्याता दीनरक्षणे लक्ष्मीः ।
जननी नः स्फुरतु सदा तेन वयं किल कृतार्थाः स्मः ॥ ४

निर्वाणाङ्कुरजननी काले सा सार्वभौमपददोग्ध्री ।
निरसतिमोहसमूहा मम दैवतमादृतं गुरुभिः ॥ ५

विष्णोर्वक्षसि लसिता शीतमयूखस्य सोदरी कमला ।
कमलायतनयना नः पातु सदा पापराशिभ्यः ॥ ६

कविपरिषदा च वेदैः नित्यं स्तुतनिजमहोदया कमला ।
मनसि मम संनिधत्तां त्वमितानन्दाय लोकनाथेन ॥ ७

दुग्धोदधितनया सा दुरितनिहन्त्री कृतप्रणामानाम् ।
आनन्दपदविधात्री पत्या साकं पदे पदे लोके ॥ ८

मन्मथजननी सा मामवतु सरोजा(क्ष)गेहिनी कमला ।
यामाराध्य बुधेन्द्रा विशन्ति परमं तु तत् पदं विष्णोः ॥ ९

सत्सूक्तिकृतिविधात्री नमतामम्बा त्रिलोक्यास्तु ।
नित्यप्रसादभूम्ना रक्षति मामादरात् कमला ॥ १०

मम सूक्तिरञ्जलिपुटः प्रणतिश्चानेकसंख्याका ।
कुतुकात् क्षीरोदसुताममितानन्दाय गाहते कमलाम् ॥ ११

या पारमार्थ्यसरणिः सा कमला निश्चिता वेदैः ।
सैषा हि जगन्माता संसृतितापापहन्त्री च ॥ १२

मन्दस्मितमधुराननममन्दसंतोषदायि भजतां तत् ।
कमलारूपं तेजो विभातु नित्यं मदीयहृत्कमले ॥ १३

काले क्षपयति कमला कटाक्षधाट्या हि मामकं दुरितम् ।
अत एवाश्रितरक्षणदीक्षेत्येवं जनो वदति ॥ १४

नवनवहर्म्यविधात्री नाकिकिरीटार्चिता च सा देवी ।
ज्योतिर्मण्डललसिता मुनिहृदयाब्जासना च सद्गतिदा ॥ १५

संवीक्ष्य जलधितनयां भूयो भूयः प्रणम्य भक्तगणः ।
निरसितदुरितौघः सन् स्तौति मुदा मोक्षसिद्धये कमलाम् ॥ १६

राकानिशीव देव्यां दृष्टायां भक्तगणवाणी ।
भजते जलनिधिशैलीं साङ्गोपाङ्गं कृतानन्दा ॥ १७

दुर्गतिभीत्या खिन्नः सोऽहं शरणं भजामि तां कमलाम् ।
शरणार्थिनां हि रक्षाकृदिति ख्याता हि या लोके ॥ १८

न हि कलयते हृदन्ते मन्दारं कामधेनुं वा ।
यः सेवते मुकुन्दप्रियां श्रियं नित्यभावेन ॥ १९

कैटभमर्दनमहिषीं ममाञ्जलिगर्हितां काले ।
न हि नाथनीयमत्र क्षमातले सा प्रसन्नास्तु ॥ २०

संतापपीडितं मामवतु सदा श्रीहरिप्रिया माता ।
रक्षितवायसमुख्या कृपानिधिः पुण्यकृद्दृश्या ॥ २१

न हि केवलं प्रणामैः स्तुत्या भक्त्या समाराध्या ।
सत्येन धर्मनिवहैर्भावेन च कमलगेहिनी कमला ॥ २२

कदाचित्कविलोकेऽप्यक्षीणानन्ददायिनी कमला ।
रक्षतु कटाक्षकलिकाङ्कूरैर्भक्तानिहादरतः ॥ २३

कलिपापग्लपितानां मुरमर्दनदिव्यगेहिनी लक्ष्मीः ।
राजति शरणं परमं वशीकृतेशा च विबुधगणसेव्या ॥ २४

नित्योल्लसदुरुमाला वक्षसि कमला हरेर्भाति ।
निजतनुभासा द्योतितकौस्तुभमणिरम्बुधेस्तनया ॥ २५

मातर्मङ्गलदायिन्यमरेन्द्रवधूसमर्चिताङ्घ्रियुगे ।
मां पाह्यपायनिवहात् संततमकलक्ष्मामूर्ते ॥ २६

यदि कलिता चोपेक्षा नश्येत् किल तावकी महती ।
कीर्तिरतोऽम्ब कटाक्षैः परिषिञ्च मुदा मुहुः शीतैः ॥ २७

धनधान्यसुतादिरुचिग्रस्तं मां पाहि कमले त्वम् ।
तेनोर्जितकीर्तिः स्या मातस्त्वं सर्वरक्षिणी ख्याता ॥ २८

तव पादाम्बुजयुगलध्यानं मातर्मदीयमघमाशु ।
कबलीकरोति काले तेनाहं सिद्धसंकल्पः ॥ २९

अञ्जलिकलिका हि कृता यदि तस्यै मुरनिहन्तृदयितायै ।
रसनाग्रे खेलनभाक् तस्य तु पुंसो गिरां देवी ॥ ३०

मातस्तव मूर्तिरियं सुधामयी निश्चिता निपुणैः ।
यत् तद्दर्शनभूम्ना निरस्ततापा बुधा भवन्त्यचिरात् ॥ ३१

कलितजगत्त्रयरक्षाभरणि मयि देवि संविधेहि मुदा ।
त्वद्वीक्षणानि कमले तेनाहं सिद्धसंकल्पः ॥ ३२

वरदे मुरारिदयिते जयन्ति ते वीक्षणानि यानि दिवि ।
संप्राप्य तानि मघवा विजितारिर्देवसंघवन्द्यश्च ॥ ३३

मोहान्धकारभास्करमम्ब कटाक्षं विधेहि मयि कमले ।
येनाप्नज्ञानकलाः स्तुवन्ति विबुधास्त्वदीयसदसि कलम् ॥ ३४

कामक्रोधादिमहासत्त्वनिरासं कृपासारात् ।
कुरु मातर्मम संसृतिभीतिं च निराकुरु त्वमेवारात् ॥ ३५

मूढानामपि हृद्यां कवितां दातुं यदीयपरिचर्या ।
प्रभवति काले सा हि श्रीरम्बा नः प्रसन्नास्तु ॥ ३६

दिव्यक्षेत्रेषु बुधा दिनकरमध्ये च वेदमौलौ च ।
यत्स्थानमिति वदन्ति श्रीरेषा भाति संश्रितहरिरिह ॥ ३७

निजलीलाक्रान्तहरी रक्षति कमला कटाक्षधाट्या नः ।
शरणार्थिनश्च काले विहगोरगपशुमुखानुव्र्याम् ॥ ३८

समराङ्गणेषु जयदा त्रिदशानां मौलिभिर्मान्या ।
आपदि रक्षणदक्षा सा कमला नः प्रसन्नास्तु ॥ ३९

नित्यानन्दासनभाङ् नवनिधिवन्द्या च सागरेन्द्रसुता ।
विलसति माधववक्षसि पालितलोकत्रया च जननी नः ॥ ४०

मुनिनुतनिजपरिपाटी वाग्धाटी दानलोलुपा भजताम् ।
शिक्षितरिपुजनकोटी विलसति धृतशातकुम्भमयशाटी ॥ ४१

निखिलागमवेद्यपदा नित्यं सद्भिः समाराध्या ।
संसृतिपाशनिहन्त्री या तस्यै चाञ्जलिः क्रियते ॥ ४२

भूयांसि नमांसि मया भक्तेन कृतानि कमलजाङ्घ्रियुगे ।
नित्यं लगन्तु तेन हि सर्वा राजन्ति संपदो मान्याः ॥ ४३

नित्यं निर्मलरूपे बरदे वाराशिकन्यके मातः ।
सद्गुणरक्षणदीक्षे पाहीति वदन्तमाशु मां पाहि ॥ ४४

भुवनजननि त्वमारात् कृतरक्षणसंततिः क्षमामूर्ते ।
प्रतिवस्तु रमे कलितस्वरूपशक्त्या हि राजसे जगति ॥ ४५

जय जय कलशाब्धिसुते जय जय हरिवल्लभे रमे मातः ।
प्रातरिति विबुधवर्याः पठन्ति नामानि ते हि मे गुरवः ॥ ४६

नेत्ररुचिविजितशारदपद्मे पद्मे नमस्तुभ्यम् ।
तेन वयं गतविपदः सा मुक्तिः करगता कलिता ॥ ४७

सततं बद्धाञ्जलिपुटमुपास्महे तच्छुभप्रदं तेजः ।
यत् कमलोदरनिलयं कमलाक्षप्रीतिवीचिकापूरम् ॥ ४८

स्फुरतु मम वचसि कमले त्वदीयवैभवसुधाधारा ।
नित्यं व्यक्तिं प्राप्ता धुतनुतजनखेदजालका महती ॥ ४९

कमले तव नुतिविषये बुद्धिर्जाता हि मे सहसा ।
तेन मम भागधेयं परिणतमित्येव नित्यसंतुष्टः ॥ ५०

कवितारसपरिमलितं करोति वदनं नतानां या ।
स्तोतुं तां मे ह्यारात् सा देवी सुप्रसन्नास्तु ॥ ५१

हरिगृहिणि तावकं नुतरूपं ये भुवि निजे हृदम्भोजे ।
ध्यायन्ति तेषु विबुधा अपि कल्पककुसुममर्पयन्ति मुदा ॥ ५२

नानावरदानकलालोलुपहृदये हृदम्भुजस्थे माम् ।
रक्षापायात् सहसा कुरु भक्तं दोषहीनं च ॥ ५३

निजघनकेशरुचा जितनीलाम्बुधरे शशाङ्ककसहजन्मन् ।
पद्मे त्वदीयरूपं मनोहरं भातु मे हृदये ॥ ५४

घनकुङ्कुमलसिताङ्गं मुक्ताहारादिभूषितं मधुरम् ।
मन्दस्मितमधुरास्यं सूर्येन्दुविलोचनं च बुधमान्यम् ॥ ५५

निबिडकुचकुम्भयुगलं निजदृग्जितहरिणशाबकाक्षियुगम् ।
लीलागतिजितकलभं मधुवैरिमनोहरं च सुरमान्यम् ॥ ५६

दिशि दिशि विस्तृतसंपद्विलासमधुरं च कुन्ददन्तालि ।
मदनजनकं च विष्णोः सर्वस्वं सर्वदानचणम् ॥ ५७

कुलदैवतमस्माकं संविद्रूपं नतार्तिहररूपम् ।
नानादुर्गतिहरणक्षममममरीसेवितं सकलम् ॥ ५८

पञ्चदशवर्णमानं पयोजवक्त्रं पितामहसमर्च्यम् ।
जगदवनजागरूकं हरिहरसंमान्यवैभवं किमपि ॥ ५९

करुणापूरितनयनं परमानन्दप्रदं च परिशुद्धम् ।
आगमगणसंवेद्यं कोशगृहं सर्वसंपदां नित्यम् ॥ ६०

मातस्तावकपादाम्बुजयुगलं सततं स्फुरतु ।
तेनाहं तव रूपं द्रक्ष्याम्यानन्दसिद्धये सकलम् ॥ ६१

देव्या कटाक्षिताः किल पुरुषा वा योषितः पशवः ।
मान्यन्ते सुरसंसदि कल्पककुसुमैः कृतार्हणाः काले ॥ ६२

सुमनोवाञ्छादाने कृतावधानं धनं विष्णोः ।
धिषणाजाड्यादिहरं यद्वीक्षणमामनन्ति जगति बुधाः ॥ ६३

अन्तरपि बहिरुदारं तव रूपं मन्त्रदेवतोपास्यम् ।
जननि स्फुरतु सदा नः संमान्यं श्रेयसे काले ॥ ६४

मुररिपुपुण्यश्रेणीपरिपाकं तावकं रूपम् ।
कमले जननि विशुद्धं दद्याच्छ्रेयो मुहुर्भजताम् ॥ ६५

पुण्यश्रेणी कमला सा जननी भक्तमानसे स्थितिभाक् ।
तेजस्ततिभिर्मोहितभुवना भुवनाधिनाथगृहिणीयम् ॥ ६६

जलनिधिकन्यारूपं हरिमान्यं सर्वसंपदां हेतुः ।
चिरकृतसुकृतविशेषान्नयनयुगे भाति सर्वस्य ॥ ६७

जलनिधितपःफलं यन्मुनिजनहृदयाब्जनित्यकृतनृत्तम् ।
करुणालोलापाङ्गं तत् तेजो भातु निःसमं वदने ॥ ६८

शमितनतदुरितसंघा हरये निजनेत्रकल्पितानङ्गा ।
कृतसुरशात्रवभङ्गा सा देवी मङ्गलैस्तुङ्गा ॥ ६९

निखिलागमसिद्धान्तं हरिशुद्धान्तं सदा नौमि ।
तेनैव सर्वसिद्धिः शास्त्रेषु विनिश्चिता विबुधैः ॥ ७०

कृष्णकृतविविधलीलं तव रूपं मातरादरान्मान्यम् ।
स्फुरतु विलोचनयुगले नित्यं संपत्समृद्ध्यै नः ॥ ७१

करुणाकटाक्षलहरी कामायास्तु प्रकामकृतरक्षा ।
लक्ष्म्या माधवमान्या सत्सुखदाने दिशि ख्याता ॥ ७२

अपवर्गसिद्धये त्वामम्बामम्भोजलोचनां लक्ष्मीम् ।
अवलम्बे हरिदयिते पद्मासनमुखसुरेन्द्रकृतपूजाम् ॥ ७३

तावककटाक्षलहरीं निधेहि मयि देवि कमले त्वम् ।
तेन मनोरथसिद्धिर्भुवि परमे धामनि प्रचुरा ॥ ७४

त्वामादरेण सततं वीक्षेमहि मातरब्जकृतवासाम् ।
विष्णोर्वक्षोनिलयामक्षयसुखसिद्धये लोके ॥ ७५

सा नः सिध्यतु सिद्ध्यै देवानां वाङ्मनोऽतीता ।
हरिगृहिणी हरिणाक्षी पालितलोकत्रया च जननीयम् ॥ ७६

सकलचराचरचिन्मयरूपं यस्या हि देवतोपास्यम् ।
सा ददतु मङ्गलं मे नित्योज्ज्वलमादराज्जननी ॥ ७७

शीतमयूखसहोदरि तां त्वामम्बां हि शीलये नित्यम् ।
निरसितवैरिगणोऽहं हरिचरणन्यस्तरक्षश्च ॥ ७८

दिक्षि विदिक्षु कृतश्रीः सा मे जननी नदीशतनयेयम् ।
हरिणा साकं भजतु प्राकाश्यं हृदि सतां समृद्ध्यै नः ॥ ७९

वारिनिधिवंशसंपद् दिव्या काचिद्धरेर्मान्या ।
अर्चन्ति यां तु मुनयो योगारम्भे तथान्ते च ॥ ८०

धृतसुममधुपक्रीडास्थानायितकेशभारायै ।
नम उक्तिरस्तु मात्रे वाग्जितपीयूषधारायै ॥ ८१

संदेहे सिद्धान्ते वादे वा समरभूमिभागे वा ।
या राजति बहुरूपा सा देवी विष्णुवल्लभा ख्याता ॥ ८२

प्रतिफलतु मे सदा तन्मुनिमानसपेटिकारत्नम् ।
विष्णोर्वक्षोभूषणमादृतनिर्गतिजनावनं तेजः ॥ ८३

बालकुरङ्गविलोचनधाटीरक्षितसुरादि मनुजानाम् ।
नयनयुगासेव्यं तद् भातीह धरातले तेजः ॥ ८४

माधवदृक्साफल्यं भक्तावलिदृश्यकामधेनुकला ।
लक्ष्मीरूपं तेजो विभातु मम मानसे वचसि ॥ ८५

हरिसरसक्रीडार्थं या विधृतानेकरूपिका माता ।
सा गेहभूषणं नः स्फुरतु सदानित्यसंपूज्या ॥ ८६

द्वारवतीपुरभागे मैथिलनगरे च यत्कथासारः ।
सा देवी जलधिसुता विहरणभाङ् मामके मनसि ॥ ८७

जलनिधितपोमहिम्ने देव्यै परमात्मनः श्रियै सततम् ।
भूयांसि नमांसि पुनः सर्वा नः संपदः सन्तु ॥ ८८

परमौषधं हि संसृतिव्याधेर्यत् कीर्तितं निपुणैः ।
तदहं भजामि सततं लक्ष्मीरूपं सदानन्दम् ॥ ८९

दशरथसुतकोदण्डप्रभावसाक्षात्कृते कृतानन्दा ।
सीतारूपा माते जज्ञे यज्ञक्षितौ हि सा सिद्ध्यै ॥ ९०

मुनिजनमानसनिलये कमले ते चरणपङ्कजं शिरसि ।
अवतंसयन्नुदारं विशामि देवैः सुधर्मा वा ॥ ९१

धनमदमेदुरसेवां त्यक्त्वाहं ते पदाम्भोजम् ।
शरणं यामि पुमर्थस्फूर्तिकलायै भृशं दीनः ॥ ९२

न घटय कुत्सितसेवां दुष्टैर्वा संगमं मातः ।
कुरु मां दासं संसृतिपापं च हर शीघ्रम् ॥ ९३

मयि नमति विष्णुकान्ते तवाग्रतस्तापभारार्ते ।
मातः सहसा सुमुखी भव बाले दोषनिलये च ॥ ९४

हन्त कदा वा मातस्तव लोचनसेचनं भवेन्मयि भोः ।
इत्थं प्रातः स्तुवतां त्वमेव रक्षाकरी नियतम् ॥ ९५

संसाररोगशान्तिप्रदमेतल्लोचनं मातः ।
तावत्कमहमुपासे दिव्यौषधमाशु सागरेन्द्रसुते ॥ ९६

संसृतिरोगार्तानां तव नामस्मरणमत्र धरणितले ।
पूजाप्रदक्षिणादिकमार्या मुख्यौषधं वदन्ति किल ॥ ९७

मातर्विना धरण्यां सुकृतानां खण्डमिह जन्तुः ।
ध्यानं वा न हि लभते प्रणतिं वा संपदां जननीम् ॥ ९८

गुरुवरकटाक्षविभवाद् देवि त्वाङ्घ्रिप्रणामधुतपापः ।
तव च हरेर्दासः सन् विशामि देवेश मानितां च सभाम् ॥ ९९

मुरहरनेत्रमहोत्सवतारुण्यश्रीर्निरस्तनतशत्रुः ।
ललितलिकुचाभकुचभरयुगला दृग्विजितहरिणसंदोहा ॥ १००

कारुण्यपूर्णनयना कलिकल्मषहारिणी च सा कमला ।
मुखजितशारदकमला वक्त्राम्भोजे सदा स्फुरतु माता ॥ १०१

तावककटाक्षसेचनविभवां निर्धूतदुरितसंघा हि ।
परमं सुखं लभन्ते परे तु लोके च सूरिभिः सार्धम् ॥ १०२

तव पादपद्मविसृमरकान्तिझरीं मनसि कलयंस्तु ।
निरसितनरकादिभयो विराजते नाकिसदसि सुरवन्द्यः ॥ १०३

हन्त सहस्त्रेष्वथ वा शतेषु सुकृती पुमान् मातः ।
तावकपादपयोरुहवरिवस्यां कलयते सकलम् ॥ १०४

जननि तरङ्गय नयने मयि दीने ते दयास्निग्धे ।
तेन वयं तु कृतार्था नातःपरमस्तिः नः प्रार्थ्यम् ॥ १०५

तावककृपावशादिह नानायोगादिनाशितभया ये ।
तेषां स्मरणमपि द्राक् श्रियावहं नित्यमाकलये ॥ १०६

नैव प्रायश्चित्तं दुरितानां मामकानां हि ।
त्वामेव यामि शरणं तस्माल्लक्ष्मि क्षमाधारे ॥ १०७

मुरवैरिमान्यचरिते मातस्त्वामखिललोकसाम्राज्ये ।
पश्यन्ति दिवि सुरेन्द्रा मुनयस्तत्त्वार्थिनश्च नित्यकलाम् ॥ १०८

स्वीयपदप्राप्त्यै ननु विबुधेशा जलधिकन्यके मातः ।
आराध्य दिव्यकुसुमैस्तव पादाब्जं परं तुष्टाः ॥ १०९

सृष्टिस्थित्यादौ हरिरम्ब तवापाङ्गवीक्षणादरवान् ।
जगदेतदवति काले त्वं च हरिर्नः क्रमात् पितरौ ॥ ११०

राज्यसुखलाभसंपत्प्राप्त्यै क्षितिपाश्च ये च विप्राद्याः ।
गाङ्गजलैरपि कुसुमैर्वरिवस्यां ते क्रमेण कलयन्ति ॥ १११

संत्यक्तकामतदनुजडम्भासूयादयो नराः कमले ।
आराध्य त्वां च हरिं काले चैकासनस्थितां धन्याः ॥ ११२

जननी कदा पुनीते मम लोचनमार्गमादरादेषा ।
ये किल वदन्ति धन्यास्तेषां दर्शनमहं कलये ॥ ११३

करधृतलीलापद्मा पद्मा पद्माक्षगेहिनी नयने ।
सिञ्चति सकलश्रेयःप्राप्त्यै निर्व्याजकारुण्या ॥ ११४

नानाविधविद्यानां लीलासदनं सरोजनिलयेयम् ।
कविकुलवचःपयोजद्युमणिरुचिर्भाति नः पुरतः ॥ ११५

अतसीकुसुमद्युतिभाङ् नाकिगणैर्वन्द्यपादपद्मयुगा ।
सरसिजनिलया सा मे प्रसीदतु क्षिप्रमादरात् सिद्ध्यै ॥ ११६

जगदीशवल्लभे त्वयि विन्यस्तभरः पुमान् सहसा ।
तीर्त्वा नाकिस्थानं विशति परं वैष्णवं सुरैर्मान्यम् ॥ ११७

मातर्ज्ञानविकासं कारय करुणावलोकनैर्मधुरैः ।
तेनाहं धन्यतमो भवेयमार्यावृते सदसि ॥ ११८

हरिवक्षसि मणिदीपप्रकाशवत्यान्या मात्रा ।
नित्यं वयमिह दासाः श्रिया सनाथा मुदा परं नौमः ॥ ११९

विद्रावयतु सरोजासने त्वदीया कटाक्षधाटी नः ।
अज्ञानाङ्कुरमुद्रां पुनरपि संसारभीतिदां सहसा ॥ १२०

तावककटाक्षसूर्योदये मदीयं हृदम्भोजम् ।
भजते विकासमचिरात् तमोविनाशश्च निश्चितो विबुधैः ॥ १२१

लक्ष्मीकटाक्षलहरी लक्ष्मीं पक्ष्मलयति क्रमान्नमताम् ।
पादपयोरुहसेवा परं पदं चित्सुखोल्लासम् ॥ १२२

चिद्रूपा परमा सा कमलेक्षणनायिका मुदे भजताम् ।
यत्प्रणयकोपकाले जगदीशः किंकरो भवति ॥ १२३

कांचन देवी विहरतु मम चित्ते संततं सिद्ध्यै ।
यापत्यं कलशाब्धेरुरगेशयसत्कलत्रं च ॥ १२४

अष्टसु महिषीष्वेका कमला मुख्या हि निर्दिष्टा ।
अनयैव सर्वजगतामुदयादिस्तन्यते काले ॥ १२५

कैवल्यानन्दकलाकन्दमहं संततं वन्दे ।
तत्तु मुकुन्दकलत्रं चिन्तितफलदानदीक्षितं किमपि ॥ १२६

ईक्षे कमलामेनामम्बामम्भोजलोचनां सततम् ।
मन्दस्मितमधुरास्यां नित्यं चाज्ञातकोपमुखदोषाम् ॥ १२७

अङ्कितमाधववक्षःस्थला सरोजेक्षणा च हरिकान्ता ।
कबलयति मानसं मे दयाप्रसारादिभिर्नित्यम् ॥ १२८

भूत्यै मम भवतु द्रागज्ञानध्वंसिनी नमताम् ।
नाथानुरूपरूपा श्रुत्यन्तेड्या दशावतारेषु ॥ १२९

सकलजनरक्षणेषु प्रणिहितनयना त्रिलोकमाता नः ।
पुष्णाति मङ्गलानां निकरं सेवाक्रमेण ॥ १३०

पद्मासनजननी मां पातु मुदा सुन्दरापाङ्गैः ।
सर्वैश्वर्यनिदानं यामाहुर्वैदिका दीप्ताम् ॥ १३१

नानालंकारवती मुनिमानसवासिनी हरेः पत्नी ।
त्रैलोक्यविनुतविभवा मां पायादापदां निचयात् ॥ १३२

विद्रावयतु भयं नः सा कमला विष्णुवल्लभा माता ।
अब्धिः संक्षुभितोऽभूत् यदर्थमार्येण रामेण ॥ १३३

भूयो यदर्थमिन्द्रः सुरतरुकुसुमार्थिना च कृष्णेन ।
हतगर्वोऽजनि युद्धे सा नित्यं श्रेयसे भूयात् ॥ १३४

त्वामाराध्य जना अपि धनहीनाः सौधमध्यतलभाजः ।
नानादेशावनीपकजनस्तुता भान्ति नित्यमेव रमे ॥ १३५

संसृतितापो न भवति पुनरपि यत्पादपङ्कजं नमताम् ।
सा मयि कलितदया स्यादम्बा विष्णोः कलत्रमनुरूपम् ॥ १३६

जननीकटाक्षभाजामिह मर्त्यानां सुरास्तु किंकरताम् ।
रिपवो गिरितटवासं भजन्ति वेश्मानि सिद्धयः सर्वाः ॥ १३७

स्मरणाद्वा भजनाद्वा यस्याः पादाम्बुजस्य भुवि धन्याः ।
हन्त रमन्ते स्तम्बेरमनिवहावृतगृहाङ्गणे मनुजाः ॥ १३८

चिरकृतसुकृतनिषेव्या सा देवी विष्णुवल्लभा ख्याता ।
यस्याः प्रसादभूम्ना जाताः पश्वादयो वदान्या हि ॥ १३९

अम्ब मधुरान् कटाक्षान् तापहरान् विकिर मयि कृपाजलधे ।
ये विन्यस्ताः करिवरमारुतिमुखभक्तवर्येषु ॥ १४०

अमृतलहरीव मधुरा जलधररुचिरा नतार्तिहरशीला ।
सर्वश्रेयोदात्री काचिद् देवी सदा विभातु हृदि ॥ १४१

गीताचार्यपुरन्ध्री त्वदीयनामप्रभावकलनाद्यैः ।
यमभयवार्ता दूरे हरिसांनिध्यं कुतो न स्यात् ॥ १४२

जलनिधितनये कान्ते विष्णोरुष्णांशुचन्द्रनयने ते ।
चतुराननादयस्तु ख्याता बालाः श्रुतौ चोक्ताः ॥ १४३

मनसिजवैरं गात्रं वाणी सौधारसी च यद्व्रजताम् ।
श्लाध्या संपत् सज्जनसमागमश्चाशु सिध्यन्ति ॥ १४४

सफलयतु नेत्रयुगलं हतनतदुरिता च सा परा देवी ।
जलनिधिकन्या मान्या पत्यवतारानुकूलनिजचरिता ॥ १४५

नित्यं स्मरामि देवीं नमतां सर्वार्थदायिनीं कमलाम् ।
यामाहुर्भवनिगलध्वंसनदीक्षां च ॥ १४६

सकलजगदघनिवारणसंकल्पां मधुजितो दयिताम् ।
जीवातुमेव कलये मोक्षार्थिजनस्य भूमिसुताम् ॥ १४७

मन्दानामपि दयया तमोनिरासं वितन्वन्ती ।
सर्वत्र भाति कमला तनुरिव विष्णोर्निरस्ताघा ॥ १४८

बालमरालीगीत्यै सुरपुरकन्यादिमहितकलगीत्यै ।
विरचितनानानीत्यै चेतो मे स्पृहयते बहुलकीर्त्यै ॥ १४९

अभिलषितदानकुशला वाग्देवीवन्दिता च सा कमला ।
नित्यं मानसपद्मे संचारं कलयते मुहुः कुतुकात् ॥ १५०

मुरमथननयनपङ्कजविलासकलिका सुरेशमुखसेव्या ।
भूतमयी सावित्री गयत्री सर्वदेवता जयति ॥ १५१

सा हि परा विद्या मे लक्ष्मीरक्षोभणीयकीर्तिकला ।
हृद्यां विद्यां दयादद्य श्रेयःपरंपरासिद्ध्यै ॥ १५२

कामजननी हि लक्ष्मीः नानालीलादिभिर्निजं नाथम् ।
मोहयति विष्णुमचिरात् प्रकृतीनां क्षेमसिद्ध्यर्थम् ॥ १५३

मनसिजसाम्राज्यकलानिदानमार्याभिवन्दितं किमपि ।
लक्ष्मीरूपं तेजो विलसति मम मनसि विष्णुसंक्रान्तम् ॥ १५४

विष्णुमनोरथपात्रं संतप्तस्वर्णकाम्यनिजगात्रम् ।
आश्रितजलनिधिगोत्रं रक्षितनतबाहुजच्छात्रम् ॥ १५५

कविकुलजिह्वालोलं मुरमर्दनकलितरम्यबहुलीलम् ।
निरसितनतदुष्कालं वन्दे तेजः सदालिनुतशीलम् ॥ १५६

आदिमपुरुषपुरन्ध्रीमम्बामम्भोजलोचनां वन्दे ।
यां नत्वा गततापास्त्यक्त्वा देहं विशन्ति परमपदम् ॥ १५७

लक्ष्म्या हरिरपि भाति प्रकृतिक्षेमाय दीक्षितायासौ ।
मम लोचनयोः पुरतो लसतु गभीरं क्रियासिद्ध्यै ॥ १५८

जननि कदा वा नेष्याम्यहमारादर्चितत्वदीयपदः ।
निमिषमिव हन्त दिवसन् दृष्ट्वा त्वामादरेण कल्याणीम् ॥ १५९

संपूर्णयौवनोज्ज्वलदेहां यां वीक्ष्य शौरिरपि ।
कुसुमशरविद्धचेताः किंकरभावं स्वयं प्राप्तः ॥ १६०

अनुनयशीलस्तदनु प्रणयक्रोधादिना भीतः ।
आदिमपुरुषः सोऽयं सा लक्ष्मीर्न श्रियै भवतु ॥ १६१

मणिकुण्डललसितास्यं कृपाकरं किमपि कुङ्कुमच्छायम् ।
हरिणा कृतसंचारं तेजो मे भातु सर्वदा सिद्ध्यै ॥ १६२

साम्राज्यमङ्गलश्रीः श्रीरेषा पुष्कराक्षस्य ।
गन्धर्वकन्यकाद्यैर्गङ्गातीरेषु गीतकीर्तिर्हि ॥ १६३

कविताभाग्यविधात्री परिमलसंक्रान्तमधुपगणकेशा ।
मम नयनयोः कदा वा सा देवी कलितसंनिधानकला ॥ १६४

कीर्तिः स्वयं वृणीते वाग्देवी चापि विजयलक्ष्मीश्च ।
तं नरमचिराल्लोके यो लक्ष्मीपादभक्तस्तु ॥ १६५

सन्मित्रं पाण्डित्यं सद्दाराः सत्सुताद्याश्च ।
जायन्ते तस्य भुवि श्रीभक्तो यश्च निर्दिष्टः ॥ १६६

परमाचार्यैर्विनुतां तामम्बामादरान्नौमि ।
परमैश्वर्यं विष्णोरपि या वेदेषु निर्दिष्टा ॥ १६७

कविकुलसूक्तिश्रेणीश्रवणानन्दोल्लसद्वतंससुमा ।
सा देवी मम हृदये कृतसांनिध्या विराजते परमा ॥ १६८

तापार्तास्तु तटाकं यथा भजन्ते रमां देवीम् ।
संसृतितप्ताः सर्वे यान्ति हि शरणं शरण्यां ताम् ॥ १६९

सर्वज्ञत्वं श्लाध्यं धराधिपत्यं रमे देवि ।
यद्यत् प्रार्थ्यं दयया तद् दिश मोक्षं च मे जननि ॥ १७०

विद्युतमचञ्चलां त्वां कृष्णे मेघे पयोधिवरकन्ये ।
नित्यमवैमि श्रेयःसिध्य मातः प्रसन्ने नः ॥ १७१

त्वामम्ब संततरुचिं कृष्णो मेघः समासाद्य ।
सद्वर्त्मनि वर्षति किल काङ्क्षाधिकमादरेण वार्धिसुते ॥ १७२

अम्ब त्वमेव काले मुकुन्दमपि दर्शयन्तीह ।
श्रेयःसिद्ध्यै नमतां भासि हृदि श्रुतिशिरःसु सल्लोके ॥ १७३

विनमदमरेशसुदतीकचसुममकरन्दधारया स्निग्धम् ।
तव पादपद्ममेतत् कदा नु मम मूर्ध्नि भूषणं जननि ॥ १७४

अपवर्गसौख्यदे ते दयाप्रसारः कथं वर्ण्यः ।
यामवलम्ब्य हि यष्टिं न पतति संसारपङ्किले मार्गे ॥ १७५

सूक्ष्मात् सूक्ष्मतरं ते रूपं पश्यन्ति योगिनो हृदये ।
तां त्वामहं कदा वा द्रक्ष्येऽलंकारमण्डितां मातः ॥ १७६

चिरतरतपसा क्लिष्टे योगिहृदि स्थानभाग् रमा देवी ।
दर्शनमचिराद् दयया ददाति योगादिहीनानाम् ॥ १७७

तीरं संसृतिजलधेः पूरं कमलाक्षलोचनप्रीतेः ।
सारं निगमान्तानां दूरं दुर्जनततेर्हि तत्तेजः ॥ १७८

लक्ष्मीरूपं तेजो ममाविरस्तु श्रियै नित्यम् ।
यन्नित्यधर्मदारान् विष्णोरमितौजसः प्राहुः ॥ १७९

जलधिसुते त्वं जननी स वासुदेवः पिता च नः कथितः ।
शरणं युवांप्रपन्ना नातो दुर्गतिपरिस्फूर्तिः ॥ १८०

हरिनीलरत्नभासा प्रकशितात्मा समुद्रवरकन्या ।
मङ्गलमातनुतेयं कटाक्षकलिकाप्रसारैस्तु ॥ १८१

मच्चित्तमत्तवारणबन्धनमधुना त्वदीयपादयुगे ।
कलयामि रमे मातर्मा रक्ष क्षिप्रमेव संसृतितः ॥ १८२

मोचय संसृतिबन्धं कटाक्षकलिकाङ्कुरै रमे मातः ।
नातः परमर्थ्यमिह क्षमातले त्वं दयामूर्तिः ॥ १८३

मञ्जुलकवितासंततिबीजाङ्कुरदायिसारसालोका ।
जननि तवापाङ्गश्रीः जयति जगत्त्राणकलितदीक्षेयम् ॥ १८४

अम्ब तवापाङ्गश्रीरपाङ्गकेलीशतानि जनयन्ती ।
मुरहन्तुहृदि जयति व्रीडामदमोहकामसारकरी ॥ १८५

बद्धमपि चित्तमेतद् यमनियमाद्यैः परिष्कारैः ।
धावति बलाद् रमे तव पादाब्जं यामि शरणमहम् ॥ १८६

मत्तगजमान्यगमना मधुरालापा च मान्यचरिता सा ।
मन्दस्मेरमुखाब्जा कमला मे हृदयसारसे लसतु ॥ १८७

शास्त्रस्मरणविहीनं पापिनमेनं जनं रमा देवी ।
दयया रक्षति काले तस्यास्तेन प्रथा महती ॥ १८८

मुखविजितचन्द्रमण्डलमिदमम्भोरुहविलोचनं तेजः ।
ध्याने जपे च सुदृशां चकास्ति हृदये कवीश्वराणां च ॥ १८९

अम्ब विवेकविदूं जनमेनं शिशिरलोचनप्रसरैः ।
शिशिरय कृपया देवि त्वमेव माता हि लोकस्य ॥ १९०

कोपदुपेक्षसे यदि मातर्मे रक्षकः कः स्यात् ।
मयि दीने को लाभस्तव तु दयायाः प्रसारिण्याः ॥ १९१

भवचण्डकिरणतप्तः श्रान्तोऽहं ज्ञानवारिदूरस्थः ।
शिशिरामङ्घ्रिच्छायां तव मातर्यामि शरणमारात्तु ॥ १९२

मातरशोकोल्लासं प्रकटय तव कोमलकटाक्षैः ।
यैर्दीना नरपतयः कलिता वारणशतावृते गेहे ॥ १९३

जयति रमे तव महती कृपाझरी सर्वसंमान्या ।
क्षेमंकरी यदेषा प्रतिकल्पं सर्वजगतां च ॥ १९४

अज्ञानकूपकुहरे पतितं मां पाहि कमले त्वम् ।
नगरे वा ग्रामे वा वनमध्ये दिक्षु रक्षिणी त्वमसि ॥ १९५

तव चरणौ शरणमिति ब्रुवन्नहं मातरब्धितनये त्वम् ।
हरिणा सहिता दयया प्राह्वविलम्बेन दीनं माम् ॥ १९६

परिसरनतविबुधालीकिरीटमणिकान्तिवल्लरीविसरैः ।
कृतनीराजनविधि ते मम तु शिरोभूषणं हि पदयुगलम् ॥ १९७

मम हृदयपङ्कजवनीविकासहेतौ दिनाधिपायेताम् ।
तव तु कटाक्षप्रसरः दीपायेतां तमोनिराकरणे ॥ १९८

यावच्छरणं याति क्षितितनये त्वां हि जन्तुरिह मूढः ।
तावत् तस्य तु रसनाङ्गणे तु वाणी समाकलितनृत्ता ॥ १९९

पङ्कजनिलये तावकचरणं शरणं समाकलये ।
तेन हि सर्वकृतानां भविष्यतां हानिरेव दुरितानाम् ॥ २००

श्रुत्यन्तसेवितं ते चरणसरोजं प्रणम्य किल जन्तुः ।
छत्रोल्लसितशिराः सन् वनीपकान् दानवारिणा सिञ्चन् ॥ २०१

विष्वक्सेनमुखाद्यैः सेवितमम्ब त्वदीयपादयुगम् ।
अवतंसयन्ति सन्तः कलितापप्रशमनायास्तु ॥ २०२

दुग्धोदधितनये त्वां दिशागजेन्द्राः सुवर्णघटतोयैः ।
मणिमण्टपमध्यतले समभ्यषिञ्चन् हरिप्रीत्यै ॥ २०३

दिग्गजपुष्पकरकुम्भैरभिषिक्तां त्वां हरिः प्रीत्या ।
उदवहदारान्मुनिगणमध्ये सर्वश्रियो मूलम् ॥ २०४

जातपराक्रमकलिका दिशि दिशि किंनरसुगीतनिजयशसः ।
धन्या भान्ति हि मनुजाः यद्दीक्षालववविशेषतः काले ॥ २०५

नमदमरीकचभरसुममरन्दधाराभिषिक्तं ते ।
पदकमलयुगलमेतच्छ्रेयःस्फूर्त्यै सदा भवतु ॥ २०६

रागद्वेषादिहतं मामव कमले हरेः कान्ते ।
दर्शय दयया काले ह्यपवर्गस्थानमार्गं च ॥ २०७

न हि जाने वर्णयितुं परमे स्थने त्वदीयविभवमहम् ।
मुनयश्च सुरा वेदा यतो निवृत्ताः क्षमातनये ॥ २०८

मनुजाः कटाक्षिताः किल तथाम्बया मेदिनीपुत्र्या ।
सत्सुतकलत्रसहिताः सुरभिं कालेन निर्विशान्ति मुदा ॥ २०९

जलधीशकन्यका सा लसतु पुरोऽस्माकमादरकृतश्रीः ।
यत्प्रणमनाज्जनानां कवितोन्मेषः सदीडिते भाति ॥ २१०

दूरिकरोतु दुरितं त्वद्भक्तिर्मामकं कमले ।
अहमपि सुरेशसेव्ये तव सदसि विशामि कीर्तिगानपरः ॥ २११

परमज्ञानविधात्री तव पादपयोजभक्तिरस्माकम् ।
किं वाशास्यमतोऽन्यत् समुद्रतनये हरेजाये ॥ २१२

अम्ब कदा वा लप्स्ये मदीयपापापनोदाय ।
तव पादकमलसेवामम्बुजभवाद्यैस्तु संप्रार्थ्याम् ॥ २१३

मन्दानामपि मञ्जुलकवित्वरसदायिनी जननी ।
कापि करुणामयी सा लसतु पुरस्तात् सदास्माकम् ॥ २१४

सकलकविलोकविनुते कमले कमलाक्षि वल्लभे विष्णोः ।
त्वन्नामानि हि कलये वने जले शत्रुपीडायाम् ॥ २१५

दिवि वा भुवि दिक्षु जले वह्नौ वा सर्वतः कमले ।
जन्तूनां किल रक्षा त्वदधीना कीर्त्यते विबुधैः ॥ २१६

कुशलविधये तदस्तु त्रिविक्रमासेव्यरम्यनिजकेलि ।
कबलितपदनतदैन्यं तरुणाम्बुजलोचनं तेजः ॥ २१७

जननी सुवर्णवृष्टिप्रदायिनी भाति विष्णुवक्षःस्था ।
कमला कलितक्षेमा प्रकृतीनां शीतलापाङ्गैः ॥ २१८

जगतामादिमजननी लसति कवेरात्मजापुलिने ।
क्षेत्रेषूत्तमजुष्टेष्वयोनिजा लोकरक्षायै ॥ २१९

कुचशोभाजितविष्णुः कुङ्कुमपङ्काङ्किता कमला ।
काञ्च्यां राजति काञ्चीमणिगणनीराजिताङ्घ्रियुगा ॥ २२०

मन्दारकुसुममदहरमन्दस्मितमधुरवदनपङ्करुहा ।
हृद्यतमनित्ययौवनमण्डितगात्री विराजते कमला ॥ २२१

कंसरिपुगेहिनी सा हंसगतिर्हंसमान्यनिजचरिता ।
संसारतापहानिं कलयतु काले रमास्माकम् ॥ २२२

मनसिजजननी जननी चास्माकमिहादरात् काले ।
शीतललोलापाङ्गैस्तरङ्गयति श्रेयसां सरिणम् ॥ २२३

तव मन्दहासकलिकां भजे भुजङ्गे शयानं तम् ।
या कलयति गतकोपं बालानां नः कृतापराधानाम् ॥ २२४

सा साधयेदभीष्टं कमला श्रीर्विष्णुवक्षःस्था ।
यस्याः पदविन्यासः श्रुतिमौलिषु तन्यते महालक्ष्म्याः ॥ २२५

शान्तिरसनित्यशेवधिमम्बां सेवे मनोरथावाप्त्यै ।
यामाराध्य सुरेशाः स्वपदं प्रापुर्हि तादृक्षम् ॥ २२६

धातुरपि वेदवचसां दूरे यत्स्थानमामनन्ति बुधाः ।
सास्तु मुदे श्रीरेषा मुरमर्दनसत्कलत्रममितौजः ॥ २२७

भवदुःखराशिजलधेर्हठात् तरित्रीं परं विद्मः ।
तामम्बां कमलस्थां मुरारिवक्षोमणिप्रदीपां च ॥ २२८

मुनिसार्वभौमवर्णितमहाचरित्रं हरेः कलत्रं तत् ।
पथि मङ्गलाय भवतु प्रस्थानजुषां कृपाधारम् ॥ २२९

खण्डितवैरिगणेयं मण्डितभक्ता सुताद्यैश्च ।
भासुरकीर्तिर्जयति क्षोणीसुरवन्द्यचरणाब्जा ॥ २३०

नतपालिनि मां पाहि त्रिजगद्वन्द्ये निधेहि मयि दयया ।
तावककटाक्षलहरीः शक्तिमये सकलसिद्धीनाम् ॥ २३१

भवसागरं तितीर्षुस्तव चरणाब्जं महासेयुम् ।
मातः कदा नु लप्स्ये घनतापोम्र्यादिपीडितो दीनः ॥ २३२

कविवाग्वासन्तीनां वसन्तलक्ष्मीर्मुरारिदयिता नः ।
परमां मुदं विधत्ते काले काले महाभूत्यै ॥ २३३

सुरहरपरतन्त्रं तद् गततन्द्रं वस्तु निस्तुलमुपासे ।
तेनैवाहं धन्यो मद्दृश्या निरसितात्मतापभराः ॥ २३४

तृष्णां शमयति देवी राघवदयिता नतालिसुरवल्ली ।
इत्यार्यवचो धैर्यं जनयति काले धरापुत्रि ॥ २३५

रघुपतिदयिते मातः काकासुररक्षणादिना लोके ।
तावककरुणामहिमा प्रथितः किल भूतिदायी नः ॥ २३६

प्रचुरतदुरितपालीसमावृतानां कलौ हि तन्मानाम् ।
तावकदया हि मातः शरणं वरमिति सतां गणः स्तौति ॥ २३७

अत्यन्तशीतलां तां कटाक्षधाटीमुपासेऽहम् ।
तेन मम त्रिदशानां न कोऽपि भेदो धरातनये ॥ २३८

यैः सेवा संकलिता तव पादाब्जे धरातनये ।
तेषामज्ञानझरी याति हि विलयं क्षणेनैव ॥ २३९

ज्ञानारविन्दविलसनमचिरादस्य स्तुतौ हि कविवर्याः ।
संपद् दिव्या च तथा विबुधावलिमाननीयात्र ॥ २४०

मातस्तव पादाब्जं यस्य ललाटे कृतोरुनिजकान्ति ।
तत्पादपद्ममचिराद् विमानगा देवता वहति ॥ २४१

आज्ञावशेन देव्या लसन्ति दिवि देवतामान्याः ।
इन्द्राद्याः स च धाता दिक्पालाश्चापि गन्धर्वाः ॥ २४२

कैवल्यानन्दकलादात्रीं कमलामहर्निशं नौमि ।
तेनैव जन्म सफलं तीर्थादिनिषेवणाद्यच्च ॥ २४३

यच्च हरिपादपङ्केरुहपरिचरणादिना लोके ।
तत् सर्वमाशु घटयति सहसा मन्दस्य मेमाता ॥ २४४

नानाश्रुत्यन्तकलापरिमलपरिवाहवासितं मातः ।
तव चरणकमलयुगलं ममावतंसः क्षणं भातु ॥ २४५

नतदेवनगरनारीधम्मिल्ललसत्सुमालिकृतनादाः ।
प्रातर्मुरजविलासं कलयन्ति भृशं तवाग्रतो भृङ्गाः ॥ २४६

पापप्रशमनदीक्षाकलाधुरीणाः पयोजनिलये ते ।
मां च पवित्रीकुर्युः पादपरागाः कृपावशतः ॥ २४७

हन्त कदा वा लप्स्ये तवाङ्घ्रिशुश्रूषणासक्तिम् ।
सहजानन्दं तेन हि पदं क्रमात् प्राप्यमादिष्टम् ॥ २४८

नलिनीविलासरुचिरां मयि देवि त्वत्कटाक्षलहरीं हि ।
काले निधेहि दयया स्फीता ते कीर्तिरादृता सर्वैः ॥ २४९

विनिहतदुरितस्तोमा कापि मदीये हृदम्भोजे ।
लसतु परदेवताख्या माधवनेत्रप्रियंकरी कलिका ॥ २५०

पञ्चायुधगुरुमन्त्रं कलनूपुरनिनदमादरात् कमले ।
कलयति रमाधवगृहं यातुं काले त्वयि प्रवृत्तायाम् ॥ २५१

नतनाकिलोकवनिताललाटसिन्दूरशोणकान्तिभृतोः ।
कलये नमांसि कमले तव पादपयोजयोर्नित्यम् ॥ २५२

कमलसुषुमानिवासस्थानकटाक्षं चिराय कृतरक्षम् ।
रक्षोगणभीतिकरं तेजो भाति प्रकाममिह मनसि ॥ २५३

ज्योत्स्नेव शिशिरपाता कटाक्षधाटी त्वदीया हि ।
अम्ब मुकुन्द कुरुते ॥ २५४

तापहररसविवर्षंअधृतकुतुका कापि नीलनलिनरुचिः ।
कादम्बिनी पुरस्तदास्तां नः संततं जननी ॥ २५५

सफलयतु नेत्रयुगलं मामकमेतत् त्वदीयरूपमहो ।
यत् कमलनेत्रसुचरितपचेलिमं वैदिकी श्रुतिर्ब्रूते ॥ २५६

माधवनेत्रपयोजामृतलहरी भाति तावकं रूपम् ।
अम्ब युवामाद्यौ नः पितरौ वने सुखावाप्त्यै ॥ २५७

सरसकवितादिसंपद्विलसनमाराद्शान्ति कविवर्याः ।
यत्प्रीणनेन सा मे भवतु विभूत्यै हि सा कमला ॥ २५८

मनसिजजयादिकार्यं यदपाङ्गलवान्नृणां भवति ।
तत्पदमानन्दकलं सेव्यं च भजे रमां जननीम् ॥ २५९

शिथिलततमःसमूहा भक्तानां सा रमा देवी ।
जनयति धैर्यं च हरेः काले या सर्वदा सेव्या ॥ २६०

यद्भ्रूविलासवशतः शक्तः सृष्ट्यादिकं कर्तुम् ।
हरिरपि लोके ख्यातः सा नः शरणं जगन्माता ॥ २६१

नयनयुगलीं कदा मे सिञ्चति एव्याः परं रूपम् ।
यद्ब्रजनान्न हि लोके दृष्टं श्लाध्यं परं वस्तु ॥ २६२

सुचरितफलं त्वदीयं रूपं नः कलितभक्तीनाम् ।
अत एव मामकानां पापानां विरतिरूर्जिता कमले ॥ २६३

सुकृतिविभवादुपास्या कमला सा सर्वकल्याणा ।
हरिवक्षसि कृतवासा रक्षति लोकानहोरात्रम् ॥ २६४

संविद्रूपा हि हरेः कुटुम्बिनी भाति भक्तहृदयेषु ।
सर्वश्रेयःप्राप्त्यै यां विदुरार्या रमां कमलाम् ॥ २६५

विषयलहरीप्रशान्त्यै कमलापादाम्बुजं नौमि ।
पूर्वं शुकादिसुधियो यद्ध्यानाद् गलितशत्रुभयाः ॥ २६६

ललितगमनं त्वदीयं कलनूपुरनादपूरितं मातः ।
नौमि पदाम्बुजयुगलं भवतापनिरासनायाद्य ॥ २६७

विरलीकरोति तापं कमलाया मन्दहासझरी ।
यत्सेवनेषु समुदितकौतुकरसनिर्भरो हरिर्जयति ॥ २६८

प्रतिफलतु संततं मे पुरतोमातस्त्वदीयरूपमिदम् ।
यद्दर्शनरसभूम्ना हरिरपि नानास्वरूपभाक् काले ॥ २६९

अम्ब तव चरणसेवां संततमहमादरात् कलये ।
तेन मम जन्म सफलं त्रिदशानामिव मुनीन्द्राणाम् ॥ २७०

दुर्वारगर्वदुर्मतिदुरर्थनिरसनकलानिपुणाः ।
तव चरणसेवयैव हि कमले मातर्बुधा जगति ॥ २७१

आनदमेति मातस्तव नामोच्चारणेन सिन्धुभवे ।
संप्राप्त्वद्रूपं मम मानसमात्तयोगकलम् ॥ २७२

तव दृष्टिपातविभवात् सर्वे लोके विधूततापभराः ।
यान्ति मुदा त्रिदशैः सह विभानमारुह्य मातरहो ॥ २७३

को वा न श्रयति बुधः श्रेयोऽर्थी तामिमां कमलाम् ।
यां पन्नगारिवाहनसद्धर्मिणीमर्चयन्ति सुरनाथाः ॥ २७४

तामरविन्दनिवासामम्बां शरणार्थिनां कलितरक्षाम् ।
बहुरूपेष्वघनिचयेष्वपि निश्चित्यात्मनो धैर्यम् ॥ २७५

करुणाप्रवाहझर्या गतपङ्क भूतलं मातः ।
सत्त्वाङ्कुरादिलसितं जयति पयोराशिककन्यके कमले ॥ २७६

विधिशिववासवमुख्यैर्वन्द्यपदाब्जे नमस्तुभ्यम् ।
मातर्विष्णोर्दयिते सर्वज्ञत्वं च मे कलय ॥ २७७

परदेवते प्रसीद प्रसीद हरिवल्लभे मातः ।
त्वामाहुः श्रुतयः किल कल्याणगुणाकरां नित्याम् ॥ २७८

क्षन्तव्यमम्ब मामकमघराशिं क्षपय वीक्षणतः ।
सत्त्वोन्मेषं देहि प्रिये हरेर्दासमपि कुरु माम् ॥ २७९

वाञ्छितसिद्धिर्न स्याद् यदि पादाब्जे कृतप्रणामानाम् ।
हानिस्त्वदीययशसामिति केचिद्धैर्यवन्तश्च ॥ २८०

सदसदनुग्रहदक्षां त्वां मातः संततं नौमि ।
ग्रहपीडा नैव भवेद्यमपीडा दूतः काले ॥ २८१

विद्याः कलाश्च काले कृपया कलय प्रसीदाशु ।
मातस्त्वमेव जगतां सर्वेषां रक्षणंत्वया क्रियते ॥ २८२

उच्छेष्वपि नीचेषु प्रकाशते तुल्यमेव तव रूपम् ।
एतद् दृष्ट्वा धैर्यं घनागसोऽप्यम्ब जायते ननु मे ॥ २८३

का शङ्का तव वैभवजालं वक्तुं दिगन्तरे मातः ।
वरहारालंकारां सेवन्ते त्वां हरित्पतयः ॥ २८४

कमलायाश्च हरेरपि संदृष्यं दिव्यदांपत्यम् ।
तावेव नः पती किल जन्मान्तरपुण्यपरिपाकात् ॥ २८५

सर्वासामुपनिषदां विद्यानां त्वंपरं स्थानम् ।
अल्पधियो वयमेते त्वत्स्तोत्रे भोः कथं शक्ताः ॥ २८६

साष्टाङ्गप्रणतिरियं प्रकल्पिता मातरद्य तव चरणे ।
तेनाहं हि कृतार्थः किं प्रार्थ्यं वस्त्वतः कमले ॥ २८७

स्तोत्रमिदं हि मया ते चरणाम्भोजे समर्पितं भक्त्या ।
तव च गुरोरपि वीक्षा तत्र निदानं परं नान्यत् ॥ २८८

देहान्ते ननु मातर्मोक्षं त्रिदशैः समं देहि ।
अहमपि साम पठन् सन् त्वां च हरिं यामि शरणार्थी ॥ २८९

शुकवाणीमिव मातर्निरर्थकां मद्वचोभङ्गीम् ।
आराच्छृणोषि दयया तदेव चोत्तमपदव्यक्त्यै ॥ २९०

विद्यां कलां वरिष्ठां अम्ब त्वां संततं वन्दे ।
या व्याकरोषि काले विद्वद्भिर्वेदतत्त्वादि ॥ २९१

वैदुष्यं वाण्याः सत्संपज्झर्यो यदीयवीक्षणतः ।
सिध्यन्त्यपि देवानां सा नः शरणं रमा देवी ॥ २९२

विपुलं श्रियोविलासं श्रद्धां भक्त्यादिकं देहि ।
अम्ब प्रसीद काले तव पादाब्जैकसेविनामिह नः ॥ २९३

केचित् प्राञ्चः कमलां प्राप्य हि शरणं विपत्काले ।
झटिति विधूनिततापाः सा मे देवी प्रसन्नास्तु ॥ २९४

मरकतकान्तिमनोहरमूर्तिः सैषा रमा देवी ।
पाति सकलानि काले जगन्ति करुणावलोकाद्यैः ॥ २९५

भागीरथीव वाणी तव नुतिरूपा विराजते परमा ।
इह मातर्यद्भजनं सर्वेषां सर्वसंपदां हेतुः ॥ २९६

कलशपयोदधितनये हरिप्रिये लक्ष्मि मातरम्बेति ।
तव नामानि जपन् सन् त्वद्दासोऽहं तु मुक्तये सिद्धः ॥ २९७

निखिलचराचररक्षां वितन्वती विष्णुवल्लभा कमला ।
मम कुलदैवतमेषा जयति सदाराध्यमान्यपादकमला ॥ २९८

सर्वजन्नुतविभवे संततमपि वाञ्छितप्रदे देवि ।
अम्ब त्वमेव शरणं तेनाहं प्राप्तसर्वकार्यार्थः ॥ २९९

कमले कथं नु वर्ण्यस्तव महिमा निगममौलिगणवेद्यः ।
इति निश्चित्य पदाब्जं तव वन्दे मोक्षकामोऽहम् ॥ ३००

त्वामम्ब बालिशोऽहं त्वचमत्कारैर्गिरां गुम्भैः ।
अयथायथक्रमं हि स्तुवन्नपि प्राप्तजन्मसाफल्यः ॥ ३०१

इति श्री कमला त्रिशती समाप्ता ।

*****

Śrī Kamalātmikā Sahasranāma Stotram

Dhyānam

Kāntyā Kāmchanasannibhām Himagiriprakhyaiśchaturbhirgajaiḥ |
Hastokśipta Hiranmayāmruta Ghatairāsichyamānām Śriyam ||
Bibhrānāmvaramabja Yugmamabhayam Hastaiḥ Kireetojvalām |
Kśou Mābadhdanidambhabimba Lasitām Vanderavindastitām ||

Oṃ Tāmāhvayāmi Subhagāṃ Lakṣmīṃ Trailokyapūjitām |
Ehyehi Devi Padmākṣi Padmākarakṛtālaye || 1

Āgacchāgaccha Varade Paśya Māṃ Svena Cakṣuṣā |
Āyāhyāyāhi Dharmārthakāmamokṣamaye Śubhe || 2

Evaṃvidhaiḥ Stutipadaiḥ Satyaiḥ Satyārthasaṃstutā |
Kanīyasī Mahābhāgā Candreṇa Paramātmanā || 3

Niśākaraśca Sā Devī Bhrātarau Dvau Payonidheḥ |
Utpannamātrau Tāvāstāṃ Śivakeśavasaṃśritau || 4

Sanatkumārastamṛṣiṃ Samābhāṣya Purātanam |
Proktavānitihāsaṃ Tu Lakṣmyāḥ Stotramanuttamam || 5

Athedṛśānmahāghorād Dāridryānnarakātkatham |
Muktirbhavati Loke'smin Dāridryaṃ Yāti Bhasmatām || 6

Sanatkumāra Uvāca -

Pūrvaṃ Kṛtayuge Brahmā Bhagavān Sarvalokakṛt |
Sṛṣṭiṃ Nānāvidhāṃ Kṛtvā Paścācci Ntāmupeyivān || 7

Kimāhārāḥ Prajāstvetāḥ Sambhaviṣyanti Bhūtale |
Tathaiva Cāsāṃ Dāridryātkathamuttaraṇaṃ Bhavet || 8

Dāridryānmaraṇaṃ Śreyastivati Sañcintya Cetasi |
Kṣīrodasyottare Kūle Jagāma Kamalodbhavaḥ || 9

Tatra Tīvraṃ Tapastaptvā Kadācitparameśvaram |
Dadarśa Puṇḍarīkākṣaṃ Vāsudevaṃ Jagadgurum || 10

Sarvajñaṃ Sarvaśaktīnāṃ Sarvāvāsaṃ Sanātanam |
Sarveśvaraṃ Vāsudevaṃ Viṣṇuṃ Lakṣmīpatiṃ Prabhum || 11

Somakoṭipratīkāśaṃ Kṣīroda Vimale Jale |
Anantabhogaśayanaṃ Viśrāntaṃ Śrīniketanam || 12

Koṭisūryapratīkāśaṃ Mahāyogeśvareśvaram |
Yoganidrārataṃ Śrīśaṃ Sarvāvāsaṃ Sureśvaram || 13

Jagadutpattisaṃhārasthitikāraṇakāraṇam |
Lakṣmyādi Śaktikaraṇajātamaṇḍalamaṇḍitam || 14

Āyudhairdehavadbhiśca Cakrādyaiḥ Parivāritam |
Durnirīkṣyaṃ Suraiḥ Siddhaḥ Mahāyoniśatairapi || 15

Ādhāraṃ Sarvaśaktīnāṃ Paraṃ Tejaḥ Sudussaham |
Prabuddha Devamīśānaṃ Dṛṣṭvā Kamalasambhavaḥ || 16

Śirasyañjalimādhāya Stotraṃ Pūrvamuvāca Ha |
Manovāñchitasiddhi Tvaṃ Pūrayasva Maheśvara || 17

Jitaṃ Te Puṇḍarīkṣa Namaste Viśvabhāvana |
Namaste'stu Hṛṣīkeśa Mahāpuruṣapūrvaja || 18

Sarveśvara Jayānanda Sarvāvāsa Parātpara |
Prasīda Mama Bhaktasya Chindhi Sandehajaṃ Tamaḥ || 19

Evaṃ Stutaḥ Sa Bhagavān Brahma Ṇā'vyaktajanmanā |
Prasādābhimukhaḥ Prāha Harirviśrāntalocanaḥ || 20

Śrī Bhagavānuvāca -

Hiraṇyagarbha Tuṣṭo'smi Brūhi Yatte'bhivāñchitam |
Tadvakṣyāmi Na Sandeho Bhakto'si Mama Suvrata || 21

Keśavādvacanaṃ Śrutvā Karuṇāviṣṭacetanaḥ |

Pratyuvāca Mahābuddhirbhagavantaṃ Janārdanam ‖ 22

Caturvidhaṃ Bhavasyāsya Bhūtasargasya Keśava |

Paritrāṇāya Me Brūhi Rahasyaṃ Paramādbhutam ‖ 23

Dāridryaśamanaṃ Dhanyaṃ Manojñaṃ Pāvanaṃ Param |

Sarveśvara Mahābuddha Svarūpaṃ Bhairavaṃ Mahat ‖ 24

Śriyaḥ Sarvātiśāyinyāstathā Jñānaṃ Ca Śāśvatam |

Nāmāni Caiva Mukhyāni Yāni Gauṇāni Cācyuta ‖ 25

Tvadvaktrakamalotthāni Śretumicchāmi Tattvataḥ |

Iti Tasya Vacaḥ Śrutvā Prativākyamuvāca Saḥ ‖ 26

Śrī Bhagavānuvāca -

Mahāvibhūtisaṃyuktā Ṣāḍguṇyavapuṣaḥ Prabho |

Bhagavadvāsudevasya Nityaṃ Caiṣā'napāyinī ‖ 27

Ekaiva Vartate'bhinnā Jyotsneva Himadīdhiteḥ |

Sarvaśaktyātmikā Caiva Viśvaṃ Vyāpya Vyavasthitā ‖ 28

Sarvaiśvaryaguṇopetā Nityaśuddhasvarūpiṇī |

Prāṇaśaktiḥ Parā Hyeṣā Sarveṣāṃ Prāṇināṃ Bhuvi ‖ 29

Śaktīnāṃ Caiva Sarvāsāṃ Yonibhūtā Parā Kalā |

Ahaṃ Tasyāḥ Paraṃ Nāmnāṃ Sahasramidamuttamam ‖ 30

Śṛṇuṣvāvahito Bhūtvā Paramaiśvaryabhūtidam |

Devyākhyāsmṛtimātreṇa Dāridryaṃ Yāti Bhasmatām ‖ 31

Atha Kamalā Sahasranāma Stotram |

Śrīḥ Padmā Prakṛtiḥ Sattvā Śāntā Cicchaktiravyayā |

Kevalā Niṣkalā Śuddhā Vyāpinī Vyomavigrahā ‖ 1

Vyomapadmakṛtādhārā Parā Vyomāmṛtodbhavā |

Nirvyomā Vyomamadhyasthā Pañcavyomapadāśritā ‖ 2

Acyutā Vyomanilayā Paramānandarūpiṇī |

Nityaśuddhā Nityatṛptā Nirvikārā Nirīkṣaṇā || 3

Jñānaśaktiḥ Kartṛśaktirbhoktṛśaktiḥ Śikhāvahā |

Snehābhāsā Nirānandā Vibhūtirvimalācalā || 4

Anantā Vaiṣṇavī Vyaktā Viśvānandā Vikāsinī |

Śaktirvibhinnasarvārtiḥ Samudraparitoṣiṇī || 5

Mūrtiḥ Sanātanī Hārdī Nistaraṅgā Nirāmayā |

Jñānajñeyā Jñānagamyā Jñānajñeyavikāsinī || 6

Svacchandaśaktirgahanā Niṣkampārciḥ Sunirmalā |

Svarūpā Sarvagā Pārā Bṛmhiṇī Suguṇorjitā || 7

Akalaṅkā Nirādhārā Niḥsaṃkalpā Nirāśrayā |

Asaṃkīrṇā Suśāntā Ca Śāśvatī Bhāsurī Sthirā || 8

Anaupamyā Nirvikalpā Niyantrī Yantravāhinī |

Abhedyā Bhedinī Bhinnā Bhāratī Vaikharī Khagā || 9

Agrāhyā Grāhikā Gūḍhā Gambhīrā Viśvagopinī |

Anirdeśyā Pratihatā Nirbījā Pāvanī Parā || 10

Apratarkyā Parimitā Bhavabhrāntivināśinī |

Ekā Dvirūpā Trividhā Asaṃkhyātā Sureśvarī || 11

Supratiṣṭhā Mahādhātrī Sthitirvṛddhirdhruvā Gatiḥ |

Īśvarī Mahimā Ṛddhiḥ Pramodā Ujjvalodyamā || 12

Akṣayā Varddhamānā Ca Suprakāśā Vihaṅgamā |

Nīrajā Jananī Nityā Jayā Rociṣmatī Śubhā || 13

Taponudā Ca Jvālā Ca Sudīptiścāṃśumālinī |

Aprameyā Tridhā Sūkṣmā Parā Nirvāṇadāyinī || 14

Avadātā Suśuddhā Ca Amoghākhyā Paramparā |

Saṃdhānakī Śuddhavidyā Sarvabhūtamaheśvarī || 15

Lakṣmīstuṣṭirmahādhīrā Śāntirāpūraṇānavā |
Anugrahā Śaktirādyā Jagajjyeṣṭhā Jagadvidhiḥ || 16

Satyā Prahvā Kriyā Yogyā Aparṇā Hlādinī Śivā |
Sampūrṇāhlādinī Śuddhā Jyotiṣmatyamṛtāvahā || 17

Rajovatyarkapratibhā"karṣiṇī Karṣiṇī Rasā |
Parā Vasumatī Devī Kāntiḥ Śāntirmatiḥ Kalā || 18

Kalā Kalaṅkarahitā Viśāloddīpanī Ratiḥ |
Sambodhinī Hāriṇī Ca Prabhāvā Bhavabhūtidā || 19

Amṛtasyandinī Jīvā Jananī Khaṇḍikā Sthirā |
Dhūmā Kalāvatī Pūrṇā Bhāsurā Sumatīrasā || 20

Śuddhā Dhvaniḥ Sṛtiḥ Sṛṣṭirvikṛtiḥ Kṛṣṭireva Ca |
Prāpaṇī Prāṇadā Prahvā Viśvā Pāṇḍuravāsinī || 21

Avanirvajranalikā Citrā Brahmāṇḍavāsinī |
Anantarūpānantātmānantasthānantasambhavā || 22

Mahāśaktiḥ Prāṇaśaktiḥ Prāṇadātrī Ṛtambharā |
Mahāsamūhā Nikhilā Icchādhārā Sukhāvahā || 23

Pratyakṣalakṣmīrniṣkampā Prarohābuddhigocarā |
Nānādehā Mahāvartā Bahudehavikāsinī || 24

Sahasrāṇī Pradhānā Ca Nyāyavastuprakāśikā |
Sarvābhilāṣapūrṇecchā Sarvā Sarvārthabhāṣiṇī || 25

Nānāsvarūpaciddhātrī Śabdapūrvā Purātanī |
Vyaktāvyaktā Jīvakeśā Sarvecchāparipūritā || 26

Saṃkalpasiddhā Sāṃkhyeyā Tattvagarbhā Dharāvahā |
Bhūtarūpā Citsvarūpā Triguṇā Guṇagarvitā || 27

Prajāpatīśvarī Raudrī Sarvādhārā Sukhāvahā |
Kalyāṇavāhikā Kalyā Kalikalmaṣanāśinī || 28

Nirūpodbhinnasaṃtānā Suyantrā Triguṇālayā |
Mahāmāyā Yogamāyā Mahāyogeśvarī Priyā || 29

Mahāstrī Vimalā Kīrtirjayā Lakṣmīrnirañjanā |
Prakṛtirbhagavanmāyā Śaktirnidrā Yaśaskarī || 30

Cintā Buddhiryaśaḥ Prajñā Śāntiḥ Suprītivarddhinī |
Pradyumnamātā Sādhvī Ca Sukhasaubhāgyasiddhidā || 31

Kāṣṭhā Niṣṭhā Pratiṣṭhā Ca Jyeṣṭhā Śreṣṭhā Jayāvahā |
Sarvātiśāyinī Prītirviśvaśaktirmahābalā || 32

Variṣṭhā Vijayā Vīrā Jayantī Vijayapradā |
Hṛdgṛhā Gopinī Guhyā Gaṇagandharvasevitā || 33

Yogīśvarī Yogamāyā Yoginī Yogasiddhidā |
Mahāyogeśvaravṛtā Yogā Yogeśvarapriyā || 34

Brahmendrarudranamitā Surāsuravarapradā |
Trivartmagā Trilokasthā Trivikramapadodbhavā || 35

Sutārā Tāriṇī Tārā Durgā Saṃtāriṇī Parā |
Sutāriṇī Tārayantī Bhūritāreśvaraprabhā || 36

Guhyavidyā Yajñavidyā Mahāvidyā Suśobhitā |
Adhyātmavidyā Vighneśī Padmasthā Parameṣṭhinī || 37

Ānvīkṣikī Trayī Vārtā Daṇḍanītirnayātmikā |
Gaurī Vāgīśvarī Goptrī Gāyatrī Kamalodbhavā || 38

Viśvambharā Viśvarūpā Viśvamātā Vasupradā |
Siddhiḥ Svāhā Svadhā Svastiḥ Sudhā Sarvārthasādhinī || 39

Icchā Sṛṣṭirdyutirbhūtiḥ Kīrtiḥ Śraddhā Dayāmatiḥ |
Śrutirmedhā Dhṛtirhrīḥ Śrīrvidyā Vibudhavanditā || 40

Anasūyā Ghṛṇā Nītirnirvṛtiḥ Kāmadhukkarā |
Pratijñā Saṃtatirbhūtirdyauḥ Prajñā Viśvamāninī || 41

Smṛtirvāgviśvajananī Paśyantī Madhyamā Samā |
Saṃdhyā Medhā Prabhā Bhīmā Sarvākārā Sarasvatī || 42

Kāṅkṣā Māyā Mahāmāyā Mohinī Mādhavapriyā |
Saumyābhogā Mahābhogā Bhoginī Bhogadāyinī || 43

Sudhautakanakaprakhyā Suvarṇakamalāsanā |
Hiraṇyagarbhā Suśroṇī Hāriṇī Ramaṇī Ramā || 44

Candrā Hiraṇmayī Jyotsnā Ramyā Śobhā Śubhāvahā |
Trailokyamaṇḍanā Nārī Nareśvaravarārcitā || 45

Trailokyasundarī Rāmā Mahāvibhavavāhinī |
Padmasthā Padmanilayā Padmamālāvibhūṣitā || 46

Padmayugmadharā Kāntā Divyābharaṇabhūṣitā |
Vicitraratnamukuṭā Vicitrāmbarabhūṣaṇā || 47

Vicitramālyagandhāḍhyā Vicitrāyudhavāhanā |
Mahānārāyaṇī Devī Vaiṣṇavī Vīravanditā || 48

Kālasaṃkarṣiṇī Ghorā Tattvasaṃkarṣiṇīkalā |
Jagatsampūraṇī Viśvā Mahāvibhavabhūṣaṇā || 49

Vāruṇī Varadā Vyākhyā Ghaṇṭākarṇavirājitā |
Nṛsiṃhī Bhairavī Brāhmī Bhāskarī Vyomacāriṇī || 50

Aindrī Kāmadhenuḥ Sṛṣṭiḥ Kāmayonirmahāprabhā |
Dṛṣṭā Kāmyā Viśvaśaktirbījagatyātmadarśanā || 51

Garuḍārūḍhahṛdayā Cāndrī Śrīrmadhurānanā |
Mahograrūpā Vārāhī Nārasiṃhī Hatāsurā || 52

Yugāntahutabhugjvālā Karālā Piṅgalākalā |
Trailokyabhūṣaṇā Bhīmā Śyāmā Trailokyamohinī || 53

Mahotkaṭā Mahāraktā Mahācaṇḍā Mahāsanā |
Śaṅkhinī Lekhinī Svasthā Likhitā Khecareśvarī || 54

Bhadrakālī Caikavīrā Kaumārī Bhavamālinī |
Kalyāṇī Kāmadhugjvālāmukhī Cotpalamālikā || 55

Bālikā Dhanadā Sūryā Hṛdayotpalamālikā |
Ajitā Varṣiṇī Rītirbharuṇḍā Garuḍāsanā || 56

Vaiśvānarī Mahāmāyā Mahākālī Vibhīṣaṇā |
Mahāmandāravibhavā Śivānandā Ratipriyā || 57

Udrītiḥ Padmamālā Ca Dharmavegā Vibhāvanī |
Satkriyā Devasenā Ca Hiraṇyarajatāśrayā || 58

Sahasāvartamānā Ca Hastinādaprabodhinī |
Hiraṇyapadmavarṇā Ca Haribhadrā Sudurddharā || 59

Sūryā Hiraṇyaprakaṭasadṛśī Hemamālinī |
Padmānanā Nityapuṣṭā Devamātā Mṛtodbhavā || 60

Mahādhanā Ca Yā Śṛṅgī Karddamī Kambukandharā |
Ādityavarṇā Candrābhā Gandhadvārā Durāsadā || 61

Varācitā Varārohā Vareṇyā Viṣṇuvallabhā |
Kalyāṇī Varadā Vāmā Vāmeśī Vindhyavāsinī || 62

Yoganidrā Yogaratā Devakī Kāmarūpiṇī |
Kaṃsavidrāviṇī Durgā Kaumārī Kauśikī Kṣamā || 63

Kātyāyanī Kālarātrirniśitṛptā Sudurjayā |
Virūpākṣī Viśālākṣī Bhaktānāṃparirakṣiṇī || 64

Bahurūpā Svarūpā Ca Virūpā Rūpavarjitā |
Ghaṇṭāninādabahulā Jīmūtadhvaniniḥsvanā || 65

Mahādevendramathinī Bhrukuṭīkuṭilānanā |
Satyopayācitā Caikā Kauberī Brahmacāriṇī || 66

Āryā Yaśodā Sutadā Dharmakāmārthamokṣadā |
Dāridryaduḥkhaśamanī Ghoradurgārtināśinī || 67

Bhaktārtiśamanī Bhavyā Bhavabhargāpahāriṇī |

Kṣīrābdhitanayā Padmā Kamalā Dharaṇīdharā || 68

Rukmiṇī Rohiṇī Sītā Satyabhāmā Yaśasvinī |

Prajñādhārāmitaprajñā Vedamātā Yaśovatī || 69

Samādhirbhāvanā Maitrī Karuṇā Bhaktavatsalā |

Antarvedī Dakṣiṇā Ca Brahmacaryaparāgatiḥ || 70

Dīkṣā Vīkṣā Parīkṣā Ca Samīkṣā Vīravatsalā |

Ambikā Surabhiḥ Siddhā Siddhavidyādharārcitā || 71

Sudīkṣā Lelihānā Ca Karālā Viśvapūrakā |

Viśvasaṃdhāriṇī Dīptistāpanī Tāṇḍavapriyā || 72

Udbhavā Virajā Rājñī Tāpanī Bindumālinī |

Kṣīradhārāsuprabhāvā Lokamātā Suvarcasā || 73

Havyagarbhā Cājyagarbhā Juhvatoyajñasambhavā |

Āpyāyanī Pāvanī Ca Dahanī Dahanāśrayā || 74

Mātṛkā Mādhavī Mukhyā Mokṣalakṣmīrmaharddhidā |

Sarvakāmapradā Bhadrā Subhadrā Sarvamaṅgalā || 75

Śvetā Suśuklavasanā Śuklamālyānulepanā |

Haṃsā Hīnakarī Haṃsī Hṛdyā Hṛtkamalālayā || 76

Sitātapatrā Suśroṇī Padmapatrāyatekṣaṇā |

Sāvitrī Satyasaṃkalpā Kāmadā Kāmakāminī || 77

Darśanīyā Dṛśā Dṛśyā Spṛśyā Sevyā Varāṅganā |

Bhogapriyā Bhogavatī Bhogīndraśayanāsanā || 78

Ārdrā Puṣkariṇī Puṇyā Pāvanī Pāpasūdanī |

Śrīmatī Ca Śubhākārā Paramaiśvaryabhūtidā || 79

Acintyānantavibhavā Bhavabhāvavibhāvanī |

Niśreṇiḥ Sarvadehasthā Sarvabhūtanamaskṛtā || 80

Balā Balādhikā Devī Gautamī Gokulālayā |

Toṣiṇī Pūrṇacandrābhā Ekānandā Śatānanā ‖ 81

Udyānanagaradvāraharmyopavanavāsinī |

Kūṣmāṇḍā Dāruṇā Caṇḍā Kirātī Nandanālayā ‖ 82

Kālāyanā Kālagamyā Bhayadā Bhayanāśinī |

Saudāmanī Megharavā Daityadānavamardinī ‖ 83

Jaganmātā Bhayakarī Bhūtadhātrī Sudurlabhā |

Kāśyapī Śubhadātā Ca Vanamālā Śubhāvarā ‖ 84

Dhanyā Dhanyeśvarī Dhanyā Ratnadā Vasuvarddhinī |

Gāndharvī Revatī Gaṅgā Śakunī Vimalānanā ‖ 85

Iḍā Śāntikarī Caiva Tāmasī Kamalālayā |

Ājyapā Vajrakaumārī Somapā Kusumāśrayā ‖ 86

Jagatpriyā Ca Sarathā Durjayā Khagavāhanā |

Manobhavā Kāmacārā Siddhacāraṇasevitā ‖ 87

Vyomalakṣmīrmahālakṣmīstejolakṣmīḥ Sujājvalā |

Rasalakṣmīrjagadyonirgandhalakṣmīrvanāśrayā ‖ 88

Śravaṇā Śrāvaṇī Netrī Rasanāprāṇacāriṇī |

Viriñcimātā Vibhavā Varavārijavāhanā ‖ 89

Vīryā Vīreśvarī Vandyā Viśokā Vasuvarddhinī |

Anāhatā Kuṇḍalinī Nalinī Vanavāsinī ‖ 90

Gāndhāriṇīndranamitā Surendranamitā Satī |

Sarvamaṅgalyamāṅgalyā Sarvakāmasamṛddhidā ‖ 91

Sarvānandā Mahānandā Satkīrtiḥ Siddhasevitā |

Sinīvālī Kuhū Rākā Amā Cānumatirdyutiḥ ‖ 92

Arundhatī Vasumatī Bhārgavī Vāstudevatā |

Māyūrī Vajravetālī Vajrahastā Varānanā ‖ 93

Anaghā Dharaṇirdhīrā Dhamanī Maṇibhūṣaṇā |
Rājaśrī Rūpasahitā Brahmaśrīrbrahmavanditā || 94

Jayaśrīrjayadā Jñeyā Sargaśrīḥ Svargatiḥ Satām |
Supuṣpā Puṣpanilayā Phalaśrīrniṣkalapriyā || 95

Dhanurlakṣmīstvamilitā Parakrodhanivāriṇī |
Kadrūrddhanāyuḥ Kapilā Surasā Suramohinī || 96

Mahāśvetā Mahānīlā Mahāmūrtirviṣāpahā |
Suprabhā Jvālinī Dīptistṛptirvyāptiḥ Prabhākarī || 97

Tejovatī Padmabodhā Madalekhāruṇāvatī |
Ratnā Ratnāvalī Bhūtā Śatadhāmā Śatāpahā || 98

Triguṇā Ghoṣiṇī Rakṣyā Narddinī Ghoṣavarjitā |
Sādhyā Ditirditidevī Mṛgavāhā Mṛgāṅkagā || 99

Citranīlotpalagatā Vṛṣaratnakarāśrayā |
Hiraṇyarajatadvandvā Śaṅkhabhadrāsanāsthitā || 100

Gomūtragomayakṣīradadhisarpirjalāśrayā |
Marīciścīravasanā Pūrṇā Candrārkaviṣṭarā || 101

Susūkṣmā Nirvṛtiḥ Sthūlā Nivṛttārātireva Ca |
Marīcijvālinī Dhūmrā Havyavāhā Hiraṇyadā || 102

Dāyinī Kālinī Siddhiḥ Śoṣiṇī Samprabodhinī |
Bhāsvarā Saṃhatistīkṣṇā Pracaṇḍajvalanojjvalā || 103

Sāṅgā Pracaṇḍā Dīptā Ca Vaidyutiḥ Sumahādyutiḥ |
Kapilā Nīlaraktā Ca Suṣumṇā Visphuliṅginī || 104

Arciṣmatī Ripuharā Dīrghā Dhūmāvalī Jarā |
Sampūrṇamaṇḍalā Pūṣā Sraṃsinī Sumanoharā || 105

Jayā Puṣṭikarīcchāyā Mānasā Hṛdayojjvalā |
Suvarṇakaraṇī Śreṣṭhā Mṛtasaṃjīvinīraṇe || 106

Viśalyakaraṇī Śubhrā Saṃdhinī Paramauṣadhiḥ |
Brahmiṣṭhā Brahmasahitā Aindavī Ratnasambhavā || 107

Vidyutprabhā Bindumatī Trisvabhāvaguṇāmbikā |
Nityoditā Nityahṛṣṭā Nityakāmakarīṣiṇī || 108

Padmāṅkā Vajracihnā Ca Vakradaṇḍavibhāsinī |
Videhapūjitā Kanyā Māyā Vijayavāhinī || 109

Māninī Maṅgalā Mānyā Mālinī Mānadāyinī |
Viśveśvarī Gaṇavatī Maṇḍalā Maṇḍaleśvarī || 110

Haripriyā Bhaumasutā Manojñā Matidāyinī |
Pratyaṅgirā Somaguptā Mano'bhijñā Vadanmatiḥ || 111

Yaśodharā Ratnamālā Kṛṣṇā Trailokyabandhanī |
Amṛtā Dhāriṇī Harṣā Vinatā Vallakī Śacī || 112

Saṃkalpā Bhāminī Miśrā Kādambaryamṛtaprabhā |
Agatā Nirgatā Vajrā Suhitā Saṃhitākṣatā || 113

Sarvārthasādhanakarī Dhāturdhāraṇikāmalā |
Karuṇādhārasambhūtā Kamalākṣī Śaśipriyā || 114

Saumyarūpā Mahādīptā Mahājvālā Vikāśinī |
Mālā Kāñcanamālā Ca Sadvajrā Kanakaprabhā || 115

Prakriyā Paramā Yoktrī Kṣobhikā Ca Sukhodayā |
Vijṛmbhaṇā Ca Vajrākhyā Śṛṅkhalā Kamalekṣaṇā || 116

Jayaṃkarī Madhumatī Haritā Śaśinī Śivā |
Mūlaprakṛtirīśānī Yogamātā Manojavā || 117

Dharmodayā Bhānumatī Sarvābhāsā Sukhāvahā |
Dhurandharā Ca Bālā Ca Dharmasevyā Tathāgatā || 118

Sukumārā Saumyamukhī Saumyasambodhanottamā |
Sumukhī Sarvatobhadrā Guhyaśaktirguhālayā || 119

Halāyudhā Caikavīrā Sarvaśastrasudhāriṇī |

Vyomaśaktirmahādehā Vyomagā Madhumanmayī || 120

Gaṅgā Vitastā Yamunā Candrabhāgā Sarasvatī |

Tilottamorvaśī Rambhā Svāminī Surasundarī || 121

Bāṇapraharaṇāvālā Bimboṣṭhī Cāruhāsinī |

Kakudminī Cārupṛṣṭhā Dṛṣṭādṛṣṭaphalapradā || 122

Kāmyācarī Ca Kāmyā Ca Kāmācāravihāriṇī |

Himaśailendrasaṃkāśā Gajendravaravāhanā || 123

Aśeṣasukhasaubhāgyasampadā Yoniruttamā |

Sarvotkṛṣṭā Sarvamayī Sarvā Sarveśvarapriyā || 124

Sarvāṅgayoniḥ Sāvyaktā Sampradhāneśvareśvarī |

Viṣṇuvakṣaḥsthalagatā Kimataḥ Paramucyate || 125

Parā Nirmahimā Devī Harivakṣaḥsthalāśrayā |

Sā Devī Pāpahantrī Ca Sānnidhyaṃ Kurutānmama || 126

Phalaśrutiḥ ||

Iti Nāmnāṃ Sahasraṃ Tu Lakṣmyāḥ Proktaṃ Śubhāvaham |

Parāvareṇa Bhedena Mukhyagauṇena Bhāgataḥ || 127

Yaścaitat Kīrtayennityaṃ Śṛṇuyād Vāpi Padmaja |

Śuciḥ Samāhito Bhūtvā Bhaktiśraddhāsamanvitaḥ || 128

Śrīnivāsaṃ Samabhyarcya Puṣpadhūpānulepanaiḥ |

Bhogaiśca Madhuparkādyairyathāśakti Jagadgurum || 129

Tatpārśvasthāṃ Śriyaṃ Devīṃ Sampūjya Śrīdharapriyām |

Tato Nāmasahasroṇa Toṣayet Parameśvarīm || 130

Nāmaratnāvalīstotramidaṃ Yaḥ Satataṃ Paṭhet |

Prasādābhimukhīlakṣmīḥ Sarvaṃ Tasmai Prayacchati || 131

Yasyā Lakṣmyāśca Sambhūtāḥ Śaktayo Viśvagāḥ Sadā |
Kāraṇatve Na Tiṣṭhanti Jagatyasmim̐ścarācare || 132

Tasmāt Prītā Jaganmātā Śrīryasyācyutavallabhā |
Suprītāḥ Śaktayastasya Siddhimiṣṭāṃ Diśanti Hi || 133

Eka Eva Jagatsvāmī Śaktimānacyutaḥ Prabhuḥ |
Tadaṃśaśaktimanto'nye Brahmeśānādayo Yathā || 134

Tathaivaikā Parā Śaktiḥ Śrīstasya Karuṇāśrayā |
Jñānādiṣāṅguṇyamayī Yā Proktā Prakṛtiḥ Parā || 135

Ekaiva Śaktiḥ Śrīstasyā Dvitīyātmani Vartate |
Parā Pareśī Sarveśī Sarvākārā Sanātanī || 136

Anantanāmadheyā Ca Śakticakrasya Nāyikā |
Jagaccarācaramidaṃ Sarvaṃ Vyāpya Vyavasthitā || 137

Tasmādekaiva Paramā Śrīrjñeyā Viśvarūpiṇī |
Saumyā Saumyena Rūpeṇa Saṃsthitā Naṭajīvavat || 138

Yo Yo Jagati Pumbhāvaḥ Sa Viṣṇuriti Niścayaḥ |
Yā Yā Tu Nārībhāvasthā Tatra Lakṣmīrvyavasthitā || 139

Prakṛteḥ Puruṣāccānyastṛtīyo Naiva Vidyate |
Atha Kiṃ Bahunoktena Naranārīmayo Hariḥ || 140

Anekabhedabhinnastu Kriyate Parameśvaraḥ |
Mahāvibhūtiṃ Dayitāṃ Ye Stuvantyacyutapriyām || 141

Te Prāpnuvanti Paramāṃ Lakṣmīṃ Saṃśuddhacetasaḥ |
Padmayoniridaṃ Prāpya Paṭhan Stotramidaṃ Kramāt || 142

Divyamaṣṭaguṇaiśvaryaṃ Tatprasādācca Labdhavān |
Sakāmānāṃ Ca Phaladāmakāmānāṃ Ca Mokṣadām || 143

Pustakākhyāṃ Bhayatrātrīṃ Sitavastrāṃ Trilocanām |
Mahāpadmaniṣaṇṇāṃ Tāṃ Lakṣmīmajaratāṃ Namaḥ || 144

Karayugalagṛhītaṃ Pūrṇakumbhaṃ Dadhānā

Kvacidamalagatasthā Śaṅkhapadmākṣapāṇiḥ |

Kvacidapi Dayitāṅge Cāmaravyagrahastā

Kvacidapi Sṛṇipāśaṃ Bibhratī Hemakāntiḥ || 145

|| Ityādipadma Purāṇe Kāśmīravarṇane Hiraṇyagarbhahṛdaye

Sarvakāmapradāyakaṃ Puruṣottamaproktaṃ Śrī Kamalātmikā

Sahasranāma Stotraṃ Samāptam ||

श्री कमलात्मिका सहस्रनाम स्तोत्रम्

ध्यानम्

कान्त्या कांचनसन्निभां हिमगिरिप्रख्यैश्चतुर्भिर्गजैः ।

हस्तोक्षिप्त हिरण्मयामृत घटैरासिच्यमानां श्रियम् ॥

बिभ्राणां वरमब्ज युग्ममभयं हस्तैःकिरीटोज्वलां ।

क्षौमाबध्दनिदंभबिम्ब लसिताम् वन्देरविन्दस्तिताम् ॥

अथ सहस्रनाम स्तोत्रम्

ॐ तामाह्वयामि सुभगां लक्ष्मीं त्रैलोक्यपूजिताम् ।

एह्येहि देवि पद्माक्षि पद्माकरकृतालये ॥ १

आगच्छागच्छ वरदे पश्य मां स्वेन चक्षुषा ।

आयाह्यायाहि धर्मार्थिकाममोक्षमये शुभे ॥ २

एवंविधैः स्तुतिपदैः सत्यैः सत्यार्थसंस्तुता ।

कनीयसी महाभागा चन्द्रेण परमात्मना ॥ ३

निशाकरश्च सा देवी भ्रातरौ द्वौ पयोनिधेः ।

उत्पन्नमात्रौ तावास्तां शिवकेशवसंश्रितौ ॥ ४

सनत्कुमारस्तमृषिं समाभाष्य पुरातनम् ।

प्रोक्तवानितिहासं तु लक्ष्म्याः स्तोत्रमनुत्तमम् ॥ ५

अथेदृशान्महाघोराद् दारिद्र्यान्नरकात्कथम् ।

मुक्तिर्भवति लोकेऽस्मिन् दारिद्रयं याति भस्मताम् ॥ ६

सनत्कुमार उवाच –

पूर्वं कृतयुगे ब्रह्मा भगवान् सर्वलोककृत् ।
सृष्टिं नानाविधां कृत्वा पश्चाच्चि न्तामुपेयिवान् ॥ ७

किमाहाराः प्रजास्त्वेताः सम्भविष्यन्ति भूतले ।
तथैव चासां दारिद्र्यात्कथमुत्तरणं भवेत् ॥ ८

दारिद्र्यान्मरणं श्रेयस्त्विति सञ्चिन्त्य चेतसि ।
क्षीरोदस्योत्तरे कूले जगाम कमलोद्भवः ॥ ९

तत्र तीव्रं तपस्तप्त्वा कदाचित्परमेश्वरम् ।
ददर्श पुण्डरीकाक्षं वासुदेवं जगद्गुरुम् ॥ १०

सर्वज्ञं सर्वशक्तीनां सर्वावासं सनातनम् ।
सर्वेश्वरं वासुदेवं विष्णुं लक्ष्मीपतिं प्रभुम् ॥ ११

सोमकोटिप्रतीकाशं क्षीरोद विमले जले ।
अनन्तभोगशयनं विश्रान्तं श्रीनिकेतनम् ॥ १२

कोटिसूर्यप्रतीकाशं महायोगेश्वरेश्वरम् ।
योगनिद्रारतं श्रीशं सर्वावासं सुरेश्वरम् ॥ १३

जगदुत्पत्तिसंहारस्थितिकारणकारणम् ।
लक्ष्म्यादि शक्तिकरणजातमण्डलमण्डितम् ॥ १४

आयुधैर्देहवद्भिश्च चक्राद्यैः परिवारितम् ।
दुर्निरीक्ष्यं सुरैः सिद्धैः महायोनिशतैरपि ॥ १५

आधारं सर्वशक्तीनां परं तेजः सुदुस्सहम् ।
प्रबुद्ध देवमीशानं दृष्ट्वा कमलसम्भवः ॥ १६

शिरस्यञ्जलिमाधाय स्तोत्रं पूर्वमुवाच ह ।
मनोवाञ्छितसिद्धिं त्वं पूरयस्व महेश्वर ॥ १७

जितं ते पुण्डरीक्ष नमस्तेविश्वभावन ।
नमस्तेऽस्तु हृषीकेश महापुरुषपूर्वज ॥ १८

सर्वेश्वर जयानन्द सर्वावास परात्पर ।
प्रसीद मम भक्तस्य छिन्धि सन्देहजं तमः ॥ १९

एवं स्तुतः स भगवान् ब्रह्म णाऽव्यक्तजन्मना ।
प्रसादाभिमुखः प्राह हरिर्विश्रान्तलोचनः ॥ २०

श्रीभगवानुवाच -

हिरण्यगर्भ तुष्टोऽस्मि ब्रूहि यत्तेऽभिवाञ्छितम् ।
तद्दक्ष्यामि न सन्देहो भक्तोऽसि मम सुव्रत ॥ २१

केशवाद्वचनं श्रुत्वा करुणाविष्टचेतनः ।
प्रत्युवाच महाबुद्धिर्भगवन्तं जनार्दनम् ॥ २२

चतुर्विधं भवस्यास्य भूतसर्गस्य केशव ।
परित्राणाय मे ब्रूहि रहस्यं परमाद्भुतम् ॥ २३

दारिद्र्यशमनं धन्यं मनोज्ञं पावनं परम् ।
सर्वेश्वर महाबुद्ध स्वरूपं भैरवं महत् ॥ २४

श्रियः सर्वातिशायिन्यास्तथा ज्ञानं च शाश्वतम् ।
नामानि चैव मुख्यानि यानि गौणानि चाच्युत ॥ २५

त्वद्वक्त्रकमलोत्थानि श्रेतुमिच्छामि तत्त्वतः ।
इति तस्य वचः श्रुत्वा प्रतिवाक्यमुवाच सः ॥ २६

श्रीभगवानुवाच -

महाविभूतिसंयुक्ता षाड्गुण्यवपुषः प्रभो ।
भगवद्वासुदेवस्य नित्यं चैषाऽनपायिनी ॥ २७

एकैव वर्ततेऽभिन्ना ज्योत्स्नेव हिमदीधितेः ।
सर्वशक्त्यात्मिका चैव विश्वं व्याप्य व्यवस्थिता ॥ २८

सर्वैश्वर्यगुणोपेता नित्यशुद्धस्वरूपिणी ।
प्राणशक्तिः परा ह्येषा सर्वेषां प्राणिनां भुवि ॥ २९

शक्तीनां चैव सर्वासां योनिभूता परा कला ।
अहं तस्याः परं नाम्नां सहस्रमिदमुत्तमम् ॥ ३०

शृणुष्वावहितो भूत्वा परमैश्वर्यभूतिदम् ।
देव्याख्यास्मृतिमात्रेण दारिद्र्यं याति भस्मताम् ॥ ३१

अथ कमला सहस्रनाम स्तोत्रम् ।

श्रीः पद्मा प्रकृतिः सत्त्वा शान्ता चिच्छक्तिरव्यया ।
केवला निष्कला शुद्धा व्यापिनी व्योमविग्रहा ॥ १

व्योमपद्मकृताधारा परा व्योमामृतोद्भवा ।
निर्व्योमा व्योममध्यस्था पञ्चव्योमपदाश्रिता ॥ २

अच्युता व्योमनिलया परमानन्दरूपिणी ।
नित्यशुद्धा नित्यतृप्ता निर्विकारा निरीक्षणा ॥ ३

ज्ञानशक्तिः कर्तृशक्तिर्भोक्तृशक्तिः शिखावहा ।
स्नेहाभासा निरानन्दा विभूतिर्विमलाचला ॥ ४

अनन्ता वैष्णवी व्यक्ता विश्वानन्दा विकासिनी ।
शक्तिर्विभिन्नसर्वार्तिः समुद्रपरितोषिणी ॥ ५

मूर्तिः सनातनी हार्दी निस्तरङ्गा निरामया ।
ज्ञानज्ञेया ज्ञानगम्या ज्ञानज्ञेयविकासिनी ॥ ६

स्वच्छन्दशक्तिर्गहना निष्कम्पार्चिः सुनिर्मला ।
स्वरूपा सर्वगा पारा बृंहिणी सुगुणोर्जिता ॥ ७

अकलङ्का निराधारा निःसंकल्पा निराश्रया ।
असंकीर्णा सुशान्ता च शाश्वती भासुरी स्थिरा ॥ ८

अनौपम्या निर्विकल्पा नियन्त्री यन्त्रवाहिनी ।
अभेद्या भेदिनी भिन्ना भारती वैखरी खगा ॥ ९

अग्राह्या ग्राहिका गूढा गम्भीरा विश्वगोपिनी ।
अनिर्देश्या प्रतिहता निर्बीजा पावनी परा ॥ १०

अप्रतर्क्या परिमिता भवभ्रान्तिविनाशिनी ।
एका द्विरूपा त्रिविधा असंख्याता सुरेश्वरी ॥ ११

सुप्रतिष्ठा महाधात्री स्थितिर्वृद्धिर्ध्रुवा गतिः ।
ईश्वरी महिमा ऋद्धिः प्रमोदा उज्ज्वलोद्यमा ॥ १२

अक्षया वर्द्धमाना च सुप्रकाशा विहङ्गमा ।
नीरजा जननी नित्या जया रोचिष्मती शुभा ॥ १३

तपोनुदा च ज्वाला च सुदीप्तिश्चांशुमालिनी ।
अप्रमेया त्रिधा सूक्ष्मा परा निर्वाणदायिनी ॥ १४

अवदाता सुशुद्धा च अमोघाख्या परम्परा ।
संधानकी शुद्धविद्या सर्वभूतमहेश्वरी ॥ १५

लक्ष्मीस्तुष्टिर्महाधीरा शान्तिरापूरणानवा ।
अनुग्रहा शक्तिराद्या जगज्ज्येष्ठा जगद्विधिः ॥ १६

सत्या प्रह्वा क्रिया योग्या अपर्णा ह्लादिनी शिवा ।
सम्पूर्णाह्लादिनी शुद्धा ज्योतिष्मत्यमृतावहा ॥ १७

रजोवत्यर्कप्रतिभाऽऽकर्षिणी कर्षिणी रसा ।
परा वसुमती देवी कान्तिः शान्तिर्मतिः कला ॥ १८

कला कलङ्करहिता विशालोद्दीपनी रतिः ।
सम्बोधिनी हारिणी च प्रभावा भवभूतिदा ॥ १९

अमृतस्यन्दिनी जीवा जननी खण्डिका स्थिरा ।
धूमा कलावती पूर्णा भासुरा सुमतीरसा ॥ २०

शुद्धा ध्वनिः सृतिः सृष्टिर्विकृतिः कृष्टिरेव च ।
प्रापणी प्राणदा प्रह्वा विश्वा पाण्डुरवासिनी ॥ २१

अवनिर्वज्रनलिका चित्रा ब्रह्माण्डवासिनी ।
अनन्तरूपानन्तात्मानन्तस्थानन्तसम्भवा ॥ २२

महाशक्तिः प्राणशक्तिः प्राणदात्री ऋतम्भरा ।
महासमूहा निखिला इच्छाधारा सुखावहा ॥ २३

प्रत्यक्षलक्ष्मीर्निष्कम्पा प्ररोहाबुद्धिगोचरा ।
नानादेहा महावर्ता बहुदेहविकासिनी ॥ २४

सहस्राणी प्रधाना च न्यायवस्तुप्रकाशिका ।
सर्वाभिलाषपूर्णेच्छा सर्वा सर्वार्थभाषिणी ॥ २५

नानास्वरूपचिद्धात्री शब्दपूर्वा पुरातनी ।
व्यक्ताव्यक्ता जीवकेशा सर्वेच्छापरिपूरिता ॥ २६

संकल्पसिद्धा सांख्येया तत्त्वगर्भा धरावहा ।
भूतरूपा चित्स्वरूपा त्रिगुणा गुणगर्विता ॥ २७

प्रजापतीश्वरी रौद्री सर्वाधारा सुखावहा ।
कल्याणवाहिका कल्या कलिकल्मषनाशिनी ॥ २८

नीरूपोद्भिन्नसंताना सुयन्त्रा त्रिगुणालया ।
महामाया योगमाया महायोगेश्वरी प्रिया ॥ २९

महास्त्री विमला कीर्तिर्जया लक्ष्मीर्निरञ्जना ।
प्रकृतिर्भगवन्माया शक्तिर्निद्रा यशस्करी ॥ ३०

चिन्ता बुद्धिर्यशः प्रज्ञा शान्तिः सुप्रीतिवर्द्धिनी ।
प्रद्युम्नमाता साध्वी च सुखसौभाग्यसिद्धिदा ॥ ३१

काष्ठा निष्ठा प्रतिष्ठा च ज्येष्ठा श्रेष्ठा जयावहा ।
सर्वातिशायिनी प्रीतिर्विश्वशक्तिर्महाबला ॥ ३२

वरिष्ठा विजया वीरा जयन्ती विजयप्रदा ।
हृद्दृहा गोपिनी गुह्या गणगन्धर्वसेविता ॥ ३३

योगीश्वरी योगमाया योगिनी योगसिद्धिदा ।
महायोगेश्वरवृता योगा योगेश्वरप्रिया ॥ ३४

ब्रह्मेन्द्ररुद्रनमिता सुरासुरवरप्रदा ।
त्रिवर्त्मगा त्रिलोकस्था त्रिविक्रमपदोद्भवा ॥ ३५

सुतारा तारिणी तारा दुर्गा संतारिणी परा ।
सुतारिणी तारयन्ती भूरितारेश्वरप्रभा ॥ ३६

गुह्यविद्या यज्ञविद्या महाविद्या सुशोभिता ।
अध्यात्मविद्या विघ्नेशी पद्मस्था परमेष्ठिनी ॥ ३७

आन्वीक्षिकी त्रयी वार्ता दण्डनीतिर्नयात्मिका ।
गौरी वागीश्वरी गोप्त्री गायत्री कमलोद्भवा ॥ ३८

विश्वम्भरा विश्वरूपा विश्वमाता वसुप्रदा ।
सिद्धिः स्वाहा स्वधा स्वस्तिः सुधा सर्वार्थसाधिनी ॥ ३९

इच्छा सृष्टिर्द्युतिर्भूतिः कीर्तिः श्रद्धा दयामतिः ।
श्रुतिर्मेधा धृतिर्ह्रीः श्रीर्विद्या विबुधवन्दिता ॥ ४०

अनसूया घृणा नीतिर्निर्वृतिः कामधुक्करा ।
प्रतिज्ञा संततिर्भूतिर्द्यौः प्रज्ञा विश्वमानिनी ॥ ४१

स्मृतिर्वाग्विश्वजननी पश्यन्ती मध्यमा समा ।
संध्या मेधा प्रभा भीमा सर्वाकारा सरस्वती ॥ ४२

काङ्क्षा माया महामाया मोहिनी माधवप्रिया ।
सौम्याभोगा महाभोगा भोगिनी भोगदायिनी ॥ ४३

सुधौतकनकप्रख्या सुवर्णकमलासना ।
हिरण्यगर्भा सुश्रोणी हारिणी रमणी रमा ॥ ४४

चन्द्रा हिरण्मयी ज्योत्स्ना रम्या शोभा शुभावहा ।
त्रैलोक्यमण्डना नारी नरेश्वरवरार्चिता ॥ ४५

त्रैलोक्यसुन्दरी रामा महाविभववाहिनी ।
पद्मस्था पद्मनिलया पद्ममालाविभूषिता ॥ ४६

पद्मयुग्मधरा कान्ता दिव्याभरणभूषिता ।
विचित्ररत्नमुकुटा विचित्राम्बरभूषणा ॥ ४७

विचित्रमाल्यगन्धाढ्या विचित्रायुधवाहना ।
महानारायणी देवी वैष्णवी वीरवन्दिता ॥ ४८

कालसंकर्षिणी घोरा तत्त्वसंकर्षिणीकला ।
जगत्सम्पूरणी विश्वा महाविभवभूषणा ॥ ४९

वारुणी वरदा व्याख्या घण्टाकर्णविराजिता ।
नृसिंही भैरवी ब्राह्मी भास्करी व्योमचारिणी ॥ ५०

ऐन्द्री कामधेनुः सृष्टिः कामयोनिर्महाप्रभा ।
दृष्टा काम्या विश्वशक्तिर्बीजगत्यात्मदर्शना ॥ ५१

गरुडारूढहृदया चान्द्री श्रीर्मधुरानना ।
महोग्ररूपा वाराही नारसिंही हतासुरा ॥ ५२

युगान्तहुतभुग्ज्वाला कराला पिङ्गलाकला ।
त्रैलोक्यभूषणा भीमा श्यामा त्रैलोक्यमोहिनी ॥ ५३

महोत्कटा महारक्ता महाचण्डा महासना ।
शङ्खिनी लेखिनी स्वस्था लिखिता खेचरेश्वरी ॥ ५४

भद्रकाली चैकवीरा कौमारी भवमालिनी ।
कल्याणी कामधुग्ज्वालामुखी चोत्पलमालिका ॥ ५५

बालिका धनदा सूर्या हृदयोत्पलमालिका ।
अजिता वर्षिणी रीतिर्भरुण्डा गरुडासना ॥ ५६

वैश्वानरी महामाया महाकाली विभीषणा ।
महामन्दारविभवा शिवानन्दा रतिप्रिया ॥ ५७

उद्रीतिः पद्ममाला च धर्मवेगा विभावनी ।
सत्क्रिया देवसेना च हिरण्यरजताश्रया ॥ ५८

सहसावर्तमाना च हस्तिनादप्रबोधिनी ।
हिरण्यपद्मवर्णा च हरिभद्रा सुदुर्द्धरा ॥ ५९

सूर्या हिरण्यप्रकटसदृशी हेममालिनी ।
पद्मानना नित्यपुष्टा देवमाता मृतोद्भवा ॥ ६०

महाधना च या शृङ्गी कर्दमी कम्बुकन्धरा ।
आदित्यवर्णा चन्द्राभा गन्धद्वारा दुरासदा ॥ ६१

वराचिता वरारोहा वरेण्या विष्णुवल्लभा ।
कल्याणी वरदा वामा वामेशी विन्ध्यवासिनी ॥ ६२

योगनिद्रा योगरता देवकी कामरूपिणी ।
कंसविद्राविणी दुर्गा कौमारी कौशिकी क्षमा ॥ ६३

कात्यायनी कालरात्रिर्निशितृप्ता सुदुर्जया ।
विरूपाक्षी विशालाक्षी भक्तानांपरिरक्षिणी ॥ ६४

बहुरूपा स्वरूपा च विरूपा रूपवर्जिता ।
घण्टानिनादबहुला जीमूतध्वनिनिःस्वना ॥ ६५

महादेवेन्द्रमथिनी भ्रुकुटीकुटिलानना ।
सत्योपयाचिता चैका कौबेरी ब्रह्मचारिणी ॥ ६६

आर्या यशोदा सुतदा धर्मकामार्थमोक्षदा ।
दारिद्र्यदुःखशमनी घोरदुर्गार्तिनाशिनी ॥ ६७

भक्तार्तिशमनी भव्या भवभर्गापहारिणी ।
क्षीराब्धितनया पद्मा कमला धरणीधरा ॥ ६८

रुक्मिणी रोहिणी सीता सत्यभामा यशस्विनी ।
प्रज्ञाधारामितप्रज्ञा वेदमाता यशोवती ॥ ६९

समाधिर्भावना मैत्री करुणा भक्तवत्सला ।
अन्तर्वेदी दक्षिणा च ब्रह्मचर्यपरागतिः ॥ ७०

दीक्षा वीक्षा परीक्षा च समीक्षा वीरवत्सला ।
अम्बिका सुरभिः सिद्धा सिद्धविद्याधरार्चिता ॥ ७१

सुदीक्षा लेलिहाना च कराला विश्वपूरका ।
विश्वसंधारिणी दीप्तिस्तापनी ताण्डवप्रिया ॥ ७२

उद्भवा विरजा राज्ञी तापनी बिन्दुमालिनी ।
क्षीरधारासुप्रभावा लोकमाता सुवर्चसा ॥ ७३

हव्यगर्भा चाज्यगर्भा जुह्वतोयज्ञसम्भवा ।
आप्यायनी पावनी च दहनी दहनाश्रया ॥ ७४

मातृका माधवी मुख्या मोक्षलक्ष्मीर्महर्द्धिदा ।
सर्वकामप्रदा भद्रा सुभद्रा सर्वमङ्गला ॥ ७५

श्वेता सुशुक्लवसना शुक्लमाल्यानुलेपना ।
हंसा हीनकरी हंसी हृद्या हृत्कमलालया ॥ ७६

सितातपत्रा सुश्रोणी पद्मपत्रायतेक्षणा ।
सावित्री सत्यसंकल्पा कामदा कामकामिनी ॥ ७७

दर्शनीया दृशा दृश्या स्पृश्या सेव्या वराङ्गना ।
भोगप्रिया भोगवती भोगीन्द्रशयनासना ॥ ७८

आर्द्रा पुष्करिणी पुण्या पावनी पापसूदनी ।
श्रीमती च शुभाकारा परमैश्वर्यभूतिदा ॥ ७९

अचिन्त्यानन्तविभवा भवभावविभावनी ।
निश्रेणिः सर्वदेहस्था सर्वभूतनमस्कृता ॥ ८०

बला बलाधिका देवी गौतमी गोकुलालया ।
तोषिणी पूर्णचन्द्राभा एकानन्दा शतानना ॥ ८१

उद्याननगरद्वारहर्म्योपवनवासिनी ।
कूष्माण्डा दारुणा चण्डा किराती नन्दनालया ॥ ८२

कालायना कालगम्या भयदा भयनाशिनी ।
सौदामनी मेघरवा दैत्यदानवमर्दिनी ॥ ८३

जगन्माता भयकरी भूतधात्री सुदुर्लभा ।
काश्यपी शुभदाता च वनमाला शुभावरा ॥ ८४

धन्या धन्येश्वरी धन्या रत्नदा वसुवर्द्धिनी ।
गान्धर्वी रेवती गङ्गा शकुनी विमलानना ॥ ८५

इडा शान्तिकरी चैव तामसी कमलालया ।
आज्यपा वज्रकौमारी सोमपा कुसुमाश्रया ॥ ८६

जगत्प्रिया च सरथा दुर्जया खगवाहना ।
मनोभवा कामचारा सिद्धचारणसेविता ॥ ८७

व्योमलक्ष्मीर्महालक्ष्मीस्तेजोलक्ष्मीः सुजाज्वला ।
रसलक्ष्मीर्जगद्योनिर्गन्धलक्ष्मीर्वनाश्रया ॥ ८८

श्रवणा श्रावणी नेत्री रसनाप्राणचारिणी ।
विरिञ्चिमाता विभवा वरवारिजवाहना ॥ ८९

वीर्या वीरेश्वरी वन्द्या विशोका वसुवर्द्धिनी ।
अनाहता कुण्डलिनी नलिनी वनवासिनी ॥ ९०

गान्धारिणीन्द्रनमिता सुरेन्द्रनमिता सती ।
सर्वमङ्गल्यमाङ्गल्या सर्वकामसमृद्धिदा ॥ ९१

सर्वानन्दा महानन्दा सत्कीर्तिः सिद्धसेविता ।
सिनीवाली कुहू राका अमा चानुमतिर्द्युतिः ॥ ९२

अरुन्धती वसुमती भार्गवी वास्तुदेवता ।
मायूरी वज्रवेताली वज्रहस्ता वरानना ॥ ९३

अनघा धरणिर्धीरा धमनी मणिभूषणा ।
राजश्री रूपसहिता ब्रह्मश्रीर्ब्रह्मवन्दिता ॥ ९४

जयश्रीर्जयदा ज्ञेया सर्गश्रीः स्वर्गतिः सताम् ।
सुपुष्पा पुष्पनिलया फलश्रीर्निष्कलप्रिया ॥ ९५

धनुर्लक्ष्मीस्त्वमिलिता परक्रोधनिवारिणी ।
कद्रूर्द्धनायुः कपिला सुरसा सुरमोहिनी ॥ ९६

महाश्वेता महानीला महामूर्तिर्विषापहा ।
सुप्रभा ज्वालिनी दीप्तिस्तृप्तिव्यप्तिः प्रभाकरी ॥ ९७

तेजोवती पद्मबोधा मदलेखारुणावती ।
रत्ना रत्नावली भूता शतधामा शतापहा ॥ ९८

त्रिगुणा घोषिणी रक्ष्या नर्दिनी घोषवर्जिता ।
साध्या दितिर्दितिदेवी मृगवाहा मृगाङ्कगा ॥ ९९

चित्रनीलोत्पलगता वृषरत्नकराश्रया ।
हिरण्यरजतद्वन्द्वा शङ्खभद्रासनास्थिता ॥ १००

गोमूत्रगोमयक्षीरदधिसर्पिर्जलाश्रया ।
मरीचिश्रीरवसना पूर्णा चन्द्रार्कविष्ठरा ॥ १०१

सुसूक्ष्मा निर्वृतिः स्थूला निवृत्तारातिरेव च ।
मरीचिज्वालिनी धूम्रा हव्यवाहा हिरण्यदा ॥ १०२

दायिनी कालिनी सिद्धिः शोषिणी सम्प्रबोधिनी ।
भास्वरा संहतिस्तीक्ष्णा प्रचण्डज्वलनोज्ज्वला ॥ १०३

साङ्गा प्रचण्डा दीप्ता च वैद्युतिः सुमहाद्युतिः ।
कपिला नीलरक्ता च सुषुम्णा विस्फुलिङ्गिनी ॥ १०४

अर्चिष्मती रिपुहरा दीर्घा धूमावली जरा ।
सम्पूर्णमण्डला पूषा स्रंसिनी सुमनोहरा ॥ १०५

जया पुष्टिकरीच्छाया मानसा हृदयोज्ज्वला ।
सुवर्णकरणी श्रेष्ठा मृतसंजीविनीरणे ॥ १०६

विशल्यकरणी शुभ्रा संधिनी परमौषधिः ।
ब्रह्मिष्ठा ब्रह्मसहिता ऐन्दवी रत्नसम्भवा ॥ १०७

विद्युत्प्रभा बिन्दुमती त्रिस्वभावगुणाम्बिका ।
नित्योदिता नित्यहृष्टा नित्यकामकरीषिणी ॥ १०८

पद्माङ्का वज्रचिह्ना च वक्रदण्डविभासिनी ।
विदेहपूजिता कन्या माया विजयवाहिनी ॥ १०९

मानिनी मङ्गला मान्या मालिनी मानदायिनी ।
विश्वेश्वरी गणवती मण्डला मण्डलेश्वरी ॥ ११०

हरिप्रिया भौमसुता मनोज्ञा मतिदायिनी ।
प्रत्यङ्गिरा सोमगुप्ता मनोऽभिज्ञा वदन्मतिः ॥ १११

यशोधरा रत्नमाला कृष्णा त्रैलोक्यबन्धनी ।
अमृता धारिणी हर्षा विनता वल्लकी शची ॥ ११२

संकल्पा भामिनी मिश्रा कादम्बर्यमृतप्रभा ।
अगता निर्गता वज्रा सुहिता संहिताक्षता ॥ ११३

सर्वार्थसाधनकरी धातुर्धारणिकामला ।
करुणाधारसम्भूता कमलाक्षी शशिप्रिया ॥ ११४

सौम्यरूपा महादीप्ता महाज्वाला विकाशिनी ।
माला काञ्चनमाला च सद्वज्रा कनकप्रभा ॥ ११५

प्रक्रिया परमा योक्त्री क्षोभिका च सुखोदया ।
विजृम्भणा च वज्राख्या शृङ्खला कमलेक्षणा ॥ ११६

जयंकरी मधुमती हरिता शशिनी शिवा ।
मूलप्रकृतिरीशानी योगमाता मनोजवा ॥ ११७

धर्मोदया भानुमती सर्वाभासा सुखावहा ।
धुरन्धरा च बाला च धर्मसेव्या तथागता ॥ ११८

सुकुमारा सौम्यमुखी सौम्यसम्बोधनोत्तमा ।
सुमुखीसर्वतोभद्रा गुह्यशक्तिर्गुहालया ॥ ११९

हलायुधा चैकवीरा सर्वशस्त्रसुधारिणी ।
व्योमशक्तिर्महादेहा व्योमगा मधुमन्मयी ॥ १२०

गङ्गा वितस्ता यमुना चन्द्रभागा सरस्वती ।
तिलोत्तमोर्वशी रम्भा स्वामिनी सुरसुन्दरी ॥ १२१

बाणप्रहरणावाला बिम्बोष्ठी चारुहासिनी ।
ककुद्मिनी चारुपृष्ठा दृष्टादृष्टफलप्रदा ॥ १२२

काम्याचरी च काम्या च कामाचारविहारिणी ।
हिमशैलेन्द्रसंकाशा गजेन्द्रवरवाहना ॥ १२३

अशेषसुखसौभाग्यसम्पदा योनिरुत्तमा ।
सर्वोत्कृष्टा सर्वमयी सर्वा सर्वेश्वरप्रिया ॥ १२४

सर्वाङ्गयोनिः साव्यक्ता सम्प्रधानेश्वरेश्वरी ।
विष्णुवक्षःस्थलगता किमतः परमुच्यते ॥ १२५

परा निर्महिमा देवी हरिवक्षःस्थलाश्रया ।
सा देवी पापहन्त्री च सान्निध्यं कुरुतान्मम ॥ १२६

फलश्रुतिः ॥

इति नाम्नां सहस्रं तु लक्ष्म्याः प्रोक्तं शुभावहम् ।
परावरेण भेदेन मुख्यगौणेन भागतः ॥ १२७

यश्चैतत् कीर्तयेन्नित्यं शृणुयाद् वापि पद्मज ।
शुचिः समाहितो भूत्वा भक्तिश्रद्धासमन्वितः ॥ १२८

श्रीनिवासं समभ्यर्च्य पुष्पधूपानुलेपनैः ।
भोगैश्च मधुपर्काद्यैर्यथाशक्ति जगद्गुरुम् ॥ १२९

तत्पार्श्वस्थां श्रियं देवीं सम्पूज्य श्रीधरप्रियाम् ।
ततो नामसहस्रेण तोषयेत् परमेश्वरीम् ॥ १३०

नामरत्नावलीस्तोत्रमिदं यः सततं पठेत् ।
प्रसादाभिमुखीलक्ष्मीः सर्वं तस्मै प्रयच्छति ॥ १३१

यस्या लक्ष्म्याश्च सम्भूताः शक्तयो विश्वगाः सदा ।
कारणत्वे न तिष्ठन्ति जगत्यस्मिंश्चराचरे ॥ १३२

तस्मात् प्रीता जगन्माता श्रीर्यस्याच्युतवल्लभा ।
सुप्रीताः शक्तयस्तस्य सिद्धिमिष्टां दिशन्ति हि ॥ १३३

एक एव जगत्स्वामी शक्तिमानच्युतः प्रभुः ।
तदंशशक्तिमन्तोऽन्ये ब्रह्मेशानादयो यथा ॥ १३४

तथैवैका परा शक्तिः श्रीस्तस्य करुणाश्रया ।
ज्ञानादिषाड्गुण्यमयी या प्रोक्ता प्रकृतिः परा ॥ १३५

एकैव शक्तिः श्रीस्तस्या द्वितीयात्मनि वर्तते ।
परा परेशी सर्वेशी सर्वाकारा सनातनी ॥ १३६

अनन्तनामधेया च शक्तिचक्रस्य नायिका ।
जगच्चराचरमिदं सर्वं व्याप्य व्यवस्थिता ॥ १३७

तस्मादेकैव परमा श्रीर्ज्ञेया विश्वरूपिणी ।
सौम्या सौम्येन रूपेण संस्थिता नटजीववत् ॥ १३८

यो यो जगति पुम्भावः स विष्णुरिति निश्चयः ।
या या तु नारीभावस्था तत्र लक्ष्मीर्व्यवस्थिता ॥ १३९

प्रकृतेः पुरुषाच्चान्यस्तृतीयो नैव विद्यते ।
अथ किं बहुनोक्तेन नरनारीमयो हरिः ॥ १४०

अनेकभेदभिन्नस्तु क्रियते परमेश्वरः ।
महाविभूतिं दयितां येस्तु वन्त्यच्युतप्रियाम् ॥ १४१

ते प्राप्नुवन्ति परमां लक्ष्मीं संशुद्धचेतसः ।
पद्मयोनिरिदं प्राप्य पठन् स्तोत्रमिदं क्रमात् ॥ १४२

दिव्यमष्टगुणैश्वर्यं तत्प्रसादाच्च लब्धवान् ।
सकामानां च फलदामकामानां च मोक्षदाम् ॥ १४३

पुस्तकाख्यां भयत्रात्रीं सितवस्त्रां त्रिलोचनाम् ।
महापद्मनिषण्णां तां लक्ष्मीमजरतां नमः ॥ १४४

करयुगलगृहीतं पूर्णकुम्भं दधानाक्वचिदमलगतस्था शङ्खपद्माक्षपाणिः ।
क्वचिदपि दयिताङ्गे चामरव्यग्रहस्ताक्वचिदपि सृणिपाशं बिभ्रती हेमकान्तिः॥१४५

॥ इत्यादिपद्मपुराणे काश्मीरवर्णिने हिरण्यगर्भहृदये सर्वकामप्रदायकं पुरुषोत्तमप्रोक्तं
श्री लक्ष्मीसहस्रनामस्तोत्रं समाप्तम् ॥

*****

Śrī Kamalātmikā Sahasra Nāmāvaliḥ

1,000 divine names on *Śrī Kamalātmikā Devi.*

Dhyānam |

Kāntyā Kāñcanasannibhāṃ Himagiriprakhyaiścaturbhirgajaiḥ

Hastotkṣiptahiraṇmayāmṛtaghaṭairāsicyamānāṃ Śriyam |

Bibhrāṇāṃ Varamabjayugmamabhayaṃ Hastaiḥ Kirīṭojjvalāṃ

Kṣaumābaddha Nitambabimbalalitāṃ Vande'ravindasthitām ‖ 1

Māṇikyapratimaprabhāṃ Himanibhaistuṅgaiścaturbhirgajaiḥ

Hastāgrāhitaratnakumbhasalilairāsicyamānāṃ Mudā |

Hastābjairvaradānamambujayugābhītīrdadhānāṃ Hareḥ

Kāntāṃ Kāṅkṣitapārijātalatikāṃ Vande Sarojāsanām ‖ 2

Āsīnā Sarasīruhesmitamukhī Hastāmbujairbibhratī

Dānaṃ Padmayugābhaye Ca Vapuṣā Saudāminīsannibhā |

Muktāhāravirājamānapṛthulottuṅgastanodbhāsinī

Pāyādvaḥ Kamalā Kaṭākṣavibhavairānandayantī Harim ‖ 3

Sindūrāruṇakāntimabjavasatiṃ Saundaryavārānnidhiṃ

Koṭīrāṅgadahārakuṇḍalakaṭīsūtrādibhirbhūṣitām |

Hastābjairvasupatramabjayugalādarśau Vahantīṃ Parāṃ

Āvītāṃ Paricārikābhiraniśaṃ Seve Priyāṃ Śārṅgiṇaḥ ‖ 4

Bālārkadyutimindukhaṇḍavilasatkoṭīrahārojjvalāṃ

Ratnākalpavibhūṣitāṃ Kucanatāṃ Śāleḥ Karairmañjarīm |

Padmaṃ Kaustubharatnamapyaviratam Sambibhratīṃ Sasmitāṃ

Phullāmbhojavilocanatrayayutāṃ Vande Parāṃ Devatām ‖ 5

श्री कमला सहस्र नामावलिः ।

ध्यानम् ।

कान्त्या काञ्चनसन्निभां हिमगिरिप्रख्यैश्चतुर्भिर्गजैः
हस्तोत्क्षिप्तहिरण्मयामृतघटैरासिच्यमानां श्रियम् ।
बिभ्राणां वरमब्जयुग्ममभयं हस्तैः किरीटोज्ज्वलां
क्षौमाबद्ध नितम्बबिम्बललितां वन्देऽरविन्दस्थिताम् ॥ १

माणिक्यप्रतिमप्रभां हिमनिभैस्तुङ्गैश्चतुर्भिर्गजैः
हस्ताग्राहितरत्नकुम्भसलिलैरासिच्यमानां मुदा ।
हस्ताब्जैर्वरदानमम्बुजयुगाभीतीर्दधानां हरेः
कान्तां काङ्क्षितपारिजातलतिकां वन्दे सरोजासनाम् ॥ २

आसीना सरसीरुहेस्मितमुखी हस्ताम्बुजैर्बिभ्रती
दानं पद्ययुगाभये च वपुषा सौदामिनीसन्निभा ।
मुक्ताहारविराजमानपृथुलोत्तुङ्गस्तनोद्भासिनी
पायाद्वः कमला कटाक्षविभवैरानन्दयन्ती हरिम् ॥ ३

सिन्दूरारुणकान्तिमब्जवसतिं सौन्दर्यवारान्निधिं
कोटीराङ्गदहारकुण्डलकटीसूत्रादिभिर्भूषिताम् ।
हस्ताब्जैर्वसुपत्रमब्जयुगलादशौ वहन्तीं परां
आवीतां परिचारिकाभिरनिशं सेवे प्रियां शार्ङ्गिणः ॥ ४

बालार्कद्युतिमिन्दुखण्डविलसत्कोटीरहारोज्ज्वलां
रत्नाकल्पविभूषितां कुचनतां शालेः करैर्मञ्जरीम् ।
पद्मं कौस्तुभरत्नमप्यविरतं सम्बिभ्रती सस्मितां
फुल्लाम्भोजविलोचनत्रययुतां वन्दे परां देवताम् ॥ ५

Atha Sahasranāmāvaliḥ । अथ सहस्र नामावलिः ।

1.	*Oṃ Śriyai Namaḥ* ।	ॐ श्रियै नमः ।
2.	*Oṃ Padmāyai Namaḥ* ।	ॐ पद्मायै नमः ।
3.	*Oṃ Prakṛtyai Namaḥ* ।	ॐ प्रकृत्यै नमः ।
4.	*Oṃ Sattvāyai Namaḥ* ।	ॐ सत्त्वायै नमः ।
5.	*Oṃ Śāntāyai Namaḥ* ।	ॐ शान्तायै नमः ।
6.	*Oṃ Cicchaktyai Namaḥ* ।	ॐ चिच्छक्त्यै नमः ।
7.	*Oṃ Avyayāyai Namaḥ* ।	ॐ अव्ययायै नमः ।
8.	*Oṃ Kevalāyai Namaḥ* ।	ॐ केवलायै नमः ।
9.	*Oṃ Niṣkalāyai Namaḥ* ।	ॐ निष्कलायै नमः ।
10.	*Oṃ Śuddhāyai Namaḥ* ।	ॐ शुद्धायै नमः ।
11.	*Oṃ Vyāpinyai Namaḥ* ।	ॐ व्यापिन्यै नमः ।
12.	*Oṃ Vyomavigrahāyai Namaḥ* ।	ॐ व्योमविग्रहायै नमः ।

13.	*Oṃ Vyomapadmakṛtādhārāyai Namaḥ*	ॐ व्योमपद्मकृताधारायै नमः ।
14.	*Oṃ Parasmai Vyomne Namaḥ*	ॐ परस्मै व्योम्ने नमः ।
15.	*Oṃ Matodbhavāyai Namaḥ*	ॐ मतोद्भवायै नमः ।
16.	*Oṃ Nirvyomāyai Namaḥ*	ॐ निर्व्योमायै नमः ।
17.	*Oṃ Vyomamadhyasthāyai Namaḥ*	ॐ व्योममध्यस्थायै नमः ।
18.	*Oṃ Pañcavyomapadāśritāyai Namaḥ*	ॐ पञ्चव्योमपदाश्रितायै नमः ।
19.	*Oṃ Acyutāyai Namaḥ*	ॐ अच्युतायै नमः ।
20.	*Oṃ Vyomanilayāyai Namaḥ*	ॐ व्योमनिलयायै नमः ।
21.	*Oṃ Paramānandarūpiṇyai Namaḥ*	ॐ परमानन्दरूपिण्यै नमः ।
22.	*Oṃ Nityaśuddhāyai Namaḥ*	ॐ नित्यशुद्धायै नमः ।
23.	*Oṃ Nityatṛptāyai Namaḥ*	ॐ नित्यतृप्तायै नमः ।
24.	*Oṃ Nirvikārāyai Namaḥ*	ॐ निर्विकारायै नमः ।
25.	*Oṃ Nirīkṣaṇāyai Namaḥ*	ॐ निरीक्षणायै नमः ।
26.	*Oṃ Jñānaśaktyai Namaḥ*	ॐ ज्ञानशक्त्यै नमः ।
27.	*Oṃ Kartṛśaktyai Namaḥ*	ॐ कर्तृशक्त्यै नमः ।
28.	*Oṃ Bhoktṛśaktyai Namaḥ*	ॐ भोक्तृशक्त्यै नमः ।
29.	*Oṃ Śikhāvahāyai Namaḥ*	ॐ शिखावहायै नमः ।
30.	*Oṃ Snehābhāsāyai Namaḥ*	ॐ स्नेहाभासायै नमः ।
31.	*Oṃ Nirānandāyai Namaḥ*	ॐ निरानन्दायै नमः ।
32.	*Oṃ Vibhūtyai Namaḥ*	ॐ विभूत्यै नमः ।
33.	*Oṃ Vimalāyai Namaḥ*	ॐ विमलायै नमः ।
34.	*Oṃ Calāyai Namaḥ*	ॐ चलायै नमः ।
35.	*Oṃ Anantāyai Namaḥ*	ॐ अनन्तायै नमः ।
36.	*Oṃ Vaiṣṇavyai Namaḥ*	ॐ वैष्णव्यै नमः ।
37.	*Oṃ Vyaktāyai Namaḥ*	ॐ व्यक्तायै नमः ।
38.	*Oṃ Viśvānandāyai Namaḥ*	ॐ विश्वानन्दायै नमः ।
39.	*Oṃ Vikāśinyai Namaḥ*	ॐ विकाशिन्यै नमः ।
40.	*Oṃ Śaktyai Namaḥ*	ॐ शक्त्यै नमः ।

41.	Oṃ Vibhinnasarvārtyai Namaḥ		ॐ विभिन्नसर्वार्त्यै नमः ।
42.	Oṃ Samudraparitoṣiṇyai Namaḥ	ॐ समुद्रपरितोषिण्यै नमः ।
43.	Oṃ Mūrtyai Namaḥ		ॐ मूर्त्यै नमः ।
44.	Oṃ Sanātanyai Namaḥ		ॐ सनातन्यै नमः ।
45.	Oṃ Hārdyai Namaḥ		ॐ हार्द्यै नमः ।
46.	Oṃ Nistaraṅgāyai Namaḥ		ॐ निस्तरङ्गायै नमः ।
47.	Oṃ Nirāmayāyai Namaḥ		ॐ निरामयायै नमः ।
48.	Oṃ Jñānajñeyāyai Namaḥ		ॐ ज्ञानज्ञेयायै नमः ।
49.	Oṃ Jñānagamyāyai Namaḥ		ॐ ज्ञानगम्यायै नमः ।
50.	Oṃ Jñānajñeyavikāsinyai Namaḥ		ॐ ज्ञानज्ञेयविकासिन्यै नमः ।
51.	Oṃ Svacchandaśaktyai Namaḥ		ॐ स्वच्छन्दशक्त्यै नमः ।
52.	Oṃ Gahanāyai Namaḥ		ॐ गहनायै नमः ।
53.	Oṃ Niṣkampārcyai Namaḥ		ॐ निष्कम्पार्च्यै नमः ।
54.	Oṃ Sunirmalāyai Namaḥ		ॐ सुनिर्मलायै नमः ।
55.	Oṃ Svarūpāyai Namaḥ		ॐ स्वरूपायै नमः ।
56.	Oṃ Sarvagāyai Namaḥ		ॐ सर्वगायै नमः ।
57.	Oṃ Apārāyai Namaḥ		ॐ अपारायै नमः ।
58.	Oṃ Bṛṃhiṇyai Namaḥ		ॐ बृंहिण्यै नमः ।
59.	Oṃ Suguṇorjitāyai Namaḥ		ॐ सुगुणोर्जितायै नमः ।
60.	Oṃ Akalaṅkāyai Namaḥ		ॐ अकलङ्कायै नमः ।
61.	Oṃ Nirādhārāyai Namaḥ		ॐ निराधारायै नमः ।
62.	Oṃ Nissaṅkalpāyai Namaḥ		ॐ निस्सङ्कल्पायै नमः ।
63.	Oṃ Nirāśrayāyai Namaḥ		ॐ निराश्रयायै नमः ।
64.	Oṃ Asaṅkīrṇāyai Namaḥ		ॐ असङ्कीर्णायै नमः ।
65.	Oṃ Suśāntāyai Namaḥ		ॐ सुशान्तायै नमः ।
66.	Oṃ Śāśvatyai Namaḥ		ॐ शाश्वत्यै नमः ।
67.	Oṃ Bhāsuryai Namaḥ		ॐ भासुर्यै नमः ।
68.	Oṃ Sthirāyai Namaḥ		ॐ स्थिरायै नमः ।
69.	Oṃ Anaupamyāyai Namaḥ		ॐ अनौपम्यायै नमः ।
70.	Oṃ Nirvikalpāyai Namaḥ		ॐ निर्विकल्पायै नमः ।

71.	Oṃ Niryantrāyai Namaḥ		ॐ निर्यन्त्रायै नमः ।
72.	Oṃ Yantravāhinyai Namaḥ		ॐ यन्त्रवाहिन्यै नमः ।
73.	Oṃ Abhedyāyai Namaḥ		ॐ अभेद्यायै नमः ।
74.	Oṃ Bhedinyai Namaḥ		ॐ भेदिन्यै नमः ।
75.	Oṃ Bhinnāyai Namaḥ		ॐ भिन्नायै नमः ।
76.	Oṃ Bhāratyai Namaḥ		ॐ भारत्यै नमः ।
77.	Oṃ Vaikharyai Namaḥ		ॐ वैखर्यै नमः ।
78.	Oṃ Khagāyai Namaḥ		ॐ खगायै नमः ।
79.	Oṃ Agrāhyāyai Namaḥ		ॐ अग्राह्यायै नमः ।
80.	Oṃ Grāhikāyai Namaḥ		ॐ ग्राहिकायै नमः ।
81.	Oṃ Gūḍhāyai Namaḥ		ॐ गूढायै नमः ।
82.	Oṃ Gambhīrāyai Namaḥ		ॐ गम्भीरायै नमः ।
83.	Oṃ Viśvagopinyai Namaḥ		ॐ विश्वगोपिन्यै नमः ।
84.	Oṃ Anirdeśyāyai Namaḥ		ॐ अनिर्देश्यायै नमः ।
85.	Oṃ Apratihatāyai Namaḥ		ॐ अप्रतिहतायै नमः ।
86.	Oṃ Nirbījāyai Namaḥ		ॐ निर्बीजायै नमः ।
87.	Oṃ Pāvanyai Namaḥ		ॐ पावन्यै नमः ।
88.	Oṃ Parāyai Namaḥ		ॐ परायै नमः ।
89.	Oṃ Apratarkyāyai Namaḥ		ॐ अप्रतक्र्यायै नमः ।
90.	Oṃ Aparimitāyai Namaḥ		ॐ अपरिमितायै नमः ।
91.	Oṃ Bhavabhrāntivināśinyai Namaḥ	ॐ भवभ्रान्तिविनाशिन्यै नमः ।
92.	Oṃ Ekāyai Namaḥ		ॐ एकायै नमः ।
93.	Oṃ Dvirūpāyai Namaḥ		ॐ द्विरूपायै नमः ।
94.	Oṃ Trividhāyai Namaḥ		ॐ त्रिविधायै नमः ।
95.	Oṃ Asaṅkhyātāyai Namaḥ		ॐ असङ्ख्याताये नमः ।
96.	Oṃ Sureśvaryai Namaḥ		ॐ सुरेश्वर्यै नमः ।
97.	Oṃ Supratiṣṭhāyai Namaḥ		ॐ सुप्रतिष्ठायै नमः ।
98.	Oṃ Mahādhātryai Namaḥ		ॐ महाधात्र्यै नमः ।
99.	Oṃ Sthityai Namaḥ		ॐ स्थित्यै नमः ।
100	Oṃ Vṛddhyai Namaḥ		ॐ वृद्ध्यै नमः ।

101.	Oṃ Dhruvāyai Gatyai Namaḥ l	ॐ ध्रुवायै गत्यै नमः l
102.	Oṃ Īśvaryai Namaḥ l	ॐ ईश्वर्यै नमः l
103.	Oṃ Mahimāyai Namaḥ l	ॐ महिमायै नमः l
104.	Oṃ Ṛddhyai Namaḥ l	ॐ ऋद्ध्यै नमः l
105.	Oṃ Pramodāyai Namaḥ l	ॐ प्रमोदायै नमः l
106.	Oṃ Ujjvalodyamāyai Namaḥ l	ॐ उज्ज्वलोद्यमायै नमः l
107.	Oṃ Akṣayāyai Namaḥ l	ॐ अक्षयायै नमः l
108.	Oṃ Vardhamānāyai Namaḥ l	ॐ वर्धमानायै नमः l
109.	Oṃ Suprakāśāyai Namaḥ l	ॐ सुप्रकाशायै नमः l
110.	Oṃ Vihaṅgamāyai Namaḥ l	ॐ विहङ्गमायै नमः l
111.	Oṃ Nīrajāyai Namaḥ l	ॐ नीरजायै नमः l
112.	Oṃ Jananyai Namaḥ l	ॐ जनन्यै नमः l
113.	Oṃ Nityāyai Namaḥ l	ॐ नित्यायै नमः l
114.	Oṃ Jayāyai Namaḥ l	ॐ जयायै नमः l
115.	Oṃ Rociṣmatyai Namaḥ l	ॐ रोचिष्मत्यै नमः l
116.	Oṃ Śubhāyai Namaḥ l	ॐ शुभायै नमः l
117.	Oṃ Tamonudāyai Namaḥ l	ॐ तमोनुदायै नमः l
118.	Oṃ Jvālāyai Namaḥ l	ॐ ज्वालायै नमः l
119.	Oṃ Sudīptyai Namaḥ l	ॐ सुदीप्त्यै नमः l
120.	Oṃ Aṃśumālinyai Namaḥ l	ॐ अंशुमालिन्यै नमः l
121.	Oṃ Aprameyāyai Namaḥ l	ॐ अप्रमेयायै नमः l
122.	Oṃ Tridhā Sūkṣmāyai Namaḥ l	ॐ त्रिधा सूक्ष्मायै नमः l
123.	Oṃ Parāyai Namaḥ l	ॐ परायै नमः l
124.	Oṃ Nirvāṇadāyinyai Namaḥ l	ॐ निर्वाणदायिन्यै नमः l
125.	Oṃ Avadātāyai Namaḥ l	ॐ अवदातायै नमः l
126.	Oṃ Suśuddhāyai Namaḥ l	ॐ सुशुद्धायै नमः l
127.	Oṃ Amoghākhyāyai Namaḥ l	ॐ अमोघाख्यायै नमः l
128.	Oṃ Paramparāyai Namaḥ l	ॐ परम्परायै नमः l
129.	Oṃ Sandhānakyai Namaḥ l	ॐ सन्धानक्यै नमः l
130.	Oṃ Śuddhavidyāyai Namaḥ l	ॐ शुद्धविद्यायै नमः l

131	Oṃ Sarvabhūtamaheśvaryai Namaḥ	ॐ सर्वभूतमहेश्वर्यै नमः ।
132	Oṃ Lakṣmyai Namaḥ ।	ॐ लक्ष्म्यै नमः ।
133	Oṃ Tuṣṭyai Namaḥ ।	ॐ तुष्ट्यै नमः
134	Oṃ Mahādhīrāyai Namaḥ ।	ॐ महाधीरायै नमः ।
135	Oṃ Śāntyai Namaḥ ।	ॐ शान्त्यै नमः ।
136	Oṃ Āpūraṇe Navāyai Namaḥ ।	ॐ आपूरणे नवायै नमः ।
137	Oṃ Anugrahāśaktyai Namaḥ ।	ॐ अनुग्रहाशक्त्यै नमः ।
138	Oṃ Ādyāyai Namaḥ ।	ॐ आद्यायै नमः ।
139	Oṃ Jagajjyeṣṭhāyai Namaḥ ।	ॐ जगज्ज्येष्ठायै नमः ।
140	Oṃ Jagadvidhyai Namaḥ ।	ॐ जगद्विध्यै नमः ।
141	Oṃ Satyāyai Namaḥ ।	ॐ सत्यायै नमः ।
142	Oṃ Prahvāyai Namaḥ ।	ॐ प्रह्वायै नमः ।
143	Oṃ Kriyāyogyāyai Namaḥ ।	ॐ क्रियायोग्यायै नमः ।
144	Oṃ Aparṇāyai Namaḥ ।	ॐ अपर्णायै नमः ।
145	Oṃ Hlādinyai Namaḥ ।	ॐ ह्लादिन्यै नमः ।
146	Oṃ Śivāyai Namaḥ ।	ॐ शिवायै नमः ।
147	Oṃ Sampūrṇāhlādinyai Namaḥ ।	ॐ सम्पूर्णाह्लादिन्यै नमः ।
148	Oṃ Śuddhāyai Namaḥ ।	ॐ शुद्धायै नमः ।
149	Oṃ Jyotiṣmatyai Namaḥ ।	ॐ ज्योतिष्मत्यै नमः ।
150	Oṃ Amatāvahāyai Namaḥ ।	ॐ अमतावहायै नमः ।
151	Oṃ Rajovatyai Arkapratibhāyai Namaḥ ।	ॐ रजोवत्यै अर्कप्रतिभायै नमः ।
152	Oṃ Ākarṣiṇyai Namaḥ ।	ॐ आकर्षिण्यै नमः ।
153	Oṃ Karṣiṇyai Namaḥ ।	ॐ कर्षिण्यै नमः ।
154	Oṃ Rasāyai Namaḥ ।	ॐ रसायै नमः ।
155	Oṃ Parāyai Namaḥ ।	ॐ परायै नमः ।
156	Oṃ Vasumatyai Namaḥ ।	ॐ वसुमत्यै नमः ।
157	Oṃ Devyai Namaḥ ।	ॐ देव्यै नमः ।
158	Oṃ Kāntyai Namaḥ ।	ॐ कान्त्यै नमः ।
159	Oṃ Śāntyai Namaḥ ।	ॐ शान्त्यै नमः ।

160	Oṃ Matyai Namaḥ l	ॐ मत्यै नमः l
161	Oṃ Kalāyai Namaḥ l	ॐ कलायै नमः l
162	Oṃ Kalaṅkarahitāyai Namaḥ l	ॐ कलङ्करहितायै नमः l
163	Oṃ Viśāloddīpanyai Namaḥ l	ॐ विशालोद्दीपन्यै नमः l
164	Oṃ Ratyai Namaḥ l	ॐ रत्यै नमः l
165	Oṃ Sambodhinyai Namaḥ l	ॐ सम्बोधिन्यै नमः l
166	Oṃ Hāriṇyai Namaḥ l	ॐ हारिण्यै नमः l
167	Oṃ Prabhāvāyai Namaḥ l	ॐ प्रभावायै नमः l
168	Oṃ Bhavabhūtidāyai Namaḥ l	ॐ भवभूतिदायै नमः l
169	Oṃ Amṛtasyandinyai Namaḥ l	ॐ अमृतस्यन्दिन्यै नमः l
170	Oṃ Jīvāyai Namaḥ l	ॐ जीवायै नमः l
171	Oṃ Jananyai Namaḥ l	ॐ जनन्यै नमः l
172	Oṃ Khaṇḍikāyai Namaḥ l	ॐ खण्डिकायै नमः l
173	Oṃ Sthirāyai Namaḥ l	ॐ स्थिरायै नमः l
174	Oṃ Dhūmāyai Namaḥ l	ॐ धूमायै नमः l
175	Oṃ Kalāvatyai Namaḥ l	ॐ कलावत्यै नमः l
176	Oṃ Pūrṇāyai Namaḥ l	ॐ पूर्णायै नमः l
177	Oṃ Bhāsurāyai Namaḥ l	ॐ भासुरायै नमः l
178	Oṃ Sumatyai Namaḥ l	ॐ सुमत्यै नमः l
179	Oṃ Rasāyai Namaḥ l	ॐ रसायै नमः l
180	Oṃ Śuddhāyai Namaḥ l	ॐ शुद्धायै नमः l
181	Oṃ Dhvanyai Namaḥ l	ॐ ध्वन्यै नमः l
182	Oṃ Sṛtyai Namaḥ l	ॐ सृत्यै नमः l
183	Oṃ Sṛṣṭyai Namaḥ l	ॐ सृष्ट्यै नमः l
184	Oṃ Vikṛtyai Namaḥ l	ॐ विकृत्यै नमः l
185	Oṃ Kṛṣṭyai Namaḥ l	ॐ कृष्ट्यै नमः l
186	Oṃ Prāpaṇyai Namaḥ l	ॐ प्रापण्यै नमः l
187	Oṃ Prāṇadāyai Namaḥ l	ॐ प्राणदायै नमः l
188	Oṃ Prahvāyai Namaḥ l	ॐ प्रह्वायै नमः l
189	Oṃ Viśvāyai Namaḥ l	ॐ विश्वायै नमः l

190	Oṃ Pāṇḍuravāsinyai Namaḥ		ॐ पाण्डुरवासिन्यै नमः	
191	Oṃ Avanyai Namaḥ		ॐ अवन्यै नमः	
192	Oṃ Vajranalikāyai Namaḥ		ॐ वज्रनलिकायै नमः	
193	Oṃ Citrāyai Namaḥ		ॐ चित्रायै नमः	
194	Oṃ Brahmāṇḍavāsinyai Namaḥ		ॐ ब्रह्माण्डवासिन्यै नमः	
195	Oṃ Anantarūpāyai Namaḥ		ॐ अनन्तरूपायै नमः	
196	Oṃ Anantātmane Namaḥ		ॐ अनन्तात्मने नमः	
197	Oṃ Anantasthāyai Namaḥ		ॐ अनन्तस्थायै नमः	
198	Oṃ Anantasambhavāyai Namaḥ	ॐ अनन्तसम्भवायै नमः	
199	Oṃ Mahāśaktyai Namaḥ		ॐ महाशक्त्यै नमः	
200	Oṃ Prāṇaśaktyai Namaḥ		ॐ प्राणशक्त्यै नमः	
201	Oṃ Prāṇadātryai Namaḥ		ॐ प्राणदात्र्यै नमः	
202	Oṃ Ratimbharāyai Namaḥ		ॐ रतिम्भरायै नमः	
203	Oṃ Mahāsamūhāyai Namaḥ		ॐ महासमूहायै नमः	
204	Oṃ Nikhilāyai Namaḥ		ॐ निखिलायै नमः	
205	Oṃ Icchādhārāyai Namaḥ		ॐ इच्छाधारायै नमः	
206	Oṃ Sukhāvahāyai Namaḥ		ॐ सुखावहायै नमः	
207	Oṃ Pratyakṣalakṣmyai Namaḥ		ॐ प्रत्यक्षलक्ष्म्यै नमः	
208	Oṃ Niṣkampāyai Namaḥ		ॐ निष्कम्पायै नमः	
209	Oṃ Prarohāyai Namaḥ		ॐ प्ररोहायै नमः	
210	Oṃ Buddhigocarāyai Namaḥ		ॐ बुद्धिगोचरायै नमः	
211	Oṃ Nānādehāyai Namaḥ		ॐ नानादेहायै नमः	
212	Oṃ Mahāvartāyai Namaḥ		ॐ महावर्तायै नमः	
213	Oṃ Bahudehavikāsinyai Namaḥ	ॐ बहुदेहविकासिन्यै नमः	
214	Oṃ Sahasrāṇyai Namaḥ		ॐ सहस्राण्यै नमः	
215	Oṃ Pradhānāyai Namaḥ		ॐ प्रधानायै नमः	
216	Oṃ Nyāyavastuprakāśikāyai Namaḥ	ॐ न्यायवस्तुप्रकाशिकायै नमः
217	Oṃ Sarvābhilāṣapūrṇāyai Namaḥ		ॐ सर्वाभिलाषपूर्णायै नमः	
218	Oṃ Icchāyai Namaḥ		ॐ इच्छायै नमः	
219	Oṃ Sarvāyai Namaḥ		ॐ सर्वायै नमः	

220.	Oṃ Sarvārthabhāṣiṇyai Namaḥ		ॐ सर्वार्थभाषिण्यै नमः ।
221.	Oṃ Nānāsvarūpaciddhātryai Namaḥ	ॐ नानास्वरूपचिद्धात्र्यै नमः ।
222.	Oṃ Śabdapūrvāyai Namaḥ		ॐ शब्दपूर्वायै नमः ।
223.	Oṃ Purātanāyai Namaḥ		ॐ पुरातनायै नमः ।
224.	Oṃ Vyaktāyai Namaḥ		ॐ व्यक्तायै नमः ।
225.	Oṃ Avyaktāyai Namaḥ		ॐ अव्यक्तायै नमः ।
226.	Oṃ Jīvakeśāyai Namaḥ		ॐ जीवकेशायै नमः ।
227.	Oṃ Sarvecchāparipūritāyai Namaḥ		ॐ सर्वेच्छापरिपूरितायै नमः ।
228.	Oṃ Saṅkalpasiddhāyai Namaḥ		ॐ सङ्कल्पसिद्धायै नमः ।
229.	Oṃ Sāṅkhyeyāyai Namaḥ		ॐ साङ्ख्येयायै नमः ।
230.	Oṃ Tattvagarbhāyai Namaḥ		ॐ तत्त्वगर्भायै नमः ।
231.	Oṃ Dharāvahāyai Namaḥ		ॐ धरावहायै नमः ।
232.	Oṃ Bhūtarūpāyai Namaḥ		ॐ भूतरूपायै नमः ।
233.	Oṃ Citsvarūpāyai Namaḥ		ॐ चित्स्वरूपायै नमः ।
234.	Oṃ Triguṇāyai Namaḥ		ॐ त्रिगुणायै नमः ।
235.	Oṃ Guṇagarvitāyai Namaḥ		ॐ गुणगर्विताये नमः ।
236.	Oṃ Prajāpatīśvaryai Namaḥ		ॐ प्रजापतीश्वर्यै नमः ।
237.	Oṃ Raudryai Namaḥ		ॐ रौद्र्यै नमः ।
238.	Oṃ Sarvādhārāyai Namaḥ		ॐ सर्वाधारायै नमः ।
239.	Oṃ Sukhāvahāyai Namaḥ		ॐ सुखावहायै नमः ।
240.	Oṃ Kalyāṇavāhikāyai Namaḥ		ॐ कल्याणवाहिकायै नमः ।
241.	Oṃ Kalyāyai Namaḥ		ॐ कल्यायै नमः ।
242.	Oṃ Kalikalmaṣanāśinyai Namaḥ	ॐ कलिकल्मषनाशिन्यै नमः ।
243.	Oṃ Nirūpāyai Namaḥ		ॐ नीरूपायै नमः ।
244.	Oṃ Udbhinnasantānāyai Namaḥ	ॐ उद्भिन्नसन्तानायै नमः ।
245.	Oṃ Suyantrāyai Namaḥ		ॐ सुयन्त्रायै नमः ।
246.	Oṃ Triguṇālayāyai Namaḥ		ॐ त्रिगुणालयायै नमः ।
247.	Oṃ Mahāmāyāyai Namaḥ		ॐ महामायायै नमः ।
248.	Oṃ Yogamāyāyai Namaḥ		ॐ योगमायायै नमः ।
249.	Oṃ Mahāyogeśvaryai Namaḥ		ॐ महायोगेश्वर्यै नमः ।

250	Oṃ Priyāyai Namaḥ		ॐ प्रियायै नमः ।
251	Oṃ Mahāstryai Namaḥ		ॐ महास्त्रयै नमः ।
252	Oṃ Vimalāyai Namaḥ		ॐ विमलायै नमः ।
253	Oṃ Kīrtyai Namaḥ		ॐ कीर्त्यै नमः ।
254	Oṃ Jayāyai Namaḥ		ॐ जयायै नमः ।
255	Oṃ Lakṣmyai Namaḥ		ॐ लक्ष्म्यै नमः ।
256	Oṃ Nirañjanāyai Namaḥ		ॐ निरञ्जनायै नमः ।
257	Oṃ Prakṛtyai Namaḥ		ॐ प्रकृत्यै नमः ।
258	Oṃ Bhagavanmāyāśaktyai Namaḥ		ॐ भगवन्मायाशक्त्यै नमः ।
259	Oṃ Nidrāyai Namaḥ		ॐ निद्रायै नमः ।
260	Oṃ Yaśaskaryai Namaḥ		ॐ यशस्कर्यै नमः ।
261	Oṃ Cintāyai Namaḥ		ॐ चिन्तायै नमः ।
262	Oṃ Buddhyai Namaḥ		ॐ बुद्ध्यै नमः ।
263	Oṃ Yaśase Namaḥ		ॐ यशसे नमः ।
264	Oṃ Prajñāyai Namaḥ		ॐ प्रज्ञायै नमः ।
265	Oṃ Śāntyai Namaḥ		ॐ शान्त्यै नमः ।
266	Oṃ Āprītivardhinyai Namaḥ		ॐ आप्रीतिवर्धिन्यै नमः ।
267	Oṃ Pradyumnamātre Namaḥ		ॐ प्रद्युम्नमात्रे नमः ।
268	Oṃ Sādhvyai Namaḥ		ॐ साध्व्यै नमः ।
269	Oṃ Sukhasaubhāgyasiddhidāyai Namaḥ		ॐ सुखसौभाग्यसिद्धिदायै नमः।
270	Oṃ Kāṣṭhāyai Namaḥ		ॐ काष्ठायै नमः ।
271	Oṃ Niṣṭhāyai Namaḥ		ॐ निष्ठायै नमः ।
272	Oṃ Pratiṣṭhāyai Namaḥ		ॐ प्रतिष्ठायै नमः ।
273	Oṃ Jyeṣṭhāyai Namaḥ		ॐ ज्येष्ठायै नमः ।
274	Oṃ Śreṣṭhāyai Namaḥ		ॐ श्रेष्ठायै नमः ।
275	Oṃ Jayāvahāyai Namaḥ		ॐ जयावहायै नमः ।
276	Oṃ Sarvātiśāyinyai Prītyai Namaḥ		ॐ सर्वातिशायिन्यै प्रीत्यै नमः ।
277	Oṃ Viśvaśaktyai Namaḥ		ॐ विश्वशक्त्यै नमः ।
278	Oṃ Mahābalāyai Namaḥ		ॐ महाबलायै नमः ।

279	Oṃ Variṣṭhāyai Namaḥ ।	ॐ वरिष्ठायै नमः ।
280	Oṃ Vijayāyai Namaḥ ।	ॐ विजयायै नमः ।
281	Oṃ Vīrāyai Namaḥ ।	ॐ वीरायै नमः ।
282	Oṃ Jayantyai Namaḥ ।	ॐ जयन्त्यै नमः ।
283	Oṃ Vijayapradāyai Namaḥ ।	ॐ विजयप्रदायै नमः ।
284	Oṃ Hṛdgṛhāyai Namaḥ ।	ॐ हृद्गृहायै नमः ।
285	Oṃ Gopinyai Namaḥ ।	ॐ गोपिन्यै नमः ।
286	Oṃ Guhyāyai Namaḥ ।	ॐ गुह्यायै नमः ।
287	Oṃ Gaṇagandharvasevitāyai Namaḥ	ॐ गणगन्धर्वसेवितायै नमः ।
288	Oṃ Yogīśvaryai Namaḥ ।	ॐ योगीश्वर्यै नमः ।
289	Oṃ Yogamāyāyai Namaḥ ।	ॐ योगमायायै नमः ।
290	Oṃ Yoginyai Namaḥ ।	ॐ योगिन्यै नमः ।
291	Oṃ Yogasiddhidāyai Namaḥ ।	ॐ योगसिद्धिदायै नमः ।
292	Oṃ Mahāyogeśvaravṛtāyai Namaḥ ।	ॐ महायोगेश्वरवृतायै नमः ।
293	Oṃ Yogāyai Namaḥ ।	ॐ योगायै नमः ।
294	Oṃ Yogeśvarapriyāyai Namaḥ ।	ॐ योगेश्वरप्रियायै नमः ।
295	Oṃ Brahmendrarudranamitāyai Namaḥ ।	ॐ ब्रह्मेन्द्ररुद्रनमितायै नमः ।
296	Oṃ Surāsuravarapradāyai Namaḥ ।	ॐ सुरासुरवरप्रदायै नमः ।
297	Oṃ Trivartmagāyai Namaḥ ।	ॐ त्रिवर्त्मगायै नमः ।
298	Oṃ Trilokasthāyai Namaḥ ।	ॐ त्रिलोकस्थायै नमः ।
299	Oṃ Trivikramapadodbhavāyai Namaḥ ।	ॐ त्रिविक्रमपदोद्भवायै नमः ।
300	Oṃ Sutārāyai Namaḥ ।	ॐ सुतारायै नमः ।
301	Oṃ Tāriṇyai Namaḥ ।	ॐ तारिण्यै नमः ।
302	Oṃ Tārāyai Namaḥ ।	ॐ तारायै नमः ।
303	Oṃ Durgāyai Namaḥ ।	ॐ दुर्गायै नमः ।
304	Oṃ Santāriṇyai Parāyai Namaḥ ।	ॐ सन्तारिण्यै परायै नमः ।
305	Oṃ Sutāriṇyai Namaḥ ।	ॐ सुतारिण्यै नमः ।
306	Oṃ Tārayantyai Namaḥ ।	ॐ तारयन्त्यै नमः ।
307	Oṃ Bhūritāreśvaraprabhāyai Namaḥ	ॐ भूरितारेश्वरप्रभायै नमः ।

308	Oṃ Guhyavidyāyai Namaḥ ǀ	ॐ गुह्यविद्यायै नमः ǀ
309	Oṃ Yajñavidyāyai Namaḥ ǀ	ॐ यज्ञविद्यायै नमः ǀ
310	Oṃ Mahāvidyāsuśobhitāyai Namaḥ	ॐ महाविद्यासुशोभितायै नमः
311	Oṃ Adhyātmavidyāyai Namaḥ ǀ	ॐ अध्यात्मविद्यायै नमः ǀ
312	Oṃ Vighneśyai Namaḥ ǀ	ॐ विघ्नेश्यै नमः ǀ
313	Oṃ Padmasthāyai Namaḥ ǀ	ॐ पद्मस्थायै नमः ǀ
314	Oṃ Parameṣṭhinyai Namaḥ ǀ	ॐ परमेष्ठिन्यै नमः ǀ
315	Oṃ Ānvīkṣikyai Namaḥ ǀ	ॐ आन्वीक्षिक्यै नमः ǀ
316	Oṃ Trayyai Namaḥ ǀ	ॐ त्रय्यै नमः ǀ
317	Oṃ Vārtāyai Namaḥ ǀ	ॐ वार्तायै नमः ǀ
318	Oṃ Daṇḍanītyai Namaḥ ǀ	ॐ दण्डनीत्यै नमः ǀ
319	Oṃ Nayātmikāyai Namaḥ ǀ	ॐ नयात्मिकायै नमः ǀ
320	Oṃ Gauryai Namaḥ ǀ	ॐ गौर्यै नमः ǀ
321	Oṃ Vāgīśvaryai Namaḥ ǀ	ॐ वागीश्वर्यै नमः ǀ
322	Oṃ Goptryai Namaḥ ǀ	ॐ गोप्त्र्यै नमः ǀ
323	Oṃ Gāyatryai Namaḥ ǀ	ॐ गायत्र्यै नमः ǀ
324	Oṃ Kamalodbhavāyai Namaḥ ǀ	ॐ कमलोद्भवायै नमः ǀ
325	Oṃ Viśvambharāyai Namaḥ ǀ	ॐ विश्वम्भरायै नमः ǀ
326	Oṃ Viśvarūpāyai Namaḥ ǀ	ॐ विश्वरूपायै नमः ǀ
327	Oṃ Viśvamātre Namaḥ ǀ	ॐ विश्वमात्रे नमः ǀ
328	Oṃ Vasupradāyai Namaḥ ǀ	ॐ वसुप्रदायै नमः ǀ
329	Oṃ Siddhyai Namaḥ ǀ	ॐ सिद्ध्यै नमः ǀ
330	Oṃ Svāhāyai Namaḥ ǀ	ॐ स्वाहायै नमः ǀ
331	Oṃ Svadhāyai Namaḥ ǀ	ॐ स्वधायै नमः ǀ
332	Oṃ Svastyai Namaḥ ǀ	ॐ स्वस्त्यै नमः ǀ
333	Oṃ Sudhāyai Namaḥ ǀ	ॐ सुधायै नमः ǀ
334	Oṃ Sarvārthasādhinyai Namaḥ ǀ	ॐ सर्वार्थिसाधिन्यै नमः ǀ
335	Oṃ Icchāyai Namaḥ ǀ	ॐ इच्छायै नमः ǀ
336	Oṃ Sṛṣṭyai Namaḥ ǀ	ॐ सृष्ट्यै नमः ǀ
337	Oṃ Dyutyai Namaḥ ǀ	ॐ द्युत्यै नमः ǀ

338	Om Bhūtyai Namaḥ		ॐ भूत्यै नमः ।
339	Om Kīrtyai Namaḥ		ॐ कीर्त्यै नमः ।
340	Om Śraddhāyai Namaḥ		ॐ श्रद्धायै नमः ।
341	Om Dayāyai Namaḥ		ॐ दयायै नमः ।
342	Om Matyai Namaḥ		ॐ मत्यै नमः ।
343	Om Śrutyai Namaḥ		ॐ श्रुत्यै नमः ।
344	Om Medhāyai Namaḥ		ॐ मेधायै नमः ।
345	Om Dhṛtyai Namaḥ		ॐ धृत्यै नमः ।
346	Om Hriyai Namaḥ		ॐ हियै नमः ।
347	Om Śriyai Namaḥ		ॐ श्रियै नमः ।
348	Om Vidyāyai Namaḥ		ॐ विद्यायै नमः ।
349	Om Vibudhavanditāyai Namaḥ		ॐ विबुधवन्दितायै नमः ।
350	Om Anasūyāyai Namaḥ		ॐ अनसूयायै नमः ।
351	Om Ghṛṇāyai Namaḥ		ॐ घृणायै नमः ।
352	Om Nītyai Namaḥ		ॐ नीत्यै नमः ।
353	Om Nirvṛtyai Namaḥ		ॐ निर्वृत्यै नमः ।
354	Om Kāmadhukkarāyai Namaḥ		ॐ कामधुक्करायै नमः ।
355	Om Pratijñāyai Namaḥ		ॐ प्रतिज्ञायै नमः ।
356	Om Santatyai Namaḥ		ॐ सन्तत्यै नमः ।
357	Om Bhūtyai Namaḥ		ॐ भूत्यै नमः ।
358	Om Dive Namaḥ		ॐ दिवे नमः ।
359	Om Prajñāyai Namaḥ		ॐ प्रज्ञायै नमः ।
360	Om Viśvamāninyai Namaḥ		ॐ विश्वमानिन्यै नमः ।
361	Om Smṛtyai Namaḥ		ॐ स्मृत्यै नमः ।
362	Om Vāce Namaḥ		ॐ वाचे नमः ।
363	Om Viśvajananyai Namaḥ		ॐ विश्वजनन्यै नमः ।
364	Om Paśyantyai Namaḥ		ॐ पश्यन्त्यै नमः ।
365	Om Madhyamāyai Namaḥ		ॐ मध्यमायै नमः ।
366	Om Samāyai Namaḥ		ॐ समायै नमः ।
367	Om Sandhyāyai Namaḥ		ॐ सन्ध्यायै नमः ।

368.	Oṃ Medhāyai Namaḥ		ॐ मेधायै नमः ।
369.	Oṃ Prabhāyai Namaḥ		ॐ प्रभायै नमः ।
370.	Oṃ Bhīmāyai Namaḥ		ॐ भीमायै नमः ।
371.	Oṃ Sarvākārāyai Namaḥ		ॐ सर्वाकाराये नमः ।
372.	Oṃ Sarasvatyai Namaḥ		ॐ सरस्वत्यै नमः ।
373.	Oṃ Kāṅkṣāyai Namaḥ		ॐ काङ्क्षायै नमः ।
374.	Oṃ Māyāyai Namaḥ		ॐ मायायै नमः ।
375.	Oṃ Mahāmāyāmohinyai Namaḥ	ॐ महामायामोहिन्यै नमः ।
376.	Oṃ Mādhavapriyāyai Namaḥ		ॐ माधवप्रियायै नमः ।
377.	Oṃ Saumyābhogāyai Namaḥ		ॐ सौम्याभोगायै नमः ।
378.	Oṃ Mahābhogāyai Namaḥ		ॐ महाभोगायै नमः ।
379.	Oṃ Bhoginyai Namaḥ		ॐ भोगिन्यै नमः ।
380.	Oṃ Bhogadāyinyai Namaḥ		ॐ भोगदायिन्यै नमः ।
381.	Oṃ Sudhautakanakaprakhyāyai Namaḥ		ॐ सुधौतकनकप्रख्यायै नमः ।
382.	Oṃ Suvarṇakamalāsanāyai Namaḥ		ॐ सुवर्णकमलासनायै नमः ।
383.	Oṃ Hiraṇyagarbhāyai Namaḥ		ॐ हिरण्यगर्भायै नमः ।
384.	Oṃ Suśroṇyai Namaḥ		ॐ सुश्रोण्यै नमः ।
385.	Oṃ Hāriṇyai Namaḥ		ॐ हारिण्यै नमः ।
386.	Oṃ Ramaṇyai Namaḥ		ॐ रमण्यै नमः ।
387.	Oṃ Ramāyai Namaḥ		ॐ रमायै नमः ।
388.	Oṃ Candrāyai Namaḥ		ॐ चन्द्रायै नमः ।
389.	Oṃ Hiraṇmayyai Namaḥ		ॐ हिरण्मय्यै नमः ।
390.	Oṃ Jyotsnāyai Namaḥ		ॐ ज्योत्स्नायै नमः ।
391.	Oṃ Ramyāyai Namaḥ		ॐ रम्यायै नमः ।
392.	Oṃ Śobhāyai Namaḥ		ॐ शोभायै नमः ।
393.	Oṃ Śubhāvahāyai Namaḥ		ॐ शुभावहायै नमः ।
394.	Oṃ Trailokyamaṇḍanāyai Namaḥ		ॐ त्रैलोक्यमण्डनायै नमः ।
395.	Oṃ Nārīnareśvaravarārcitāyai Namaḥ		ॐ नारीनरेश्वरवरार्चिताये नमः ।
396.	Oṃ Trailokyasundaryai Namaḥ		ॐ त्रैलोक्यसुन्दर्यै नमः ।

397.	Oṃ Rāmāyai Namaḥ		ॐ रामायै नमः ।
398.	Oṃ Mahāvibhavavāhinyai Namaḥ		ॐ महाविभववाहिन्यै नमः ।
399.	Oṃ Padmasthāyai Namaḥ		ॐ पद्मस्थायै नमः ।
400.	Oṃ Padmanilayāyai Namaḥ		ॐ पद्मनिलयायै नमः ।
401.	Oṃ Padmamālāvibhūṣitāyai Namaḥ	ॐ पद्ममालाविभूषितायै नमः ।
402.	Oṃ Padmayugmadharāyai Namaḥ		ॐ पद्मयुग्मधरायै नमः ।
403.	Oṃ Kāntāyai Namaḥ		ॐ कान्तायै नमः ।
404.	Oṃ Divyābharaṇabhūṣitāyai Namaḥ	ॐ दिव्याभरणभूषितायै नमः ।
405.	Oṃ Vicitraratnamukuṭāyai Namaḥ		ॐ विचित्ररत्नमुकुटायै नमः ।
406.	Oṃ Vicitrāmbarabhūṣitāyai Namaḥ	ॐ विचित्राम्बरभूषितायै नमः ।
407.	Oṃ Vicitramālyagandhāḍhyāyai Namaḥ		ॐ विचित्रमाल्यगन्धाढ्यायै नमः ।
408.	Oṃ Vicitrāyudhavāhanāyai Namaḥ		ॐ विचित्रायुधवाहनायै नमः ।
409.	Oṃ Mahānārāyaṇīdevyai Namaḥ		ॐ महानारायणीदेव्यै नमः ।
410.	Oṃ Vaiṣṇavyai Namaḥ		ॐ वैष्णव्यै नमः ।
411.	Oṃ Vīravanditāyai Namaḥ		ॐ वीरवन्दितायै नमः ।
412.	Oṃ Kālasaṅkarṣiṇyai Namaḥ		ॐ कालसङ्कर्षिण्यै नमः ।
413.	Oṃ Ghorāyai Namaḥ		ॐ घोरायै नमः ।
414.	Oṃ Tattvasaṅkarṣiṇyai Kalāyai Namaḥ		ॐ तत्त्वसङ्कर्षिण्यै कलायै नमः ।
415.	Oṃ Jagatsampūraṇyai Namaḥ		ॐ जगत्सम्पूरण्यै नमः ।
416.	Oṃ Viśvāyai Namaḥ		ॐ विश्वायै नमः ।
417.	Oṃ Mahāvibhavabhūṣaṇāyai Namaḥ		ॐ महाविभवभूषणायै नमः ।
418.	Oṃ Vāruṇyai Namaḥ		ॐ वारुण्यै नमः ।
419.	Oṃ Varadāyai Namaḥ		ॐ वरदायै नमः ।
420.	Oṃ Vyākhyāyai Namaḥ		ॐ व्याख्यायै नमः ।
421.	Oṃ Ghaṇṭākarṇavirājitāyai Namaḥ		ॐ घण्टाकर्णविराजितायै नमः ।
422.	Oṃ Nṛsiṃhyai Namaḥ		ॐ नृसिंह्यै नमः ।
423.	Oṃ Bhairavyai Namaḥ		ॐ भैरव्यै नमः ।
424.	Oṃ Brāhmyai Namaḥ		ॐ ब्राह्म्यै नमः ।

425	Oṃ Bhāskaryai Namaḥ		ॐ भास्कर्यै नमः ।
426	Oṃ Vyomacāriṇyai Namaḥ		ॐ व्योमचारिण्यै नमः ।
427	Oṃ Aindryai Namaḥ		ॐ ऐन्द्र्यै नमः ।
428	Oṃ Kāmadhanussṛṣṭyai Namaḥ		ॐ कामधनुस्सृष्ट्यै नमः ।
429	Oṃ Kāmayonyai Namaḥ		ॐ कामयोन्यै नमः ।
430	Oṃ Mahāprabhāyai Namaḥ		ॐ महाप्रभायै नमः ।
431	Oṃ Dṛṣṭāyai Namaḥ		ॐ दृष्टायै नमः ।
432	Oṃ Kāmyāyai Namaḥ		ॐ काम्यायै नमः ।
433	Oṃ Viśvaśaktyai Namaḥ		ॐ विश्वशक्त्यै नमः ।
434	Oṃ Bījagatyātmadarśanāyai Namaḥ	ॐ बीजगत्यात्मदर्शनायै नमः ।
435	Oṃ Garuḍārūḍhahṛdayāyai Namaḥ		ॐ गरुडारूढहृदयायै नमः ।
436	Oṃ Cāndryai Śriye Namaḥ		ॐ चान्द्र्यै श्रिये नमः ।
437	Oṃ Madhurānanāyai Namaḥ		ॐ मधुराननायै नमः ।
438	Oṃ Mahograrūpāyai Namaḥ		ॐ महोग्ररूपायै नमः ।
439	Oṃ Vārāhīnārasiṃhīhatāsurāyai Namaḥ		ॐ वाराहीनारसिंहीहतासुराये नमः ।
440	Oṃ Yugāntahutabhugjvālāyai Namaḥ		ॐ युगान्तहुतभुग्ज्वालाये नमः ।
441	Oṃ Karālāyai Namaḥ		ॐ करालाये नमः ।
442	Oṃ Piṅgalāyai Kalāyai Namaḥ		ॐ पिङ्गलाये कलाये नमः ।
443	Oṃ Trailokyabhūṣaṇāyai Namaḥ		ॐ त्रैलोक्यभूषणाये नमः ।
444	Oṃ Bhīmāyai Namaḥ		ॐ भीमाये नमः ।
445	Oṃ Śyāmāyai Namaḥ		ॐ श्यामाये नमः ।
446	Oṃ Trailokyamohinyai Namaḥ		ॐ त्रैलोक्यमोहिन्ये नमः ।
447	Oṃ Mahotkaṭāyai Namaḥ		ॐ महोत्कटाये नमः ।
448	Oṃ Mahāraktāyai Namaḥ		ॐ महारक्ताये नमः ।
449	Oṃ Vyahācaṇḍāyai Namaḥ		ॐ व्यहाचण्डाये नमः ।
450	Oṃ Mahāsanāyai Namaḥ		ॐ महासनाये नमः ।
451	Oṃ Śaṅkhinyai Namaḥ		ॐ शङ्खिन्ये नमः ।
452	Oṃ Lekhinyai Namaḥ		ॐ लेखिन्ये नमः ।

453	Oṃ Svasthālikhitāyai Namaḥ		ॐ स्वस्थालिखितायै नमः ।
454	Oṃ Khecareśvaryai Namaḥ		ॐ खेचरेश्वर्यै नमः ।
455	Oṃ Bhadrakālyai Namaḥ		ॐ भद्रकाल्यै नमः ।
456	Oṃ Ekavīrāyai Namaḥ		ॐ एकवीरायै नमः ।
457	Oṃ Kaumāryai Namaḥ		ॐ कौमार्यै नमः ।
458	Oṃ Bhagamālinyai Namaḥ		ॐ भगमालिन्यै नमः ।
459	Oṃ Kalyāṇyai Namaḥ		ॐ कल्याण्यै नमः ।
460	Oṃ Kāmadhugjvālāmukhyai Namaḥ	ॐ कामधुग्ज्वालामुख्यै नमः ।
461	Oṃ Utpalamālikāyai Namaḥ		ॐ उत्पलमालिकायै नमः ।
462	Oṃ Bālikāyai Namaḥ		ॐ बालिकायै नमः ।
463	Oṃ Dhanadāyai Namaḥ		ॐ धनदायै नमः ।
464	Oṃ Sūryāyai Namaḥ		ॐ सूर्यायै नमः ।
465	Oṃ Hṛdayotpalamālikāyai Namaḥ		ॐ हृदयोत्पलमालिकायै नमः ।
466	Oṃ Ajitāyai Namaḥ		ॐ अजितायै नमः ।
467	Oṃ Varṣiṇyai Namaḥ		ॐ वर्षिण्यै नमः ।
468	Oṃ Rītyai Namaḥ		ॐ रीत्यै नमः ।
469	Oṃ Bheruṇḍāyai Namaḥ		ॐ भेरुण्डायै नमः ।
470	Oṃ Garuḍāsanāyai Namaḥ		ॐ गरुडासनायै नमः ।
471	Oṃ Vaiśvānarīmahāmāyāyai Namaḥ	ॐ वैश्वानरीमहामायायै नमः ।
472	Oṃ Mahākālyai Namaḥ		ॐ महाकाल्यै नमः ।
473	Oṃ Vibhīṣaṇāyai Namaḥ		ॐ विभीषणायै नमः ।
474	Oṃ Mahāmandāravibhavāyai Namaḥ		ॐ महामन्दारविभवायै नमः ।
475	Oṃ Śivānandāyai Namaḥ		ॐ शिवानन्दायै नमः ।
476	Oṃ Ratipriyāyai Namaḥ		ॐ रतिप्रियायै नमः ।
477	Oṃ Udṛtyai Namaḥ		ॐ उद्रीत्यै नमः ।
478	Oṃ Padmamālāyai Namaḥ		ॐ पद्ममालायै नमः ।
479	Oṃ Dharmavegāyai Namaḥ		ॐ धर्मवेगायै नमः ।
480	Oṃ Vibhāvanyai Namaḥ		ॐ विभावन्यै नमः ।
481	Oṃ Satkriyāyai Namaḥ		ॐ सत्क्रियायै नमः ।

482	Oṃ Devasenāyai Namaḥ		ॐ देवसेनायै नमः ।
483	Oṃ Hiraṇyarajatāśrayāyai Namaḥ		ॐ हिरण्यरजताश्रयायै नमः ।
484	Oṃ Sahasāvartamānāyai Namaḥ		ॐ सहसावर्तमानायै नमः ।
485	Oṃ Hastinādaprabodhinyai Namaḥ	ॐ हस्तिनादप्रबोधिन्यै नमः ।
486	Oṃ Hiraṇyapadmavarṇāyai Namaḥ	ॐ हिरण्यपद्मवर्णायै नमः ।
487	Oṃ Haribhadrāyai Namaḥ		ॐ हरिभद्रायै नमः ।
488	Oṃ Sudurdharāyai Namaḥ		ॐ सुदुर्धरायै नमः ।
489	Oṃ Sūryāyai Namaḥ		ॐ सूर्यायै नमः ।
490	Oṃ Hiraṇyaprakaṭasadṛśyai Namaḥ	ॐ हिरण्यप्रकटसदृश्यै नमः ।
491	Oṃ Hemamālinyai Namaḥ		ॐ हेममालिन्यै नमः ।
492	Oṃ Padmānanāyai Namaḥ		ॐ पद्माननायै नमः ।
493	Oṃ Nityapuṣṭāyai Namaḥ		ॐ नित्यपुष्टायै नमः ।
494	Oṃ Devamātre Namaḥ		ॐ देवमात्रे नमः ।
495	Oṃ Amṛtodbhavāyai Namaḥ		ॐ अमृतोद्भवायै नमः ।
496	Oṃ Mahādhanāyai Namaḥ		ॐ महाधनायै नमः ।
497	Oṃ Śṛṅgyai Namaḥ		ॐ शृङ्ग्यै नमः ।
498	Oṃ Kārdamyai Namaḥ		ॐ कार्दम्यै नमः ।
499	Oṃ Kambukandharāyai Namaḥ		ॐ कम्बुकन्धरायै नमः ।
500	Oṃ Ādityavarṇāyai Namaḥ		ॐ आदित्यवर्णायै नमः ।
501	Oṃ Candrābhāyai Namaḥ		ॐ चन्द्राभायै नमः ।
502	Oṃ Gandhadvārāyai Namaḥ		ॐ गन्धद्वारायै नमः ।
503	Oṃ Durāsadāyai Namaḥ		ॐ दुरासदायै नमः ।
504	Oṃ Varārcitāyai Namaḥ		ॐ वरार्चितायै नमः ।
505	Oṃ Varārohāyai Namaḥ		ॐ वरारोहायै नमः ।
506	Oṃ Vareṇyāyai Namaḥ		ॐ वरेण्यायै नमः ।
507	Oṃ Viṣṇuvallabhāyai Namaḥ		ॐ विष्णुवल्लभायै नमः ।
508	Oṃ Kalyāṇyai Namaḥ		ॐ कल्याण्यै नमः ।
509	Oṃ Varadāyai Namaḥ		ॐ वरदायै नमः ।
510	Oṃ Vāmāyai Namaḥ		ॐ वामायै नमः ।
511	Oṃ Vāmeśyai Namaḥ		ॐ वामेश्यै नमः ।

512	Oṃ Vindhyavāsinyai Namaḥ I	ॐ विन्ध्यवासिन्यै नमः I
513	Oṃ Yoganidrāyai Namah I	ॐ योगनिद्रायै नमः I
514	Oṃ Yogaratāyai Namah I	ॐ योगरतायै नमः I
515	Oṃ Devakīkāmarūpiṇyai Namah	ॐ देवकीकामरूपिण्यै नमः I
516	Oṃ Kaṃsavidrāviṇyai Namah I	ॐ कंसविद्राविण्यै नमः I
517	Oṃ Durgāyai Namah I	ॐ दुर्गायै नमः I
518	Oṃ Kaumāryai Namah I	ॐ कौमार्यै नमः I
519	Oṃ Kauśikyai Namah I	ॐ कौशिक्यै नमः I
520	Oṃ Kṣamāyai Namah I	ॐ क्षमायै नमः I
521	Oṃ Kātyāyanyai Namah I	ॐ कात्यायन्यै नमः I
522	Oṃ Kālarātryai Namah I	ॐ कालरात्र्यै नमः I
523	Oṃ Niśitṛptāyai Namah I	ॐ निशितृप्तायै नमः I
524	Oṃ Sudurjayāyai Namah I	ॐ सुदुर्जयायै नमः I
525	Oṃ Virūpākṣyai Namah I	ॐ विरूपाक्ष्यै नमः I
526	Oṃ Viśālākṣyai Namah I	ॐ विशालाक्ष्यै नमः I
527	Oṃ Bhaktānāṃ Parirakṣiṇyai Namaḥ I	ॐ भक्तानां परिरक्षिण्यै नमः I
528	Oṃ Bahurūpāsvarūpāyai Namah	ॐ बहुरूपास्वरूपायै नमः I
529	Oṃ Virūpāyai Namah I	ॐ विरूपायै नमः I
530	Oṃ Rūpavarjitāyai Namah I	ॐ रूपवर्जितायै नमः I
531	Oṃ Ghaṇṭāninādabahulāyai Namah	ॐ घण्टानिनादबहुलायै नमः I
532	Oṃ Jīmūtadhvaninisvanāyai Namah	ॐ जीमूतध्वनिनिस्वनायै नमः I
533	Oṃ Mahāsurendramathinyai Namah	ॐ महासुरेन्द्रमथिन्यै नमः I
534	Oṃ Bhrukuṭīkuṭilānanāyai Namah I	ॐ भ्रुकुटीकुटिलाननायै नमः I
535	Oṃ Satyopayācitāyai Ekāyai Namaḥ I	ॐ सत्योपयाचितायै एकायै नमः I
536	Oṃ Kauberyai Namah I	ॐ कौबेर्यै नमः I
537	Oṃ Brahmacāriṇyai Namah I	ॐ ब्रह्मचारिण्यै नमः I
538	Oṃ Āryāyai Namah I	ॐ आर्यायै नमः I
539	Oṃ Yaśodāsutadāyai Namah I	ॐ यशोदासुतदायै नमः I

540	Oṃ Dharma Kāmārthamokṣa Dāyai Namaḥ ǀ	ॐ धर्मकामार्थमोक्षदाये नमः ǀ
541	Oṃ Dāridryaduḥkhaśamanyai Namaḥ ǀ	ॐ दारिद्र्यदुःखशमन्यै नमः ǀ
542	Oṃ Ghoradurgārtināśinyai Namaḥ ǀ	ॐ घोरदुर्गार्तिनाशिन्यै नमः ǀ
543	Oṃ Bhaktārtiśamanyai Namaḥ ǀ	ॐ भक्तार्तिशमन्यै नमः ǀ
544	Oṃ Bhavyāyai Namaḥ ǀ	ॐ भव्यायै नमः ǀ
545	Oṃ Bhavabhargāpahāriṇyai Namaḥ	ॐ भवभर्गापहारिण्यै नमः ǀ
546	Oṃ Kṣīrābdhitanayāyai Namaḥ ǀ	ॐ क्षीराब्धितनयायै नमः ǀ
547	Oṃ Padmāyai Namaḥ ǀ	ॐ पद्मायै नमः ǀ
548	Oṃ Kamalāyai Namaḥ ǀ	ॐ कमलायै नमः ǀ
549	Oṃ Dharaṇīdharāyai Namaḥ ǀ	ॐ धरणीधरायै नमः ǀ
550	Oṃ Rukmiṇyai Namaḥ ǀ	ॐ रुक्मिण्यै नमः ǀ
551	Oṃ Rohiṇyai Namaḥ ǀ	ॐ रोहिण्यै नमः ǀ
552	Oṃ Sītāyai Namaḥ ǀ	ॐ सीतायै नमः ǀ
553	Oṃ Satyabhāmāyai Namaḥ ǀ	ॐ सत्यभामायै नमः ǀ
554	Oṃ Yaśasvinyai Namaḥ ǀ	ॐ यशस्विन्यै नमः ǀ
555	Oṃ Prajñādhārāyai Namaḥ ǀ	ॐ प्रज्ञाधारायै नमः ǀ
556	Oṃ Amitaprajñāyai Namaḥ ǀ	ॐ अमितप्रज्ञायै नमः ǀ
557	Oṃ Vedamātre Namaḥ ǀ	ॐ वेदमात्रे नमः ǀ
558	Oṃ Yaśovatyai Namaḥ ǀ	ॐ यशोवत्यै नमः ǀ
559	Oṃ Samādhyai Namaḥ ǀ	ॐ समाध्यै नमः ǀ
560	Oṃ Bhāvanāyai Namaḥ ǀ	ॐ भावनायै नमः ǀ
561	Oṃ Maitryai Namaḥ ǀ	ॐ मैत्र्यै नमः ǀ
562	Oṃ Karuṇāyai Namaḥ ǀ	ॐ करुणायै नमः ǀ
563	Oṃ Bhaktavatsalāyai Namaḥ ǀ	ॐ भक्तवत्सलायै नमः ǀ
564	Oṃ Antarvedīdakṣiṇāyai Namaḥ	ॐ अन्तर्वेदीदक्षिणायै नमः ǀ
565	Oṃ Brahmacaryaparāgatyai Namaḥ	ॐ ब्रह्मचर्यपरागत्यै नमः ǀ
566	Oṃ Dīkṣāyai Namaḥ ǀ	ॐ दीक्षायै नमः ǀ
567	Oṃ Vīkṣāyai Namaḥ ǀ	ॐ वीक्षायै नमः ǀ
568	Oṃ Parīkṣāyai Namaḥ ǀ	ॐ परीक्षायै नमः ǀ

569.	Oṃ Samīkṣāyai Namaḥ ।	ॐ समीक्षायै नमः ।
570.	Oṃ Vīravatsalāyai Namaḥ ।	ॐ वीरवत्सलायै नमः ।
571.	Oṃ Ambikāyai Namaḥ ।	ॐ अम्बिकायै नमः ।
572.	Oṃ Surabhyai Namaḥ ।	ॐ सुरभ्यै नमः ।
573.	Oṃ Siddhāyai Namaḥ ।	ॐ सिद्धायै नमः ।
574.	Oṃ Siddhavidyādharārcitāyai Namaḥ ।	ॐ सिद्धविद्याधरार्चितायै नमः ।
575.	Oṃ Sudīptāyai Namaḥ ।	ॐ सुदीप्तायै नमः ।
576.	Oṃ Lelihānāyai Namaḥ ।	ॐ लेलिहानायै नमः ।
577.	Oṃ Karālāyai Namaḥ ।	ॐ करालायै नमः ।
578.	Oṃ Viśvapūrakāyai Namaḥ ।	ॐ विश्वपूरकायै नमः ।
579.	Oṃ Viśvasaṃhāriṇyai Namaḥ ।	ॐ विश्वसंहारिण्यै नमः ।
580.	Oṃ Dīptyai Namaḥ ।	ॐ दीप्त्यै नमः ।
581.	Oṃ Tapinyai Namaḥ ।	ॐ तपिन्यै नमः ।
582.	Oṃ Tāṇḍavapriyāyai Namaḥ ।	ॐ ताण्डवप्रियायै नमः ।
583.	Oṃ Udbhavāyai Namaḥ ।	ॐ उद्भवायै नमः ।
584.	Oṃ Virajārājñyai Namaḥ ।	ॐ विरजाराज्ञ्यै नमः ।
585.	Oṃ Tāpanyai Namaḥ ।	ॐ तापन्यै नमः ।
586.	Oṃ Bindumālinyai Namaḥ ।	ॐ बिन्दुमालिन्यै नमः ।
587.	Oṃ Kṣīradhārāsuprabhāvāyai Namaḥ ।	ॐ क्षीरधारासुप्रभावायै नमः ।
588.	Oṃ Lokamātre Namaḥ ।	ॐ लोकमात्रे नमः ।
589.	Oṃ Suvarcalāyai Namaḥ ।	ॐ सुवर्चलायै नमः ।
590.	Oṃ Havyagarbhāyai Namaḥ ।	ॐ हव्यगर्भायै नमः ।
591.	Oṃ Ājyagarbhāyai Namaḥ ।	ॐ आज्यगर्भायै नमः ।
592.	Oṃ Juhvato Yajñasambhavāyai Namaḥ ।	ॐ जुह्वतो यज्ञसम्भवायै नमः ।
593.	Oṃ Āpyāyanyai Namaḥ ।	ॐ आप्यायन्यै नमः ।
594.	Oṃ Pāvanyai Namaḥ ।	ॐ पावन्यै नमः ।
595.	Oṃ Dahanyai Namaḥ ।	ॐ दहन्यै नमः ।
596.	Oṃ Dahanāśrayāyai Namaḥ ।	ॐ दहनाश्रयायै नमः ।

597	Oṃ Mātṛkāyai Namaḥ		ॐ मातृकायै नमः ।
598	Oṃ Mādhavyai Namaḥ		ॐ माधव्यै नमः ।
599	Oṃ Mucyāyai Namaḥ		ॐ मुच्यायै नमः ।
600	Oṃ Mokṣalakṣmyai Namaḥ		ॐ मोक्षलक्ष्म्यै नमः ।
601	Oṃ Maharddhidāyai Namaḥ		ॐ महर्द्धिदायै नमः ।
602	Oṃ Sarvakāmapradāyai Namaḥ		ॐ सर्वकामप्रदायै नमः ।
603	Oṃ Bhadrāyai Namaḥ		ॐ भद्रायै नमः ।
604	Oṃ Subhadrāyai Namaḥ		ॐ सुभद्रायै नमः ।
605	Oṃ Sarvamaṅgalāyai Namaḥ		ॐ सर्वमङ्गलायै नमः ।
606	Oṃ Śvetāyai Namaḥ		ॐ श्वेतायै नमः ।
607	Oṃ Suśuklavasanāyai Namaḥ		ॐ सुशुक्लवसनायै नमः ।
608	Oṃ Śuklamālyānulepanāyai Namaḥ	ॐ शुक्लमाल्यानुलेपनायै नमः
609	Oṃ Haṃsāyai Namaḥ		ॐ हंसायै नमः ।
610	Oṃ Hīnakaryai Namaḥ		ॐ हीनकर्यै नमः ।
611	Oṃ Haṃsyai Namaḥ		ॐ हंस्यै नमः ।
612	Oṃ Hṛdyāyai Namaḥ		ॐ हृद्यायै नमः ।
613	Oṃ Hṛtkamalālayāyai Namaḥ		ॐ हृत्कमलालयायै नमः ।
614	Oṃ Sitātapatrāyai Namaḥ		ॐ सितातपत्रायै नमः ।
615	Oṃ Suśreṇyai Namaḥ		ॐ सुश्रेण्यै नमः ।
616	Oṃ Padmapatrāyatekṣaṇāyai Namaḥ		ॐ पद्मपत्रायतेक्षणायै नमः ।
617	Oṃ Sāvitryai Namaḥ		ॐ सावित्र्यै नमः ।
618	Oṃ Satyasaṅkalpāyai Namaḥ		ॐ सत्यसङ्कल्पायै नमः ।
619	Oṃ Kāmadāyai Namaḥ		ॐ कामदायै नमः ।
620	Oṃ Kāmakāminyai Namaḥ		ॐ कामकामिन्यै नमः ।
621	Oṃ Darśanīyāyai Namaḥ		ॐ दर्शनीयायै नमः ।
622	Oṃ Dṛśyādṛśyāyai Namaḥ		ॐ दृश्यादृश्यायै नमः ।
623	Oṃ Spṛśyāyai Namaḥ		ॐ स्पृश्यायै नमः ।
624	Oṃ Sevyāyai Namaḥ		ॐ सेव्यायै नमः ।
625	Oṃ Varāṅganāyai Namaḥ		ॐ वराङ्गनायै नमः ।

626	Oṃ Bhogapriyāyai Namaḥ		ॐ भोगप्रियायै नमः ।
627	Oṃ Bhogavatyai Namaḥ		ॐ भोगवत्यै नमः ।
628	Oṃ Bhogīndraśayanāsanāyai Namaḥ		ॐ भोगीन्द्रशयनासनायै नमः ।
629	Oṃ Ārdrāyai Namaḥ		ॐ आर्द्रायै नमः ।
630	Oṃ Puṣkariṇyai Namaḥ		ॐ पुष्करिण्यै नमः ।
631	Oṃ Puṇyāyai Namaḥ		ॐ पुण्यायै नमः ।
632	Oṃ Pāvanyai Namaḥ		ॐ पावन्यै नमः ।
633	Oṃ Pāpasūdanyai Namaḥ		ॐ पापसूदन्यै नमः ।
634	Oṃ Śrīmatyai Namaḥ		ॐ श्रीमत्यै नमः ।
635	Oṃ Śubhākārāyai Namaḥ		ॐ शुभाकारायै नमः ।
636	Oṃ Paramaiśvaryabhūtidāyai Namaḥ		ॐ परमैश्वर्यभूतिदायै नमः ।
637	Oṃ Acintyānantavibhavāyai Namaḥ	ॐ अचिन्त्यानन्तविभवायै नमः
638	Oṃ Bhavabhāvavibhāvanyai Namaḥ	ॐ भवभावविभावन्यै नमः ।
639	Oṃ Niśreṇyai Namaḥ		ॐ निश्रेण्यै नमः ।
640	Oṃ Sarvadehasthāyai Namaḥ		ॐ सर्वदेहस्थायै नमः ।
641	Oṃ Sarvabhūtanamaskṛtāyai Namaḥ		ॐ सर्वभूतनमस्कृतायै नमः ।
642	Oṃ Balāyai Namaḥ		ॐ बलायै नमः ।
643	Oṃ Balādhikāyai Devyai Namaḥ	ॐ बलाधिकायै देव्यै नमः ।
644	Oṃ Gautamyai Namaḥ		ॐ गौतम्यै नमः ।
645	Oṃ Gokulālayāyai Namaḥ		ॐ गोकुलालयायै नमः ।
646	Oṃ Toṣiṇyai Namaḥ		ॐ तोषिण्यै नमः ।
647	Oṃ Pūrṇacandrābhāyai Namaḥ	ॐ पूर्णचन्द्राभायै नमः ।
648	Oṃ Ekānandāyai Namaḥ		ॐ एकानन्दायै नमः ।
649	Oṃ Śatānanāyai Namaḥ		ॐ शतानिनायै नमः ।
650	Oṃ Udyānanagara Dvāra Harmyo Pavana vāsinyai Namaḥ	ॐ उद्याननगर द्वार हर्म्यो पवनवासिन्यै नमः ।
651	Oṃ Kūṣmāṇḍyai Namaḥ		ॐ कूष्माण्ड्यै नमः ।
652	Oṃ Dāruṇāyai Namaḥ		ॐ दारुणायै नमः ।

653.	Oṃ Caṇḍāyai Namaḥ		ॐ चण्डायै नमः ।
654.	Oṃ Kirātyai Namaḥ		ॐ किरात्यै नमः ।
655.	Oṃ Nandanālayāyai Namaḥ		ॐ नन्दनालयायै नमः ।
656.	Oṃ Kālāyanāyai Namaḥ		ॐ कालायनायै नमः ।
657.	Oṃ Kālagamyāyai Namaḥ		ॐ कालगम्यायै नमः ।
658.	Oṃ Bhayadāyai Namaḥ		ॐ भयदायै नमः ।
659.	Oṃ Bhayanāśinyai Namaḥ		ॐ भयनाशिन्यै नमः ।
660.	Oṃ Saudāminyai Namaḥ		ॐ सौदामिन्यै नमः ।
661.	Oṃ Megharavāyai Namaḥ		ॐ मेघरवायै नमः ।
662.	Oṃ Daityadānavamardinyai Namaḥ	ॐ दैत्यदानवमर्दिन्यै नमः ।
663.	Oṃ Jaganmātre Namaḥ		ॐ जगन्मात्रे नमः ।
664.	Oṃ Abhayakaryai Namaḥ		ॐ अभयकर्यै नमः ।
665.	Oṃ Bhūtadhātryai Namaḥ		ॐ भूतधात्र्यै नमः ।
666.	Oṃ Sudurlabhāyai Namaḥ		ॐ सुदुर्लभायै नमः ।
667.	Oṃ Kāśyapyai Namaḥ		ॐ काश्यप्यै नमः ।
668.	Oṃ Śubhadānāyai Namaḥ		ॐ शुभदानायै नमः ।
669.	Oṃ Vanamālāyai Namaḥ		ॐ वनमालायै नमः ।
670.	Oṃ Śubhāyai Namaḥ		ॐ शुभायै नमः ।
671.	Oṃ Varāyai Namaḥ		ॐ वरायै नमः ।
672.	Oṃ Dhanyāyai Namaḥ		ॐ धन्यायै नमः ।
673.	Oṃ Dhanyeśvaryai Namaḥ		ॐ धन्येश्वर्यै नमः ।
674.	Oṃ Dhanyāyai Namaḥ		ॐ धन्यायै नमः ।
675.	Oṃ Ratnadāyai Namaḥ		ॐ रत्नदायै नमः ।
676.	Oṃ Vasuvardhinyai Namaḥ		ॐ वसुवर्धिन्यै नमः ।
677.	Oṃ Gāndharvyai Namaḥ		ॐ गान्धर्व्यै नमः ।
678.	Oṃ Revatyai Namaḥ		ॐ रेवत्यै नमः ।
679.	Oṃ Gaṅgāyai Namaḥ		ॐ गङ्गायै नमः ।
680.	Oṃ Śakunyai Namaḥ		ॐ शकुन्यै नमः ।
681.	Oṃ Vimalānanāyai Namaḥ		ॐ विमलाननायै नमः ।
682.	Oṃ Iḍāyai Namaḥ		ॐ इडायै नमः ।

683.	Oṃ Śāntikaryai Namaḥ		ॐ शान्तिकर्यै नमः ।
684.	Oṃ Tāmasyai Namaḥ		ॐ तामस्यै नमः ।
685.	Oṃ Kamalālayāyai Namaḥ		ॐ कमलालयायै नमः ।
686.	Oṃ Ājyapāyai Namaḥ		ॐ आज्यपायै नमः ।
687.	Oṃ Vajrakaumāryai Namaḥ		ॐ वज्रकौमार्यै नमः ।
688.	Oṃ Somapāyai Namaḥ		ॐ सोमपायै नमः ।
689.	Oṃ Kusumāśrayāyai Namaḥ		ॐ कुसुमाश्रयायै नमः ।
690.	Oṃ Jagatpriyāyai Namaḥ		ॐ जगत्रियायै नमः ।
691.	Oṃ Sarathāyai Namaḥ		ॐ सरथायै नमः ।
692.	Oṃ Durjayāyai Namaḥ		ॐ दुर्जयायै नमः ।
693.	Oṃ Khagavāhanāyai Namaḥ		ॐ खगवाहनायै नमः ।
694.	Oṃ Manobhavāyai Namaḥ		ॐ मनोभवायै नमः ।
695.	Oṃ Kāmacārāyai Namaḥ		ॐ कामचारायै नमः ।
696.	Oṃ Siddhacāraṇasevitāyai Namaḥ		ॐ सिद्धचारणसेवितायै नमः ।
697.	Oṃ Vyomalakṣmyai Namaḥ		ॐ व्योमलक्ष्म्यै नमः ।
698.	Oṃ Mahālakṣmyai Namaḥ		ॐ महालक्ष्म्यै नमः ।
699.	Oṃ Tejolakṣmyai Namaḥ		ॐ तेजोलक्ष्म्यै नमः ।
700.	Oṃ Sujājvalāyai Namaḥ		ॐ सुजाज्वलायै नमः ।
701.	Oṃ Rasalakṣmyai Namaḥ		ॐ रसलक्ष्म्यै नमः ।
702.	Oṃ Jagadyonaye Namaḥ		ॐ जगद्योनये नमः ।
703.	Oṃ Gandhalakṣmyai Namaḥ		ॐ गन्धलक्ष्म्यै नमः ।
704.	Oṃ Vanāśrayāyai Namaḥ		ॐ वनाश्रयायै नमः ।
705.	Oṃ Śravaṇāyai Namaḥ		ॐ श्रवणायै नमः ।
706.	Oṃ Śrāvaṇīnetrāyai Namaḥ		ॐ श्रावणीनेत्रायै नमः ।
707.	Oṃ Rasanāprāṇacāriṇyai Namaḥ		ॐ रसनाप्राणचारिण्यै नमः ।
708.	Oṃ Viriñcimātre Namaḥ		ॐ विरिञ्चिमात्रे नमः ।
709.	Oṃ Vibhavāyai Namaḥ		ॐ विभवायै नमः ।
710.	Oṃ Varavārijavāhanāyai Namaḥ	ॐ वरवारिजवाहनायै नमः ।
711.	Oṃ Vīryāyai Namaḥ		ॐ वीर्यायै नमः ।
712.	Oṃ Vīreśvaryai Namaḥ		ॐ वीरेश्वर्यै नमः ।

713.	Oṃ Vandyāyai Namaḥ		ॐ वन्द्यायै नमः	
714.	Oṃ Viśokāyai Namaḥ		ॐ विशोकायै नमः	
715.	Oṃ Vasuvardhinyai Namaḥ		ॐ वसुवर्धिन्यै नमः	
716.	Oṃ Anāhatāyai Namaḥ		ॐ अनाहतायै नमः	
717.	Oṃ Kuṇḍalinyai Namaḥ		ॐ कुण्डलिन्यै नमः	
718.	Oṃ Nalinyai Namaḥ		ॐ नलिन्यै नमः	
719.	Oṃ Vanavāsinyai Namaḥ		ॐ वनवासिन्यै नमः	
720.	Oṃ Gāndhāriṇyai Namaḥ		ॐ गान्धारिण्यै नमः	
721.	Oṃ Indranamitāyai Namaḥ		ॐ इन्द्रनमितायै नमः	
722.	Oṃ Surendranamitāyai Namaḥ		ॐ सुरेन्द्रनमितायै नमः	
723.	Oṃ Satyai Namaḥ		ॐ सत्यै नमः	
724.	Oṃ Sarvamaṅgalamāṅgalyāyai Namaḥ		ॐ सर्वमङ्गलमाङ्गल्यायै नमः	
725.	Oṃ Sarvakāmasamṛddhidāyai Namaḥ		ॐ सर्वकामसमृद्धिदायै नमः	
726.	Oṃ Sarvānandāyai Namaḥ		ॐ सर्वानन्दायै नमः	
727.	Oṃ Mahānandāyai Namaḥ		ॐ महानन्दायै नमः	
728.	Oṃ Satkīrtyai Namaḥ		ॐ सत्कीर्त्यै नमः	
729.	Oṃ Siddhasevitāyai Namaḥ		ॐ सिद्धसेवितायै नमः	
730.	Oṃ Sinīvālyai Namaḥ		ॐ सिनीवाल्यै नमः	
731.	Oṃ Kuhvai Namaḥ		ॐ कुह्वै नमः	
732.	Oṃ Rākāyai Namaḥ		ॐ राकायै नमः	
733.	Oṃ Amāyai Namaḥ		ॐ अमायै नमः	
734.	Oṃ Anumatyai Namaḥ		ॐ अनुमत्यै नमः	
735.	Oṃ Dyutyai Namaḥ		ॐ द्युत्यै नमः	
736.	Oṃ Arundhatyai Namaḥ		ॐ अरुन्धत्यै नमः	
737.	Oṃ Vasumatyai Namaḥ		ॐ वसुमत्यै नमः	
738.	Oṃ Bhārgavyai Namaḥ		ॐ भार्गव्यै नमः	
739.	Oṃ Vāstudevatāyai Namaḥ		ॐ वास्तुदेवतायै नमः	
740.	Oṃ Mayūryai Namaḥ		ॐ मयूर्यै नमः	

741.	Oṃ Vajravetālyai Namaḥ ।	ॐ वज्रवेताल्यै नमः ।
742.	Oṃ Vajrahastāyai Namaḥ ।	ॐ वज्रहस्तायै नमः ।
743.	Oṃ Varānanāyai Namaḥ ।	ॐ वराननायै नमः ।
744.	Oṃ Anaghāyai Namaḥ ।	ॐ अनघायै नमः ।
745.	Oṃ Dharaṇyai Namaḥ ।	ॐ धरण्यै नमः ।
746.	Oṃ Dhīrāyai Namaḥ ।	ॐ धीरायै नमः ।
747.	Oṃ Dhamanyai Namaḥ ।	ॐ धमन्यै नमः ।
748.	Oṃ Maṇibhūṣaṇāyai Namaḥ ।	ॐ मणिभूषणायै नमः ।
749.	Oṃ Rājaśrīrūpasahitāyai Namaḥ ।	ॐ राजश्रीरूपसहितायै नमः ।
750.	Oṃ Brahmaśriye Namaḥ ।	ॐ ब्रह्मश्रिये नमः ।
751.	Oṃ Brahmavanditāyai Namaḥ ।	ॐ ब्रह्मवन्दितायै नमः ।
752.	Oṃ Jayaśriyai Namaḥ ।	ॐ जयश्रियै नमः ।
753.	Oṃ Jayadāyai Namaḥ ।	ॐ जयदायै नमः ।
754.	Oṃ Jñeyāyai Namaḥ ।	ॐ ज्ञेयायै नमः ।
755.	Oṃ Sargaśriyai Namaḥ ।	ॐ सर्गश्रिये नमः ।
756.	Oṃ Svargatyai Namaḥ ।	ॐ स्वर्गत्यै नमः ।
757.	Oṃ Supuṣpāyai Namaḥ ।	ॐ सुपुष्पायै नमः ।
758.	Oṃ Puṣpanilayāyai Namaḥ ।	ॐ पुष्पनिलयायै नमः ।
759.	Oṃ Phalaśriyai Namaḥ ।	ॐ फलश्रिये नमः ।
760.	Oṃ Niṣkalapriyāyai Namaḥ ।	ॐ निष्कलप्रियायै नमः ।
761.	Oṃ Dhanurlakṣmyai Namaḥ ।	ॐ धनुर्लक्ष्म्यै नमः ।
762.	Oṃ Amilitāyai Namaḥ ।	ॐ अमिलितायै नमः ।
763.	Oṃ Parakrodhanivāriṇyai Namaḥ ।	ॐ परक्रोधनिवारिण्यै नमः ।
764.	Oṃ Kadrvai Namaḥ ।	ॐ कद्र्वै नमः ।
765.	Oṃ Dhanāyave Namaḥ ।	ॐ धनायवे नमः ।
766.	Oṃ Kapilāyai Namaḥ ।	ॐ कपिलायै नमः ।
767.	Oṃ Surasāyai Namaḥ ।	ॐ सुरसायै नमः ।
768.	Oṃ Suramohinyai Namaḥ ।	ॐ सुरमोहिन्यै नमः ।
769.	Oṃ Mahāśvetāyai Namaḥ ।	ॐ महाश्वेतायै नमः ।
770.	Oṃ Mahānīlāyai Namaḥ ।	ॐ महानीलायै नमः ।

771	Oṃ Mahāmūrtyai Namaḥ		ॐ महामूर्त्यै नमः ।
772	Oṃ Viṣāpahāyai Namaḥ		ॐ विषापहायै नमः ।
773	Oṃ Suprabhāyai Namaḥ		ॐ सुप्रभायै नमः ।
774	Oṃ Jvālinyai Namaḥ		ॐ ज्वालिन्यै नमः ।
775	Oṃ Dīptyai Namaḥ		ॐ दीप्त्यै नमः ।
776	Oṃ Tṛtyai Namaḥ		ॐ तृत्यै नमः ।
777	Oṃ Vyāptyai Namaḥ		ॐ व्याप्त्यै नमः ।
778	Oṃ Prabhākaryai Namaḥ		ॐ प्रभाकर्यै नमः ।
779	Oṃ Tejovatyai Namaḥ		ॐ तेजोवत्यै नमः ।
780	Oṃ Padmabodhāyai Namaḥ		ॐ पद्मबोधायै नमः ।
781	Oṃ Madalekhāyai Namaḥ		ॐ मदलेखायै नमः ।
782	Oṃ Aruṇāvatyai Namaḥ		ॐ अरुणावत्यै नमः ।
783	Oṃ Ratnāyai Namaḥ		ॐ रत्नायै नमः ।
784	Oṃ Ratnāvalībhūtāyai Namaḥ		ॐ रत्नावलीभूतायै नमः ।
785	Oṃ Śatadhāmāyai Namaḥ		ॐ शतधामायै नमः ।
786	Oṃ Śatāpahāyai Namaḥ		ॐ शतापहायै नमः ।
787	Oṃ Triguṇāyai Namaḥ		ॐ त्रिगुणायै नमः ।
788	Oṃ Ghoṣiṇyai Namaḥ		ॐ घोषिण्यै नमः ।
789	Oṃ Rakṣyāyai Namaḥ		ॐ रक्ष्यायै नमः ।
790	Oṃ Nardinyai Namaḥ		ॐ नर्दिन्यै नमः ।
791	Oṃ Ghoṣavarjitāyai Namaḥ		ॐ घोषवर्जितायै नमः ।
792	Oṃ Sādhyāyai Namaḥ		ॐ साध्यायै नमः ।
793	Oṃ Adityai Namaḥ		ॐ अदित्यै नमः ।
794	Oṃ Dityai Namaḥ		ॐ दित्यै नमः ।
795	Oṃ Devyai Namaḥ		ॐ देव्यै नमः ।
796	Oṃ Mṛgavāhāyai Namaḥ		ॐ मृगवाहायै नमः ।
797	Oṃ Mṛgāṅkagāyai Namaḥ		ॐ मृगाङ्कगायै नमः ।
798	Oṃ Citranīlotpalagatāyai Namaḥ		ॐ चित्रनीलोत्पलगतायै नमः ।
799	Oṃ Vṛtaratnākarāśrayāyai Namaḥ		ॐ वृतरत्नाकराश्रयायै नमः ।

800.	Oṃ Hiraṇyarajatadvandvāyai Namaḥ		ॐ हिरण्यरजतद्वन्द्वायै नमः ।
801.	Oṃ Śaṅkhabhadrāsanasthitāyai Namaḥ		ॐ शङ्खभद्रासनस्थितायै नमः ।
802.	Oṃ Gomūtra Gomaya Kṣīra Dadhi Sarpirjalāśrayāyai Namaḥ	ॐ गोमूत्र गोमय क्षीर दधि सर्पिर्जलाश्रयायै नमः ।
803.	Oṃ Marīcaye Namaḥ		ॐ मरीचये नमः ।
804.	Oṃ Cīravasanāyai Namaḥ		ॐ चीरवसनायै नमः ।
805.	Oṃ Pūrṇacandrārkaviṣṭarāyai Namaḥ		ॐ पूर्णचन्द्रार्कविष्टरायै नमः ।
806.	Oṃ Susūkṣmāyai Namaḥ		ॐ सुसूक्ष्मायै नमः ।
807.	Oṃ Nirvṛtyai Namaḥ		ॐ निर्वृत्यै नमः ।
808.	Oṃ Sthūlāyai Namaḥ		ॐ स्थूलायै नमः ।
809.	Oṃ Nivṛttārātyai Namaḥ		ॐ निवृत्तारात्यै नमः ।
810.	Oṃ Marīcyai Namaḥ		ॐ मरीच्यै नमः ।
811.	Oṃ Jvālinyai Namaḥ		ॐ ज्वालिन्यै नमः ।
812.	Oṃ Dhūmrāyai Namaḥ		ॐ धूम्रायै नमः ।
813.	Oṃ Havyavāhāyai Namaḥ		ॐ हव्यवाहायै नमः ।
814.	Oṃ Hiraṇyadāyai Namaḥ		ॐ हिरण्यदायै नमः ।
815.	Oṃ Dāyinyai Namaḥ		ॐ दायिन्यै नमः ।
816.	Oṃ Kālinīsiddhyai Namaḥ		ॐ कालिनीसिद्ध्यै नमः ।
817.	Oṃ Śoṣiṇyai Namaḥ		ॐ शोषिण्यै नमः ।
818.	Oṃ Samprabodhinyai Namaḥ		ॐ सम्प्रबोधिन्यै नमः ।
819.	Oṃ Bhāsvarāyai Namaḥ		ॐ भास्वरायै नमः ।
820.	Oṃ Saṃhatyai Namaḥ		ॐ संहत्यै नमः ।
821.	Oṃ Tīkṣṇāyai Namaḥ		ॐ तीक्ष्णायै नमः ।
822.	Oṃ Pracaṇḍajvalanojjvalāyai Namaḥ		ॐ प्रचण्डज्वलनोज्ज्वलायै नमः ।
823.	Oṃ Sāṅgāyai Namaḥ		ॐ साङ्गायै नमः ।
824.	Oṃ Pracaṇḍāyai Namaḥ		ॐ प्रचण्डायै नमः ।
825.	Oṃ Dīptāyai Namaḥ		ॐ दीप्तायै नमः ।

826	Oṃ Vaidyutyai Namaḥ l	ॐ वैद्युत्यै नमः l
827	Oṃ Sumahādyutyai Namaḥ l	ॐ सुमहाद्युत्यै नमः l
828	Oṃ Kapilāyai Namaḥ l	ॐ कपिलायै नमः l
829	Oṃ Nīlaraktāyai Namaḥ l	ॐ नीलरक्तायै नमः l
830	Oṃ Suṣumnāyai Namaḥ l	ॐ सुषुम्नायै नमः l
831	Oṃ Visphuliṅginyai Namaḥ l	ॐ विस्फुलिङ्गिन्यै नमः l
832	Oṃ Arciṣmatyai Namaḥ l	ॐ अर्चिष्मत्यै नमः l
833	Oṃ Ripuharāyai Namaḥ l	ॐ रिपुहरायै नमः l
834	Oṃ Dīrghāyai Namaḥ l	ॐ दीर्घायै नमः l
835	Oṃ Dhūmāvalyai Namaḥ l	ॐ धूमावल्यै नमः l
836	Oṃ Jarāyai Namaḥ l	ॐ जरायै नमः l
837	Oṃ Sampūrṇamaṇḍalāyai Namaḥ l	ॐ सम्पूर्णमण्डलायै नमः l
838	Oṃ Pūṣāyai Namaḥ l	ॐ पूषायै नमः l
839	Oṃ Sraṃsinyai Namaḥ l	ॐ स्रंसिन्यै नमः l
840	Oṃ Sumanoharāyai Namaḥ l	ॐ सुमनोहरायै नमः l
841	Oṃ Jayāyai Namaḥ l	ॐ जयायै नमः l
842	Oṃ Puṣṭikaryai Namaḥ l	ॐ पुष्टिकर्यै नमः l
843	Oṃ Cchāyāyai Namaḥ l	ॐ च्छायायै नमः l
844	Oṃ Mānasāyai Namaḥ l	ॐ मानसायै नमः l
845	Oṃ Hṛdayojjvalāyai Namaḥ l	ॐ हृदयोज्ज्वलायै नमः l
846	Oṃ Suvarṇakaraṇyai Namaḥ l	ॐ सुवर्णकरण्यै नमः l
847	Oṃ Śreṣṭhāyai Namaḥ l	ॐ श्रेष्ठायै नमः l
848	Oṃ Mṛtasañjīvanyai Namaḥ l	ॐ मृतसञ्जीवन्यै नमः l
849	Oṃ Viśalyakaraṇyai Namaḥ l	ॐ विशल्यकरण्यै नमः l
850	Oṃ Śubhrāyai Namaḥ l	ॐ शुभ्रायै नमः l
851	Oṃ Sandhinyai Namaḥ l	ॐ सन्धिन्यै नमः l
852	Oṃ Paramauṣadhyai Namaḥ l	ॐ परमौषध्यै नमः l
853	Oṃ Brahmiṣṭhāyai Namaḥ l	ॐ ब्रह्मिष्ठायै नमः l
854	Oṃ Brahmasahitāyai Namaḥ l	ॐ ब्रह्मसहितायै नमः l
855	Oṃ Aindavyai Namaḥ l	ॐ ऐन्दव्यै नमः l

856	Oṃ Ratnasambhavāyai Namaḥ		ॐ रत्नसम्भवायै नमः ।
857	Oṃ Vidyutprabhāyai Namaḥ		ॐ विद्युत्प्रभायै नमः ।
858	Oṃ Bindumatyai Namaḥ		ॐ बिन्दुमत्यै नमः ।
859	Oṃ Trisvabhāvaguṇāyai Namaḥ		ॐ त्रिस्वभावगुणायै नमः ।
860	Oṃ Ambikāyai Namaḥ		ॐ अम्बिकायै नमः ।
861	Oṃ Nityoditāyai Namaḥ		ॐ नित्योदितायै नमः ।
862	Oṃ Nityadṛṣṭāyai Namaḥ		ॐ नित्यदृष्टायै नमः ।
863	Oṃ Nityakāmāyai Namaḥ		ॐ नित्यकामायै नमः ।
864	Oṃ Karīṣiṇyai Namaḥ		ॐ करीषिण्यै नमः ।
865	Oṃ Padmāṅkāyai Namaḥ		ॐ पद्माङ्कायै नमः ।
866	Oṃ Vajrajihvāyai Namaḥ		ॐ वज्रजिह्वायै नमः ।
867	Oṃ Vakradaṇḍāyai Namaḥ		ॐ वक्रदण्डायै नमः ।
868	Oṃ Vibhāsinyai Namaḥ		ॐ विभासिन्यै नमः ।
869	Oṃ Videhapūjitāyai Namaḥ		ॐ विदेहपूजितायै नमः ।
870	Oṃ Kanyāyai Namaḥ		ॐ कन्यायै नमः ।
871	Oṃ Māyāyai Namaḥ		ॐ मायायै नमः ।
872	Oṃ Vijayavāhinyai Namaḥ		ॐ विजयवाहिन्यै नमः ।
873	Oṃ Māninyai Namaḥ		ॐ मानिन्यै नमः ।
874	Oṃ Maṅgalāyai Namaḥ		ॐ मङ्गलायै नमः ।
875	Oṃ Mānyāyai Namaḥ		ॐ मान्यायै नमः ।
876	Oṃ Māninyai Namaḥ		ॐ मानिन्यै नमः ।
877	Oṃ Mānadāyinyai Namaḥ		ॐ मानदायिन्यै नमः ।
878	Oṃ Viśveśvaryai Namaḥ		ॐ विश्वेश्वर्यै नमः ।
879	Oṃ Gaṇavatyai Namaḥ		ॐ गणवत्यै नमः ।
880	Oṃ Maṇḍalāyai Namaḥ		ॐ मण्डलायै नमः ।
881	Oṃ Maṇḍaleśvaryai Namaḥ		ॐ मण्डलेश्वर्यै नमः ।
882	Oṃ Haripriyāyai Namaḥ		ॐ हरिप्रियायै नमः ।
883	Oṃ Bhaumasutāyai Namaḥ		ॐ भौमसुतायै नमः ।
884	Oṃ Manojñāyai Namaḥ		ॐ मनोज्ञायै नमः ।
885	Oṃ Matidāyinyai Namaḥ		ॐ मतिदायिन्यै नमः ।

886.	Oṃ Pratyaṅgirāyai Namaḥ		ॐ प्रत्यङ्गिरायै नमः ।
887.	Oṃ Somaguptāyai Namaḥ		ॐ सोमगुप्तायै नमः ।
888.	Oṃ Manobhijñāyai Namaḥ		ॐ मनोभिज्ञायै नमः ।
889.	Oṃ Vadanmatyai Namaḥ		ॐ वदन्मत्यै नमः ।
890.	Oṃ Yaśodharāyai Namaḥ		ॐ यशोधरायै नमः ।
891.	Oṃ Ratnamālāyai Namaḥ		ॐ रत्नमालायै नमः ।
892.	Oṃ Kṛṣṇāyai Namaḥ		ॐ कृष्णायै नमः ।
893.	Oṃ Trailokyabandhinyai Namaḥ	ॐ त्रैलोक्यबन्धिन्यै नमः ।
894.	Oṃ Amṛtāyai Namaḥ		ॐ अमृतायै नमः ।
895.	Oṃ Dhāriṇyai Namaḥ		ॐ धारिण्यै नमः ।
896.	Oṃ Harṣāyai Namaḥ		ॐ हर्षायै नमः ।
897.	Oṃ Vinatāyai Namaḥ		ॐ विनतायै नमः ।
898.	Oṃ Vallakyai Namaḥ		ॐ वल्लक्यै नमः ।
899.	Oṃ Śacyai Namaḥ		ॐ शच्यै नमः ।
900.	Oṃ Saṅkalpāyai Namaḥ		ॐ सङ्कल्पायै नमः ।
901.	Oṃ Bhāminyai Namaḥ		ॐ भामिन्यै नमः ।
902.	Oṃ Miśrāyai Namaḥ		ॐ मिश्रायै नमः ।
903.	Oṃ Kādambaryai Namaḥ		ॐ कादम्बर्यै नमः ।
904.	Oṃ Amṛtāyai Namaḥ		ॐ अमृतायै नमः ।
905.	Oṃ Prabhāyai Namaḥ		ॐ प्रभायै नमः ।
906.	Oṃ Āgatāyai Namaḥ		ॐ आगतायै नमः ।
907.	Oṃ Nirgatāyai Namaḥ		ॐ निर्गतायै नमः ।
908.	Oṃ Vajrāyai Namaḥ		ॐ वज्रायै नमः ।
909.	Oṃ Suhitāyai Namaḥ		ॐ सुहितायै नमः ।
910.	Oṃ Sahitāyai Namaḥ		ॐ सहितायै नमः ।
911.	Oṃ Akṣatāyai Namaḥ		ॐ अक्षतायै नमः ।
912.	Oṃ Sarvārthasādhanakaryai Namaḥ	ॐ सर्वार्थसाधनकर्यै नमः ।
913.	Oṃ Dhātave Namaḥ		ॐ धातवे नमः ।
914.	Oṃ Dhāraṇikāyai Namaḥ		ॐ धारणिकायै नमः ।
915.	Oṃ Amalāyai Namaḥ		ॐ अमलायै नमः ।

916.	Oṃ Karuṇādhārasambhūtāyai Namaḥ		ॐ करुणाधारसम्भूतायै नमः ।
917.	Oṃ Kamalākṣyai Namaḥ		ॐ कमलाक्ष्यै नमः ।
918.	Oṃ Śaśipriyāyai Namaḥ		ॐ शशिप्रियायै नमः ।
919.	Oṃ Saumyarūpāyai Namaḥ		ॐ सौम्यरूपायै नमः ।
920.	Oṃ Mahādīptāyai Namaḥ		ॐ महादीप्तायै नमः ।
921.	Oṃ Mahājvālāyai Namaḥ		ॐ महाज्वालायै नमः ।
922.	Oṃ Vikāsinyai Namaḥ		ॐ विकासिन्यै नमः ।
923.	Oṃ Mālāyai Namaḥ		ॐ मालायै नमः ।
924.	Oṃ Kāñcanamālāyai Namaḥ		ॐ काञ्चनमालायै नमः ।
925.	Oṃ Sadvajrāyai Namaḥ		ॐ सद्वज्रायै नमः ।
926.	Oṃ Kanakaprabhāyai Namaḥ		ॐ कनकप्रभायै नमः ।
927.	Oṃ Prakriyāyai Namaḥ		ॐ प्रक्रियायै नमः ।
928.	Oṃ Paramāyai Namaḥ		ॐ परमायै नमः ।
929.	Oṃ Yoktryai Namaḥ		ॐ योक्त्यै नमः ।
930.	Oṃ Kṣebhikāyai Namaḥ		ॐ क्षेभिकायै नमः ।
931.	Oṃ Sukhodayāyai Namaḥ		ॐ सुखोदयायै नमः ।
932.	Oṃ Vijṛmbhaṇāyai Namaḥ		ॐ विजृम्भणायै नमः ।
933.	Oṃ Vajrākhyāyai Namaḥ		ॐ वज्राख्यायै नमः ।
934.	Oṃ Śṛṅkhalāyai Namaḥ		ॐ शृङ्खलायै नमः ।
935.	Oṃ Kamalekṣaṇāyai Namaḥ		ॐ कमलेक्षणायै नमः ।
936.	Oṃ Jayaṅkaryai Namaḥ		ॐ जयङ्कर्यै नमः ।
937.	Oṃ Madhumatyai Namaḥ		ॐ मधुमत्यै नमः ।
938.	Oṃ Haritāyai Namaḥ		ॐ हरितायै नमः ।
939.	Oṃ Śaśinyai Namaḥ		ॐ शशिन्यै नमः ।
940.	Oṃ Śivāyai Namaḥ		ॐ शिवायै नमः ।
941.	Oṃ Mūlaprakṛtyai Namaḥ		ॐ मूलप्रकृत्यै नमः ।
942.	Oṃ Īśānāyai Namaḥ		ॐ ईशानायै नमः ।
943.	Oṃ Yogamātre Namaḥ		ॐ योगमात्रे नमः ।
944.	Oṃ Manojavāyai Namaḥ		ॐ मनोजवायै नमः ।

945.	Oṃ Dharmodayāyai Namaḥ ǀ	ॐ धर्मोदयायै नमः ǀ
946.	Oṃ Bhānumatyai Namaḥ ǀ	ॐ भानुमत्यै नमः ǀ
947.	Oṃ Sarvābhāsāyai Namaḥ ǀ	ॐ सर्वाभासायै नमः ǀ
948.	Oṃ Sukhāvahāyai Namaḥ ǀ	ॐ सुखावहायै नमः ǀ
949.	Oṃ Dhurandharāyai Namaḥ ǀ	ॐ धुरन्धरायै नमः ǀ
950.	Oṃ Bālāyai Namaḥ ǀ	ॐ बालायै नमः ǀ
951.	Oṃ Dharmasevyāyai Namaḥ ǀ	ॐ धर्मसेव्यायै नमः ǀ
952.	Oṃ Tathāgatāyai Namaḥ ǀ	ॐ तथागतायै नमः ǀ
953.	Oṃ Sukumārāyai Namaḥ ǀ	ॐ सुकुमारायै नमः ǀ
954.	Oṃ Saumyamukhyai Namaḥ ǀ	ॐ सौम्यमुख्यै नमः ǀ
955.	Oṃ Saumyasambodhanāyai Namaḥ	ॐ सौम्यसम्बोधनायै नमः ǀ
956.	Oṃ Uttamāyai Namaḥ ǀ	ॐ उत्तमायै नमः ǀ
957.	Oṃ Sumukhyai Namaḥ ǀ	ॐ सुमुख्यै नमः
958.	Oṃ Sarvatobhadrāyai Namaḥ ǀ	ॐ सर्वतोभद्रायै नमः ǀ
959.	Oṃ Guhyaśaktyai Namaḥ ǀ	ॐ गुह्यशक्त्यै नमः ǀ
960.	Oṃ Guhālayāyai Namaḥ ǀ	ॐ गुहालयायै नमः ǀ
961.	Oṃ Halāyudhāyai Namaḥ ǀ	ॐ हलायुधायै नमः ǀ
962.	Oṃ Kāvīrāyai Namaḥ ǀ	ॐ कावीरायै नमः ǀ
963.	Oṃ Sarvaśāstrasudhāriṇyai Namaḥ ǀ	ॐ सर्वशास्त्रसुधारिण्यै नमः ǀ
964.	Oṃ Vyomaśaktyai Namaḥ ǀ	ॐ व्योमशक्त्यै नमः ǀ
965.	Oṃ Mahādehāyai Namaḥ ǀ	ॐ महादेहायै नमः ǀ
966.	Oṃ Vyomagāyai Namaḥ ǀ	ॐ व्योमगायै नमः ǀ
967.	Oṃ Madhumanmayyai Namaḥ ǀ	ॐ मधुमन्मय्यै नमः ǀ
968.	Oṃ Gaṅgāyai Namaḥ ǀ	ॐ गङ्गायै नमः ǀ
969.	Oṃ Vitastāyai Namaḥ ǀ	ॐ वितस्तायै नमः ǀ
970.	Oṃ Yamunāyai Namaḥ ǀ	ॐ यमुनायै नमः ǀ
971.	Oṃ Candrabhāgāyai Namaḥ ǀ	ॐ चन्द्रभागायै नमः ǀ
972.	Oṃ Sarasvatyai Namaḥ ǀ	ॐ सरस्वत्यै नमः ǀ
973.	Oṃ Tilottamāyai Namaḥ ǀ	ॐ तिलोत्तमायै नमः ǀ
974.	Oṃ Ūrvaśyai Namaḥ ǀ	ॐ ऊर्वश्यै नमः ǀ

975.	Oṃ Rambhāyai Namaḥ ।	ॐ रम्भायै नमः ।
976.	Oṃ Svāminyai Namaḥ ।	ॐ स्वामिन्यै नमः ।
977.	Oṃ Surasundaryai Namaḥ ।	ॐ सुरसुन्दर्यै नमः ।
978.	Oṃ Bāṇapraharaṇāyai Namaḥ ।	ॐ बाणप्रहरणायै नमः ।
979.	Oṃ Bālāyai Namaḥ ।	ॐ बालायै नमः ।
980.	Oṃ Bimboṣṭhyai Namaḥ ।	ॐ बिम्बोष्ठ्यै नमः ।
981.	Oṃ Cāruhāsinyai Namaḥ ।	ॐ चारुहासिन्यै नमः ।
982.	Oṃ Kakudminyai Namaḥ ।	ॐ ककुद्मिन्यै नमः ।
983.	Oṃ Cārupṛṣṭhāyai Namaḥ ।	ॐ चारुपृष्ठायै नमः ।
984.	Oṃ Dṛṣṭādṛṣṭaphalapradāyai Namaḥ ।	ॐ दृष्टादृष्टफलप्रदायै नमः ।
985.	Oṃ Kāmyācāryai Namaḥ ।	ॐ काम्याचार्यै नमः ।
986.	Oṃ Kāmyāyai Namaḥ ।	ॐ काम्यायै नमः ।
987.	Oṃ Kāmācāravihāriṇyai Namaḥ ।	ॐ कामाचारविहारिण्यै नमः ।
988.	Oṃ Himaśailendrasaṅkāśāyai Namaḥ ।	ॐ हिमशैलेन्द्रसङ्काशायै नमः ।
989.	Oṃ Gajendravaravāhanāyai Namaḥ	ॐ गजेन्द्रवरवाहनायै नमः ।
990.	Oṃ Aśeṣa Sukha Saubhāgya Sampadāṃ Yonaye Namaḥ ।	ॐ अशेषसुखसौभाग्यसम्पदां योनये नमः ।
991.	Oṃ Uttamāyai Namaḥ ।	ॐ उत्तमायै नमः ।
992.	Oṃ Sarvotkṛṣṭāyai Namaḥ ।	ॐ सर्वोत्कृष्टायै नमः ।
993.	Oṃ Sarvamayyai Namaḥ ।	ॐ सर्वमय्यै नमः ।
994.	Oṃ Sarvāyai Namaḥ ।	ॐ सर्वायै नमः ।
995.	Oṃ Sarveśvarapriyāyai Namaḥ ।	ॐ सर्वेश्वरप्रियायै नमः ।
996.	Oṃ Sarvāṅgayonyai Namaḥ ।	ॐ सर्वाङ्गयोन्यै नमः ।
997.	Oṃ Avyaktāyai Namaḥ ।	ॐ अव्यक्तायै नमः ।
998.	Oṃ Sampradāneśvareśvaryai Namaḥ ।	ॐ सम्प्रदानेश्वरेश्वर्यै नमः ।
999.	Oṃ Viṣṇuvakṣaḥsthalagatāyai Namaḥ ।	ॐ विष्णुवक्षःस्थलगतायै नमः ।

Thus ends *Śrī Kamalātmikā Sahasranāmāvaliḥ* ।

इति श्रीकमलासहस्रनामावलिः सम्पूर्णा ॥

*****

About the Author
(http://Ramamurthy.jaagruti.co.in)

Dr. Ramamurthy is a versatile personality having experience and expertise

in various areas of banking, related IT solutions, information security, IT audit, Vedas, Samskrutam and so on.

His thirst for continuous learning does not subside. Even at the age of late fifties, he did research on a unique topic "Information Technology and Samskrutam" and obtained Ph.D. – doctorate degree from University of Madras. He is into a project of developing a Samskrutam based compiler.

It is his passion to spread his knowledge and experience through conducting classes, training programs and writing books.

He has already published books as detailed below. Further books are in pipe-line.

#	Title	Remarks	Pages
		Indology Related	
1.	*Shrī Lalitā Sahasranāmam*	English Translation of Shrī *Bhāskararāya's Bhāśyam*	750
2.	Power of *Shrī Vidyā*	The Secrets Demystified – With Lucid English Rendering and Commentaries	80
3.	ஸ்ரீ வித்யையின் ஶக்தி	ஸ்ரீ வித்யா ரகசியங்கள்	100
4.	*Samatā* – समता	An Exposition of Similarities in *Lalitā Sahasranāma* with *Soundaryalaharī, Saptaśatī, Viṣṇu Sahasranāma* and *Shrīmad Bhagavad Gīta*	172
5.	ஸமதா – समता	ஸ்ரீ லலிதா ஸஹஸ்ரநாமம் ஸௌந்தர்யலஹரீ, ஸப்தஶதீ, ஸ்ரீ விஷ்ணு ஸஹஸ்ரநாமம் மற்றும் ஸ்ரீமத் பகவத் கீதைகளில் ஒற்றுமையின் ஒரு வெளிப்பாடு	266
6.	*Advaita* In *Shākta*	Advaita Philosophy Discussed in Shakta Related Books	80
7.	*Shrī Lalitā Triśatī*	300 Divine Names of The Celestial Mother – **English** Translation of *Shrī Ādhi Śaṅkara's Bhāśyam*	193
8.	ஸ்ரீ லலிதா த்ரிஶதி	300 Divine Names of The Celestial Mother – Tamil Translation of *Shrī Ādi Śaṅkara's Bhāśyam*	234

#	Title	Remarks	Pages
65.	*Śrī Bhuvaneshwari Devī*	4th Devi of Dasha Maha Vidya	137
66.	ஸ்ரீ புவனேஸ்வரீ தேவீ	4th Devi of Dasha Maha Vidya	151
67.	*Śrī Tripura Bhairavi Devi*	5th Devi of Dasha Maha Vidya	132
68.	ஸ்ரீ த்ரிபுர பைரவீதேவீ	5th Devi of Dasha Maha Vidya	146
69.	*Śrī Kamalātmikā Devi*	6th Devi of Dasha Maha Vidya	138
70.	ஸ்ரீ சின்ன மஸ்தா தேவீ	6th Devi of Dasha Maha Vidya	164
71.	*Śrī Dhūmāvatī Devī*	7th Devi of Dasha Maha Vidya	141
72.	ஸ்ரீ தூமாவதீ தேவீ	7th Devi of Dasha Maha Vidya	166
73.	*Śrī Bhagalāmukhī Devī*	8th Devi of Dasha Maha Vidya	158
74.	ஸ்ரீ பகலாமுகீ தேவீ	8th Devi of Dasha Maha Vidya	186
75.	*Śrī Mātangī Devī*	9th Devi of Dasha Maha Vidya	145
76.	ஸ்ரீ மாதங்கீ³ தே³வீ	9th Devi of Dasha Maha Vidya	171
77.	*Śrī Kamalātmikā Devī*	10th Devi of Dasha Maha Vidya	170
78.	ஸ்ரீ கமலாத்மிகா தே³வீ	10th Devi of Dasha Maha Vidya	226
79.	*Chaṇḍī Homa Vidhānam*	Process of Performing Chandi Homam	60
80.	சண்டி ஹோம விதானம்	Process of Performing Chandi Homam	80
81.	ஸ்ரீ ருத்³ர ந்யாசம் & த்ரிஸதீ	300 Divine names of Lord Rudra and Japa Nyasam	224
82.	*Śrī Rudra Nyāsa & Triśati*	300 Divine names of Lord Rudra and Japa Nyasam	160
83.	ஸ்ரீ ஸௌர்ய ஸஹஸ்ர நாமம்	கருத்துக்களுடன் ஒரு விளக்கம்	404
84.	*Śrī Sūrya Sahasranāmam*	Explanation with Comments	320
85.	Kaliviḍambanam	An explanation	97
86.	கலிவிட³ம்ப³னம்	ஒரு விளக்கம்	100
87.	*Mūka Pancaśatī*	An Understanding	428
88.	மூக பஞ்ச ஸதி	ஒரு புரிதல்	577
89.	*Śrī Dattatreyar*	*Ādi Guru*	154
90.	ஸ்ரீ த³த்தாத்ரேயர்	ஆதி³ கு³ரு	174
91.	தெய்வீகத் தாயின் பத்து பிரபஞ்ச வடிவங்கள்	ஒருங்கிணைந்த த3ஸ மஹா வித்3யா	1,400
92.	Ten Cosmic Forms of the Divine Mother	Integrated *Daśa Mahā Vidyā*	1,402
93.	Ten Cosmic Forms of the Divine Mother – Volume 1	Integrated *Daśa Mahā Vidyā*	751
94.	Ten Cosmic Forms of the Divine Mother – Volume 1	Integrated *Daśa Mahā Vidyā*	678
Applied Samskrutam Based			
95.	*Paribhāshā Stora–S*	An Exploration of *Lalitā Sahasranāmam*	96
96.	பரிபாஷா ஸ்தோத்ரங்கள்	ஸ்ரீ லலிதா ஸஹஸ்ரநாமம் - ஒரு ஆய்வு	135

#	Title	Remarks	Pages
97.	*Shrī Cakra*, An Esoteric Approach	Mathematical Construction to Draw *Shrī Cakra*	64
98.	ஸ்ரீ சக்கரம் வரையும் முறை	ஸ்ரீ சக்கரம் வரைய கணித கட்டுமானம்	84
99.	Number System in Samskrutam	An Overview of Mathematics Based on Samskrutam	123
100.	ஸமஸ்க்ருதத்தில் எண்ணியல்	ஸமஸ்க்ருதத்தில் பொதிந்துள்ள எண் கணிதம்	140
101.	*Vedic* Mathematics	30 Formulae Elucidated	146
102.	Vedic IT	Information Technology and Samskrutam	162
IT Based			
103.	Orthogonal Array	A Statistical Tool for Software Testing	180
Banking Based			
104.	Retail Banking	A Guide Book for Novice	213
105.	Corporate Banking	A Guide Book for Novice	232
106.	Dictionary of Financial Terms	A Guide Book for All – Demystifying Myriad Global Financial Terms	215
107.	GRC In BFS Industry	(**G**overnance, **R**isk Management and **C**ompliance by Banking & Finance Industry)	200

＊＊＊＊＊